T0211712

Lecture Notes in Artificial Intelligence 8953

Subseries of Lecture Notes in Computer Science

More information about this series at http://www.springer.com/series/1244

Nils Bulling (Ed.)

Multi-Agent Systems

12th European Conference, EUMAS 2014
Prague, Czech Republic, December 18–19, 2014
Revised Selected Papers

Editor
Nils Bulling
Delft University of Technology
Delft
The Netherlands

ISSN 0302-9743 ISSN 1611-3349 (electronic)
Lecture Notes in Artificial Intelligence
ISBN 978-3-319-17129-6 ISBN 978-3-319-17130-2 (eBook)
DOI 10.1007/978-3-319-17130-2

Library of Congress Control Number: 2015935051

LNCS Sublibrary: SL7 – Artificial Intelligence

Springer Cham Heidelberg New York Dordrecht London

Printed on acid-free paper

Springer International Publishing AG Switzerland is part of Springer Science+Business Media
(www.springer.com)

Preface

This volume contains the papers accepted at the 12th European Conference on Multi-Agent Systems (EUMAS 2014) held during December 18–19, 2014, in Prague, Czech Republic.

Multi-agent systems are systems of interacting, intelligent, and autonomous agents that pursue their goals alone, in collaboration with others, or against others. In order to solve complex problems, agents must have a variety of skills, e.g., they need to communicate and to negotiate with their peers and humans. Also, they need to be able to take good, often strategic, decisions. This requires sophisticated tools and techniques. Such being the case, the research field of multi-agent systems is very interdisciplinary with connections to, for example, logic, mathematics, economics, and psychology. Also, engineering aspects have been becoming increasingly important for the deployment of multi-agent systems for real-world and industrial applications.

This interdisciplinarity is very much in the spirit of EUMAS. Following the tradition of previous editions (Oxford 2003, Barcelona 2004, Brussels 2005, Lisbon 2006, Hammamet 2007, Bath 2008, Agia Napa 2009, Paris 2010, Maastricht 2011, Dublin 2012, Toulouse 2013), the aim of EUMAS 2014 was to encourage and support activity in the research and development of multi-agent systems, and to provide a forum for researchers from academia as well as from industry to meet, to present their work, and to discuss ideas in a friendly and professional environment. Sticking to these renowned traditions, this year's edition also brought a change: EUMAS 2014 was run, for the first time, as a conference, with formal proceedings in the form of an LNCS/LNAI volume—the present one.

As a consequence of the new format, the reviewing process was more selective when compared to previous editions. EUMAS 2014 attracted a good number of 79 submissions: 57 papers were submitted to the full paper track, 17 to the short paper track, and five additional submissions reported on already published work. Each submission was peer-reviewed by at least three members of the Program Committee which consisted of 80 top-level researchers and 22 additional reviewers who helped in the process. The reviewing process was selective: 21 papers were accepted as full papers and eight as short papers. The acceptance rate was 37 %. In addition to these papers, the proceedings includes abstracts of two invited talks, given by Michael Fisher (University of Liverpool, UK) on "Verifiable Autonomy – (how) can you trust your robots"? and by Carles Sierra (IIIA-CSIC, Spain) on "Agreement Computing," respectively.

There are many people who helped to make EUMAS 2014 a successful event. First, I would like to thank all authors for submitting to EUMAS, all participants, the invited speakers, the members of the Program Committee, and the additional reviewers for putting together a strong program. Second, I would like to thank the EURAMAS board, especially Thomas Ågotnes (Chair of the EUMAS liaison) and Jordi Sabater-Mir (Chair of the EURAMAS board) for their support, and the Local Organizing Committee, especially the Local Chairs Michal Jakob and Jiri Vokrinek, for the great organization of this event. Last but not least, I very much appreciate the financial support of the European Coordination Committee of Artificial Intelligence (ECCAI, http://www.eccai.org) for sponsoring the invited speakers and, on behalf of the local organizers, the financial support of the Office of Naval Research (Global Collaborative Support Program Grant No. N62909-15-1-C008)—many thanks to these sponsors!

I hope you enjoy reading.

January 2015   Nils Bulling

Organization

Program Committee Chair

Nils Bulling   Delft University of Technology, The Netherlands

Local Organizers

Jiri Vokrinek   Czech Technical University, Czech Republic
Michal Jakob   Czech Technical University, Czech Republic

Program Committee

Natasha Alechina	University of Nottingham, UK
Fred Amblard	IRIT - Université Toulouse 1 Capitole, France
Leila Amgoud	IRIT - CNRS, France
Luis Antunes	Universidade de Lisboa, Portugal
Katie Atkinson	University of Liverpool, UK
Bernhard Bauer	University of Augsburg, Germany
Ana L.C. Bazzan	Universidade Federal do Rio Grande do Sul, Brazil
Elizabeth Black	King's College London, UK
Olivier Boissier	ENS Mines Saint-Etienne, France
Elise Bonzon	LIPADE - Université Paris Descartes, France
Nils Bulling	Delft University of Technology, The Netherlands
Dídac Busquets	Imperial College London, UK
Cristiano Castelfranchi	Institute of Cognitive Sciences and Technologies, CNR, Italy
Amit Chopra	Lancaster University, UK
Massimo Cossentino	ICAR-CNR, Italy
Mehdi Dastani	Utrecht University, The Netherlands
Paul Davidsson	Malmö University, Sweden
Tiago De Lima	University of Artois and CNRS, France
Marina De Vos	University of Bath, UK
Frank Dignum	Utrecht University, The Netherlands
Juergen Dix	Clausthal University of Technology, Germany
Amal El Fallah Seghrouchni	LIP6 - University of Pierre and Marie Curie, France
Klaus Fischer	DFKI GmbH, Germany
Nicola Gatti	Politecnico di Milano, Italy
Valentin Goranko	Technical University of Denmark, Denmark
Davide Grossi	University of Liverpool, UK
Koen Hindriks	Delft University of Technology, The Netherlands
Anthony Hunter	University College London, UK

Wiebe Van Der Hoek	University of Liverpool, UK
Leon van der Torre	University of Luxembourg, Luxembourg
Wamberto Vasconcelos	University of Aberdeen, UK
Laurent Vercouter	LITIS Laboratory, INSA de Rouen, France
Serena Villata	Inria Sophia Antipolis, France
Danny Weyns	Linnaeus University, Sweden
Cees Witteveen	Delft University of Technology, The Netherlands
Neil Yorke-Smith	American University of Beirut, Lebanon
Thomas Ågotnes	University of Bergen, Norway

Additional Reviewers

Ahlbrecht, Tobias	Persson, Jan A.
Billhardt, Holger	Popovici, Matei
Craciun, Matei	Ribino, Patrizia
Dignum, Virginia	Riccio, Daniel
Fiosins, Maksims	Rossi, Silvia
Knobbout, Max	Sabatucci, Luca
Lujak, Marin	Schlesinger, Federico
Niewiadomski, Artur	Seidita, Valeria
Nunes, Davide	Skaruz, Jaroslaw
O'Riordan, Colm	Testerink, Bas
Olsson, Carl Magnus	Wáng, Yì N.

Verifiable Autonomy—(How) Can You Trust Your Robots? (Invited Talk)

Michael Fisher

Department of Computer Science
University of Liverpool, Liverpool, UK
mfisher@liverpool.ac.uk
http://intranet.csc.liv.ac.uk/~michael

Abstract. As the use of autonomous systems and robotics spreads, the need for their activities to not only be understandable and explainable, but even verifiable, is increasing. But how can we be sure what such a system will decide to do, and can we really formally verify this behaviour?

Practical autonomous systems are increasingly based on some form of hybrid agent architecture, at the heart of which is an agent that makes many, and possibly all, of the decisions that the human operator used to make. However it is important that these agents are "rational", in the sense that they not only make decisions, but have explicit and explainable reasons for making those decisions.

In this talk, I will examine these "rational" agents, discuss their role at the heart of autonomous systems, and explain how we can formally verify their behaviours. This then allows us: to be more confident about what our autonomous systems will decide to do; to use formal arguments in system certification and safety; and even to analyse ethical decisions our systems might make.

Acknowledgement. The work described in this talk has involved *many* others, for example my thanks go to

- Louise Dennis (Computer Science, Univ. Liverpool)
- Matt Webster (Computer Science, Univ. Liverpool)
- Clare Dixon (Computer Science, Univ. Liverpool)
- Rafael Bordini (UFRGS, Brazil)
- Alexei Lisitsa (Computer Science, Univ. Liverpool)
- Sandor Veres (Engineering, Univ. Sheffield)
- Mike Jump (Engineering, Univ. Liverpool)
- Richard Stocker (NASA Ames Research Center, USA)
- Neil Cameron (Virtual Engineering Centre, Daresbury)
- Marija Slavkovik (Univ. Bergen, Norway)
- Alan Winfield (Bristol Robotics Lab)

Thanks also to the UK's Engineering and Physical Sciences Research Council (EPSRC) for funding much of this research, particularly through the projects

- *Model-Checking Agent Programming Languages* (EP/D052548; 2006–2009)
- *Engineering Autonomous Space Software* (EP/F037201; 2008–2012)
- *Trustworthy Robotic Assistants* (EP/K006193; 2013–2016)
- *Verifiable Autonomy* (EP/L024845; 2014–2018)

References

1. Dennis, L.A, Fisher, M., Lincoln, N.K., Lisitsa, A., Veres, S.M.: Practical verification of decision-making in agent-based autonomous systems. Autom. Softw. Eng. (2014)
2. Dennis, L.A., Fisher, M., Slavkovik, M., Webster, M.: Ethical choice in unforeseen circumstances. In: Natraj, A., Cameron, S., Melhuish, C., Witkowski, M. (eds.) TAROS 2013. LNCS (LNAI), vol. 8069, pp. 433–445. Springer, Heidelberg (2013)
3. Dennis, L.A., Fisher, M., Webster, M., Bordini, R.H.: Model checking agent programming languages. Autom. Softw. Eng. **19**(1), 5–63 (2012)
4. Dixon, C., Webster, M., Saunders, J., Fisher, M., Dautenhahn, K.: "The fridge door is open" — temporal verification of a robotic assistant's behaviours. In: Mistry, M., Leonardis, A., Witkowski, M., Melhuish, C. (eds.) AROS 2014. LNCS (LNAI), vol. 8717, pp. 97–108. Springer, Heidelberg (2014)
5. Fisher, M., Dennis, L.A., Webster, M.: Verifying autonomous systems. ACM Commun. **56**(9), 84–93 (2013)
6. Konur, S., Fisher, M., Schewe, S.: Combined model checking for temporal, probabilistic, and real-time logics. Theoret. Comput. Sci., **503**, 61–88 (2013)
7. Lincoln, N., Veres, S., Dennis, L., Fisher, M., Lisitsa, A.: Autonomous asteroid exploration by rational agents. IEEE Comput. Intell. Mag. **8**(4), 25–38 (2013)
8. Stocker, R., Dennis, L.A., Dixon, C., Fisher, M.: Verification of Brahms human-robot teamwork models. In: del Cerro, L.F., Herzig, A., Mengin, J. (eds.) JELIA 2012. LNCS, vol. 7519, pp. 385–397. Springer, Heidelberg (2012)
9. Webster, M., Cameron, N., Fisher, M., Jump, M.: Generating certification evidence for autonomous unmanned aircraft using model checking and simulation. J. Aerosp. Inf. Syst. **11**(5), 258–279 (2014)
10. Webster, M., Dixon, C., Fisher, M., Salem, M., Saunders, J., Koay, K.L., Dautenhahn, K.: Formal verification of an autonomous personal robotic assistant. In: Formal Verification and Modeling in Human-Machine Systems: Papers from the AAAI Spring Symposium (FVHMS 2014) (2014)

Agreement Computing
(Invited Talk)

Carles Sierra

IIA-CSIC, Barcelona, Spain
sierra@iiia.csic.es
http://www.iiia.csic.es/~sierra/public/Home.html

In modern IT-enabled societies, the human user is being assisted with an increasing number of tasks by computational communicating entities/software (usually called agents). Agents interact with and act on behalf of their human users. Their assistance could take different forms, starting with simple technical support such as email filtering, information retrieval, shopping, etc., and moving towards full delegation of more complex tasks, such as service composition for travel organization, dispute resolution in the context of divorces, labour controversies, traffic accidents, etc. To support the agents with the more complex tasks, we argue that the concept of "agreement" lies at the basis of agent communication and interaction. Interacting agents will need to base their decisions and actions on explicit agreements. Agreement Computing aims at proposing a plethora of adequate theoretical methods and applied techniques in order to allow for the design and implementation of those new generation "intelligent" communicating artefacts that will form the basis of future modern "mixed" societies populated by interconnected and mutually interacting humans and artefacts.

Agreements are an explicit description of the interoperation between two independent pieces of code that is generated by the two pieces of code themselves. Agreements are to be computed by a particular type of built-in interaction between software entities. Software components willing to participate in open systems will therefore require to include extra capabilities to explicitly represent and compute these agreements, on top of the simpler capacity to interoperate, once the agreements are set. That is, agreements should become the basic run-time structures that determine whether a certain interaction is correct, in a similar way as type-checking currently determines if the values in a call to a procedure are correct. Agreement-checking is a run-time analysis of whether a particular interaction between two entities satisfies certain agreements. Agreements are multi-faceted: on meaning of the exchanged variables, on constraints to be respected during the interactions between the entities, on properties of the values exchanged, on the particular protocol to follow, etc. In summary, this view proposes that the interaction between software components consists of (1) the computation (or perhaps selection) of their interoperation agreement, and then (2) the actual agreement-compliant interoperation of those software components.

Acknowledgement. This research is been supported by the EU funded research project PRAISE (EU FP7 grant number 388770).

Contents

Agent-Based Models, Trust and Reputation

Ants in the OCEAN: Modulating Agents with Personality for Planning with Humans

Sebastian Ahrndt[✉], Armin Aria, Johannes Fähndrich, and Sahin Albayrak

DAI-Laboratory of the Technische Universität Berlin,
Faculty of Electrical Engineering and Computer Science,
Ernst-Reuter-Platz 7, 10587 Berlin, Germany
sebastian.ahrndt@dai-labor.de

Abstract. This work introduces a prototype that demonstrates the idea of using a psychological theory of personality types known as the Five-Factor Model (FFM) in planning for human-agent teamwork scenarios. FFM is integrated into the BDI model of agency leading to variations in the interpretation of inputs, the decision-making process and the generation of outputs. This is demonstrated in a multi-agent simulation. Furthermore, it is outlined how these variations can be used for the planning process in collaborative settings.

Keywords: User/machine systems · Human factors · Software psychology

1 Introduction

Human-Aware Planning (HAP) is mainly required when the situation involves artificial and natural agents in the same environment, the actions of the artificial agents being planned and those of the natural agents being predicted [10, p. 15:2]. We find such situations in collaborative application areas like Smart Homes inhabited by agents, robots and humans, e.g., when addressing the ageing of the population with socially assistive robotics [34]. Although making artificial agents a constituent part of human activities leads to more affiliated teamwork scenarios on the one hand, it also introduces several new challenges on the other (cf. [3,6,17,18]). One of those challenges is the *predictability* of an agent's actions during the planning process. Predictability addresses the condition that an agent can only plan its own actions—which includes coordination activities—effectively if it is assessable what the others collaborators will do [6]. To address this challenge in human-agent teamwork the use of human-behavioural models provided by psychology studies was proposed as being beneficial, e.g., when determining the most likely next action of a person [1,17].

Taking that into consideration, this work introduces a prototype that integrates a psychological theory of personality types into a popular computational model for the conceptualisation of human behaviour (see Sect. 5). The work is intended to show that the integration of personality leads to variations in

© Springer International Publishing Switzerland 2015
N. Bulling (Ed.): EUMAS 2014, LNAI 8953, pp. 3–18, 2015.
DOI: 10.1007/978-3-319-17130-2_1

the interpretation of inputs, the decision-making process and the generation of outputs (see Sect. 6). In fact, it is essential to prove this assumption prior to applying it to the more complex problem of planning with humans. Afterwards, it is outlined how this model can be used to enhance HAP by using the information about the personality as a kind of heuristic during the actual planning process (see Sect. 7). However, before describing the applied mechanism and the future work we will first introduce the psychological theory of personality types used within the work, which is known as the Five-Factor Model [22] (FFM) (see Sect. 2). Subsequently, we will provide a literature overview exploring the use of personality theories in agent-based systems (see Sect. 3). After introducing the state-of-the-art we compare the two most-popular personality theories and explain the reason for applying the FFM, finally justifying the motivation for presenting this work (see Sect. 4).

2   Five-Factor Model

The Five-Factor Model of personality [21,22] is a psychological theory that can be used to model human personality types and their influences on the decision-making process of humans. As suggested by the name, the FFM introduces five dimensions characterising an individual, which are briefly described in the following:

- *Openness to experience* describes a person's preference to vary their activities over keeping a strict routine and is also related to their creativity (e.g., inventive, emotional and curious behaviour vs. consistent, conservative and cautious behaviour).
- *Conscientiousness* describes a person's preference to act duteously over spontaneously. This directly relates to the level of self-discipline when aiming for achievements (e.g., efficient, planned and organised behaviour vs. easy-going, spontaneous and careless behaviour).
- *Extraversion* describes a person's preference to interact with other people and to gain energy from this interaction over being more independent of social interaction (e.g., outgoing, action-oriented and energetic behaviour vs. solitary, inward and reserved behaviour).
- *Agreeableness* describes a person's preference to trust others, to act helpful and to be optimistic over an antagonistic and sceptical mind set. This trait directly influences the quality of relationships with other individuals (e.g., friendly, cooperative and compassionate behaviour vs. analytical, antagonistic and detached behaviour).
- *Neuroticism* describes a person's preference to interpret external stimuli such as stress as minatory over confidence and emotional stability. Neuroticism addresses the level of emotional reaction to events (e.g., sensitive, pessimistic and nervous behaviour vs. secure, emotionally stable and confident behaviour).

These dimensions are also named the Big Five personality traits leading to acronyms such as OCEAN, NEOAC, NEO-PI and NEO-PI-R, which are frequently used when referring to the FFM theory. To some extent the different acronyms indicate different assessment instruments. The characteristic of each dimension is defined as a variation from the norm, whereas each dimension is an overarching container subsuming different lower-level personality traits. For example, neuroticism is associated with subordinated traits such as anxiety, hostility and impulsiveness [22]. Taking this observation into account, one can argue that the FFM theory is a conceptual framework about human personality traits that can, for example, be used to integrate other theories about human personalities into its structure [16,24].

3   Related Work

In the following we will explore the use of personality theories in agent-based systems. In particular we want to carve out whether or not there is existing work aiming to prove that different personalities act in different ways and how the cooperation between agents is affected by this.

In research on agent-based systems, formal models of human personality are comprehensively used for the implementation of (microscopic) traffic simulation frameworks [20] and the agent-based simulation/visualisation of groups of people [8,13]. The work of *Durupinar et al.* [13] shows how the introduction of different personalities into agents influences the behaviour of a crowd. For this simulation the authors applied the OCEAN model. Other areas include human-machine interaction [11], in particular conversational agents/virtual humans [4,14] and life-like characters [5]. The latter outlines three projects that apply two dimensions of the FFM (extraversion and agreeableness). The effects are interpreted in a rule-based or scripted manner.

The mentioned approaches focus either on supplying personality to agents that interact with human users or applying personality theories to simulation environments to analyse more global effects. They implement the effects of personalities specifically for the individual use-case, without proving that this can be done in a more generic manner. Another branch of research focuses on modelling and examining the effects of personalities on interactions between agents and their environments. In particular, the effects of personalities in cooperative settings as addressed by this work are examined.

Talman et al. [33] present a work that illustrates the use of a rather simple abstraction of personality types. Personalities of agents are determined by the two dimensions cooperation and reliability, which are used to measure the helpfulness of an agent. The agents have to negotiate and cooperate as cooperation is an inherent part of the game they play. During repeatedly played games the agents reason about each other's helpfulness along the two dimensions. As an effect they try to respond more effectively by customising their behaviour appropriately for different personalities. *Campos et al.* [7] present a work employing the Myers-Briggs Type Indicator [23] (MBTI) model, which is here restricted to two of its dichotomies. It is integrated into the reasoning process of a BDI agent and the work proves that different personality characteristics lead to variations in the decision-making process in a simulation specifically designed for the paper's use-case. In an early work, *Castelfranchi et al.* [9] present a framework to investigate the effects of personalities on social interactions between agents, such as delegation and help. The agents apply opponent modelling in terms of personality traits to motivate interactions. However, the work discusses personality traits as an abstract concept without relation to psychological theories. The work that is most closely related to our work, answering the question whether individuals with different personalities act in different ways, is presented by *J. Salvit* and *E. Sklar* [29, 30]. That is the case because the authors established an experiment validating the impact of the MBTI onto the decision-making process of agents. In order to do so, the MBTI is integrated into a sense-plan-act structure and the behaviour of each MBTI type is analysed in a simulation environment called the 'Termite World'. The results underline the hypothesis of the paper that the different personality types act in quite different ways. One consequence is 'that some agent personality types are better suited to particular tasks—the same observation that psychologists make about humans' [30, p. 147].

To conclude, there is evidence that proves the hypothesis addressed. Nevertheless, the literature overview also shows that the majority of works addressing the hypothesis apply the MBTI theory. The others use simplified models that are not based on psychology findings. In the following, we will carve out why we applied the OCEAN model and explain why MBTI should no longer be used within the agent community, thus giving the motivation for presenting this work.

4   Comparison of OCEAN and MBTI

To start with, the FFM emerged from empirical observations and analysis leading to the introduced formal model of human personality, whereas MBTI emerged from theoretical considerations, which were proven through user studies [26]. Another difference is the use of personality types on the one hand and personality traits on the other. The use of types presents the advantage of being distinct, but at the same time presents the disadvantage of being disjoint. This means that being classified as extrovert (E) clearly distinguish an individual from being introvert (I) and adds such an individual to its specific cluster, without giving any hint about the degree of extroversion. Still, this information might be important when this individual was close to the 'artificial' border that disjoints the dichotomies or when someone wants to compare persons of the same type. At this point a continuous scale as presented by FFM delivers more information, but misses the advantage of introducing standardised clusters to compare groups of people, making the implementation of FFM into agents challenging.

The completeness of a theory is another important characteristic that implies whether such a theory is broad enough to understand/describe the different human personalities. Here, it was shown that there are some characteristics of humans that the MBTI fails to cover [15, 22]. In particular the missing preference of being emotionally stable is criticised. In contrast, FFM presents a more generic structure, which is nevertheless also criticised for neglecting some domains of a human personality like honesty or religiosity [25] (also applies to MBTI). In both cases, these criticisms are still an open discussion among psychologists and are subject to further investigation.

Beside the completeness of a theory, reliability is at least equally important. On the one hand, reliability addresses the consistency of the results when assessing an individual using self-assessment, questionnaires and professional assessments. On the other hand, it addresses the consistency when performing the same assessment repeatedly with some temporal distance, which is also named test-retest reliability. MBTI suffers in both categories, as it does not deliver constant results using the different assessment techniques. Also, experiments about the test-retest reliability have shown that there is a chance of 50 % to be classified as another MBTI type when repeating the test after a period of only five weeks [26]. Here, FFM delivers more accurate results for short term intervals (1 week) [19] and long-term intervals (10 years) [35], which supports the finding that a developed personality is stable over the life span of a human [36].

Balancing the presented arguments and taking into account the possibility to integrate MBTI into FFM comes down to the point 'that it may be better [...] to reinterpret the MBTI in terms of the five factor model' [21, p. 37, according to [15]]. This is an advice we follow and that should be recognised by the agent community. One argument here might be that the use of psychological theories is not of relevance when the goal is to produce different artificial agent traits. We want to respond to this by highlighting the fairly long tradition of knowledge transfer between psychology and agent research and that newer findings should not be ignored.

5   Modulating BDI Agents with Personality

To integrate the personality of humans we embed the FFM theory into the BDI model of agency [28], a popular model for the conceptualisation of human behaviour. BDI agents separate the current execution of a plan from the activity of selecting a plan using the three mental concepts belief, desire and intention. The life-cycle of a BDI agent comprises four phases, namely the *Belief Revision*, the *Option Generation*, the *Filter Process*, and the *Actuation*. In our model, the phases of the BDI cycle are influenced by the characteristics of a personality in different ways. For instance, the trait conscientiousness strongly influences the goal-driven behaviour of an agent, whereas the trait extraversion influences the agent's preference to interact with others. Table 1 lists the influences of the different characteristics of FFM on the different phases of the BDI life-cycle. These influences address the intensity by which one personality trait influences a phase and thus (only) highlights the traits that are most influential.

In the following, to explain the model, we represent a BDI cycle as a sequence of states. Therefore let each state be a set of variables (syntax follows $\mathcal{LORA}$ [37]):

- P: *Per* is the collection of personality traits the agent has, *i.e.* the actual characteristics for this agent according to the dimensions of the FFM;
- ρ : *Percepts* is the information that the agent perceives/receives in its environment;

Table 1. In order not to value the influence in terms of being negative or positive, the list only highlights the traits that are most influential in each phase. Indeed, this classification is discussable as it reflects our own interpretation of the FFM traits in comparison with the BDI phases.

	O	C	E	A	N
Belief revision	×			×	
Option generation		×		×	×
Filter process	×	×	×	×	×
Actuation		×	×	×	

- $B : \wp(Bel)$ is the set of beliefs, *i.e.* the current assumptions about the state of the environment;
- $D : \wp(Des)$ is the set of desires, *i.e.* the set of intended goals the agent wants to fulfil;
- $I : \wp(Int)$ is the set of intentions, *i.e.* the set of desires the agent is committed to fulfil;
- $\pi : Act^*$ is the current sequence of actions taken from the set of plans over some set of actions Act this agent has chosen, *i.e.* the current plan; and
- $\alpha : Act$ is the action that is executed.

Algorithm 1 shows an adapted BDI life-cycle that involves personality as an influence during the different stages. All personality traits are considered during the process. Furthermore, we assume that the personality does not change during the life-cycle of an agent. This assumption is based on the finding that we as humans have a stable personality over our lifespan as adults [36].

Algorithm 1. A BDI cycle that incorporates personality into the decision making process.

Input: B_{init}, I_{init}, P; **Output:** -

```
 1:  B ← B_init, I ← I_init
 2:  while true do
 3:      ρ ← percept(Env, Msg)
 4:      B ← beliefRevision(B, ρ, P)
 5:      D ← options(B, I, P)
 6:      I ← filter(B, D, I, P)
 7:      π ← plan(B, I, P)
 8:      while not empty(π) do
 9:          α ← hd(π)
10:          execute(α, P)
11:          π ← tail(π)
12:      end while
13:  end while
```

The cycle starts with the perception of information. During this stage the agent receives new information from the environment (Env) using its sensors, which also comprises messages (Msg) from other agents (communication acts). The perception is not affected by the personality, as humans are not able to restrict their perception during the cognition. This is a deliberate process taking place in the next step of the cycle. Formally, the signature of the perception function *percept* is defined as:

$$percept : Env \times Msg \rightarrow Percepts.$$

The next step of the BDI life-cycle is the *Belief Revision*. That means that given the new perceptions (ρ) an updated belief set (B) is computed with respect to the current personality (P). The belief revision function *beliefRevision* is defined as:

$$beliefRevision : \wp(Bel) \times Percepts \times Per \rightarrow \wp(Bel).$$

After this step the set of beliefs can contain information about the environment, the state of the agent itself (e.g., energy level, injuries like sensory malfunctions) and facts that were received via communication. In our model the **O** and **A** characteristics influence this phase most frequently, as they influence the interpretation of what the new measurement means for the agent and how trustful the agent is when receiving information from others. One essential reason to distinguish between perceptions/beliefs derived from the environment and perceptions/beliefs derived from other agents is the characteristic of the personality trait agreeableness, which indicates the preference to trust others.[1] We implemented this behaviour (the influence of the trait **A** during the belief revision) for our simulation environment using the characteristic of the personality trait as likelihood. For example, an agent with $A = 1.0$ would always trust information received via communication acts, whereas an agent with $A = 0.0$ would always reject them.

The next step is the *Option Generation*, where the agent generates its desires (D) taking into account the updated beliefs, the currently selected intentions (I) and the personality. The option generation is mainly influenced by the **C**, **A** and **N** characteristics, as these traits indicate the preferences to follow picked goals, the tendency to act selfishly or generously, and the reaction of the agent to external influences. This deliberation process is represented by the function *options* with the following signature:

$$options : \wp(Bel) \times \wp(Int) \times Per \rightarrow \wp(Des).$$

The generated desires are a set of alternatives (goals) an agent wants to fulfil, which are often mutually exclusive. As the option generation should produce all options available to the agent, the influence of the personality is restricted

---

[1] In fact, it might be hard to clearly distinguish the information sources. That is because other agents are part of the environment and the observation of the behaviour of other agents might thus be both an observation of the environment and an (implicit) communication act.

to the persistence of already selected intentions. Again, we implemented this by interpreting the traits as likelihood, e.g. an agent with $C = 1.0$ will always maintain an intention as an option regardless of the current beliefs about the world.

The third stage is the *Filter Process* where the agent chooses between competing desires and commits to achieve some of them next. The filter process is influenced by the preference to vary activities over keeping a strict routine (**O**) and the level of self-discipline (**C**), the need to act in harmony with other agents (**A, N**) and even the tendency to generally interact with others (**E**). For example, variations of **C** influence an agent's preference to detach the previously selected intentions. As another example, variations of **A** and **E** influence an agent's preference to commit to selfish/altruistic goals. The *filter* function is defined as:

$$filter : \wp(Bel) \times \wp(Des) \times \wp(Int) \times Per \rightarrow \wp(Int).$$

The personality helps to prioritise the different intentions and for example indicates to what extent an agent acts goal-driven, prefers interaction and varies the activities. It selects the best option from the agent's point of view based on the current beliefs, with respect to the previously selected option. Again interpreting the traits as likelihood, the filter process was implemented by, e.g., prioritising intentions that imply interaction with others using the characteristic of **E**.

The last stage is the *Actuation*, in which the agent creates/selects the plan (π) and influences the environment performing actions (α). This phase is mainly influenced by the creativity level of the agent (**O**), the tendency to apply actions in a decent manner (**C**) and the preference to interact with others (**E**). The actual plan is then generated for the selected intentions and executed, which is defined as:

$$plan : \wp(Bel) \times \wp(Int) \times Per \rightarrow Act^*.$$

The execution of actions as plan-elements directly influences the environment and the personality indicates how accurately an agent behaves (**C**), which however is a rather vague argument for agents. To set an example, imagine a robot that performs a motion from one point to another in a specific time frame. The level of conscientiousness can then be used to implement a noise level added to the target location or time frame borders. Indeed, this seems to be curious when considering artificial agents but is one important difference between humans. The actuation function *execute* is formally defined as:

$$execute : Act \times Per$$

The algorithm explained here is one variant of a BDI agent following a blind-commitment strategy and being overcommitted to both the ends and means. As the chosen evaluation domain is tick-based and the plans are rather short, this commitment strategy is acceptable. However, using the provided explanation the algorithm can be adapted to produce reactive and single- or open-minded behaviour, which might be either bold or cautious. These variations of the BDI life-cycle are described by *M. Wooldridge* [37, pp. 31] and the modifications are straightforward.

6   Evaluation

To evaluate the model we implemented it for the multi-agent simulation environment AntMe![2]. The main objective of each ant colony is to collect as much food (apples, sugar) as possible and to defend their own anthill from enemies such as other ant colonies and bugs. Each simulation run encompassed 5000 time-steps, where each ant in each time-step completes the BDI cycle of sensing its environment, updating its beliefs, desires and intentions and executing. The ants are able to sense their location, to recognise whether or not they are transporting food, and to determine the location of food, other ants, scent-marks, and enemies within their range of sight. The scent-marks are used to determine what other ants of the own colony are targeting and to highlight the occurrence of enemies. The possible actions are goStraight, goAwayFromPOI, goToPOI, goToNest, turnToPOI, turnByAngle, turnAround, turnToGoal ('turn actions'), pick-up and drop-off food, attack, and put scent-mark. Figure 1 shows a screenshot of the simulation environment.

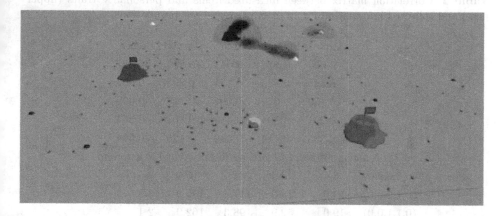

Fig. 1. Screenshot from an AntMe! simulation with three ant colonies (red, blue, black). Carrying apples (green) is a teamwork task and white cubes are sugar. The black dust is the visualisation of scent-marks, here used to highlight sugar. Such scent-marks disappear after a while (Color figure online).

Using the introduced model we expect that the ants' behaviours vary when adjusting the personality traits. In particular we expect that an ant population with high values in the trait openness (O+) does more exploration than a population with low values (O-).[3] That means that O+ ants are expected to find sugar and apples earlier. At the same time, we expect the O- ants to harvest sugar faster as a consistent behaviour is favourable for this task, which includes

---

[2] For further information about the simulation environment the interested reader is referred to http://www.antme.net/.

[3] The −, + label represent a value in the interval $[0.0, 0.5]$, $[0.5, 1.0]$ respectively.

walking the same route multiple times. We expect that high values in the trait conscientiousness (C+) lead to more collected food, as such ants will not drop food when facing other goals such as attacking/running away from bugs. At the same time, we expect low valued ants (C-) to have a lower chance of starving during the search for food as collecting food is the most important desire. Extroverted ants (E+) are expected to communicate more frequently with other ants by putting scent-marks as markers for the occurrence of sugar, apples and bugs more frequently. However, this effect correlates with the effect of the trait agreeableness, indicating whether an ant trusts information received from other ants (A+) or not (A-). We expect that high valued ants in both traits collect food more frequently. The neuroticism trait indicates the ants' emotional stability. We expect high valued ants (N+) to avoid dangerous situations such as bugs and hostile ants – resulting in lower numbers of eaten ants and killed bugs. However, the effect of this trait correlates with the level of trust (A+ vs. A-) and the level of self-discipline (C+ vs. C-).

Table 2. Correlation matrix between measured items and personality traits (upper part) and collected information for an example set of ant populations.

	Apple	Sugar	Eaten	Starved	Bugs
O	−0.068	−0.444	−0.043	−0.209	0.027
C	0.545	0.425	−0.454	0.893	−0.027
E	−0.150	0.072	0.002	−0.119	−0.009
A	0.261	0.501	−0.430	0.107	−0.554
N	0.305	0.114	−0.436	0.125	−0.554
values below are ordered according to the OCEAN acronym					
(0,0,0,0,0)	8.4	18.4	281.6	6.0	2.5
(0,1,0,0,0)	19.0	75.6	117.4	146.9	3.3
(0,1,1,0,0)	19.0	52.9	98.3	162.9	2.1
(0,1,1,1,0)	16.5	181.0	65.9	174.6	0.0
(0,1,1,1,1)	16.0	175.7	64.2	175.9	0.0
(1,0,0,0,0)	8.5	8.1	285.4	0.0	3.0
(1,0,1,0,0)	7.9	6.5	283.9	0.1	3.5
(1,0,1,1,1)	15.8	39.9	75.0	0.0	0.0
(1,1,1,1,1)	19.3	75.8	54.2	188.4	0.0
$(\frac{1}{2},\frac{1}{2},\frac{1}{2},\frac{1}{2},\frac{1}{2})$	9.7	17.1	270.8	19.5	1.5

Table 2 shows the correlation matrix for all personality traits and the measurable features of an AntMe! simulation. For this we simulated the permutation of the minimum and maximum values for each trait, resulting in $2^5 = 32$ ant populations. The features comprise the collected apples and the collected sugar, the number of eaten and starved ants, and the number of killed bugs.

For each permutation the values were averaged over 50 simulation runs, where each simulation run started with the same point of origin of the ant hill, apples, and sugar. Occurrence of bugs is randomised and each deceased ant is instantly replaced with a new one. As indicated in the correlation matrix, the majority of effects that were postulated are observable in the simulation. To start with, the matrix indicates that O+ ants collect less food than O- ants and that this behaviour is most notable for the collected sugar. Still, we postulated that O+ ants will find sugar earlier. This effect is illustrated in Fig. 2, where the process of collecting sugar is depicted tick-wise.

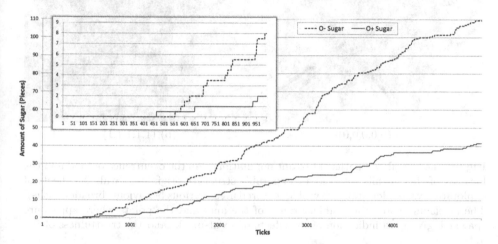

Fig. 2. Tick-based cumulation of O+ (average for 10000, 11111) and O- (average for 00000, 01111) ant populations and their process of collecting sugar. The values are averaged over the 50 simulation runs performed for each population. One can see that O+ ant populations start approximately 2 % earlier with the collection (the smaller diagram shows the relevant segment) but collect food slower than O- ant populations.

Table 2 also lists the results for some selected ant populations and emphasises that different types of personality lead to different simulation results. For example, an ant population with maximum values (1,1,1,1,1) collects more apples and sugar, kills fewer bugs and loses fewer ants because of bugs than an ant population with minimum values (0,0,0,0,0). Still, for the latter a lower number of starved ants can be observed. Here, the traits **E** and **A** influence the occurrence of scent-marks and the interpretation (trust) of the very same thing. The trait **C** implies that already picked-up food is not dropped because of new percepts, as collecting food is the most important goal for the ants. The trait **N** affects the flight behaviour of the ants leading to fewer/more eaten ants/killed bugs, respectively.

The effects of the personality traits are also visible in the paths an ant population takes. Figure 3 shows the path heat maps for the two discussed populations. It emphasises the effects of the trait **O**, which affects an ant's preference of acting exploratively vs. exploitatively or following a conservative vs. curious behaviour (*i.e.* staying in known areas vs. eager to explore new areas). At the same point, the figure visualises how cooperatively the ants act, visible through the round artefacts highlighting the occurrence of apples – collecting apples is a cooperative task.

(a) (0,0,0,0,0)   (b) (1,1,1,1,1)

Fig. 3. The cumulated paths of two ant populations. As the occurrence of food and the location of the ant hill are fixed a comparable structure originates. Still, the effects of exploration vs. exploitation are visible (covered area, curious behaviour, broader paths). The artefacts denote the visibility range of the ants and the points where apples are spawned, giving an indication of the effects of scent-marks and the trustfulness of the ants.

Taking these results into account we can conclude that different personalities affect the result of the simulation and that some personalities are better suited for particular tasks than others. That confirms the finding of *J. Salvit* and *E. Sklar* [30] with respect to the Five-Factor Model of personality. One implication might be that personality is a kind of basic heuristic that influences an agent's performance during the lifetime as it influences the interpretation of perceptions, the interaction with other agents, the decision-making process and even the actual actuation.

7   Personality and Human-Aware Planning

The basic idea to forward the information about the personality to the planning process is to provide a cost estimate for the capabilities. We refer to this idea as Dynamic Heuristic of Human-Behaviour (DHHB). DHHB is used to determine the likelihood that a task will be performed, *i.e.* lower cost indicates a higher likelihood and vice versa. Indeed, *Sisbot et al.* [32] already showed the usefulness of this idea in a human-aware robot motion planning setting. Such robots should avoid to approach humans from behind during the motion. To accomplish this the authors attached higher cost to actions in the back of humans and thus influenced the path-finding of the applied A* algorithm without changing it.

To enable this idea for HAP, we represent each natural agent as an avatar in the computing system that provides information for the actual planning process to the artificial agents. Doing this, we are enabled to use existing planning components and to influence the action selection of a planning process, while the actual planning procedure remains a black box. In a prior work [2], we already showed that this is possible; influencing the action selection process using an estimate of how helpful (in terms of cooperation and reliability) a human might be as an additional actor in a multi-actor Blocks-World domain. In particular, it is planned to integrate the model introduced within this work into the development environment presented in published work [2]. To provide some more details: The BDI model introduced here builds a decision-tree during the life-cycle as shown elsewhere [31]. In the current prototype this tree contains weights for the intentions, which are used to remember previously selected intentions and which depend upon the personality. Such weights can also be interpreted as likelihoods indicating which intention will be satisfied next by the represented human. In HTN planning, these intentions can be seen as either primitive or non-primitive tasks. Thus, such weights can also be used as one of the factors determining the likelihood of the next action. However, other factors like familiarization with specific actions or the timely execution of an action must be learned and added here. This leads to a theory- and data-driven approach, such as postulated by *R. Prada* and *A. Paiva* [27] for encouraging human-agent interaction. Thus major part of the integration will be experiments with real users to find a way to accurately infer the likelihood of a human's next steps from the proposed model.

8 Conclusion

This work demonstrated that the integration of the FFM into the BDI model of agency leads to variations in the interpretation of inputs and generation of outputs. The observation indicates that the decision-making process is influenced by the personality type and that agents with different personalities behave differently. That is the same observation that psychologists make about humans and was proven for the MBTI in a related work. It was argued why we applied the FFM and that psychologists tend to accept the FFM as a conceptual framework for describing human personality. The evaluation comprises the implementation of the model into the multi-agent based simulation environment AntMe!. Despite the fact that ants were simulated, the environment provides a completely adaptable test-bed for behavioural studies, which were used to show that personality affects all relevant phases of decision-making processes. Still, the actual implementation has shortcomings and it is important to mention that we presented a stepping-stone rather than a holistic solution. First of all, the effect of a personality is only based on the characteristic of the trait that decides how often such a trait influences the current stages in one of two ways. But in fact, the influence of a personality is always subject to the context of the individual. For instance, persons that are very calm in general, can become very temperamental given the right circumstance. Here a more realistic method must be found that includes the current context of the agent, which also comprises the effects of emotions or moods. Surprisingly, agent-based research that particularly emphasises the effects of emotions abandons the fact that emotions and its influences are contingent upon the personality. However, finding solutions for both problems is an open topic and requires both further theoretical work and empirical results obtained within user-studies. A first step in this direction is presented by H. Du and M. Huhns [12]. The authors examine whether the interaction of humans with both humans and agents depends on the humans' personality type according to the MBTI. The experiments done using the cake-cutting game show that the different personalities act in different ways, but also show that there is only little evidence that can be used to make correct predictions about possible behaviour based on information about personality. In future work, it will be interesting to examine whether a combination of theory-driven and data-driven approaches leads to more accurate results in the prediction of the next actions a human takes.

References

1. Ahrndt, S.: Improving human-aware planning. In: Klusch, M., Thimm, M., Paprzycki, M. (eds.) MATES 2013. LNCS (LNAI), vol. 8076, pp. 400–403. Springer, Heidelberg (2013)
2. Ahrndt, S., Ebert, P., Fähndrich, J., Albayrak, S.: HPLAN: facilitating the implementation of joint human-agent activities. In: Demazeau, Y., Zambonelli, F., Corchado, J.M., Bajo, J. (eds.) PAAMS 2014. LNCS (LNAI), vol. 8473, pp. 1–12. Springer, Heidelberg (2014). http://dx.doi.org/10.1007/978-3-319-07551-8_1
3. Ahrndt, S., Fähndrich, J., Albayrak, S.: Human-aware planning: a survey related to joint human-agent activities. In: Bajo Perez, J., et al. (eds.) Trends in Practical Applications of Heterogeneous Multi-agent Systems. The PAAMS Collection. AISC, vol. 293, pp. 95–102. Springer, Heidelberg (2014). http://dx.doi.org/10.1007/978-3-319-07476-4_12
4. Allbeck, J., Badler, N.: Toward representing agent behavior modified by personality and emotion. In: Proceedings of the Workshop on Embodied Conversational Agents at the 1st International Conference on Autonomous Agents and Multiagent Systems (AAMAS). ACM Press, April 2002
5. Andre, E., Klesen, M., Gebhard, P., Allen, S., Rist, T.: Integrating models of personality and emotions into lifelike characters. In: Paiva, A.C.R. (ed.) IWAI 1999. LNCS (LNAI), vol. 1814, pp. 150–165. Springer, Heidelberg (2000)
6. Bradshaw, J.M., et al.: From tools to teammates: joint activity in human-agent-robot teams. In: Kurosu, M. (ed.) Human Centered Design, HCII 2009. LNCS, vol. 5619, pp. 935–944. Springer, Heidelberg (2009). http://dx.doi.org/10.1007/978-3-642-02806-9_107
7. Campos, A., Dignum, F., Dignum, V., Signoretti, A., Magaly, A., Fialho, S.: A process-oriented approach to model agent personality. In: Sierra, C., Castelfranchi, C., Decker, K.S., Sichman, J.S. (eds.) Proceedings of the 8th International Conference on Autonomous Agents and Multiagent Systems (AAMAS 2009), pp. 1141–1142. IFAAMAS, Budapest, Hungary, May 2009

8. Canuto, A.M.P., Campos, A.M.C., Santos, A.M., Moura, E.C.M., Santos, E.B., Soares, R.G., Dantas, K.A.A.: Simulating working environments through the use of personality-based agents. In: Sichman, J.S., Coelho, H., Rezende, S.O. (eds.) IBERAMIA 2006 and SBIA 2006. LNCS (LNAI), vol. 4140, pp. 108–117. Springer, Heidelberg (2006)
9. Castelfranchi, C., de Rosis, F., Falcone, R., Pizzutilo, S.: Personality traits and social attitudes in multi-agent cooperation. Appl. Artif. Intell. 12(7–8), 649–675 (1998). Special Issue on 'Socially Intelligent Agents'
10. Cirillo, M., Karlsson, L., Saffiotti, A.: Human-aware task planning: An application to mobile robots. ACM Trans. Intell. Syst. Technol. 1(2), 15:1–15:26 (2010). http://doi.acm.org/10.1145/1869397.1869404
11. Dryer, C.: Getting personal with computers: how to design personalities for agents. Appl. Artif. Intell. 13(3), 273–295 (1999)
12. Du, H., Huhns, M.N.: Determining the effect of personality types on human-agent interactions. In: 2013 IEEE/WIC/ACM International Joint Conferences on Web Intelligence (WI) and Intelligent Agent Technologies (IAT), vol. 2, pp. 239–244. IEEE, November 2013
13. Durupinar, F., Allbeck, J., Pelechano, N., Badler, N.: Creating crowd variation with the OCEAN personality model. In: Padgham, Parkes, Müller, Parsons (eds.) Proceedings of the 7th International Conference on Autonomous Agents and Multiagent Systems (AAMAS 2008), pp. 1217–1220. IFAAMAS (2008)
14. Egges, A., Kshirsagar, S., Magnenat-Thalmann, N.: Generic personality and emotion simulation for conversational agents. Comput. Anim. Virtual Worlds 15, 1–13 (2004)
15. Furnham, A.: The big five versus the big four: the relationship between the Myers-Briggs type indicator (MBTI) and NEO-PI five factor model of personality. Pers. Individ. Differ. 21(2), 303–307 (1996)
16. John, O.P., Srivastava, S.: The big-five trait taxonomy: history, measurement, and theoretical perspectives. In: Pervin, L.A., John, O.P. (eds.) Handbook of Personality: Theory and Research, pp. 102–138. The Guilford Press, New York (1999)
17. Kirsch, A., Kruse, T., Sisbot, E.A., Alami, R., Lawitzky, M., Brscic, D., Hirche, S., Basili, P., Glasauer, S.: Plan-based control of joint human-robot activities. KI - Künstliche Intelligenz 24(3), 223–231 (2010)
18. Klein, G., Woods, D.D., Bradshaw, J.M., Hoffmann, R.R., Feltovich, P.J.: Ten challenges for making automation a 'team player' in joint human-agent activity. Hum. Cent. Comput. 19(6), 91–95 (2004)
19. Kurtz, J.E., Parrish, C.L.: Semantic response consistency and protocol validity in structured personality assessment: the case of the NEO-PI-R. J. Pers. Assess. 76(2), 315–332 (2001)
20. Lützenberger, M., Albayrak, S.: Current frontiers in reproducing human driver behavior. In: Proceedings of the 46th Summer Computer Simulation Conference 2014, pp. 514–521 (2014)
21. McCrea, R.R., Costa, P.: Reinterpreting the Myers-Briggs type indicators from the perspective of the five-factor model of personality. J. Pers. 57(1), 17–40 (1989)
22. McCrea, R.R., John, O.P.: An introduction to the five-factor model and its applications. J. Pers. 60(2), 175–215 (1992)
23. Myers, I.B., Byers, P.B.: Gifts Differing: Understanding Personality Type, 2nd edn. Nicholas Brealey Publishing, Boston (1995)
24. O'Connor, B.P.: A quantitative review of the comprehensiveness of the five-factor model in relation to popular personality inventories. Assessment 9, 188–203 (2002)

25. Paunonen, S.V., Jackson, D.N.: What is beyond the big five? plenty!. J. Pers. **68**(5), 821–835 (2000)
26. Pittenger, D.J.: Cautionary comments regarding the Myers-Briggs type indicator. Consult. Psychol. J. Pract. Res. **57**(3), 210–221 (2005)
27. Prada, R., Paiva, A.: Human-agent interaction: challenges for bringing humans and agents together. In: Proceedings of the 3rd International Workshop on Human-Agent Interaction Design and Models (HAIDM 2014) at the 13th International Conference on Agent and Multi-Agent Systems (AAMAS 2014), pp. 1–10. IFAA-MAS (2014)
28. Rao, A.S., Georgeff, M.P.: BDI agents: from theory to practice. In: Lesser, V., Gasser, L. (eds.) Proceedings of the First International Conference on Multiagent Systems (ICMAS 1995), pp. 312–319. AAAI, The MIT Press, April 1995
29. Salvit, J., Sklar, E.: Toward a Myers-Briggs type indicator model of agent behavior in multiagent teams. In: Bosse, T., Geller, A., Jonker, C.M. (eds.) MABS 2010. LNCS, vol. 6532, pp. 28–43. Springer, Heidelberg (2011). http://dl.acm.org/citation.cfm?id=1946224.1946228
30. Salvit, J., Sklar, E.: Modulating agent behavior using human personality type. In: Proceedings of the Workshop on Human-Agent Interaction Design and Models (HAIDM) at Autonomous Agents and MultiAgent Systems (AAMAS), pp. 145–160 (2012)
31. de Silva, L., Padgham, L.: A comparison of BDI based real-time reasoning and HTN based planning. In: Webb, G.I., Yu, X. (eds.) AI 2004. LNCS (LNAI), vol. 3339, pp. 1167–1173. Springer, Heidelberg (2004)
32. Sisbot, E.A., Marin-Urias, L.F., Alami, R., Simeon, T.: A human aware mobile robot motion planner. IEEE Trans. Robot. **23**(5), 874–883 (2007)
33. Talman, S., Hadad, M., Gal, Y., Kraus, S.: Adapting to agents' personalities in negotiation. In: Pechoucek, M., Steiner, D., Thompson, S. (eds.) Proceedings of the 4th International Joint Conference on Autonomous Agents and Multiagent Systems (AAMAS), pp. 383–389. ACM, New York (2005)
34. Tapus, A., Matarić, M.J., Scassellati, B.: The grand challenges in socially assistive robotics. IEEE Robot. Autom. Mag. **14**(1), 35–42 (2007)
35. Terracciano, A., Costa Jr., P.T., McCrae, R.R.: Personality plasticity after age 30. Pers. Soc. Psychol. B **32**(8), 999–1009 (2006)
36. Wilks, L.: The stability of personality over time as a function of personality trait dominance. Griffith Univ. Undergrad. Stud. Psychol. J. **1**, 1–9 (2009)
37. Wooldridge, M.: Reasoning About Rational Agents. Intelligent robotics and autonomous agents. The MIT Press, Cambridge (2000)

A Trust-Based Situation Awareness Model

Reyhan Aydoğan[1]([✉]), Alexei Sharpanskykh[2], and Julia Lo[3]

[1] Interactive Intelligence Group,
Delft University of Technology, Delft, The Netherlands
R.Aydogan@tudelft.nl
[2] Aerospace Engineering Department,
Delft University of Technology, Delft, The Netherlands
O.A.Sharpanskykh@tudelft.nl
[3] Policy, Organization, Law and Gaming,
Delft University of Technology, Delft, The Netherlands
J.C.Lo@tudelft.nl

Abstract. Trust is a social phenomenon that impacts the situation awareness of individuals and indirectly their decision-making. However, most of the existing computational models of situation awareness do not take interpersonal trust into account. Contrary to those models, this study introduces a computational, agent-based situation awareness model incorporating trust to enable building more human-like decision making tools. To illustrate the proposed model, a simulation case study has been conducted in the airline operation control domain. According to the results of this study, the trustworthiness of information sources had a significant effect on airline operation controller's situation awareness.

Keywords: Situation awareness · Trust · Agent-based modeling

1 Introduction

Decision makers in complex sociotechnical systems, such as airline operation control and train traffic control centers, often encounter complex and dynamic situations that require optimal decisions to be made rapidly based on the available information. The sustainability of such complex systems is highly dependent on the quality of decisions made in these situations. The concept of *situation awareness* has been identified as an important contributor to the quality of decision-making in complex, dynamically changing environments [6,12]. According to one of the most cited definitions, provided by Endsley [5], the concept of situation awareness refers to the level of awareness that an individual has of a situation and an operator's dynamic understanding of 'what is going on'.

In complex and dynamic environments, there is a vast amount of information flows that shape the decision maker's situation awareness. To understand how situation awareness is formed in such environments, it is crucial to understand how decision makers treat the information received from diverse sources. Imagine that information gathered from two information sources is conflicting.

© Springer International Publishing Switzerland 2015
N. Bulling (Ed.): EUMAS 2014, LNAI 8953, pp. 19–34, 2015.
DOI: 10.1007/978-3-319-17130-2_2

Which information source should be taken into account in decision making? In general, the choice would depend not only on the content of information, but also on the trustworthiness of the information source [11]. As the trustworthiness of information sources affects decision maker's assessment of the situation, it is important to incorporate interpersonal trust in computational models of situation awareness.

To the best of our knowledge, interpersonal trust has not been taken into account while modeling the situation awareness (SA) of an intelligent software agent. To address this gap, in this paper we propose a novel, computational agent-based model of SA, which integrates SA with trust. Our model is based on the theoretical three-level SA model of Endsley [5]. Level 1 involves the perception by an individual of elements in the situation. At Level 2 data perceived at Level 1 are being interpreted and understood in relation to the individual's tasks and goals. At Level 3 the individual predicts future states of the systems and elements in the environment based on his/her current state.

In the proposed model, SA of an agent is represented by a belief network, in which beliefs are activated by communicated or observed information, as well as by propagation of belief activation in the network. The perceived trustworthiness of an information source and the degree of (un)certainty of information provided by this source determine to what extent the communicated or observed information contributes to the activation level of the corresponding belief. The perceived trustworthiness of a source can be evaluated by taking into account direct experience with the source, categorization, and reputation [7]. Furthermore, trust is context dependent. For example, when the context is "repairing an instrument problem of a particular aircraft" one's trust in an aircraft maintenance engineer would probably be higher than one's trust in a pilot. However, one's trust in a pilot might be higher in another context such as "landing an aircraft in a rainy weather". Moreover, a similarity between opinions of individuals has a high impact on their trust relationship [9]. These arguments are also in line with Morita and Burns' model on trust and situation awareness formation [13]. Following these arguments, an experience based trust model from the literature has been adopted in our paper to model the trustworthiness of information sources [8,18].

A case study in the airline operation control domain has been conducted to validate the applicability of our model, and an agent-based simulation has been developed to investigate the effect of trust on the airline operation controller's situation awareness in the case study. The results of our study support that the trustworthiness of the information sources has a significant influence on decision maker's situation awareness.

The rest of this paper is organized as follows. In Sect. 2 related work is discussed. The proposed situation awareness model is explained in Sect. 3. Section 4 describes the case study and experimental results. Section 5 provides conclusions with a review of the contribution of this research and future work.

2   Related Work

In simple terms situation awareness (SA) refers to knowing what is happening around oneself [6]. The specific definition and operationalization of SA has been strongly debated amongst researchers in the nineties, whereas two main streams could be identified: the traditional information-processing approach in psychology versus ecological psychology [21]. Basically, these two theoretical views differentiate on the extent the natural environment plays a role in relation to an individual's cognition and the relationship between perception and action. Thus, in accordance with the information-processing school, SA and performance can be seen as separable concepts, whereas the ecological school considers them as inseparable. Another disagreement is whether situation awareness is seen as respectively a product or state, or as a process. Following the debate on the different approaches, Endsley's three-level model of situation awareness has received the predominant support for defining and operationalizing the situation awareness of individual operators [17]. This approach takes upon the information-processing perspective, in which situation awareness is seen as a state and mental models are identified to provide an input to the development of the comprehension of elements in the situation (level 2) and the projection of these elements in the near future (level 3 SA) [5]. Mental models can be seen as long-term memory structures [5]. More specifically, they can be defined as "mechanisms whereby humans are able to generate descriptions of system purpose and form, explanations of system functioning and observed system states, and predictions of future states" (p. 7) [16].

   The role of mental models in developing SA as defined by this psychological approach have been the basis in developing computational models for software agents. In particular, in developing a computational agent-based model of SA, Hoogendoorn et al. [10] connected the observation, belief formation in the current situation and related mental models of an agent to the formation of the agent's belief in the future situation. So et al. [19] proposed another agent-based model of SA, in which SA is considered as a form of a meta-level control over deliberation of agents about their intentions, plans and actions. Another computational model developed by Aydoğan et al. [1] considers formation of SA as interplay between possible actions and predicted consequences. To the best of our knowledge, integration of SA and trust has not been considered in agent-based modelling before. However, recently experimental studies on relationships between trust and SA were performed involving human subjects in the context of social games [14,20]. These studies have indeed confirmed that trust plays an important role in formation and maintenance of SA of humans. In particular, they established that trust impacted the reasoning of subjects of the experiment about the strategy choices in the game. Previously, an important role of trust for SA was also acknowledged by researchers from the human factors area [15]. In particular, they argued that trust in automation has important consequences for the quality of mental models and SA of operators, and thus should be taken seriously by system designers.

3   Situation Awareness Model

In the proposed model, the SA of an agent is represented by a belief network - a directed graph with the nodes representing agent's beliefs and the edges representing dependencies between beliefs. In our model belief networks have similarities with neural networks in the way that beliefs may contribute positively (reinforce) or negatively (inhibit) to the activation of other beliefs. As such, the activation of beliefs is propagated through the network. In line with the model of Endsley, based on the perceived information (Level 1), some nodes of the network will be activated. This activation will spread further through the network, representing the process of comprehension (Level 2) and projection (Level 3). We assume that the perception of the information is performed via sensors, through which the agent receives observations from the environment and communication from diverse information sources. This information is incorporated into the agent's belief network to the extent the agent trusts the information source providing the information.

Similar to the Hoogendoorn *et al.*'s situation awareness model [10], two types of beliefs, *simple beliefs* and *complex beliefs* are distinguished in our model. Simple beliefs are leaf nodes in a belief network. They may be generated by the perception of observed or communicated information. Complex beliefs are obtained by aggregating multiple beliefs, e.g. by using mental models and reasoning. Both simple and complex beliefs are updated after obtaining relevant observed or communicated information. To illustrate this, consider an example depicted in Fig. 1. In this example the airline operation controller observes that a storm is approaching Canberra airport. Based on this observation a simple belief is created. Similarly, based on the information communicated by the engineer "the repair of the aircraft NBO takes longer than four hours" another simple belief is generated. These two beliefs activate the controller's complex belief, "the repair of the aircraft NBO will be delayed". Note that according to the domain expert the second simple belief is a better predictor for the complex belief than the first simple belief, which is indicated in the weights of the corresponding edges. Furthermore, to generate a conclusive complex belief both simple beliefs need to be activated.

Fig. 1. An example of a complex belief in the airline traffic control domain

Each belief has a confidence value denoting to what extent the agent is certain of that belief. Over time, the confidence of some beliefs may change (e.g. increase or decrease depending on environmental inputs about the content of the belief). Equation 1 shows how the belief confidence value is updated in general, regardless of its type. In this formula, $C_{i,B}(t + \Delta t)$ represents *Agent i*'s updated confidence value about the belief B at time point $t + \Delta t$ and $C_{i,B}(t)$ denotes the confidence of that belief at time t. B is a belief state property expressed using some state language, e.g., a predicate logic. As both past and current experiences play a role in the situation assessment of an individual, this is taken into account in updating the confidence of a belief in our model. The parameter α determines to what extent the past experiences are taken into account in the updated confidence value of a belief. This parameter may be set dynamically for each particular application by taking the environmental factors into consideration. For instance, the faster the environment changes, the lower value α will take. Moreover, the more sensitive the belief system to changes, the lower value this parameter should be assigned. $F_{i,B}(t)$ denotes *Agent i*'s *confidence value change* at time point t. This change is based on the perceived environmental inputs at time t.

$$C_{i,B}(t + \Delta t) = (\alpha * C_{i,B}(t)) + ((1 - \alpha) * F_{i,B}(t)) \tag{1}$$

$F_{i,B}(t)$ is calculated differently for simple and complex beliefs. First let us consider how it is calculated for simple beliefs. Information supporting a simple belief might be received from different sources at the same time. This means that the confidence value change of a belief should be evaluated by aggregating information from all information sources.

Assume that there are inputs from n sources regarding belief B at time t, then the confidence value change of this belief is estimated as specified in Eq. 2, where $EI_{i,B,j}(t)$ denotes the evaluated information, which was gathered from the jth source by *Agent i* regarding the belief B.

$$F_{i,B}(t) = Aggr(EI_{i,B,1}(t), ..., EI_{i,B,n}(t)) \tag{2}$$

Note that the type of aggregation of the evaluated information components EI may vary according to the person's personality traits. Following one of the Big Five dimensions, the trait "agreeableness" has been related to being tolerant, cooperative and trusting [2]. Thus, if the person is skeptical or uncooperative, then MIN function could be used for aggregation, while MAX function would be more appropriate for trusting or positively thinking people. Alternatively, we may aggregate EI values by means of a weighted sum, where different weights may be assigned to each information source. In particular, the weights may be assigned according to the extent to which the agent is inclined to trust those information sources. Note that when the agent observes information in the environment, the corresponding weight may be determined by the trust of the agent to itself. There could be situations in which an agent does not trust its observations fully (e.g. when the agent is stressed). For instance, consider that the airline operation controller observes the weather himself and he also receives weather forecast information from a service point. All this information is aggregated to determine the confidence value of the belief "A storm is approaching". This example is illustrated in Fig. 2 where the information fusion box represents the aggregation function.

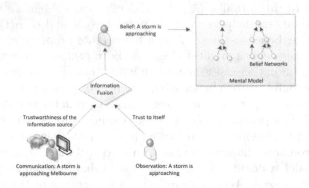

Fig. 2. A belief update by aggregating information from different information sources

Equation 3 shows how to evaluate information received from j^{th} source. If the information is obtained by communication from an information source $Agent j$, then ω_j is equal to 1 and the evaluated information is defined by multiplying $Agent$ i's trust in $Agent$ j w.r.t. domain D by $Agent$ j's confidence of belief B where $j \neq i$. If the information is observed, then ω_j is equal to 0 and the evaluated information is defined by multiplying $Agent$ i's trust in itself w.r.t. domain D by $Agent$ i's confidence of its observation ($O_B(t)$). In this formula, domain D is a set of state properties B, over which beliefs could be formed. For example, if B is "the technical problem in the aircraft can be fixed in one hour", then D may be the aircraft maintenance domain. Note that state properties are expressed using a standard multi-sorted first-order predicate language. An agent may have a high trust in another agent w.r.t. some domain D (e.g., driving a car) and at the same time a low trust in the same agent w.r.t. another domain D (e.g. flying an aircraft).

$$EI_{i,B,j}(t) = (\omega_j * T_{i,j,D}(t) * C_{j,B}(t)) + ((1 - \omega_j) * T_{i,i,D} * O_B(t))) \qquad (3)$$

Here, one of the important issues is how to model the trustworthiness of an information source ($T_{i,j,D}(t)$) in the specific sense that it determines to what extent the information provided by the information source is incorporated in the agent's belief network.

A variety of trust models have been proposed in trust literature. Many of these models identify experience as an essential basis of trust, e.g., [8,11,18]. The models differ in the way how they represent experience and how different experiences are aggregated over time. In this study, we adopt the experience-based trust as shown in Eq. 4 proposed by Şensoy et $al.$ [18] where $r(w)$ and $s(w)$ denotes the functions that map the opinion w to positive and negative evidence respectively. That corresponds to the ratio of positive evidence to the all evidence, which takes the prior trust value, a, into account.

$$E(w,a) = \frac{r(w) + a * 2}{r(w) * s(w) * 2} \qquad (4)$$

To define the mapping functions, we adopt the approach introduced in [8], where the authors estimated the trust based on the difference between the agent's own belief and the information source's belief. This is also supported by the principle from social science that the closer the opinions of the interacting agents, the higher the mutual influence of the agents is or will be, and, thus, the more the tendency of the agents to accept information will be [4]. Additionally, it is proposed that a higher similarity between individuals is related to a higher degree of trust [22].

In our model the belief differences are calculated according to Eq. 5. Here, Agent i believes that Agent j believes B with the confidence $C_{i,belief(j,B)}(t)$. An option is to infer an agent's estimation of a confidence value is through observation. Alternatively, through communication the agent can directly ask the other agent for its confidence value.

$$L_{i,j,B}(t) = |C_{i,B}(t) - C_{i,belief(j,B)}(t)| \qquad (5)$$

To decide whether $L_{i,j,B}(t)$ represents a positive or negative evidence that can be used in Eq. 4, a threshold value μ is introduced. If $(1 - L_{i,j,P}(t))$ is greater than μ, it is taken as a positive evidence (see Eq. 7); otherwise, it is taken as a negative evidence (see Eq. 8). Thus, trust $T_{i,j,D}(t)$ is estimated according to Eq. 6.

$$T_{i,j,D}(t) = \frac{r(i,j,D,t) + a * 2}{r(i,j,D,t) * s(i,j,D,t) * 2} \qquad (6)$$

$$r(i,j,D,t) = \frac{\sum_{P \in D} x_{i,j,P,t}}{|D|}, \text{ where } x_{i,j,P,t} = \begin{cases} 1 \text{ if } (1 - L_{i,j,P}(t)) > \mu \\ 0 \text{ otherwise} \end{cases} \qquad (7)$$

$$s(i,j,D,t) = \frac{\sum_{P \in D} y_{i,j,P,t}}{|D|} \text{ where } y_{i,j,P,t} = \begin{cases} 0 \text{ if } (1 - L_{i,j,P}(t)) > \mu \\ 1 \text{ otherwise} \end{cases} \qquad (8)$$

For complex beliefs, confidence value change $F_{i,B}(t)$ is calculated based on two types of updates. When an agent receives information regarding complex belief S, $F_{i,B}(t)$ is calculated in the same way as for the simple beliefs, according to Eq. 2. When B is activated by a propagation in the belief network, $F_{i,B}(t)$ is estimated by Eq. 9 proposed by Farrahi et al. [8]. In this formula, θ denotes the set of beliefs which contribute positively or negatively to complex belief B, $w_{r,B}$ is the weight of the edge between contributing belief r and belief B in the belief network, and β and γ are respectively the steepness and threshold parameters of the logistic function. Weights of edges may have negative values; in such a casethey represent inhibition edge in a belief network. Note that trust is implicitly included in Eq. 9 through aggregation of simple belief confidence values.

$$F_{i,B}(t) = \frac{1}{1 + e^{-\gamma \sum\limits_{r \in \theta \wedge r \neq B} C_{i,r}(t) * w_{r,B} + \beta}} \tag{9}$$

4 Case Study

To analyze the proposed situation awareness model, a case study has been constructed by drawing on airline operations control scenarios that Bruce designed and conducted [3]. These scenarios aimed at understanding the decision making process of airline operation controllers who guide domestic and international flights in airline Operations Control Centers (OCC). In the case study, our focus is to model the airline operation controller's situation awareness with the proposed approach. Figure 3 illustrates the belief network of the airline operation controller (AOC) according to the scenario explained below.

1. The aircraft NBO with flight number 876 took off from Melbourne to Canberra. At this moment, the airline operation controller believes that flight 876 will land in Canberra on time (AOC-B1) and the passengers will be able to catch their transit flight in Canberra (AOC-B2).
2. During the flight, the pilot encounters an instrument problem and he recalls that they had the same problem before taking off. Therefore, he informs the airline operation controller about this problem. When the airline operation controller learns about this problem, the following beliefs are activated:
   - AOC-B3: Aircraft NBO has the instrument problem during the flight from Melbourne (MEL) to Canberra (CBR).
   - AOC-B4: The problem of this type should be fixed before the next flight according to the Minimum Equipment List describing possible problems, how and when they should be fixed.
   - The controller does not know whether this problem can be fixed in Canberra; therefore, under high uncertainty he will believe the following two beliefs related to two possible decision options, which are in conflict with each other:
     • AOC-B5: The problem can be fixed in Canberra (CBR).
     • AOC-B9: The problem should be fixed in Melbourne (MEL).
   - Therefore, his confidence about the belief AOC-B6: The flight can continue to CBR, will decrease.
   - That also decreases his confidence about AOC-B1 and AOC-B2.
3. After that, the airline operation controller contacts a maintenance engineer in Melbourne to inquire about the instrument problem. The engineer is aware that NBO had the same problem before taking off and believes that the reparation of the reoccurred instrument problem would take about four hours. The engineer believes that the instrument problem is significantly more complex and needs an expert who would be able to fix it. He believes that the engineer in Canberra has not done this type of repair before; therefore, the problem

should be fixed in Melbourne. That means the flight 876 should return to Melbourne for a proper fix. After obtaining this information, the airline operation controller does the following modification of his belief network:
- This communicated information reduces the confidence of AOC-B6 and increases the confidence of AOC-B8, AOC-B9 and AOC-B10.
- AOC-B8: There is no expert to fix the problem in CBR.
- AOC-B9: The problem should be fixed in MEL.
- AOC-B10: The aircraft NBO needs to turn back to Melbourne. That decreases the confidence of AOC-B1 and AOC-B2.

4. After taking into consideration the information from the maintenance engineer in Melbourne, the airline operation controller decides to contact the OCC maintenance engineer as a second opinion in order to make the right decision. It is worth noting that returning the aircraft to Melbourne is a very costly option since the passengers will not arrive on time and some of them will not be able to catch their transit flight. The OCC maintenance engineer confirms the estimated reparation time, but he also thinks that it is possible to send a more experienced maintenance engineer from Sydney to Canberra to fix the problem. Through this way, the instrument problem can be fixed in Canberra. Furthermore, he also believes that the problem is not sufficiently severe to restrain the flight from continuing to its destination. Thus, the flight can continue to CBR. After this conversation, the airline operation controller maintains his belief network in the following way:
   - Two following beliefs are added:
     • AOC-B11: An experienced engineer from Sydney can be sent to CBR to fix the problem.
     • AOC-B7: An expert can fix the problem in Canberra.
   - These beliefs trigger the following beliefs:
     • AOC-B5: The problem can be fixed in CBR.
     • AOC-B6: The flight can continue to CBR.
     • AOC-B1: The flight 876 will land in CBR on time.
     • AOC-B2: Passengers will catch their transit flight in CBR.
   - At the same time, the controller decreases the confidence of AOC-8, AOC-9, and AOC-10.

5. Lastly, the airline operation controller receives weather forecast information from the flight planning controller about a potential fog problem in Sydney. Based on the communicated information, the airline operation controller maintains his belief network as follows:
   - AOC-B12: There is fog in Sydney.
   - AOC-B13: An experienced maintenance engineer from Sydney cannot be sent to CBR to fix the problem.
   - This information decreases the belief confidence of AOC-B11, AOC-B7, AOC-B5, AOC-B6, AOC-B1, and AOC-B2 while it causes an increase in AOC-B8, AOC-B9, and AOC-10.

To analyze this case study in detail, we have developed an agent-based simulation in Java. The belief network depicted in Fig. 3 has been used to model

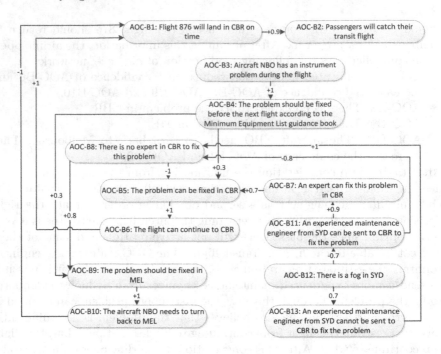

Fig. 3. Belief network of the Airline Operation Controller (AOC) for the given scenario

the airline operation controller's situation awareness. Note that the initial belief network was built based on the empirical information from Bruce [3] and interviews with domain experts in which operators' reasoning about the problem was captured. At runtime, information required to build the belief network is retrieved from the mental model, where it's stored, to the working memory [10]. The initial confidence values for AOC-B1, AOC-B2, AOC-B6 are taken as 1, while 0 is assigned to the rest (see the first row of Table 1). Since the environment in which the airline controller operates changes rapidly, a low value (0.05) has been assigned to the parameter α. This parameter determines to what extent the past experiences are taken into account in the update of the beliefs. The parameters for updating the complex beliefs - γ and β - are taken as 5 and 2.5 respectively. These values correspond to an unbiased agent (i.e., an agent without strong under- or overestimation of the belief confidence values). In the first test setting, it is assumed that the airline operation controller trusts all information sources fully and equally. Note that to focus on the gradual formation of situation awareness based on information from different sources, constant trust values were used in this case study; however, in a more complex scenario having multiple interactions between the same agents, the trust values can be updated after each interaction as explained in Sect. 3. At each simulation time step, the information described in the scenario above is communicated to the airline operation controller and based on this communication, s/he maintains his/her belief network. The details of this communication is listed below:

- At $t = 1$, the pilot informs the airline operation controller about AOC-B3. The controller's trust in the pilot is taken as $T_{AOC,pilot,Aircraft}(1) = 1.0$, and the confidence of the pilot about AOC-B3 is taken as $C_{pilot,AOC-B3}(1) = 0.90$.
- At $t = 2$ the maintenance engineer in Melbourne informs the controller about AOC-B8. The controller's trust in the maintenance engineer is taken as $T_{AOC,ME,Repair}(2) = 1.0$, and the confidence of the maintenance engineer is taken as $C_{ME,AOC-B8}(2) = 0.85$.
- At $t = 3$, the OCC maintenance engineer informs the controller about AOC-B11. The controller's trust in the OCC maintenance engineer is taken as $T_{AOC,OCC,Repair}(3) = 1.0$, and the confidence of the OCC engineer is taken as $C_{OCC,AOC-B11}(3) = 0.90$.
- At $t = 4$, the flight planning controller informs the airline operation controller about AOC-B12. The controller's trust in the planning controller is taken as $T_{AOC,PC,Weather}(4) = 1)$, and the confidence of the planning controller is taken as $C_{PC,AOC-B12}(4) = 0.95$.

Table 1 shows the estimated belief confidence values of the controller agent at each time step. As seen from Table 1, the generated belief confidence values are consistent with the given scenario. When the pilot informed the airline operation controller about the instrument problem ($t = 2$), the controller's confidence about AOC-B1 and AOC-B2 drastically decreased (0.14 and 0.18 respectively). The confidence values for AOC-B5 and AOC-B9 are the same since at that moment the controller does not know where exactly the problem can be fixed. When the maintenance engineer in Melbourne informed the controller that there was no expert to fix this problem in Canberra ($t = 3$), the controller's belief confidence about AOC-B8, AOC-B9 and AOC-B10 increased. That means that he believes that the aircraft NBO needs to turn back to Melbourne. After the OCC maintenance engineer's advice ($t = 4$), the airline operation controllers started to believe that the problem can be fixed in Canberra and the flight can continue to Canberra with the confidence of 0.72. After that, the flight planning controller noticed that there is a fog in Sydney, which means that the experienced engineer could not be sent from Sydney to Canberra. This information reduced the airline operation controller's confidence of AOC-B5 and AOC-B6 while increasing his confidence on AOC-B9 and AOC-B10. As the result, the controller was more inclined to make the decision of returning the aircraft to Melbourne.

Table 1. Belief confidence values at each time step when $\beta = 2.5$ and $\gamma = 5$

Time	C1	C2	C3	C4	C5	C6	C7	C8	C9	C10	C11	C12	C13
1	1.00	1.00	0.00	0.00	0.00	1.00	0.00	0.00	0.00	0.00	0.00	0.00	0.00
2	0.14	0.18	0.86	0.81	0.21	0.23	0.00	0.00	0.21	0.18	0.00	0.00	0.00
3	0.01	0.08	0.86	0.81	0.01	0.09	0.00	0.81	0.84	0.81	0.00	0.00	0.00
4	0.41	0.33	0.86	0.81	0.72	0.72	0.75	0.04	0.28	0.28	0.86	0.00	0.00
5	0.02	0.10	0.86	0.81	0.06	0.13	0.12	0.58	0.72	0.72	0.05	0.90	0.63

C_i stands for $C_{AOC,AOC-Bi}(t)$ in our belief system.

4.1   Studying the Effect of β and γ Parameters

In this section, the effect of β and γ parameters has been studied. Recall that β and γ are the parameters adjusting the shape of the logistic function that is used in the calculation of the agent's confidence value change of a given complex belief as seen in Eq. 9. When β and γ are taken as 2.5 and 5.0, respectively, this corresponds to an unbiased agent, i.e., an agent without strong under- or over-estimation of the belief confidence values. When β and γ are taken as 5 and 10 respectively, this corresponds to a biased agent that is more inclined to under-estimate the beliefs with a low confidence value and to overestimate the beliefs with a high confidence value. For instance, when the weighted sum of the belief confidence values supporting the given complex belief is equal to 0.3, the biased agent updates the confidence value change as 0.12 (an example for underestimation) while the unbiased agent updates as 0.27. However, when the weighted sum of belief confidence values is high, for example 0.85, the biased agent estimates it as 0.97. Figure 4 depicts the shape of this function with different values of these parameters.

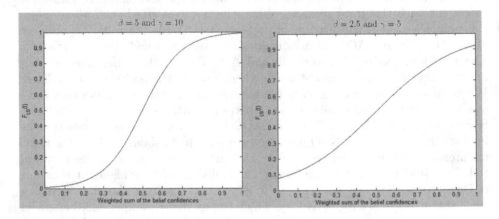

Fig. 4. Agent's confidence value change function for a complex belief

To analyze how biases of the agent would affect the simulation results, we run the same scenario with only β and γ parameters changed to 5 and 10 respectively. Table 1 represents the belief confidence values for the unbiased agent, while Table 2 shows the corresponding results for the biased agent. Since our case study is sensitive to the incoming information, α is taken as 0.05 in both settings. When we compare the results for both agents, it can be seen that the biased agent has higher belief confidence values for the complex beliefs, which confidence values are high, than the unbiased agent (e.g. 0.94 versus 0.72 for AOC-B10 at $t = 5$, 0.92 versus 0.72 for AOC-B5 at $t = 4$). For the beliefs with low confidence values the opposite can be observed, since the biased agent under-estimates them (e.g. 0.06 versus 0.14 for AOC-B1 at $t = 2$, 0.08 versus 0.28 for AOC-B9 at $t = 4$).

Table 2. Belief confidence values at each time step when $\beta = 5$ and $\gamma = 10$

Time	C1	C2	C3	C4	C5	C6	C7	C8	C9	C10	C11	C12	C13
1	1.00	1.00	0.00	0.00	0.00	1.00	0.00	0.00	0.00	0.00	0.00	0.00	0.00
2	0.06	0.06	0.86	0.92	0.09	0.07	0.00	0.00	0.09	0.02	0.00	0.00	0.00
3	0.00	0.01	0.86	0.92	0.00	0.01	0.00	0.81	0.94	0.94	0.00	0.00	0.00
4	0.92	0.92	0.86	0.92	0.92	0.94	0.89	0.04	0.17	0.08	0.86	0.00	0.00
5	0.05	0.06	0.86	0.92	0.05	0.06	0.05	0.85	0.95	0.94	0.04	0.90	0.75

C_i stands for $C_{AOC,AOC-Bi}(t)$ in our belief system.

4.2 Investigating the Effect of α Parameter

In this section we analyze how the value of parameter α influences the belief update and, by implication, the situation awareness of the controller. Basically, this parameter determines to what extent the information perceived by the controller agent changes its beliefs. The low values should be chosen for the cases where the belief maintenance system is sensitive to the incoming information, while high values may be preferred for the cases where the agent should be more conservative w.r.t. belief update. Furthermore, this parameter may also reflect a personal characteristic such as openness to experience from the Five Factor Model [2]. Choosing the right value for the given scenario is crucial.

Table 3 shows the belief confidence values of the airline operation controller at the last time point of the simulation obtained using different α values. Here, we adopt the unbiased agent type where β and γ are 2.5 ad 5.0 respectively. According to the scenario we consider the confidence values for AOC-B8, AOC-B9 and AOC-10, in which they are expected to be high. As seen from the results, the most appropriate values are obtained when α is equal to 0.05 and 0.1 (low values). This is because the airline operation controller in the examined scenario is very sensitive to new information. The results are not well aligned with the case study, when α is 0.5 (high value), i.e. a conservative agent.

4.3 Analyzing the Effect of Trustworthiness of Information Sources

In order to study how the controller agent's trust in information sources affects its situation awareness, we run the same scenario with varying trust values, when

Table 3. The belief confidence values of the AOC for different values of α at t = 5

Case	C1	C2	C3	C4	C5	C6	C7	C8	C9	C10	C11	C12	C13
$\alpha = 0.05$	0.02	0.10	0.86	0.81	0.06	0.13	0.12	<u>0.58</u>	<u>0.72</u>	<u>0.72</u>	0.05	0.90	0.63
$\alpha = 0.1$	0.03	0.09	0.81	0.74	0.10	0.16	0.16	<u>0.45</u>	<u>0.57</u>	<u>0.56</u>	0.08	0.86	0.56
$\alpha = 0.2$	0.04	0.09	0.72	0.60	0.15	0.17	0.22	<u>0.25</u>	<u>0.35</u>	<u>0.33</u>	0.15	0.76	0.43
$\alpha = 0.5$	0.18	0.29	0.45	0.22	0.07	0.16	0.19	<u>0.14</u>	<u>0.19</u>	<u>0.17</u>	0.23	0.48	0.15

C_i stands for $C_{AOC,AOC-Bi}(5)$ in our belief system.

Table 4. The airline operation controller's trust value to each information source

Case	[Pilot]	[Engineer in MEL]	[OCC engineer]	[Planning controller]
1	1.0	1.0	1.0	1.0
2	1.0	0.2	1.0	1.0
3	1.0	1.0	0.2	1.0
4	1.0	1.0	1.0	0.2
5	1.0	0.2	1.0	0.2
6	1.0	1.0	0.2	0.2

α is taken equal to 0.1. Table 4 describes the test cases that we investigated and Table 5 shows the belief confidence values for each test case at t = 5.

It can be seen that for the first three cases the confidence values of beliefs AOC-B9 and AOC-10 are much higher than the confidence values of AOC-B5 and AOC-B6. In these cases the controller's trust in the flight planning controller is equal to one ($T_{AOC,PC,Weather}(4) = 1.0$). Since the airline operation controller trusts the planning controller fully, the information about the weather conditions in Sydney will have a negative influence on the confidence of AOC-B5 and AOC-B6 while activating AOC-B9 and AOC-B10. However, in the forth and fifth test cases, it is observed that the confidence values of AOC-B5 and AOC-B6 are a bit higher than those for AOC-B9 and AOC-10. This means that in these test cases the airline operation controller is more inclined to allow the flight to continue to Canberra. The airline operation controller's trust in the flight planning controller in these cases is low; therefore, it does not have a positive effect on the activation of AOC-B9 and AOC-B10. On the contrary, such an effect has not been observed in the last case because the airline operation controller's trust in the OCC maintenance in this case is low. This low value of trust causes a decrease in the confidence values of AOC-B5 and AOC-B6, while increasing the confidence of AOC-B9 and AOC-10. These results support our hypothesis that trust in information sources of an agent plays a crucial role in the development of the agent's situation awareness.

Table 5. The belief confidence values for the test cases in Table 4 at t = 5

Case	C1	C2	C3	C4	C5	C6	C7	C8	C9	C10	C11	C12	C13
1	0.03	0.09	0.81	0.74	0.10	0.16	0.16	0.45	0.57	0.56	0.08	0.86	0.56
2	0.05	0.11	0.81	0.74	0.11	0.17	0.16	0.44	0.56	0.53	0.08	0.86	0.56
3	0.01	0.08	0.81	0.74	0.04	0.10	0.09	0.51	0.62	0.62	0.02	0.86	0.56
4	0.10	0.12	0.81	0.74	0.27	0.27	0.18	0.08	0.26	0.24	0.12	0.17	0.12
5	0.13	0.14	0.81	0.74	0.28	0.29	0.18	0.08	0.25	0.22	0.12	0.17	0.12
6	0.05	0.09	0.81	0.74	0.17	0.16	0.10	0.11	0.28	0.26	0.06	0.17	0.12

C_i stands for $C_{AOC,AOC-Bi}(5)$ in our belief system.

5   Conclusion

In this paper a novel computational model for situation awareness of an intelligence agent has been proposed. The model is based on the theoretical three-level SA model of Endsley and Hoogendoorn's computational model of SA. The contribution of this work is threefold. First, a computational model for situation awareness that incorporates interpersonal trust is introduced. Second, a case study to validate the applicability of the model in real life domains has been conducted. Lastly, it has been shown for the given scenario that the trustworthiness of information sources has a significant impact on agent's situation awareness and by implication on its decision-making.

The proposed model can be used to develop a decision support tool for human operators in complex and dynamic sociotechnical systems to increase the quality of their decisions. To develop such a tool, the following aspects need to be addressed: (1) representing an extensive domain knowledge to capture diverse situations over which SA may be formed, (2) perceiving inputs from the environment, (3) reasoning about incoming information, and lastly (4) foreseeing the consequences of the actions to be taken. The focus was of this paper was on individual SA. As a future work, we shall study SA in teams, since it has a significant impact on the team performance. Another challenge for our future research is measuring individual and team SA in real life settings.

Acknowledgments. We thank Soufiane Bouarfa for his involvement and contribution in the development of the paper and especially the case study.

References

1. Aydoğan, R., Lo, J.C., Meijer, S.A., Jonker, C.M.: Modeling network controller decisions based upon situation awareness through agent-based negotiation. In: Meijer, S.A., Smeds, R. (eds.) ISAGA 2013. LNCS, vol. 8264, pp. 191–200. Springer, Heidelberg (2014)
2. Barrick, M.R., Mount, M.K.: The big five personality dimensions and job performance: a meta-analysis. Pers. Psychol. **1**(44), 1–26 (1991)
3. Bruce, P.J.: Understanding Decision-Making Processes in Airline Operations Control. Ashgate, Burlington (2011)
4. Byrne, D., Clore, G., Smeaton, G.: The attraction hypothesis: do similar attitudes affect anything? J. Pers. Soc. Psychol. **51**(6), 1167–1170 (1986)
5. Endsley, M.R.: Towards a theory of situation awareness in dynamic systems. Hum. Factors **37**(1), 32–64 (1995)
6. Endsley, M.R.: Theoretical underpinnings of situation awareness: a critical review. In: Endsley, M.R., Garland, D.J. (eds.) Situation Awareness Analysis and Measurement. Lawrence Erlbaum Associates, Mahwah (2000)
7. Falcone, R., Castelfranchi, C.: Generalizing trust: inferencing trustworthiness from categories. In: Falcone, R., Barber, S.K., Sabater-Mir, J., Singh, M.P. (eds.) TRUST 2008. LNCS (LNAI), vol. 5396, pp. 65–80. Springer, Heidelberg (2008)

8. Farrahi, K., Zia, K., Sharpanskykh, A., Ferscha, A., Muchnik, L.: Agent perception modeling for movement in crowds. In: Demazeau, Y., Ishida, T., Corchado, J.M., Bajo, J. (eds.) PAAMS 2013. LNCS (LNAI), vol. 7879, pp. 73–84. Springer, Heidelberg (2013)

9. Golbeck, J.A.: Computing and applying trust in web-based social networks. Ph.D. thesis, College Park, MD, USA (2005)

10. Hoogendoorn, M., Van Lambalgen, R.M., Treur, J.: Modeling situation awareness in human-like agents using mental models. In: Proceedings of the Twenty-Second International Joint Conference on Artificial Intelligence, IJCAI 2011, vol. 2, pp. 1697–1704. AAAI Press (2011)

11. Josang, A., Ismail, R., Boyd, C.: A survey of trust and reputation systems for online service provision. Decis. Support Syst. **43**(2), 618–644 (2007). Emerging Issues in Collaborative Commerce

12. Klein, G.: Sources of Power: How People Make Decisions. MIT Press, Cambridge (1998)

13. Morita, P.P., Burns, C.M.: Understanding interpersonal trust from a human factors perspective: insights from situation awareness and the lens model. Theor. Issues Ergon. Sci. **15**(1), 88–110 (2014)

14. ODonovan, J., Jones, R.E., Marusich, L.R., Teng, Y., Gonzalez, C., Höllerer, T.: A model-based evaluation of trust and situation awareness in the diners dilemma game. In: Proceedings of the 22nd Behavior Representation in Modeling & Simulation (BRIMS) Conference, pp. 11–14 (2013)

15. Parasuraman, R., Sheridan, T.B., Wickens, C.D.: Situation awareness, mental workload, and trust in automation: viable, empirically supported cognitive engineering constructs. J. Cogn. Eng. Decis. Making **2**(2), 140–160 (2008)

16. Rouse, W., Morris, N.: On looking into the black box: prospects and limits in the search for mental models. Technical report 85–2, Center for Man-Machine Systems Research (1985)

17. Salmon, P.M., Stanton, N.A., Walker, G.H., Jenkins, D.P.: What really is going on? review of situation awareness models for individuals and teams. Theor. Issues Ergon. Sci. **9**(4), 297–323 (2008)

18. Sensoy, M., Yilmaz, B., and Norman, T.J.: Stage: Stereotypical trust assessment through graph extraction. Comput. Intell. (2014)

19. So, R., Sonenberg, L.: Situation awareness in intelligent agents: foundations for a theory of proactive agent behavior. In: IEEE/WIC/ACM International Conference on Intelligent Agent Technology, (IAT 2004), pp. 86–92 (2004)

20. Teng, Y., Jones, R., Marusich, L., O'Donovan, J., Gonzalez, C., Hollerer. T.: Trust and situation awareness in a 3-player diner's dilemma game. In: 2013 IEEE International Multi-Disciplinary Conference on Cognitive Methods in Situation Awareness and Decision Support (CogSIMA), pp. 9–15, February 2013

21. Tenney, Y.J., Pew, R.W.: Situation awareness catches on: what? so what? now what? Rev. Hum. Factors Ergon. **2**, 1–34 (2006)

22. Winter, F., Kataria, M.: You are who your friends are: An experiment on trust and homophily in friendship networks. Jena Economic Research Papers 2013–044, Friedrich-Schiller-University Jena, Max-Planck-Institute of Economics, October 2013

Angerona - A Flexible Multiagent Framework for Knowledge-Based Agents

Patrick Krümpelmann[✉], Tim Janus, and Gabriele Kern-Isberner

Technische Universität Dortmund, Dortmund, Germany
patrick.kruempelmann@cs.tu-dortmund.de

Abstract. We present the ANGERONA framework for the implementation of knowledge-based agents with a strong focus on flexibility, extensibility, and compatibility with diverse knowledge representation formalisms. As the basis for this framework we propose and formalize a general concept of *compound agents* in which we consider agents to consist of hierarchies of interacting epistemic and functional components. Each epistemic component is instantiated by a knowledge representation formalism. Different knowledge representation formalisms can be used within one agent and different agents in the same system can be based on different agent architectures and can use different knowledge representation formalisms. Partially instantiations define sub-frameworks for, e. g., the development of BDI agents and variants thereof. The ANGERONA framework realizes this concept by means of a flexible *JAVA* plug-in architecture for the epistemic and the functional components of an agent. The epistemic plug-ins are based on the TWEETY *library* for knowledge representation, which provides various ready-for-use implementations and knowledge representation formalisms and a framework for the implementation of additional ones. ANGERONA already contains several partial and complete instantiations that implement several approaches. ANGERONA also features an environment plug-in for communicating agents and a flexible GUI to monitor the multiagent system and the inner workings of the agents, particularly the inspection of the dynamics of their epistemic states. ANGERONA and TWEETY are ready to use, well documented, and open source.

1 Introduction

A variety of logical formalisms with different expressivity and computational properties have been developed for knowledge representation with the agent paradigm in mind [1,2]. Especially non-monotonic formalisms are designed to deal with incomplete information and to enable an agent to act in uncertain environments. Moreover, the field of research on belief change has been working for over 25 years already on solutions on how to change an agent's beliefs in the light of new information [3]. Yet, very little of the approaches developed in these two fields of research are available in actual multiagent frameworks.

Our concept of component based agents and its realisation in the ANGERONA framework are designed to reduce this gap, to support the development of knowledge based, i. e. epistemic, agents based on logical formalisms for knowledge

© Springer International Publishing Switzerland 2015
N. Bulling (Ed.): EUMAS 2014, LNAI 8953, pp. 35–50, 2015.
DOI: 10.1007/978-3-319-17130-2_3

representation and reasoning, and to support the use of belief change operators based on belief change theory. Moreover, it facilitates the development of
divers agents with respect to their architecture and knowledge representation.
It allows the formation of multiagent systems comprising heterogeneous agents
which interact by communicating or in a common simulated environment.

The ANGERONA framework is based on the conceptual work on a hierarchical component-based agent model. In this, an agent comprises an epistemic state
and a functional component that can both be composed. This model is realized
on the basis on a plug-in architecture. These are based on knowledge representation plug-ins and on operator plug-ins respectively, and tied together by an
XML based script language and configuration files. The plug-in for the functional component is based on the general ANGERONA operator interface and the
corresponding operators provided by the angerona framework. For the knowledge representation plug-ins we integrated the TWEETY *library* for knowledge
representation [4]. The TWEETY library contains interfaces and implementations
for divers knowledge representation formalisms and inference and change operators for them. TWEETY is under active development, in which we participate.
It currently contains implementations for: first-order logic, ordinal conditional
functions, relational conditional logic, probabilistic conditional logic, relational
probabilistic conditional logic, markov logic, epistemic logic, description logic,
deductive argumentation, structured argumentation frameworks, defeasible logic
programming, probabilistic argumentation, answer set programming. Confer to
[4] for details and references. ANGERONA is open source and available on *github*[1],
as is TWEETY on *sourceforge*[2].

The ANGERONA agent architecture can be freely defined by specifying the
types of operators to be used and their order of execution. This way ANGERONA
allows to easily design different types of agents. Not only the used language for
knowledge representation can differ, but also to which amount an agent's functionality is logic based. It is, for instance, easily possible to realize the agent's
deliberation and means-ends reasoning by JAVA operators and simple data components, or by simple JAVA operators which make use of logical formalisms,
e. g. answer set programming (ASP) [5], ordinal conditional functions (OCF)
[6], argumentation formalisms [7], or propositional logic or horn logic, or any
other formalism from the TWEETY library.

While the general ANGERONA framework allows for a high degree of flexibility it also allows to define partially instantiated plug-ins and default agent
configurations, which represent sub-frameworks with more predefined structure
and functionality. The latter might fix the general agent cycle by specifying the
types of operators to be used and provide different implementations for these.
Hence, the sub-frameworks provide more support for easy and rapid development
of agents. We distinguish three different types of users in the ANGERONA framework: the *core developer* that uses ANGERONA as a toolkit to define its own agent
types; the *plug-in developer* that uses provided agent types and instantiates them

---

[1] https://github.com/Angerona.
[2] http://sourceforge.net/projects/tweety/.

with given or its own plug-ins; and the *knowledge engineer* that defines the background and initial knowledge, and all other initial instances of the components of the agents.

ANGERONA provides default implementations for BDI style agents and diverse extensions that can be modularly used to build agents. Complete multiagent systems of communicating agents using answer set programming, propositional logic and ordinal conditional functions for knowledge representation, including change operators for these based on belief change theory are implemented and available. These are used in the context of secrecy preserving agents for which scenarios and simulations are available. ANGERONA also features a plug-in interface for different environments, with a communication environment for agents implemented. A graphical user interface (GUI) allows the selection, execution, observation, and inspection of multi-agent simulations. The GUI can be extended by plug-ins to feature displays of specific knowledge representation formalisms, for instance dependency graphs.

In the next section we introduce the concept of compound agents that underlies the ANGERONA framework. Following on this we describe how this is realized in the agent framework of ANGERONA. Then we describe the multiagent framework of ANGERONA in the following section. Afterwards, we briefly describe how we used ANGERONA to build secrecy preserving agents. Finally, we discuss our framework and its relation to other frameworks, and we conclude.

2   Concept of Compound Agents

ANGERONA agents are based on a concept of hierarchical, component-based agent models with the goal of capturing a variety of agent architectures in a flexible and extensible way. In the following we give an overview of the main concepts of it. In this, a general *agent* instance is a tuple $(\mathcal{K}, \xi)$ comprising of an epistemic state $\mathcal{K} \in \mathcal{L}_{ES}$ from a given language $\mathcal{L}_{ES}$ and a functional component $\xi = (\circ, \mathsf{act})$. Further, we assume the set of possible actions Act and perceptions Per to be given. These might, for instance, be speech acts that are interchanged by the agents. Then, we require the operators of the functional component to be of the following types:

$$\circ : Per \times \mathcal{L}_{ES} \to \mathcal{L}_{ES} \text{ and } \mathsf{act} : \mathcal{L}_{ES} \to Act.$$

The language of the epistemic state might be a logical language, e. g. an answer set program or a conditional belief base, or a Cartesian product of (logical) languages, e. g. to represent the BDI components of an agent by the language $\mathcal{L}_B \times \mathcal{L}_D \times \mathcal{L}_I$. The epistemic state of an agent contains representations of its background knowledge about how the world works, and information coming from its perceptions, as well as its goals and know-how, and potentially more. The functional component of an agent consists of a change operator $\circ$, which adapts the current epistemic state of the agent upon reception of a perception, and an action operator act, which executes the next action based on the current epistemic state. The change of the epistemic state might involve different types of reasoning, such as non-monotonic reasoning, deliberation and means-ends reasoning. These are partially or completely based on logical inference. This means, that an agent's behavior is realized in parts by the functional component, and in parts by the knowledge representation and reasoning based on the epistemic state. How much of the agents behavior is defined by the epistemic state and how much by the functional component might differ largely; a pure deductive agent's behavior is entirely defined by its epistemic state, and a stateless agent entirely by its functional component. To capture these different types of agents we consider the epistemic state as well as the functional component to consist of hierarchical components. Compositions thereof define more structured agent models and can be further refined.

A compound epistemic state is a component, which again can either be atomic or compound. An atomic component $\mathcal{C}_a$ is an element from the components language $\mathcal{L}_{\mathcal{C}_a}$, e. g. a belief base BB from the language $\mathcal{P}(\mathcal{L}_{BB})$, such as an OCF-base or an answer set program. Belief operators of the form $Bel : \mathcal{P}(\mathcal{L}_{BB}) \rightarrow \mathcal{P}(\mathcal{L}_{BS})$ are applied by other operators to belief bases to determine the current belief set for it. For example, the (sceptical) ASP belief operator $Bel : \mathcal{P}(\mathcal{L}_{At}^{asp}) \rightarrow Lit$ is defined as $Bel(P) = \cap AS(P)$, with $AS(P)$ being the answer sets of P. Other operators for ASP might make use of preferences or might be defined for sequences of logic programs.

A compound component is a tuple of components, $\mathcal{C} = \langle \mathcal{C}_1, \ldots, \mathcal{C}_n \rangle$, and each component is an element of its language such that the language of a compound component is a cartesian product of languages: $\mathcal{L}_{\mathcal{C}} = \mathcal{L}_{\mathcal{C}_1} \times \cdots \times \mathcal{L}_{\mathcal{C}_n}$. In particular, each component can potentially have a different representation. The interaction of the components is realized by the functional component of the agent. In particular, for an epistemic state $\mathcal{K} \in \mathcal{L}_{ES}$ and functional component $\xi = (\circ, \mathsf{act})$ the change operator $\circ : Per \times \mathcal{L}_{ES} \rightarrow \mathcal{L}_{ES}$ can be realized by a single function or by a composition of explicit sub-functions. In the latter case sub-functions are applied to the epistemic state in sequential order. Each sub-function modifies a single component or a set of components of the epistemic state. The next function operates on the epistemic state that results from the modifications of the previous functions. This concept realizes the idea of an agent cycle. Typical agent cycles as the one of the BDI architecture can be easily formalized. For example, first the beliefs of the agent are modified given a perception by some function, then another function modifies the goals of the agent and then yet another function modifies the current plan of the agent, or revises the agent's plan library. Inner loops or concurrent execution of operators can be modeled by single operators which contain loops or concurrency. The resulting hierarchical agent model with compound epistemic state and compound functional component is illustrated in Fig. 1. Formally, a compound functional component consists of a change operator $\circ$ that is a composition of operators, i. e. $\circ =_{def} \circ_1 \cdot \ldots \cdot \circ_{n'}$, and an action function act.

We exemplify this model by showing how a basic BDI agent model can be realized. A *BDI agent* is a tuple $(\mathcal{K}_{BDI}, \xi_{BDI})$. The epistemic state is of the form $\mathcal{K}_{BDI} = \langle \mathcal{B}, \Delta, \mathcal{I} \rangle$ with the agent's beliefs $\mathcal{B} \subseteq \mathcal{L}_{\mathcal{B}}$, a set of desires $\Delta \subseteq \mathcal{L}_{\Delta}$ and a set of intentions $\mathcal{I} \subseteq \mathcal{L}_{\mathcal{I}}$, all of which might be belief bases of a

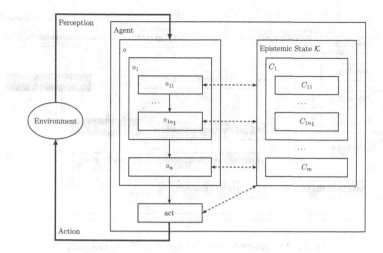

Fig. 1. Hierarchical agent model

knowledge representation formalism. We define the language of BDI epistemic states as $\mathcal{L}_{BDI}$. A functional BDI component $\xi_{BDI} = (\circ, \mathsf{act})$ consists of a change operator $\circ$ and an action operator act of the type $\circ : Per \times \mathcal{L}_{BDI} \to \mathcal{L}_{BDI}$ and $\mathsf{act} : \mathcal{L}_{BDI} \to Act$. The change operation can then be represented as $\circ_{BDI} =_{def} \circ_{\mathcal{B}} \cdot \circ_{\Delta} \cdot \circ_{\mathcal{I}}$. That is, an *BDI-epistemic-state* $\mathcal{K}_{BDI} = \langle \mathcal{B}, \Delta, \mathcal{I} \rangle$ is changed by a perception p such that $\mathcal{K}_{BDI} \circ_{BDI} p = \circ_{\mathcal{I}}(\circ_{\Delta}(\mathcal{K}_{BDI} \circ_{\mathcal{B}} p))$. More details about the concept of compound agents can be found in [8], here we continue with the presentation of its realization in the ANGERONA framework.

3   Agent Framework

ANGERONA agents consist of *agent components* which can be *epistemic components*, i.e. belief bases and associated operators, and other data components, or *functional components*, i.e. operators used for the agent cycle. Logic based components are based on the *belief base plug-in*. Operators for the agent cycle are based on the *operator plug-in*. For the realization of plug-ins in ANGERONA we use the *Java Simple Plugin Framework (JSPF)* [9].

The class diagram in Fig. 2 illustrates the realization of the conceptual model in the ANGERONA framework. An ANGERONA agent contains an epistemic state and a list of operators. An epistemic state consists of agent components. One type of agent components are belief bases which are defined via a belief base plug-in. The belief base plug-in implements the interfaces of the TWEETY library, in particular those for a belief base, a formula, a revision operator and a belief operator. Different belief operators might be available for the same formalism. Different agents might use the same knowledge representation formalism but different belief operators, and each agent might use different belief operators in different situations. We use, for example, families of belief operators that are ordered by

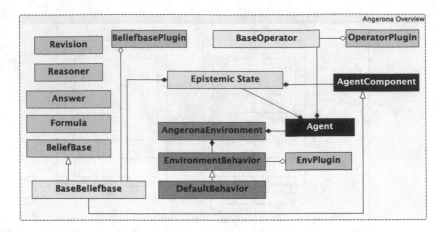

Fig. 2. ANGERONA agent simplified class diagram

their credulity, e. g. skeptical reasoning vs. credulous reasoning, in the setting of secrecy preserving agents. More on this can be found in [8].

The agent cycle is realized by a sequence of operators provided by operator plug-ins. Operators in ANGERONA exist on two fundamental levels of abstraction. *Operation types* represent types of operators and have three parameters, a unique name, a set of input parameters and an output type. By means of operation types we can define the agent cycle for an agent class without instantiating the concrete operators to be used. An operator is a class that implements a particular *operation type*, e. g. an ASP change operator. There might be several operators with the same operation type implemented, e. g. those of [10–13]. The *knowledge engineer* can select which operator shall be used for which of its agents in the respective agent configuration files.

The agent cycle of an ANGERONA agent is specified by means of the ANGERONA Script Markup Language (*ASML*). *ASML* is an *XML* format, which features operator invocation and basic control structures to design sequences of these. It also supports access to variables in a given context, which is normally provided by the agent. For the operator invocation in *ASML* only the operator type is specified in the *ASML* file, the concrete operator instance is specified in the agent configuration file. Listing 1.1 shows a simple *ASML* example script for a BDI-style agent. The *ASML* language also features basic control structures such as assertions, conditions and loops. For a full reference of *ASML* refer to [8].

Listing 1.1. Simple BDI Agent Cycle in *ASML*

```
<asml-script name="BDICycle">
    <operation type="ChangeBeliefs">
        <param name="perception" value="$perception"/>
        <param name="beliefs" value="$beliefs"/>
        <output>beliefs</output>
    </operation>
```

```
<operation type="ChangeDesires">
    <param name="beliefs"value="$beliefs"/>
    <param name="desires"value="$desires"/>
    <output>desires</output>
</operation>

<operation type="ChangeIntentions">
    <param name="desires"value="$desires"/>
    <param name="intentions"value="$intentions"/>
    <output>intentions</output>
</operation>

<execute action="$action" />
</asml-script>
```

We implemented BDI-style agents and default operators for these. We also implemented elaborate approaches for the generation and ordering of desires based on the approach to motivated BDI agents presented in [14]. Further, for the implementation of hierarchical planning for BDI agents we implemented the approach of know-how as presented in [15] by means of answer set programming as presented in [16]. Here, we focus on the presentation of the novel features of the ANGERONA framework; that is, its support and use of knowledge representation formalisms, non-monotonic reasoning and belief change theory. As explained above, a belief base plug-in provides the languages to be used and the reasoning and change operators for them. Each belief operator corresponds to the implementation of a *reasoner* of the TWEETY library.

ANGERONA provides change operators that handle incoming perceptions as illustrated in Fig. 3. It determines the affected belief bases of the agent and calls the specialized change operators for each of these, provided by the specific plug-ins. Each belief base change operator uses an interpretation operator and a change operator. A perception might represent an act of communication between agents and comprise of information about the sender of the information, the addressees, a timestamp, and some logical content. The interpretation operator has to process this complex information into some sentence or set of sentences in the belief base language. The belief base is then revised by the preferred belief base change operator as specified in the agent configuration file. After all changes have been made, the agent's epistemic state gets a *changed beliefs event*, which might trigger further operations. That is, after all directly affected belief bases have been changed other belief bases that are dependent on these might be changed.

We implemented general types of belief change operators in the TWEETY library. These include a selective revision operator that allow to evaluate the new information and decide if and to what extent it should be accepted [17,18]. The result of the selection operator represents the information which shall be accepted and thus be incorporated into the belief base with priority over the information in the belief base. This is exactly the task mainly studied in classic belief revision theory such that we can make use of results from that field.

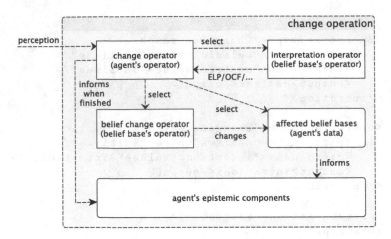

Fig. 3. Change operator in detail

Moreover, we implemented a full fledged belief base plug-in for *ASP*. It is capable of using several *ASP* solver such as *clasp*, *DLV*, *DLV-Complex*, and *smodels*. It provides parsers for the different language versions by means of *ASP*. Different belief operators and belief change operators are implemented and can be used, including those of [10–13]. Moreover, *ASP*-based version of know-how for hierarchical planning and reasoning about know-how as presented in [16] is implemented. For the visualization of ASPs extended dependency graphs and explanations graphs, based on [19], are implemented as a GUI plug-in.

4   Multiagent Framework

The multiagent framework of ANGERONA is what is commonly referred to as the *middleware* of agent programming frameworks. It organizes and starts the execution of the individual agents and the environment and implements the interaction between these. The execution order of the agents, the *multiagent cycle*, is flexible. The default is the sequential execution of agents such that each agent gets the perceptions from the previous multiagent cycle, and not those created by the execution of agents in the same cycle. This way the order of the execution of agents does not matter.

The environment in ANGERONA is formed by the set of agents in the system and the environment behavior. The environment behavior might range from a communication infrastructure that delegates the speech acts between agents, to a simulator for physical environments. It is implemented in form of an environment plug-in which allows to use external environment simulators, or to develop new ones. The interrelation of the environment classes is shown in Fig. 2. The default environment behavior of ANGERONA is a communication infrastructure based on FIPA-style, [20], speech acts. The actions of agents are speech-acts which are transmitted to the receiver agents as their perception. Since different agents might use different knowledge representation formalisms in ANGERONA a common logical language has to be determined for which each agent has an appropriate translation operator. As a language which is appropriate for agents that use such different formalisms as *ASP* and OCF we chose *nested logic programs* [21] as common language for the agents. It supports both, propositional logic and its connectives as well as conditional or rule like connectives, and default negation. However, this is only the default implementation, any other language might be used as common communication language.

ANGERONA also features a versatile graphical user interface (GUI). It is based on a docking panes approach which allows to display various aspect in different panes and tiles the entire window with these panes. The tiling can be changed individually. Panes can be grouped by means of tabs or be detached from the main window to form new windows that might be moved to a secondary screen. The plug-in architecture of ANGERONA allows for UI plug-ins which allow the development of plug-ins for the specific visualization of components stemming from plug-ins such as the representation of belief bases specific to the used formalism, potentially with alternative views such as text-based and graph-based perspectives. For example for ASP we implemented a representation based on explanation and extended dependency graphs, as presented in [19].

Another important feature of the user interface is the *report system* used in ANGERONA. The *report* defines an interface to post new *report entries* and to query the existing ones. A report entry consists of the identifier of its poster, the tick (number of multiagent cycle) and the realtime (system time) in which it was posted, a call-stack and an optional attachment in form of an epistemic component. Poster of report entries can be the agent, one of its operators or one of its epistemic components. The queries to the report then allow to construct

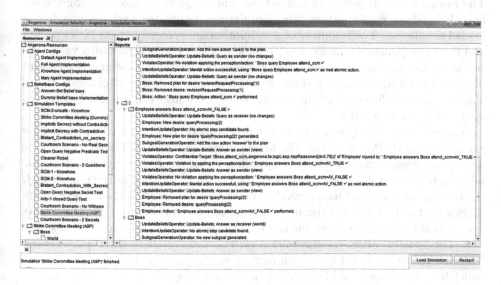

Fig. 4. Angerona GUI - overview

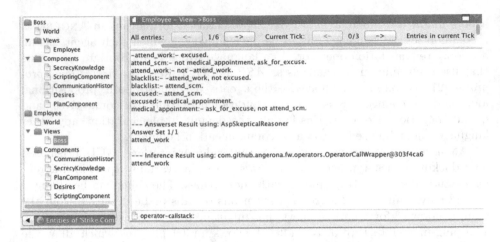

Fig. 5. Secrecy scenario ressources (left), *ASP* belief base UI component (right)

a timeline of posts with filters based on the poster, the type of attachment and the call-stack; for instance to inspect the changes of an agent's beliefs during runtime. The report system is extensively used by the GUI to allow for the inspection on the level of an agent cycle and of a multiagent cycle. Every pane that displays the content of an epistemic component uses the report system to provide a timeline for its displayed component.

Figure 4 shows the GUI in its start configuration after a simulation has been selected and run. The window is tiled by three docking panes, the resource pane to the left, the workspace pane to the right and the status pane at the bottom. The resources are displayed in a tree-view and are given by agent configuration files, belief base configuration files, simulations templates and resources of a loaded simulation. The resources of a simulation are typically given by its agents and their components. The workspace pane has its default tab, which views the report for the current simulation. Resources of the resource pane are opened and displayed as an additional tab of the workspace pane by double-clicking on them. The status pane displays the current status of Angerona and holds buttons to load and run a simulation.

Figure 5 shows how an agent component can be selected and inspected by example of an *ASP* belief base. The logic program of the belief base is shown as well as its answer sets and the corresponding belief set that is produced by the selected belief operator. The controls at the top allow for the navigation through the timeline of the belief base given by the current report. It is shown how many entries for the belief base exist in the entire report, how many ticks the report covers, and how many entries for the belief base exist in the currently selected tick. The controls allow the navigation on the basis of these three parameters. The changes to the belief base with respect to the previous report entry for the belief base are shown by highlighting new parts in green and missing parts in red. These controls and the form of display allows to not only inspect the belief base but also to track its evolution throughout the simulation.

5 Case Study - Secrecy Preserving Agents

We use the ANGERONA framework to implement and experiment with secrecy preserving agents according to the concepts presented in [22–24]. The following example illustrates one of the scenarios we use.

Example 1. An employee *Emma* is working in a company for her boss *Beatriz*. She wants to attend a strike committee meeting (*scm*) next week and has to ask *Beatriz* for a day off in order to attend. She knows that *Beatriz* puts everyone who attends the *scm* on her list of employees to be fired next. Thus, *Emma* wants to keep her attendance to the *scm* secret from *Beatriz*, but has to communicate with her in order to achieve her goal of getting that day off.

The intuitive formulation of our notion of secrecy preservation can be formulated as follows:

> *An agent $\mathcal{D}$ preserves secrecy if, from its point of view, none of its secrets Φ that it wants to hide from agent $\mathcal{A}$ is, from $\mathcal{D}$'s perspective, believed by $\mathcal{A}$ after any of $\mathcal{D}$'s actions (given that $\mathcal{A}$ does not believe Φ already).*

Hence, an agent has to model other agents, the information available to them and their reasoning capabilities. To implement such agents we use the architecture depicted in Fig. 6. It refines the belief component of BDI agents that now consists of the agent's view on the world, its own beliefs, views on the world-views of other agents and a representation of its secrets. The belief change operator then changes all components of the beliefs. In particular, the views on the information available to other agents has to be adapted after each execution

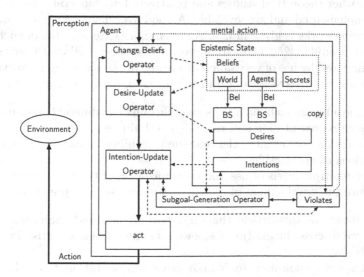

Fig. 6. Angerona BDI secrecy instance

of an action. In the deliberation process an agent has to evaluate potential sub-goals with respect to secrecy. To this end we implemented a *violates* operator which performs internal change operations on copies of the belief components to determine the degrees of violation of secrets. This agent model can then be instantiated by use of different knowledge representation formalisms. This far, we use propositional logic, ordinal conditional functions, and answer set programming to instantiate it and run simulations.

In this scenario we make use of several of ANGERONA's particular features. We build on the BDI sub-framework provided by ANGERONA and refine the composition of the epistemic state. The views on other agents are belief bases such that for each agent a different knowledge representation formalism and different belief operators can be used. Changes to the views on other agents are performed by operators from the belief base plug-in used for the respective view. We also implemented operators that change the secrets of an agent in the light of new information. We used different knowledge representation plug-ins for the agent instantiations. For the ASP instance we build on the ASP know-how [16] implementation of the intention-update operator in ANGERONA and extended it to take the secrets into consideration. The report system and the GUI serve well to inspect the evaluation process of actions with respect to secrecy since the internal, temporary, change operations can be observed. Figure 5 shows the resource view and an example ASP belief base view from the described secrecy scenario. For more details on the secrecy instance refer to [8, 23].

6   Related Work

A plethora of multiagent programming frameworks have been proposed. Most of these are rather theoretical studies and relatively few, but still a lot, have been actually implemented and are available. A good overview of the most prominent available frameworks is given in [25]. An even more extensive list of such frameworks can be found in [26]. These frameworks haven been build with very different goals in mind and by use of very different means. In the following we survey those coming closest to the ANGERONA frameworks main features. These are:

1. to provide a means to build agents capable of using (different) non-monotonic knowledge representation and reasoning techniques,
2. to allow for flexible agent cycles and the possibility to use widely logic based realizations of agent cycles,
3. to allow multiple levels of use and customization of the framework,
4. to feature the development of secrecy aware and secrecy preserving agents.

We have shown in this article that and how we realized these goals. In the following, we discuss the existing frameworks being closest to satisfying some of these goals.

With respect to non-monotonic knowledge representation, to our knowledge, the only formalism that has been used in actual multiagent systems is ASP. But most implemented works on ASP agents treat only the planning problem independently of the rest of the agent, e. g. in the APLAgent Manager [27] or the DLV^K system [28]. In the literature several proposals for the design of an agent entirely based on ASP have been made, e. g. [29,30]. However, for these no implemented systems or documentation on how to implement such a system are available. To the best of our knowledge, there are only two complete and available multiagent programming frameworks that facilitate the use of ASP for knowledge representation, namely *Jazzyk* [31] and *GOAL* [32,33]. Both of these also feature a modular approach wrt. knowledge representation.

A *Jazzyk* agent consist of several knowledge bases which are realized by knowledge representation modules and an agent program. The agent program consists of a set of rules of the form "when *Query*, then *Update*". The knowledge representation modules implement the *Query* and *Update* methods. The semantics of the agent programs is based on the *Behavioural State Machines* approach developed for *Jazzyk*, on the basis of abstract state machines. The knowledge representation modules allow to use different knowledge representation formalisms and an implemented ASP module is available. With respect to belief operators it implements credulous and skeptical ASP querying. But with respect to belief change it only supports a pure addition of new formulas to the knowledge base and no actual belief change. The only other existing available KR module is based on the *Ruby* programming language which cannot be considered as a logic based knowledge representation formalism.

The *GOAL* Framework [32,33] also allows the specification of modules for knowledge representation and allows, in principle, for the use of different knowledge representation formalisms. There are general interfaces for knowledge representation, but we could not find implementations or examples for any formalism other than *prolog*. The agent programs used in *GOAL* feature a clear syntax and semantics, but are rather inflexible with respect to the use of different agent cycles and architectures. The structure is fixed, goals are defined explicitly and are blindly committed to.

There are no other multiagent frameworks that consider the development of secrecy aware and secrecy preserving agents with explicitly represented secrets and views on other agents, as considered in ANGERONA. The closest implemented frameworks on the consideration of privacy in multiagent systems consider rather specific problem in distributed problem solving. The $DAREC^2$ system [34] considers the problem of a group of agents that have to collaboratively compute consistent answers to a query and protect their private information at the same time. Confidentiality is expressed by means of the specification of *private* and *askable* literals which are used in a distributed abduction algorithm based on state passing. In [35] quantitative privacy loss is considered in distributed constraint satisfaction problems.

7   Conclusion

We presented the ANGERONA framework for the implementation of knowledge-based agents. The agent cycle in ANGERONA can be specified by means of the

ASML script in combination with the operator interface. The distinction between operator types and their implementation in combination with predefined agent cycles, e. g. the BDI cycle, allows for multiple levels of use and customization. The ANGERONA framework ASP Plug-in supports the use of various ASP solvers and different extensions thereof, such as *DLV-complex*. On the basis of the latter a planning component on the basis of know-how [15,16] is implemented. Sophisticated change operators on the basis of belief change theory such as [10–13] are implemented. For the ANGERONA framework, plug-ins for ASP, OCF and propositional logic are actively used in several available complete simulations.

The ANGERONA framework is under constant development. We are planning to extend it and to use it as a platform for the development and evaluation of knowledge representation and belief change formalisms in multiagent systems. Our current focus is on the development of secrecy preserving agents. ANGERONA is also already used in other domains, for instance to experiment with logic-based reasoning on strategies for soccer robots.

Acknowledgements. This work has been supported by the DFG, Collaborative Research Center SFB876, Project A5. (http://sfb876.tu-dortmund.de).

References

1. Brachman, R.J., Levesque, H.J.: Knowledge Representation and Reasoning. Elsevier and Morgan Kaufmann Publishers, Amsterdam (2004)
2. van Harmelen, F., van Harmelen, F., Lifschitz, V., Porter, B.: Handbook of Knowledge Representation. Elsevier Science, San Diego (2007)
3. Fermé, E., Hansson, S.: AGM 25 years. J. Philos. Logic **40**, 295–331 (2011). doi: 10.1007/s10992-011-9171-9
4. Thimm, M.: Tweety - a comprehensive collection of java libraries for logical aspects of artificial intelligence and knowledge representation. In: Proceedings of the 14th International Conference on Principles of Knowledge Representation and Reasoning (KR 2014), July 2014
5. Gelfond, M., Leone, N.: Logic programming and knowledge representation: the A-Prolog perspective. Artif. Intell. **138**, 3–38 (2002)
6. Spohn, W.: Ordinal conditional functions: a dynamic theory of epistemic states. In: Harper, W., Skyrms, B. (eds.) Causation in Decision, Belief Change, and Statistics, vol. 2, pp. 105–134. Kluwer Academic Publishers, Dordrecht (1988)
7. Bench-Capon, T.J.M., Dunne, P.E.: Argumentation in artificial intelligence. Artif. Intell. **171**(10–15), 619–641 (2007)
8. Krümpelmann, P., Janus, T., Kern-Isberner, G.: Angerona - a multiagent framework for logic based agents. Technical report, Technische Universität Dortmund, Department of Computer Science (2014)
9. Biedert, R., Delsaux, N., Lottermann, T.: Java simple plugin framework. http://code.google.com/p/jspf/. Accessed 10 December 2012
10. Delgrande, J.P., Schaub, T., Tompits, H.: A preference-based framework for updating logic programs. In: Baral, C., Brewka, G., Schlipf, J. (eds.) LPNMR 2007. LNCS (LNAI), vol. 4483, pp. 71–83. Springer, Heidelberg (2007)

11. Delgrande, J.P., Schaub, T., Tompits, H., Woltran, S.: A general approach to belief change in answer set programming. Comput. Res. Repository (CoRR). abs/0912.5511 (2009)

12. Krümpelmann, P., Kern-Isberner, G.: Propagating credibility in answer set programs. In: Schwarz, S., (ed.) Proceedings of the 22nd Workshop on (Constraint) Logic Programming WLP 2008). Technische Berichte, Martin-Luther-Universität Halle-Wittenberg, Germany (2008)

13. Krümpelmann, P., Kern-Isberner, G.: Belief base change operations for answer set programming. In: del Cerro, L.F., Herzig, A., Mengin, J. (eds.) JELIA 2012. LNCS, vol. 7519, pp. 294–306. Springer, Heidelberg (2012)

14. Krümpelmann, P., Thimm, M., Kern-Isberner, G., Fritsch, R.: Motivating agents in unreliable environments: a computational model. In: Klügl, F., Ossowski, S. (eds.) MATES 2011. LNCS, vol. 6973, pp. 65–76. Springer, Heidelberg (2011)

15. Thimm, M., Krümpelmann, P.: Know-how for motivated BDI agents (extended abstract). In: Decker, S., Sierra, C. (eds.) Proceedings of the 8th International Conference on Autonomous Agents and Multiagent Systems (AAMAS 2009). Accessed 10–15 May 2009

16. Krümpelmann, P., Thimm, M.: A logic programming framework for reasoning about know-how. In: Proceedings of the 13th International Workshop on Non-monotonic Reasoning (NMR 2010) (2010)

17. Fermé, E.L., Hansson, S.O.: Selective revision. Stud. Logica. 63(3), 331–342 (1999)

18. Tamargo, L.H., Thimm, M., Krümpelmann, P., Garcia, A.J., Falappa, M.A., Simari, G.R., Kern-Isberner, G.: Credibility-based selective revision by deductive argumentation in multi-agent systems. In: Ferme, E., Gabbay, D., Simari, G. (eds.) Trends in Belief Revision and Argumentation Dynamics. College Publications, London (2013)

19. Albrecht, E., Krümpelmann, P., Kern-Isberner, G.: Construction of explanation graphs from extended dependency graphs for answer set programs. In: Hanus, M., Rocha, R. (eds.) KDPD 2013. LNCS, vol. 8439, pp. 1–16. Springer, Heidelberg (2014)

20. Foundation for Intelligent Physical Agents: Fipa communicative act library specification (12 2002)

21. Lifschitz, V., Tang, L.R., Turner, H.: Nested expressions in logic programs. Ann. Math. Artif. Intell. 25(3–4), 369–389 (1999)

22. Krümpelmann, P., Kern-Isberner, G.: On agent-based epistemic secrecy. In: Rossi, R., Woltran, S. (eds.) Proceedings of the 14th International Workshop on Non-Monotonic Reasoning (NMR 2012) (2012)

23. Krümpelmann, P., Kern-Isberner, G.: Secrecy preserving BDI agents based on answerset programming. In: Klusch, M., Thimm, M., Paprzycki, M. (eds.) MATES 2013. LNCS, vol. 8076, pp. 124–137. Springer, Heidelberg (2013)

24. Biskup, J., Tadros, C.: Preserving confidentiality while reacting on iterated queries and belief revisions. Ann. Math. Artif. Intell., 73(1-2), 75–123 (2015)

25. Bordini, R.H., Braubach, L., Dastani, M., Seghrouchni, A.E.F., Gomez-Sanz, J.J., Leite, J., O'Hare, G., Pokahr, A., Ricci, A.: A survey of programming languages and platforms for multiagent systems. Informatica 30, 33–44 (2006)

26. Agentprogramming.com: Agent platforms

27. Baral, C., Gelfond, M.: Reasoning Agents in Dynamic Domains, pp. 257–279. Kluwer Academic Publishers, Norwell (2000)

28. Eiter, T., Faber, W., Leone, N., Pfeifer, G., Polleres, A.: Planning under incomplete knowledge. In: Palamidessi, C., Moniz Pereira, L., Lloyd, J.W., Dahl, V., Furbach, U., Kerber, M., Lau, K.-K., Sagiv, Y., Stuckey, P.J. (eds.) CL 2000. LNCS (LNAI), vol. 1861, pp. 807–821. Springer, Heidelberg (2000)
29. Leite, J., Alferes, J., Pereira, L.: $\mathcal{MINERVA}$ - a dynamic logic rogramming agent architecture. In: Meyer, J.-J.C., Tambe, M. (eds.) ATAL 2001. LNCS (LNAI), vol. 2333, pp. 141–157. Springer, Heidelberg (2002)
30. Móra, M.d.C., Lopes, J.G.P., Vicari, R.M., Coelho, H.: BDI models and systems: bridging the gap. In: Proceedings of the 5th International Workshop on Intelligent Agents V, Agent Theories, Architectures, and Languages (ATAL 1998), pp. 11–27. Springer, London (1999)
31. Novák, P.: Jazzyk: a programming language for hybrid agents with heterogeneous knowledge representations. In: Hindriks, K.V., Pokahr, A., Sardina, S. (eds.) ProMAS 2008. LNCS, vol. 5442, pp. 72–87. Springer, Heidelberg (2009)
32. Hindriks, K.V., de Boer, F.S., van der Hoek, W., Meyer, J.-J.C.: Agent programming with declarative goals. In: Castelfranchi, C., Lespérance, Y. (eds.) ATAL 2000. LNCS (LNAI), vol. 1986, pp. 228–243. Springer, Heidelberg (2001)
33. Koen, V., Hindriks, W.P.: GOAL User Manual. Delft University of Technology, Delft (2014)
34. Ma, J., Russo, A., Broda, K., Lupu, E.: Multi-agent abductive reasoning with confidentiality. In: AAMAS, pp. 1137–1138 (2011)
35. Wallace, R.J., Freuder, E.C.: Constraint-based reasoning and privacy/efficiency tradeoffs in multi-agent problem solving. Artif. Intell. 161(1–2), 209–227 (2005). Distributed Constraint Satisfaction

Affordance-Based Interaction Design for Agent-Based Simulation Models

Franziska Klügl[✉]

School of Science and Technology, Örebro University, Örebro, Sweden
franziska.klugl@oru.se

Abstract. When designing and implementing an Agent-Based Simulation model a major challenge is to formulate the interactions between agents and between agents and their environment. In this contribution we present an approach for capturing agent-environment interactions based on the "affordance" concept. Originated in ecological psychology, affordances represent relations between environmental objects and potential actions that an agent may perform with those objects and thus offer a higher abstraction level for dealing with potential interaction. Our approach has two elements: a methodology for using the affordance concept to identify interactions and secondly, a suggestion for integrating affordances into agents' decision making. We illustrate our approach indicating an agent-based model of after-earthquake behavior.

1 Introduction

Identification of interactions plus their particular design in a way that the overall system behaves as intended, is a central challenge when developing agent-based simulation models. This is due to the generative nature of this kind of models [3]: the individual agents' behavior and interaction makeup the system level behavior during simulation. In only few cases, the system level behavior can be a priori determined. Often it just can be analyzed after running the model. Thus, for efficient modeling it is important to determine interactions between agents and between agents and their environment in a systematic and grounded way.

This contribution presents an approach for designing interaction between an agent and its environment based on the "affordance" concept. Originating in ecological psychology, this idea ties perception of environmental features to potential agent activity. Relevant environmental features are hereby perceived by the agents as such, not after processing sensor data to symbols that the agent then reasons about to determine their relevance.

We assume that the affordance concept may provide an appropriate abstraction for model development. Appropriate abstractions form the centerpiece for each methodology supporting the development of agent-based simulation models. They provide guidelines what elements of the original system need to be modeled and how those elements can be used in a model. Too low level elements do hardly help – at least not more than a high-level programming language would. Too restrictive, high-level concepts may be confusing for modelers if they

N. Bulling (Ed.): EUMAS 2014, LNAI 8953, pp. 51–66, 2015.
DOI: 10.1007/978-3-319-17130-2_4

leave room for interpretation or do not perfectly fit to what the modeler actually wants to formulate.

In the following, we first introduce the affordance concept and justify why we think that it is useful for agent-based simulation model development. This is followed by a description of how we suggest to use affordances in Sect. 4 elaborating on a generic agent architecture and a related environmental model concept. After a short sketch of a development process for designing a model, we exemplify the process with a short glance on a rather complex model capturing how a population of agents may behave after a disaster that radically disturbed daily life. The contribution ends with a discussion of critical issues to be tackled in the future.

2 Affordances

The question how (human) agents are situated in their environment perceiving environmental features and elements and interacting with them, is a central one in psychology. Originally introduced by Gibson [4], the concept of "affordances" is the basic element of one of the two major research directions for explaining situatedness. An affordance denotes some perceivable element in the environment that invites a particular activity of an animal or human. This idea forms the basis for a theory of direct perception which states that a perception is tied to a something existing in the environment per se, instead of being produced by sensor data processing that results in symbols that the agent can use for reasoning [21]. The original affordance concept was quite fuzzy and left room for discussions and various more different elaborations. So, for example Chemero [1] presents his view on affordances as intuitively perceivable relations between abilities of organisms and features of an environmental situation. A perceivable constellation in the environment with particular features *enables* the execution of a particular ability of the organism. It does not automatically trigger an activity. The organism – the agent – has the choice to actually perform a particular behavior. The idea of affordances can be well illustrated using examples such as a bench that affords sitting on it. But also some horizontal plank which is sufficiently fixed on an appropriate height affords that.

Over the years, the affordance idea has gained importance in several areas in which interaction plays a central role: In human computer interaction it forms the basis for the idea that a user must be able to perceive what he/she can do with a particular element. It also plays an important role in applications of geo-information science where ontologies for capturing potential agent activities and observations are proposed and used for fast and user-friendly information retrieval [16], for enhanced analysis of the spatial environment, as e.g. in the "walkability" or accessibility analysis of [7] or for a methodology to capture "places" based on what humans can do at that place in [9]. Other application areas are natural language understanding and dialog [5] or in studies about autonomous robot control (such as [20]) where the idea of a direct connection between robot and rich environment representations was proposed in the area of behaviour-based, reactive robotics emerging towards the end of the 1980ies (for a recent survey see [6] or not so recent case studies in [15]).

During the last years, the idea of affordances formed the basic concept for a number of approaches and applications in agent-based simulation, mainly for capturing environmental aspects that enable agent mobility: Raubal [18] focuses on identifying the right ontological concepts – determining the elements of the environment – and epistemological concepts – determining what the agent might know. His application is the identification where and wayfinding might be problematic for humans in complex environments such as airports. Clearly, the correspondence between concepts used in the simulation model and the ones used by real humans is essential. Aligned to the original terminology of Gibson and based on interviews with travelers, Raubal identifies categories of "substances", i.e. environmental entities, and "affordances" which represent what the substances may offer. He analyzed affordances more deeply and categorized them into physical, socio-institutional and mental affordances. Interesting is also that other travelers can afford talking-to. In that way he does not restrict his affordance model to the agent-environment interaction, but also includes simple agent-agent interaction, basically treating other agents as environmental entities. In [19], Raubal and Moratz elaborate these ideas further into a functional model of how affordances could be embedded into the abstract reasoning of an agent. They locate reasoning about them between the skill layer and the deliberative layer of a robotic agent architecture. Joo et al. propose in [8] affordance-based finite state automata for modeling human behavior in complex and dynamic environments. Hereby, they use affordance-effect pairs to structure the transitions between states in which a simulated human may be. In an evacuation scenario, an agent follows a given route to the exit, but checks at every step that necessary affordances are fulfilled using affordances to evaluate different local options. Kapadia et al. [10] use "affordance fields" for representing the suitability of possible actions in a simulation of pedestrian steering and path-planning behavior. An affordance is hereby a potential steering action. The affordance field is calculated from a combination of multiple fields filled with different kinds of perception data. The agent selects the action with the best value in the affordance field. A particular interesting approach is suggested by Ksontini et al. [12] They use affordances in traffic simulation generating virtual lanes of occupy-able space. This is an important advance for agent-based mobility simulation for capturing realistic human decision making beyond strict adherence to legislation as it enables shared usage of road space, overtaking, avoiding badly parked cars, etc. The agents reason about what behavior is enabled by the environmental situation. The affordances offered by the environment are explicitly represented by those virtual objects that offer driving on them. Papasimeon [17] connects affordances to a BDI architecture for identifying options for space occupation supporting navigation and movement for pilots.

Cornwell et al. [2] argue that based on affordance theory a semantic decoupling of the agents' individual point of view (as necessary for a believable emotional behavior) and the scenario setup can be achieved. Their goal behind using affordances was to easily feed knowledge about how to behave and with whom and why to interact into an emotional agent architecture. An agent may perceive environmental objects in different ways captured by perceptual types.

Each of these perceptual types affords actions at the perceiving agent. Those actions have anticipate-able effects on the goals of the agent. Cornwell et al. demonstrate that this concept embedded into the PMFServ agent architecture makes scenario modeling more efficient because fixed predefinition of scenario-specific behavioral and emotional models is avoided and building new scenarios is facilitated.

3   Why Affordances?

Similar to [2], we came across affordance theory not because of theoretical predisposition, but because it helps us to solve an engineering problem. The idea of decoupling and making agent-environment relations more flexible the center of our proposal for interaction engineering. Affordances enable a way of structuring interaction based on the reason why an agent interacts with a particular entity. Thus it lifts the engineering of interactions to a higher level beyond physical interaction of sensing and acting. That higher level may result in using natural language descriptions of particular affordances[1]. We assume that explicitly capturing affordances is suitable for facilitating identification of reasons for interactions in the original system as well as designing the interaction for the simulated environment when formulation based on low-level sensing and information processing appears to be too detailed for modeling. Affordances, as we use them here, enable formulating the reason for interaction by capturing the environmental features relevant for agent decision making and activity. Thus, it is a mean to establish a high-level relation between agent and its environment that then produce actual interactions during a simulation run.

As interaction formulation happens on a higher abstraction level, we assume that this supports

- A higher level of complexity in behavior formulation than would be possible than in reactive approaches. It also helps integrating agent-environment interaction into more sophisticated agent architectures. This supports not only adaptivity of behavior with environmental changes, but also flexibility of modeling as agent and its environment are explicitly coupled with the affordance relation.
- Clarity in model design as it lifts interaction engineering from programming to higher, more knowledge-engineering like levels.
- Extension of models as interaction is clearly motivated and flexible. Introducing new object types comes with the explicit handling of what role these objects can play in the agents' activities. Knowledge about when and how agents interact is explicit.
- Reusability of models, in the same way as their extension. When and where interactions happen is justified based on their connection to agent activity; this facilitates documentation of agent behavior in their environmental context.

---

[1] Using symbols for capturing a particular affordance – ignoring any potential conflict between approaches from ecological psychology to which original affordance theory was assigned to and representational approaches based on symbolic reasoning.

The affordance concept – as we understand it – is not connected to a particular agent architecture. So, it is not obvious how affordances could be practically used for producing those positive consequences. This will be elaborated in the next sections.

4 Using Affordances

Following the ideas of Sahin et al. [20], one can identify three perspectives on affordances:

- The perspective of an agent who searches for a particular affordance in the environment: for example an agent have encountered that there is no milk in his fridge and thus searches for a place (environmental entity) where he can get milk.
- The environment perspective which offers a particular affordance to a particular agent. So that is the perspective of the supermarket which may offer to agents buying milk, a neighbor may offer to "borrow" milk or a cow may offer to produce milk.
- The observer perspective ascribing an affordance in an agent-environment system

A modeler must capture all three perspectives: the first two need to be designed and implemented in the simulation model for generating the appropriate outcome of the third. Affordances and interactions of the original system must both be observable in the model. Yet in principle, the modeler faces a similar challenge as without affordances: interaction needs to be formulated from the point of view of an agent and its interaction partners, as interactions originate from their individual behavior; these interactions must end up in an observable (potentially only temporary) relation between the partners. We assume that the gains of lifting interaction design to such an affordance-based level facilitate their systematic development.

To achieve that, we have to consider two questions:

1. How the overall model framework must look like to integrate affordance-based behavior?
2. What is the appropriate process to actually fill such a framework in a particular scenario?

4.1 Agent Architecture

It is obvious that affordances alone do not create agent behavior per se, but they need to be integrated into an overall architecture or process for managing the agent's decision making: An affordance represents an agent-specific offer for action. Consequently it is not hard wired to an actual action. The agent has the choice whether or not to trigger the actions or may select between different actions that are possible at the same time. There is no standard way for integrating the affordance concept into the agent's behavior generation: [17] integrates affordances into a BDI architecture, [20] use affordances for capturing scenario specific information in PMFServ, [12] create options that afford driving on that driver agents evaluate and select, etc. In some models - also shortly described above, affordances are used as preconditions in rule-like structure, etc. Affordance-based robotics is often associated with reactive, behavior-based robotic agents directly connecting perception and action.

On a rather technical level, agents' decision making consists of two parts which are deeply linked: determining what is the next action, and secondly with which entity to interact when performing that action. An agent may decide to now sit down, but on which of the available chairs? If there would be no chair – or no other object that affords the action of sitting on it – the agent may not consider sitting down at all.

These thoughts are summarized in Fig. 1 presenting an abstract architecture. Some aspects of this need more explanation: In contrast to affordance-based robotics, we assume that an agent can remember situations that it has previously perceived as offering some activity. For example, the agent while walking through the museum, may be able to remember that there was a something to sit down in one of the previously passed exhibition rooms. This is not supported by the original affordance concept as it focuses on direct perception. Nevertheless, it makes sense to assume that an agent can memorize what it has perceived in some belief set organizing previous perceptions or communicated information about its environment. Whether an affordance is actually perceived is depending on the agent's situation awareness including its physical, social, emotional, etc. state. Thus, there

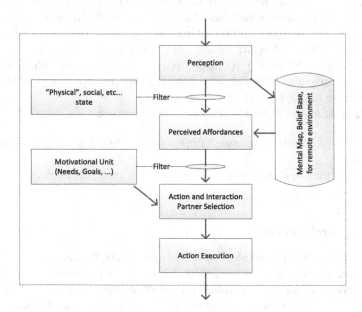

Fig. 1. General architecture for an agent based on affordances in interaction with its environment

must be some form of a filter, so that the agent just considers affordances that make sense for it. Whether it actually follows an affordance relation and performs a particular activity with the part of the environment, is depending on what the agent wants to do actually; that means, it depends on its motivational state to evaluate and select the relevant actions and interactions which are then actually performed. In principle, one could need to consider different forms of motivational concepts and their dynamics and combinations for producing rich agent behavior in a rich simulated environment. Yet, this opens an additional thread of discussion about necessary and sufficient complexity of agent architecture to be traded against transparency of produced behavior.

4.2 Model and Structure of the Environment

In the original psychological literature [1, 4], the perceivable "environment" is seen as the scene or situation the agent (human/animal) is in. Affordances is what parts of that situation offer connected to the agent context and potential actions. So, it is not a single object that is to be considered, but a constellation of objects. For example, a cup only affords grasping, if it is accessible for the agent's hand. If it has fallen behind the shelf, the agent may need to move some furniture before the situation affords grasping the cup. Another example that illustrates why it may be too restrictive to associate affordance information to single environmental objects is: A soup in a pot just affords being eaten by an agent, if there are devices available like a spoon (if the soup is not too hot and the pot is too large to be directly attached to the mouth. Clearly, it would be possible to reduce the situation with multiple objects to a sequence of tackling single objects: In such a case, the agent would need to do planning: first it shall take the spoon which affords grasping and then the agent can perceive that the soup alone is now eatable. This would be naturally done in for example robotic applications. Yet, for modeling the scenario in a simulation, it forms a question of the level of detail in which an agents' perception and activities are handled. What is the appropriate level of detail should be handled by the modeler who uses the affordance-based approach and not enforced by restrictive details of the approach.

We assume that a group of environmental objects including other agents together may contribute with different features to an environment constellation. This composition together affords particular actions of the perceiving agent. In the simplest case, such a group contains only one object. Whether a constellation really affords some agent activity is depending on the agent, its configuration and dynamic context. Figure 2 illustrates the overall assumed environmental structure for our affordance-based approach.

An alternative approach would be to generate a particular virtual object for representing the environmental constellation if and when necessary. This is proposed by Ksontini et al. in [12] who generate virtual lanes that an agent may drive on. Virtual objects may be a clean solution for capturing "constellations", but belong to a more technical level than we currently discuss an affordance-based approach. In the technical design of the example model sketched below, generation was not necessary. Yet, the situations in which a virtual lane is generated, contain much more geometric details and constraints to be handled than in our more coarse-grained model.

4.3 Individual Context

The individual agents context influences what action opportunities it actually perceives and which it finds relevant to consider. This is clearly shown in the architecture as well as in the concept of the environmental structure above. The question remains what are the particular influences that are relevant from the agents' side. In principle it can be every detailed feature of the situation and state the agent:

- Physical state of the agent: If the agent has no hands or it may currently not have sufficient energy for lifting things, no affordance of being grasp-able is relevant for the agent.
- Mental state: If an agents' reasoning is overloaded, it cannot process incoming information that information source such as for example a newspaper would afford. If an agent does not believe that a supermarket is reachable, it may not consider the groceries that the supermarket affords to buy. In simulation models that explicitly involve agent beliefs about their environment, the perception of affordances must be filtered based on what the agent believes to be feasible.
- Motivational and emotional state: The goals of an agent determine what it finds relevant in its environment. The motivational state is so relevant that it was even shown as an extra component in Fig. 1. It determines not just what

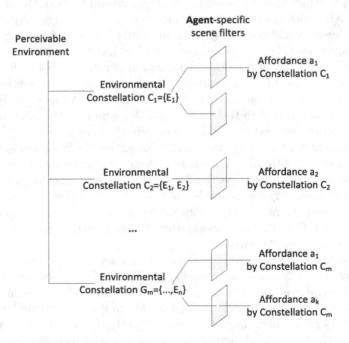

Fig. 2. Illustration of the assumed environmental structure

the agent may select to pursue, but it influences what the agent expects to perceive.

– Social and institutional state: If the agent is member of a group or organization, playing a particular role, this also influences what expectations the agent may have about its environment. Raubal [18] found this context so relevant that he introduced institutional affordances in his airport scenario: a border official affords the activity of passport control due to its role in the overall institutional setting.

5   Model Development Process

The idea of affordances is based on psychological theories how humans (and animals) perceive interaction possibilities. We assume that - if interactions are formulated in a way related to how humans think -, this might make this process easier for a human modeler. This might offer a good starting point for identification of both, agent-environment interactions and agent-agent interactions. Additionally, the level of abstraction when dealing with affordances is higher than specifying that an particular protocol is used for realizing interactions. Affordances express not just that there can be interactions, but also why, with whom and under which conditions. So, potential interactions are meaningful and the definition of types and features of environmental entities, which determines the level of detail of the environmental model, are linked to agent activities using those features.

Basically one can interpret this approach as an elaboration of the vague interaction-oriented design strategy for model development sketched in [11]. A process starting from affordances is different from interaction-oriented model development approaches such as suggested in [13]. Focusing on reactive agents, they assume that full behavior can be described based on interactions; complex behavior in which interactions serve a particular purpose and are intentionally selected are hardly supported.

A process centered around affordance-based interaction design might contain the following steps:

1. Specify intentions and/or behavioural repertoire of the agents.
2. Develop a list of affordances that are needed for this behavioral repertoire or to fulfill the intentions, determining what the environment in general must provide to the agent so that it can do what it wants to do.
3. For each affordance, write down the conditions and constraints under which it actually may fulfill its reason to be.
4. Decide what shall be the elements of the environment: What object-types shall be there and assign them to affordances fulfilling the constraints and conditions.
5. Fill the behavioral gaps in the agents decision making/behavior program - e.g. planning to move to the locations at which an affordance can be used.

Later phases of such a development process then should deal with data structures, organizations and especially with protocols stating what exactly shall happen if an interaction takes place. Those elements depend on the actual agent architecture.

6   Illustration: The After-Disaster Scenario

We used the described concepts for developing a simulation of civilian behavior during the first 24 h after an earthquake. Instead of analyzing evacuation processes, we focus on what people might do and where they might move to after a catastrophic event which dramatically changed their environment. The final vision consists of a decision support tool for disaster helpers enabling them to evaluating the best location for establishing support equipment, distribution of goods, etc. This decision support tool shall be based on predicting how the population might be distributed in the destroyed area. We cannot give a full description of the model here, a more elaborated characterization with simulation results is currently under preparation.

6.1   Intentions and Behavioral Repertoire of the Agents

Starting point is the question what activities the agents could perform. We based our motivational model of the agents onto Maslow's Theory of Human Motivation [14] which formulates a hierarchy of needs. We assumed that directly after a catastrophic event – that does not require immediate evacuation of the population – basic physiological and safety-related needs (on the two lower levels of Maslow's hiearachy of needs) are the most relevant. After discussions with experts we added needs related to information acquisition. Thus, we came to the following list:

- Need for information about family
- Need for medical help
- Need for self-medication
- Need for food and water (physiological needs)
- Need for security of health, body, safe sleep
- Need for security of property
- Need for general information
- Need for mobile phone charging

Clearly, this is just a first draft of needs and can be easily extended due to the underlying affordance-based approach. For now it is sufficient for illustrating the overall approach. Depending on the particular agent architecture, these needs form the basic goals of the agent or motivate some other form of behavior program. In our case we decide for an architecture of competing needs and associated each need with an urgency, thresholds and functions describing the dynamics of the needs' urgency. So for example the need for food or water linearly increases over time; when the agent executes some activity fulfilling the need, it is nulled again. Each need is connected to a list of potentially satisficing places in the environment, at which the need may be fulfilled.

6.2   Affordances for Needs

The next question is what properties the locations might have that the agents might want to go for fulfilling which need. For that aim, we need to setup a

Table 1. Assigning affordances to needs

Need for	Corresponding affordance
Information about family	Meeting family members
Medical help	Meeting doctors and nurses
Self-medication	Provides medicaments
Food and water	Provides food and water
Security of body,	Provides shelter
Security of property	Enables protection
General information	Provides Internet access, enables broadcast listening, provides talking to
Mobile phone charging	Provides electricity

list of affordances describing what an environmental constellation might need to offer so that the agent can perform activities that fulfill each of its needs. For the needs listed above, the list of affordances might look like in Table 1. The relation is not a 1:1 relation. Most of the needs have exactly one affordance. The need for general information about for example the location of the epicenter or the general state of the road network, destructions, etc. can be acquired either by searching in the Internet, more conservative sources such as radio or television or by talking to other agents.

So, for finding a place where the agent may find need fulfillment, it may identify place that in an environmental constellation provides the corresponding affordance. In the simulation, the agent might not know that a particular place actually affords a particular activity, but if the agent believes, it will plan its way to that place.

6.3 Conditions and Constraints on Affordances

The next step is to determine under which circumstances an affordance can be offered. In our example, most affordances can be realized by a particular place in a particular state, only few affordances needs more than one entity to be fulfill-able, that means they need a true constellation of environmental objects and agents. Table 2 gives an impression about how this could look like informally.

6.4 Environmental Model

The next question is how the environment may look like for providing the affordances listed in Table 2. Thus, the relevant types of objects that should be there – and consequently the level of abstraction of the environmental model – can be derived from that list. It is clear that we may assume that a place of type supermarket or pharmacy is relevant whereas a place of type clothes shop only in its role as a particular workplace. So, the overall environmental model does not need to explicitly show clothes shops. An example list of places that may

Table 2. Conditions for affordances to be provided

Affordance	Constraints
Meeting family members	Other family member(s) must be located at place
Meeting doctors and nurses	Doctors/nurses are not overloaded, place is not destroyed
Provides medicaments	Sufficient medication storage available
Provides food and water	Sufficient storage
Provides shelter	Building is not destroyed
Enables protection	Something of value left
Provides Internet access	Electricity available, Internet accessible
Provides broadcast access	Electricity available, receiver accessible
Provides talking to	Other (knowledgeable) person at the agents' location
Provides electricity	Electricity available

Table 3. What affordances need to be satisfied, determines what kind of environmental entities need to be provided

Affordance	Providing Places
Meeting family members	Family Residence(A), Workplace/School(A)
Meeting doctors and nurses	Hospital, Ambulance
Provides medicaments	Pharmacy
Provides food and water	Restaurant, Supermarket, Family Residence(A)
Provides shelter	Family Residence(A), Public Building
Enables protection	Family Residence(A)
Provides Internet access	Family Residence(A), Public Building, some Restaurants
Provides broadcast access	Family Residence(A), Public Building, some Restaurants
Provides talking to	Other Agent
Provides electricity	Family Residence(A), Public Building

provide a particular affordance is given in Table 3. Places that are agent-specific are marked with (A).

With that model concept, the coupling between environmental entities (buildings, places, other agents) and the agents is determined, yet not fixed. The agent decides about which is the most urgent need and thus on the related activity it wants to perform. Then, it checks what type of object or particular provides a relevant affordances, and searches for it.

Whether an environmental object affords something, is not necessarily a boolean decision. In our scenario, we assigned a degree of availability to every affordances of an (environmental) entity. This availability may have changed due to disaster-based destructions or over time depending on the load, tiredness of the personal, available storages, etc. Yet, the agent first assumes that a place with a particular type is fully available, until it perceives (or is told) what the place actually can afford. The coupling between agent and environment is flexible. Affordances are there to match agent activities and location and interaction partner. Also other agents are treated similar to "environmental objects". They can afford talking to for acquiring more information about the general situation or about blocked roads or unavailable distant places. Interaction to other agents is not only triggered when the need for general information becomes the most urgent one, but when an agent meets other agents.

6.5   Filling the Behavioral Gaps and Next Steps

Affordance theory per se covers perception linked to agent activity. Yet, in a spatially explicit, extended scenario, an agent may not perceive the environmental constellation that would afford the activity it intents to do at a certain time. Also, there might be more than one environmental constellation with which it makes sense for the agent to interact. In the disaster scenario this means, the agent needs to select a place out of the potentially satisficing locations and plan its activities for going there for need fulfillment. This place selection and mobility form behavioral gaps not tackled so far, but that need to be filled for complete agent behavior and interaction.

Using its (individual) "mental map", that means its believe about location and road network linking places, the agent can start from information about what places exist and potentially provide relevant affordances. Based on that, the agent determines which place is reachable within what time and selects the one at which it believes to reach within the shortest time. Having determined a path, it moves there for need fulfillment. We also used the affordance idea for determining the availability of a road segment for moving across it. Also the road network might be affected by the disaster. The agent takes only the believed availability of links into considerations when determining the route to a place. While moving, the agent updates its mental map with its perceived state of the environment. Interaction for information exchange happens with other agents that it meets during movement or at places. This communicated information is also used for updating mental maps with more accurate information on affordance availability. While moving, the perception of affordances for moving at the different road segments may also trigger re-routing, re-selection of places for relevant affordance or even for need reconsideration (as it does not make sense to search for fulfilling a need that the agent does not believe is fulfill-able). When finally reaching the place that was chosen as destination, the agent starts an activity for the satisfaction of the particular need. Actually, the need for protecting its properties has some low yet constant urgency that will lead the agent to its residence when there is no other important need, unless the home cannot fulfill that affordance any more because it is fully destroyed - that means has no availability for protecting valuable items any more.

Designing data structures and decision making processes, as well as implementing them is rather straight forward given the concepts described here after some more formal and detailed specification. A first prototype of the model is implemented using the standard means and language of the SeSAm simulation system[2]. SeSAm was hereby used on a level of abstraction that also an

---

[2] www.simsesam.org.

object oriented programming language would provide in terms of construction of complex data structures. We used predefined plugins for shortest-path algorithms as well as for road network data structures, etc.

7   Discussion and Next Steps

In the example, we illustrated a model design strategy around an abstract coupling between agents and their environment based on a high-level idea of affordances. We focused on conceptually showing how agent motivational concepts can be connected with environmental objects. Clearly, for understanding how the example works, a much more detailed description would be necessary. Also, for a precise methodology a more formally complete description of our particular affordance-based interaction framework would be essential. Yet, this contribution aimed at giving an impression what can be possible and motivate why it is important to have a look onto the affordance concept for developing model design strategies. Several interconnected aspects need to be discussed and addressed in future work:

In how far, an affordance-based approach really makes modeling more accessible is something that must be tested. We basically re-allocated behavioral elements to be formulated in the agent behavior to the specification of the environmental entities. That might not be useful for all modelers in all domains. We will undertake tests about usefulness after we ourselves made more experiences with this way of formulating the model in at least one other – sufficiently different project. This leads to the question about generalizability: The question about whether that, what we have presented here, is transferable to other modeling problems, is still open.

Another issue concerns the question whether classes of affordances can be formulated that - during the actual model design - can be identified and this classification is useful for modeling. Our approach presented so far also does not distinguish between passive environmental entities and other agents. It is not clear whether we – from the perspective of one agent need to create a distinct approach and whether that would result in different types of affordances. In general the idea has some relations to design pattern for agent-environment interactions. It might be interesting to consider the question how far affordances as a high-level intermediate concept can serve as the basis for interaction patterns connecting agent behavior and environmental structure.

As indicated above, for implementation, we developed all the data structures for needs, affordances, environmental entities as well as mental map structures using the standard toolset provided by SeSAm. In general, a modeler should not need to create his own need structures, affordance data types or environmental structure, but reuse given abstractions on the appropriate level. It would be clearly an important next step to formalize the concepts and make the single phases more precise and clear. This could lead to modeling support starting with simple implementation tools to maybe even support for model-driven simulation engineering.

Acknowledgements. The author wants to thank Sabine Timpf for introducing her to the affordance idea, as well as Per-Olof Persson and Sepideh Pashami for valuable discussions of the topics addressed in the paper. The work was funded by KKS (the Knowledge Foundation) in the RM4RS (Rapid Mapping for Realistic Simulation) project.

References

1. Chemero, A.: An outline of a theory of affordances. Ecol. Psychol. **15**(2), 181–195 (2003)
2. Cornwell, J.B., O'Brien, K., Silverman, B.G., Toth, J.A.: Affordance theory for improving the rapid generation, composability, and reusability of synthetic agents and objects. In: Presented at 2003 BRIMS Conference (Behavior Representation in Modelling and Simulation) (2003). http://repository.upenn.edu/ese_papers/291
3. Epstein, J.M.: Generative Social Science: Studies in Agent-Based Computational Modeling. Princeton University Press, Princeton (2007)
4. Gibson, J.J.: The Ecological Approach to Visual Perception. Houghton Mifflin, Boston (1979)
5. Gorniak, P.J.: The Affordance-Based Concept. Ph.D. thesis, School of Architecture and Planning, MIT (2005)
6. Horton, T.E., Chakraborty, A., Amant, R.S.: Affordances for robots: a brief survey. AVANT **2**, 70–84 (2012)
7. Jonietz, D., Timpf, S.: An affordance-based simulation framework for assessing spatial suitability. In: Tenbrink, T., Stell, J., Galton, A., Wood, Z. (eds.) COSIT 2013. LNCS, vol. 8116, pp. 169–184. Springer, Heidelberg (2013)
8. Joo, J., Kim, N., Wysk, R.A., Rothrock, L., Son, Y.-J., Gwang Oh, Y., Lee, S.: Agent-based simulation of affordance-based human behaviors in emergency evacuation. Simul. Model. Pract. Theory **13**, 99–115 (2013)
9. Jordan, T., Raubal, M., Gartrell, B., Egenhöfer, M.J.: An affordance-based model of place in GIS. In: Poiker, T., Chrisman, N. (eds.) Proceeding of 8th International Symposium on Spatial Data Handling, pp. 98–109. Vancouver, CA (1998)
10. Kapadia, M., Singh, S., Hewlett, W., Faloutsos, P.: Egocentric affordance fields in pedestrian steering. In: Proceedings of the 2009 Symposium on Interactive 3D Graphics and Games (I3D 2009), pp. 215–223. ACM, New York (2009)
11. Klügl, F.: Multiagent simulation model design strategies. In: Proceedings of the Second Multi-Agent Logics, Languages, and Organisations Federated Workshops (MALLOW), Turin, Italy, September 7–10, 2009, vol. 494 of CEUR Workshop Proceedings (2009)
12. Ksontini, F., Mandiau, R., Guessoum, Z., Espié, S.: Affordance-based agent model for traffic simulation. J. Auton. Agent. Multi-Agent Syst. (2014)
13. Kubera, Y., Mathieu, P., Picault, S.: IODA: an interaction-oriented approach for multi-agent based simulations. Auton. Agent. Multi-Agent Syst. **23**(3), 303–343 (2011)
14. Maslow, A.H.: A theory of human motivation. Psychol. Rev. **50**(4), 370–396 (1943)
15. Murphy, R.R.: Case studies of applying Gibson's ecological approach to mobile robotics. IEEE Trans. Syst. Man Cybern. B Cybern. Part A Syst. Hum. **29**(1), 105–111 (1999)
16. Ortmann, J., Kuhn, W.: Affordances as qualities. In: Galton, A., Mizoguchi, R. (eds.) Proceedings of the 2010 Conference on Formal Ontology in Information Systems (FOIS 2010), pp. 117–130. IOS Press, The Netherlands (2010)

17. Papasimeon, M.: Modelling agent-environment interaction in multi-agent simulations with affordances. Ph.D. thesis, Melbourne School of Engineering, University of Melbourne (2009)
18. Raubal, M.: Ontology and epistemology for agent-based wayfinding simulation. Int. J. Geog. Inform. Sci. **15**, 653–665 (2001)
19. Raubal, M., Moratz, R.: A functional model for affordance-based agents. In: Rome, E., Hertzberg, J., Dorffner, G. (eds.) Towards Affordance-Based Robot Control. LNCS (LNAI), vol. 4760, pp. 91–105. Springer, Heidelberg (2008)
20. Şahin, E., Çakmak, M., Doğar, M.R., Uğur, E., Üçoluk, G.: To afford or not to afford: a new formalism of affordances towards affordance-based robot control. Adapt. Behav. **15**(4), 447–472 (2007)
21. Shaw, R.: The agent-environment interface: Simon's indirect or Gibson's direct coupling. Ecol. Psychol. **15**(1), 37–106 (2003)

MORE: Merged Opinions Reputation Model

Nardine Osman[1]([✉]), Alessandro Provetti[2], Valerio Riggi[2], and Carles Sierra[1]

[1] Artificial Intelligence Research Institute (IIIA-CSIC), Barcelona, Spain
nardine@iiia.csic.es
[2] Department of Math and Informatics, University of Messina, Messina, Italy

Abstract. Reputation is generally defined as the opinion of a group on an aspect of a thing. This paper presents a reputation model that follows a probabilistic modeling of opinions based on three main concepts: (1) the value of an opinion decays with time, (2) the reputation of the opinion source impacts the reliability of the opinion, and (3) the certainty of the opinion impacts its weight with respect to other opinions. Furthermore, the model is flexible with its opinion sources: it may use explicit opinions or implicit opinions that can be extracted from agent behaviour in domains where explicit opinions are sparse. We illustrate the latter with an approach to extract opinions from behavioral information in the sports domain, focusing on football in particular. One of the uses of a reputation model is predicting behaviour. We take up the challenge of predicting the behavior of football teams in football matches, which we argue is a very interesting yet difficult approach for evaluating the model.

Keywords: Trust · Reliability · Reputation

1 Introduction

This paper is concerned with the classic, yet crucial, issue of reputation. We propose MORE, the *Merged Opinions REputation model*, to compute reputation on the basis of opinions collected over time. MORE uses a probabilistic modelling of reputation; adopts the notion of information decay; considers the reliability of an opinion as a function of the reputation of the opinion holder; and assesses the weight of an opinion based on its certainty. This latter feature constitutes the most novel feature of our algorithm.

Furthermore, MORE may be applied to fields with varying abundancy of explicit opinions available. In other words, if explicit opinions are available, as it is the case with so-called *eMarkets,* then those opinions may directly be used by MORE. In other cases, where such opinions are sparse, behavioral information can be translated into opinions that MORE can then use. For example, if Barcelona beats Real Madrid at football, then this may be translated into *mutual opinions* where Barcelona expresses Real Madrid's inadequate skills and Real Madrid acknowledges Barcelona's superior skills. This paper also proposes an approach for extracting opinions from behavioural information in the sports domain.

© Springer International Publishing Switzerland 2015
N. Bulling (Ed.): EUMAS 2014, LNAI 8953, pp. 67–81, 2015.
DOI: 10.1007/978-3-319-17130-2_5

MORE's calculated reputation measures may then be used for different objectives, from ranking performance to predicting behaviour and sports results.

Evaluating reputation is a notoriously tricky task, since there seldom is an objective measure to compare to. For instance, how can we prove which opinion is correct and which is biased? In this paper, we present an extensive validation effort that has sought to assess MORE's predictive abilities in the football domain, where accurate predictions are notoriously hard to make [4].

The rest of this paper is divided as follows: Sect. 2 presents the MORE model, Sect. 3 introduces the necessary approximations, Sect. 4 summarizes the MORE algorithm; Sects. 5, 6, and 7 presents our evaluation, before concluding with Sect. 8.

2   The MORE Model

We define the opinion that agent β may form about agent α at time t as: $o_\beta^t(\alpha) = \{e_1 \mapsto v_1, \ldots, e_n \mapsto v_n\}$, where $G = \{\alpha, \beta, \ldots\}$ is a set of agents; $t \in T$ and T represents calendar time; $E = \{e_1, \ldots, e_n\}$ is an ordered evaluation space where the terms e_i may account for terms such as *bad*, *good*, *very good* and so on; and $v_i \in [0, 1]$ represents the value assigned to each element $e_i \in E$ under the condition that $\sum_{i \in [1, |E|]} v_i = 1$. In other words, the opinion $o_\beta^t(\alpha)$ is specified as a discrete probability distribution over the evaluation space E. We note that the opinion one holds with respect to another may change with time, hence various instances of $o_\beta^t(\alpha)$ may exist for the same agents α and β but for distinct time instants t.

Now assume that at time t, agent β forms an opinion $o_\beta^t(\alpha)$ about agent α. To be able to properly interpret the opinion, we need to consider how reliable β is in giving opinions. We reckon that the overall reliability of any opinion is the reliability of the person holding this opinion, which changes along time. That is the more reliable an opinion is, the closer its reviewed value is to the original one; inversely, the less reliable an opinion is, the closer its reviewed value is to the flat (or uniform) probability distribution $\mathbb{F}$, which represents complete ignorance and is defined as $\forall e_i \in E \cdot \mathbb{F}(e_i) = 1/|E|$. This reliability value $\mathcal{R}$ is defined later on in Sect. 2.3. However, in this section, we use this value to assess the reviewed value $\mathbb{O}_\beta^t(\alpha)$ of the expressed opinion $o_\beta^t(\alpha)$, which we define accordingly:

$$\mathbb{O}_\beta^t(\alpha) = \mathcal{R}_\beta^t \times o_\beta^t(\alpha) + (1 - \mathcal{R}_\beta^t) \times \mathbb{F} \tag{1}$$

2.1   Opinion Decay

Information loses its value with time. Opinions are no exception, and their integrity decreases with time as well. Based on the work of [9], we say the value of an opinion should tend to ignorance, which may be represented by the flat distribution $\mathbb{F}$. In other words, given a distribution $\mathbb{O}^{t'}$ created at time t', we say at time $t > t'$, $\mathbb{O}^{t'}$ would have decayed to $\mathbb{O}^t = \Lambda(t, \mathbb{F}, \mathbb{O}^{t'})$, where Λ is the *decay function* satisfying the property $\lim_{t' \to \infty} \mathbb{O}^{t'} = \mathbb{F}$.

One possible definition, used by MORE, for Λ is the following:

$$\mathbb{O}^{t'\to t} = \nu^{\Delta_t}\,\mathbb{O}^{t'} + (1 - \nu^{\Delta_t})\,\mathbb{F} \tag{2}$$

where $\nu \in [0,1]$ is the decay rate, and:

$$\Delta_t = \begin{cases} 0, \text{ if } t - t' < \kappa \\ 1 + \frac{t-t'}{\kappa}, \text{ otherwise} \end{cases} \tag{3}$$

Δ_t serves the purpose of establishing a minimum *grace* period during which the information does not decay and that once reached the information starts decaying. This period of grace is determined by the parameter κ, which is also used to control the pace of decay.

2.2 Certainty and its Impact on Group Opinion

A group opinion on something at some moment is based on the aggregation of all the previously-expressed individual opinions. However, the certainty of each of these individual opinions has a crucial impact on the aggregation. This is a concept that, to our knowledge, has not been used in existing aggregation methods for reputation. We say, the more uncertain an opinion is then the smaller its effect on the final group opinion is. The maximum uncertainty is defined in terms of the flat distribution $\mathbb{F}$. Hence, we define this certainty measure, which we refer to as the opinion's value of information, as follows:

$$\mathcal{I}(\mathbb{O}_\beta^t(\alpha)) = \mathcal{H}(\mathbb{O}_\beta^t(\alpha)) - \mathcal{H}(\mathbb{F}) \tag{4}$$

where, $\mathcal{H}$ represents the entropy of a probability distribution, or the value of information of a probability distribution. In other words, the certainty of an opinion is the difference in entropies of the opinion and the flat distribution.

Then, when computing the group opinion, we say that any agent can give opinions about another at different moments in time. We define $T_\beta(\alpha) \subseteq T$ to describe the set of time points at which β has given opinions about α. The group opinion about α at time t, $\mathbb{O}_G^t(\alpha)$, is then calculated as follows:

$$\mathbb{O}_G^t(\alpha) = \frac{\displaystyle\sum_{\beta \in G}\sum_{t' \in T_\beta(\alpha)} \mathbb{O}_\beta^{t'\to t}(\alpha)\cdot\mathcal{I}(\mathbb{O}_\beta^{t'\to t}(\alpha))}{\displaystyle\sum_{\beta \in G}\sum_{t' \in T_\beta(\alpha)} \mathcal{I}(\mathbb{O}_\beta^{t'\to t}(\alpha))} \tag{5}$$

This equation states that the group opinion is an aggregation of all the decayed individual opinions $\mathbb{O}_\beta^{t'\to t}(\alpha)$ that represent the view of every agent β that has expressed an opinion about α at some point t' in the past. However, different views are given different weights, depending on the value of their information $\mathcal{I}(\mathbb{O}_\beta^{t'\to t}(\alpha))$.

Note that in the proposed approach, one's latest opinion does not override previous opinions. This choice to override previous opinions or not is definitely context dependent. For example, consider one providing an opinion about a certain product on the market, then changing his opinion after using the product for some time. In such a case, only the latest opinion should be considered and it should override the previous opinion. However, in our experiments, we use the sports domain, where winning football matches are interpreted as opinions formed by the teams about each others strength in football. In such a case, the opinions obtained from the latest match's score should not override opinions obtained from previous matches. In such a context, past opinions resulting from previous matches will still need to be considered when assessing a team's reputation.

Finally, we note that initially, at time t_0, we have $\forall \alpha \in G \cdot \mathbb{O}_G^{t_0}(\alpha) = \mathbb{F}$. In other words, in the absence of any information, the group opinion is equivalent to the flat distribution accounting for maximum ignorance. As individual opinions are expressed, the group opinion starts changing following Eq. 5.

2.3 Reliability and Reputation

An essential point in evaluating the opinions held by someone is considering how reliable they are. This is used in the interpretation of the opinions issued by agents (Eq. 1). The idea behind the notion of reliability is very simple. A person who is considered very good at solving a certain task, i.e. has a high reputation with respect to that task, is usually considered an expert in *assessing* issues related to that task. This is a kind of *ex-cathedra* argument. An example of current practice supported by this argument is the selection of members of committees or advisory boards.

But how is reputation calculated? First, given an evaluation space E, it is easy to see what could be the best opinion about someone: the 'ideal' distribution, or the 'target', which is defined as $\mathbb{T} = \{e_n \mapsto 1\}$, where e_n is the top term in the evaluation space. Then, the reputation of β within a group G at time t may be defined as the distance between the current aggregated opinion of the group $\mathbb{O}_G^t(\beta)$ and the ideal distribution $\mathbb{T}$, as follows:

$$\mathcal{R}_\beta^t = 1 - emd(\mathbb{O}_G^t(\beta), \mathbb{T}) \tag{6}$$

where emd is the earth movers distance that measures the distance between two probability distributions [7] (although other distance measurements may also be used). The range of the emd function is $[0,1]$, where 0 represents the minimum distance (i.e. both distributions are identical) and 1 represents the maximum distance possible between the two distributions.

As time passes and opinions are formed, the reputation measure evolves along with the group opinion. Furthermore, at any moment in time, the measure $\mathcal{R}^t$ can be used to rank the different agents as well as assess their reliability.

3   Necessary Approximation

As Eq. 5 illustrates, the group opinion is calculated by aggregating the decayed individual opinions and normalizing the final aggregated distribution by considering the value of the information of each decayed opinion $(\mathcal{I}(\mathbb{O}_\beta^{t' \to t}(\alpha)))$. This approach imposes severe efficiency constraints as it demands exceptional computing power: each time the group opinion needs to be calculated, all past opinions need to decay to the time of the request, and the value of the information of these decayed opinions should be recomputed.

We suggest an approximation to Eq. 5 that allows us to apply the algorithm over a much longer history of opinions. To achieve this, when a group opinion is requested, its value is calculated by obtaining the latest group opinion and decaying it accordingly. In other words, we assume the group opinion to decay just like any other source of information. Instead of recalculating them over and over again, we simply decay the latest calculated value following Eq. 2 as follows:

$$\mathbb{O}_G^t(\alpha) = \nu^{\Delta_t} \, \mathbb{O}_G^{t'}(\alpha) + (1 - \nu^{\Delta_t}) \, \mathbb{F}$$

When a new opinion is added, the new group opinion is then updated by adding the new opinion to the decayed group opinion. In this case, normalisation is still achieved by considering the value of the information of the opinions being aggregated; however, it also considers the number of opinions used to calculate the latest group opinion. This is because one new opinion should not have the exact weight as all the previous opinions combined. In other words, more weight should be given to the group opinion, and this weight should be based on the number of individual opinions contributing to that group opinion. As such, when a new opinion $o_\beta^t(\alpha)$ is added, Eq. 5 is replaced with Eq. 7:

$$\mathbb{O}_G^t(\alpha) = \frac{n_\alpha \, \mathbb{O}_G^{t' \to t}(\alpha) \cdot \mathcal{I}(\mathbb{O}_G^{t' \to t}(\alpha)) + \mathbb{O}_\beta^t(\alpha) \cdot \mathcal{I}(\mathbb{O}_\beta^t(\alpha))}{n_\alpha \, \mathcal{I}(\mathbb{O}_G^{t' \to t}(\alpha)) + \mathcal{I}(\mathbb{O}_\beta^t(\alpha))} \tag{7}$$

where n_α represents the number of opinions used to calculate the group opinion about α.

Of course, this approach provides an approximation that is not equivalent to the exact group opinion calculated following Eq. 5. This is mainly because the chosen decay function (Eq. 2) is not a linear function since the decay parameter ν is raised to the exponent of Δ_t, which is time dependent. In other words, decaying the group opinion as a whole results in a different probability distribution than decaying all the individual opinions separately and aggregating the results following Eq. 5. Hence, there is a need to know how close is the approximate group opinion to the exact one. In what follows, we introduce the test used for comparing the two, along with the results of this test.

3.1   The Approximation Test

To test the proposed approximation, we generate a number of random opinions $\mathbb{O}_{\beta_i}^t(\alpha)$ over a number of years, where α is fixed, β_i is an irrelevant variable (although we do count the number of opinion sources every year, the identity of the source itself is irrelevant in this specific experiment), and t varies according to the constraints set by each experiment. For example, if 4 opinions were generated every year for a period of 15 years, then the following is the set of opinion sets that will be generated over the years:

$$\{\{\mathbb{O}^1_{\beta_1}(\alpha),\ldots,\mathbb{O}^1_{\beta_4}(\alpha)\},\ldots,\{\mathbb{O}^{15}_{\beta_1}(\alpha),\ldots,\mathbb{O}^{15}_{\beta_4}(\alpha)\}\}$$

With every generated opinion, the group opinion is calculated following both the exact model (Eq. 5) and the approximate model (Eq. 7). We then plot the distance between the exact group opinion and the approximate one. The distance between those two distributions is calculated using the earth mover's distance method outlined earlier. We note that a good approximation is an approximation where the earth mover's distance (EMD) is close to 0.

Two different experiments were executed. In the first, 10 opinions were being generated every year over a period of 6 years. In the second, 4 opinions where being generated every year over a period of 15 years. Each of these experiments were repeated several times to test a variety of decay parameters. The final results of these experiments are presented in the following section.

3.2   Results of the Approximation Test

Figure 1 presents the results of the first experiment introduced above. The results show that the approximation error increases to around 11 % in the first few rounds, and after 12 opinions have been introduced. The approximation error then starts to decrease steadily until it reaches 0.3 % when 60 opinions have been added. Experiment 2 has the exact same results, although spanning over 15 years instead of 6. For this reason, as well as well as lack of space, we do not present the second experiment's results here. However, we point that both experiments illustrate that it is the number of opinions that affect the increase/decrease in the EMD distance, rather than the number of years and the decay parameters. In fact, undocumented results illustrate that the results of Fig. 1 provide a good estimate of the worst case scenarios, since the earth mover's distance does not grow much larger for smaller ν values, but starts decreasing towards 0. When $\nu = 0$ and the decay is maximal (i.e. opinions decay to the flat distribution at every time-step), the EMD distance is 0. However, when the decay is minimal (i.e. opinions never decay), then the results are very close to the case of $\nu = 0.98$ and $\kappa = 5$.

We conclude that the larger the available number of opinions, then the more precise the approximation is. This makes this approximation suitable for applications where more and more opinions are available.

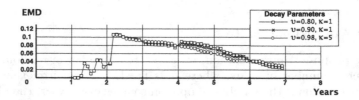

Fig. 1. Distance between the exact and approximate $\mathbb{O}^t_G$

4   The MORE Algorithm

The merged opinions reputation model, MORE, is implemented using the approximation of Sect. 3 and formalized by Algorithm 1.

Algorithm 1. The MORE Algorithm

Require: $E = \{e_1, \ldots, e_n\}$ to be an evaluation space
Require: $G = \{\alpha, \beta, \ldots\}$ to be a group of agents
Require: $t \in \mathbb{N}$ to be a point in time
Require: ODB to describe the database of all opinions
Require: $o_\beta^{t'}(\alpha) \preceq o_\delta^t(\gamma) = \{\top, \text{ if } t' \preceq t; \bot, \text{ otherwise}\}$
Require: $\mathbb{O}_X^{t' \to t}(\alpha) = (\mathbb{O}_X^{t'}(\alpha) - \mathbb{F})\nu^{1+(t-t')/\kappa} + \mathbb{F}$, where $\nu \in [0,1]$ is the decay parameter and $\kappa \in \mathbb{N}$ is the pace of decay
Require: $emd : 2^{\mathbb{P}(E)} \times 2^{\mathbb{P}(E)} \to [0,1]$ to represent the earth mover's distance function that calculates the distance between two probability distributions
$\forall e_i \in E \cdot \mathbb{F}(e_i) = 1/n$
$\forall e_i \in E \cdot (i < |E| \Rightarrow \mathbb{T}(e_i) = 0) \wedge (i = |E| \Rightarrow \mathbb{T}(e_i) = 1)$
$\mathcal{H}(\mathbb{F}) = -\log(1/n)$
$\forall \alpha \in G \cdot \mathbb{O}_G^{t_0}(\alpha) = \mathbb{F}$
$\forall \alpha \in G \cdot n_\alpha = 0$
while $\exists o_\beta^t(\alpha) \in \text{ODB} \cdot (\forall o \in \text{ODB} \cdot o_\beta^t(\alpha) \preceq o)$ **do**
$\quad \mathcal{R}_\beta^t = 1 - emd(\mathbb{O}_G^{t' \to t}(\beta), \mathbb{T})$
$\quad \mathbb{O}_\beta^t(\alpha) = \mathcal{R}_\beta^t \times o_\beta^t(\alpha) + (1 - \mathcal{R}_\beta^t) \times \mathbb{F}$
$\quad \mathcal{I}(\mathbb{O}_\beta^t(\alpha)) = -\sum_{e_i \in E} \mathbb{O}_\beta^t(\alpha)(e_i) \cdot \log \mathbb{O}_\beta^t(\alpha)(e_i) - \mathcal{H}(\mathbb{F})$
$\quad \mathcal{I}(\mathbb{O}_G^{t' \to t}(\alpha)) = -\sum_{e_i \in E} \mathbb{O}_G^{t' \to t}(\alpha)(e_i) \cdot \log \mathbb{O}_G^{t' \to t}(\alpha)(e_i) - \mathcal{H}(\mathbb{F})$
$\quad \mathbb{O}_G^t(\alpha) = \dfrac{n_\alpha \, \mathbb{O}_G^{t' \to t}(\alpha) \cdot \mathcal{I}(\mathbb{O}_G^{t' \to t}(\alpha)) + \mathbb{O}_\beta^t(\alpha) \cdot \mathcal{I}(\mathbb{O}_\beta^t(\alpha))}{n_\alpha \, \mathcal{I}(\mathbb{O}_G^{t' \to t}(\alpha)) + \mathcal{I}(\mathbb{O}_\beta^t(\alpha))}$
$\quad \mathcal{R}_\alpha^t = 1 - emd(\mathbb{O}_G^t(\alpha), \mathbb{T})$
$\quad n_\alpha = n_\alpha + 1$
end while

In summary, the algorithm is called with a predefined set of opinions, or the opinions database ODB. For each opinion in ODB, the reviewed value is calculated following Eq. 1, the informational value of the opinion as well as that of the decayed latest group opinion are calculated following Eq. 4, the updated group opinion is then calculated following Eq. 7, and the reputation of the agent is calculated via Eq. 6. These steps are repeated for all opinions in ODB in an ascending order of time, starting from the earliest given opinion and moving towards the latest given opinion.

We note that the complexity of this algorithm is constant ($\mathcal{O}(1)$). Whereas if we were using Eq. 5 as opposed to the proposed approximation, then the complexity would have been linear w.r.t. the number of opinions n ($\mathcal{O}(n)$). For very large datasets, such as those used in the experiment of Sect. 7, the approximation does provide a great advantage.

5   From Raw Scores to Opinions

This section describes the extraction of opinions from behavioural information. While we focus on football, we note that these methods may easily be applied to other domains. We say the possible outcomes of a match between teams α and β are as follows: *(i)* α wins, *(ii)* α loses, or *(iii)* the match ends up in a draw. We denote as $ng(\alpha)$ (resp., $ng(\beta)$) the number of goals scored by α (resp., β). We then define three methods to convert match results into opinions. Generated opinions belongs to a binary evaluation space consisting of two outcomes, namely bad (B) and good (G): $E = \{B, G\}$.

5.1   The Naive Conversion

In this first strategy, we simply look for the winner. If α wins, then it receives an opinion from β equal to $o^t_\beta(\alpha) = \{B \mapsto 0, G \mapsto 1\}$, and β will get an opinion from α equal to $o^t_\alpha(\beta) = \{B \mapsto 1, G \mapsto 0\}$. In case of a draw, they both get the same opinion: $o^t_\beta(\alpha) = o^t_\alpha(\beta) = \{B \mapsto 0.5, G \mapsto 0.5\}$. The method is quite simple and it does not take into account important aspects such as the final score of the match. For instance, losing 0 to 3 is equivalent to losing 2 to 3.

5.2   Margin-of-Victory Conversion

A second strategy we consider is called *Margin of Victory – MV*. The margin of victory of a match involving clubs α and β is defined as the difference of goals $M = ng(\alpha) - ng(\beta)$ scored by α and β. Of course $M > 0$ if α wins. The main idea here is this: if we know α beats β, this tells us something about the relative strength of α against β. If we know α scored more than 3 goals against β (which is rather unusual in many professional leagues), we could probably have a better picture of the relative strength of the two clubs. We believe that including more data in the process of generating opinions should produce more accurate results and, ultimately, this should help us in better predicting the outcome of a football match. The rules we used to include the number of goals scored by each club are as follows:

$$o^t_\alpha(\beta) = \begin{cases} \{B \mapsto 0.5, G \mapsto 0.5\}, & \text{for a 0-0 tie} \\ \left\{B \mapsto \frac{ng(\alpha)}{ng(\alpha)+ng(\beta)}, G \mapsto \frac{ng(\beta)}{ng(\alpha)+ng(\beta)}\right\}, & \text{otherwise} \end{cases} \tag{8}$$

In analogous fashion we can compute the opinion of β on α. Equation 8 tells us that if the margin of victory $ng(\alpha) - ng(\beta)$ is large, then $ng(\alpha)$ is higher than $ng(\beta)$ and the ratio $\frac{ng(\alpha)}{ng(\alpha)+ng(\beta)}$ will be closer to 1. As a consequence, the larger the margin of victory between α and β, the more likely α will get an evaluation biased towards good. In case of a 0-0 tie, the terms $\frac{ng(\alpha)}{ng(\alpha)+ng(\beta)}$ and $\frac{ng(\beta)}{ng(\alpha)+ng(\beta)}$ are undefined. To manage such a configuration, we assume that the probability that α (resp., β) gets the evaluation good is equal to the probability it gets the evaluation bad.

A potential drawback of the *MV* strategy is that different scores may be translated into the same distribution. This happens every time one of the clubs does not score any goal. For instance, the winners in two matches that end with the scores $1-0$ and $4-0$ would received an opinion $\{B \mapsto 0, G \mapsto 1\}$, as calculated by the *MV* strategy.

5.3 Gifted Margin of Victory

The third strategy we propose is called the *Gifted Margin of Victory – GMV*. It has been designed to efficiently handle the case of football matches in which one of the clubs does not score any goal. The *GMV* strategy computes opinions accordingly:

$$o^t_\beta(\alpha) = \left\{ B \mapsto \frac{ng(\alpha)+X}{ng(\alpha)+ng(\beta)+2X}, G \mapsto \frac{ng(\beta)+X}{ng(\alpha)+ng(\beta)+2X} \right\} \tag{9}$$

$$o^t_\alpha(\beta) = \left\{ B \mapsto \frac{ng(\beta)+X}{ng(\alpha)+ng(\beta)+2X}, G \mapsto \frac{ng(\alpha)+X}{ng(\alpha)+ng(\beta)+2X} \right\} \tag{10}$$

In other words, we give as a gift both clubs with a bonus of $X > 0$ goals in order to manage all matches in which one (or possibly both) of the two clubs does not score goal. Here X is any positive real number. If $X \to 0$, then the *GMV* strategy would collapse to the *MV* strategy. On the other hand, if X is extremely large then the constant X would dominate over both $ng(\alpha)$ and $ng(\beta)$ and the terms $\frac{ng(\beta)+X}{ng(\alpha)+ng(\beta)+2X}$ and $\frac{ng(\alpha)+X}{ng(\alpha)+ng(\beta)+2X}$ would converge to 0.5. This result is potentially negative because the probability that any team is evaluated as **good** is substantially equivalent to the probability that it is evaluated as **bad** and, therefore, all the opinions would be intrinsically uncertain. An experimental analysis was carried out to identify the value of X guaranteeing the highest prediction accuracy. Due to space limitations we omit the discussion on the experimental tuning of the X parameter and we suffice with the results of our experiment that show that the best value found for X was 1.

A further improvement of the *GMV* strategy comes from normalization. Normalization is motivated by the observation that, since $X > 0$, term $ng(\alpha) + X$ (resp., $ng(\beta) + X$) is strictly less than $ng(\alpha) + ng(\beta) + 2X$. Hence, α (resp., β) will never get an opinion where the probability of **good** comes close to 1, even if it has scored much more goals than β (resp., α). At the same time, since $ng(\alpha) + X > 0$, there is no chance that α will get an opinion where the probability of **bad** is close to 0.

Let $p^{GMV}_{\alpha,\beta}(G)$ be the probability of α being evaluated **good** by β, according to the *GMV* strategy. We then normalize $p^{GMV}_{\alpha,\beta}(G)$ to the [0,1] range by considering, for a given set S of teams, the highest and lowest probabilities of being evaluated **good** according to the calculations of the GMV strategy, which we denote as $M(S)$ and $m(S)$, respectively. We then define the normalized probability $\hat{p}_G(\alpha)$ of team α being evaluated **good** by β as follows:

$$\hat{p}_G(\alpha) = \frac{p^{GMV}_{\alpha,\beta}(G) - m(S)}{M(S) - m(S)} \tag{11}$$

And the probability of team α being evaluation **bad** by β becomes: $\hat{p}_B(\alpha) = 1 - \hat{p}_G(\alpha)$.

6   From Reputation to Predictions

This section illustrates how we can use MORE to predict the outcome of a football match. We note that a football match may be depicted as an *ordered pair* $\langle \alpha, \beta \rangle$, where α and β are opponent clubs. We will follow this convention: we will let α be the 'home club' whereas β will be the 'visiting club'. To compute the reputation of teams α and β, we define the *relative strength* of α w.r.t. β at time t as follows:

$$r_{\alpha,\beta}(t) = \frac{\mathcal{R}_\alpha^t}{\mathcal{R}_\alpha^t + \mathcal{R}_\beta^t} \tag{12}$$

In what follows, and for simplification, we omit the reference to time t and we use the simplified notation $r_{\alpha,\beta}$. Notice that $0 \le r_{\alpha,\beta} \le 1$ and the higher (resp., lower) $r_{\alpha,\beta}$ is, the stronger (resp., weaker) the club α is at playing and winning a football match. We shall adopt the following rules to predict the outcome of a match:[1]

1. If $r_{\alpha,\beta} \gtrsim \frac{1}{2}$, then the winner will be α.
2. If $r_{\alpha,\beta} \approx \frac{1}{2}$, then the match will end up in a draw.
3. If $r_{\alpha,\beta} \lesssim \frac{1}{2}$, then the winner will be β.

7   Experimental Results

In this section, we test the effectiveness of our approach. In detail, we designed our experiments to answer the following questions:

Q_1. What is the accuracy of the MORE algorithm in correctly predicting the outcome of a football match?
Q_2. Which score-to-opinion strategy is reliably the most accurate?
Q_3. To what extent does information decay impact the accuracy of MORE?

7.1   Datasets and Experimental Procedure

To answer questions Q_1–Q_3, we ran several experiments, drawn on a large dataset of match scores that we collected from public sources.[2] Our dataset contains the complete scores of several seasons of the Spanish *Primera División* (*Liga*), the top football league in Spain. At the moment of writing, 20 clubs play

---

[1] We note that we look for values that are approximately greater ($\gtrsim$), approximately less than ($\lesssim$), or approximately equal ($\approx$) to $\frac{1}{2}$. In practice, this is achieved by defining three different intervals to describe this.
[2] Data were extracted from http://www.lfp.es/LigaBBVA/Liga_BBVA_Resultados. aspx.

in the Liga. Each club plays every other club twice, once at home and once when visiting the other club. Points are assigned according to the 3/1/0 schema: 3 for win, 1 for draw and 0 for loss. Clubs are ranked by the total number of points they accumulate and the highest-ranked club at the end of the season is crowned champion. The dataset consists of 8182 matches from the 1928–29 season until the 2011–12 season. Overall, the home club won 3920 times and lost 2043 times, and the number of ties amounted to 2119.

For the football domain, a major goal of our experimental tests was to check MORE's predicting accuracy. For each match in our database involving clubs α (home club) and β (visiting club) we separately applied the *Naive, MV* and *GMV* strategies to convert the outcomes of a football match into opinions. We then applied the MORE algorithm and computed the relative strength $r_{\alpha,\beta}$ of α against β. We tried various configurations of the decay parameter ν in order to study how the tuning of this parameter influences the overall predictive performance of MORE. The usual 3/1/0 scoring system for football rankings (and other games) provided us with a baseline to study the predictive accuracy of MORE.

The experimental procedure we followed to compare the predictive accuracy of MORE and 3/1/0 was as follows. We partitioned the dataset containing football matches into 10 intervals, $\mathcal{I}_1, \mathcal{I}_2, \ldots, \mathcal{I}_{10}$, on the basis of the relative strength of opponent clubs. In detail, for an arbitrary pair of clubs α and β, the first interval $\mathcal{I}_1$ was formed by the matches such that $0 \leq r_{\alpha,\beta} < 0.1$, the second interval $\mathcal{I}_2$ contained the matches for which $0.1 \leq r_{\alpha,\beta} < 0.2$ and so on until the tenth interval $\mathcal{I}_{10}$ (consisting of the matches in which $0.9 \leq r_{\alpha,\beta} \leq 1$). Observe that the intervals may have different sizes (because, for instance, the number of matches in $\mathcal{I}_1$ could differ from those in $\mathcal{I}_2$). Given an interval $\mathcal{I}_k$, we have that the larger k, the better the skills of α are and, then, the more likely α should be able to beat β.

For different strategies and parameter settings, we computed the percentage of times $(F_H(k))$ that MORE accurately predicted the outcome of matches in the $\mathcal{I}_k$ interval that ended with the victory of the home club. Accordingly, we refer to $F_H(k)$ as the *home success frequency*. In an analogous fashion, we computed the percentage of times $(F_A(k))$ that MORE accurately predicted the outcome of matches in the $\mathcal{I}_k$ interval that ended with the victory of the visiting club. Accordingly, we refer to $F_A(k)$ as the *visiting success frequency*. We would expected that the higher $r_{\alpha,\beta}$ the higher $F_H(k)$. In fact, as $r_{\alpha,\beta} \to 1$ MORE becomes more and more confident on the ability of α of beating β and, therefore, we expect that $F_H(k)$ is consequently large. The situation for $r_{\alpha,\beta}$ is similar: its increase corresponds to a decrease of $r_{\beta,\alpha}$ and, therefore, an increase of $r_{\beta,\alpha}$ should correspond to a decrease in the frequency of (home club) α wins.

In the following, when it does not generate confusion, we shall use the simplified notation F_H (resp., F_A) in place of $F_H(k)$ (resp., $F_A(k)$) because, for a fixed match $\langle \alpha, \beta \rangle$ we can immediately identify the interval $\mathcal{I}_k$ to which $\langle \alpha, \beta \rangle$ belongs to and, therefore, the $F_H(k)$ (resp., $F_A(k)$) becomes redundant.

7.2   Assessing the Quality of Predictions

The first series of experiments we performed aimed at assessing the accuracy of the predictions with respect to the different strategies. The results are plotted

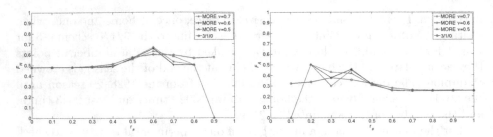

Fig. 2. Naive strategy: success frequencies for F_H and F_A (resp.) over relative strength.

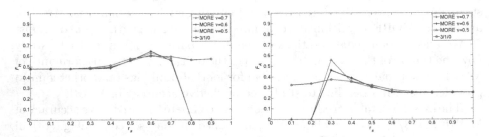

Fig. 3. MV strategy: success frequencies for F_H and F_A (resp.) over relative strength.

in Figs. 2, 3 and 4 for the Naive, MV, and GMV strategies, respectively. In each figure, the plot on the left represents the frequency of successful predictions for the home team winning, and that on the right represents the frequency of successful predictions for the visiting team winning.

From the analysis of these results we can draw some relevant conclusions. The Naive strategy, despite its simplicity and independence from the final outcome of the match, is able to generate accurate predictions. In fact, Naive is ofter a better forecaster than ranking-based prediction (i.e., using the 3/1/0 point system). For home victories, the maximum value of F_H is around 66 % whereas the 3/1/0 algorithm peaks at around 59 %. For away victories, the values of F_A range between 25 % and 50 % whereas the 3/1/0 algorithm has its success frequency flat around 0.3.

It is also interesting to observe that the decay factor ν has little impact on the values of both F_H and F_A. In particular, the peak value of F_H is obtained when $\nu = 0.7$ but the value $\nu = 0.5$ provides more stable results. In contrast, setting $\nu = 0.5$ is the best option for visiting victories, even if the curves describing the evolution of F_A tend to coincide when the relative strength (depicted as r_s in Figs. 2, 3 and 4) is greater than 0.5.

Let us now consider the MV strategy, whose results are reported in Fig. 3. This second experiment provides evidence of an increase in the accuracy of MORE, as the highest value of F_H is now equal to 64 % and the highest value of F_A is equal to 46 %. This suggests that including the number of goals scored by each team in the process of generating opinions is effective in better computing the strength of each club and, ultimately, in producing more accurate predictions. From these

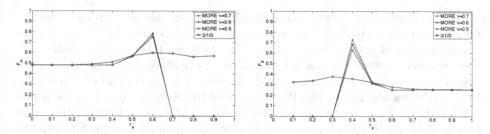

Fig. 4. GMV strategy: success frequencies for F_H and F_A (resp.) over relative strength.

figures we can also conclude that for both home and visiting victories, F_H and F_A achieve their peak when $\nu = 0.6$. But the trends of the curves depicted in Fig. 3 are quite similar. This implies that information decay has little impact when the MV strategy is chosen.

Finally, we consider the GMV strategy. Once again, we computed F_H and F_A for different values of ν and the corresponding results are graphically reported in Fig. 4.

This last experiment illustrates that the GMV strategy (with $X = 1$) provides the highest values of F_H and F_A. The best value of F_H is around 78 % (while F_H associated with the 3/1/0 algorithm does not exceed 59 %). Analogously, in case of visiting victories, the best value of F_A is equal to 68 % (while the 3/1/0 algorithm is not able to go beyond 37 %).

The value of ν providing the peak values of F_H and F_A was 0.6 even though the information decay has little impact, as in the case of MV strategy.

We conclude this section by observing that when $r_{\alpha,\beta}$ is less than 0.3, the value of F_H is around 0.5, independently of the adopted strategy. This result is clearly superior to a merely guess-and-check strategy, where choices are chosen uniformly at random and the probability of guessing the correct result is $\frac{1}{3}$ (as there are three possible outcomes: α winning, β winning, or neither - having a draw).

8   Conclusion

This paper proposed a reputation model based on a probabilistic modelling of opinions, a notion of information decay, an understanding that the reputation of an opinion holder provides an insight on how reliable his/her opinions are, as well as an understanding that the more certain an opinion is, the more its weight, or impact.

An interesting aspect of this model is that it may be used in domains rich with explicit opinions, as well as in domains where explicit opinions are sparse. In the latter case, implicit opinions are extracted from the behavioural information. This paper has also proposed an approach for extracting opinions from behavioural information in the sports domain, focusing on football in particular.

In the literature, several ranking algorithms exist that are also based on the notion of implicit opinions. For instance, PageRank [1] and HITS [6] compute the reputation of entities based on the links between these entities. Indirectly, their approach assumes that a link describes a positive opinion: one links to the "good" entities. Both have been applied successfully in the context of web search. In [11], ranking algorithms like PageRank and HITS were applied to the social network to find experts in the network based on who is replying to the posts of whom. In [2], HITS has been used in a similar manner to help find experts based on who is replying to the emails of whom. EigenTrust [5] calculates the reputation of peers in P2P networks by relying on the number of downloads that one peer downloads files from another. In [3], a personalized version of PageRank that also relies on the download history is used to find trustworthy peers in P2P networks. Also, CiteRank [10] and SARA [8] are algorithms that rank research work by interpreting a citation as a positive opinion about the cited work.

In comparison, we note that MORE is more generic than existing ranking algorithms, since it has the power to incorporate both explicit and implicit opinions in one system. Although built upon previous work, MORE also introduces the novel idea of considering the certainty of an opinion as a measure of its weight, or impact, when aggregating the group members' opinions. Finally, the model is validated by evaluating its performance in predicting the scores of football matches. We consider the football league scenario particularly interesting because it describes well the opportunities and limitations of the mechanisms by which we would like to evaluate reputation, and thus estimate the true strength of agents in general. Furthermore, we note that unlike the sophisticated predictive models in use today, (e.g., Goldman Sachs' model that was used for World Cup 2014, and relied on around a dozen statistical/historical parameters), MORE relies solely on game scores. In other words, it requires no tuning of complex parameters, and yet its predictions are reasonably accurate.

Acknowledgements. This work is supported by the Agreement Technologies project (CONSOLIDER CSD2007-0022, INGENIO 2010) and the PRAISE project (EU FP7 grant number 388770).

References

1. Brin, S., Page, L.: The anatomy of a large-scale hypertextual web search engine. Comput. Netw. ISDN Syst. **30**(1–7), 107–117 (1998). http://dx.doi.org/10.1016/S0169-7552(98)00110-X
2. Campbell, C.S., Maglio, P.P., Cozzi, A., Dom, B.: Expertise identification using email communications. In: Proceedings of the Twelfth International Conference on Information and Knowledge Management, CIKM 2003, pp. 528–531. ACM, New York (2003). http://doi.acm.org/10.1145/956863.956965
3. Chirita, P.A., Nejdl, W., Schlosser, M.T., Scurtu, O.: Personalized reputation management in p2p networks. In: Golbeck, J., Bonatti, P.A., Nejdl, W., Olmedilla, D., Winslett, M. (eds.) ISWC Workshop on Trust, Security, and Reputation on the Semantic Web. CEUR Workshop Proceedings, vol. 127. CEUR-WS.org (2004)

4. Hill, I.: Association football and statistical inference. Appl. Stat. **23**, 203–208 (1974)
5. Kamvar, S.D., Schlosser, M.T., Garcia-Molina, H.: The eigentrust algorithm for reputation management in p2p networks. In: Proceedings of the 12th International Conference on World Wide Web, WWW 2003, pp. 640–651. ACM, New York (2003). http://doi.acm.org/10.1145/775152.775242
6. Kleinberg, J.M.: Authoritative sources in a hyperlinked environment. J. ACM **46**(5), 604–632 (1999). http://doi.acm.org/10.1145/324133.324140
7. Peleg, S., Werman, M., Rom, H.: A unified approach to the change of resolution: space and gray-level. IEEE Trans. Pattern Anal. Mach. Intell. **11**(7), 739–742 (1989). http://dx.doi.org/10.1109/34.192468
8. Radicchi, F., Fortunato, S., Markines, B., Vespignani, A.: Diffusion of scientific credits and the ranking of scientists. Phys. Rev. E **80**, 056103 (2009). http://link.aps.org/doi/10.1103/PhysRevE.80.056103
9. Sierra, C., Debenham, J.: Information-based reputation. In: First International Conference on Reputation: Theory and Technology (2009)
10. Walker, D., Xie, H., Yan, K.K., Maslov, S.: Ranking scientific publications using a model of network traffic. J. Stat. Mech: Theory Exp. **2007**(06), P06010 (2007), http://stacks.iop.org/1742-5468/2007/i=06/a=P06010
11. Zhang, J., Ackerman, M.S., Adamic, L.: Expertise networks in online communities: structure and algorithms. In: Proceedings of the 16th International Conference on World Wide Web, WWW 2007, pp. 221–230. ACM, New York (2007). http://doi.acm.org/10.1145/1242572.1242603

Coordination, Coalitions and Teamwork

Computing Coalitions in Multiagent Systems: A Contextual Reasoning Approach

Antonis Bikakis[1]([⊠]) and Patrice Caire[2]

[1] Department of Information Studies, UCL, London, UK
a.bikakis@ucl.ac.uk
[2] SnT and CSC, University of Luxembourg, Luxembourg City, Luxembourg
patrice.caire@uni.lu

Abstract. In multiagent systems, agents often have to rely on other agents to reach their goals, for example when they lack a needed resource or do not have the capability to perform a required action. Agents therefore need to cooperate. Some of the questions then raised, such as, which agent to cooperate with, are addressed in the field of coalition formation. In this paper we go further and first, address the question of how to compute the solution space for the formation of coalitions using a contextual reasoning approach. We model agents as contexts in Multi-Context Systems (MCS) and dependence relations among agents as bridge rules. We then systematically compute all potential coalitions using algorithms for MCS equilibria. Finally, given a set of functional and non-functional requirements, we propose ways to select the best solutions. We illustrate our approach with an example from robotics.

1 Introduction

In multiagent systems, agents have goals to satisfy. Typically, agents cannot reach all their goals by themselves, without any help. Instead, agents need to cooperate with other agents, for example because they need a specific resource to satisfy a goal, or do not have the capability required to perform a task.

The questions then, are: Which agent to cooperate with? Which group of agents to join? The problem of assembling a group of cooperating agents in order for all agents to reach their goals, shared or not, is referred to as coalition formation, and has been on the focus of many recent works in the area of multiagent systems (e.g., [3,7,17,18,30–32]). This paper introduces a novel contextual reasoning approach to address the problem based on the use of Multi-Context Systems (MCS).

Multi-Context Systems (MCS) [6,15,16] are logical formalizations of distributed context theories connected through a set of bridge rules, which enable information flow between different contexts. A *context* can be thought of as a logical theory - a set of axioms and inference rules - that models local knowledge of an agent. Intuitively, MCS can be used to represent any information system that consists of heterogeneous knowledge agents including peer-to-peer systems,

© Springer International Publishing Switzerland 2015
N. Bulling (Ed.): EUMAS 2014, LNAI 8953, pp. 85–100, 2015.
DOI: 10.1007/978-3-319-17130-2_6

distributed ontologies or Ambient Intelligence systems. Several applications have already been developed on top of MCS or other similar formal models of context including (a) CYC common sense knowledge base [21], (b) contextualized ontology languages, such as Distributed Description Logics [4] and C-OWL [5], (c) context-based agent architectures [25,26], and (d) distributed reasoning algorithms for Mobile Social Networks [1] and Ambient Intelligence systems [2].

Here we address the question of how to find and evaluate coalitions among agents while taking advantage of the MCS model and algorithms. The main advantages of this approach are: (a) MCS can represent heterogenous multiagent systems, i.e. systems containing agents with different knowledge representation models; (b) bridge rules can represent different kinds of inter-agent relationships such as dependencies, constraints and conflicting goals; (c) there are both centralized and distributed algorithms that can be used for computing the potential coalitions. We formulate our main research question as:

How to find and evaluate coalitions among agents in multiagent systems using MCS tools?

This breaks down into the following two sub-questions:

1. *How to formally compute the solution space for coalition formation using MCS tools?*
2. *How to select the best solution given a set of requirements?*

Our methodology is the following. We start with modeling dependencies among agents using dependence relations as described in [32]. We then model the system as a MCS: each agent is modeled as a context with a knowledge base with an underlying logic and dependence relations are modeled as bridge rules. Third, we use appropriate algorithms to compute MCS equilibria. Each equilibrium corresponds to a different coalition. Finally, given a set of requirements, we show how to select the best solutions. The requirements we consider may be of two kinds. They may be domain related. For example in robotics, power consumption is a key concern that must be carefully dealt with. They may also be system related. For example in multiagent systems, the efficiency and conviviality of the system may be considered.

The rest of the paper is structured as follows. Section 2 introduces our running example from robotics. Section 3 presents background information on dependence networks, coalition formation and MCS. Section 4 describes our approach: how we use MCS to represent agents and their dependencies; how we systematically compute the coalitions; and how we then select the best coalitions with respect to given requirements. Section 5 presents related research, and Sect. 6 concludes with a summary and a perspective on future works.

2 Running Example

We now present a scenario to illustrate how our approach works. Consider an office building, where robots assist human workers. As typically, there are not enough office supplies, such as cutters, glue, etc., for everyone, they have to be shared among the workers. Furthermore, as it is considered inefficient and unproductive for a worker to contact other colleagues and get supplies by themselves, the worker can submit a request to the robots to get and/or deliver the needed supplies for her, while she/he keeps on working at her desk. We refer to a request submitted to the robots as a task.

Workers and robots communicate via a simple web-based application, which transmits the workers' requests to the robots and keeps track of their status. The robots have limited computational resources: they only keep track of their recent past. Furthermore, not all robots know about the exact locations of supplies. Therefore, robots rely on each other for information about the location of the supplies: the last robot having dealt with a supply is the one knowing where it is. We assume the availability of such an application, and a stable and reliable communication network. A depiction of the scenario is presented in Fig. 1.

Fig. 1. A depicted scenario of robots in office building.

We consider a set of 4 robots $A = \{ag_1, ag_2, ag_3, ag_4\}$ and four tasks: $T = \{t_1, t_2, t_3, t_4\}$, where: t_1 is to deliver a pen to desk A, t_2 is to deliver a piece of paper to desk A, t_3 is to deliver a tube of glue to desk B, and t_4 is to deliver a cutter to desk B. We assume that a robot can perform a task if it can carry the relevant supply and knows its source and destination. Due to their functionalities, robots can carry the following supplies: ag_1 the pen or the glue, ag_2 the paper, ag_3 the glue or the cutter, and ag_4 the pen or the cutter. Each robot knows who has the information about the source and the destination of each supply, but the actual coordinates are only revealed after an agreement on a coalition among the robots has been made. This involves interdependency among robots.

To start, robots get the information concerning the locations of the supplies and the distances between the supplies and their destinations. Tables 1 and 2 present the knowledge of the robots about the tasks and the current distances among the robots, the supplies and the destinations, respectively. The table should be read as follows. Robot ag_1, regarding task t_1, knows nothing about

Table 1. Robots' knowledge and capabilities

Robot	ag_1				ag_2			
Task	t_1	t_2	t_3	t_4	t_1	t_2	t_3	t_4
Source		x			x			
Destination	x	x						x
Robot	ag_3				ag_4			
Task	t_1	t_2	t_3	t_4	t_1	t_2	t_3	t_4
Source			x		x			
Destination		x						

Table 2. Distances among locations

Robot	Pen	Paper	Glue	Cutter
ag_1	10	15	9	12
ag_2	14	8	11	13
ag_3	12	14	10	7
ag_4	9	12	15	11
Destination	Pen	Paper	Glue	Cutter
Desk A	11	16	9	8
Desk B	14	7	12	9

the source of the pen, i.e., where it currently is, but does know the destination for the pen, i.e., where it must be delivered. Regarding task t_2, robot ag_1 knows where the paper is, but knows nothing about its destination.

Upon receiving information about the tasks, robots generate plans to carry out the tasks based on the knowledge and the capabilities of each robot. For example, there are two different plans for delivering the pen to desk A) t_1: ag_1 can deliver it after receiving information about its location from robot ag_2; alternatively, ag_4 can deliver it after receiving information about its location from ag_2 and about its destination from ag_1. Given the plans, the robots then need to decide how to form coalitions to execute the tasks. We refer to a coalition as a group of robots executing a task. For example to accomplish all tasks t_1, t_2, t_3, t_4, the following coalitions may be formed: C_0 : $\{(ag_1, t_3), (ag_2, t_2), (ag_3, t_4), (ag_4, t_1)\}$ and C_1 : $\{(ag_1, t_1), (ag_2, t_2), (ag_3, t_3), (ag_4, t_4)\}$.

After forming coalitions, each robot has to generate its own plan to carry out the assigned tasks, e.g. plan the optimal route to get the supply and carry it to its destination. Optimal route planning is a typical shortest path finding algorithm, i.e., implementations are available and can be deployed on the robots. Therefore, the robots can generate plans for themselves after they have been given tasks. Details about generating plans for the robots is out of the scope of the paper.

3   Background

3.1   Dependence Networks and Coalition Formation

Our model for dependencies among agents in multiagent systems is based on dependence networks. According to Conte and Sichman [34], dependence networks can be used to represent the pattern of relationships that exist between agents, and more specifically, interdependencies among agents goals and actions. They can be used to study emerging social structures such as aggregates of heterogeneous agents. They are based on a social reasoning mechanism, on social dependence and on power [32]. Power, in this context, means the ability to fulfill a goal. Multi-agent dependence allows one to express a wide range of interdependent situations between agents.

A dependence network consists of a finite set or sets of actors and the relation or relations between them [33]. Actors can be people or organizations. They are linked together by goals, behaviors and exchanges such as hard currency or information. The structural similarity between dependence networks and directed graphs is such that a dependence network can be represented as a dependence graph. Informally, the nodes in the graph represent both the agents themselves, and the actions they have to perform to reach a goal. The directed edges in the graph are labelled with goals, and link agents with actions.

When agents cooperate to achieve some of their goals, they form groups or coalitions. Coalitions are topological aspects of a dependence network. They are indicative of some kind of organization, for example, the cooperation between agents in the dependence network. The coalition is supposed to ensure individual agents a sufficient payoff to motivate them to collaborate. In a coalition, agents coordinate their behaviors to reach their shared or reciprocal goals, for example in [27, 34]. All the agents in the coalition somehow benefit from the goals being reached. A coalition can achieve its purpose if its members are cooperative, i.e., if they adopt the goals of the coalition in addition to their own goals.

3.2 Multi-context Systems

Multi-Context Systems (MCS) [6, 15, 16] has been the main effort to formalize context and contextual reasoning in Artificial Intelligence. We use here the definition of heterogeneous nonmonotonic MCS given in [6]. The main idea is to allow different logics to be used in different contexts, and to model information flow among contexts via bridge rules. According to [6], a MCS is a set of contexts, each composed of a knowledge base with an underlying logic, and a set of bridge rules. A logic $L = (\mathbf{KB}_L, \mathbf{BS}_L, \mathbf{ACC}_L)$ consists of the following components:

- $\mathbf{KB}_L$ is the set of well-formed knowledge bases of L. Each element of $\mathbf{KB}_L$ is a set of formulae.
- $\mathbf{BS}_L$ is the set of possible belief sets, where the elements of a belief set is a set of formulae.
- $\mathbf{ACC}_L: \mathbf{KB}_L \rightarrow 2^{\mathbf{BS}_L}$ is a function describing the semantics of the logic by assigning to each knowledge base a set of acceptable belief sets.

As shown in [6], this definition captures the semantics of many different logics both monotonic, e.g. propositional logic, description logics and modal logics, and nonmonotonic, e.g. default Logic, circumscription, defeasible logic and logic programs under the answer set semantics.

A *bridge rule* refers in its body to other contexts and can thus add information to a context based on what is believed or disbelieved in other contexts. Bridge rules are added to those contexts to which they potentially add new information. Let $L = (L_1, \ldots, L_n)$ be a sequence of logics. An L_k-bridge rule r over L, $1 \leq k \leq n$, is of the form

$$r = (k : s) \leftarrow (c_1 : p_1), \ldots, (c_j : p_j),$$
$$\mathbf{not}(c_{j+1} : p_{j+1}), \ldots, \mathbf{not}(c_m : p_m). \tag{1}$$

where c_i, $1 \leq i \leq n$, refers to a context, p_i is an element of some belief set of L_{c_i}, and k refers to the context receiving information s. We denote by $h_b(r)$ the belief formula s in the head of r.

A *MCS* $M = (C_1, \ldots, C_n)$ is a set of contexts $C_i = (L_i, kb_i, br_i)$, $1 \leq i \leq n$, where $L_i = (\mathbf{KB}_i, \mathbf{BS}_i, \mathbf{ACC}_i)$ is a logic, $kb_i \in \mathbf{KB}_i$ a knowledge base, and br_i a set of L_i-bridge rules over $(L_1, \ldots, L_n)$. For each $H \subseteq \{h_b(r) | r \in br_i\}$ it holds that $kb_i \cup H \in \mathbf{KB}_{L_i}$, meaning that bridge rule heads are compatible with knowledge bases.

A belief state of a MCS is the set of the belief sets of its contexts. Formally, a *belief state* of $M = (C_1, \ldots, C_n)$ is a sequence $S = (S_1, \ldots, S_n)$ such that $S_i \in \mathbf{BS}_i$. Intuitively, S is derived from the knowledge of each context and the information conveyed through applicable bridge rules. A bridge rule of form (1) is applicable in a belief state S iff for $1 \leq i \leq j$: $p_i \in S_{c_i}$ and for $j < l \leq m$: $p_l \notin S_{c_l}$. Equilibrium semantics selects certain belief states of a MCS $M = (C_1, \ldots, C_n)$ as acceptable. Intuitively, an equilibrium is a belief state $S = (S_1, \ldots, S_n)$ where each context C_i respects all bridge rules applicable in S and accepts S_i. Formally, $S = (S_1, \ldots, S_n)$ is an equilibrium of M, iff for $1 \leq i \leq n$,

$$S_i \in \mathbf{ACC}_i(kb_i \cup \{h_b(r) | r \in br_i \text{ applicable in } S\}).$$

Paper [6] presents also an analysis on computational complexity, focusing on MCS with logics that have *poly-size kernels* such as propositional logic, propositional Defeasible Logic, Autoepistemic Logic and Nonmonotonic Logic Programs. According to this analysis, for a MCS M, deciding whether a literal p is in a belief set S_i for some (or each) equilibrium of M is in Σ_{k+1}^p (resp. $\Pi_{k+1}^p = co - \Sigma_{k+1}^p$).

4   Computing and Evaluating Coalitions

One question that arises in scenarios such as the one that we present in Sect. 2 is how to compute the alternative coalitions that may be formed to achieve a set of given goals. Here we present a solution based on the use of heterogeneous nonmonotonic MCS [6], described in Sect. 3. The main reasons for choosing the MCS model are: (a) it enables representing systems consisting of agents with different knowledge representation models; (b) it can represent different kinds of relationships among agents such as goal-based dependencies, constraints and conflicting goals; and (c) it provides both centralized and distributed reasoning algorithms, which can be used for computing goal-based coalitions. Our solution consists, roughly, of representing agent dependencies and inter-agent constraints using *bridge rules* and computing the potential coalitions using algorithms for MCS equilibria.

4.1 Modeling Dependencies

We model each agent in a multiagent system as a context in a MCS. The knowledge base of the context describes the goals of the agent and the actions that it can perform. Goals and actions are represented as literals of the form g_k, a_j, respectively. Bridge rules represent the dependencies of the agent on other agents to achieve its goals. According to the definition given by [34], a dependence relation

$$dp : basic\_dep(ag_i, ag_j, g_k, p_l, a_m)$$

denotes that agent ag_i depends on agent ag_j to achieve goal g_k, because ag_j may perform action a_m needed in the plan p_l, which achieves the goal. For a goal g_k of agent ag_i, which is achieved through plan $p_l = (ag_1 : a_1, ag_2 : a_2, ..., ag_n : a_n)$, where $ag_j : a_j$ represents action a_j performed by agent ag_j, the following dependence relations hold:

$$dp_j : basic\_dep(ag_i, ag_j, g_k, p_l, a_j), j = \{1, ..., n\}$$

We denote this set of dependencies as $DP(ag_i, g_k, p_l)$. One way to represent dependencies is by using rules of the form: $Head \leftarrow Body$, where the $Head$ denotes the goal of agent ag_i that is to be achieved (g_k), and the $Body$ describes the actions of plan p_l that will lead to the achievement of the goal. Based on this intuition, we define bridge rules representing dependence relations among agents as follows:

Definition 1. *For an agent ag_i with goal g_k achieved through plan $p_l = (ag_1 : a_1, ag_2 : a_2, ..., ag_n : a_n)$, the set of dependencies $DP(ag_i, g_k, p_l)$ is represented by a bridge rule of the form:*

$$(c_i : g_k) \leftarrow (c_1 : a_1), (c_2 : a_2), ..., (c_n : a_n)$$

where c_j, $j = 1, ..., i, ..., n$ is the context representing agent ag_j.

Based on the above representation of agents as contexts, and goal-based dependencies among agents as bridge rules, we represent multiagent systems as MCS as follows.

Definition 2. *A MCS $M(A)$ corresponding to a multiagent system A is a set of contexts $c_i = \{L_i, kb_i, br_i\}$, where $L_i = (KB_i, BS_i, ACC_i)$ is the logic of agent $ag_i \in A$, $kb_i \in KB_i$ is a knowledge base that describes the actions that ag_i can perform and its goals, and br_i is a set of bridge rules, a subset of which represents the dependencies $DP(ag_i, g_k, p_l)$ of ag_i on other agents in A for all goals g_k of ag_i and all plans p_l, with which these goals can be achieved.*

Example 1. In our example, we assume that all four robots use propositional logic as their knowledge representation model. We model the four robots, ag_1–ag_4, as contexts c_1–c_4, respectively, with the following knowledge bases:

$$kb_1 = \{a_{2s}, a_{1d}, a_{3d}, a_{1c} \lor a_{3c}\}$$
$$kb_2 = \{a_{1s}, a_{4d}, a_{2c}\}$$
$$kb_3 = \{a_{4s}, a_{2d}, a_{3c} \lor a_{4c}\}$$
$$kb_4 = \{a_{3s}, a_{1c} \lor a_{4c}\}$$

where a_{ij} represents the actions that a robot can perform. i stands for the object to be delivered: 1 stands for the pen, 2 for the paper, 3 for the glue and 4 for the cutter. j stands for the kind of action that the agent can perform: c stands for carrying the object, s stands for providing information about the current location (source) of the object, while d stands for providing information about the destination of the object. For example, ag_1 can provide information about the source of the paper (a_{2s}) and the destinations of the pen (a_{1d}) and the glue (a_{3d}), and can carry the pen and the glue ($a_{1c} \lor a_{3c}$).

We represent the four tasks that the robots are requested to perform, t_i, as goals, g_i. For example g_1 represents the task of delivering the pen to desk A (t_1). We also assume that a robot ag_j can fulfil goal g_i, i.e. deliver object i to its destination, if it can perform action a_{ic}, i.e. carry object i. For example, g_1 can be fulfilled by robots ag_1 and ag_4, because these robots can carry the pen (a_{1c}).

Given the knowledge and capabilities of robots, as described in Table 1, the robots can fulfil goals g_1–g_4 as follows. For g_1, there are two alternative plans:

$$p_{11} =(ag_2 : a_{1s}, ag_1 : a_{1c})$$
$$p_{12} =(ag_2 : a_{1s}, ag_1 : a_{1d}, ag_4 : a_{1c})$$

According to p_{11}, robot ag_2 must provide information about the source of the pen ($ag_2 : a_{1s}$) and ag_1 must carry the pen to its destination ($ag_1 : a_{1c}$). According to p_{12}, robot ag_2 must provide information about the source of the pen ($ag_2 : a_{1s}$), ag_1 must provide information about its destination ($ag_1 : a_{1d}$), and ag_4 must carry the pen to its destination ($ag_4 : a_{1c}$).

For g_2 there is only one plan, p_{21}; for g_3 there are two alternative plans: p_{31} and p_{32}; and for g_4 there are two plans as well: p_{41} and p_{42}:

$$p_{21} =(ag_1 : a_{2s}, ag_3 : a_{2d}, ag_2 : a_{2c})$$
$$p_{31} =(ag_4 : a_{3s}, ag_1 : a_{3c})$$
$$p_{32} =(ag_4 : a_{3s}, ag_1 : a_{3d}, ag_3 : a_{3c})$$
$$p_{41} =(ag_2 : a_{4d}, ag_3 : a_{4c})$$
$$p_{42} =(ag_3 : a_{4s}, ag_2 : a_{4d}, ag_4 : a_{4c})$$

Each plan implies dependencies among robots. For example, from p_{11} the following dependency is derived: $dp_1 : basic\_dep(ag_1, ag_2, g_1, p_{11}, a_{1s})$, namely ag_1 depends on ag_2 to achieve goal g_1, because ag_2 can provide information about the source of the pen (a_{1s}). Figure 2 represents the dependencies derived from all plans, abstracting from plans, similarly to [32]. The figure should be read as follows: The pair of arrows going from node ag_1 to the rectangle box labeled a_{1s} and then to node ag_2 indicates that agent ag_1 depends on agent ag_2 to achieve goal g_1, because the latter can perform action a_{1s}.

Bridge rules r_1–r_7 represent the same dependencies. Each rule represents the dependencies derived by a different plan. For example r_1 corresponds to plan p_{11} and represents dependency dp_1.

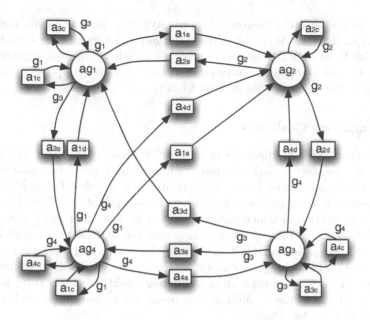

Fig. 2. Dependencies among the four robot agents.

$$r_1 = (ag_1 : g_1) \leftarrow (ag_1 : a_{1c}), (ag_2 : a_{1s})$$
$$r_2 = (ag_4 : g_1) \leftarrow (ag_4 : a_{1c}), (ag_2 : a_{1s}), (ag_1 : a_{1d})$$
$$r_3 = (ag_2 : g_2) \leftarrow (ag_2 : a_{2c}), (ag_1 : a_{2s}), (ag_3 : a_{2d})$$
$$r_4 = (ag_1 : g_3) \leftarrow (ag_1 : a_{3c}), (ag_4 : a_{3s})$$
$$r_5 = (ag_3 : g_3) \leftarrow (ag_3 : a_{3c}), (ag_4 : a_{3s}), (ag_1 : a_{3d})$$
$$r_6 = (ag_3 : g_4) \leftarrow (ag_3 : a_{4c}), (ag_2 : a_{4d})$$
$$r_7 = (ag_4 : g_4) \leftarrow (ag_4 : a_{4c}), (ag_3 : a_{4s}), (ag_2 : a_{4d})$$

One system constraint is that two robots cannot carry the same object at the same time. This can be described with bridge rules of the form:

$$\neg ag_l : a_{ic} \leftarrow ag_k : a_{ic}$$

where $i, k, l = \{1...4\}$ and $k \neq l$. For example, the following rules describe that ag_1 will not carry the pen if one of the other three robots is already carrying it.

$$\neg(ag_1 : a_{1c}) \leftarrow (ag_2 : a_{1c})$$
$$\neg(ag_1 : a_{1c}) \leftarrow (ag_3 : a_{1c})$$
$$\neg(ag_1 : a_{1c}) \leftarrow (ag_4 : a_{1c})$$

Note that using MCS enables us to represent agents that are heterogeneous with respect to the knowledge representation model that they use. In our running example, we assumed (for reasons of simplicity) that the four agents use propositional logic. However, we can also represent any agent using a logic that can be captured by Definition 2. Note also that we use a rather simplistic representation for plans, because our goal is not to represent and reason with plans; we are only interested in the dependencies derived from plans.

4.2   Computing Coalitions

An equilibrium in MCS represents an acceptable belief state of the system. Each belief set in this state is derived from the knowledge base of the corresponding context and is compatible with the applicable bridge rules. For a MCS $M(A)$ that corresponds to a multiagent system A, an equilibrium $S = \{S_1, ..., S_n\}$ represents a coalition in which agents of A can achieve their goals. Specifically, each belief set S_i in the equilibrium contains the actions that agent ag_i can perform and the goals that it will achieve in this coalition. If there is more than one ways with which the goals can be achieved, the MCS will have more than one equilibria, each one representing a different coalition. If a certain goal does not appear in any of the equilibria, this means that there is no coalition with which the goal can be achieved.

In order to compute the potential coalitions in a multiagent system A, one then has to formulate the MCS $M(A)$ that corresponds to A, and compute the equilibria S of $M(A)$. The computation of equilibria can either be done by a central entity that monitors the bridge rules of all agents [6]; or in a distributed fashion using the distributed algorithm proposed in [11].

Example 2. In our example, the MCS that corresponds to the system of the four robots, $M(A)$, has two equilibria: S_0 and S_1:

$$S_0 = \{\{a_{2s}, a_{1d}, a_{3d}, a_{3c}, g_3\}, \{a_{1s}, a_{4d}, a_{2c}, g_2\},$$
$$\{a_{4s}, a_{2d}, a_{4c}, g_4\}, \{a_{3s}, a_{1c}, g_1\}\}$$
$$S_1 = \{\{a_{2s}, a_{1d}, a_{3d}, a_{1c}, g_1\}, \{a_{1s}, a_{4d}, a_{2c}, g_2\},$$
$$\{a_{4s}, a_{2d}, a_{3c}, g_3\}, \{a_{3s}, a_{4c}, g_4\}\}$$

S_0 represents coalition C_0, according to which ag_1 delivers the glue to desk B (g_3), ag_2 delivers the paper to desk A (g_2), ag_3 delivers the cutter to desk B (g_4) and ag_4 delivers the pen to desk A (g_1). S_1 represents coalition C_1, according to which ag_1 delivers the pen to desk A (g_1), ag_2 delivers the paper to desk A (g_2), ag_3 delivers the glue to desk B (g_3) and ag_4 delivers the cutter to desk B (g_4). Using the previous abstraction of plans, the two coalitions are graphically represented in Fig. 3.

In order to achieve their goals, the robots then have to carry out the actions in the plans that are associated to these goals. For example, for coalition C_0 the associated plans are: p_{12} (for goal g_1), p_{21} (for g_2), p_{31} (for g_3) and p_{41} (for g_4), while the plans associated to C_1 are p_{11}, p_{21}, p_{32} and p_{42}.

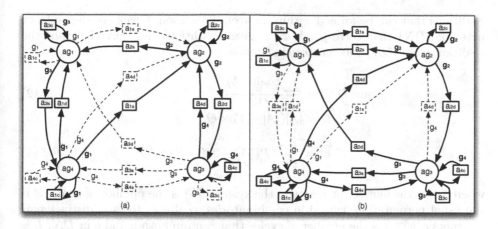

Fig. 3. Coalitions C_0 (a), and C_1 (b) in bold; remaining dependencies in dotted lines.

4.3   Selecting the Best Coalition

Selecting the best among the coalitions in which agents can achieve their goals requires evaluating and comparing them. Efficiency and stability metrics are commonly used to evaluate coalitions (e.g., [19,24,28,29]). The former giving an assurance on the economical gain reached by being in the coalition, the later giving a certainty that the coalition is viable on the long term.

Generally speaking, efficiency in a coalition is a relation between what agents can achieve as part of the organization compared to what they can do alone or in different coalitions. Furthermore, a coalition is economically efficient iff (i) no one can be made better off without making someone else worse off, (ii) no additional output can be obtained without increasing the amount of inputs, (iii) production proceeds at the lowest possible per-unit cost [24].

In our example, we can associate efficiency to the distances that the four robots must cover to perform the required actions. From Table 2 we can compute the distance for each robot to do each task, and, by adding them up, the cost of executing tasks in a given coalition. For instance, the cost of C_0 is $Cost(C_0) = 81$ whereas the cost of C_1 is $Cost(C_1) = 87$. If we compare C_0 and C_1, C_0 is economically efficient as at least one agent is better off without making anyone worse off, all else being equal; C_0 is also more cost efficient than C_1.

Stability of coalitions is related to the potential gain in staying in the coalition or quitting the coalition for more profit (i.e., free riding). Hence, several elements come to play for the evaluation of a coalition's stability such as the characteristic function [23], Shapley value [29], nucleolus [28], Satisfactory Nucleolus [19] and others.

Depending on the application domain, other functional and non-functional requirements, e.g., security, user-friendliness or conviviality, may also play an important role in the choice of a coalition. In [8], we compared coalitions in terms of conviviality, which we measured by the number of reciprocity based coalitions that can be formed within an overall coalition. Given the dependence network (DN) that corresponds to a given coalition, the conviviality of the coalition $Conv(DN)$ was measured as follows:

$$Conv(DN) = \frac{\sum coal(a, b)}{\Omega}, \tag{2}$$

$$\Omega = |A|(|A| - 1) \times \Theta, \tag{3}$$

$$\Theta = \sum_{L=2}^{L=|A|} P(|A| - 2, L - 2) \times |G|^L, \tag{4}$$

where $|A|$ is the number of agents in the system, $|G|$ is the number of goals, P is the usual permutation defined in combinatorics, $coal(a, b)$ for any distinct pair of agents $a, b \in A$ is the number of cycles that contain both a and b in DN, L is the cycle length, and Ω denotes the maximal number of pairs of agents in cycles.

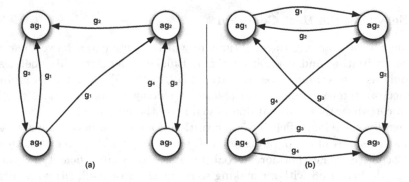

Fig. 4. Goal dependencies in coalitions C_0 (a), and C_1 (b).

Abstracting from plans and actions, Fig. 4a and b represent the dependence networks for coalitions C_0 and C_1 respectively. By applying formula 2 on the two dependence networks, we can compute the conviviality of the two coalitions: $Conv(C_0) = 0.0000897$, $Conv(C_1) = 0.000143$. C_1 is therefore preferred to C_0 in terms of conviviality.

In cases of agents with conflicting goals, coalitions differ in the set of goals that they can fulfil and the selection of a coalition depends on the priorities among the conflicting goals. It is among our future plans to integrate in the proposed model a preference relation on the set of goals to represent such priorities and develop algorithms for preference-based coalition formation.

5   Related Works

This is not the first work that brings together agents and context logics. Previous studies [25,26] used Multi-Context Systems as a means of specifying and implementing agent architectures. Both studies propose *breaking* the logical description of an agent into a set of contexts, each of which represents a different component of the architecture, and the interactions between these components are specified by means of bridge rules between the contexts. Study [25] followed this approach to simplify the construction of a BDI agent, while [26] extended it to handle more efficiently implementation issues such as grouping together contexts in modules, and enabling inter-context synchronization. The main difference of our approach is that its focus is not on the internal representation of agents, but rather on their interactions with other agents and the coalitions that they can form.

Our previous work on evaluating information exchange in distributed information systems was based on modeling MCS as dependence networks where bridge rules are represented as dependencies [9]. Here we do the opposite: we use bridge rules to represent dependencies among agents, and model agents as contexts in MCS.

Several works from different research areas have focused on the problem of coalition formation including variants of the contract net protocol [14,20], according to which agents break down composite tasks into simpler subtasks and subcontract subtasks to other agents via a bidding mechanism; formal approaches from multiagent systems, e.g. [18,30]; and solutions from the field of robotics based on schema theory, e.g. [35,36] or synergy [22]. The distinct characteristics of our approach are: (a) it allows agents to use different knowledge representation models; (b) based on a non-monotonic reasoning model, it enables representing and reasoning with agents with conflicting goals; and (c) it provides both centralized and distributed algorithms for computing coalitions, and can hence be applied in settings with different requirements for information hiding and sharing.

6   Summary and Future Work

In multiagent systems agents often depend on each other and need to cooperate in order to achieve their goals. In this paper we deal with the problem of computing the alternative coalitions in which the agents may fulfil their goals. Specifically, we propose a MCS-based representation of multiagent systems, in which agents are modeled as contexts, and dependence relations among agents as bridge rules. Based on this representation, we then compute the equilibria of the MCS, which represent the coalitions in which the agents may fulfil their goals. Finally, given a set of functional and non-functional requirements such as efficiency, stability and conviviality, we select the best coalitions. We demonstrate the proposed approach using an example from robotics, in which four different robots need to cooperate in order to perform a given set of tasks. For simplicity we assumed that all four robots use propositional logic. However, being based on MCS, the proposed solution may also handle agents using different knowledge representation models.

In further research, we contemplate the need to integrate preferences on agents and goals into our model. Building on previous work on preference-based inconsistency resolution in MCS [2,12,13], we will develop algorithms for preference-based coalition formation in the presence of conflicting goals. We also plan to extend our approach with elements of dynamic MCS [10], i.e. schematic bridge rules that are instantiated at run time with concrete contexts. This will enable us handling changes such as the failure of an agent, the arrival of a new agent or any change in the operating environment. We will also look into applying and testing our methods in different kinds of agent-based systems characterized by heterogeneity of the participating agents, openness and dynamicity, such as ubiquitous robots and Ambient Intelligence systems. To achieve this we will use existing MCS implementations, such as DMCS[1], a distributed solver for MCS, and MCS-IE[2], a tool for explaining inconsistencies in MCS.

References

1. Antoniou, G., Papatheodorou, C., Bikakis, A.: Reasoning about context in ambient intelligence environments: a report from the field. In: Principles of Knowledge Representation and Reasoning: Proceedings of the 12th International Conference, KR 2010, Toronto, Ontario, Canada, 9–13 May 2010, pp. 557–559. AAAI Press (2010)
2. Bikakis, A., Antoniou, G., Hassapis, P.: Strategies for contextual reasoning with conflicts in ambient intelligence. Knowl. Inf. Syst. **27**(1), 45–84 (2011)
3. Boella, G., Sauro, L., van der Torre, L.: Algorithms for finding coalitions exploiting a new reciprocity condition. Logic J. IGPL **17**(3), 273–297 (2009)
4. Borgida, A., Serafini, L.: Distributed description logics: assimilating information from peer sources. J. Data Semant. **1**, 153–184 (2003)
5. Bouquet, P., Giunchiglia, F., van Harmelen, F., Serafini, L., Stuckenschmidt, H.: C-OWL: contextualizing ontologies. In: Fensel, D., Sycara, K., Mylopoulos, J. (eds.) ISWC 2003. LNCS, vol. 2870, pp. 164–179. Springer, Heidelberg (2003)
6. Brewka, G., Eiter, T.: Equilibria in heterogeneous nonmonotonic multi-context systems. In: Proceedings of the 22nd AAAI Conference on Artificial Intelligence, July 22–26 2007, Vancouver, British Columbia, Canada, pp. 385–390 (2007)
7. Caire, P., Villata, S., Boella, G., van der Torre, L.: Conviviality masks in multiagent systems. In: 7th International Joint Conference on Autonomous Agents and Multiagent Systems (AAMAS 2008), Estoril, Portugal, 12–16 May 2008, vol. 3, pp. 1265–1268 (2008)
8. Caire, P., Alcade, B., van der Torre, L., Sombattheera, C.: Conviviality measures. In: 10th International Joint Conference on Autonomous Agents and Multiagent Systems (AAMAS 2011), Taipei, Taiwan, 2–6 May 2011 (2011)
9. Caire, P., Bikakis, A., Le Traon, Y.: Information dependencies in MCS: Conviviality-based model and metrics. In: Boella, G., Elkind, E., Savarimuthu, B.T.R., Dignum, F., Purvis, M.K. (eds.) PRIMA 2013. LNCS, vol. 8291, pp. 405–412. Springer, Heidelberg (2013)

---

[1] http://www.kr.tuwien.ac.at/research/systems/dmcs/.
[2] http://www.kr.tuwien.ac.at/research/systems/mcsie/.

10. Dao-Tran, M., Eiter, T., Fink, M., Krennwallner, T.: Dynamic distributed non-monotonic multi-context systems. Nonmonotonic Reasoning, Essays Celebrating its 30th Anniversary, Studies in Logic 31
11. Dao-Tran, M., Eiter, T., Fink, M., Krennwallner, T.: Distributed nonmonotonic multi-context systems. In: Principles of Knowledge Representation and Reasoning: Proceedings of the Twelfth International Conference, KR 2010, Toronto, Ontario, Canada, 9–13 May 2010 (2010)
12. Eiter, T., Fink, M., Schüller, P., Weinzierl, A.: Finding explanations of inconsistency in multi-context systems. In: Principles of Knowledge Representation and Reasoning: Proceedings of the Twelfth International Conference, KR 2010, Toronto, Ontario, Canada, 9–13 May 2010. AAAI Press (2010)
13. Eiter, T., Fink, M., Weinzierl, A.: Preference-based inconsistency assessment in multi-context systems. In: Janhunen, T., Niemelä, I. (eds.) JELIA 2010. LNCS, vol. 6341, pp. 143–155. Springer, Heidelberg (2010)
14. Gerkey, B.P., Matarić, M.J.: Sold!: auction methods for multi-robot coordination. IEEE Trans. Robot. Autom. Spec. Issue Multi-Robot Syst. 18(5), 758–768 (2002). http://robotics.usc.edu/publications/10/ (Also Technical report IRIS-01-399)
15. Ghidini, C., Giunchiglia, F.: Local models semantics, or contextual reasoning = locality + compatibility. Artif. Intell. 127(2), 221–259 (2001)
16. Giunchiglia, F., Serafini, L.: Multilanguage hierarchical logics, or: how we can do without modal logics. Artif. Intell. 65(1), 29–70 (1994)
17. Grossi, D., Turrini, P.: Dependence theory via game theory. In: van der Hoek, W., Kaminka, G.A., Lespérance, Y., Luck, M., Sen, S. (eds.) AAMAS, pp. 1147–1154. IFAAMAS (2010)
18. Klusch, M., Gerber, A.: Dynamic coalition formation among rational agents. IEEE Intell. Syst. 17(3), 42–47 (2002)
19. Kronbak, L.G., Lindroos, M.: Sharing rules and stability in coalition games with externalities. Mar. Resour. Econ. 22, 137–154 (2007)
20. Lemaire, T., Alami, R., Lacroix, S.: A distributed tasks allocation scheme in multi-uav context. In: Proceedings of the 2004 IEEE International Conference on Robotics and Automation, ICRA 2004, April 26 - May 1 2004, New Orleans, LA, USA, pp. 3622–3627 (2004)
21. Lenat, D.B., Guha, R.V.: Building Large Knowledge-Based Systems; Representation and Inference in the Cyc Project. Addison-Wesley Longman Publishing Co., Inc., Boston (1989)
22. Liemhetcharat, S., Veloso, M.M.: Weighted synergy graphs for effective team formation with heterogeneous ad hoc agents. Artif. Intell. 208, 41–65 (2014)
23. Mesterton-Gibbons, M.: An Introduction to Game-Theoretic Modelling. Addison-Wesley, Redwood (1992)
24. O'Sullivan, A., Sheffrin, S.M.: Economics: Principles in Action. Pearson Prentice Hall, Needham (2006)
25. Parsons, S., Sierra, C., Jennings, N.R.: Agents that reason and negotiate by arguing. J. Logic Comput. 8(3), 261–292 (1998)
26. Sabater, J., Sierra, C., Parsons, S., Jennings, N.R.: Engineering executable agents using multi-context systems. J. Logic Comput. 12(3), 413–442 (2002)
27. Sauro, L.: Formalizing Admissibility Criteria in Coalition Formation among Goal Directed Agents. Ph.D. thesis, University of Turin, Italy (2006)
28. Schmeidler, D.: The nucleolus of a characteristic functional game. SIAM J. Appl. Math. 17, 1163–1170 (1969)
29. Shapley, L.S.: A value for n-person games. Ann. Math. Stud. 28, 307–317 (1953)

30. Shehory, O., Kraus, S.: Methods for task allocation via agent coalition formation. Artif. Intell. **101**(1–2), 165–200 (1998)
31. Sichman, J.S.: Depint: dependence-based coalition formation in an open multi-agent scenario. J. Artif. Soc. Soc. Simul. **1**(2) (1998)
32. Sichman, J.S., Conte, R.: Multi-agent dependence by dependence graphs. In: Proceedings of The First International Joint Conference on Autonomous Agents and Multiagent Systems, AAMAS 2002, pp. 483–490. ACM (2002)
33. Sichman, J.S., Conte, R., Castelfranchi, C., Demazeau, Y.: A social reasoning mechanism based on dependence networks. In: Proceedings of the Eleventh European Conference on Artificial Intelligence, Amsterdam, The Netherlands, 8–12 August 1994, pp. 188–192 (1994)
34. Sichman, J.S., Demazeau, Y.: On social reasoning in multi-agent systems. Revista Iberoamericana de Inteligencia Artificial **13**, 68–84 (2001)
35. Tang, F., Parker, L.E.: Asymtre: automated synthesis of multi-robot task solutions through software reconfiguration. In: Proceedings of the 2004 IEEE International Conference on Robotics and Automation, ICRA 2004, April 26 - May 1 2004, New Orleans, LA, USA, pp. 1501–1508 (2005)
36. Zhang, Y., Parker, L.E.: Iq-asymtre: forming executable coalitions for tightly coupled multirobot tasks. IEEE Trans. Robot. **29**(2), 400–416 (2013)

Comparison of Task-Allocation Algorithms in Frontier-Based Multi-robot Exploration

Jan Faigl[1]([⊠]), Olivier Simonin[2], and Francois Charpillet[3]

[1] Czech Technical University in Prague, Prague, Czech Republic
faiglj@fel.cvut.cz
[2] INSA de Lyon, CITI-Inria Laboratory, Université de Lyon, Lyon, France
[3] Inria, Université de Lorraine, Nancy, France

Abstract. In this paper, we address the problem of efficient allocation of the navigational goals in the multi-robot exploration of unknown environment. Goal candidate locations are repeatedly determined during the exploration. Then, the assignment of the candidates to the robots is solved as the task-allocation problem. A more frequent decision-making may improve performance of the exploration, but in a practical deployment of the exploration strategies, the frequency depends on the computational complexity of the task-allocation algorithm and available computational resources. Therefore, we propose an evaluation framework to study exploration strategies independently on the available computational resources and we report a comparison of the selected task-allocation algorithms deployed in multi-robot exploration.

Keywords: Multi-robot exploration · Task-allocation · Planning

1 Introduction

The robotic exploration of unknown environment can be formulated as a problem to create a map of the environment as quickly as possible, e.g., to find eventual victims during search and rescue missions, and the main objective function considered in this paper is the time to create such a map. The fundamental approach to address the exploration problem is based on an iterative determination of possible goal candidates from which new information about the unknown part of the environment can be acquired. These candidates are assigned to the particular exploring units to maximize their utilization regarding the mission objective. This assignment problem can be formulated as the *task-allocation* problem [3]. After the assignment, each robot is navigated towards the assigned goal while its sensor system is used to perceive its surroundings and update the map being built.

J. Faigl—The presented work is supported by the Czech Science Foundation (GAČR) under research project No. 13-18316P. The travel support of the Czech Ministry of Education under the project No. 7AMB14FR019 is also gratefully acknowledged.
O. Simonin and F. Charpillet—This work is supported by the French-Czech PHC "Murotex" project.

N. Bulling (Ed.): EUMAS 2014, LNAI 8953, pp. 101–110, 2015.
DOI: 10.1007/978-3-319-17130-2_7

This process is repeated until the whole map is created, which is indicated by an empty set of the determined goal candidates.

During the exploration, new information about the environment being explored can be exploited by a more frequent determination of the goal candidates and their assignment to the robots that can improve the mission performance [4]. However, it may not necessarily be the case if robots oscillate between the assigned goals and do not explore new areas, because the location of the newly assigned goals are significantly different from the previous one. In such a case, a stable behaviour can be achieved with a less frequent assignment, e.g., after a robot reaches the previously assigned goal. Moreover, in robotics, the performance of the exploration is usually considered in a practical deployment, which even more emphasizes a less frequent decision-making because of limited on-board computational resources that are shared with other tasks like localization. Therefore, a poor behaviour of the exploration strategy might not be observed, while it can be an issue for more computationally powerful systems.

In this paper, we consider five task-allocation algorithms [1,2,6,8] dealing with the multi-robot exploration and we compare their performance under different mission execution constraints. The results indicate the frequency of the decision-making can change conclusions about the performance of the algorithms. Thus a consideration of the limiting cases of the frequency of the decision-making loop allows to provide a more general results and to identify particular constraints for a good expected performance of the algorithms in practical deployments.

Based on these findings, we propose to consider simulation to tackle robotic problems and thus we aim to encourage researchers in the field of multi-agent system and artificial intelligence to consider their task-allocation algorithms also in the multi-robot exploration missions, which can be currently considered as a problem that is more studied by the robotic community.

2 Multi-robot Exploration Framework

Three main decision-making parts can be identified in the exploration approaches based on frontier cells determination [7]. The first is the method to determine new goal candidates from the frontier cells in the actual map of the environment. The second important decision-making process is the assignment of the goal candidates to the robots together with the selection of the next navigational goal for each robot. The third part is the condition when to perform new assignment and how often the first two parts are repeated.

For simplicity, the multi-robot exploration is considered for a homogeneous group of m mobile robots $R = \{r_1, \ldots, r_m\}$, each equipped with an omnidirectional sensor with the sensing range ρ. The control architecture for the exploration is an iterative procedure where new sensor measurements are integrated into the common map represented as the occupancy grid Occ. The procedure can be implemented in a centralized or distributed way as follows:

1. Initialize the occupancy grid Occ and set the initial plans to $\mathcal{P} = (P_1, \ldots, P_m)$, where $P_i = \{\emptyset\}$ for each robot $1 \leq i \leq m$.

2. Repeat
   (a) Navigate robots towards their goals using the plans $\mathcal{P}$, i.e., move each robot to the next cell from the plan;
   (b) Collect new measurements with the range ρ to the occupancy grid $\mathcal{O}cc$;
   Until **replanning condition is meet**.
3. Update a navigation map $\mathcal{M}$ from the current occupancy grid $\mathcal{O}cc$.
4. Detect all frontiers $\mathcal{F}$ in the current map $\mathcal{M}$.
5. **Determine goal candidates G from the frontiers $\mathcal{F}$.**
6. If $|G| > 0$ **assign goals to the robot**
   - $(\langle r_1, g_{r_1} \rangle, \ldots, \langle r_m, g_{r_m} \rangle) = \mathrm{assign}(\boldsymbol{R}, \boldsymbol{G}, \mathcal{M})$, $r_i \in \boldsymbol{R}$, $g_{r_i} \in \boldsymbol{G}$;
   - Plan paths to the assigned goals (as sequences of grid cells) $\mathcal{P} = \mathrm{plan}$ $(\langle r_1, g_{r_1} \rangle, \ldots, \langle r_m, g_{r_m} \rangle, \mathcal{M})$;
   - Go to Step 2.
7. Stop all robots (all reachable parts of the environment are explored).

The navigation part (Step 2(a) and Step 2(b)) is repeated according to the specified condition. Two basic variants of the condition can be distinguished: (1) a robot reaches its goal; (2) a new assignment is performed whenever an assigned goal will no longer be a frontier cell, e.g., a surrounding unknown area becomes explored. In this paper, we call the first variant as the *goal replanning* (**GR**) condition and the second variant the *immediate replanning* (**IR**) condition. The second variant is more computationally demanding as surrounding cells of the frontier can be explored once the robot moves towards the goal about a distance equal to the size of the grid cell, e.g., 0.05 m; hence, new goals and their assignment have to be determined as quickly as possible.

A frequency of the assignment influences the performance of the exploration, but it depends on the computational complexity of the assignment procedure. Therefore, we consider a discrete time simulator to provide an evaluation setup that is independent on available computational power. An average velocity of the robot is assumed and the robot motion is restricted to traverse a single grid cell per one simulation step. Furthermore, we consider the robots have omnidirectional wheels and can move in arbitrary direction in the grid.

3 Exploration Strategies

Five task-allocation algorithms have been used in this evaluation study of the exploration strategies. All assignment procedures assign one or several goal candidates to each robot from which a single goal candidate is then assigned as the navigational goal. Thus, each goal candidate can be assigned only to one robot.

Greedy Assignment (GA) – A modified greedy assignment is utilized rather than the original approach proposed by Yamauchi in [8]. The closest not yet assigned goal is assigned to each robot sequentially; however, the assignment is performed for a random order of the robots to avoid preference of the first robots like in the original Yamauchi's approach.

Iterative Assignment (IA) – is based on the *Broadcast of Local Eligibility* [6], which is implemented in a centralized environment. The assignment is an iterative procedure, where all robot–goal pairs $\langle r, g \rangle$ are ordered by the associated distance cost. Then, the first not assigned goal from the sequence is assigned to the particular robot without an assigned goal.

Hungarian Assignment (HA) – is an optimal task-allocation algorithm for the given $m \times n$ cost matrix in which each cell value is a distance cost of particular robot–goal assignment for m robots and n goal candidates. If $m > n$ the IA algorithm is used, while for $m < n$ the cost matrix is enlarged and virtual robots are added with a very high distance cost for the goals.

Multiple Traveling Salesman Assignment (MA) – is an extension of the TSP distance cost approach [5] in which the next robot goal is selected as the first goal on the route found as a solution of the Traveling Salesman Problem (TSP). In MA, this distance cost is utilized in the multiple traveling salesman problem (MTSP) that is addressed by the $\langle$*cluster first, route second*$\rangle$ heuristic [2]. First, the goal candidates are clustered by the K-means algorithm to m clusters. Then, each cluster is assigned to a particular robot and the next robot goal is determined according to the TSP distance cost [5].

MinPos – is based on a computation of the rank $r_{i,j}$ for each goal i and robot j [1]. The rank $r_{i,j}$ is the number of robots that are closer to the goal candidate i than the robot j. Then, each robot selects the goal for which its rank is minimal. If several goal candidates have the same minimal rank for the robot i, the closest goal candidate to the robot is selected as the goal.

3.1   Proposed Goal Candidates Determination

The proposed goal candidates determination method is an extension of the method [5] developed for a single robot exploration. The method is based on selection of representatives of the frontiers cells from which all frontier cells can be covered. However, we found out that for a group of robots, the original procedure [5] can provide less representatives than the number of robots, which may decreases the mission performance. Therefore, we modified the procedure to adaptively adjust the number of the determined goal candidates and call the new procedure as the *Adaptive Number of Representatives* (ANR) method.

It is assumed the freespace cells in the map $\mathcal{M}$ of the environment always form a single connected component and all frontier cells $\boldsymbol{F}$ are organized into a set of o sets (called free edges) of the single connected components $\mathcal{F} = \{\boldsymbol{F}_1, \ldots, \boldsymbol{F}_o\}$ such that $\boldsymbol{F} = \bigcup_{i=1}^{o} \boldsymbol{F}_i$ and $\boldsymbol{F}_i \cap \boldsymbol{F}_j = \emptyset$ for $i \neq j$, $1 \leq i, j \leq o$. Then, representatives are determined by the K-means clustering algorithm. n_r clusters are determined for each free edge $\boldsymbol{F}_i$ and the mean of each cluster is one goal candidate. In [5], authors determined n_r as $n_r = 1 + \lfloor |\boldsymbol{F}_i|/1.8\rho_g + 0.5 \rfloor$, where ρ_g is the sensor range (in the number of grid cells). However, for many robots in the team and small n_r a goal candidate can be assigned to several robots or there will be a robot without the assigned goal. Therefore, we propose to adjust particular n_r of the largest free edges to have at least m goal candidates in total.

We experimentally verified improvement of this method over the original method of the goal candidates determination [5] for all scenarios considered in this paper. Due to limited space we consider ANR as the only goal candidates determination method and do not present the supporting results here.

4   Results

The task-allocation algorithms have been studied in four environments: *em*, *auto-lab*, *jh*, and *potholes*; with dimensions 21 m × 24 m, 30 m × 30 m, and 21 m × 24 m, and 40 m × 40 m, respectively, that represent office-like and open space environments, see Fig. 1. The studied performance indicator is the required time to explore the whole environment that is measured using the proposed discrete-time simulator as the number of the simulation steps denoted as T. Notice that for this criterion, it does not make sense if one robot stop its activity sooner while other robots still need to visit remaining frontiers.

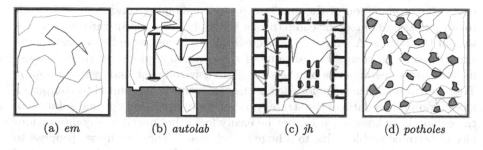

(a) *em*   (b) *autolab*   (c) *jh*   (d) *potholes*

Fig. 1. Final exploration paths in the evaluated environments and for the number of robots $m = 3$ and sensor range $\rho = 3\,\mathrm{m}$

The comparison of algorithms performance is made for a set of scenarios, where each scenario consists of the environment with the defined starting positions of the robots, the number of robots m selected from the set $m \in \{3, 5, 7\}$, and the sensor range ρ from the set $\rho \in \{3\,\mathrm{m}, 5\,\mathrm{m}, 7\,\mathrm{m}\}$. A small random perturbation (in tenths of meters) is introduced to the initial positions of the robots to consider sensitivity of the algorithms to the initial conditions. Therefore, 20 variants of each environment are considered, which gives $4 \times 3 \times 3 \times 20 = 720$ variants, and T is evaluated as the average value.

Two limiting replanning conditions **GR** and **IR** of the exploration procedure are considered. For the **GR** condition new goal candidates are determined once a robot reaches its goal, while **IR** is the fastest replanning possible as new goal candidates are determined and assigned to the robots immediately once an assigned goal is no longer frontier. Besides, based on the results in [2], we consider replanning after 7 discrete steps, or sooner when a robot reaches its goal, which is denoted as **S7R**.

Table 1. Reference exploration times T_{ref}

Map	$\rho = 3\,\mathrm{m}$			$\rho = 5\,\mathrm{m}$			$\rho = 7\,\mathrm{m}$		
	$m=3$	$m=5$	$m=7$	$m=3$	$m=5$	$m=7$	$m=3$	$m=5$	$m=7$
autolab	1204	854	827	837	719	654	686	624	601
em	726	527	475	456	405	410	366	343	356
jh	864	660	613	857	654	588	782	624	588
potholes	2578	1679	1205	1678	1058	916	1301	928	829

The evaluation framework is deterministic and also IA, HA, and MinPos algorithms are deterministic procedures and thus only a single trial of each algorithm for a particular scenario is performed. On the other hand, GA and MA strategies are stochastic, and therefore, 20 trials are performed for these strategies and each scenario. Thus, the total number of performed trials is 92 880.

Evaluation Methodology – The performance of each exploration strategy may differs in a particular scenario, which requires an individual comparison for the particular combination of the map, m, ρ, and replanning condition. This leads to an excessive number of comparisons without a straightforward generalization of the results. A summary of the overall performance indicator cannot be simply computed as an average value of the required exploration time, because its absolute value depends on the size of the environment and sensor range ρ. Therefore, a reference value for each particular scenario is required to compute a global competitive ratio of the strategy. A reference can be an optimal solution of the exploration; however, it cannot be easily found because it is a computationally intractable problem due to a huge search space. That is why we propose to determine the reference value as the best found solution from the large set of the results we computed. The found references are depicted in Table 1.

Influence of the Replanning Condition – Two scenarios are selected to show the influence of the replanning conditions and particular five-point summaries are depicted in Fig. 2. The MA strategy is considered with **GR** and **IR** conditions (see Sect. 2) denoted as MA–GR and MA–IR, respectively. These results clearly show that with the IR condition, the performance of all exploration strategies (including the greedy assignment) is better than the MA strategy with a lower replanning frequency under the GR condition. Therefore, a deployment of the exploration strategy on different computational platforms may results to different conclusions about the algorithms' performance.

Overall Comparison of the Exploration Strategies – is computed as the average value of the competitive ratio between the required exploration time T and the reference time, see Table 1. Selected aggregated results over all environments are presented in Figs. 3, 4, and 5 for particular sensor range ρ.

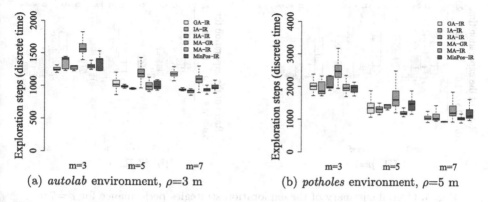

(a) *autolab* environment, ρ=3 m   (b) *potholes* environment, ρ=5 m

Fig. 2. Required exploration time to explore the *autolab* and *potholes* environments with m robots, sensor range $\rho = 3$ m and **IR** or **GR** replanning condition

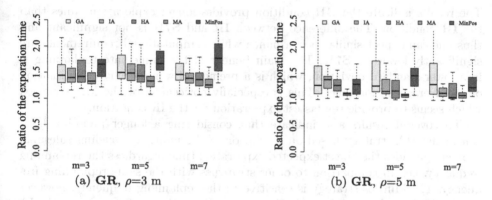

(a) **GR**, ρ=3 m   (b) **GR**, ρ=5 m

Fig. 3. Overall summary of the exploration strategies performance for **GR** condition

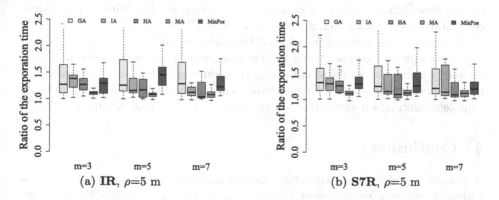

(a) **IR**, ρ=5 m   (b) **S7R**, ρ=5 m

Fig. 4. Overall summary of the exploration strategies performance for $\rho = 5$ m

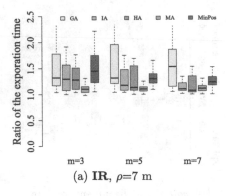
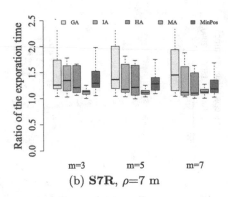

<table>
<tr><td>(a) IR, ρ=7 m</td><td>(b) S7R, ρ=7 m</td></tr>
</table>

Fig. 5. Overall summary of the exploration strategies performance for $\rho = 7\,\mathrm{m}$

4.1 Discussion

The results indicate the **GR** condition provides longer exploration times than the **IR** condition. The difference between **IR** and **S7R** is not significant and thus one can expect similar performance while computational requirements are significantly lower for **S7R**. The main benefit of the immediate replanning is in a lower standard deviation, which is a premise of a more reliable estimation of the average performance. This is especially noticeable for the MA strategy, which seems to provide the fastest exploration for the IR condition.

The overall results also indicate that considering a longer planning horizon in the MA strategy based on a solution of the multiple traveling salesman problem provides the lowest expected exploration time regardless the replanning frequency, i.e., in comparison to other strategies with the same replanning frequency. The MinPos strategy is sensitive to the replanning frequency; however for the **S7R** condition, it provides better or competitive performance to the IA and HA strategies. The main advantage of the MinPos strategy is the ability to be implemented in a distributed environment, which is not straightforward for implementation of the goal candidates clustering in MA. MinPos is also less computationally demanding, which can be an additional benefit.

A relative comparison of the IA and HA strategies can be concluded that both approaches provide competitive overall performance. Here, we can also highlight an ability to implement decision-making procedure in a distributed environment that is straightforward for IA using only local information, while HA may need complete information about the robots positions and all goal candidates.

5   Conclusion

A comparison of five task-allocation algorithms employed in multi-robot exploration of unknown environment is presented in this paper. The algorithms are accompanied with a new improved goal candidates determination called *adaptive number of representatives* (ANR). The used evaluation methodology is based on

a reference solution of the particular exploration scenario that allows to aggregate results among different scenarios and evaluate the performance indicators
statistically. Moreover, we propose to evaluate the exploration strategies using
precisely defined computational environment that does not depend on the available computational resources, and which allows to obtain statistically significant
results using thousands of trials.

The presented results indicate the performance of the exploration strategy
depends on the frequency of replanning, and therefore, an evaluation methodology that is not dependent on a particular setup of the evaluation environment
may provide a more general results and conclusions. In particular, we consider
a limit case with the immediate replanning condition to validate scalability of
the decision-making procedure with a more powerful computational resources.
Although this may not be achieved in a practical deployment, such an evaluation
allows to identify if the exploration strategy is "stable" in the taken decisions
with increasing replanning frequency or if it needs a specific limit to exhibit the
taken decision before another decision will be made.

Our future work can be divided into two research streams. The first stream
aims to deliver a methodology for benchmarking exploration algorithms that will
allow to compare different approaches in a unified and easily replicable setup,
which will not only compare algorithm performance using particular hardware
setup but will also provide a more general conclusion about the expected performance. The proposed evaluation framework, task-allocation algorithms, and
the limiting replanning conditions are the initial building blocks for such benchmarking. The second research stream aims to consider the exploration problem
in a distributed setup with a limited communication. Here, we aim to employ the
proposed evaluation methodology and extend it for distributed task-allocation
algorithms and their evaluation using the proposed simulator and practical verification using real mobile robots.

Acknowledgments. Computational resources were provided by the MetaCentrum
under the program LM2010005 and the CERIT-SC under the program Centre CERIT
Scientific Cloud, part of the Operational Program Research and Development for Innovations, Reg. no. CZ.1.05/3.2.00/08.0144.

References

1. Bautin, A., Simonin, O., Charpillet, F.: *MinPos*: a novel frontier allocation algorithm for multi-robot exploration. In: Su, C.-Y., Rakheja, S., Liu, H. (eds.) ICIRA
   2012, Part II. LNCS, vol. 7507, pp. 496–508. Springer, Heidelberg (2012)
2. Faigl, J., Kulich, M., Přeučil, L.: Goal assignment using distance cost in multi-robot
   exploration. In: IEEE/RSJ International Conference of the Intelligent Robots and
   Systems (IROS), pp. 3741–3746 (2012)
3. Gerkey, B.P., Mataric, M.J.: A formal analysis and taxonomy of task allocation in
   multi-robot systems. Int. J. Robot. Res. **23**(9), 939–954 (2004)
4. Holz, D., Basilico, N., Amigoni, F., Behnke, S.: Evaluating the efficiency of frontier-
   based exploration strategies. In: ISR/ROBOTIK, pp. 1–8 (2010)

5. Kulich, M., Faigl, J., Přeučil, L.: On distance utility in the exploration task. In: IEEE International Conference on Robotics and Automation (ICRA), pp. 4455–4460 (2011)
6. Werger, B.B., Mataric, M.J.: Broadcast of local eligibility: behavior-based control for strongly cooperative robot teams. In: 4th International Conference on Autonomous Agents, AGENTS 2000, pp. 21–22. ACM, New York (2000)
7. Yamauchi, B.: A frontier-based approach for autonomous exploration. In: IEEE International Symposium on Computational Intelligence in Robotics and Automation (CIRA), pp. 146–151 (1997)
8. Yamauchi, B.: Decentralized coordination for multirobot exploration. Robot. Auton. Syst. 29, 111–118 (1999)

Homecoming: A Multi-robot Exploration Method for Conjunct Environments with a Systematic Return Procedure

Shervin Ghasemlou[1(✉)], Ali Mohades[2], Taher Abbas Shangari[2], and Mohammadreza Tavassoli[2]

[1] Amirkabir Robotics Center, Amirkabir University of Technology, Tehran, Iran
`Shervin.ghasemloo@aut.ac.ir`
[2] Faculty of Mathematics and Computer Science,
Amirkabir University of Technology, Tehran, Iran
`{mohades,taher.abbasi,tavassoli.mreza}@aut.ac.ir`

Abstract. The present work proposes a multi-robot exploration method for conjunct environments, based on one of the state-of-the-art algorithms. In many exploration missions, after the subject is found, it is beneficial if the discoverer robot returns back to the base station, in order to report, delivery or recharge. In addition, the exploration might need a long time to be finished or has to be done over and over. Returning back to the base station enables robots to get recharged, fixed, or even substituted with other robots. Furthermore, the equilibrium in task allocation to robots is this work's other concern. The presented algorithm also reduces the maximum energy consumption of robots, as a good side effect. The efficiency of the proposed algorithm is demonstrated by providing simulation results for a variety of obstacle densities and different number of robots.

Keywords: Multi-robot exploration · Conjunct environment · Task allocation

1 Introduction

In the multi-robot exploration field of research, the most important objective is to provide an efficient method to explore unknown environments using a team of robots. The method should lead robots to visit every accessible region in the area, usually under connectivity constraints. The application fields of the algorithms vary from demining [1] to rescue [2] and mapping [3]. The communication type is usually dynamic and robots are equipped with Bluetooth [4], Wi-Fi [5] or ZigBee [6] technologies in order to communicate with each other.

There are two research fields in the literature which have very similar concepts to the multi-robot exploration study field: terrain coverage and foraging. For the terrain coverage studies, two main differences distinguish them from multi-robot exploration researches. Firstly, in terrain coverage studies it is not essential to have permanent communication between robots. The main concern is to visit every corner of the environment at least once. Since usually there is no communication range limitations, the

© Springer International Publishing Switzerland 2015
N. Bulling (Ed.): EUMAS 2014, LNAI 8953, pp. 111–127, 2015.
DOI: 10.1007/978-3-319-17130-2_8

configuration space can be visited completely with-out any worry about breaking the connection. In terrain coverage problems, robots also don't have to report their situation to the base center or other robots during the process. Secondly, since the map of the environment is not available in multi-robot exploration problems, these algorithms should work online. On the other hand, in terrain coverage studies robots usually have access to the map of the environment, therefore every move can be computed before beginning of the process. In a survey paper from Choset [7], all researches in the field of terrain coverage are classified as heuristic algorithms, approximate algorithms, partial-approximate algorithms, and exact cellular decomposition ones. To show the intractability of this problem, in a paper from Zheng et al. [8], authors have shown those coverage problem versions which try to minimize the coverage time, are NP-hard problems. Authors also have provided a polynomial time algorithm based on another work [9] and claimed that the coverage time of their algorithm is close to the optimal solution. In several papers authors also consider sensor-based cover-age [10–13], where a robot doesn't have to move into a cell to add that cell to set of visited ones, it is sufficient to observe that cell via sensors.

In the foraging problems, the number of employed robots are comparatively much more than both multi-robot exploration and terrain coverage fields of study. Another distinguishing characteristic of foraging researches is that the employed robots are often equipped with very limited tools. In foraging problems providing an effective task allocation scheme, usually based on swarm intelligence algorithms, is the main purpose. Similar to multi-robot exploration studies, robots communicate with each other, but in a different manner. In most of the studies communication is not dynamic and permanent. Based on the way ants communicate with each other by means of a chemical called "pheromone", robots communicate through virtual pheromone with each other [14]. In a paper by Couceiro et al. [15] the authors combine a biology inspired algorithm with a potential field method to explore the area. In other work [16], two distributed exploration algorithms are provided, gradient and sweeper algorithms. The first one is able to quickly return robots back to the base station, while the sweeper algorithm has the ability to find food in farther distances, albeit with a slower speed.

In spite of having different properties mentioned above, there is no exact boundary to separate these three categories from each other. For instance, in [17] the authors provide a swarm navigating method in which robots are in contact with each other by means of a wireless connection. The presented algorithm in this paper, as a multi-robot exploration algorithm, has common properties with both terrain coverage and foraging algorithms. In the next section, we investigate the multi-robot exploration literature more thoroughly.

2   Previous Works

In an early work [18] a method was proposed in which a center makes decisions for all robots. In [19] authors presented a centralized method too, which considers the cost of reaching a particular point along with the efficiency of the same point. This algorithm always tries to assign a point to a robot as its next position, if reaching to that point makes the best possible balance between cost and efficiency. In this study efficiency is based on the probability of visibility of the assigned target point to a robot, from the assigned target points to the other robots.

Although centralized methods are able to provide complete solutions, they act slowly. On the other hand decentralized algorithms are faster, but lack completeness and optimality. In [20] a decentralized method is proposed which considers range constraints. In this study, robots are able to decide whether to keep persistency of the communication with other robots or to avoid obstacles. The lack of prior knowledge about the environment makes it hard to provide a robust method, or to guarantee the performance. In [21] a decentralized multi-robot exploration method is provided which guarantees the performance of the algorithm under some assumptions. In another work [22] as a market-based one, a hierarchical task allocation method is provided that uses coalitions. The authors claim that such methods act better than greedy or coalition-free ones. In another work [23] two strategies for task allocation is provided. In the first strategy as a decentralized method, while the performance is good, the energy consumption is more than the second strategy, which is a centralized one. In [24] the authors have studied two different kinds of explorations where in both cases robots have to be in touch with each other. In one case, robots have to be connected with a fixed base station also, which delimitates exploration area, similar to the present work.

Performance measures vary widely. Different papers use total path lengths [25], balance in workload distribution [25], total steps of the algorithm [26], algorithm's overload [27, 28], energy consumption [28, 29] and time complexity [8, 23] to measure the efficiency of provided algorithms. In our work, distribution of exploration task, maximum energy consumption, traveled distance and number of step-moves for each robot are considered.

In the literature, there are several studies which have considered energy consumption [10, 27, 28, 30]. None of these works provide a scheme to recharge robots. If the exploration process is ongoing, as in a surveillance system [31], robots have to be charged or exchanged with other charged ones to continue the exploration task. In a paper from Koveos et al. [32], authors have studied multi-robot exploration in space missions. In their work robots are in touch with the base station and the base station is responsible for tracking and recharging them. In their study robots are getting recharged by radiations emitted from a laser. The distance of robots from the base station, environmental conditions and also the amount of energy needed for robots can affect the efficiency of recharge procedure in their work.

In a paper by Kovacs, Pásztor and Istenes [33] authors have proposed an algorithm to explore the environment under connectivity constraints. In this work robots have to be connected to each other and a fixed base station using a Blue-tooth communication system. The algorithm guarantees the communication persistency during exploration. The authors have shown that in obstacle-free environments, their algorithm works optimally, in the terms of the number of step-moves. The way we define conjunct environments in this paper, enables the presented algorithm to see conjunct environments similar to obstacle free environments, from a global planner point of view. This property is the result of leaving the obstacle avoidance duty to the local planner. The optimality of the provided algorithm in [33], makes it suitable to be used as a basis for our global planner.

Three major contributions of this paper to the field are as follows. First, a systematic procedure for returning robots back to the base station have been provided. The return procedure executes simultaneous with the exploration task and doesn't interrupt it. The provided method also keeps the communication persistency as long as robots explore the environment. Second, the proposed method makes the system balanced in assigning the exploration task to robots and also reduces the maximum energy consumption. Simulation results show that the presented algorithm works close to the optimal solution for reducing maximum energy consumption and balancing the system. Third, the provided global planner works independent from local planners of each robot. Therefore the provided algorithm has the ability to be used in any conjunct environment with any type of robot.

3 Preliminaries

Similar to most studies, we use a grid to divide the environment into square cells. Two cells are considered neighbors if they share a common edge. In this part our aim is to define conjunct environments in a way that, regardless of where obstacles lie, each robot is able to move to any neighbor cell, or swap its position with neighbor robots, only through the common edge.

Conjunct environment: If in the environment E, the length of the edge of cells is A, and we have:

$$d_o + 2d_r + 4\mu \leq A \tag{1}$$

$$\forall \text{Obstacle O:}\quad \text{Distance}\,(O, O_c) \geq 2d_r + 4\mu \tag{2}$$

then we call E a conjunct environment.

In this definition d_o is the maximum diameter of excircles of obstacles, d_r is the diameter of robots, O_c is the closest obstacle to obstacle O and $\mu \geq 0$ is the prudential margin. The Distance function returns the closest distance between two obstacles by the Euclidean metric.

Figure 1 left illustrates the worst possible case for migration of a robot from one cell to a neighbor cell in a conjunct environment. Two robots R_1 and R_2 are in two neighbor cells and an obstacle lies in the middle of the common edge. Even in this case, there is enough room on both sides of the obstacle for each robot to pass through and go to the other cell. The grey tube indicates the obstacle-free area between the obstacle and the closest possible obstacle.

For flying robots when the altitude of flight is constant, it is usually easy to classify the workspace as conjunct. It is almost the same for marine robots too, because in both cases most of the times there is actually no obstacle in the work space. But the definition of conjunct environment also covers obstructed areas. For instance, in a forest the maximum diameter of trees is available. The density of trees in the area is also available for many forests (see [34]). This makes it possible to estimate the closest possible distance between trees. Our definition of conjunct environment also covers some extra-terrestrial environments. There are papers which have studied the spatial distribution of

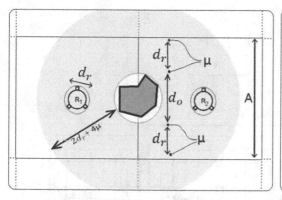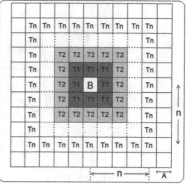

Fig. 1. Left: two neighbor cells of the environment and position of robots and obstacles in one possible worst case. Red circles are indicating excircles of robots and the obstacle. Right: the exploration Environment, the base station's cell (in the center) and Toruses (Color figure online).

rocks on mars [35] and size of rocks on it [36]. This information is adequate to decide whether the environment is conjunct or not.

Step-move: robots' migration from one cell to a neighbor one is called step-move.

Team-move: migration of all robots together to their next assigned positions is called *team-move*. Next assigned position for a robot can be its current position, but in a *team-move* at least one robot goes to a non-visited cell.

In the *kovacs algorithm*, the length of a cell's edge is a function of the communication range. If we denote the radius of the communication range by r_c, the edge length of each square shaped cell is determined using this formula:

$$A = \frac{2r_c}{\sqrt{26}} \tag{3}$$

This equation is based on the definition of three subareas [33] (Fig. 2. Up):

E_c**:** is a set of cells that neighbor robots of each robot are only allowed to be in them during the exploration process. In other words, neighbors are not allowed to leave the coverage range of the robot.

E_s**:** is a set of cells that neighbor robots of each robot are only allowed to be in them after the completion of a *team-move*, and before executing the next team-move.

E_n**:** is a set of cells that a robot can only go to them, during its current *team-move*.

Torus: is a set of cells which their distance from the base cell (B) is equal. Here distance is measured using the infinite norm:

$$Torus_i = \left\{ c \mid c \in E \parallel c - B \parallel_\infty = i \right\} \tag{4}$$

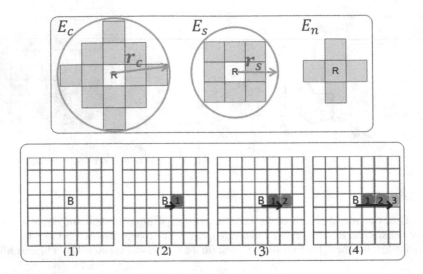

Fig. 2. Up: three subareas in the *kovacs algorithm*. All cells of each subarea is shown by grey. Note that in all of these three subareas the center cell is the location of the robot which the area is defined for. Only for E_n the occupied cell by the robot (center cell) is also a subset of the subarea. Down: result of running initialize position algorithm for three robots.

It can easily be shown that there are 8i cells in the **Torus**$_i$ (see Fig. 1. Right). In the presented algorithm, since the first Torus is the closest Torus to the base station, robots return back to this torus in order to get recharged or deliver an object.

4   The Base Algorithm

In this section we rewrite the *kovacs algorithm* in our own words, and call it the *base algorithm*. The *base algorithm* is written in a way that imitates the Kovacs' algorithm's behavior in obstacle free environments, but in a simpler and clearer manner. For the sake of simplicity, we didn't put any code in the algorithm concerning connectivity and its constraints. All constraints are implicitly covered and satisfied in the *base algorithm*.

In the base algorithm, Lines 1–6 are initializations. Line 6 is a call to initialize position algorithm, which brings out all robots from the base station and builds up the exploration chain, as Fig. 2. Down illustrates.

In the base algorithm (Table 1), if we set aside the number of step-moves caused by initialize position algorithm, the number of team-moves will be equal to the number of step-moves of the farthest robot at the end. Farthest robot has to do 8 N step-moves, since the last torus has the same number of cells within. As an exception, the result of executing initialize position algorithm is considered as the first team-move.

Table 1. The *base algorithm*

Algorithm Base algorithm
1 $N_r \leftarrow$ number of robots
2 Robot [] $\leftarrow$ new Robot [N_r]
3 Torus [] $\leftarrow$ new Torus [N_r]
4 Search_Direction $\leftarrow$ choose from {cw, ccw} // cw=clockwise,ccw=counter clockwise
5 Initialize_Direction $\leftarrow$ choose from {right, up, left, down}
6 Initialize_position (N_r , Initialize_Direction, Torus, Robot)
7 SFP $\leftarrow$ 0 // SFP = swap feasibility pointer
8 for i=N_r down to 1
9   for j=1 to 8
10   if i is equal to 1 and j is equal to 8
11   break;//means one round of exploration is done
12   end if
13   for k=N_r down to SFP
14   Torus[k]. Robot. next_position_in_grid$\leftarrow$ next neighbor cell in the Torus (k)
15   end for
16   for k=SFP down to 1
17   Torus[k]. Robot. next_position_in_grid $\leftarrow$ Torus[k]. Robot. position_in_grid
18   end for
19   move robots together to their next assigned positions
20   for k=1 to N_r
21   Robot[k]. position_in_grid $\leftarrow$ Robot[k]. next_ position_in_grid
22   end for
23 SFP=N_r-	(N_r-i) %(2N_r) - N_r|
24   end for
25 end for

In the rest of the *base algorithm*, the main loop lies between lines 8–25. The result of running the *base algorithm* for 3 robots is shown in the Fig. 3. It can be seen that except for the first robot, all other robots never touch the first torus again during the process. In addition the distribution of exploration task in this algorithm is very disparate. The initialize position algorithm forces i-th robot to do i *step-moves*. Thereafter ro-bots visit remaining non-visited cells of their current torus in order to complete the exploration. Therefore first robot does 8 *step-moves*, second one 17 *step-moves* and the N-th one 9 N–1 steps. It is obvious that farther robots carry the burden of the exploration task much more than the closer ones.

In order to have a simpler maintenance system, it will be much better if we use same hardware for all robots, particularly for locomotion parts and power sources. The main consumer of the power is the locomotion part. Other parts consume less in comparison.

In the *base algorithm*, if we choose the capacity of the power source according to requirements of farther robots, it results in forcing closer ones to carry a power source much heavier than their needs. On the other hand, if we choose the power source capacity according to the closer robots, the farther ones soon will get out of energy. In the next section we provide the idea to solve these problems.

5   The Homecoming Algorithm

Assume that the *base algorithm* runs till the end of the initialize position algorithm. Then after every *team-move*, and before executing the next *team-moves*, the

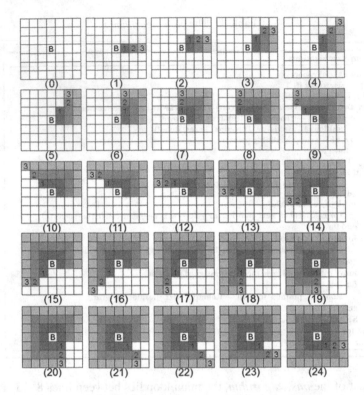

Fig. 3. The result of running the *base algorithm* for three robots. In the state zero, positions are being initialized (Fig. 2. right), which results in the first *team-move*, state 1. Explored cells of each robot has shown in different colors, red for first robot, blue for second one and grey for third one (Color figure online).

last robot R_N, is swapped c_i times with its predecessors, first time with R_{N-1}, then R_{N-2} and the same way till R_{N-c_i}. By doing so, if $c_i < N$, then R_N goes to previous position of R_{N-c_i} and robots $R_{N-c_1+1}, R_{N-c_1+2}, \dots, R_{N-1}$ go to the previous positions of $R_{N-c_1+1}, R_{N-c_1+2}, \dots, R_N$ with no change in the order. Positions of other robots don't change. If $\sum_1^8 c_i = N - 1$ and above procedure is repeated eight times using $c_1, c_2, \dots, c_8$ for robot R_N, after these 8 team-moves R_N goes to R_1's previous cell, which lies at the first torus. All other robots are shifted one cell further.

Thereafter, if we repeat the whole procedure using the same c_i values for the current last robot, R_{N-1}, which its current position is R_N's previous position, all other robots are shifted one cell further, and R_{N-1} goes to the first cell. If this procedure is repeated totally N times, at the end 8N team-moves will be done, and all robots experience the first torus at least once. The flowchart of this process, which we call it *Homecoming* is shown in Fig. 4. left.

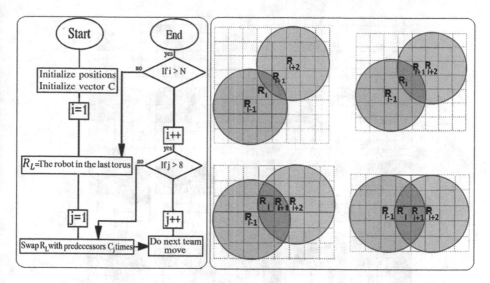

Fig. 4. Left: The flow chart of the Homecoming procedure. Right: Four possible situation of swap. In two upper situation, if R_i and R_{i+1} do swap, R_i gets out of the coverage area of R_{i-1} and R_{i+1} gets out of coverage area of R_{i+2}, which results in breaking the connection. But for two lower situations at least one cell is common between coverage areas of R_{i+2} and R_{i-1}, which is highlighted in green. Swap can be done by means of this common cell (Color figure online).

To initialize vector C we use a formula which distributes N − 1 swaps almost uniformly between $c_1, c_2, \ldots, c_8$. This formula plays the main role in distributing the exploration task between robots equally:

$$c_i = \begin{cases} 0 & i = 1 \\ K_i - K_{i-1} & i > 1 \end{cases} \quad i = 1, 2 \ldots 8 \quad Where\ K_i = \left\lfloor \frac{(i-1) \cdot (N-1)}{7} \right\rfloor \tag{5}$$

The provided scheme for return procedure is very effective. For example if during the exploration process a subject is found and the discoverer decides to send it back to the base station, there is always a further robot which is returning to the base, and the object can be given to this returning robot.

The connection between robots shouldn't be broken. When two robot have to swap, if cells which they occupy have a common edge, the connection is not broken, otherwise it will (Fig. 4. Right, two upper cases). In case of a connection-breaking swap, it is post-poned until the state of occupied cells change into a non-connection-breaking state (Fig. 4. Right, two lower cases). After every 2 N *team-moves*, the chain of robots becomes completely straight and swaps can be done without breaking the connection (Fig 5).

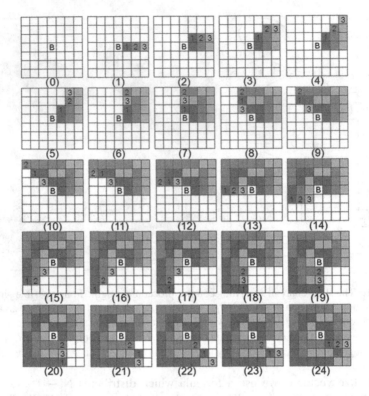

Fig. 5. The result of running the proposed algorithm for three robots. In each state the positions of robots after doing swaps are shown.

6 Simulation Results

In the first part of this section we provide the simulation results of the proposed algorithm without taking into account the effects of obstacle avoidance. In the second part, we provide a very simple obstacle avoidance method based on the Bug2 [38] algorithm in order to study the effects of the obstacle avoidance on the global planner's performance. All major parts of the simulator code, including the global planner (*base algorithm* and *Homecoming algorithm*) and some parts of the local planner module are implemented in the visual studio 2010 using C#.net. The rest of the local planner codes are implemented in Matlab.

6.1 The Global Planner

In these experiments, both kovacs and the proposed algorithm was executed for 1–32 robots. To measure how much these algorithm are successful in uniform task allocation, the number of *step-move*s of each robot was counted and the standard deviation around the average was computed. To measure the maximum energy consumption of robots, maximum number of *step-move*s of all robots was calculated. The results are shown in Fig. 6.

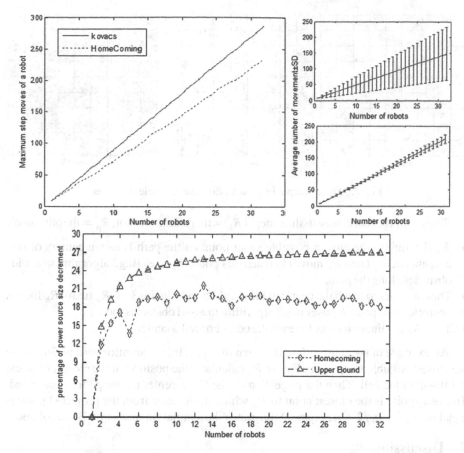

Fig. 6. Up-left: Maximum number of *step-move*s in kovacs and *Homecoming algorithm* s. Up-right: Average number of *step-move*s (mean) with standard deviation around it for *kovacs algorithm* (up) and *Homecoming algorithm* (down). Down: Percentage of reduction in maximum energy consumption for the *Homecoming algorithm*.

6.2 The Local Planner

In this section, maps of three set of different conjunct environments was generated. We generated 100 maps with the obstacle density d = 2 %, 100 maps with d = 5 % and 100 maps with d = 8 %. The spatial distribution of obstacles is uniform, but for the size of obstacles we used Gaussian distribution with mean = 1 m and standard-deviation = 0.25 m. Figure 7 illustrates one sample map of each density.

According to Eq. 3, the size of cell's edge is determined by the range of the communication device. Most of the communication devices provide a connectivity range of 10–100 m, therefore the size of the edge can be 3.9–39 m of robots = 50 cm, and the prudential margin μ = 10 cm. Our simulated robots are equipped with range finders, which are able to detect obstacles up to 7 m in distance.

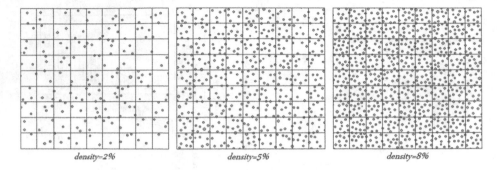

density≈2%   density≈5%   density≈8%

Fig. 7. Three sample maps with different obstacle densities

The swap procedure consists three steps (R_b = the returning robot, R_a = the other one):

- R_b determines the closest possible swap point on the path between centers of two neighbor cells. Then R_b moves to reach this point. R_b uses Bug2 algorithm to avoids obstacles along the path.
- Then R_a goes to reach the center of the neighbor cell. In this step R_a treats R_b like an obstacle on its path. R_a uses Bug2 algorithm to avoid obstacles too.
- Then R_b continues its way to reach the neighbor cell's center.

An example of swap procedure is shown in Fig. 8. It is straightforward to determine the closest possible swap point. Firstly R_a calculates the position of the closest obstacle (CO) within the cell. Then the projection of the CO's center on the path is computed. The swap point is the closest point to R_a which its distance from the projected point is equal to $d_r/2 + d_r/2 + \mu$. Figure 9 illustrates the simulation results for 3–10 robots.

7   Discussion

If we put aside the base station's cell, the reachable environment has $(2N + 1)^2 - 1$ cells. Reachability here refers to ability to reach a point without breaking the connection. The initialize position algorithm does $\frac{N(N+1)}{2}$ step-moves, which results in visiting N unexplored cells. To visit the rest of the environment $(2N + 1)^2 - N - 1$ other step-moves, totally $4.5N^2 + 3.5N$ step-moves have to be done.

Here we show that for each algorithm which tries to return robots from the last torus to the first one during one complete round of exploration, at least $6.5N^2 + 1.5N$ total step-moves are required. Such an algorithm has to do at least $4.5N^2 + 3.5N$ step-moves to visit the whole area. Then for return procedure, if robots returns back to the first torus in a monotonic manner [37] N − 1 swaps are required; otherwise robots should do more swaps. Each swap is equal to two step-moves, therefore totally $2(N − 1)$ step-moves are needed. Thus return procedure for all robots takes 2N (N − 1) moves. Therefore the optimal algorithm requires at least $6.5N^2 + 1.5N$ step-moves, as a lower bound to visit the whole area. As described before, the provided algorithm acts in the same way.

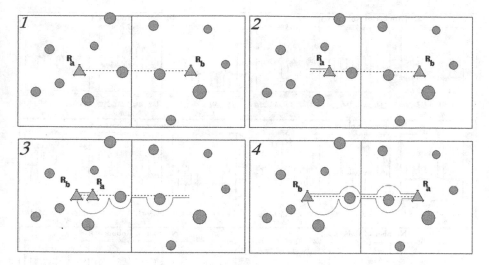

Fig. 8. State 1 represents positions of obstacles and robots (R_1 in the left cell, R_2 in the right cell) and the connecting line of centers. Other states represent three steps of the swap procedure respectively. The traveled paths of R_1 and R_2 are shown by red and purple trajectories. Robots always choose left turn in case of facing an obstacle, as a part of Bug2 algorithm. Robots keep their distance from obstacles equal to the prudential margin (μ) (Color figure online).

The ideal equilibrium in task allocation is achieved when all robots travel same distance, equal to the mean. The mean for *kovacs algorithm* is 4.5N + 3.5 and for provided algorithm is 6.5N + 1.5. The increment in average number of *step-moves* is because of the Homecoming procedure. As Fig. 6. Up-right shows, the task allocation in provided algorithm is very close to the optimal and the standard deviation is very intensive around the mean. As a result of equalization in the task allocation, the maximum number of *step-moves* (NSM) is also less than the *kovacs algorithm* (Fig. 6. Up-left).

Since the robot with maximum NSM, consumes the energy more than the others, it is possible to set an upper bound on how much an algorithm is able to reduce the maximum energy consumption of robots, in comparison with the best non-returning algorithm (the *kovacs algorithm*). Obviously the maximum NSM can't be less than the average number of *step-moves* (6.5 N + 1.5). In the *kovacs algorithm* the maximum NSM is 9N − 1, then the maximum percentage of reduction (MPR) will be:

$$\text{MPR (N)} = \frac{(9N - 1) - 6.5N + 1.5}{9N - 1} = \frac{2.5N - 2.5}{9N - 1} * 100 \tag{6}$$

By approaching the number of robots to infinity, MPR_{max} is derived:

$$\text{MPR}_{\text{max}} = \lim_{i \to \infty} \frac{2.5i - 2.5}{9i - 1} * 100 = 27.78\% \tag{7}$$

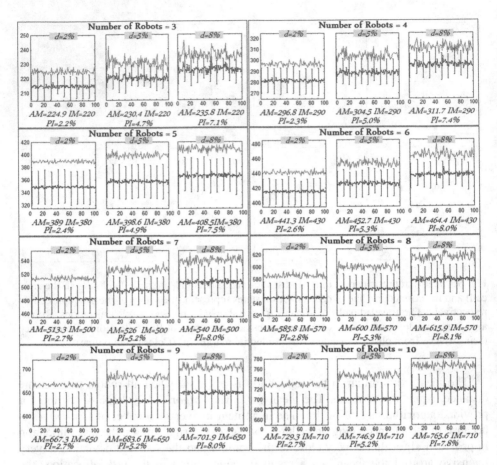

Fig. 9. Simulation results for *Homecoming algorithm* using the provided local planner. The Y axis represents the traveled distance and the X axis represents number of the map. Blue plots show average traveled distance and the standard deviation around the mean. Red plots show the maximum traveled distance in each map. For each density and for each number of robots, the Average of maximum traveled distance (AM), the ideal maximum traveled distance(IM) and the percentage of increment in the traveled distance (PI) comparing with the ideal traveled distance are computed and written under each plot. Ideal situation occurs in obstacle-free environments (Color figure online).

The size of the power source is directly related to the maximum energy consumption of robots. As Fig. 6. Down shows, the maximum possible energy consumption needed to accomplish the exploration is decreased in the provided algorithm up to 21.5 %, close to the maximum possible theoretical reduction.

The Fig. 9 illustrates the effects of the local planner on the global planner's performance. For density = 2 %, the maximum travelled distance by 3–10 robots are between 2.2 % to 2.8 % longer than the ideal situation. For densities 5 % and 8 % these numbers are 4.7 % to 5.3 % and 7.1 % to 8.1 % respectively. With a slight difference, the same goes for the average travelled distance.

The provided global planner reduces the maximum energy consumption up to 21.5 % in compare with the *kovacs algorithm*, and the local planner affects the global planner's performance up to 8.1 %. This means even when the density of the obstacles in the environment is 8 %, the provided algorithm is able to reduce the maximum energy consumption up to 20 % in compare with the *kovacs algorithm*.

8 Conclusion and Future Works

In this work, firstly an exact definition of conjunct environments was provided. Then based on a referenced work, a new algorithm having two main features was provided, return procedure and uniform task allocation. To evaluate the efficiency of the presented algorithm, several simulation experiments was done. The experiments show the efficiency of the provided algorithm. The provided algorithm acts very close to the optimal solution. As a good side effect, the maximum energy consumption of robots was decreased up to 21.5 %. Then, a simple local planner was designed and the performance for different numbers of robots was evaluated. Results show that the obstacle avoidance task, doesn't affect the global planners overall performance in a drastic manner.

In this work we distributed $N - 1$ swaps almost uniformly among the entries of C. A more intellectual method should take the initial position of robots into account to assign an independent vector C to each robot. This may result in a more uniform task allocation scheme. Designing enhanced local planners and also studying the applications of the presented algorithm on different types of robots, can be considered for future works.

References

1. Rogge, J., Aeyels, D.: A novel strategy for exploration with multiple robots. In 4th International Conference on Informatics in Control, Automation and Robotics, pp. 76–83. INSTICC Press, Milan (2007)
2. Kleiner, A., Prediger, J., Nebel, B.: RFID technology-based exploration and SLAM for search and rescue. In: IEEE/RSJ International Conference on Intelligent Robots and Systems, pp. 4054–4059. IEEE, Beijing (2006)
3. Ko, J., Stewart, B., Fox, D., Konolige, K., Limketkai, B.: A practical, decision-theoretic approach to multi-robot mapping and exploration. In: Proceedings IEEE/RSJ International Conference on Intelligent Robots and Systems, (IROS 2003), vol. 4, pp. 3232–3238. IEEE (2003)
4. Bell, J., Elizabeth, F., Costilla, O.: Cooperation of Autonomous NXT Robots Using Bluetooth Wireless Technology (2013)
5. Howard, A., Parker, L.E., Sukhatme, G.S.: Experiments with a large heterogeneous mobile robot team: exploration, mapping, deployment and detection. Int. J. Robot. Res. 25(5–6), 431–447 (2006)
6. Wang, Y., Alei, L., Guan, H.: Frontier-based multi-robot map exploration using particle swarm optimization. In: IEEE Symposium on Swarm Intelligence (SIS), pp. 1–6. IEEE (2011)
7. Choset, H.: Coverage for robotics–a survey of recent results. Ann. Math. Artif. Intell. 31(1–4), 113–126 (2001)

8. Zheng, X., Sven, K., Kempe, D., Jain, S.: Multirobot forest coverage for weighted and unweighted terrain. IEEE Trans. Robot. **26**(6), 1018–1031 (2010)
9. Even, G., Naveen, G., Jochen, K., Ravi, R., Sinha, A.: Min–max tree covers of graphs. Oper. Res. Lett. **32**(4), 309–315 (2004)
10. Sipahioglu, A., Kirlik, G., Parlaktuna, O., Yazici, A.: Energy constrained multi-robot sensor-based coverage path planning using capacitated arc routing approach. Robot. Auton. Syst. **58**(5), 529–538 (2010)
11. Yazici, A., Gokhan, K., Osman, P., Aydin, S.: A dynamic path planning approach for multi-robot sensor-based coverage considering energy constraints. In: IEEE/RSJ International Conference on Intelligent Robots and Systems, pp. 5930–5935 (2009)
12. Mandal, P., Barai, K.R., Maitra, M., Roy, S., Ghosh, S.: Autonomous robot coverage in rescue operation. In: International Conference on Computer Communication and Informatics (ICCCI), pp. 1–5 (2013)
13. Batsaikhan, D., Janchiv, A., Lee, S.-G.: Sensor-based incremental boustrophedon decomposition for coverage path planning of a mobile robot. In: Intelligent Autonomous Systems, vol. 12, pp. 621–628. Springer, Heidelberg (2013)
14. Senthilkumar, K.S., Bharadwaj, K.K.: Multi-robot exploration and terrain coverage in an unknown environment. Robot. Auton. Syst. **60**(1), 123–132 (2012)
15. Micael, S.C., Rocha, R.P., Figueiredo, C.M., Luz, J.A., Ferreira, N.M.F.: Multi-robot foraging based on Darwin's survival of the fittest. In: IEEE/RSJ International Conference on Intelligent Robots and Systems (IROS), pp. 801–806 (2012)
16. Hoff, N., Wood, R., Nagpal, R.: Distributed colony-level algorithm switching for robot swarm foraging. In: Distributed Autonomous Robotic Systems, pp. 417–430. Springer, Berlin (2013)
17. Ducatelle, F., Di Caro, G.A., Carlo, P., Francesco, M., Luca, G.: Communication assisted navigation in robotic swarms: self-organization and cooperation. In: IEEE/RSJ International Conference on Intelligent Robots and Systems (IROS), pp. 4981–4988 (2011)
18. Simmons, R., David, A., Wolfram, B., Dieter, F., Mark, M., Sebastian, T., Håkan, Y.: Coordination for multi-robot exploration and mapping. In: AAAI/IAAI, pp. 852–858 (2000)
19. Burgard, W., Moors, M., Stachniss, C., Schneider, F.E.: Coordinated multi-robot exploration. IEEE Trans. Robot. **21**(3), 376–386 (2005)
20. Vazquez, J., Chris, M.: Distributed multirobot exploration maintaining a mobile network. In: Proceedings 2nd International IEEE Conference on Intelligent Systems, vol. 3, pp. 113–118 (2004)
21. Low, K.H., Chen, J., Dolan, J.M., Chien, S., Thompson, D.R.: Decentralized active robotic exploration and mapping for probabilistic field classification in environmental sensing. In: Proceedings of the 11th International Conference on Autonomous Agents and Multiagent Systems, International Foundation for Autonomous Agents and Multiagent Systems, vol. 1, pp. 105–112 (2012)
22. Hawley, J., Zack, B.,: Hierarchical distributed task allocation for multi-robot exploration. In: Distributed Autonomous Robotic Systems, pp. 445–458. Springer, Heidelberg (2013)
23. Wawerla, J., Vaughan, R.T.: A fast and frugal method for team-task allocation in a multi-robot transportation system. In: IEEE International Conference on Robotics and Automation (ICRA), pp. 1432–1437 (2010)
24. Rooker, M.N., Birk, A.: Multi-robot exploration under the constraints of wireless networking. Control Eng. Pract. **15**(4), 435–445 (2007)
25. Fazli, P., Davoodi, A., Mackworth, A.K.: Multi-robot repeated area coverage. Auton. Robots **34**(4), 251–276 (2013)
26. Tanoto, A., Rückert, U.: Local navigation strategies for multi-robot exploration: from simulation to experimentation with mini-robots. Proc. Eng. **41**, 1197–1203 (2012)

27. Mei, Y., Lu, Y.-H., Hu, Y.C., Lee, C.S.G.: Deployment of mobile robots with energy and timing constraints. IEEE Trans. Robot. **22**(3), 507–522 (2006)
28. Mei, Y., Lu, Y.-H., Lee, C.S.G., Hu, Y.C.: Energy-efficient mobile robot exploration. In: Proceedings 2006 IEEE International Conference on Robotics and Automation, ICRA, pp. 505–511 (2006)
29. Stirling, T., Dario, F.: Energy-time efficiency in aerial swarm deployment. In: Distributed Autonomous Robotic Systems, pp. 5–18. Springer, Heidelberg (2013)
30. Hazon, N., Kaminka, G.A.: On redundancy, efficiency, and robustness in coverage for multiple robots. Robot. Auton. Syst. **56**(12), 1102–1114 (2008)
31. Jaimes, A., Kota, S., Gomez, J.: An approach to surveillance an area using swarm of fixed wing and quad-rotor unmanned aerial vehicles UAV (s). In: IEEE International Conference on System of Systems Engineering, SoSE 2008, pp. 1–6 (2008)
32. Koveos, Y., Athanasia, P., Efthymios, K., Vasiliki, R., Konstantinos, K., Athanasios, T., Tzes A.: An integrated power aware system for robotic-based lunar exploration. In IEEE/RSJ International Conference on Intelligent Robots and Systems, IROS, pp. 827–832 (2007)
33. Kovács, T., Pásztor, A., Istenes, Z.: A multi-robot exploration algorithm based on a static bluetooth communication chain. Robot. Auton. Syst. **59**(7), 530–542 (2011)
34. Cox, T.F.: A method for mapping the dense and sparse regions of a forest stand. Appl. Stat. **28**, 14–19 (1979)
35. Christensen, P.R.: The spatial distribution of rocks on Mars. Icarus **68**(2), 217–238 (1986)
36. Golombek, M.P., Haldemann, A.F.C., Forsberg-Taylor, N.K., DiMaggio, E.N., Schroeder, R.D., Jakosky, B.M., Mellon, M.T., Matijevic, J.R.: Rock size-frequency distributions on mars and implications for mars exploration rover landing safety and operations. J. Geophys. Res. Planets (1991–2012) **108**(E12) (2003)
37. o'Rourke, J.: Computational Geometry in C. Cambridge University Press, Cambridge (1998)
38. Choset, H.M. (ed.): Principles of Robot Motion: Theory, Algorithms, and Implementation. MIT Press, Massachusetts (2005)

Distributed Deliberation on Direct Help in Agent Teamwork

Mojtaba Malek Akhlagh$^{(\boxtimes)}$ and Jernej Polajnar

Department of Computer Science, University of Northern British Columbia,
Prince George, BC V2N 4Z9, Canada
{malekak,polajnar}@unbc.ca

Abstract. This paper explores how the members of an agent team can jointly deliberate on providing direct help to each other with an intended benefit to team performance. By direct help we mean assistance between teammates that is initiated by them as need arises, rather than being imposed by the general organization of the team or by a centralized decision. The deliberation starts with a request for help in some approaches and with an offer of help in others; it is typically effected through a bidding protocol. We examine the existing principles and designs of help deliberation and propose a new protocol, which refines and combines two existing versions into one. The new protocol allows an agent to initiate help deliberation by either a request or an offer, and to simultaneously engage in both providing and receiving assistance. We demonstrate its potential performance gains over the previous versions through simulation experiments.

Keywords: Agent teamwork · Agent interaction protocols · Helpful behavior · Mutual Assistance Protocol

1 Introduction

The interest in agent teamwork has been rising in recent years, often motivated by existing, emerging, or envisioned practical applications. The research on helpful behavior among agents often relates to teamwork context. The disposition to provide direct help to teammates is considered an important ingredient of effective human teamwork; its potential benefits to team performance are confirmed by specific studies (e.g., [6]) and recognized in management practice. The growing practical importance of teams composed purely of artificial agents motivates the investigation of whether and how much such teams could benefit in performance from incorporation of direct help mechanisms into their designs. Direct help is extended by one team member to another based on their own initiative rather than global team organization or central decision. Modeling and simulation studies such as [7–9] indicate that such benefits are possible, but practical confirmation through engineering developments is still pending.

In order to examine the practical impact of direct help upon team performance from an engineering perspective, one needs well-developed and well-understood mechanisms for help interactions. This motivated the introduction of the Mutual

© Springer International Publishing Switzerland 2015
N. Bulling (Ed.): EUMAS 2014, LNAI 8953, pp. 128–143, 2015.
DOI: 10.1007/978-3-319-17130-2_9

Assistance Protocol (MAP) in [9] and its subsequent elaboration in [7]. In MAP, two agents can jointly decide, through a bilateral distributed agreement, that one will perform an action on behalf of the other. The agents use their own beliefs to assess the team interest, and reach the agreement through a bidding protocol. Direct help is a possible team strategy for decentralized reactive adjustment to unpredictable changes in the environment [8]. Several direct help protocols derived from basic MAP have been studied using the specialized Agent Interaction Modeling Simulator (AIMS) framework [1]. The present paper continues the same line of work by focusing on the deliberation process.

The designer of a help protocol must decide whether an agent can simultaneously provide and receive help. The question has not received much attention, and we are unaware of protocols that explicitly support it. Yet an agent's next action may be less costly when performed by a teammate with better fitting skills, while the same agent may rely on its own skill profile to further lower the team's cost by simultaneously helping another member of the team. Thus it appears that letting an agent provide and receive help simultaneously could lead to performance gains, at least for teams with heterogeneous skill profiles. The simulation study in this paper suggests that this is indeed the case.

The opening message in a help protocol sequence can be a request for help, as in the Requester-Initiated Action MAP (RIAMAP) [7]. Alternatively, it can be an offer of help, as in the Helper-Initiated Action MAP (HIAMAP) [7]. It was noted in [7] that the two protocols have complementary impacts on team performance across a parameter space that involves environmental disturbance, agent resources, and communication costs; this led to the question of whether a single protocol that combines proactive requesting and offering of action help might exhibit an even better overall performance than either of the two individually.

The present paper resolves that question by introducing and analyzing a new combined protocol, the Bidirectionally Initiated Action MAP (BIAMAP). As a first step, RIAMAP and HIAMAP are refined to let an agent provide and receive help simultaneously, which leads to improved team performance in simulation experiments. The refined versions are then combined into BIAMAP, a comprehensive and general version of Action MAP, with more complex patterns of help deliberation. In the simulation experiments, BIAMAP outperforms each individual protocol, which makes it the best-performing variation of Action MAP.

In the rest of the paper, we briefly review the MAP family of help protocols in Sect. 2; discuss distributed deliberation on direct help, including the refinements of RIAMAP and HIAMAP, in Sect. 3; introduce BIAMAP in Sect. 4; describe the simulation models in Sect. 5; present the simulation experiments and resulting performance comparisons in Sect. 6; and summarize the conclusions in Sect. 7.

2   The Mutual Assistance Protocol (MAP) Family

2.1   The Agent Team Model

A team consists of agents $A_1, \ldots, A_n$, $n > 1$, that operate in an environment E by performing actions from a domain Act. The environment is dynamic in the sense that its state can be changed by events other than agents' actions. The team is assigned a task T, and each A_i is given an individual *subtask* T_i with a *budget* R_i. Each agent maintains its own belief base through perception and communication, and acts rationally in the interest of the team.

Each action performed towards T_i has a cost that is charged to R_i. The cost of performing an instance of action $a \in Act$ in a given state of environment depends on a itself, the component e of the environment state that impacts the execution of the particular action instance, and on the skill profile of the agent A_i that executes it. Formally, let $Act^E = \{\alpha_1, \ldots, \alpha_m\}$, $m > 1$, be the set of all *augmented actions* of the form $< a, e >$. Then the agent A_i performs α_k at a cost represented as a positive integer constant $cost_{ik}$. The vector $cost_i$ represents the A_i's *skill profile* with respect to the augmented actions, and the $n \times m$ matrix $cost$ represents the individual abilities of all agents. Our action cost model differs from descriptions in other MAP papers (such as [7,9]) in that it explicitly represents the impact of the environment state.

To avoid explicit modeling of synchronization details, we assume that agents perform actions in synchronous *rounds* and communicate only at the start of each round, in a sequence of synchronous *phases*, before any actions take place.

2.2   The Principles of MAP

Local Planning Autonomy (LPA). This is the principle that each team member A_i can use its own belief set B_i to generate its own local plan π_i for the subtask T_i, and assess its expected utility to the team as $u_i(\pi_i, B_i)$. The agent uses its own *team utility function* $u_i : Plans \times BeliefSets \to \mathcal{R}_+$ to decide which of its candidate plans is best for the team. LPA enables MAP deliberation, as it lets each agent rely on own beliefs in the joint decision on whether a potential help act would benefit the team.

Bilateral Distributed Agreement (BDA). Fundamental to the design of MAP is the principle that one team member helps another as a result of their joint decision, in contrast to unilateral approaches as in [5]. The agent A_i that considers receiving help for (augmented) action α calculates the *team benefit*, $\Delta_i^+ = u_i(\pi_i', B_i) - u_i(\pi_i, B_i)$, where π_i is the A_i's original plan and π_i' its new plan that excludes α; in A_i's view, the team would benefit Δ_i^+ from additional progress on subtask T_i that A_i could deliver if relieved of α. Analogously, the agent A_j that considers providing help calculates the *team loss*, $\Delta_j^- = u_j(\pi_j, B_j) - u_j(\pi_j'', B_j)$, where π_j is the A_j's original plan and π_j'' its new plan that includes α. The difference $\Delta_{ij} = \Delta_i^+ - \Delta_j^-$ is called the *net team impact (NTI)*. The help act may occur only if NTI is positive. The functions u_i and u_j must be properly mutually scaled to allow meaningful comparisons.

The Basic Protocol and its Variations. There are two generic versions of the MAP protocol: Action MAP, in which an agent performs an action on behalf of a teammate, and Resource MAP, in which an agent helps a teammate perform an action by providing budget resources. Action help is always provided by a single helper, while resource help can be combined from multiple sources [9]. All protocols in this paper are versions of Action MAP.

The Basic Action MAP uses a bidding sequence similar to the one in the Contract Net Protocol [11]. An agent A_i broadcasts a help request that includes the desired action α and the corresponding team benefit Δ_i^+; each recipient A_j calculates its team loss Δ_j^- (adding a *help overhead* h) and the net team impact (NTI) value Δ_{ij}; if $\Delta_{ij} > 0$, and A_j has not received another request with higher NTI, A_j sends a bid containing the NTI to A_i; finally, A_i selects and acknowledges the bid with the highest NTI, completing the BDA. The behavioral and performance advantages of the BDA approach to direct help over unilateral help protocols are discussed in [9]. The reasoning in the bilateral deliberation is approximate in the sense that individual beliefs of the two agents may not include all relevant information available to the team.

In general, deliberation on help can be initiated by asking for help or by offering help. The corresponding variations of Action MAP, called Requester-Initiated Action MAP (RIAMAP) and Helper-Initiated Action MAP (HIAMAP) [7,8], serve as a basis for the help protocols introduced in this paper.

2.3   Individual and Team Aspects of MAP Agents

Consider a heterogeneous agent team, in which the activity profile of an agent at run time may occasionally deviate from the agent's role expected at design time, due to environment dynamism. Limited but potentially damaging discrepancies may be alleviated effectively by a direct help mechanism, offsetting the need for costlier intervention into global team organization [8]. The corrective impact of direct help on team performance is expected to vary, depending on the flexibility of the team organization and its inherent responsiveness to change [9].

Aimed at improving the overall team performance, the Action MAP help mechanism is not concerned with the balance of help between individual agents. Nonetheless, a significantly imbalanced or excessive help pattern may indicate a need for other adjustment strategies, such as replanning or reassignment of subtasks. A comparative study of decentralized reactive strategies for adjusting to unpredictable environment changes in [8] indicates that combined strategies work best, and that combinations benefit from the inclusion of help component.

As in human multidisciplinary cooperation, the team's success depends on individual experts who, while pursuing the team's objectives, require the autonomy to individually create and evaluate their own local plans (LPA). Good "team players" must also be able to objectively compare the team impacts of their individual contributions. In MAP, this need arises in the bilateral calculation of the net team impact (NTI); it is expressed in the additional requirement for proper mutual scaling of the team utility functions, u_i and u_j, of the two agents. Thus the fact that the agents are motivated by team interest does not trivialize autonomy. Instead, the individuals rely on their autonomy to contribute their best judgment to the team, and objectively evaluate team impacts of their actions. To the extent that these requirements are met, the protocol ensures the best impact of helpful behavior on team performance.

The modeling relates to several ideas in the literature. The agents have individual ability profiles, and they expend resources based on action costs, as in cooperative boolean games [2], but act in team interest rather than self interest. Compared to dependence theory [10], the social reasoning in MAP relies on interaction rather than unilateral inference from representation of teammates. In practice, a combined approach would seek a balance between the two design principles, considering dependence maintainance costs vs. interaction costs. As MAP teamwork is conveniently modeled in a game microworld (Sect. 5), one might consider possible connections to game theory. In that respect, the recent connection of dependence theory to game theory in [4] is inspiring.

3   Distributed Deliberation on Direct Help

In this section we first briefly review the relevant deliberation criteria used by RIAMAP and HIAMAP [7], and then refine each protocol to let an agent provide and receive help simultaneously.

3.1   Criteria for Help Deliberation

Estimating the Cost of a Plan. Each agent A_i initially selects the lowest-cost plan P_i among its generated candidate plans, and remains committed to it. P_i is a sequence of action instances, whose costs are calculated relative to the current state of the environment. During the execution of P_i, the state of the environment changes dynamically, and so does the expected cost of the remainder of P_i. If the agent knows the (deterministic or stochastic) model of environment dynamism, it can compute the expected cost of its initial plan, or its remainder.

Agent's Individual Wellbeing. The *individual wellbeing* is a metric introduced in [7] to express the A_i's current prospects for completion of its plan. It is defined as:

$$\mathcal{W}_i = \frac{R_i - Ecost_i(P_i)}{(\ell + 1)\bar{c}_i} \tag{1}$$

where $Ecost_i(P_i)$ is the estimated cost of the remaining plan P_i, ℓ is the number of actions in P_i, R_i is the remaining resources, and $\bar{c}_i$ is the average expected cost of an action for A_i. The wellbeing value changes as A_i performs actions, gets involved in a help act, or as the environment state changes. An agent with positive wellbeing expects to accomplish its plan with its own resource budget and have some resources left; while a negative wellbeing indicates shortage of resources and possible need for help. Agents apply wellbeing thresholds called *watermarks* in order to deliberate on helpful behavior.

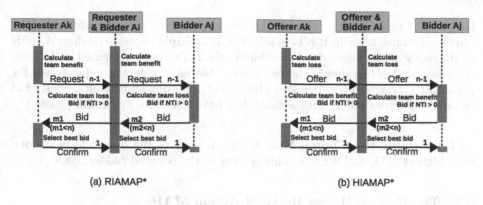

Fig. 1. RIAMAP* and HIAMAP* bidding sequences

Proximity to Significant Achievement. With a known model of dynamism, it may be possible to estimate the effect of help upon the recipient's chances of reaching an objective that is significant to the team (e.g., adding a reward to the team score). Based on such estimates, the deliberation on who should receive help can be biased in favor of team members with best prospects for immediate achievement. The bias is regulated through the selection of the proximity bias function and its coefficient values.

3.2   The Refined Requester-Initiated Action MAP

In RIAMAP [7], agents can proactively request, but not offer, action help. An agent that considers providing help can bid to requests, but may only do so if it is not currently requesting help. The refined model (RIAMAP*) removes the last restriction. The agent is now allowed to concurrently request help in one protocol session, and bid in another. A protocol session comprises three interaction phases as follows. Its interaction sequence is illustrated in Fig. 1(a).

1) Help Request Generation: At the start of every round, agent A_i deliberates on requesting help, using its next action cost, $cost_{ik}$, and its wellbeing W_i. A_i broadcasts a help request containing its next augmented action α_k and the calculated team benefit, Δ_i^+, if any of the following three conditions holds:

(i) A_i's remaining resources are below $cost_{ik}$;
(ii) $W_i < W^{LL}$ and $cost_{ik} > LowCostThreshold$;
(iii) $cost_{ik} > RequestThreshold$;

where $LowCostThreshold$ is the upper limit of the 'cheap' action range, $Request$-$Threshold$ is the lower limit of the 'expensive' action range, and W^{LL} is a fixed *low watermark* value for individual wellbeing. (For a detailed rationale see [7].)

2) Bidding to a Request: Each agent $A_j, j \neq i$, even if it has sent a request in the same round, deliberates on bidding to A_i's request. A_j calculates the team loss Δ_j^- for performing α_k, and NTI using the received team benefit, Δ_i^+. The request qualifies for help if NTI is positive. If multiple requests qualify, A_j bids to the one with the highest NTI, including the requested augmented action and the associated NTI value in the bid. (Note that an agent may request help for performing α_k, which is expensive in its own skill profile, and simultaneously bid to provide help to others with actions that have low costs in its skill profile.)

3) Confirming the Chosen Bid: Agent A_i receives the bids, selects the one with highest NTI, and sends a confirmation to the selected bidder agent A_j.

3.3   The Refined Helper-Initiated Action MAP

In HIAMAP [7], agents can proactively offer, but not request, action help. The refined model (HIAMAP*) additionally allows the agent that offers help to bid to other offers, and thus to provide and receive help simultaneously. Its three-phase interaction sequence is described below and illustrated in Fig. 1(b).

1) Help Offer Generation: At the start of every round, agent A_i calculates its individual wellbeing. If $\mathcal{W}_i$ is above the *high watermark* W^{HH}, A_i broadcasts an offer message containing pairs $[\alpha_k, \Delta_i^{(k)-}]$ for each augmented action α_k with A_i's cost below *OfferThreshold*, and its associated team loss $\Delta_i^{(k)-}$.

2) Bidding to an Offer: All agents including the ones who have sent offers, receive the offer from A_i and deliberate on bidding to it. Agent A_j whose next augmented action α_k matches the offer, calculates the team benefit $\Delta_j^{(k)+}$ for not performing the offered action, and then NTI using the received team loss, $\Delta_i^{(k)-}$. If NTI is positive and higher than in any competing offer for α_k, A_j sends a bid containing α_k and the associated NTI value to A_i. (Note that an agent may offer help for low-cost actions in its skill profile, and simultaneously bid to receive help for its next expensive action.)

3) Confirming the Chosen Bid: Agent A_i receives the bids, selects the one with highest NTI, and sends a confirmation to the selected bidder agent A_j.

In the state-machine representation of the protocols, each agent A_i ends the protocol session in a final state that determines its team-oriented behavior in the current round. Specifically, A_i may be blocked for shortage of resources and not receiving help from teammates; it may have decided to perform its own action and not engage in a help act; it may be committed to receive help from a teammate and have its next action performed at no cost; it may be committed to provide help by performing a teammate's next action instead of its own; or it may be committed to both receive and provide help simultaneously, which is a new final state specified in the refined models.

4 The Bidirectionally Initiated Action MAP

4.1 Combining Protocols with One-Sided Initiative

Simulation experiments in [7] show that the performance profiles of the requester and helper-initiated protocols are complementary. Where one performs weakly, the other often dominates. While neither of them generally outperforms the other, together they maintain superiority over simpler help protocols across the space of parameters that represent the environment dynamism, agent resources, and communication cost. This motivates the research efforts to compose these two protocols into a single interaction protocol that combines both proactive requesting and offering of action help, aiming at strong contribution to team performance across the parameter space. We next examine, based on comparative simulation studies in [7], how variations along each dimension of the parameter space impact the individual performance of requester and helper-initiated versions of Action MAP.

Environment Dynamism. Generally, a high level of environment dynamism hampers the helper-initiated protocol significantly more than the requester-initiated protocol. When environment state changes at a low rate, the helper-initiated protocol dominates with high initial resources. The estimated cost of a typical agent's plan remains close to its initial optimal value, the individual wellbeing remains high, which enables many offers of help. When the environment changes at high rate, the effects of the initial optimization of plan costs tend to disappear rapidly, individual wellbeing of most agents drops below the offer threshold, resulting in fewer offers and fewer help acts. On the other hand, the requester-initiated protocol dominates because it can adjust its teamwork to dramatic changes by broadcasting requests for help, particularly at low communication cost; while the decline of wellbeing leads to fewer bids to help requests, the overall activity is sustained and help acts continue to take place.

Initial Resources. Generally, a decrease in initial resources available to agents hampers the helper-initiated protocol significantly more than the requester-initiated protocol. Lower initial resources lead to lower wellbeing levels; the effects of that are similar to the effects in previous case, when the decline in wellbeing was caused by the rise in environment dynamism. The helper-initiated protocol experiences a decline in offers and ultimately in help acts, while the requester-initiated protocol sustains help activity and becomes dominant, especially with low communication cost. But when initial resources are high, the helper-initiated protocol dominates, as typical agent's wellbeing exceeds the offer threshold and agents can make more offers to enhance the team performance.

Communication Cost. A rise in communication cost hampers the requester-initiated protocol significantly more than the helper-initiated protocol. Hence, the helper-initiated protocol dominates with high communication cost. The reason for this is that the decline in individual wellbeing, brought about by the communication expenditures, impacts the need for communication differently in the two protocols. In the helper-initiated protocol, agents with declining wellbeing make fewer offers and communicate less, which has a stabilizing effect. In the requester-initiated protocol, the agents with declining wellbeing generate more requests and communicate more, which aggravates the problem. When communication costs are low, the requester-initiated protocol broadcasts requests with little penalty to agents' wellbeing, and help acts improve team performance. Hence, the requester-initiated protocol dominates with low communication cost.

4.2   The Bidirectionally Initiated Action MAP

To combine the strengths of proactive requesting and proactive offering of action help, we now compose the refined versions of RIAMAP and HIAMAP to form a single interaction protocol, called the Bidirectionally Initiated Action MAP (BIAMAP). Its session comprises four interaction phases, one more than in RIAMAP* or HIAMAP*. This design allows one to prioritize the redundant alternatives provided in the new protocol and thus reduce communication. For instance, an agent needing help can either bid to help offers or broadcast a request. In the current design, the agent should do the latter only if suitable offers are not available. The phases are described as follows.

1) Help Offer Generation: At the start of every round, agent A_i deliberates on offering action help to its teammates. In case of a positive decision, it broadcasts its offer.

2) Help Request Generation: Having received offers from teammates, A_i deliberates whether it needs help for its next action. If it decides to look for help, it processes the offers by calculating the NTI value for those offers which match its next action. If any of the calculated NTI values is positive, it decides to bid and does not send a help request. Otherwise, it broadcasts a help request.

3) Bidding to Requests and/or Offers: Once A_i has received all offers and requests from teammates, four different situations arise, depending on whether A_i has sent a help offer and/or help request. The protocol interaction sequences for the four cases are illustrated in Fig. 2.

Case 1. A_i has not sent any help offer or request. In this case, it considers bidding to both the received offers and requests. It deliberates and decides whether to bid to an offer, a request, or both.

Case 2. A_i has not sent a help offer, but has sent a help request. In this case, it considers bidding to the requests but not to the offers. Hence it only deliberates and decides on bidding to a request.

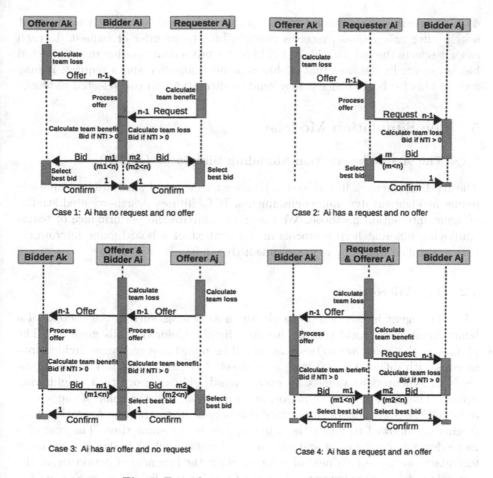

Fig. 2. Four characteristic cases of BIAMAP

The rationale for not bidding to offers in this case is that A_i has already considered the available offers in the request generation phase, but did not find a suitable one and hence decided to send a help request.

Case 3. A_i has sent an offer, but has not sent a request. In this case, it considers bidding to the offers but not to the requests. Hence, it only deliberates and decides on bidding to an offer.

The rationale for not bidding to requests in this case is that the agents who have sent requests have already considered the available offers from all agents, including A_i, but decided to send a request.

Case 4. A_i has sent both an offer and a request. In this case, it does not consider bidding to any of the received offers or requests. The rationale consists of the two reasons already given in cases 2 and 3.

4) Confirming the Chosen Bids: In this phase, the agent A_i, who has sent a help offer or a request, receives possible bids to its offer or request. In each case, it selects the bid with highest NTI and sends a confirmation to the selected bidder agent. In the case that A_i has sent both an offer and a request, it may receive bids for both, hence it may send confirmations to two selected bidders.

5   The Simulation Models

5.1   The Agent Interaction Modeling Simulator (AIMS)

The AIMS framework introduced in [1] allows concurrent simulation of multiple teams in identical dynamic environments. It facilitates design-oriented studies of agent interaction protocols. We use it to compare the performance of teams employing different help protocols in the context of a board game microworld with controlled modeling of environment dynamism.

5.2   The Microworld

We study agent interaction protocols for mutual assistance in the context of a board game microworld (Fig. 3), inspired by the Colored Trails game [3]. The players in the game are software agents. The board is a rectangle divided into squares with different colors from a color set $S = \{S_1, \ldots, S_m\}$. The game proceeds in synchronous rounds. In every round, A_i can move to a neighboring square. The move represents performing an action, and the color of the square to which the agent moves is the state component impacting the operation cost. Agents are allowed to be on the same square at the same time. The cost of a move depends on the color and not on the direction, which makes it convenient to equate the move to a field of color S_k with the augmented action α_k in the general model. For an agent A_i, the cost of moving to a field of color S_k is $cost_{ik}$. A_i's individual skill profile is represented as a vector $cost_i$. All the cost vectors are included in the $n \times m$ positive integer matrix $cost$.

At the start of the game, each agent A_i is given a subtask $T_i = (L_i, G_i, g_i, R_i)$, where L_i is the initial location on the board, G_i the goal location, g_i the *goal reward* (to be earned by reaching the goal), and R_i the *budget* equal to $\ell_i a'$, where ℓ_i is the length (in steps) of the shortest path from L_i to G_i, and a' is a positive integer constant. When the agent A_i performs α_k (i.e., moves to a field of color S_k), it pays $cost_{ik}$ from its subtask's budget R_i; if the resources are insufficient, A_i blocks. If A_i reaches the goal, it stops. The game ends when all agents are stopped or blocked, and the scores then get calculated as follows. If the agent has reached the goal, its individual score equals the goal reward, otherwise it equals $d_i a''$, where d_i is the number of steps it has made, and a'' is a positive integer constant called *cell reward*. The team performance is represented by *team score*, which is the sum of all individual scores.

The environment dynamism is represented by the changes of the board color setting: after each round, the color of any square can be replaced by a uniformly

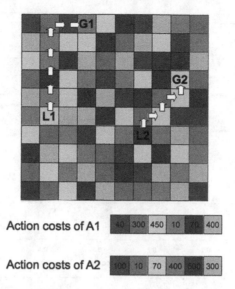

Action costs of A1 | 40 | 300 | 450 | 10 | 70 | 400 |

Action costs of A2 | 100 | 10 | 70 | 400 | 500 | 300 |

Fig. 3. The board game microworld. Each agent A_i has its individual vector $cost_i$. At the start of the game, A_i adopts a plan by selecting a least-cost path among the shortest paths, from its initial location L_i to its individual goal G_i. The colors on the board change dynamically, affecting the costs of chosen paths. [Adapted from [7].] (Color figure online)

random choice from the color set S. The replacement occurs with a fixed probability D, called the *level of disturbance*. Each agent can observe the entire board. Initially, each agent selects its *plan* as the least-cost path among the shortest paths to its goal, and commits to it for the entire game. However, the cost of the plan changes as the environment evolves, i.e., as the board colors change. The agent does not know the disturbance value, D, but can estimate it by observing the frequency of changes in the board. The formulas for estimated path cost (based on known value of D), team benefit, and team loss are given in [7].

6   Performance Comparisons

6.1   The Simulation Experiments

The Parameter Settings. The game board has the size 10×10 with six possible colors. Each agent's cost vector includes three entries randomly selected from an 'expensive' action range: $\{250, 300, 350, 500\}$ and three entries from a 'cheap' action range: $\{10, 40, 100, 150\}$. Hence, each agent's skill profile is specialized for certain actions. Each team includes eight agents. The initial subtask assignment process is random. The *goal achievement reward* is 2000 points. The *cell reward* is 100 points. The help overhead, h, is 20 points. The *RequestThreshold* and *LowCostThreshold*, used in request generation process are 351 and 50, respectively. The *OfferThreshold*, used in the offer generation process, is 299. The

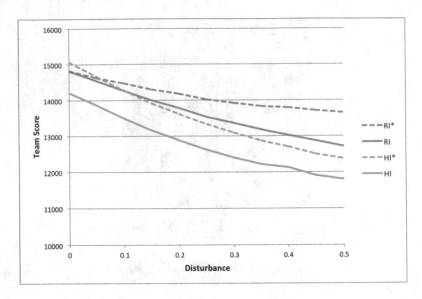

Fig. 4. Team scores vs. disturbance

experimentally optimized values of W^{LL} and W^{HH} are -0.1 and 0.1 in RIAMAP and HIAMAP; and -0.3 and 0.4 in RIAMAP* and HIAMAP*, respectively. In BIAMAP, the W^{LL} and W^{HH} optimized values are -0.3 and 0.7.

In our experiments, we vary: the *level of disturbance* in the dynamic environment, D; the *initial resources* for each step of the path, a'; and the *communication cost* of sending a unicast message, U. In the experiments with fixed value of *initial resources*, a' is 160. In the experiments with fixed value of *communication cost*, U is 9. The final team scores are averaged over 10,000 simulation runs, using random initial board settings.

6.2   The Impacts of New Protocols on Team Performance

First, we present the team performance impact of the new model that enables agents to provide and receive help act simultaneously in both requester-initiated and helper-initiated approaches. We compare four teams that employ different interaction protocols: RIAMAP, RIAMAP*, HIAMAP, and HIAMAP*. The teams are otherwise identical and operate in identical environments. Figure 4 shows the comparative team scores for varying levels of disturbance, D. One can note the significant team performance gains for the two new models (RIAMAP* and HIAMAP*) over their previous models (RIAMAP and HIAMAP). Another observation is that RI and RI* achieve same team score when there is no disturbance; but RI degrades more as disturbance increases, and RI* prevails significantly at high disturbance. Also, it can be seen that HI* scores higher than RI* at low disturbance, but HI* degrades more as disturbance increases; hence RI* outperforms it at some disturbance level and dominates significantly at high

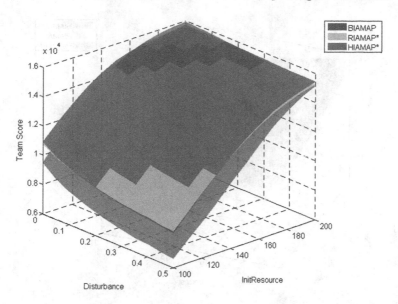

Fig. 5. Team scores vs. disturbance and initial resources (Color figure online)

disturbance. As discussed before, this occurs because high disturbance has more impact on helper-initiated protocols than requester-initiated ones. The picture also illustrates the complementary performance profiles of RI* and HI*, as there is a crossing point at which they exchange their dominance over other protocols.

Next, we present the experiment results for the team performance impact of combining the requester-initiated and helper-initiated approaches. We compare three teams employing RIAMAP*, HIAMAP*, and BIAMAP. Figure 5 shows the comparative team scores for an experiment in which we vary the level of disturbance, D, together with the initial resources for each step, a'. The immediate observation is that the team which employs BIAMAP dominates in most of the parameter space. This suggests the superiority of the model that allows initiative from both helper and requester sides. However, in two opposite corners, the other two teams dominate. In the corner which corresponds to high disturbance and low initial resources, RIAMAP* prevails as the helper-initiated component of BIAMAP is less effective in this situation; while in the other corner, HIAMAP* prevails as requester-initiated component of BIAMAP is less effective with low disturbance and high initial resources. These results are in agreement with our analysis of critical situations and confirm the complementary performance profiles of RIAMAP* and HIAMAP*.

Finally, Fig. 6 displays the results of an experiment in which we vary the level of disturbance, D, together with the communication cost, U. Again, the team with BIAMAP outperforms the other two teams, and shows superiority in most of the parameter space. The exceptions are again in the two opposite corners, where in each case one of the teams with one-sided help initiative prevails. As discussed before, these are the critical sections in which one of the two

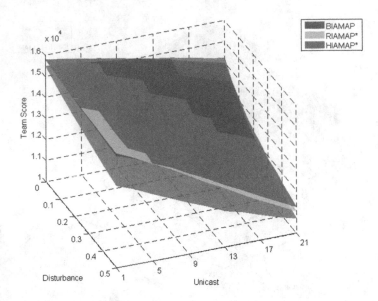

Fig. 6. Team scores vs. disturbance and communication cost (Color figure online)

one-sided approaches is significantly less effective and hence the opposite approach prevails over both the weaker one-sided approach and over the composite
BIAMAP that balances the two approaches.

7   Conclusion

Building on previous research on interaction protocols for direct help in agent
teamwork, such as the Mutual Assistance Protocol (MAP), we have analyzed
advanced deliberation patterns involving the possibility that the same agent can
simultaneously provide and receive help, as well as the possibility that members
of the same team can initiate help deliberations by both offering and requesting help. We have defined three new protocols that realize those possibilities,
including the Bidirectionally Initiated Action MAP (BIAMAP) that realizes
both. We have investigated their impacts on team performance through simulation experiments in the AIMS framework, with respect to varying levels of
environment dynamism, agent resources, and communication cost. The superior
performance of teams that employed the new protocols indicates that direct help
in agent teams works best when help can be both offered and requested within
the same protocol, and may be simultaneously provided and received by the
same agent.

Acknowledgments. We thank Narek Nalbandyan, Desanka Polajnar, and the anonymous referees for helpful comments and suggestions.

References

1. Alemi, O., Polajnar, D., Polajnar, J., Mubaiwala, D.: A simulation framework for design-oriented studies of interaction models in agent teamwork. In: Proceedings of the 2014 Agent-Directed Simulation Symposium (ADS 2014), pp. 28–35. Society for Computer Simulation International, April 2014
2. Dunne, P.E., van der Hoek, W., Kraus, S., Wooldridge, M.: Cooperative boolean games. In: Proceedings of 7th International Conference on Autonomous Agents and Multiagent Systems (AAMAS 2008), pp. 1015–1022 (2008)
3. Gal, Y., Grosz, B., Kraus, S., Pfeffer, A., Shieber, S.: Agent decision-making in open mixed networks. Artif. Intell. **174**(18), 1460–1480 (2010)
4. Grossi, D., Turrini, P.: Dependence theory via game theory. In: Proceedings of 9th International Conference on Autonomous Agents and Multiagent Systems (AAMAS 2010), pp. 1147–1154 (2010)
5. Kamar, E., Gal, Y., Grosz, B.J.: Incorporating helpful behavior into collaborative planning. In: Autonomous Agents and Multiagent Systems/Agent Theories, Architectures, and Languages, pp. 875–882 (2009)
6. LePine, J.A., Hanson, M.A., Borman, W.C., Motowidlo, S.J.: Contextual performance and teamwork: implications for staffing. In: Research in Personnel and Human Resources Management, vol. 19, pp. 53–90 (2000)
7. Nalbandyan, N., Polajnar, J., Mumbaiwala, D., Polajnar, D., Alemi, O.: Requester vs. helper-initiated protocols for mutual assistance in agent teamwork. In: The Proceedings of the 2013 IEEE International Conference on Systems, Man, and Cybernetics (SMC 2013), Manchester, UK, pp. 2741–2746, October 2013
8. Polajnar, J., Malek Akhlagh, M., Nalbandyan, N., Mumbaiwala, D., Polajnar, D.: Decentralized reactive adjustment of agent teamwork organization to changing environment. In: The Proceedings of the 2014 IEEE International Conference on Systems, Man, and Cybernetics (SMC 2014), San Diego, California, pp. 1457–1462, October 2014
9. Polajnar, J., Nalbandyan, N., Alemi, O., Polajnar, D.: An interaction protocol for mutual assistance in agent teamwork. In: Proceedings of the 6th International Conference on Complex, Interactive, and Software-Intensive Systems (CISIS 2012), Palermo, Italy, pp. 6–11, July 2012
10. Sichman, J.S., Conte, R., Demazeau, Y., Castelfranchi, C.: A social reasoning mechanism based on dependence networks. In: 11th European Conference on Artificial Intelligence (ECAI 1994), pp. 188–192 (1994)
11. Smith, R.G.: The contract net protocol: high-level communication and control in a distributed problem solver. IEEE Trans. Comput. **29**, 1104–1113 (1980)

Forming Coalitions in Self-interested Multi-agent Environments Through the Promotion of Fair and Cooperative Behaviour

Ted Scully[1]([✉]) and Michael G. Madden[2]

[1] Cork Institute of Technology, Cork, Ireland
ted.scully@cit.ie
[2] National University of Ireland, Galway, Ireland
michael.madden@nuigalway.ie

Abstract. The issue of collaboration amongst agents in a multi-agent system (MAS) represents a challenging research problem. In this paper we focus on a form of cooperation known as coalition formation. The problem we consider is how to facilitate the formation of a coalition in a competitive marketplace, where self-interested agents must cooperate by forming a coalition in order to complete a task. Agents must reach a consensus on both the monetary amount to charge for completion of a task as well as the distribution of the required workload. The problem is further complicated because different subtasks have various degrees of difficulty and each agent is uncertain of the payment another agent requires for performing specific subtasks. These complexities, coupled with the self-interested nature of agents, can inhibit or even prevent the formation of coalitions in such a real-world setting. As a solution, a novel auction-based protocol called *ACCORD* is proposed here. *ACCORD* manages real-world complexities by promoting the adoption of cooperative behaviour amongst agents. Through extensive empirical analysis we analyse the *ACCORD* protocol and demonstrate that cooperative and fair behaviour is dominant and any agents deviating from this behaviour perform less well over time.

Keywords: Agent · Coalition · Auction · Protocol · Negotiation

1 Introduction

Coalition formation is one of the fundamental research problems in multi-agent systems [1]. Coalition formation represents an important means of MAS cooperation, which has associated benefits such as enabling agents to take advantage of their complementary capabilities, resources and expertise.

We consider the problem of coalition formation in a real-world context. The real-world problem domain that we address consists of a marketplace populated by self-interested agents, where each agent represents an individual firm. In this

© Springer International Publishing Switzerland 2015
N. Bulling (Ed.): EUMAS 2014, LNAI 8953, pp. 144–158, 2015.
DOI: 10.1007/978-3-319-17130-2_10

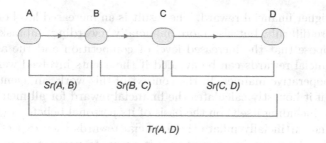

Fig. 1. Subdivision of the task $Tr(A, D)$ into its constituent subtasks

marketplace, a task consisting of multiple subtasks is proposed to all agents. We assume that no agent is capable of individually performing an entire task. Therefore, in order to successfully perform a task, agents must cooperate by forming a coalition.

We provide a context for our problem domain by considering a simplified model of a real world transport marketplace. Each agent represents a transportation firm, and the ability of an agent relates to the routes its firm can service. As an example, consider the transportation task, $Tr(A, D)$, presented in Fig. 1. This task requires the delivery of an item from point A to D. Each task can be broken into subtasks. In our model, subtasks correspond to the sub-routes that constitute the complete journey. A transportation subtask, $Sr(A, B)$, requires the transportation of an item from point A to B. For the purpose of illustration, we subdivide the example transportation task $Tr(A, D)$ into three subtasks, $Sr(A, B)$, $Sr(B, C)$ and $Sr(C, D)$.

Successful coalition formation in such a real-world setting presents a significant research challenge. Firstly, an agent must determine the optimal set of agents with whom to enter into a coalition. This activity, which we refer to as *coalition calculation*, has received significant attention in previous research work. Secondly, if a coalition of agents is to successfully form, its member agents must reach a consensus on the amount to charge for completion of the task as well as the distribution of the required workload.

To ensure the practical applicability of this work, we incorporate a number of real-world difficulties into our problem domain. We assume that agents do not possess perfect information about one another; rather, each agent is unsure of the value (monetary or otherwise) that other agents place on specific subtasks. However, we also assume that the values maintained by agents for a particular subtask are not widely distributed. For example, a transportation firm cannot precisely predict the value another firm will charge for completion of $Sr(A, B)$, however, it can make a reasonable estimate, based on details such as distance. An emergent difficulty is that agents may artificially inflate the financial reward they require for performing a subtask within a coalition.

We incorporate an additional real-world complexity into our problem domain with the assumption that subtasks may have various levels of difficulty. It is realistic to expect that agents performing the more difficult subtasks will expect to receive a higher financial reward. The result is an increased level of competition for the more difficult, but also more financially rewarding, subtasks.

We propose that the increased level of competition and the artificial inflation of financial rewards can be avoided if the agents involved were to act in a fair and cooperative manner. In the context of this work, an agent exhibits fair behaviour if it honestly calculates the financial reward for all member agents of a coalition (including itself) on the basis of its personal beliefs. Agents behaving fairly will not artificially inflate the financial rewards they expect for performing subtasks. An agent is cooperative if it agrees to participate in any coalition proposal irrespective of the subtask it is asked to perform, assuming the financial reward it receives for performing that subtask is adequate. Therefore, we hypothesize that an agent will participate in a coalition, even though it may not be optimal from that agent's perspective. While the adoption of cooperative and fair behaviour would allow agents to successfully form coalitions, the difficulty remains that such agents are self-interested and have to be motivated to adopt these behaviours.

As a solution we propose a coalition formation protocol called *ACCORD*. We perform a detailed evaluation of the *ACCORD* protocol. The results obtained confirm that cooperative and fair behaviour amongst agents is dominant.

2   Related Research

A fundamental challenge encountered in many multi-agent systems is the capability of agents to form coalitions. Agents may need to join together in a coalition in order to complete a complex task, which none of them may be able to complete independently [3]. Within the area of MASs the issue of coalition formation has generally been approached from either a macroscopic or microscopic perspective [4].

The macroscopic perspective adopts a system-level view of the entire agent population; it describes the system from the viewpoint of an external observer. Research work in this area has focused on calculating the optimal coalition structure, which is the division of all agents in the environment into exhaustive and disjoint coalitions [5–10]. When adopting the macroscopic perspective, it is typically assumed that each coalition has a fixed associated value, which is universally known and accepted by all agents [11].

The microscopic perspective adopts an agent-level view of the system. Each agent will reason about the process of forming a coalition based on its personal information and its perspective of the system. The work in this area can be broadly categorised into cooperative and self-interested multi-agent environments. A number of distributed coalition formation protocols have been proposed for cooperative agent environments [3,12,13]. However, given the self-interested nature of our environment these protocols cannot be directly applied to our problem domain.

Research has been carried out on the topic of coalition formation in self-interested buyers markets. One such example is the development of coalition formation protocols that enable buyers, interested in purchasing the same or similar products, to form coalitions [14,15]. These protocols facilitate coalition formation, however the market that they address differs significantly from that considered in this paper as the agents are not in direct competition with one another.

Kraus et al. present a microscopic coalition protocol to allow agents to form coalitions for a task consisting of multiple subtasks [16,17]. A central agent announces a task consisting of a number of subtasks and a corresponding monetary reward that will be paid to the agents that form a coalition. In our environment we assume that the price for completion of a task is unknown in advance and that agents can reach a consensus on the price to be paid for completion of the task.

Microscopic coalition formation has recently been examined in the context of hedonic games. In such a game agents are self-interested and their level of coalition satisfaction is dependent on the composition of the coalition they join. The primary objective of these agents is the maximization of their profit. A number of distributed protocols have been proposed to facilitate coalition formation in such self-interested environments [18–20]. While hedonic games adopt a macroscopic perspective in a self-interested environment the solution to a such a game is the exhaustive decomposition of all agents in an environment into coalitions. The problem scenario addressed in this paper is quite different, in that we seek to identify the best single coalition to perform a specific task.

3   ACCORD

We define a coalition formation protocol as a set of public rules that govern the behaviour of agents by specifying how they may form coalitions. We present the *ACCORD*(An Auction Integrated Coalition Formation Protocol For Dynamic Multi-Agent Environments) protocol, which will enable agents to form coalitions while simultaneously governing agent behaviour by promoting the adoption of cooperative and fair behaviour.

3.1   Overview of *ACCORD*

ACCORD consists of a single auctioneer agent and a set of independent bidder agents. Its operation can be decomposed into a series of eight distinct stages. The following points constitute a high-level description of each stage of the protocol.

1. **Task Notification:** The auctioneer sends notification of a task to all agents in the environment.
2. **Bidder Participation:** Each agent will inform the auctioneer of whether or not it is interested in participating in the protocol.
3. **Auction Commencement:** Auctioneer will commence a first-price sealed bid auction for the task. It will subsequently supply each interested agent with a list of all agents wishing to participate in the protocol coupled with the subtasks these agents are capable of performing.

The following steps 4, 5, 6 and 7 are performed by any agent interested in forming a coalition.

4. **Coalition Proposal**: Each interested agent performs coalition calculation in order to determine its optimal coalition. It subsequently proposes this coalition to the member agents involved. An agent cannot simultaneously propose multiple different coalitions. It is limited to proposing a single coalition to the member agents involved.

5. **Proposal Response**: An agent assesses each coalition proposal it receives and responds to the proposing agent with either an acceptance or rejection of the proposal.

6. **Coalition Result**: Based on the replies received to a coalition proposal, an agent will:
   - Fail to form its proposed coalition: an agent that receives one or more rejections in response to a coalition proposal must notify each of the potential member agents that the coalition could not be successfully formed.
   - Successfully form a coalition: coalition formation is successful when an agent receives an acceptance from every potential member of the proposed coalition.

7. **Bid Submission**: Assuming a coalition is successfully formed, the proposing agent will submit the coalition proposal as a bid to the auctioneer. It should be noted that an agent can submit a maximum of one bid to the auction.

8. **Winner Notification**: The auctioneer determines the coalition with the lowest collective bid and announces the winner of the auction.

At a fundamental level, $ACCORD$ is a type of auction that is extended specifically for the purpose of facilitating coalition formation amongst self-interested agents. ACCORD motivates cooperation by imposing the restriction that each agent can only submit a single bid to the auction for a task. However, an agent may receive and accept multiple coalition proposals, originating from other agents, for the same task. Therefore, we hypothesize that involvement in multiple coalitions will lead to a higher probability of being a member of a successful coalition; this in turn provides an agent with motivation to cooperate.

An agent that artificially inflates the financial reward they require for performing a subtask within a coalition is acting selfishly. Agents are provided with two disincentives against acting selfishly. Firstly, by acting selfishly, an agent reduces its probability of winning the auction. Secondly, by acting selfishly, an agent reduces its appeal to others as a potential coalition partner. When performing coalition calculation it is logical to assume that an agent will attempt to minimise the total price charged by the coalition. Therefore, selfish agents with inflated monetary requirements are less probable to be chosen as coalition partners.

3.2 Problem Description

$ACCORD$ consists of a central auctioneer agent and a set of self-interested service agents $A = \{a_1, a_2, \ldots, a_m\}$. As with most forms of real-world auctions, such as those hosted by eBay, it is assumed that the auctioneer is unbiased and will not discriminate between the participating agents in A. The set $S = \{s_1, s_2, \ldots, s_h\}$ consists of all valid subtasks that can be performed in this market. Each agent $a_i \in A$ is capable of performing a certain set of subtasks S_{a_i}, such that $S_{a_i} \subseteq S$. In addition, a_i maintains a set of private valuations for all possible subtasks. The function $mn()$ denotes the monetary valuation that a_i places on any subtask. For example, a_i's private valuation of subtask s_g is $mn(s_g)$.

In order to perform a task, a_i must cooperate with one or more agents in the form of a coalition. A coalition is represented by the tuple $\langle C, salloc, palloc \rangle$. The members of the proposed coalition are contained in the set C, such that $C \subseteq A$. In order for a coalition to form successfully, the agents in C must reach an agreement on the distribution of subtasks and finances within the coalition. The subtask distribution is specified by the allocation function $salloc()$. For any agent $a_i \in C$, $salloc(a_i)$ returns the subtask(s) within the coalition that a_i is to perform $(salloc(a_i) \subseteq S_{a_i})$. The financial distribution is specified by the allocation function $palloc()$. Therefore, the monetary amount that a_i would receive for performing its specified subtask(s) within the coalition is $palloc(a_i)$.

3.3   Protocol Description of *ACCORD*

This section formally describes *ACCORD*. The description is subdivided into the same eight stages previously described in Sect. 3.1:

1. **Task Submission**: A customer submits a task T consisting of multiple sub-tasks to the auctioneer, such that $T \subseteq S$. Subsequently, the auctioneer will send notification of T to each agent a_i.
2. **Bidder Participation**: Each agent a_i will inform the auctioneer that it will participate in the protocol iff:

$$\exists\, s_x \,:\, s_x \in S_{a_i} \wedge s_x \in T$$

In order for a_i to indicate its willingness to participate in the protocol it must submit its offers to the auctioneer. The subtask and monetary offers from a_i in relation to T are denoted by the set $B_{a_i}^T = \{S_{a_i}^T, P_{a_i}^T\}$. The set $S_{a_i}^T = \{ \langle s_1', ds_1' \rangle, \langle s_2', ds_2' \rangle, \ldots, \langle s_q', ds_q' \rangle \}$ contains the subtasks in T that a_i is capable of performing. Each tuple $\langle s_j', ds_j' \rangle$ specifies an independent subtask s_j' that a_i can perform as well as a subtask ds_j' that is dependent on a_i first performing s_j'. It is possible that s_j' has no dependent subtasks, in which case $ds_j' = null$.

The set $P_{a_i}^T$ contains a_i's private monetary valuation for each subtask specified in $S_{a_i}^T$. Therefore,
$$P_{a_i}^T = \{ \langle mn(s_1'), mn(ds_1') \rangle, \langle mn(s_2'), mn(ds_2') \rangle, \ldots \langle mn(s_q'), mn(ds_q') \rangle \}.$$
3. **Auction Commencement**: The auctioneer maintains a record, B^T, of the subtask capabilities and associated monetary fees of all agents willing to participate in the protocol. When the auctioneer receives a reply, $B_{a_i}^T$, from a_i it adds it to the record B^T.

Once all replies have been collected the auctioneer will commence a first-price sealed bid auction for T. Subsequently, the auctioneer sends notification of the auction deadline coupled with B^T to each agent a_i that is willing to participate in the protocol.

4. **Coalition Proposal**: Agents participating in the protocol will propose coalitions to each other in a peer-to-peer manner. Therefore, an a_i will initially perform coalition calculation in order to determine the optimal coalition proposal $CP_{a_i} = \langle C, salloc, palloc \rangle$. In order to construct such a coalition proposal, a_i must consider both the monetary demands and subtask capabilities of all agents. Fortunately, on receipt of B^T, a_i is aware of the subtasks in T that all other agents can perform as well as the monetary amount each agent will charge for completion of these subtasks.

   We also assume that a_i maintains a private estimation of the level of cooperation exhibited by other agents. It is reasonable to expect that a_i will incorporate these cooperation ratings into its coalition calculation process. For example, it would be less likely to include an agent that constantly refuses all coalition proposals compared to an agent that regularly demonstrates a high willingness to accept proposals.

   Once a_i has determined the optimal member agents $C = \{a'_1, a'_2, \ldots, a'_n\}$ it can construct and send CP_{a_i} to each member agent in C.

5. **Proposal Response**: An agent a_v will assess any coalition proposal CP_{a_i} that it receives. It will issue either an accept or reject notice to the proposing agent. $ACCORD$ does not control the means by which a_v evaluates a coalition proposal. However, it is reasonable to assume that a_v will consider both the subtask(s) and the monetary award it is offered in CP_{a_i}. It is also reasonable to expect that a_v will assess the value of participating in a coalition with the other member agents in C.

6. **Coalition Proposal Result**: After sending a proposal a_i must await the replies from the potential member agents of the coalition. The two possible outcomes of this stage are:

   – The failure to form the proposed coalition CP_{a_i}. If a_i receives one or more rejections from the member agents in C the coalition cannot be formed. It must subsequently inform all agents in C of the unsuccessful completion of coalition formation. If adequate time remains before the auction deadline expires a_i can recommence the coalition proposal stage and attempt to form another coalition.

   – The successful formation of the proposed coalition CP_{a_i}. If a_i receives an acceptance from each of the potential member agents then the coalition formation process has been successful. It subsequently notifies each member agent that the proposed coalition has been successfully formed.

7. **Bid Submission**: If a_i successfully forms the proposed coalition CP_{a_i} it will subsequently enter the coalition as a bid in the auction. Each agent is limited to submitting a single bid. Therefore, after a_i has submitted a bid, it can only participate in the proposal response stage. That is, it can only accept or reject coalitions proposed by other agents.

Once the auctioneer receives CP_{a_i}, it calculates the total monetary reward required by the coalition to perform T as $\sum_{d=1}^{n} palloc(a'_d)$. Subsequently, the auctioneer submits this monetary amount as a sealed-price bid in the auction.

8. **Winner Notification**: Once the auction deadline expires, the auctioneer calculates the lowest monetary bid. The member agents of the corresponding coalition are notified that they have been successful in obtaining the contract to collectively perform T.

4   Empirical Evaluation

We have developed a simulation testbed as a means to evaluate the $ACCORD$ protocol. Each experiment measures the performance of agents adopting different behaviours in the $ACCORD$ simulation environment. We observe the impact of cooperative and fair behaviour on agent performance.

4.1   Experimental Methodology

The simulation testbed has been constructed using the JADE development framework [21]. Each experiment is run on 10 randomly generated datasets. A dataset is comprised of 50 tasks, which are auctioned in sequential order. Each task consists of 8 subtasks, chosen randomly from a set of 20 possible subtasks. The duration of each auction is 4 minutes. If two bids of equal value are submitted, a winner is chosen randomly.

For each new dataset a population of 20 service agents is generated. Each agent is capable of performing 8 subtasks. By allowing each agent to perform 8 out of the possible 20 subtasks, a high level of competition occurs in our simulation environment.

The monetary amount each agent will charge for subtask completion must also be generated. For each subtask $s_z \in S$ (where S is the set of all possible subtasks), we have randomly selected a mean cost, V_{s_z}, with a uniform distribution between 10 and 99. To simulate uncertainty of information, each agent chooses the monetary amount it will charge for completion of s_z by using a Normal distribution with a standard deviation of 2 and a mean equal to V_{s_z}.

For each of the 10 datasets generated, the performance of 4 differing behaviour types (described later) is contrasted. Within the simulated marketplace of 20 agents, each agent will exhibit 1 of the 4 behaviours (5 agents for each behaviour). The subtask capabilities are also represented equally amongst agents exhibiting differing behaviours. This allows us to compare the performance of different behaviour types in an unbiased manner.

The result of a single experiment is arrived at by combining the results obtained from 10 randomly generated datasets. After each task in a dataset is auctioned, the accummulated financial reward obtained by each agent type is recorded. Therefore, the results of a single experiment are derived by summing the accumulated financial reward received by each agent type across the 10 datasets. For example, in Fig. 2 the maximum financial reward obtained by the best performing agent type is derived by summing the maximum reward obtained by that agent type in each of the 10 datasets.

We characterise each agent with a function accepting two parameters, $\lambda(\alpha, \beta)$. The level of cooperation exhibited by an agent is denoted by α, such that $0 \leq \alpha \leq 1$, $\alpha \in \mathbb{R}$. The level of selfishness displayed by an agent is defined by β, such that $0 \leq \beta \leq 4$, $\beta \in \mathbb{Z}$. The value of β is bounded to be at most 4 as empirical evaluations demonstrated that higher values resulted in a degradation in agent performance.

A fair coalition proposal offers an agent an adequate financial reward for performing a specific subtask. An adequate financial reward is greater than or equal to the minimum reward the agent would expect to receive for performing the subtask. If an agent receives a fair coalition proposal, it must subsequently decide whether it will cooperate and join the proposed coalition. It bases this decision on its value of α. The parameter α represents the minimum fraction of the most financially rewarding subtask that an agent is willing to accept. For example, consider our transportation model where the transportation task $Tr(A, D)$ consists of the sub-routes $Sr(A, B)$, $Sr(B, C)$ and $Sr(C, D)$. Assume that agent t_1 with an α value of 0.5 expects a monetary reward of 15 units for performing $Sr(A, B)$ and 40 units for performing $Sr(C, D)$. Therefore, its α value dictates that it will not accept a coaliton proposal that offers less than 20 $(0.5 * 40)$. Higher values of α imply lower cooperation. If t_1 in our above example had an α value of 0.8 then it would only accept a coalition proposal that offered it greater than or equal to 32 $(0.8 * 40)$.

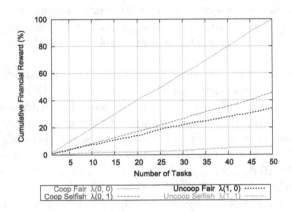

Fig. 2. Experiment 1: A Comparison between the Performance of Fair $(\beta = 0)$ and Selfish $(\beta = 1)$ Behaviour for $ACCORD$

An agent can exhibit selfish behaviour by artificially inflating its own financial rewards. The value of β signifies the amount by which an agent increases its financial reward. For example, assume the agent t_1 with $\beta = 0$ expects a financial reward of 40 units for performing $Sr(C, D)$. If the configuration of t_1 is changed so that it has $\beta = 1$ it would now expect a financial reward of 41 units for performing $Sr(C, D)$. Agents with $\beta = 0$ exhibit fair behaviour because they do not artificially inflate their own financial rewards.

4.2   Fair/Selfish Behaviour in $ACCORD$

To investigate the effect of different levels of selfishness (β) in $ACCORD$, we perform 4 experiments that contrast the performance of fair ($\beta = 0$) and selfish ($\beta > 0$) agents. In Experiment 1 we contrast the performance of selfish agents where $\beta = 1$ with fair agents ($\beta = 0$). The 4 agent types that populate the marketplace are Cooperative Fair ($\lambda(0,0)$), Cooperative Selfish ($\lambda(0,1)$), Unco-operative Fair ($\lambda(1,0)$) and Uncooperative Selfish ($\lambda(1,1)$).

The details for Experiments 2–4 are the same, except that selfish agents use $\beta = 2$ in Experiment 2, $\beta = 3$ in Experiment 3 and $\beta = 4$ in Experiment 4.

The results obtained from Experiment 1 are presented in Fig. 2. The Cooperative Fair $\lambda(0,0)$ agent type is dominant and obtains the maximum earned reward, which is depicted as 100 % in Fig. 2. The cumulative financial reward of all 4 agent types is measured as a percentage of this maximum financial reward. The Cooperative Fair $\lambda(0,0)$ agent type outperforms their selfish equivalent, $\lambda(0,1)$. Likewise, the Uncooperative Fair $\lambda(1,0)$ agent type outperforms their selfish equivalent $\lambda(1,1)$.

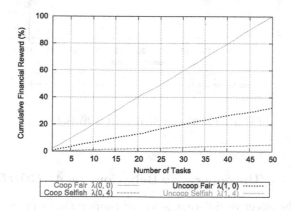

Fig. 3. Experiment 4: Comparing Performance of Fair ($\beta = 0$) and Selfish ($\beta = 4$) Behaviour for $ACCORD$

Because of space restrictions the results obtained from Experiments 2 and 3 are not included. The results obtained from Experiment 4 are depicted in Fig. 3. As with Experiment 1 the cumulative financial reward of all 4 agent types is measured as a percentage of the maximum financial reward obtained by the dominant Cooperative Fair $\lambda(0,0)$ agent type. When the results of Experiment 4 are compared with those of Experiment 1, it can be seen that an increase in β to 4 has resulted in a degradation in the performance of the selfish agent types.

An overview of the results obtained by cooperative agents in the Experiments 1–4 are presented in Fig. 4. The performance of the Cooperative Fair $\lambda(0,0)$ agent type over Experiments 1–4 is normalised as 100 %. Figure 4 measures the performance of the Cooperative Selfish agent types ($\lambda(0,1)$, $\lambda(0,2)$, $\lambda(0,3)$, $\lambda(0,4)$) in the Experiments 1–4 as a percentage of the performance of the Cooperative Fair agent type. The Cooperative Fair $\lambda(0,0)$ agent type exhibits the best performance in Fig. 4. It is evident from the results depicted that an increase in the value of β corresponds to a decrease in performance. It should be noted that agents experience a shot period of instability at the commencement of the experiments. This instability corresponds to the period in which each agent attempts to learn about the other service agents with whom it shares the marketplace. While this instability is an undesirable property of our coalition formation protocol it is necessary in order to allow agents to accurately identify coalition partners.

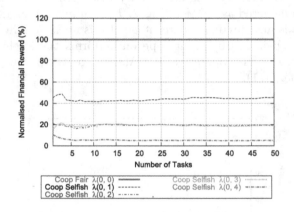

Fig. 4. Overview of Fair ($\beta = 0$) and Selfish ($\beta > 0$) Behaviour for $ACCORD$

4.3   Cooperative/Uncooperative Behaviour in $ACCORD$

To investigate the effect of different levels of cooperation (α), Experiments 5–8 are performed. The objective of these experiments is to contrast the performance of cooperative ($\alpha = 0$) and uncooperative ($0 < \alpha \leq 1$) agents. In Experiment 5, we examine the performance of uncooperative agents that use $\alpha = 0.25$ with cooperative agents ($\alpha = 0$). The 4 agent types that populate the marketplace for Experiment 5 are Cooperative Fair $\lambda(0,0)$, Cooperative Selfish $\lambda(0,2)$, Uncooperative Fair $\lambda(0.25,0)$ and Uncooperative Selfish $\lambda(0.25,2)$. The details for Experiments 6–8 are the same, except that uncooperative agents use $\alpha = 0.5$ in Experiment 6, $\alpha = 0.75$ in Experiment 7 and $\alpha = 1$ in Experiment 8.

Figure 5 contains the results of Experiment 5. Again the Cooperative Fair $\lambda(0,0)$ agent type performs best, outperforming its uncooperative equivalent

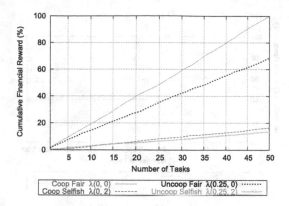

Fig. 5. Experiment 5: Comparing Performance of Cooperative ($\alpha = 0$) and Uncooperative ($\alpha = \mathbf{0.25}$) Behaviour for *ACCORD*

$\lambda(0.25, 0)$. The cooperative selfish $\lambda(0, 2)$ agent type also outperforms its uncooperative equivalent $\lambda(0.25, 2)$. Because of space restrictions the results obtained from Experiments 6 and 7 are not included.

Experiment 8 contrasts the performance of cooperative agents using $\alpha = 0$ and uncooperative agents using $\alpha = 1$. The results are presented in Fig. 6. (Note that individual graphs for Experiments $6-7$ are not presented.) Again the Cooperative Fair $\lambda(0, 0)$ agent type is dominant. It is interesting to compare the results of Experiment 5 and 8. The uncooperative agent types in Experiment 5 ($\lambda(0.25, 0)$ and $\lambda(0.25, 2)$) perform better than the uncooperative agent types in Experiment 8 ($\lambda(1, 0)$ and $\lambda(1, 2)$). This indicates that by increasing its value of α, an agent experiences a loss in performance.

This conclusion is further supported by Fig. 7, which contains an overview of the results obtained by fair agents in the Experiments 5–8. As a fair agent

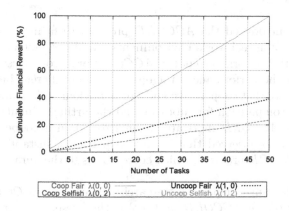

Fig. 6. Experiment 8: Comparing Performance of Cooperative ($\alpha = 0$) and Uncooperative ($\alpha = 1$) Behaviour for *ACCORD*

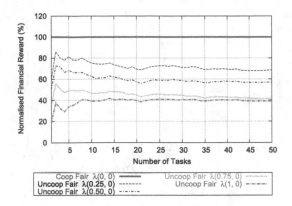

Fig. 7. Overview of Cooperative ($\alpha = 0$) and Uncooperative ($0 < \alpha \leq 1$) Behaviour for *ACCORD*

reduces its value of α it experiences a corresponding degradation in performance. This result demonstrates the dominance of cooperative behaviour ($\alpha = 0$) in *ACCORD*.

The period of instability present in Fig. 4 is repeated in Fig. 7. However, it takes longer to stabilise in Fig. 7. This suggests that it is more difficult for agents to accurately identify uncooperative agents as opposed to selfish agents. This effect can be attributed to the fact that agents participating in *ACCORD* are made immediately aware of the financial demands of the participating agents. Therefore, the identification of selfish behaviour is a relatively straight forward process. However, the level of cooperative behaviour possessed by various agents is not known in advance and must be learned through interaction. This effect manifests itself in the form of increased initial instability.

5   Conclusions

This paper has introduced the *ACCORD* protocol to facilitate the process of coalition formation in real-world environments. We developed a simulation testbed to evaluate the performance of the *ACCORD* protocol. These testbeds were used to contrast the performance of agents adopting different behaviours. The results demonstrate that cooperative and fair behaviour is dominant. This solves the problems of competition for subtasks and the artificial inflation of financial rewards because *ACCORD* motivates agents to act in a cooperative and fair manner. It was also observed that an initial period of instability was experienced in the *ACCORD* protocol, which corresponds to the duration of the agent learning process.

There is wide range of possible research avenues for *ACCORD*. An undesirable property of the *ACCORD* protocol is the presence of an initial period of instability. This has been attributed to the learning process that each agent must undergo. Such instability could potentially be exploited by uncooperative or selfish agents. Indeed, the results of the empirical evaluation show that during the initial instability the cooperative fair agent type in *ACCORD* is briefly outperformed.

Sen & Dutta encounter a similar problem with their method of reciprocative-based cooperation [5]. In their work selfish agents could initially exploit the cooperative tendency of reciprocative agents. As a solution they propose the use of a reputation mechanism. Each agent in their problem domain maintains an opinion of other agents. They demonstrated that the exploitative tendency of selfish agents could be effectively curbed if reciprocative agents share these opinions with other agents. An interesting area of future work would be to incorporate this reputation mechanism into the *ACCORD* protocols and record its effect on the initial period of instability. It would also be worthwhile to observe the level of instability that occurs in *ACCORD* for large agent populations. For example, it is possible that the period of instability will increase in line with the size of the agent population.

References

1. Wooldridge, M.: Computational aspects of cooperative game theory. In: O'Shea, J., Nguyen, N.T., Crockett, K., Howlett, R.J., Jain, L.C. (eds.) KES-AMSTA 2011. LNCS, vol. 6682, pp. 1–1. Springer, Heidelberg (2011)
2. Sim, K.M.: Agent-based cloud computing. IEEE Trans. Serv. Comput. **5**(4), 564–577 (2012)
3. Ye, D., Zhang, M., Sutanto, D.: Self-adaptation-based dynamic coalition formation in a distributed agent network: a mechanism and a brief survey. Parallel Distrib. Sys. **24**(5), 1042–1051 (2013)
4. Vassileva, J., Breban, S., Horsch, M.: Agent reasoning mechanism for long-term coalitions based on decision making and trust. Comput. Intell. **18**(4), 583–595 (2002)
5. Sen S., Dutta, P.: Searching for optimal coalition structures. In: Proceedings Fourth International Conference on MultiAgent Systems, pp. 287–292 (2000)
6. Bachrach, Y., Kohli, P., Kolmogorov, V., Zadimoghaddam, M.: Optimal coalition structure generation in cooperative graph games finding the optimal coalitional structure. In: Twenty-Seventh AAAI Conference on Artificial Intelligence, pp. 81–87 (2013)
7. Rahwan, T., Ramchurn, S.: An anytime algorithm for optimal coalition structure generation. J. Artif. Intell. **34**, 521–567 (2009)
8. Iwasaki, A., Ueda, S., Yokoo, M.: Finding the core for coalition structure utilizing dual solution. In: IEEE/WIC/ACM International Joint Conferences on Web Intelligence (WI) and Intelligent Agent Technologies (IAT), pp. 114–121 (2013)
9. Dan, W., Cai, Y., Zhou, L., Wang, J.: A cooperative communication scheme based on coalition formation game in clustered wireless sensor networks. IEEE Trans. Wirel. Commun. **11**(3), 1190–1200 (2012)
10. Xu, B., Zhang, R., Yu, J.: Improved multi-objective evolutionary algorithm for multi-agent coalition formation. J. Softw. **8**(12), 2991–2995 (2013)
11. Sandholm, T., Lesser, V.: Coalitions among computationally bounded agents. Artif. Intell. (Special Issue on Economic Principles of Multi-Agent Systems) **94**, 99–137 (1997)

12. Tošić, P.T., Ordonez, C.: Distributed protocols for multi-agent coalition formation: a negotiation perspective. In: Huang, R., Ghorbani, A.A., Pasi, G., Yamaguchi, T., Yen, N.Y., Jin, B. (eds.) AMT 2012. LNCS, vol. 7669, pp. 93–102. Springer, Heidelberg (2012)
13. Smirnov, A., Sheremetov, L.: Models of coalition formation among cooperative agents: the current state and prospects of research. Sci. Tech. Inf. Process. **39**(5), 283–292 (2012)
14. Tsvetovat, M., Sycara, K.: Customer coalitions in the electronic marketplace. In: Fourth International Conference on Autonomous Agents, pp. 263–274 (2000)
15. Shehory, O.: Coalition formation for large-scale electronic markets. In: Proceedings of the Fourth International Conference on MultiAgent Systems, pp. 167–174 (2000)
16. Kraus, S., Shehory, O., Taase, G.: Coalition formation with uncertain heterogeneous information. In: Second International Joint Conference on Autonomous Agents and Multiagent Systems, pp. 1–8 (2003)
17. Kraus, S., Shehory, O., Taase, G.: The advantages of compromising in coalition formation with incomplete information. In: Third International Joint Conference on Autonomous Agents and MultiAgent Systems, pp. 588–595 (2004)
18. Ghaffarizadeh, A., Allan, V.: History based coaliton formation in hedonic conext using trust. Int. J. Artif. Intell. Appl. **4**(4), 1 (2013)
19. Aziz, H., Brandt, F., Seedig, H.: Stable partitions in additively separable hedonic games. Auton. Agents Multiagent Sys. **1**, 183–190 (2011)
20. Genin, T., Aknine, S.: Constraining self-interested agents to guarantee pareto optimality in multiagent coalition formation problem. In: IEEE/WIC/ACM International Conferences on Web Intelligence and Intelligent Agent Technology, pp. 369–372 (2011)
21. Bellifemine, F.L., Caire, G., Greenwood, D.: Developing Multi-agent Systems with JADE, vol. 6. Wiley, Chichester (2007)

Auction-Based Dynamic Task Allocation
for Foraging with a Cooperative Robot Team

Changyun Wei$^{(\boxtimes)}$, Koen V. Hindriks, and Catholijn M. Jonker

Interactive Intelligence Group, EEMCS, Delft University of Technology,
Mekelweg 4, 2628 CD, Delft, The Netherlands
{c.wei,k.v.hindriks,c.m.jonker}@tudelft.nl

Abstract. Many application domains require search and retrieval, which is also known in the robotic domain as foraging. An example domain is search and rescue where a disaster area needs to be explored and transportation of survivors to a safe area needs to be arranged. Performing these tasks by more than one robot increases performance if tasks are allocated and executed efficiently. In this paper, we study the Multi-Robot Task Allocation (MRTA) problem in the foraging domain. We assume that a team of robots is cooperatively searching for targets of interest in an environment which need to be retrieved and brought back to a home base. We look at a more general foraging problem than is typically studied where coordination also requires to take temporal constraints into account. As usual, robots have no prior knowledge about the location of targets, but in addition need to deliver targets to the home base in a specific order. This significantly increases the complexity of a foraging problem. We use a graph-based model to analyse the problem and the dynamics of allocating exploration and retrieval tasks. Our main contribution is an extension of auction-based approaches to deal with dynamic foraging task allocation where not all tasks are initially known. We use the Blocks World for Teams (BW4T) simulator to evaluate the proposed approach.

Keywords: Multi-Robot task allocation · Foraging · Auctions

1 Introduction

Robot teams are expected to perform more complicated tasks consisting of multiple subtasks that need to be completed concurrently or in sequence [1]. In this paper, we investigate the Multi-Robot Task Allocation (MRTA) problem in the foraging domain. Foraging is a canonical task for studying multi-robot teamwork [2–5] in which a team of robots needs to search targets of interest in an environment and bring them back to a home base. Many applications need to perform this type of task such as urban search and rescue robots [6], deep-sea mineral mining robots [7] and order picking robots in warehouses [8].

Many bio-inspired, swarm-based approaches to foraging have been proposed in the literature [3,4], where, typically, robots minimally interact with one another

© Springer International Publishing Switzerland 2015
N. Bulling (Ed.): EUMAS 2014, LNAI 8953, pp. 159–174, 2015.
DOI: 10.1007/978-3-319-17130-2_11

as in [3], and, if they communicate explicitly, only basic information such as the locations of targets or their own location are exchanged [9]. Most of this work has focussed on foraging tasks where targets are not distinguished, which reduces the need for explicit cooperation and coordination. In contrast, we study a more general foraging problem where various types of targets are distinguished. Moreover, we also assume *ordering* constraints can be present that require targets to be delivered to the home base in a specific order. Ordering constraints on the types of targets that need to be retrieved are useful for modelling, for example, how urgently a victim needs assistance, how valuable a mining resource is, or how urgently a package is needed.

Task allocation has been extensively addressed in various multi-agent/robot domains over the past few years, with the aim of finding an allocation of tasks to robots that minimises the overall team cost. In general, however, even if the locations of the targets are initially known and only an optimal solution for a multi-robot routing problem [10–12] needs to be found, the problem is NP-hard [10,11,13,14]. The foraging task allocation problem that we study here, moreover, is also harder than the typical multi-robot exploration problem [14–16], where robots only need to search and locate the targets but do not need to deliver them back.

The main contribution of this paper is an auction-inspired approach for dynamic task allocation for foraging. The approach that we propose extends the Sequential-Single-Item (SSI) auctions which have been used to address the routing problem in [10,11]. Comparing with other auctions, [10,11] have shown that SSI auctions can provide a good compromise between computational complexity and solution quality for problems where the set of tasks is initially known. We build on these results but extend the approach to also handle dynamically arriving tasks that need to satisfy additional ordering constraints. In addition, an experimental study is performed to evaluate two heuristics, that is, whether or not robots should stop exploring when needed targets have been located.

This paper is organized as follows. We begin by analysing the MRTA problem for foraging and presenting a formal model of the problem we deal with in Sect. 2. The auction-inspired approach is discussed in Sect. 3. The experimental setup and results are presented in Sect. 4, and finally we conclude this work in Sect. 5.

2 Multi-robot Task Allocation for Foraging

In this section we first present a formal model of the foraging problem that we study here, and then we use it to precisely formulate the problem.

2.1 Model

Our model of the task allocation problem for multi-robot foraging is based on and extends [11,17,18] where a model of the task allocation problem for multi-robot routing is presented that requires robots to only visit target locations. We extend this model by adding retrieval and delivery tasks for target items.

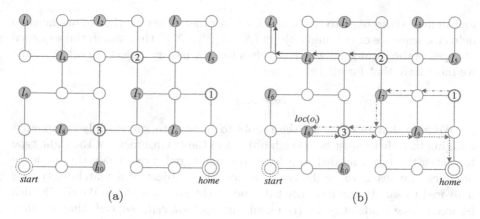

Fig. 1. Graph models of foraging tasks and the estimated costs.

For reasons of simplicity, we assume that robots need to deliver objects to a single home base (multiple bases introduce additional complexity). We use $Agt = \{1, 2, \ldots, k\}$ to denote the k robotic agents that are available for foraging. We use an undirected graph $\mathcal{G}(\mathcal{V}, \mathcal{E})$ with a non-empty set of vertices $\mathcal{V} = \{v_1, v_2, \ldots, v_p\}$ and a set of edges $\mathcal{E}$ connecting vertices for representing the robots' environment, see Fig. 1(a). Edges are assumed to have unit length.

In the environment, a non-empty set of objects $O = \{o_1, o_2, \ldots, o_n\}$ is distributed. In different application contexts, an object could be, for example, a victim in a search and rescue context, a resource to be mined in a mining context, or a package to be picked up in a warehouse context. These objects are located on a subset of vertices $L = \{l_1, l_2, \ldots, l_q\} \subseteq \mathcal{V}$ called *target locations*. We allow that no, one, or multiple objects are located at a target location, i.e., a vertex in L. We use $loc(o)$ to denote the location of an object o. In our model, objects initially can only be located at target locations, so we must have that $\bigcup_{o \in O} loc(o) \subseteq L$ initially.

Another difference which sets our work apart from that of others is that we explicitly model *object types*. As mentioned above, object types are useful for modelling the application context. In our model we abstract from the specific features of a domain and assume that objects can be differentiated by means of their color. Object types allow us to model *ordering constraints* on objects that need to be retrieved from the environment. We can say, for example, that a red object needs to be retrieved before a blue one. We thus study a more general foraging problem here where types of objects that need to be retrieved can be distinguished from those that do not need to be retrieved, and types can be used to introduce ordering constraints. We use $type(o)$ to denote the type of object o.

The goal of the foraging problem that we study here can be specified as a finite sequence of types $\langle \tau_1, \tau_2, \ldots, \tau_m \rangle$, i.e., colors of target objects that need to be delivered; $\langle red, blue, red, red, yellow, blue \rangle$ is an example goal. The idea is that the robots should search for objects in the environment of the right type and deliver these back to the home base in order. That is, the robots need to deliver a sequence of m found objects $\langle X_1, X_2, \ldots, X_m \rangle$ that match the sequence of types of the main goal, where X refers to an arbitrary object. In other words, we must have that for all $1 \leq i \leq m$:

$$type(X_i) = \tau_i. \tag{1}$$

We note that in order for the robots to be able to successfully complete a foraging task there must be enough objects in the environment of the right type to match the types needed to achieve the main goal. Over time, the sequence of types that needs to be delivered reduces if an object of a matching type is delivered to satisfy the next needed type in the goal sequence. We distinguish between three kinds of goals: (i) a goal such as $\langle red, red, red, red \rangle$ that requires all objects to be of the *same type*, i.e., $\tau_i = \tau_j$ for all i, j; (ii) a goal such as $\langle red, blue, yellow, white \rangle$ that requires objects to all have a *different type*, i.e., $\tau_i \neq \tau_j$ for any pair of indexes $i \neq j$, and (iii) a *mixed type* goal such as $\langle red, blue, red, yellow \rangle$ that requires some but not all objects to have different types, i.e., $\tau_i \neq \tau_j$ for some i, j.

In the foraging problem, robots initially have no prior knowledge about the location of objects but do know which locations are possible target locations where objects can be found (i.e., they know which locations on the map are target locations). They also do not know how many objects there are in total. Robots thus need to *explore* target locations in order to locate objects. Because robots are cooperative, throughout we assume that they will inform each other about objects that are located. Visiting a location to find out which objects are present at that location is called an *exploration task*. Exploration tasks can be identified with target locations.

Definition 1. *An* exploration task *is a target location* $l \in L$.

Exploration tasks need to be allocated to robots, so the robot team will be able to locate objects that are needed to achieve the team goal. The set of exploration tasks that have not been completed, i.e., have not been visited by any robot, is denoted by E. This set changes over time as follows. Initially, we have $E = L$ because none of the target locations has been visited. If a location l has been visited, that location is removed from E. The set E over time thus gets smaller but does not need to become empty before the team goal has been achieved. This means that it may not be necessary to visit all target locations to find all the needed objects. We use T_E^i to denote the exploration tasks that are allocated to robot i, and $T_E = \bigcup_{i \in Agt} T_E^i$ for the set of all allocated exploration tasks. Note that a robot may have multiple allocated exploration tasks to perform at a moment, so it should also consider which one to execute. Once an exploration task is completed, it will be removed from T_E^i.

To complete a foraging problem, the robots need to know what their team goal looks like. We assume that they know the goal sequence of types and understand what types of objects they need to retrieve from the environment and in which order these objects need to be delivered. For different and mixed type goals, it is important to understand the order in which objects need to be delivered, so we define retrieval tasks as pairs of objects o and indexes i into a goal sequence.

Definition 2. *A retrieval task r is a pair $\langle o, i \rangle$ where o is an object and i is an index into the goal sequence of types.*

For each retrieval task we assume that $type(o) = \tau_i$ because it does not make sense to retrieve an object in order to match the i-th type in the main goal if the object type is different from τ_i. In other words, we assume that robots only allocate retrieval tasks that at least potentially contribute to the overall goal.

We use R to denote the set of all possible retrieval tasks that can be allocated at a particular time to a robot. This set changes over time as follows. Initially, we have $R = \emptyset$ because the robots initially do not know any of the object locations. If an object o is found and $\langle \tau_j, \ldots, \tau_m \rangle$ is the remaining goal sequence of types that still need to be delivered, all retrieval tasks $\langle o, i \rangle$ such that $type(o) = \tau_i$ for $j \le i \le m$ are added to R. An object thus is associated with all indexes of the same type and R can include multiple retrieval tasks for a single object. Because we can have multiple objects of the same type, it also can be the case that R includes more than one retrieval task for a particular index. If an object has been delivered to a home base that matches the type needed for the first index j that needs to be matched next, *all* retrieval tasks for that index are removed again from R. The set R thus includes all retrieval tasks that still might contribute to achieving the team goal. For example, if the team goal is $\langle red, blue, red \rangle$ and two red objects o_4 and o_5 are found at a moment, then the retrieval tasks will be $R = \{\langle o_4, 1 \rangle, \langle o_4, 3 \rangle, \langle o_5, 1 \rangle, \langle o_5, 3 \rangle\}$. If o_4 is delivered to the home base first, R is updated to $R = \{\langle o_5, 3 \rangle\}$ because o_4 is not available any more and the first red object type in the goal has been matched.

We use T_R^i to denote the retrieval tasks allocated to robot i, and $T_R = \bigcup_{i \in Agt} T_R^i$ for the set of all allocated retrieval tasks. Similarly, a robot may have multiple allocated retrieval tasks to complete, and the retrieval tasks that have been completed by the robot will be removed again from T_R^i. We also use $T^i = T_E^i \bigcup T_R^i$ to denote the set of exploration and retrieval tasks that have been allocated to robot i but still need to be completed.

Cost Estimate for Exploration Tasks. We use $loc(i)$ to denote the real-time location of robot i. A robot is assumed to deliver objects to its home base $home(i)$. The cost function $cost_E(i, l)$ is used to indicate the travel costs for robot i to go to and explore a target location $l \in L$:

$$cost_E(i, l) = \| loc(i) - l \|, \tag{2}$$

where $\| l_1 - l_2 \|$ denotes the shortest travel cost for a robot to get from location l_1 to location l_2. Given a robot's location and the location that the robot wants to explore in the graph, we can calculate the shortest travel cost in Eq. 2 by performing a graph search, for example, using Dijkstra's algorithm. As shown in Fig. 1(b), the estimated cost for robot 2 to explore l_1 takes 4 steps.

Cost Estimate for Retrieval Tasks. We use the cost function $cost_R(i, r)$ to represent the shortest travel cost for robot i to complete the retrieval task $r = \langle o, i \rangle$ for a specific object o:

$$cost_R(i, r) = \| loc(i) - loc(o) \| + \| loc(o) - home(i) \| . \tag{3}$$

For instance, as shown in Fig. 1(b), the estimated cost for robot 1 to collect object o_1 and deliver it to the home base takes 10 steps.

2.2 Problem Formulation

The foraging problem that we study here is how a cooperative team of robots *Agt* can most efficiently locate and deliver objects in order to achieve a goal $\langle \tau_1, \ldots, \tau_m \rangle$, where the τ_i are object types. We assume that the objective is to *minimise total completion time*.

3   An Auction-Inspired Approach for Foraging

An auction-inspired coordination framework for multi-robot task allocation in the routing domain has been introduced in [10–12]. In these works, it is assumed that the robots already know the locations of the targets, and only need to visit these targets, but do not need to deliver them back to a home base. We extend these standard SSI auctions to auctions that are also able to handle *dynamic task allocation* for the foraging problem with *ordering constraints*. We first briefly discuss the standard SSI auctions and then introduce our proposed extension.

3.1 Standard Sequential-Single-Item Auctions

Standard SSI auctions are designed for *static task allocation* problems, for example, in the context of multi-robot routing [10,11,17,19], where all the tasks are known at the beginning of auctions. The tasks are allocated by a multi-round auction, in which each robot bids on *only one task in each round*, and a simple winner determination mechanism is used to allocate a task to the robot who *made the lowest bid*. The winner is typically determined by a central auctioneer, but a decentralized approach for winner determination is also possible [20]. SSI auctions can iteratively provide a complete solution to a problem, starting from a partial solution, though it is not guaranteed to find the optimal one.

When determining which task to bid on in a new round of auctions, each robot takes account of the tasks that have already been allocated to it in previous rounds because the cost for the robot to complete the new task depends on the tasks that it has already committed to. To determine which task to bid on,

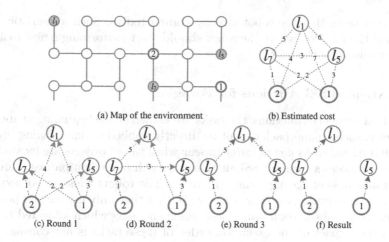

Fig. 2. With the MINMAX team objective, robots aim at minimizing the maximum cost that any of the individual robots will make.

the MINMAX team objective [16,17] can be used to minimize the *maximum travel cost of the individual robots*. With the MINMAX team objective, each robot bids the *total travel cost* for visiting both the targets allocated to it in previous rounds and the new target.

Figure 2 illustrates the effect of the MINMAX team objective on bidding for tasks by means of an example. We use a subgraph in Fig. 1(a) as the map of the environment to illustrate the details. In this example, robot 1 and 2 need to allocate locations l_1, l_5 and l_7 for exploration. The robots can obtain the estimated costs for each task using the map information. In the first round, none of the locations has been allocated, so both robots can bid on all of these. Robot 2 will take 1, 4 or 2 steps to arrive at l_7, l_1 or l_5, respectively. As the robots bid for the task with the lowest cost, robot 2 will bid 1 for l_7. Likewise, robot 1 will bid 2 for l_7 because it takes 7 or 3 steps to go to l_1 or l_5. As a result, robot 2 wins the task in this round, i.e., l_7, as its bidding cost is the lowest. In the second round, since l_7 has been allocated, the robots can only bid on l_1 or l_5. In this round robot 2 has to take into account its previous allocated tasks, i.e., l_7, when bidding on a new task. Consequently, its costs for l_1 will be $1 + 5 = 6$ (first move to l_7 then to l_1) and for l_5 will be $1 + 3 = 4$, and the robot will bid 4 for l_5. Robot 1 simply bids 3 for l_5, so it will win l_5 in this round. In the third round, only l_1 still needs to be allocated and both robots have previously allocated tasks. As a result, robot 2 will bid $1 + 5 = 6$ for l_1, while robot 1 will bid $3 + 6 = 9$ for l_1, and robot 2 gets task l_1 assigned in this round. Finally, all the tasks are allocated.

To execute the allocated tasks, a robot can be free to order those tasks in any way that it wants to perform, which is called *plan modification* [20]. Searching for an optimal execution order, however, is computationally prohibitive. Typically, some heuristics are used to determine where to insert a new task into the sequence of tasks that the robot already committed to. Such a heuristic would determine the location where the robot should start performing a new task, if it would be allocated the task.

3.2   Extended SSI Auctions for Foraging

In standard sequential auctions, the tasks are known at the beginning of auctions, and, hence, such an approach cannot be directly applied to our foraging problem in which retrieval tasks *dynamically* appear when target objects are located. The work [18] proposes a dynamic SSI auction approach to navigation tasks, focusing on the robustness of accomplishing the tasks. The robots thus are not expected to minimize the completion time in the sense that they only use current positions to bid on new tasks in each round, and when choosing which allocated tasks to execute, the impact of the execution order of these tasks is not considered. In contrast, we in particular put effort into enhancing team performance, which means that we are concerned with optimizing the allocation and execution of the tasks. In addition, since the foraging problem involves two types of tasks, in order to minimise the completion time, each robot needs to consider when and which task to be allocated and executed in the our approach.

How to Interleave Exploring and Retrieving? In the foraging problem, although it is clear that initially the robots need to explore, once they find objects that are needed, they can also start to deliver these objects. In other words, the robots need to consider how to interleave exploration and retrieval tasks. For example, suppose that robot 1 in Fig. 3 (a sub-graph of Fig. 1(b)) knows that object o_1 matches type τ_1 that needs to be matched next to achieve the goal sequence. It can then directly choose to go to collect object o_1 which will take 5 steps to collect, or it can choose to first explore locations l_9, l_3 or l_5, which are closer to its current position. Of course, the robot cannot be sure that it will find another object that matches τ_1 in these locations, but it may still be worthwhile because it may find other objects that it needs to achieve the main goal.

It is not a trivial problem to determine whether retrieval tasks should be allocated or executed first, even in a very simple instance where the number of objects n distributed in the environment is equal to the length m of the goal sequence, i.e., $n = m$, and all the objects have the same color. For instance, in Fig. 3, suppose that the main goal consists of two red boxes, and a red box o_1 has been found. Given $n = m$, o_1 must be retrieved from $loc(o_1)$ anyway, and the robots have to explore l_9, l_5 or l_3 to find another red box. If a robot has been

Fig. 3. First retrieve object o_1 or first explore locations close to the robot?

allocated the retrieval task to collect o_1 and the exploration tasks to explore l_9, l_5 and l_3, then the robot still needs to determine the optimal order for executing these tasks. In general, however, finding such an optimal order is NP-hard.

From the perspective of an individual robot, task allocation and execution take place in parallel in our approach. This means that once a robot has been allocated a task, it can start executing the task, and while performing one task, it still can bid for another available task.

– **Allocation.** In the foraging problem, since the robots do not initially know the locations of objects, they have to begin by bidding on exploration tasks. This means that only exploration tasks are available in the earlier stages of auctions, and one robot may be allocated multiple exploration tasks. Retrieval tasks appear dynamically when robots are executing their allocated exploration tasks and target objects are found. As the indexed types in the goal sequence should be retrieved in the right order, we assume that the robots only bid on a discovered object to satisfy an indexed type when other objects have also been located to satisfy the preceding indexed types in the goal sequence.

In order to distribute the workload more evenly in our approach, when determining the bidding cost for a new task, each robot bids the *total travel cost* of completing all the previously allocated tasks as well as the new task. This means that when bidding on a retrieval (or exploration) task, each robot should also take into account the costs for completing all the exploration (or retrieval) tasks allocated to it in previous rounds. Note that it is possible that a robot has both exploration and retrieval tasks that it can bid on at the start of a session (when an object has already been found before all exploration tasks have been allocated). Robots in that case will also use the MINMAX criterion to determine which task to bid on. According to the MINMAX criterion, the robot may still choose an exploration task to bid on even if there is a retrieval task available, implying that the robot would rather choose a nearby location to explore than directly go to retrieve a faraway object.

In our approach, once a task is allocated to a robot, the robot is committed to achieve it, and we do not consider re-allocating these tasks. Since *only one* task is allocated to the robot who made the lowest bid in *each* round, if there are q target locations and the team goal requires t types of objects, all the tasks can be allocated in $q + t$ rounds of auctions.

– **Execution.** Since a robot may have multiple allocated tasks to execute at any moment, we need to further prioritise the execution of allocated tasks. We give higher priority to the retrieval tasks because they directly contribute to achieving the team goal, and the robots do not have to explore all the locations in order to complete the team goal. Nevertheless, we still need to consider the execution order of each set of allocated tasks. For the retrieval tasks, since all the indexed types must be satisfied in the right order, the order of performing retrieval tasks should match the order of types in the goal sequence. For the exploration tasks, when winning an exploration task, a robot may consider re-ordering these tasks because its current location might have changed. As each robot only bids on one task in each round, it can find the optimal position to insert the new winning task into the list of previously allocated ones, which is also called *cheapest insertion heuristic* [10,20]. In such a way, when a robot has completed one task, it can pick up another allocated task from the list to perform until the team goal is accomplished.

When to Stop Exploring? As we prioritise the execution of the retrieval tasks over exploration tasks, another issue that robots need to consider is when they should stop exploring, i.e., when to terminate the execution of allocated exploration tasks. In order to complete a foraging task, we know that the robots do not have to explore all the locations if they have already found enough objects to satisfy all the required types. If the number of available objects in the environment equals the number of objects needed, of course, it is no longer useful to explore after locating these objects, but the robots do not know how many objects there are in an environment. If the robots first explore, for example, target locations that are closest to their home base, intuitively it makes sense to stop exploring when all objects needed have been located. However, since there are two types of tasks, some robots may be allocated more exploration tasks, whereas the others may be allocated more retrieval tasks. For those who only have target locations to explore, it may still be worthwhile to continue exploring the remaining allocated but unvisited locations, because they might find another object that can be retrieved more efficiently than a teammate who is assigned to retrieve an already located object.

The issue that the robots need to decide on thus is whether they should stop exploring when all the needed objects have been located, but they still have allocated exploration tasks to perform. This involves making a decision on the trade-off to explore more at a certain cost for an individual robot but with a potential efficiency gain later for the entire team versus completing the goal at a known cost using the already located objects. Continuing exploration requires an individual robot to do more, but it is not clear whether this may benefit their teamwork. Therefore, we will investigate two heuristics, *stop-exploring* and *continue-exploring*, in our experimental study.

Algorithm. We formalize our extended SSI auction approach for the foraging problem in Algorithm 1. It shows how an individual robot (e.g., robot i) performs the foraging task, mainly consisting of bidding, re-ordering and executing procedures. In order to decide which task to bid on, a robot first has to estimate the total cost of performing each available task, taking into account the previously allocated but uncompleted ones (line 14). Note that since the retrieval tasks have ordering constraints, the robot only bid on a discovered object to satisfy an indexed type when other objects have also been located to satisfy the preceding indexed types in the goal sequence. Thus, the ordering constraints must be taken into consideration when calculating the currently available unallocated retrieval

---

Algorithm 1. Extended SSI auction for the foraging problem.

1: Input: • the goal sequence $\langle \tau_1, \ldots, \tau_m \rangle$ that the robot team has to accomplish.
2: • E: the set of all currently available uncompleted exploration tasks.
3: • R: the set of all currently available uncompleted retrieval tasks.
4: • T_E^i: the exploration tasks allocated to robot i.
5: • T_R^i: the retrieval tasks allocated to robot i.
6: • T_E: all allocated exploration tasks.
7: • T_R: all allocated retrieval tasks.
8: **while** the remaining goal sequence has not been achieved **do**
9:        **Update** the currently available unallocated exploration tasks: $U_E = E \backslash T_E$.
10:        **Update** the currently available unallocated retrieval tasks: $U_R = R \backslash T_R$.
11:        **procedure** BIDDING
12:            **if** $U_E \cup U_R \neq \emptyset$ **then**   ▷ at least an exploration task or retrieval task is available.
13:                **for all** $t \in U_E \cup U_R$ **do**
14:                    Estimate $cost(i, t) = cost(T_E^i \bigcup T_R^i \bigcup \{t\})$ ▷ estimate the total travel cost.
15:                **end for**
16:                Bid on the task t^* with the smallest cost.
17:            **end if**
18:        **end procedure**
19:        **procedure** RE-ORDERING
20:            **if** received winning task t^* **then**
21:                Update $T_E^i \leftarrow T_E^i \bigcup \{t^*\}$ or $T_R^i \leftarrow T_R^i \bigcup \{t^*\}$ ▷ use *cheapest insertion heuristic.*
22:            **end if**
23:        **end procedure**
24:        **procedure** EXECUTING
25:            **if** $T_R^i \neq \emptyset$ **then**
26:                Go to retrieve the first indexed object in T_R^i
27:            **else if** $T_E^i \neq \emptyset$ **then**   ▷ can decide when to stop executing exploration tasks.
28:                Go to explore the first indexed location in T_E^i
29:            **end if**
30:        **end procedure**
31: **end while**

---

tasks U_R in line 10. With the MINMAX team objective, the robot will choose the task that minimizes the overall cost (line 16). The re-ordering procedure is used to insert a winning task announced by the auctioneer into the list of allocated but uncompleted tasks (line 19–23). In the executing procedure, the robot decides which task to execute and when to stop. In our approach, each robot gives top priority to executing the retrieval tasks as delivering objects can directly contribute the team goal. According to line 27, a robot stops executing exploration tasks if there is no exploration task to execute any more. As a result, the robot would continue with its exploration tasks until the team goal has been fulfilled by the objects delivered to the home base. If we require the robot to immediately stop executing its exploration tasks when all the required types of objects have been located, the condition of line 27 needs to be changed accordingly. According to the algorithm, if the robot is not allocated an object that it just found, it will not pick it up for delivering. This case happens when the robot has already been allocated too much tasks to complete, so it cannot offer the smallest bid to win this object.

4   Experimental Study

4.1   Simulator: The Blocks World for Teams

For the sake of repeatability and accessibility, we use a simulator, called the Blocks World for Teams (BW4T)[1], to study the foraging problem in this work. The BW4T is an office-like environment that consists of *rooms* in which coloured *blocks* are randomly distributed differently in each simulation run (see Fig. 4). The *rooms* correspond to the target locations in the foraging problem, and the colored *blocks* are the objects that can be retrieved to satisfy the team goal. Robots are supposed to search, locate, and collect blocks from the rooms and return them to a so-called *drop-zone*.

At the bottom of the simulator in Fig. 4 the team goal of a foraging mission is indicated by the sequence of the required blocks. The required blocks need to be delivered to the drop-zone in the order indicated. Access to rooms is limited in the BW4T, and at any time at most one robot can be present in a room or the drop-zone, and robots have to go through a door to enter a room.

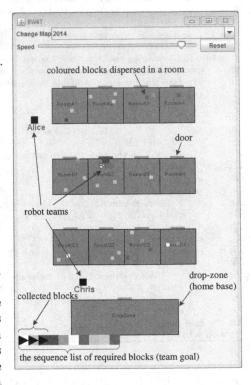

Fig. 4. The BW4T simulator.

Robots have a limited carrying capability and can only carry one block at a time.

To complete a foraging task, each robot is informed of the team goal, i.e., the sequence of the required blocks, at the start of a simulation. The robots also obtain information about room locations, but they do not initially know which blocks are present in which rooms. This knowledge is obtained for a particular room by a robot when it visits that room. While interacting with the BW4T environment, each robot gets various percepts that allow it to keep track of the current environment state. Each robot has its own localization function, which allows it to update its current location. In the BW4T, whenever a robot arrives at a place, in a room, or near a block, it will receive a corresponding percept. A robot in a room can perceive which blocks of what color are in that room. In our experiments, each robot in the BW4T is controlled by an agent written in GOAL [22], the agent programming language that we have used for

---

[1] BW4T introduced in [21] has been integrated into the agent environments in GOAL [22], http://ii.tudelft.nl/trac/goal.

implementing and evaluating our proposed approach in this paper. GOAL also facilitates communication among the agents. For simplicity, we implemented the approach with a centralized auctioneer agent for winner determination.

4.2 Experimental Setup

In the experimental study, we use our proposed approach to investigate whether the robots should stop exploring unvisited rooms when all blocks that are needed have been located, i.e., the *stop-exploring* and *continue-exploring* heuristics. We use robot teams from 2 robots to 5 robots, which start from more or less the same location near the drop-zone. We use a standard map with 12 rooms (see Fig. 4), and the team goal of the robots is to collect 10 colored blocks from the environment, which will be set randomly in each simulation. In order to allow for the possibility that robots find other blocks that can also contribute to the team goal in unvisited rooms even when all blocks that are needed have been located, we initialized the environment to randomly generate a total of 20 blocks in each simulation run. In our experiments, we have measured *completion time* and the *travel costs* which provide an indication of consumed energy. Each condition has been run for 50 times to reduce variance and to filter out random effects in our experiments.

4.3 Results

Figure 5 shows the performance of the robots that use the proposed approach to resolve the foraging problem in the BW4T simulator. Figure 5(a) depicts the completion time for various robot teams in a foraging mission, and Fig. 5(b) shows the average number of moving steps of each robot in a team. Figure 5(a) shows that more robots can indeed reduce completion time, but the speed up obtained by using more robots is sub-linear, which is consistent with the results reported in [23,24]. For example, using the *stop-exploring* heuristic, two robots take 50.51 s on average to complete the task, whereas four robots only take 38.42 s and thus yields a 23.94 % gain. In addition, more robots can share the workload more evenly, as shown in Fig. 5(b). The results, therefore, demonstrate that our proposed auction-inspired approach provides an efficient solution for a general foraging problem.

With regard to the issue about whether the robots should immediately stop exploring when required blocks have been located by the team, we can see in Fig. 5(a) that robots can indeed get benefit from continuing to explore unvisited rooms. This means that it would be worth the effort to explore the remaining unvisited rooms until the team goal has been achieve. For example, it can yield a 14.81 % gain for a team with two robots if doing so. Moreover, as shown in Fig. 5(b), we also find that, statistically, such a strategy does not increase average travel costs for each robot. Because we have simulated with more blocks available in the environment than needed, we can conclude from our results that if there is a sufficiently large chance to find more than one target object that satisfies an

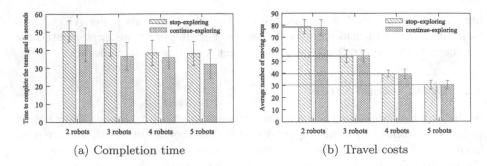

(a) Completion time   (b) Travel costs

Fig. 5. Experimental results using the BW4T simulator.

indexed type in the goal sequence, then it is more efficient to continue exploring than to stop exploring.

It is an interesting observation that continuing exploration may not increase the average travel costs. To explain this point, we first need to understand why a robot can have a chance to retrieve another block ahead of a teammate to contribute to the team goal by exploring unvisited room. We know that task allocation and task execution in our approach run in parallel. This means that each robot may have multiple allocated tasks to execute at any moment, but it needs to execute those allocated tasks one after the other. It happens that, for example, robot 1 is busy retrieving two allocated blocks (first a blue one and then a yellow one), whereas robot 2 has no block to retrieve but still has two rooms to explore. Although robot 1 can accomplish the team goal without any help from robot 2, it is possible that robot 2 can find the other yellow block when exploring its remaining allocated unvisited rooms. In this case, robot 2 has a chance to retrieve the newly found yellow block to contribute the team goal because robot 1 first has to achieve the blue color. As a consequence, robot 1 does not need to retrieve its allocated yellow one because their team goal can be finished with the active help from robot 2. In this case, indeed robot 2 increases its travel costs, but it reduces the travel costs of robot 1, which is why this strategy may not increase the average travel costs for each robot. Therefore, we can conclude that it is worth the effort to continue exploring rooms when the required blocks have been located in the foraging domain. To some extent, offering active help to teammates is a kind of altruistic cooperation, which requires an individual robot to do more but may enhance their teamwork.

5 Conclusions and Future Work

In this paper, we discussed *dynamic task allocation in a foraging problem with ordering constraints* and presented an auction-inspired approach to the problem. We performed an experimental study in the BW4T simulator to evaluate our proposed approach and investigated whether robots should stop exploring when all the required blocks have been located. Our experimental results show that the proposed approach provides an efficient approach to a general foraging problem and allow robots to share the workload in a team more evenly. In addition, a key insight into the foraging task allocation problem is that even if all the required targets have been located, robots still can reduce the time to complete their team goal by continuing to explore unvisited rooms until the team goal has been achieved. The experimental results, somewhat surprisingly, also show that such a strategy will not increase the average travel costs for each robot.

In our approach, each robot may have multiple allocated tasks to execute at any moment, and in order to distribute the workload more evenly, each robot needs to consider previously allocated tasks when bidding on a new task. In our experiments, we noticed that this may not be the most efficient task allocation strategy. For example, in the BW4T environment, when a robot explores a room and finds the next block that is needed, the associated retrieval task for this block may be allocated to another robot than the robot that found the block because it already has a heavy workload. This may happen, for example, if a robot has already been allocated many rooms to explore, which causes its bid (based on total time needed) to be rather high. In future work, we are planning to do a follow-up study in which the robots will coordinate with each other through direct communication to allocate the foraging tasks without using auctions. We aim to develop a fully decentralized coordination mechanism for the foraging task allocation, in which a robot is only allocated a new task when its previously allocated task has been completed.

References

1. Kaminka, G.A.: Autonomous agents research in robotics: a report from the trenches. In: 2012 AAAI Spring Symposium Series (2012)
2. Cao, Y.U., Fukunaga, A.S., Kahng, A.B., Meng, F.: Cooperative mobile robotics: antecedents and directions. Autono. Robots **4**, 1–23 (1997)
3. Campo, A., Dorigo, M.: Efficient multi-foraging in swarm robotics. In: Almeida e Costa, F., Rocha, L.M., Costa, E., Harvey, I., Coutinho, A. (eds.) ECAL 2007. LNCS (LNAI), vol. 4648, pp. 696–705. Springer, Heidelberg (2007)
4. Krannich, S., Maehle, E.: Analysis of spatially limited local communication for multi-robot foraging. In: Kim, J.-H., et al. (eds.) Progress in Robotics. CCIS, vol. 44, pp. 322–331. Springer, Heidelberg (2009)
5. Winfield, A.: Foraging robots. In: Meyers, R.A. (ed.) Encyclopedia of Complexity and Systems Science, pp. 3682–3700. Springer, New York (2009)
6. Davids, A.: Urban search and rescue robots: from tragedy to technology. IEEE Intell. Syst. **17**, 81–83 (2002)
7. Yuh, J.: Design and control of autonomous underwater robots: a survey. Auton. Robots **8**, 7–24 (2000)
8. Hompel, M.T., Schmidt, T.: Warehouse Management: Automation and Organisation of Warehouse and Order Picking Systems (Intralogistik). Springer-Verlag New York, Inc., Secaucus (2006)
9. Parker, L.E.: Distributed intelligence: overview of the field and its application in multi-robot systems. J. Phys. Agents **2**, 5–14 (2008)
10. Koenig, S., Keskinocak, P., Tovey, C.A.: Progress on agent coordination with cooperative auctions. In: AAAI (2010)

11. Lagoudakis, M.G., Markakis, E., Kempe, D., Keskinocak, P., Kleywegt, A., Koenig, S., Tovey, C., Meyerson, A., Jain, S.: Auction-based multi-robot routing. In: Proceedings of Robotics: Science and Systems, pp. 343–350 (2005)
12. Zheng, X., Koenig, S.: K-swaps: cooperative negotiation for solving task-allocation problems. In: Proceedings of the 21st International Jont Conference on Artifical Intelligence, pp. 373–378. Morgan Kaufmann Publishers Inc. (2009)
13. Zlot, R., Stentz, A.: Market-based multirobot coordination for complex tasks. Int. J. Robot. Res. **25**, 73–101 (2006)
14. Dasgupta, P.: Multi-robot task allocation for performing cooperative foraging tasks in an initially unknown environment. In: Jain, L.C., Aidman, E.V., Abeynayake, C. (eds.) Innovations in Defence Support Systems -2. SCI, vol. 338, pp. 5–20. Springer, Heidelberg (2011)
15. Burgard, W., Moors, M., Stachniss, C., Schneider, F.E.: Coordinated multi-robot exploration. IEEE Robot. Trans. **21**, 376–386 (2005)
16. Tovey, C., Lagoudakis, M.G., Jain, S., Koenig, S.: The generation of bidding rules for auction-based robot coordination. In: Parker, L.E., Schneider, F.E., Schultz, A.C. (eds.) Multi-Robot Systems. From Swarms to Intelligent Automata, vol. III, pp. 3–14. Springer, The Netherlands (2005)
17. Koenig, S., Zheng, X., Tovey, C., Borie, R., Kilby, P., Markakis, V., Keskinocak, P.: Agent coordination with regret clearing. In: Proceedings of the 23rd National Conference on Artificial Intelligence, AAAI 2008, vol. 1, pp. 101–107. AAAI Press (2008)
18. Nanjanath, M., Gini, M.: Performance evaluation of repeated auctions for robust task execution. In: Carpin, S., Noda, I., Pagello, E., Reggiani, M., von Stryk, O. (eds.) SIMPAR 2008. LNCS (LNAI), vol. 5325, pp. 317–327. Springer, Heidelberg (2008)
19. Koenig, S., Tovey, C., Lagoudakis, M., Markakis, V., Kempe, D., Keskinocak, P., Kleywegt, A., Meyerson, A., Jain, S.: The power of sequential single-item auctions for agent coordination. In: Proceedings of the National Conference on Artificial Intelligence, vol. 21, p. 1625. AAAI/MIT, Melano Park, Cambridge (1999, 2006)
20. Schoenig, A., Pagnucco, M.: Evaluating sequential single-item auctions for dynamic task allocation. In: Li, J. (ed.) AI 2010. LNCS, vol. 6464, pp. 506–515. Springer, Heidelberg (2010)
21. Johnson, M., Jonker, C., van Riemsdijk, B., Feltovich, P.J., Bradshaw, J.M.: Joint activity testbed: blocks world for teams (BW4T). In: Aldewereld, H., Dignum, V., Picard, G. (eds.) ESAW 2009. LNCS, vol. 5881, pp. 254–256. Springer, Heidelberg (2009)
22. Hindriks, K.: The goal agent programming language (2013). http://ii.tudelft.nl/trac/goal
23. Wei, C., Hindriks, K., Jonker, C.M.: The role of communication in coordination protocols for cooperative robot teams. In: Proceedings of International Conference on Agents and Artifical Intelligence (ICAART), pp. 28–39 (2014)
24. Balch, T., Arkin, R.C.: Communication in reactive multiagent robotic systems. Auton. Robots **1**, 27–52 (1994)

Logic and Formal Approaches

Tableaux and Complexity Bounds
for a Multiagent Justification Logic
with Interacting Justifications

Antonis Achilleos[✉]

The Graduate Center of the City University of New York,
365 Fifth Avenue, New York, NY 10016, USA
aachilleos@gc.cuny.edu

Abstract. We introduce a family of multi-agent justification logics with
interactions between the agents' justifications, by extending and generalizing the two-agent versions of the Logic of Proofs (LP) introduced by
Yavorskaya in 2008. LP, and its successor, Justification Logic, is a refinement of the modal logic approach to epistemology in which for every
belief assertion, an explicit justification is supplied. This affects the complexity of the logic's derivability problem, which is known to be in the
second level of the polynomial hierarchy (first result by Kuznets in 2000)
for all single-agent justification logics whose complexity is known. We
present tableau rules and some complexity results. In several cases
the satisfiability problem for these logics remains in the second level of
the polynomial hierarchy, while the problem becomes PSPACE-hard for
certain two-agent logics and there are EXP-hard logics of three agents.

1 Introduction

Justification Logic is a family of logics of justified beliefs. Where epistemic modal
logic treats formulas of the form $K\phi$ with the intended meaning that an agent
knows/believes ϕ, in Justification Logic we consider formulas of the form $t : \phi$
with the intended meaning that t is a justification for ϕ – or that the agent
has justification t for ϕ. The first justification logic was LP, the logic of proofs,
and appeared in [4] by Artemov to provide provability semantics for S4, but it
has since developed in a wide system of explicit epistemic logics. Justification
Logic has been successfully used to shed light to situations where an explicit
treatment of beliefs, instead of the implicit, modal treatment, is more appropriate
(for example see [6,7,17]).

The complexity properties of Justification Logic significantly differ from the
corresponding modal logics: while every single-agent justification logic whose
complexity has been studied has its derivability problem in Π_2^p (the second level
of the polynomial hierarchy), the corresponding modal logics have PSPACE-
complete derivability problems. Furthermore certain significant fragments of
these justification logics have an even lower complexity – NP, or even P in
some cases. For an overview of Justification Logic see [5,6]. For an overview
of complexity results of (single-agent) Justification Logic, see [14].

© Springer International Publishing Switzerland 2015
N. Bulling (Ed.): EUMAS 2014, LNAI 8953, pp. 177–192, 2015.
DOI: 10.1007/978-3-319-17130-2_12

In [21], Yavorskaya presents two-agent variations of LP. These logics feature interactions between the two agents' justifications: for LP$_\uparrow$, for instance, every justification for agent 1 can be converted to a justification for agent 2 for the same fact, while in LP$_!$ agent 2 is aware of agent 1's justifications.

In [3], we extended Yavorskaya's logics to two-agent variations of other justification logics, as well as to combinations of two different justification logics. We then gave tableau procedures to prove that most of these logics were in the second level of the polynomial hierarchy, an expected result which mimics the ones for single-agent justification logics from [1,13,14]. For some cases, however, we were able to prove PSPACE-completeness, which was a new phenomenon for Justification Logic.

In this paper we continue our work from [3]. It is our goal to provide a flexible system capable of modeling situations of diverse agents, or diverse types of justifications, allowing for reasonably general interactions among them. We provide a general family of multi-agent justification logics. Each member of this family is described by a tuple $(n, \subset, \hookrightarrow, F)_{\mathcal{CS}}$, where n is the number of agents and the interactions are given by $\subset, \hookrightarrow$. Furthermore, each agent i is using its own justification logic, $F(i)$, so not all agents are equally reliable: depending on each agent's underlying logic there may be agents with consistent beliefs and possibly agents with true beliefs, or perhaps agents with none of these properties. These concepts are made precise in Sect. 2.

For this family of multi-agent logics we give semantics and a general tableau procedure and then we make observations on the complexity of the derivation problem for its members. In particular, we demonstrate that all logics in this family have their satisfiability problem in NEXP – under reasonable assumptions. This family demonstrates significant variety, as it also includes PSPACE- and EXP-complete members, while we demonstrate that the members of a general class of logics have their satisfiability problem in Σ_2^p. This is a somewhat surprising result, as all single-agent justification logics whose complexity is known have their satisfiability problem in Σ_2^p.

Multimodal logics with interacting modalities have been studied before by Spaan [20], Demri [9], and Dziubiński et al. [10], achieving a corresponding complexity jump to EXP-completeness in similar cases as ours. Specifically, [10] is particularly relevant, as the system studied there (TEAMLOG) has its versions of the interactions $\subset$ and $\hookrightarrow$ that our system uses. There these are interactions between beliefs and intentions in a multiagent system, or between individual beliefs (or intentions) and group beliefs. The correspondence between the modal system from [10] and the family of justification logics we present in this paper is not strict, though, as there are differences between the axioms used and the freedom given to the interactions.

2 Multiagent Justification Logic with Interactions

We present the system we study in this paper, its semantics and the basic tools we will need later on. Most of the proofs for the claims of this section can be adjusted from the one- or two- agent versions of Justification Logic. The reader can see [6] or [14] for an overview of single-agent justification logic and [3] for a two-agent version of this system.

2.1 Syntax and Axioms

In this paper, if $n \in \mathbb{N}$, $[n]$ will be the set $\{1, 2, \ldots, n\}$. For every $n \in \mathbb{N}$, the justification terms of the language L_n include constants $c_1, c_2, c_3, \ldots$ and variables $x_1, x_2, x_3, \ldots$ and if t_1 and t_2 are terms, then the following are also terms: $(t_1 + t_2), (t_1 \cdot t_2), !t_1$. The set of terms will be referred to as Tm – notice that we use one set of terms for all agents. We use a set $Pvar$ of propositional variables, which will usually be $p_1, p_2, \ldots$. Formulas of the language L_n include all propositional variables and if ϕ, ψ are formulas, $i \in [n]$ (i.e. i is an agent) and t is a term, then the following are also formulas of L_n: $\bot, \phi \rightarrow \psi, t :_i \phi$. The remaining propositional connectives, whenever needed, are treated as constructed from $\rightarrow$ and $\bot$ in the usual way: $\neg a := a \rightarrow \bot$, $a \vee b := \neg a \rightarrow b$, and $a \wedge b := \neg(\neg a \vee \neg b)$. The operators $\cdot, +$ and $!$ are explained by the following axioms. Intuitively, $\cdot$ applies a justification for a statement $A \rightarrow B$ to a justification for A and gives a justification for B. Using $+$ we can combine two justifications and have a justification for anything that can be justified by any of the two initial terms – much like the concatenation of two proofs. Finally, $!$ is a unary operator called the proof checker. Given a justification t for ϕ, $!t$ justifies the fact that t is a justification for ϕ. A multi-agent justification logic is denoted by the quadruple $J = (n, \subset, \hookrightarrow, F)_{\mathcal{CS}}$, where $n \in \mathbb{N}$, so that $[n]$ is the set of agents, $\subset, \hookrightarrow$ are binary relations on $[n]$, and for every agent i, $F(i)$ is a (single-agent) justification logic. In this paper we assume that $F : [n] \longrightarrow \{J, JD, JT, J4, JD4, LP\}$. $\mathcal{CS}$ is called a constant specification and is explained later in this section. We also define $i \supset j$ iff $j \subset i$ and $i \leftrightarrow j$ iff $j \hookrightarrow i$.

For an agent i, $F(i)$ specifies the logic agent i is based on – and as we observe below, this mainly affects the reliability of the agent's justifications. As for the interactions, for agents i, j, if $i \supset j$, then the justifications of i are also accepted as such by agent j. If $i \leftrightarrow j$, then agent j is *aware* of agent i's justifications – but awareness does not necessarily imply acceptance. In the latter case, we also say that j can verify the justifications of i. In the original logic, LP, where justifications were proofs, if t is a proof of ϕ, then the proof of that fact comes from *verifying* t for ϕ and is denoted as $!t$. In the current system we expect that since j is aware that $t :_i \phi$, j should have a justification for the fact and this justification simply comes from verifying that t is a justification of ϕ for i.

J uses modus ponens and all agents share the following common axioms.

Propositional Axioms: Finitely many schemes of classical propositional logic;
Application: $s :_i (\phi \rightarrow \psi) \rightarrow (t :_i \phi \rightarrow (s \cdot t) :_i \psi)$;
Concatenation: $s :_i \phi \rightarrow (s + t) :_i \phi$, $s :_i \phi \rightarrow (t + s) :_i \phi$.

For every agent i, we also include a set of axioms that depend upon the logic i is based on (i.e. $F(i)$). So, if $F(i)$ has Factivity, then we include the Factivity axiom for i, if $F(i)$ has Consistency, then we include Consistency for i, while if $F(i)$ has Positive Introspection, then we include Positive Introspection for i.

Factivity: for every agent i, such that $F(i) \in \{\mathsf{JT}, \mathsf{LP}\}$, $t :_i \phi \to \phi$;
Consistency: for every agent i, such that $F(i) \in \{\mathsf{JD}, \mathsf{JD4}\}$, $t :_i \bot \to \bot$;
Positive Introspection: for every i, such that $F(i) \in \{\mathsf{J4}, \mathsf{LP}\}$, $t :_i \phi \to !t :_i t :_i \phi$;

The following, interaction axioms depend upon the binary relations $\subset$ and $\hookrightarrow$.

Conversion: for every $i \supset j$, $t :_i \phi \to t :_j \phi$;
Verification: for every $i \hookleftarrow j$, $t :_i \phi \to !t :_j t :_i \phi$.

In this context Positive introspection is a special case of Verification. From now on we assume that for every agent i, $F(i) \in \{\mathsf{J}, \mathsf{JD}, \mathsf{JT}\}$, so agent i has positive introspection iff $i \hookrightarrow i$.

To complete the description of justification logic $(n, \subset, \hookrightarrow, F)_{\mathcal{CS}}$, a *constant specification* $\mathcal{CS}$ is needed: A constant specification for $(n, \subset, \hookrightarrow, F)$ is any set of formulas of the form $c :_i A$, where c a justification constant, i an agent, and A an axiom of the logic from the ones above. We say that axiom A is justified by a constant c for agent i when $c :_i A \in \mathcal{CS}$. Then we can introduce our final axiom,

Axiom Necessitation: $t :_i \phi$, where either $t :_i \phi \in \mathcal{CS}$ or $\phi = s :_j \psi$ an instance of Axiom Necessitation and $t = !s$.

Axiom Necessitation will be called AN for short. In this paper we will be making the assumption that the constant specifications are *axiomatically appropriate:* each axiom is justified by at least one constant; and *schematic:* every constant justifies only a certain number of schemes from the ones above (as a result, if c justifies A for i and B results from A and substitution, then c justifies B for i).

As Proposition 1 demonstrates, Modal Logic's full Necessitation Rule is a derived property of Justification Logic:

Proposition 1. *For an axiomatically appropriate constant specification $\mathcal{CS}$, if $\phi_1, \ldots, \phi_k \vdash \phi$, then for any $i \in [n]$ and terms $t_1, \ldots, t_k$, there is some term t such that $t_1 :_i \phi_1, \ldots, t_k :_i \phi_k \vdash t :_i \phi$.*

Proof. By induction on the proof of ϕ: If ϕ is an axiom, then by AN, the theorem holds and it obviously holds for any ϕ_i, $i \in [k]$. This covers the base cases. Using the application axiom, if ϕ is the result of ψ, χ and modus ponens, since the theorem holds for some $r :_i \psi, s :_i \chi$, the theorem holds for ϕ and $t = (r \cdot s)$. $\square$

We fix a certain logic $\mathcal{J} = (n, \subset, \hookrightarrow, F)_{\mathcal{CS}}$ and we make certain (reasonable) assumptions. We assume that $\subset$ is transitive and $([n], \subset)$ has no cycles. This is reasonable, because if $i \subset j \subset k$, then $t :_k \phi \to t :_i \phi$ is a theorem and if $i \subset j \subset i$, then agent i and j have exactly the same justifications for the same formulas, since $t :_i \phi \leftrightarrow t :_j \phi$ is a theorem and thus the agents are indistinguishable – there may be some effect of these $\subset$-paths and cycles on the logic, depending on the constant specification, but not in any way that interests us here. We also assume that if $F(i) = \mathsf{JD}$ (resp. $F(i) = \mathsf{JT}$) and $i \subset j$, then $F(j) = \mathsf{JD}$ (resp. $F(j) = \mathsf{JT}$), that if $i \hookrightarrow j$ and $k \subset i$, then $j \hookrightarrow k$, and that if $j \hookrightarrow i$ and $F(i) = \mathsf{JT}$, then $i \subset j$ – notice that if $j \hookrightarrow i$, $F(i) = \mathsf{JT}$, and $c :_j (t :_i \phi \rightarrow \phi) \in \mathcal{CS}$, then $t :_i \phi \rightarrow (c \cdot !t) :_j \phi$ is a theorem of $\mathcal{J}$. Making these assumptions simplifies the system and often clearer the notation, as they make the behavior and interactions among the agents clearer, while it is not hard to adjust the analysis in their absence. However, the assumptions on $\mathcal{CS}$ are mostly required.

Examples. In [3], we gave two scenarios that can be formalized using a multi-agent justification logic, but when formalized in another logic we lose essential information. In the first situation we acquire two pieces of evidence: one in support of ϕ and the other in support of $\neg\phi$; after further inquiries we conclude that the first piece of evidence is compromised, while the second one is confirmed. For two "agents", $K \hookrightarrow B$, we can formalize this situation with the following set of formulas: $comp :_B \phi$, $conf :_B \neg\phi$, $inquiry :_K (conf :_B \neg\phi \rightarrow \neg\phi)$, from which we can infer $!conf :_K conf :_B \neg\phi$ (by verification) and then, $inquiry \cdot !conf :_K \neg\phi$ (by using the application axiom).

Another interesting situation arises when there are several agents who accept different views from each other, but each agent is aware of the other's views. For example, there may be three agents from three respective religions, based on three respective holy books. Each agent may be completely aware of the contents of all three books, so each agent is completely aware of every agent's beliefs, but does not necessarily embrace them. Then, the underlying logic would have three agents, a, b, c, such that $a \hookrightarrow b \hookrightarrow c \hookrightarrow a$. Furthermore, distinguishing between justifications makes sense, for example, when two (or all) of the agents accept a certain prophet's teachings (this story can be adjusted for three lawyers in a courtroom who accept different pieces of evidence, or politicians who support different policies, etc.).

2.2 Semantics

We introduce Fitting models, usually called F-models and sometimes in this paper just models. These are essentially Kripke models with an additional machinery to accommodate justification terms. They were introduced first by Fitting in [11] with further variations appearing in [16, 19].

Definition 1. *An F-model $\mathcal{M}$ for $\mathcal{J}$ is a quadruple $(W, (R_i)_{i \in [n]}, (\mathcal{E}_i)_{i \in [n]}, \mathcal{V})$, where $W \neq \emptyset$ is a set, for every $i \in [n]$, $R_i \subseteq W^2$ is a binary relation on W, $\mathcal{V} : Pvar \longrightarrow 2^W$ and for every $i \in [n]$, $\mathcal{E}_i : (Tm \times L_n) \longrightarrow 2^W$. W is called the universe of $\mathcal{M}$ and its elements are the worlds or states of the model. $\mathcal{V}$ assigns a subset of W to each propositional variable, p, and $\mathcal{E}_i$ assigns a subset of W to each pair of a justification term and a formula. $(\mathcal{E}_i)_{i \in [n]}$ will often be seen and referred to as $\mathcal{E} : [n] \times Tm \times L_n \longrightarrow 2^W$ and $\mathcal{E}$ is called an admissible evidence function. Additionally, $\mathcal{E}$ and $(R_i)_{i \in [n]}$ must satisfy the following conditions:*

Application closure: for any $i \in [n]$, formulas ϕ, ψ, and justification terms t, s,
    $\mathcal{E}_i(s, \phi \rightarrow \psi) \cap \mathcal{E}_i(t, \phi) \subseteq \mathcal{E}_i(s \cdot t, \psi).$

Sum closure: for any $i \in [n]$, formula ϕ, and justification terms t, s,
  $\mathcal{E}_i(t, \phi) \cup \mathcal{E}_i(s, \phi) \subseteq \mathcal{E}_i(t + s, \phi)$.
AN-closure: for any instance of AN, $t :_i \phi$, $\mathcal{E}_i(t, \phi) = W$.
Verification Closure: If $i \hookrightarrow j$, then $\mathcal{E}_j(t, \phi) \subseteq \mathcal{E}_i(!t, t :_i \phi)$
Conversion Closure: If $i \subset j$, then $\mathcal{E}_j(t, \phi) \subseteq \mathcal{E}_i(t, \phi)$
Distribution: for any formula ϕ, justification term t, $j \hookrightarrow i$ and $a, b \in W$, if
  $aR_j b$ and $a \in \mathcal{E}_i(t, \phi)$, then $b \in \mathcal{E}_i(t, \phi)$.

- If $F(i) = \mathsf{JT}$, then R_i must be reflexive.
- If $F(i) = \mathsf{JD}$, then R_i must be serial ($\forall a \in W \ \exists b \in W \ aR_i b$).
- If $i \hookrightarrow j$, then for any $a, b, c \in W$, if $aR_i bR_j c$, we also have $aR_j c$.[1]
- For any $i \subset j$, $R_i \subseteq R_j$.

Truth in the model is defined in the following way, given a state a:

- $\mathcal{M}, a \not\models \bot$ and if p is a propositional variable, then $\mathcal{M}, a \models p$ iff $a \in \mathcal{V}(p)$.
- $\mathcal{M}, a \models \phi \rightarrow \psi$ if and only if $\mathcal{M}, a \models \psi$, or $\mathcal{M}, a \not\models \phi$.
- $\mathcal{M}, a \models t :_i \phi$ if and only if $a \in \mathcal{E}_i(t, \phi)$ and $\mathcal{M}, b \models \phi$ for all $aR_i b$.

A way to think about the purpose of admissible evidence function is that it specifies which evidence is relevant (but not necessarily accepted) as evidence of a statement for an agent in a certain state. For example, that the sky is blue may not be relevant evidence to the claim that one has paid for an item, but a receipt is relevant, even if it is fake.

A formula ϕ is called satisfiable if there are some $\mathcal{M}, a \models \phi$; we then say that $\mathcal{M}$ satisfies ϕ in a. A pair $(W, (R_i)_{i \in [n]})$ as above is a frame for $(n, \subset, \hookrightarrow, F)_{\mathcal{CS}}$. We say that $\mathcal{M}$ has the *Strong Evidence Property* when $\mathcal{M}, a \models t :_i \phi$ iff $a \in \mathcal{E}_i(t, \phi)$.

Proposition 2. *$\mathcal{J}$ is sound and complete with respect to its F-models;[2] it is also complete with respect to F-models with the Strong Evidence property.*

Proof. Soundness is left to the reader. Completeness will be proven using a canonical model construction. Let W be the set of all maximal consistent subsets of L_n. We know that W is not empty, because J is consistent. For $\Gamma \in W$ and $i \in [n]$, let $\Gamma^{\#i} = \{\phi \in L_n | \exists t \in Tm \ t :_i \phi \in \Gamma\}$. For any $i \in [n]$, R_i is a binary relation on W, such that $\Gamma R_i \Delta$ if and only if $\Gamma^{\#i} \subseteq \Delta$. Also, for $i \in [n]$, let $\mathcal{E}_i(t, \phi) = \{\Gamma \in W | t :_i \phi \in \Gamma\}$. Finally, $\mathcal{V} : Pvar \longrightarrow \mathcal{P}(W)$ is such that $\mathcal{V}(p) = \{\Gamma \in W | p \in \Gamma\}$. The canonical model is $\mathcal{M} = (W, (R_i)_{i \in [n]}, (\mathcal{E}_i)_{i \in [n]}, \mathcal{V})$.

Define the relation between worlds of the canonical models and formulas of L_n, $\models$, as in the definition of models.

Lemma 1 (Truth Lemma). *For all $\Gamma \in W$, $\phi \in L_n$, $\mathcal{M}, \Gamma \models \phi \Longleftrightarrow \phi \in \Gamma$.*

---

[1] Thus, if i has positive introspection (i.e. $i \hookrightarrow i$), then R_i is transitive.
[2] That $\mathcal{CS}$ is axiomatically appropriate is a requirement for completeness.

Proof. By induction on the structure of ϕ. The cases for $\phi = p$, a propositional variable, $\perp$, or $\psi_1 \rightarrow \psi_2$, are immediate from the definition of $\mathcal{V}$ and $\models$.

If $\phi = t :_i \psi$, then $\mathcal{M}, \Gamma \models t :_i \psi \Rightarrow \Gamma \in \mathcal{E}_i(t, \psi) \Leftrightarrow t :_i \psi \in \Gamma$,

$t :_i \psi \in \Gamma \Rightarrow \forall \Delta \in W \ (\Gamma R_i \Delta \rightarrow \psi \in \Delta) \Rightarrow \forall \Delta \in W \ (\Gamma R_i \Delta \rightarrow \Delta \models \psi)$,

and finally, $\Gamma \in \mathcal{E}_i(t, \psi)$ and $\forall \Delta \in W \ (\Gamma R_i \Delta \rightarrow \Delta \models \psi) \Rightarrow \mathcal{M}, \Gamma \models t :_i \psi$, which completes the proof. $\square$

The canonical model is, indeed, a model for J. To establish this, we must show that the conditions expected from R_1, R_2 and $\mathcal{E}_1, \mathcal{E}_2$ are satisfied. First, the admissible evidence function conditions:

Application closure: If $\Gamma \in \mathcal{E}_i(s, \phi \rightarrow \psi) \cap \mathcal{E}_i(t, \phi)$, then $s :_i (\phi \rightarrow \psi), t :_i \phi \in \Gamma$.
  Because of the application axiom, $(s \cdot t) :_i \psi \in \Gamma$, so $\Gamma \in \mathcal{E}_i(s \cdot t, \psi)$.

Sum closure: If $\Gamma \in \mathcal{E}_i(t, \phi)$, then $t :_i \phi \in \Gamma$, so, by the Concatenation axiom, $(s + t) :_i \phi, (t + s) :_i \phi \in \Gamma$, therefore, $\Gamma \in \mathcal{E}_i(t + s, \phi) \cap \mathcal{E}_i(s + t, \phi)$.

$\mathcal{CS}$ **closure:** Any $\Gamma \in W$ includes all instances of AN, so this is satisfied.

Verification closure: If $\Gamma \in \mathcal{E}_i(t, \phi)$, then $t :_i \phi \in \Gamma$. If $i \leftrightarrow j$ then $!t :_j t :_i \phi \in \Gamma$, therefore, $\Gamma \in \mathcal{E}_j(!t, t :_i \phi)$.

Conversion closure: If $\Gamma \in \mathcal{E}_i(t, \phi)$, then $t :_i \phi \in \Gamma$. If $i \supset j$ then $t :_j \phi \in \Gamma$, therefore, $\Gamma \in \mathcal{E}_j(t, \phi)$.

Distribution: If $\Gamma R_j \Delta$ and $\Gamma \in \mathcal{E}_i(t, \phi)$, then $t :_i \phi \in \Gamma$. If $i \leftrightarrow j$ then $!t :_j t :_i \phi \in \Gamma$, thus $t :_i \phi \in \Gamma^{\#j} \subseteq \Delta$, concluding that $\Delta \in \mathcal{E}_i(t, \phi)$.

To complete the proof, we prove that $(R_i)_{i \in [n]}$ satisfy the required conditions:

If $F(i) = \mathsf{JT}$, then R_i is reflexive. For this, we just need that if $\Gamma \in W$, then $\Gamma^{\#i} \subseteq \Gamma$. If $\phi \in \Gamma^{\#i}$, then there is some justification term, t, for which $t :_i \phi \in \Gamma$. Because of the F-Factivity axiom, $\neg\phi \notin \Gamma$, since $\{t :_i \phi, \neg\phi\}$ is inconsistent. Therefore, as Γ is maximal consistent, $\phi \in \Gamma$.

If $F(i) = \mathsf{JD}$, then R_i is serial. To establish this, we just need to show that $\Gamma^{\#i}$ is consistent. If it is not, then there are formulas $\phi_1, \ldots, \phi_k \in \Gamma^{\#i}$ s.t. $\phi_1, \ldots, \phi_k \vdash \perp$. This means that there are $t_1 :_i \phi_1, \ldots t_k :_i \phi_k \in \Gamma$, s.t. $t_1 :_i \phi_1, \ldots t_k :_i \phi_k \vdash t :_i \perp$ (by Proposition 1), which is a contradiction.

If iVj and $\Gamma R_j \Delta R_i E$, then $\Gamma R_i E$. If $t :_i \phi \in \Gamma$ then $!t :_j t :_i \phi \in \Gamma$, so $t :_i \phi \in \Gamma^{\#j}$.
If $\Gamma R_j \Delta$, then $t :_i \phi \in \Delta$. So, $\Gamma^{\#i} \subseteq \Delta^{\#i}$ and if $\Delta R_i E$, then $\Gamma R_i E$.

If $i \subset j$, then $R_i \subseteq R_j$. If $i \subset j$ then for any $\Gamma \in W$, $\Gamma^{\#i} \subseteq \Gamma^{\#j}$, i.e. $R_j \subseteq R_i$.

Finally, notice that the canonical model has the Strong Evidence Property: if $\Gamma \in \mathcal{E}_i(t, \phi)$ then $t :_i \phi \in \Gamma$ and by the Truth Lemma, $\Gamma \models t :_i \phi$.[3] $\square$

Corollary 1 can be proven by altering the canonical model construction from the proof above.

Corollary 1. *If ϕ is $\mathcal{J}$-satisfiable, then ϕ is satisfiable by an F-model for $\mathcal{J}$ of at most $2^{|\phi|}$ states which has the strong evidence property.*

---

[3] In fact, it is not hard to demonstrate how to construct from a model $\mathcal{M} = (W, (R_i)_{i \in [n]}, \mathcal{E}, \mathcal{V})$ a model $\mathcal{M}' = (W, (R_i)_{i \in [n]}, \mathcal{E}', \mathcal{V})$ which has the Strong Evidence Property and for every $w \in W$ and $\phi \in L_n$, $\mathcal{M}, w \models \phi$ iff $\mathcal{M}', w \models \phi$: just define $\mathcal{E}_i(t, \phi) = \{w \in W \mid \mathcal{M}, w \models t :_i \phi\}$.

2.3   The ∗-Calculus

We present the ∗-calculus for $(n, \subset, \hookrightarrow, F)_{\mathcal{CS}}$. The ∗-calculi for the single-agent justification logics are an invaluable tool in the study of the complexity of these logics. This concept and results were adapted to the two-agent setting in [3] and here we extend them to the general multi-agent setting. Although the calculi have significant similarities to the ones of the single-agent justification logics, there are differences, notably that each calculus depends upon a frame. A ∗-calculus was first introduced in [12], but its origins can be found in [18].

∗$\mathcal{CS}(\mathcal{F})$ **Axioms:** $w \;*_i\; (t, \phi)$, where $t :_i \phi$ an instance of AN	$* \hookrightarrow (\mathcal{F})$: For any $i \hookrightarrow j$, $$\frac{w \;*_i\; (t, \phi)}{w \;*_j\; (!t, t :_i \phi)}$$
∗**App**$(\mathcal{F})$: $$\frac{w \;*_i\; (s, \phi \to \psi) \qquad w \;*_i\; (t, \phi)}{w \;*_i\; (s \cdot t, \psi)}$$	$* \subset (\mathcal{F})$: For any $i \supset j$, $$\frac{w \;*_i\; (t, \phi)}{w \;*_j\; (t, \phi)}$$
∗**Sum**$(\mathcal{F})$: $$\frac{w \;*_i\; (t, \phi)}{w \;*_i\; (s + t, \phi)} \qquad \frac{w \;*_i\; (s, \phi)}{w \;*_i\; (s + t, \phi)}$$	$* \hookrightarrow$**Dis**$(\mathcal{F})$: For any $i \hookrightarrow j$ and $(a, b) \in R_j$, $$\frac{a \;*_i\; (t, \phi)}{b \;*_i\; (t, \phi)}$$

Fig. 1. The $*^{\mathcal{F}}$-calculus for $\mathcal{J}$: where $\mathcal{F} = (W, (R_i)_{i \in [n]})$ and for every $i \in [n]$

If t is a term, ϕ is a formula, and $i \in [n]$, then $*_i(t, \phi)$ is a ∗-expression. Given a frame $\mathcal{F} = (W, (R_i)_{i \in [n]})$ for $\mathcal{J}$, the $*^{\mathcal{F}}$-calculus for $\mathcal{J}$ on the frame $\mathcal{F}$ is a calculus on ∗-expressions prefixed by worlds from W ($*^{\mathcal{F}}$-expressions from now on) with the axioms and rules that are shown in Fig. 1.

If $\mathcal{E}$ is an admissible evidence function of $\mathcal{M}$, we define $\mathcal{M}, w \models *_i (t, \phi)$ iff $\mathcal{E} \models w \;*_i\; (t, \phi)$ iff $w \in \mathcal{E}_i(t, \phi)$. Notice that the calculus rules correspond to the closure conditions of the admissible evidence functions. In fact, because of this, given a frame $\mathcal{F} = (W, (R_i)_{i \in [n]})$ and a set S of $*^{\mathcal{F}}$-expressions, the function $\mathcal{E}$ such that $\mathcal{E} \models e \Leftrightarrow S \vdash_{*^{\mathcal{F}}} e$ is an admissible evidence function. Furthermore, $\mathcal{E}$ is *minimal and unique*: if some admissible evidence function $\mathcal{E}'$ is such that for every $e \in S$, $\mathcal{E}' \models e$, then for every $*^{\mathcal{F}}$-expression e, $\mathcal{E} \models e \Rightarrow \mathcal{E}' \models e$. Therefore, given a frame $\mathcal{F} = (W, (R_i)_{i \in [n]})$ and two set X, Y of $*^{\mathcal{F}}$-expression there is an admissible evidence function $\mathcal{E}$ on $\mathcal{F}$ such that for every $e \in X$, $\mathcal{E} \models e$ and for every $e \in Y$, $\mathcal{E} \not\models e$, if and only if there is no $e \in Y$ such that $X \vdash_* e$. When $X = \emptyset$, this yields the following proposition (see also [12,14]):

Proposition 3. *For any frame $\mathcal{F}$, state w, $\mathcal{J} \vdash t :_i \phi \iff \vdash_{*^{\mathcal{F}}} w \;*_i\; (t, \phi)$.*

The required assumptions on the constant specification are made explicit in the following Proposition 4 and Corollary 2. The proof of Proposition 4 is very similar to the one that can be found in [14].

Proposition 4. *If $\mathcal{CS}$ is schematic and in* P, *then the following problem is in* NP: *Given a finite frame $\mathcal{F} = (W, (R_i)_{i \in [n]})$, a finite set S of $*$-expressions prefixed by worlds from W, a formula $t :_i \phi$, and a $w \in W$, is it the case that $S \vdash_{*\mathcal{F}} w *_i (t, \phi)$?*

The shape of a $*$-calculus derivation in mostly given away by the term t. So, we can use t to extract the general shape of the derivation – the term keeps track of the applications of all rules besides $* \subset$ and $* \hookrightarrow$Dis. We can then plug in to the leaves of the derivation either axioms of the calculus or members of S and unify ($\mathcal{CS}$ is schematic, so the derivation includes schemes) trying to reach the root. Using this result, we can conclude with the following complexity bounds.

Corollary 2.

1. *If $\mathcal{CS}$ is schematic and in* P, *then deciding for $t :_i \phi$ that $\mathcal{J} \vdash t :_i \phi$ is in* NP.
2. *If $\mathcal{CS}$ is axiomatically appropriate, in* P, *and axiomatically appropriate, then the satisfiability problem for $\mathcal{J}$ is in* NEXP.

3 Tableaux

In this section we give a general tableau procedure for every logic which varies according to each logic's parameters. We can then use the tableau for a particular logic and make observations on its complexity.

If $A_1, \ldots, A_k$ are binary relations on the same set, then $A_1 \cdots A_k$ is the binary relation on the same set, such that $x A_1 \cdots A_k y$ if and only if there are $x_1, \ldots, x_k$ in the set, such that $x = x_1 A_1 x_2 A_2 \cdots A_{k-1} x_k A_k y$. If A is a binary relation, then A^* is the reflexive, transitive closure of A; if A is a set (but not a set of pairs), then A^* is the set of strings from A. We also use the following relation on strings: $a \sqsubseteq b$ iff there is some string c such that $ac = b$.

We define $D = \{i \in [n] \mid F(i) = \mathsf{JD}\}$, $\min(D) = \{i \in D \mid \nexists j \in D \text{ s.t. } j \subset i\}$ and for every $i \in [n]$ $\min(i) = \{j \in \min(D) \mid j \subset i \text{ or } i = j\}$ (notice that if $F(i) \neq \mathsf{JD}$, then $\min(i) = \emptyset$). These are important because we can use them to identify the agents that need to contribute new states we need to consider as we construct a model during the tableau. For example, consider a situation of three agents $F(1) = F(2) = F(3) = \mathsf{JD}$, where $1 \subset 2 \subset 3$ and a state w in a model. Then, since the accessibility relations (R_1, R_2, R_3) are serial, given formulas $t_1 :_1 \phi_1$, $t_2 :_2 \phi_2$, and $t_3 :_3 \phi_3$, we need to consider some states $v_1 \models \phi_1$, $v_2 \models \phi_2$, and $v_3 \models \phi_3$. However, we also know that $R_1 \subseteq R_2 \subseteq R_3$, so v_1 is enough, as $v_1 \models \phi_1, \phi_2, \phi_3$. We will use this observation during the tableau.

The formulas used in the tableau will have the form $0.\sigma \; s \; \beta\psi$, where $\psi \in L_n$ or is a $*$-expression, $\sigma \in D^*$, β is (either the empty string or) of the form $\Box_i \Box_j \cdots \Box_k$, $i, j, \ldots, k \in D$, and $s \in \{T, F\}$. Furthermore, $0.\sigma$ will be called a world-prefix or state-prefix, s a truth-prefix and world prefixes will be denoted as $0.s_1.s_2 \ldots s_k$, instead of $0.s_1 s_2 \cdots s_k$, where for all $x \in [k]$, $s_x \in D$.

Prefixes of the form $0.\sigma$, where $\sigma \in D^*$ represent states in the constructed model ($\mathcal{M} = (W, (R_i)_{i \in [n]}, (\mathcal{E}_i)_{i \in [n]}, V)$ for this paragraph). The intuitive meaning of $\sigma \; T \; \psi$ is that $\mathcal{M}, \sigma \models \psi$ and of course, $\sigma \; F \; \psi$ declares that $\mathcal{M}, \sigma \not\models \psi$.

Then, $\sigma\ T\ *_i\ (t,\psi)$ declares that $\mathcal{E} \models \sigma\ T\ *_i\ (t,\psi)$ and $\sigma\ F\ *_i\ (t,\psi)$ declares that $\mathcal{E} \not\models \sigma\ T\ *_i\ (t,\psi)$. As one may expect, the meaning of $\sigma\ T\ \square_i\psi$ is that $\mathcal{M},\sigma' \models \psi$ for every $\sigma R_i\sigma'$. Finally, $\sigma.i$ is some state in W such that $\sigma R_i\sigma.i$.

A tableau branch is a set of formulas of the form $\sigma\ s\ \beta\psi$, as above. A branch is complete if it is closed under the tableau rules (they follow). It is propositionally closed if $\sigma\ T\ \beta\psi$ and $\sigma\ F\ \beta\psi$ are both in the branch, or if $\sigma\ T\ \bot$ is in the branch. We say that a tableau branch is constructed by the tableau rules from ϕ, if it is a closure of $\{0\ T\ \phi\}$ under the rules. The tableau rules for J can be found in Table 1, but before that we need some extra definitions.

For every $i,j \in [n]$, $i \in N(j)$ if $i,j \in D$ and there is some $j \hookrightarrow i'$ such that $i \in \min(i')$. We can say that i is a "next" agent from j – if we can reach some state in the constructed model through R_i, then we must consider a state that we can access through R_j from there. This is the essence of rule S (Table 1) and it is needed to prove correctness for the tableau (see the proof of Proposition 5).

We define the equivalence relation $i \equiv_\hookrightarrow j$ if $i \subset^*\hookrightarrow^* j \subset^*\hookrightarrow^* i$ (notice that $i \subset^* i'$ iff $i \subset i'$ or $i = i'$). As an equivalence relation, it gives equivalence classes on $D^+ = D \cup \{i \in [n] \mid F(i) = JT\}$; let the set of these classes be P. Furthermore, notice that for any $L \in P$, $\exists x, y \in L$ s.t. $x \hookrightarrow y$, or $|L| = 1$. In the first case, L is called a *V-class* of agents. For each agent $i \in D^+$, $P(i)$ is the equivalence class which contains i. The tableau we use for J-satisfiability makes use of the following lemma, which in many cases allows us to save on the number of states that are produced in the constructed frame.

Lemma 2. *Let* $\mathcal{M} = (W, (R_i)_{i\in[n]}, (\mathcal{E}_i)_{i\in[n]}, V)$ *be an F-model on a finite frame, $L \in P$ a V-class, and $u \in W$. Then, there are states of W, $(a_i)_{i\in L}$, such that*

1. *For any $i \in L$, uR_ia_i.*
2. *For any $i,j \in L$, $v,b \in W$, if a_i, bR_jv, then bR_ja_j.*

$(a_i)_{i\in L}$ will be called an L-cluster for u.

Proof. For this proof we need to define the following. Let $i \in [n]$, $w,v \in W$. An E_V-path ending at i (and starting at i') from w to v is a finite sequence $v_1,\ldots,v_{k+1}$, such that for some $j_1,\ldots,j_k \in [n]$, $E_1,\ldots,E_{k-1} \in \{\subset,\hookrightarrow\}$, where for some $j \in [k-1]$ $E_j =\hookrightarrow$ and $j_k = i$ (and $j_1 = i'$), for every $a \in [k-1]$, $j_aE_aj_{a+1}$ and if $E_a =\subset$, then $v_{a+1} = v_{a+2}$, while if $E_a =\hookrightarrow$, then $v_{a+1}R_{j_{a+1}}v_{a+2}$ and $v_1 = w$, $v_k = v$, $v_1R_1v_2$. The E_V-path *covers* a set $s \subseteq [n]$ if $\{j_1,\ldots,j_k\} = s$. For this path and $a \in [k]$, v_{a+1} is a j_a-state. Notice that if there is an E_V path ending at i from w to v and some $j \in s$ and $z \in W$ such that the path covers s and zR_jw, it must also be the case that w, zR_iv.

Let $p : [m] \longrightarrow L$ be such that $m \in \mathbb{N}$, $p[[m]] = L$ and for every $i+1 \in [m]$, either $p(i+1) \subset p(i)$ or $p(i+1)Vp(i)$ and there is some $i+1 \in [m]$ such that $p(i+1)Vp(i)$. For any $s \in W$, $x \in \mathbb{N}$ let $b_0(s), b_1(s), b_2(s),\ldots,b_m(s)$ be the following: $b_0(s) = s$, for all $k \in [m]$, $b_1(s)$ will be such that there is an E_V path ending at $p(1)$ from s to $b_1(s)$ and covering P_a and if $k > 1$, $b_k(s)$ is such that $b_0(s),b_1(s),b_2(s),\ldots,b_k(s)$ is an E_V path ending at $p(k)$. Let $(b_i^x)_{i\in[m],x\in\mathbb{N}}, (a_i^x)_{i\in[m],x\in\mathbb{N}}$ be defined in the following way. For every $i \in [m]$,

$b_i^0 = b_i(u)$ and for every $x \in \mathbb{N}$, $a_i^x = b_i(b_m^x)$. Finally, for $0 < x \in \mathbb{N}$, $(b_i^x)_{i \in [m]}$ is defined in the following way. If there are some $b_x, v \in W$, $i, j \in L$, such that $b_x R_j v$, $a_i^{x-1} R_j v$ and not $b_x R_j a_j^{x-1}$, then for all $i \in L$, $b_i^x = b_i(v)$. Otherwise, $(b_i^x)_{i \in L} = (a_i^x)_{i \in L}$. By induction on x, we can see that for every $x, y \in \mathbb{N}$, $i \in L$, if $y \geq x$, then $b_x R_i b_i^y$, a_i^y. Since the model has a finite number of states, there is some $x \in \mathbb{N}$ such that for every $y \geq x$, $(b_i^y)_{i \in L} = (a_i^y)_{i \in L}$. Therefore, we can pick appropriate $(a_i)_{i \in L}$ among $(a_i^k)_{i \in L}$ that satisfy conditions 1, 2.   □

We recursively define relation $\Rightarrow$ on $(D^+)^*$: if $i \subset j$ then $i \Rightarrow j$; if $i \hookrightarrow j$, then $ij \Rightarrow j$; if $\beta \Rightarrow \delta$, then $\alpha\beta\gamma \Rightarrow \alpha\delta\gamma$. $\Rightarrow^*$ is the reflexive, transitive closure of $\Rightarrow$. We can see that $\Rightarrow^*$ captures the closure conditions on the accessibility relations of a frame, so if for some frame $(W, (R_i)_{i \in [n]})$, $a R_{i_1} R_{i_2} \cdots R_{i_k} b$ and $i_1 i_2 \cdots i_k \Rightarrow^* j_1 j_2 \cdots j_l$, then $a R_{j_1} R_{j_2} \cdots R_{j_l} b$. Furthermore, if, in addition, $l = k$, then for every $r \in [k]$, $j_r \subset i_r$. For every agent $F(i) = \mathsf{JD}$, we introduce a new agent, $\bar{i}$ and we extend $\Rightarrow^*$, so that $\bar{i} \Rightarrow^* i.\chi$ for every $\chi \in D^*$ such that $i.\chi \Rightarrow^* i$ (notice that χ is not the empty string only if $P(i)$ a V-class). Furthermore, if $xy \in D^*$, then $\overline{xy} = \bar{x}\ \bar{y}$. This extended definition of $\Rightarrow^*$ tries to capture the closure of the conditions on the accessibility relations of a frame like the ones that will result from a tableau procedure as defined in the following.

Let $L \in P$ and $\sigma \in D^*$. Then, L is *visible* from $0.\sigma$ if and only if there is some $i \in L$ and some $\chi, \alpha \in D^*$ such that $\sigma = \tau.i.\chi$ and $\overline{\chi}\alpha \Rightarrow^* i$; $\tau.\chi(i)$ is then called the *L-view* from σ. Notice that there is a similarity between this definition and the statement of Lemma 2 – this will be made explicit later on.

This discussion above the rules should explain rules TrB, SB, FB, C, and V, as well as S. Rule TrD merely says that when we encounter $\sigma\ T\ t :_i \psi$, we need to consider the states σ' where $\sigma R_i \sigma'$ (see also the discussion on $\min(i)$ above). We do not need to produce $\sigma.j\ T\ \psi$, as this is handled by the following successive applications of the rules: TrB, C, SB. Rule Fa may seem strange, as

Table 1. The tableau rules for J

$$\frac{\sigma\ T\ t :_i \psi}{\sigma\ T\ *_i (t, \psi)}\ \mathrm{TrB}$$
$$\sigma\ T\ \Box_i \psi$$

$$\frac{\sigma\ T\ t :_i \psi}{\sigma.j\ F\ \bot}\ \mathrm{TrD}$$

if $j \in \min(i)$, $P(j)$ not a V-class visible from σ;

$$\frac{\sigma\ F\ t :_i \psi}{\sigma\ F\ *_i (t, \psi)}\ \mathrm{FA}$$

$$\frac{}{\sigma.j.i\ F\ \bot}\ \mathrm{S}$$

if $i \in N(j)$, $\sigma.i$ has appeared, and $P(i)$ is not a V-class visible from $\sigma.j$;

$$\frac{\sigma\ T\ \Box_i \psi}{\sigma.i\ T\ \psi}\ \mathrm{SB}$$

if $\sigma.i$ has already appeared;

$$\frac{\sigma\ T\ \Box_i \psi}{\sigma\ T\ \psi}\ \mathrm{FB}$$

if $F(i) = \mathsf{JT}$;

$$\frac{\sigma\ T\ \Box_i \psi}{\tau.i\ T\ \psi}\ \mathrm{SVB}$$

$$\frac{\sigma\ T\ \Box_i \psi}{\sigma\ T\ \Box_j \psi}\ \mathrm{C}$$

if $i \supset j$;

$$\frac{\sigma\ T\ \Box_i \psi}{\sigma\ T\ \Box_j \Box_i \psi}\ \mathrm{V}$$

if $i \hookrightarrow j$.

if $P(i)$ a V-class visible from σ, $\tau.j$ is the $P(i)$-view from σ and $\tau.i$ has already appeared in the tableau.

in a model there may be two reasons for which $\sigma \not\models t:_i \psi$: either because of the admissible evidence function or because of the accessibility relation. Therefore, one would expect a nondeterministic choice for this rule (see for example [14]); we use F-models with the Strong Evidence property, though, and in these models we know that $\sigma \not\models t:_i \psi$ because of the admissible evidence function.

If b is a tableau branch, then Let $(R_i)_{i \in [n]}$ be such that for every $i \in [n]$,

$$R_i = \{(\sigma, \sigma.i) \in (W(b))^2\} \cup \{(w,w) \in (W(b))^2 \mid F(i) = \mathsf{JT}\} \cup$$

$$\{(\sigma, \tau.i) \in (W(b))^2 \mid P(i) \text{ a } V\text{-class}, \tau.j \text{ the } P(i)\text{-view from } \sigma\}$$

then $\mathcal{F}(b) = (W(b), (R'_i)_{i \in [n]})$, where $(R'_i)_{i \in [n]}$ is the closure of $(R_i)_{i \in [n]}$ under the conditions of frames for the accessibility relations, except for seriality. Finally, let $X(b) = \{\sigma *_i (t, \psi) \mid \sigma \, T *_i (t, \psi) \text{ appears in } b\}$ and $Y(b) = \{\sigma *_i (t, \psi) \mid \sigma \, F *_i (t, \psi) \text{ appears in } b\}$. Branch b of the tableau is rejecting when it is propositionally closed or there is some $f \in Y(b)$ such that $X(b) \vdash_{*^{\mathcal{F}(b)}} f$. Otherwise it is an accepting branch.

Proposition 5. *Let $\phi \in L_n$. ϕ is $\mathcal{J}$-satisfiable if and only if there is a complete accepting tableau branch b that is produced from $0 \, T \, \phi$.*

Proof. We first prove the "if" direction. By induction on the construction of $\mathcal{F}(b)$, it is not hard to see that for every $(\sigma, \tau.j) \in R_i$, it must be the case that $i \subset j$ or that $F(i) = \mathsf{JT}$ and $\sigma = \tau.j$ and that if $\sigma \, T \, \Box_i \phi$ appears in b and $\sigma R_i \tau$, then $\tau \, T \, \phi$ appears in b. Let $\mathcal{M} = (W, (R_i)_{i \in [n]}, \mathcal{E}, \mathcal{V})$, where $(W, (R_i)_{i \in [n]}) = \mathcal{F}(b)$, $\mathcal{V}(p) = \{w \in W \mid w \, T \, p \in b\}$, and $\mathcal{E}_i(t, \psi) = \{w \in W \mid *_T (b) \vdash_{*^{\mathcal{F}}_{\mathcal{CS}}(V,C)} w *_i (t, \psi)\}$.

Let $\mathcal{M}' = (W, (R'_i)_{i \in [n]}, (\mathcal{E}_i)_{i \in [n]}, \mathcal{V})$, where for every $i \in [n]$, if $F(i) = \mathsf{JD}$, then $R'_i = R_i \cup \{(a,a) \in W^2 \mid \exists j \in \min(i) \, \nexists (a,b) \in R_j\}$ and $R'_i = R_i$, otherwise. $\mathcal{M}'$ is an F-model for J: $(\mathcal{E}_i)_{i \in [n]}$ easily satisfy the appropriate conditions, as the extra pairs of the accessibility relations do not affect the $*$-calculus derivation, and we can prove the same for $(R'_i)_{i \in [n]}$. If $aR'_i bR'_j c$ and $i \hookrightarrow j$, if $(a,b) \in R'_i \setminus R_i$, then $a = b$ and thus $aR'_i c$. If $(a,b) \in R_i$, then, from rule S, there must be some $(b,c') \in R_j$, so $(b,c) \in R_j$ and thus, $(a,c) \in R_j$. If $(a,b) \in R'_i$ and $i \subset j$, then, trivially, whether $(a,b) \in R_i$ or not, $(a,b) \in R'_j$.

By induction on χ, we prove that for every formula χ and $a \in W$, if $a \, T \, \chi \in b$, then $\mathcal{M}', a \models \chi$ and if $a \, F \, \chi \in b$, then $\mathcal{M}', a \not\models \chi$. Propositional cases are easy. If $\chi = t:_i \psi$ and $a \, F \, \chi \in b$, then $a \notin \mathcal{E}_i(t, \psi)$, so $\mathcal{M}', a \not\models \chi$. On the other hand, if $a \, T \, t:_i \psi \in b$, then $a \in \mathcal{E}_i(t, \psi)$ and by rule TrD, for every $j \in \min(i)$, there is some $(a,b) \in R_j$. Therefore, for every $(a,b) \in R'_j$, it is the case that $(a,b) \in R_j$, so by rule TrB and the inductive hypothesis, for every $(a,b) \in R_i$, $\mathcal{M}', b \models \psi$ and therefore, $\mathcal{M}', a \models t:_i \psi$.

We now prove the "only if" direction. Let $\mathcal{M} = (W, (R_i)_{i \in [n]}, (\mathcal{E}_i)_{i \in [n]}, \mathcal{V})$ that has the strong evidence property and a state $s \in W$ such that $\mathcal{M}, s \models \phi$. For every $a \in W$ and V-class L fix some L-cluster for a (Lemma 2). For $x \in D^*$, we define $(0.x)^{\mathcal{M}}$ to be such that $0^{\mathcal{M}} = s$ and $(0.\sigma.i)^{\mathcal{M}}$ is some element of W s.t. $((0.\sigma)^{\mathcal{M}}, (0.\sigma.i)^{\mathcal{M}}) \in R_i$; particularly, if $P(i)$ a V-class and $(a_j)_{j \in L}$ is the fixed L-cluster for $\sigma^{\mathcal{M}}$, then $(\sigma.i)^{\mathcal{M}} = a_i$.

Let $L_n^\square = \{\square_{i_1} \cdots \square_{i_k} \phi | \phi \in L_n, k \in \mathbb{N}, i_1, \ldots, i_k \in [n]\}$. Given a state a of the model, and $\square_i \psi \in sub_\square(\phi)$, $\mathcal{M}, a \models \square_i \psi$ has the usual, modal interpretation, $\mathcal{M}, a \models \square_i \psi$ iff for every $(a, b) \in R_i$, $\mathcal{M}, b \models \psi$.

Notice that if $P(i)$ a V-class visible from σ and $\tau.j$ is the $P(i)$-view from σ, then in model $\mathcal{M}$ there is some v such that $\sigma^\mathcal{M}, (\tau.j)^\mathcal{M} R_i v$, which by the definition of clusters in turn means that $\sigma^\mathcal{M} R_j (\tau.j)^\mathcal{M}$. It is then straightforward to see by induction on the tableau derivation that there is a branch, such that if $\sigma \, T \, \psi$ appears in the branch and $\psi \in L_n^\square$ or is a $*$-expression, then $\mathcal{M}, \sigma^\mathcal{M} \models \psi$ and if $\sigma \, F \, \psi$ appears, then $\mathcal{M}, \sigma^\mathcal{M} \not\models \psi$. The proposition follows. $\square$

4   Complexity Results

In the tableau we presented, if for all appearing world-prefixes $\sigma.i$, i in the same V-class L, then all prefixes are either of the form $0.j$, where $j \in L$. In this case we can simplify the box rules and in particular just ignore rule V and end up with the following result.

Corollary 3. *When* $\min(D) = \emptyset$ *or there is some* V-class $L \in P$ *such that* $\min(D) \subseteq L$, *then* $\mathcal{J}$-*satisfiability is in* Σ_2^p.

Corollary 3 may seem rather specific, but it settles that $\mathcal{J}$-satisfiability is in Σ_2^p for several cases. In particular, its assumptions are satisfied when $\mathcal{J}$ is any multi-agent version of LP ($F(i) = JT$, $i \hookrightarrow i$ for all i), or even any combination of single-agent justification logics from J, J4, JT, LP – not JD, JD4 ($F(i) \neq JD$). Other interesting cases are logics with agents that form a single V-class – we consider these logics a way of generalizing JD4. For example, consider all agents in D such that $i \sqsubset j$ iff $i < j$ and $\hookrightarrow = \{(n, i) \mid i \in [n]\}$. Then, we can think of the agent i's justifications as increasing in reliability as i increases and thus can model a situation where the agents are degrees of the belief of some other agent. Thus if the agent believes something with degree n, then the agent is aware of their belief with degree 1. On the other hand, if they believe something with degree 1, then they may not be aware of the fact that their belief is so reliable, so they are aware only of their least reliable belief. It would also make sense that for some $i_T < n$, for every $i < i_T$, $F(i) = JT$ instead of JD, so the most reliable beliefs could actually be knowledge. Furthermore, even if we have $\hookrightarrow = \{(n, 1)\}$, the complexity of satisfiability remains in Σ_2^p.

We look into some more specific cases of multi-agent justification logics and demonstrate certain jumps in the complexity of the satisfiability problem for these logics. We first revisit the two-agent logics from [3]. As before, we assume our constant specifications are schematic and axiomatically appropriate (and in P for upper bounds). Our definition here of $(n, \sqsubset, \hookrightarrow, F)_{\mathcal{CS}}$ allows for more two-agent logics than the ones that were studied in [3]. It is not hard, though, to extend those results to all two-agent cases of $(n, \sqsubset, \hookrightarrow, F)_{\mathcal{CS}}$: when there are $\{i, j\} = [2]$, $F(i) = JD$, $\emptyset \neq \hookrightarrow \subseteq \{(i, j), (j, i)\}$, and $i \sqsubset j$, then $(2, \sqsubset, \hookrightarrow, F)_{\mathcal{CS}}$-satisfiability is PSPACE-complete; otherwise it is in Σ_2^p (see [3]).

We will further examine the following two cases. $\mathcal{J}_1, \mathcal{J}_2$ are defined in the following way. $n_1 = n_2 = 3$; $F(1) = F(2) = F(3) = JD$; $\hookrightarrow_1 = \emptyset$, $\hookrightarrow_2 = \{(3, 3)\}$;

Table 2. Tableau rules for J_1, J_2. V and S are used only for J_2

$$\frac{\sigma\,T\ t:_i\psi}{\sigma\,T\ *_i\,(t,\psi)}\ \text{TRB}$$
$$\sigma\,T\ \Box_i\psi$$

$$\frac{\sigma\,T\ t:_j\psi}{\sigma.i\ F\perp}\ \text{TRD}$$

$$\frac{\sigma\,F\ t:_i\psi}{\sigma\,F\ *_i\,(t,\psi)}\ \text{FA}$$

$$\text{if } i = j < 3 \text{ or } j = 3;$$

$$\frac{\sigma\,T\ \Box_i\psi}{\sigma.i\ T\ \psi}\ \text{SB}$$

$$\frac{\sigma\,T\ \Box_3\psi}{\sigma\,T\ \Box_1\psi}\ \text{C}$$
$$\sigma\,T\ \Box_2\psi$$

$$\frac{\sigma\,T\ \Box_1\psi}{\sigma\,T\ \Box_1\Box_1\psi}\ \text{V}$$

$$\frac{}{\sigma.i\ F\perp}\ \text{S}$$

if $\sigma.i$ has already appeared;

where $\sigma \neq \emptyset$ has appeared

$\supset = \{(3,1),(3,2)\}$; finally, for $i \in [2]$, $J_i = (3, \subset, \hookrightarrow_i, F)_{\mathcal{CS}_i}$, where $\mathcal{CS}_i$ is some axiomatically appropriate and schematic constant specification.

By an adjustment of the reductions in [2], as it was done in [3], it is not hard to prove that $\mathcal{J}_1$ is PSPACE-hard and $\mathcal{J}_2$ is EXP-hard.[4] Notice that the way we prove PSPACE-hardness for $\mathcal{J}_1$ is different in character from the way we prove the same result for the two-agent logics in [3]. For $\mathcal{J}_1$ we use the way the tableau prefixes for it branch, while for $\mathcal{J}_2$ the prefixes do not branch, but they increase to exponential length. In fact, we can see that $\mathcal{J}_1$ is PSPACE-complete, while $\mathcal{J}_2$ is EXP-complete (Table 2).

Notice that in the tableau for J_1, the maximum length of a world prefix is at most $|\phi|$, since the depth (nesting of terms) of the formulas decrease whenever we move from σ to $\sigma.i$. Also notice that when we run the $*$-calculus, there is no use for rule $* \hookrightarrow$Dis, so we can simply run the calculus on one world-prefix at the time, without needing the whole frame. Therefore, we can turn the tableau into an alternating polynomial time procedure, which uses a non-deterministic choice when the tableau would make a nondeterministic choice (when we apply the propositional rules) and uses a universal choice to choose whether to increase prefix σ to $\sigma.2$ or to $\sigma.3$. This means that J_1-satisfiability is PSPACE-complete.

For the tableau procedure of J_2 we have no such bound on the size of the largest world-prefix, so we cannot have an alternating polynomial time procedure. As before, though, the $*$-calculus does not use rule $* \hookrightarrow$Dis, so again we can run the calculus on one world-prefix at the time. Furthermore, for every prefix w, $|\{w\ a \in b\}|$ is polynomially bounded (observe that we do not need more than two boxes in front of any formula), so in turn we have an alternating polynomial space procedure. Therefore, J_2-satisfiability is EXP-complete.

---

[4] $\mathcal{J}_1$ would correspond to what is defined in [3] as $\mathsf{D}_2 \oplus_{\subset} \mathsf{K}$ and $\mathcal{J}_2$ to $\mathsf{D}_2 \oplus_{\subset} \mathsf{D4}$. Then we can pick a justification variable x and we can either use the same reductions and substitute $\Box_i$ by $x :_i$, or we can just translate each diamond-free fragment to the corresponding justification logic in the same way. It is not hard to see then that the original modal formula behaves exactly the same way as the result of its translation with respect to satisfiability – just consider F-models where always $\mathcal{E}_i(t,\phi) = W$.

5   Final Remarks

We introduced a family of multi-agent justification logics with two types of inter-actions among the agents to provide a general framework capable of modeling situations of multiple agents of different cognitive abilities and interdependencies, in a setting where we are also interested in the agents' justifications. We gave a general tableau procedure and an upper complexity bound for the general satisfiability problem: for each of these logics, satisfiability is in NEXP. Then we identified a class of logics for which satisfiability remains in the second level of the Polynomial Hierarchy, as it is the case for all single-agent justification logics on which the current system is based (J, JD, JT, J4, JD4, LP). This class nat-urally includes all single-agent cases, all cases where no agent is based on JD (or JD4), the case where every aent is aware of every other agent's justifications (i.e. for all agents i, j, $i \hookrightarrow j$), and several others. Finally, we demonstrated that this family presents certain genuine complexity jumps: for logics J_1, J_2 as defined in Sect. 4, the satisfiability problem is PSPACE-complete and EXP-complete respectively. A complexity jump to PSPACE-completeness was already proven in [3], but for a different logic, using different reasoning. For all these results we used certain assumptions about the constant specification. These were mainly that the constant specification is axiomatically appropriate, schematic and in P, all of which we consider to be reasonable – and often necessary.

Several issues remain to be settled. For the NEXP upper bound for satisfi-ability, we have not provided a NEXP-complete logic in this family. In fact all logics we have examined were in EXP, so it is not clear whether there is another complexity jump, or the general upper bound can be lowered to EXP. We con-jecture that there is in fact another complexity jump and a logic in this family has a NEXP-complete satisfiability problem. We also need to characterize in a satisfactory manner when each complexity jump occurs. The results we have provided may give an idea of what to expect from certain logics, but it is defi-nitely not a complete picture. We need to provide a general Σ_2^p-hardness result for these logics the way it was done in [8]. It would be important to the study of the complexity of Justification Logic in general to determine the complexity of more single-agent justification logics (for example the ones with negative intro-spection) and then extend the system to include agents based on these logics and perhaps include further interactions. Finally, we need to identify more areas where this paper's system can be used effectively to provide solutions.

References

1. Achilleos, A.: A complexity question in justification logic. J. Comput. Syst. Sci. **80**(6), 1038–1045 (2014)
2. Achilleos, A.: Modal logics with hard diamond-free fragments. CoRR, abs/1401.5846 (2014)
3. Achilleos, A.: On the complexity of two-agent justification logic. In: Bulling, N., van der Torre, L., Villata, S., Jamroga, W., Vasconcelos, W. (eds.) CLIMA 2014. LNCS, vol. 8624, pp. 1–18. Springer, Heidelberg (2014)

4. Artemov, S.: Explicit provability and constructive semantics. Bull. Symbolic Logic **7**(1), 1–36 (2001)
5. Artemov, S.: Justification logic. In: Hölldobler, S., Lutz, C., Wansing, H. (eds.) JELIA 2008. LNCS (LNAI), vol. 5293, pp. 1–4. Springer, Heidelberg (2008)
6. Artemov, S.: The logic of justification. Rev. Symbolic Logic **1**(4), 477–513 (2008)
7. Artemov, S., Kuznets, R.: Logical omniscience as infeasibility. Ann. Pure Appl. Logic **165**(1), 6–25 (2014). http://dx.doi.org/10.1016/j.apal.2013.07.003
8. Buss, S.R., Kuznets, R.: Lower complexity bounds in justification logic. Ann. Pure Appl. Logic **163**(7), 888–905 (2012)
9. Demri, S.: Complexity of simple dependent bimodal logics. In: Dyckhoff, R. (ed.) TABLEAUX 2000. LNCS, vol. 1847, pp. 190–204. Springer, Heidelberg (2000)
10. Dziubiński, M., Verbrugge, R., Dunin-Kęplicz, B.: Complexity issues in multiagent logics. Fundamenta Informaticae **75**(1), 239–262 (2007)
11. Fitting, M.: The logic of proofs, semantically. Ann. Pure Appl. Logic **132**(1), 1–25 (2005)
12. Krupski, N.V.: On the complexity of the reflected logic of proofs. Theor. Comput. Sci. **357**(1–3), 136–142 (2006)
13. Kuznets, R.: On the complexity of explicit modal logics. In: Clote, P.G., Schwichtenberg, H. (eds.) CSL 2000. LNCS, vol. 1862, pp. 371–383. Springer, Heidelberg (2000). Errata concerning the explicit counterparts of $\mathcal{D}$ and $\mathcal{D}\triangle$ are published as [15]
14. Kuznets, R.: Complexity Issues in Justification Logic. Ph.D. thesis, CUNY Graduate Center, May 2008
15. Kuznets, R.: Complexity through tableaux in justification logic. In: Plenary Talks, Tutorials, Special Sessions, Contributed Talks of Logic Colloquium (LC 2008), Bern, Switzerland, pp. 38–39 (2008)
16. Kuznets, R.: Self-referentiality of justified knowledge. In: Hirsch, E.A., Razborov, A.A., Semenov, A., Slissenko, A. (eds.) Computer Science – Theory and Applications. LNCS, vol. 5010, pp. 228–239. Springer, Heidelberg (2008)
17. Kuznets, R., Studer, T.: Update as evidence: belief expansion. In: Artemov, S., Nerode, A. (eds.) LFCS 2013. LNCS, vol. 7734, pp. 266–279. Springer, Heidelberg (2013)
18. Mkrtychev, A.: Models for the logic of proofs. In: Adian, S., Nerode, A. (eds.) Logical Foundations of Computer Science. LNCS, vol. 1234, pp. 266–275. Springer, Heidelberg (1997)
19. Pacuit, E.: A note on some explicit modal logics. In: Proceedings of the 5th Panhellenic Logic Symposium, Athens, Greece, University of Athens (2005)
20. Spaan, E.: Complexity of modal logics. Ph.D. thesis, University of Amsterdam (1993)
21. Yavorskaya (Sidon), T.: Interacting explicit evidence systems. Theor. Comput. Syst. **43**(2), 272–293 (2008)

A Framework for Epistemic Gossip Protocols

Maduka Attamah[1]([✉]), Hans van Ditmarsch[2], Davide Grossi[1],
and Wiebe van der Hoek[1]

[1] Department of Computer Science, University of Liverpool, Liverpool, UK
m.k.attamah@liverpool.ac.uk
[2] LORIA—CNRS, University of Lorraine, Nancy, France
hans.van-ditmarsch@loria.fr

Abstract. We implement a framework to evaluate epistemic gossip protocols. Gossip protocols spread information within a network of agents by pairwise communications. This tool, Epistemic Gossip Protocol (EGP), is applied to epistemic gossip protocols presented in [1]. We introduce a programming language for epistemic gossip protocols. We describe an interpreter for this language, together with a model generator and model checker, for a dynamic model of the protocol. The tool EGP outputs key dynamic properties of such protocols, thus facilitating the process of protocol design and planning. We conclude with some experimental results.

Keywords: Epistemic gossip protocol · Epistemic gossip framework · Gossip tree · Protocol engineering

1 Introduction

Epistemic gossip protocols are gossip protocols [1,4] in which an agent chooses to communicate with another agent based on its own knowledge, or ignorance, of the distribution of factual information among the agents in the scenario. The initial setting of the gossip scenarios we consider is as follows. There are a finite number of agents, and each agent knows a unique piece of information called a secret. Only pairwise communications between the agents are allowed. These communications are known as *calls*, and only one call is allowed in a round. In each call, the calling pair exchange all the secrets they know. The goal of such communications is to reach a state where all the agents know all the secrets in the scenario.

Each epistemic gossip protocol can be considered as a rule whose condition is an epistemic property that has to be satisfied for one agent to call another agent. We call these rules epistemic calling conditions. In each round, a pair of agents is chosen non-deterministically from the set of pairs for which the calling condition is satisfied, and allowed to make a call. This call can be made in one of several modes. For example, the calling pair can make the call publicly such that every other agent knows who is calling who in any round. This mode is referred to as the *non-epistemic synchronous* mode (while there is no uncertainty about who is calling whom in each round, the contents of the calls, namely the secrets,

© Springer International Publishing Switzerland 2015
N. Bulling (Ed.): EUMAS 2014, LNAI 8953, pp. 193–209, 2015.
DOI: 10.1007/978-3-319-17130-2_13

are not observed). Another mode is that in which the calls are made in private such that, apart from the pair involved in the call, the other agents may not be sure which pair of agents is making the call, but all the agents are sure a call is made in each round. This mode is referred to as the *epistemic synchronous* mode. The *epistemic asynchronous* mode is like the epistemic synchronous mode except that the agents consider it possible that no call is made in a round even though there is some pair for which the calling condition is satisfied.

In this paper we assume that the protocols are based on the epistemic synchronous call mode. Therefore the agents would have to reason about possible situations which are due to all the possible calls in the previous round. For example: at the initial situation of a gossip scenario comprising of four agents, no other situation is considered possible. But after one round there could be up to twelve new and different possible situations due to possible calls at the initial situation. Note that the call $a_i a_j$ is different from the call $a_j a_i$, where $a_i a_j$ denotes the call from agent a_i to another agent, a_j. Hence after a maximal series of rounds we can think of a tree structure in which each path is an execution sequence of calls in accordance with the protocol in use. We refer to this tree as the *call tree* or *gossip tree* of the corresponding protocol, and the set of all the paths of this tree is the *extension* of the protocol.

The gossip tree offers a platform to protocol designers for the evaluation and comparison of epistemic gossip protocols. In the gossip protocol literature it is typical to measure the performance of a protocol by considering the length of its execution sequence, that is, the number of calls in the execution sequence [4]. Correspondingly we measure the performance of epistemic gossip protocols by considering the average length of the execution sequences in the protocol's extension, together with the size of the extension of the given protocol. Whereas the size of the extension gives an idea of the computational memory required by an agent to reason about possible situations, the average execution length gives an idea of how fast it will take for all agents to know all secrets under the given protocol. We also make use of the definitions as follows:

Given a set $Ag = \{a_1, \ldots, a_n\}$ of agents and a set $P = \{A_1, \ldots, A_n\}$ of secrets. Let secret A_i be the unique secret of a_i, and let S_i be the set of secrets known by a_i where $a_i \in Ag$, and where initially $S_i = \{A_i\}$. Then, a *gossip situation* is a n-tuple $\langle S_1, \ldots, S_n \rangle$, the *initial state* is $\langle \{A_i\}, \ldots, \{A_n\} \rangle$, and the *goal state* is $\langle P, \ldots, P \rangle$ (see also Definition 3, later.)

A gossip protocol gives rise to a collection of execution sequences of gossip calls. A protocol is *terminating* if all its execution sequences are finite. Otherwise it is *non-terminating*. An execution sequence is *successful* if the first gossip situation is the initial state and the last gossip situation is the goal state. An epistemic gossip protocol is *successful* if all its execution sequences are successful. The following protocols were described in [1], reproduced informally here.

Protocol 1 (Learn New Secrets). *An agent a_i can call another agent a_j if a_i does not know the secret of a_j.*

Protocol 2 (Known Information Growth de Dicto). *An agent a_i can call another agent a_j if a_i knows that there is some secret A_k that would be learnt in the call $a_i a_j$.*

Protocol 3 (Known Information Growth de Re). *An agent a_i can call another agent a_j if there is some secret A_k such that a_i knows that it would be learnt in the call $a_i a_j$.*

Protocol 4 (Possible Information Growth de Dicto). *An agent a_i can call another agent a_j if a_i considers it possible that there is some secret A_k that would be learnt in the call $a_i a_j$.*

Protocol 5 (Possible Information Growth de Re). *An agent a_i can call another agent a_j if there is some secret A_k such that a_i considers it possible that it would be learnt in the call $a_i a_j$.*

Whereas Protocols 1, 2 and 3 are terminating, Protocols 4 and 5 are non-terminating. Take a scenario with four agents a, b, c, d and consider the following execution sequence of Protocol 4: $ab; cd; ab; cd; \ldots$. After the first two calls, agent a considers it possible that agent b learnt some new secret in the second round, therefore a calls b in the third round, which turns out to be redundant. Likewise in the fourth round agent c considers it possible that agent d learnt some new secret in the third round, so c calls d in the fourth round. In this way the loop $ab; cd; \ldots$ could go on infinitely. The same example works for Protocol 5. See [7] for the De Re / De Dicto distinction.

The protocol extension and gossip tree are convenient for design and planning purposes. However they are not easy to construct manually, even for a small number of agents. The difficulty of such a task naturally increases with the number of agents and with the complexity of the epistemic property comprising the calling condition for the given protocol. Therefore it is desirable to have a tool that automates the process of gossip tree generation and the evaluation of epistemic gossip protocols by means of their extension. Given a high level description of an epistemic gossip protocol, the tool outputs the characteristics of the protocol by analysing the extension of the given protocol. In this paper we describe the implementation of such a tool, and present some experimental results obtained by using this tool to evaluate the above epistemic gossip protocols.

In Sect. 2 we present the design of the EGP tool. In Sect. 3 we present experimental results, and in Sect. 4 we discuss related works.

2   The EGP Tool

In this section we present the implementation structure of EGP tool, describing each of its components. Figure 1 shows the structural overview of the EGP tool.

Definition 1. *The language $\mathcal{L}_{cc}$ is defined as*

$$\mathcal{L}_{cc} \ni \quad \varphi ::= Kw_{a_i} A_j \mid \neg\varphi \mid (\varphi \wedge \varphi) \mid (\varphi \vee \varphi) \mid (\varphi \rightarrow \varphi) \mid K_{a_i}\varphi, \ \text{where } a_i \neq a_j.$$

Note that A_j is a propositional atom, and the formula $Kw_{a_i}A_j$ stands for 'agent a_i knows whether secret A_j (is true)', and $K_{a_i}\varphi$ stands for 'agent a_i knows that φ (is true)'.

2.1 Structural Overview

For the protocol designer we provide a high level language for describing epistemic gossip protocols within the EGP tool. We call this language Epistemic Gossip Protocol Language (EGPL). The language $\mathcal{L}_{cc}$ of epistemic calling condition is embedded within the language of EGPL such that any calling condition $\varphi_{a_i a_j} \in \mathcal{L}_{cc}$ can also be expressed within EGPL.

Next we present a language interpreter for EGPL. Given a protocol description expressed in EGPL, the EGPL interpreter generates the gossip tree corresponding to the described protocol, and outputs the characteristics of the protocol. The terminating protocols are characterised in terms of success, average execution length, shortest and longest execution lengths and extension size. Also, samples of execution sequences of various lengths are displayed by the tool, whereas the entire extension of the protocol is stored in a file.

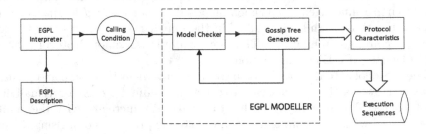

Fig. 1. Structural Overview of EGP Tool.

To generate the possible situations in a round, the EGPL interpreter employs an epistemic model checker to check the calling conditions for each pair of agents at each possible situation.

2.2 Epistemic Gossip Protocol Language (EGPL)

EGPL is a programming language for describing epistemic gossip protocols in terms of the epistemic calling conditions of such protocols. Any calling condition in the language of $\mathcal{L}_{cc}$ can be expressed in EGPL. An EGPL protocol description must begin with the keyword **begin** and finish with the keyword **end**. Between these two keywords lies the core of the protocol specification which consists of the epistemic calling condition. The following code listing is an example protocol specification using EGPL. The protocol described is Protocol 1.

```
1     begin
2          /* epistemic calling condition */
3          let ai call aj if {
4               ai knows (init(aj) \notin secret(ai));
5          }
6     end
```

Listing 1.1. EGPL Description for Protocol 1

In Listing 1.1, the epistemic calling condition is given in lines 3–5. It says that agent ai can call agent aj if ai knows that it does not know aj's unique secret. In the EGPL description in Listing 1.1, ai and aj are agent name variables. They are substituted by agent names when the description is parsed.

2.3   The EGPL Interpreter

As shown in Fig. 1, the framework tool accepts an EGPL protocol description, and outputs a set of protocol characteristics and execution sequences for the described protocol.

An EGPL description is interpreted in two stages, namely, expansion stage and model checking stage. The expansion stage produces an instance of the epistemic calling condition for every valid agent combination. A valid agent combination is obtained by substituting a unique and real agent name for each unique agent name variable appearing in the description. The output of the expansion stage is the set of all the calling condition instances, over all the agents in the scenario. See listing 1.2 for a sample output from the expansion stage for the description shown in listing 1.1. In this example the names for the agents in the scenario are a, b, c, d.

```
c  knows(init(b)\notinsecret(c));
c  knows(init(a)\notinsecret(c));
b  knows(init(a)\notinsecret(b));
d  knows(init(a)\notinsecret(d));
        (...)
```

Listing 1.2. Expansion Stage Output (Four-Agent Scenario)

The set of all the calling condition instances is fed into the model checking stage where they are checked on all the possible situations in the round to determine which pair of agents satisfy the epistemic calling condition at the considered situation.

The parsers are implementations of the LALR parsing technique described in [2], using the CUP parser generator [5].

2.4   Gossip Tree Generator

The EGPL Modeller is the component which constructs and updates the gossip tree for the specified protocol. It consists of two main components, namely, a gossip tree generator and a model checker. The model we refer to is a partial gossip tree which is an abstraction of the gossip model described in [1]. Given the *initial* or *root node* of the gossip tree, the gossip tree generator constructs the successor nodes of the gossip tree for the specified protocol. Each successor node in the gossip tree is a result of a possible call at some *parent node*. Such a call is considered possible at the parent node if the calling condition given by the specified protocol is satisfied at the parent node. Thus the model checker is needed to construct the gossip tree because it checks the epistemic calling conditions on the nodes of the gossip tree to determine successor nodes. In what follows in this section we describe the gossip tree and provide the semantics of the language of epistemic calling conditions based on the gossip tree.

Definition 2 (History, h). *A history h, or an execution sequence, is defined inductively as: $h ::= e \mid h; a_i a_j$ where e is the empty sequence and $a_i \neq a_j \in Ag$.*

Definition 3 (Situation Label, F). *A gossip situation is a tuple $\theta = \langle S_1, \ldots, S_n \rangle$. We let Θ be the set of every θ. Given a non-empty set H of histories, a situation label is a function $F : H \to \Theta$ which returns the gossip situation corresponding to a given history. The function F is defined as $F(e) = \langle \{A_1\}, \ldots, \{A_n\} \rangle$ where A_i is the secret of agent a_i, and if $F(h) = \langle S_1, \ldots, S_n \rangle$ then $F(h; a_i a_j) = \langle S'_1, \ldots, S'_n \rangle$, where $S'_i = S_i \cup S_j = S'_j$ and $S'_k = S_k, k \notin \{i, j\}$.*

Definition 4 (Equivalence Relation, $\equiv$). *Let $F(h; a_i a_j) = \langle S_1, \ldots, S_n \rangle$ and $F(h'; a_k a_l) = \langle S'_1, \ldots, S'_n \rangle$, we inductively define an equivalence relation between histories as follows: $e \equiv_{a_m} e$, and $h; a_i a_j \equiv_{a_m} h'; a_k a_l$ iff: $S_m = S'_m$, and $h \equiv_{a_m} h'$, where $a_m \in \{a_i, a_j\} = \{a_k, a_l\}$ or $a_m \notin \{a_i, a_j\} \cup \{a_k, a_l\}$, for all $a_m \in Ag$.*

Definition 5 (Tree). *A tree is a tuple $\mathcal{T} = \langle H, R \rangle$, where H is a finite set of histories closed under prefixes, and R is a parent relation over H such that $h' R h$ if there exists a_i, a_j such that $h = h'; a_i a_j$. We call h' the parent node of such h. The node e is the root node of the tree.*

Definition 6 (Epistemic Tree). *An epistemic tree is a tree which is of the form $\langle H, R, F, \{Z_{a_m}\} \rangle$. The function $Z_{a_m} : H \to 2^H$ assigns an equivalence class to agent $a_m \in Ag$ from the domain of histories such that $h \equiv_{a_m} h'$ for all $h' \in Z_{a_m}(h)$. Furthermore, we define a parent relation R_c over the codomain of all Z_{a_m} such that $Z_{a_m}(h'') R_c Z_{a_m}(h)$ iff for every node $h' \in Z_{a_m}(h)$, the parent node of h' is in $Z_{a_m}(h'')$.*

We will sometimes refer to such equivalence class $Z_{a_m}(h)$ of the node h as the *cell* of h. If $Z_{a_m}(h'') R_c Z_{a_m}(h)$, then $Z_{a_m}(h'')$ is called the *parent cell* of $Z_{a_m}(h)$, and $Z_{a_m}(h)$ is called the *child cell* of $Z_{a_m}(h'')$.

Definition 7 (Gossip Tree, $\mathcal{T}_g$). *Given an epistemic gossip protocol Π, an epistemic tree is a gossip tree for Π if it is compliant with Π and complete with respect to Π. An epistemic tree is compliant with Π if $\Sigma_\Pi \subseteq H$. An epistemic tree is complete with respect to a protocol Π if $H \subseteq \Sigma_\Pi$, where Σ_Π is the extension of Π.*

Definition 8 (Gossip Tree Layer). *Given a gossip tree* $\mathcal{T}_g$, *let* $k = l(h)$ *be the length of* $h \in H$; *let* $l(e) = 0$ *and* $l(h; a_i a_j) = l(h) + 1$. *Then the layers* λ *of* $\mathcal{T}_g$ *is defined as a tuple* $\lambda = \langle \lambda_0, \lambda_1, \dots \rangle$ *where* $\lambda_k = \{h \mid h \in H \text{ and } l(h) = k\}$.

For any λ_k of a gossip tree $\mathcal{T}_g$, and for any $h \in \lambda_k$, the equivalence class of h for all agents, the parent relations involving h, and the situation label of h are the same as in $\mathcal{T}_g$. Finally, we define a labelling function L over λ such that $L_{a_m}(\lambda_k) = \bigcup_{h \in \lambda_k} \{Z_{a_m}(h)\}$, for all $a_m \in Ag$.

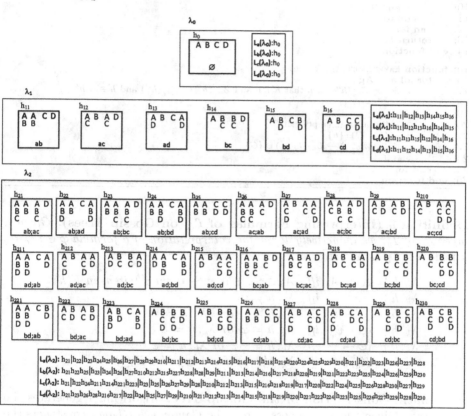

Fig. 2. Gossip Tree Layers (4 Agents)

The labelling function L defines a partition, for each agent, over the nodes in a given layer. Hence $Z_{a_i}(h)$ returns the cell of h in the partition corresponding to agent a_i in a given gossip tree layer. For illustration, in Fig. 2 we show the first three layers of the gossip tree for Protocol 1. In Fig. 2 we use names a, b, c, d for the agents in the scenario, with corresponding secrets A, B, C, D. In each layer shown we omit reverse calls for the sake of visual clarity.

In order to construct layer λ_{k+1}, only layer λ_k is required. Given the initial layer λ_0 of the gossip tree of a specified protocol, it possible to automatically construct the entire gossip tree layer by layer. Algorithm 1 presents a procedure to this end.

Algorithm 1. Automatic Construction of a Gossip Tree Layer

```
 1: function COMPUTENEXTLAYER(λₖ, φₐᵦ)
 2:     C ← {aᵢaⱼ | aᵢ, aⱼ ∈ Ag, aᵢ ≠ aⱼ}
 3:     if λₖ = ∅ then λₖ ← {e}, Lₐᵢ(λₖ) ← ∅ and Lₐᵢ(λₖ) ← Lₐᵢ(λₖ) ∪ {{e}}, ∀aᵢ ∈ Ag end if
 4:     Lₐᵢ(λₖ₊₁) ← ∅
 5:     for all h' ∈ λₖ do
 6:         for all aᵢaⱼ ∈ C do
 7:             if SAT(φₐᵢaⱼ, h') holds then
 8:                 h ← h'; ab, and F(h) is computed accordingly
 9:                 LAYERLABEL(λₖ₊₁, h', h)
10:             end if
11:         end for
12:     end for
13:     return λₖ₊₁
14: end function

15: function LAYERLABEL(λₖ₊₁, h', h)
16:     for all aᵢ ∈ Ag :
17:         if ∃C' = Zₐᵢ(h'') such that h'R h and Zₐᵢ(h')Rᴄ Zₐᵢ(h'') and h ≡ₐᵢ h''
18:             C' ← C' ∪ {h}
19:         else
20:             Initialise an empty cell C
21:             C ← C ∪ {h}
22:             Lₐᵢ(λₖ₊₁) ← Lₐᵢ(λₖ₊₁) ∪ {C}
23:         end if
24:     end for
25: end function
```

Definition 9 (Interpreting Formulas of $\mathcal{L}_{cc}$ on Gossip Trees). *Given a layer λ_k of $\mathcal{T}_g$, we inductively define the interpretation of a formula $\varphi \in \mathcal{L}_{cc}$ on a node $h \in \lambda_k$ as follows[1]:*

$$\lambda_k, h \models Kw_{a_i}A_j \quad \textit{iff} \quad A_j \in S_i, \textit{ where } S_i \textit{ is the } i^{th} \textit{ item in } F(h)$$
$$\lambda_k, h \models \neg\varphi \quad\quad \textit{iff} \quad \lambda_k, h \not\models \varphi$$
$$\lambda_k, h \models (\varphi \wedge \psi) \quad \textit{iff} \quad \lambda_k, h \models \varphi \textit{ and } \lambda_k, h \models \psi$$
$$\lambda_k, h \models (\varphi \vee \psi) \quad \textit{iff} \quad \lambda_k, h \models \varphi \textit{ or } \lambda_k, h \models \psi$$
$$\lambda_k, h \models (\varphi \rightarrow \psi) \quad \textit{iff} \quad \lambda_k, h \models \neg\varphi \textit{ or } \lambda_k, h \models \psi$$
$$\lambda_k, h \models K_{a_i}\varphi \quad \textit{iff} \quad \lambda_k, h' \models \varphi \textit{ for every } h' \in Z_{a_i}(h)$$

Automatic Construction of the Gossip Tree. Algorithm 1 generates the gossip tree. Given a layer of a gossip tree, the *ComputeNextLayer* constructs the next layer of the tree, whereas *LayerLabel* updates the layer label of the gossip tree layer under construction. Therefore, beginning with an initial layer, we can build the gossip tree up to a desired finite layer. Given a layer of the gossip tree we compute all the calls that are possible at each node by model checking the calling condition $\varphi_{a_i a_j}$ for each pair of agents at the node. For each possible call at a node, we produce a successor node which is naturally in the next layer from the given node. Algorithm 1 exploits the following properties of gossip trees:

Proposition 1. *Given any two layers λ_k and λ_{k+1} of a gossip tree $\mathcal{T}_g$, and given any $h' \in \lambda_k$ and $h \in \lambda_{k+1}$, then $h'Rh$ iff $Z_{a_i}(h')R_c Z_{a_i}(h)$, for all $a_i \in Ag$.*

---

[1] Note that the truth value of A_j is irrelevant here, what is important is whether the truth value is known.

Proof. Let $p(h) = \hat{h}$, such that $\hat{h}Rh$. Choose an arbitrary agent $a_i \in Ag$.
$\Longrightarrow$ Suppose $h'Rh$.
Consider an arbitrary $\bar{h} \in Z_{a_i}(h)$. One of the conditions for equivalence of $\bar{h}$ and h is that $p(h) \equiv_{a_i} p(\bar{h})$ (from Definition 4). But $h \in Z_{a_i}(h)$ and $p(h) = h'$, so $h' \equiv_{a_i} p(\bar{h})$. Since $\bar{h}$ is an arbitrary element of $Z_{a_i}(h)$, and from the definition of R_c in Definition 6, we conclude that $Z_{a_i}(h')R_cZ_{a_i}(h)$.
$\Longleftarrow$ Suppose $Z_{a_i}(h')R_cZ_{a_i}(h)$.
Choose an arbitrary $\bar{h} \in Z_{a_i}(h)$, then there must be a $\bar{h}' \in Z_{a_i}(h')$ such that $\bar{h}'R\bar{h}$ (from the definition of R_c in Definition 6). For every $h'' \in Z_{a_i}(h')$, $Z_{a_i}(h'') = Z_{a_i}(h')$. We chose $\bar{h}$ arbitrarily, so now we fix a node $h \in Z_{a_i}(h)$ and call its parent h'. Then $Z_{a_i}(h')R_cZ_{a_i}(h)$ implies $h'Rh$. $\square$

Proposition 2. *Let h and h' be as in Proposition 1. If h is assigned to any child cell of $Z_{a_i}(h')$, then h is not in any other child cell of $Z_{a_i}(h')$.*

Proof. Choose an arbitrary agent a_i from the given set of agents. Let C' and C'' be two distinct child cells of $Z_{a_i}(h')$. Suppose that h is assigned to C' and h is also assigned to C'', then it follows that for all $\bar{h} \in C'$ and for all $\bar{\bar{h}} \in C''$, $h \equiv_{a_i} \bar{h} \equiv_{a_i} \bar{\bar{h}}$. Then from the definition of cell it follows that $C' = C''$ for agent a_i and therefore C' and C'' are not distinct, contrary to the assumption. $\square$

Given a parent node h' and its successor h, the LayerLabel function assigns h to a cell within the partition for each agent, as follows. Consider the partition for an arbitrary agent $a_i \in Ag$. Since the cell of h, for agent a_i, is a child cell of $Z_{a_i}(h')$ (Proposition 1), the LayerLabel function first checks whether $Z_{a_i}(h')$ already has any child cells. Let such a child cell be called C'. The node h can be assigned to such C' if there exists an $h'' \in C'$ such that $h'' \equiv_{a_i} h$. If h cannot be assigned to any currently existing child cell of $Z_{a_i}(h')$ then we create a new empty child cell C for $Z_{a_i}(h')$ and assign h to it. Moreover, LayerLabel function ensures that h is assigned to only one cell (Proposition 2).

Furthermore, for any $h \in \lambda_{k+1}$, where $k \geq 0$, the condition under which h is assigned to a cell is equivalent to that given in Definition 4. Given λ_{k+1}, and given h' and h such that $h'Rh$, where $h \in \lambda_{k+1}$, the history h is assigned to some $C' = Z_{a_i}(h'')$ such that $Z_{a_i}(h')R_cZ_{a_i}(h'')$ and $h \equiv_{a_i} h''$. Again let $p(h) = \hat{h}$, such that $\hat{h}Rh$. The condition $\eta = (h'Rh$ and $Z_{a_i}(h')R_cZ_{a_i}(h''))$ implies that $p(h'') \equiv_{a_i} h' = p(h)$, since $p(h'') \in Z_{a_i}(h')$ by the definition of R_c. Therefore η ensures that $p(h) \equiv_{a_i} p(h'')$, which is required by Definition 4. Based on the fact that $p(h) \equiv_{a_i} p(h'')$, the condition $h \equiv_{a_i} h''$ is then checked according to Definition 4.

The SAT Function. Our model checking algorithm combines the bottom-up approach and the top-down approach similar to that employed in temporal-epistemic model checking (see Algorithm 4). In the bottom-up approach, a given formula φ is checked in a state of the model by iteratively obtaining all the states where the subformulas of φ are true, beginning with the smallest subformula of

φ, and increasing the size of the subformulas in a step-wise manner in each iteration, until the set of states satisfying the largest subformula, namely φ itself, is obtained. Each subformula of φ is checked on the states obtained from the previous iteration [6]. This approach is called the bottom-up approach because model checking starts with the smallest subformula of φ. In the top-down approach, the reverse is the case. At the given state of the model, φ is checked by recursively checking its subformulas in order of decreasing size until the smallest subformula is checked [10]. Our model checking algorithm is with respect to the language $\mathcal{L}_{cc}$. In the general temporal and epistemic setting, the top-down approach is more computationally expensive than the bottom-up approach. However, in our experiments we show that by combining the top-down and the bottom-up approach we take advantage of the peculiarities of the equivalence classes obtained from the gossip tree to obtain a better performance in practice, than by using the bottom-up approach (see subsection *Equivalence Class Analysis*, later). We also obtain added performance by means of our representation of the gossip tree and the layer labelling procedure, which introduces a caching technique for faster computation of equivalence classes by reusing equivalence class information from previous rounds.

We now describe our SAT function as used in Algorithm 1, but first we give some ancillary definitions as follows:

Definition 10 (Model Checking). *Given $h \in \lambda_k$ of a gossip tree $\mathcal{T}_g$, and a formula $\varphi \in \mathcal{L}_{cc}$, the model checking problem is whether φ is satisfied at h, i.e., whether $\lambda_k, h \models \varphi$. The output is "yes" if φ is satisfied at the given h, and otherwise "no". The model checking algorithm is defined in Algorithm 4.*

Definition 11 (Relevant Set). *Let the language $\mathcal{L}'_{cc}$ be equal to $\mathcal{L}_{cc}$ without the fragment $K_{a_i}\varphi$. Let $\varphi' \in \mathcal{L}'_{cc}$ be called epistemic propositional formula. Given a formula $\varphi \in \mathcal{L}_{cc}$, and $h \in \lambda_k$, let Relevant Set QQ with respect to φ and h be defined in Algorithm 2, with $QQ = \{h\}$, initially.*

Intuitively, the relevant set is the largest set of gossip tree nodes needed for the model checking of φ at the designated node h.

Definition 12 (Truth Set). *The Truth Set TT is defined in Algorithm 3, with $TT = \emptyset$, initially.*

Here, the *TopDownSAT* function mitigates the state-space explosion by narrowing down the set of nodes to relevant ones. We then employ the *BottomUp-SAT*, which is an adaptation of the CTL labelling algorithm, on the relevant set. We show that this two-step approach is better in practice than the bottom-up or top-down approach.

We sketch an argument to establish the correctness of the SAT function as follows. From the semantics of $\mathcal{L}_{cc}$ it is easy to see that *TopDownSAT* computes the set of all nodes needed to model-check the given formula φ on the designated node h. By the case basis, if φ is epistemic propositional, then we need only the designated node h; if φ is $K_{a_i}\varphi'$ then we need the set QQ' of nodes which agent a_i cannot distinguish from each of the nodes contained in QQ, in order to check

---

Algorithm 2. Definition of Relevant Set

```
 1: function TOPDOWNSAT(φ, QQ)
 2:     begin case
 3:         φ is epistemic propositional: return QQ
 4:         φ is K_{a_i}φ_1:
 5:             QQ' ← ∅
 6:             for every h' ∈ QQ
 7:                 QQ' ← QQ' ∪ Z_{a_i}(h')
 8:             end for
 9:             QQ ← QQ'
10:             TOPDOWNSAT(φ_1, QQ)
11:         φ is ¬φ_1:
12:             QQ ← TOPDOWNSAT(φ_1, QQ)
13:         φ is (φ_1 ∨ φ_2):
14:             QQ ← TOPDOWNSAT(φ_1, QQ) ∪ TOPDOWNSAT(φ_2, QQ)
15:         φ is (φ_1 ∧ φ_2):
16:             QQ ← TOPDOWNSAT(φ_1, QQ) ∪ TOPDOWNSAT(φ_2, QQ)
17:         φ is (φ_1 → φ_2):
18:             QQ ← TOPDOWNSAT((¬φ_1 ∨ φ_2), QQ)
19:     end case
20: end function
```

Algorithm 3. Definition of Truth Set

```
 1: function BOTTOMUPSAT(φ, TT, QQ)
 2:     begin case
 3:         φ is epistemic propositional:
 4:             TT ← {h| h ∈ QQ and φ is true at h}
 5:             return TT
 6:         φ is K_{a_i}φ_1:
 7:             TT ← SAT_k(a, φ_1, TT, QQ)
 8:             return TT
 9:         φ is ¬φ_1:
10:             TT ← QQ \ BOTTOMUPSAT(φ_1, TT, QQ)
11:             return TT
12:         φ is (φ_1 ∨ φ_2):
13:             TT ← BOTTOMUPSAT(φ_1, TT, QQ) ∪ BOTTOMUPSAT(φ_2, TT, QQ)
14:             return TT
15:         φ is (φ_1 ∧ φ_2):
16:             TT ← BOTTOMUPSAT(φ_1, TT, QQ) ∩ BOTTOMUPSAT(φ_2, TT, QQ)
17:             return TT
18:         φ is (φ_1 → φ_2):
19:             TT ← BOTTOMUPSAT((¬φ_1 ∨ φ_2), TT, QQ)
20:             return TT
21:     end case
22: end function

23: function SAT_k(a, φ, TT, QQ)
24:     TT' ← ∅
25:     for every h ∈ QQ:
26:         if Z_{a_i}(h) ⊆ TT, then TT' ← TT' ∪ {h}
27:     end for
28:     return TT'
29: end function
```

---

whether $K_{a_i}\varphi'$. Note that due to the reflexivity property of the accessibility relation (a node is equivalent to itself, for all the agents) $QQ \subseteq QQ'$. If φ is $\neg K_{a_i}\varphi'$ then we need *at most* the same nodes as for $K_{a_i}\varphi$. If φ is $(\varphi' \wedge \varphi'')$ or $(\varphi' \vee \varphi'')$, we need the set of relevant nodes for φ' *union* the set of relevant nodes for φ''.

To prove the correctness of the *BottomUpSAT* function, we note that in order to check the formula φ on the given node h we do not require any node that is not in QQ, as returned by *TopDownSAT*.

Time Complexity of the SAT Function

Definition 13 (Iterated-K Subformula). *An iterated-K subformula is a subformula of the language $\mathcal{L}_{itk}$ such that $\varphi ::= Kw_{a_i}A_j \mid (\varphi \wedge \varphi) \mid (\varphi \vee \varphi) \mid \neg\varphi$, and $\mathcal{L}_{itk} \ni \psi ::= K_{a_i}\varphi \mid \neg\psi$. The length of an iterated-K subformula ψ is the number of K operators (that is, K or $\neg K$ operator) in ψ.*

Proposition 3. *The time complexity of the SAT function shown in Algorithm 4 is $O((m+|Ag|).|\lambda_k|^2)$, where m is the length of the longest iterated-K subformula in φ.*

Considering *TopDownSAT* (shown in Algorithm 2), we obtain the equivalence class of a node for an agent in constant time, and for each K operator in an iterated-K formula, the relevant set is computed in time $O(|\lambda_k|)$. For the "leftmost" K operator, at the designated node h, we can obtain $QQ = Z_{a_i}(h)$ in constant time, where a_i is the agent associated with the K operator. For each subsequent K operator, left-to-right, we compute $Z_{a_i}(h')$ for each $h' \in QQ$ in time $O(|QQ|)$ which is in turn at most $|\lambda_k|$. For m iterated-K operators we can compute QQ in $O(1) + O((m-1).|\lambda_k|) = O((m-1).|\lambda_k|)$. The time complexity of epistemic propositional formulae is $O(|\lambda_k|)$ since we would have to check all the nodes in the relevant set, which are at most $|\lambda_k|$ nodes. For a conjunctive or disjunctive formula the worst-case complexity is that of its most expensive term. Therefore the time complexity of a given $\varphi \in \mathcal{L}_{cc}$ is the complexity of the longest iterated-K subformula, that is, the iterated-K subformula with the most number of K operators. Considering *BottomUpSAT* (shown in Algorithm 3), we compute the truthset TT in time $O(|\lambda_k|)$, and for each non-negated iterated-K operator $(K_{a_i}\varphi')$ associated with some agent $a_i \in Ag$, we compute the truthset TT' of all nodes h in QQ whose equivalence class is a subset of TT, in time $O(|\lambda_k|)$ for each node h; this gives $O(|\lambda_k|^2)$ for all nodes in QQ. For each negated iterated-K operator $(\neg K_{a_i}\varphi)$ we compute TT' as for the non-negated iterated-K operator, and take the complement of the obtained TT'. So, the time complexity of *BottomUpSAT* algorithm is $O(m.|\lambda_k|^2)$. Considering the *LayerLabel* algorithm, we create $|\lambda_k|$ nodes, and update the layer label, for each of the nodes created and for each of the agents. We process each node h' as follows: the parent cell is retrieved in constant time; child cells of the parent cell are also retrieved in constant time; we compare a member from each child cell, with h', to determine membership of h'. This is achieved in $(|\lambda_k|)$. Inclusion of h' into a cell is done in constant time. This gives a time complexity of $O(|Ag|.|\lambda_k|^2)$ for the *LayerLabel* algorithm.

We will see in the next section that, given the nature of gossip models, the size of the equivalence classes are very small with respect to the size of the λ_k, as such the actual size of the relevant set is small compared to the size of λ_k, thus lending space and time efficiency in practical terms.

Algorithm 4. The SAT Function

```
1: function SAT(φ, h)
2:     QQ' ← h
3:     TT' ← ∅
4:     QQ ← TopDownSAT(φ, QQ')
5:     TT ← BottomUpSAT(φ, TT', QQ)
6:     if h ∈ TT then return true                          ▷ true is "Yes"
7:     else return false                                    ▷ false is "No"
8:     end if
9: end function
```

Table 1. Equivalence class summary for Protocol 3 (Five Agents)

k	$|\lambda_k|$	Number of Cells	Min. Cell Size	Max. Cell Size	Average Cell Size
0	1	1	1	1	1
1	20	5	2	12	4
2	360	33	4	120	11
3	6,000	217	4	1,056	28
4	86,880	1,161	8	6,912	75
5	993,600	5,029	8	23,232	198
6	7,764,480	17,325	8	44,448	448
7	36,969,600	48,556	16	80,256	761
8	107,021,392	108,655	16	160,512	985
9	239,439,360	190,312	16	321,024	1,258
10	325,891,200	167,644	16	617,472	1,944

Equivalence Class Analysis. The data presented in Table 1 is the summary of an equivalence class analysis for one of five agents in Protocol 3, beginning from the root layer to the terminal layer of the gossip tree. We chose only one of the agents because we observed that the cell sizes (and their distribution) for other agents are symmetrical variants of each other. From Table 1 we observe that the cell or equivalence class sizes in each layer is indeed very small compared to the layer size. The same trend is found when the experiment is repeated for three and four agents, and for Protocol 2. We did not carry out the analysis for Protocol 1 because, strictly speaking, to check its epistemic calling condition on a given situation we require only the information contained in that same situation, namely the secrets known by the agents in the situation - hence there is no need to reason about other possible situations. The results shown in Table 1 indicate that indeed the relevant set obtained through the *TopDownSAT* is significantly small compared to the size of the corresponding layer, and hence lends added performance to the *SAT* function in practice.

Implementation Note. To implement the *ComputeNextLayer* procedure, we create μ threads (lightweight processes), $\mu \geq 1$, and then create as many parallel *tasks* as the number of tree nodes h' in λ_k. A task generates all the successor nodes h at h'. We place each of the newly created tasks in a *task pool*, from where the threads take tasks to execute in parallel. The list of successor nodes is returned by each thread, and all such lists are merged to produce the nodes in the next layer λ_{k+1} of the gossip tree. Program execution stops after $n(n-1)/2$ rounds of calls. This corresponds to the maximum number of rounds needed to attain the goal state if there is no redundant call in an execution sequence, that is, in each call some agent learns some new secret.

3   Results of Experiments

In Tables 2, 3 and 4 we present the protocol characteristics obtained from the EGP tool for Protocols 1, 2 and 3, respectively. The tables show the number of length x sequences for $3, 4, 5$ agents, where $3 \leq x \leq 10$. We also show the extension size and average execution length for the protocols. (Protocols 4 and 5 are non-terminating and omitted.) All execution sequences reach the goal state for the respective protocol scenarios, hence they are successful after $n(n-1)/2$ rounds, and therefore do not allow redundant calls to be made. From the figures for average execution length and extension size, respectively, it is clear that Protocol 1 performs better than Protocol 2 and Protocol 3. It is also interesting to note that Protocol 3 proves significantly better in terms of extension size, and slightly better in terms of average execution length, than Protocol 2.

Table 2. Protocol characteristics for Protocol 1

Execution Sequence Length	Three Agents	Four Agents	Five Agents
3	24		
4		384	
5		2,496	
6		2,688	103,680
7			1,614,720
8			5,285,760
9			6,913,920
10			3,492,480
Extension Size	24	5,568	17,410,560
Average Execution Length	3	5.41379	8.69365
Successful Sequences	24	5,568	17,410,560
% Successful Sequences	100.00 %	100.00 %	100.00 %

Let us consider some extension analysis for a scenario which consists of four agents a, b, c, d. For Protocol 2 it is expected that after a first call bc, followed by three rounds in which b is not involved in any call, then in the fifth round b knows that there is some secret to learn from c (an example sequence is $bc; cd; ac; ad; bc$). But using the tool we see that already in the fourth round b knows that there is some secret to learn from c (an example sequence is $bc; cd; ad; bc; ab; bc$). Also, we

Table 3. Protocol characteristics for Protocol 2

Execution Sequence Length	Three Agents	Four Agents	Five Agents
3	96		
4		384	
5		15,744	
6		64,896	195,840
7			7,958,400
8			61,155,840
9			220,404,480
10			472,988,160
Extension Size	96	81,024	762,702,720
Average Execution Length	3	5.79621	9.51833
Successful Sequences	96	81,024	762,702,720
% Successful Sequences	100.00 %	100.00 %	100.00 %

Table 4. Protocol characteristics for Protocol 3

Execution Sequence Length	Three Agents	Four Agents	Five Agents
3	96		
4		384	
5		13,824	
6		53,952	149,760
7			5,798,400
8			37,975,680
9			172,362,240
10			325,891,200
Extension Size	96	68,160	542,177,280
Average Execution Length	3	5.78592	9.50882
Successful Sequences	96	68,160	542,177,280
% Successful Sequences	100.00 %	100.00 %	100.00 %

can check whether a given sequence is in the extension of a given protocol. For example the execution sequence $ab; ac; bd; ad; ab; bc$ is in Σ_{Π_2} but not in Σ_{Π_3}.

4 Related Work

The gossip tree and the EGP tool implement the epistemic gossip protocols described in [1]. The EGP tool can be seen as a dedicated model checker, based on the standard procedures for CTL model checking [6]. The technique of combining the *TopDownSAT* and *BottomUpSAT* procedures is similar to the Bounded Model Checking technique described in [9], which mitigates the state explosion problem by narrowing down the set of situations to the relevant set, that is, the set of those situations which are required to check the satisfiability of a formula at a given situation. We further optimise the computation of the relevant set by introducing a gossip tree layer labelling, which in effect maintains a cache of the equivalence class information from previous rounds. Other, general purpose, model checkers for epistemic scenarios include DEMO [11], MCK [3] and MCMAS [8]. In principle, our protocols could also be implemented in such environments. For this investigation however we focused on a dedicated tool for epistemic gossip protocols.

5   Conclusion

In this paper we presented an end-to-end description of the tool EGP — a framework for epistemic gossip protocols. We introduced EGPL — a high level language for describing epistemic gossip protocols, and we described the design of EGPL interpreter which translates a given protocol description into a gossip tree on which the protocol is evaluated. We also presented experimental results obtained by using EGP. We intend to extend the framework to incorporate the asynchronous epistemic call mode, with network topologies for agent interaction, and with epistemic gossip protocols with rounds of parallel calls.

Acknowledgements. We thank the reviewers for their comments. Hans van Ditmarsch is also affiliated to IMSc, Chennai, as research associate. He acknowledges support from ERC project EPS 313360.

References

1. Attamah, M., van Ditmarsch, H., Grossi, D., van der Hoek, W.: Knowledge and gossip. In: ECAI 2014, Frontiers in Artificial Intelligence and Applications, vol. 263, pp. 21–26. IOS Press (2014)
2. DeRemer, F.L.: Practical translators for LR (k) languages. Ph.D. thesis, Massachusetts Institute of Technology (1969)
3. Gammie, Peter, van der Meyden, Ron: MCK: model checking the logic of knowledge. In: Alur, Rajeev, Peled, Doron A. (eds.) CAV 2004. LNCS, vol. 3114, pp. 479–483. Springer, Heidelberg (2004)
4. Hedetniemi, S.M., Hedetniemi, S.T., Liestman, A.L.: A survey of gossiping and broadcasting in communication networks. Networks **18**, 319–349 (1988)
5. Hudson, S.E., Flannery, F., Ananian, C.S., Wang, D.: Cup LALR parser generator for java (1999). http://www2.cs.tum.edu/projects/cup/ (Online accessed 24-July-2014)
6. Huth, M., Ryan, M.: Logic in Computer Science: Modelling and Reasoning about Systems. Cambridge University Press, Cambridge (2004)
7. Jamroga, W., van der Hoek, W.: Agents that know how to play. Fundamenta Informaticae **63**, 185–219 (2004)
8. Lomuscio, Alessio, Qu, Hongyang, Raimondi, Franco: MCMAS: a model checker for the verification of multi-agent systems. In: Bouajjani, Ahmed, Maler, Oded (eds.) CAV 2009. LNCS, vol. 5643, pp. 682–688. Springer, Heidelberg (2009)

9. Penczek, W., Lomuscio, A.: Verifying epistemic properties of multi-agent systems via bounded model checking. In: Proceedings of 2nd AAMAS, pp. 209–216. ACM (2003)
10. Ruan, J.: Reasoning about Time, Action and Knowledge in Multi-Agent Systems. Ph.D. thesis, University of Liverpool (2008)
11. van Eijck, J.: DEMO – a demo of epistemic modelling. In: van Benthem, J., Gabbay, D., Löwe, B. (eds.) Interactive Logic – Proceedings of the 7th Augustus de Morgan Workshop, pp. 305–363. Amsterdam University Press (2007). Texts in Logic and Games 1

Compliance Games

Piotr Kaźmierczak[(✉)]

Department of Computing, Mathematics and Physics,
Bergen University College, Bergen, Norway
phk@hib.no

Abstract. In this paper we analyze *compliance games*, which are games induced by agent-labeled Kripke structures, goal formulas in the language of CTL and behavioral constraints. In compliance games, players are rewarded for achieving their goals while complying to social laws, and punished for non-compliance. Design of these games is an attempt at incentivizing agents to be compliant. We analyze the core and properties of compliance games, and study the connection between underlying logical framework and their properties.

1 Introduction

Normative systems or *social laws* are a framework for coordinating agents in multi-agent systems initially proposed by Shoham and Tennenholtz in [12,13]. The idea has been extensively studied in the multi-agent systems literature since. While in Shoham and Tennenholtz's seminal papers the framework consisted of synchronous transition systems with first order logic language for goals, in further work other semantic structures and goal languages were used. In a series of papers, Ågotnes et al. [1–5] presented social laws implemented on agent-labeled Kripke structures with Computation Tree Logic (CTL) as a language for goals, while Van der Hoek et al. [14] used Alternating-time Transition Systems with Alternating-time Temporal Logic (ATL) [6], and a similar framework was used in [8,11]. Each of these approaches uses the same idea, namely that we impose *restrictions* on agents' behavior,[1] and check which goals (expressed by our language of choice) are satisfied when agents comply with these restrictions.

A number of interesting decision problems are usually studied in the social laws literature, such as *compliance sufficiency* (given a structure, a set of constraints, and a goal, which coalition's compliance to the constraints is sufficient in order for the goal to be achieved?), *k-robustness* (how many agents can deviate from complying to the normative system and still not break goal satisfiability?), *feasibility* (is it feasible for the agents to satisfy their goals while complying with the restrictions?), or social law *synthesis* (can we synthesize a set of restrictions such that when complied with they guarantee goal satisfaction?).

However, the key problem in social laws is how to assure that agents comply with a given social law. Our approach here is to make compliance the rational choice for our agents. While in principle similar to the games presented by

---

[1] Thus social laws are sometimes also called "behavioral constraints."

N. Bulling (Ed.): EUMAS 2014, LNAI 8953, pp. 210–218, 2015.
DOI: 10.1007/978-3-319-17130-2_14

Ågotnes et al. in [2] where agents had preferences over goals and normal form games were induced based on the *utility* of laws, we employ cooperative games to incentivize agents. The mechanism is simple: agents are rewarded for achieving goals while complying with laws, and punished (by means of null payoffs) for non-compliance. Formally, compliance games are induced by well-known agent-labeled Kripke structures, goal formulas expressed in the language of CTL and social laws understood as black-listed transitions of the Kripke structure. Our main contribution here is the representation theorem for compliance games and the analysis of stability (the core), which is a particularly problematic concept in this formal setting.

The paper is structured as follows. In Sect. 2 we provide the necessary formal background, Sect. 3 presents main definition of compliance games together with analysis of their properties, and in Sect. 4 we discuss stability of said games. We conclude and discuss future work in Sect. 5.

2   Technical Background

We begin by concisely presenting all the formal background for our work. This paper brings temporal logic, cooperative game theory and social laws together, thus we will present a rather concise introduction to all the necessary technicalities.

2.1   Kripke Structures and CTL

We start by defining agent-labelled Kripke structures, in the same way as defined by Ågotnes et al. in [3]:

Definition 2.1 (Agent-labelled Kripke Structure).   *An* agent-labeled Kripke structure *(henceforth referred to simply as* Kripke structure*) K is a tuple $\langle S, S^0, R, V, \Phi, \mathcal{A}, \alpha \rangle$ where:*

- *S is the non-empty, finite set of* states *and S^0 is the initial state,*
- *$R \subseteq S \times S$ is the serial ($\forall s \exists t \ (s,t) \in R$) relation between elements of S that captures transitions between states,*
- *Φ is a non-empty, finite set of propositional symbols,*
- *$V : S \to 2^\Phi$ is a labeling function which assigns propositions to states in which they are satisfied,*
- *$\mathcal{A}$ is a non-empty finite set of agents, and*
- *$\alpha : R \to \mathcal{A}$ is a function that labels edges with agents.[2]*

A *path* π over a relation R is an infinite sequence of states $s_0, s_1, s_2, \ldots$ such that $\forall u \in \mathbb{N} : (s_u, s_{u+1}) \in R$. $\pi[0]$ denotes the first element of the sequence, $\pi[1]$ the second, and so on. An *s-path* is a path π such that $\pi[0] = s$. $\Pi_R(s)$ is the set of *s*-paths over R, and we write $\Pi(s)$, if R is clear from the context.

---

[2] While formally not necessary, throughout the paper we assume that an agent has to "own" at least one transition.

Objectives are specified using the language of *Computation Tree Logic* (CTL), a popular branching-time temporal logic. We use an adequate fragment of the language defined by the following grammar:

$$\varphi ::= \top \mid p \mid \neg\varphi \mid \varphi \vee \varphi \mid \mathsf{E}\bigcirc\varphi \mid \mathsf{E}(\varphi\mathcal{U}\varphi) \mid \mathsf{A}(\varphi\mathcal{U}\varphi)$$

where p is a propositional symbol. The standard derived propositional connectives are used, in addition to standard derived CTL connectives such as $\mathsf{A}\bigcirc\varphi$ for $\neg\mathsf{E}\bigcirc\neg\varphi$ (see [9] for details). We distinguish two fragments of the language defined above – a *universal* L^u (with a typical element u) and an *existential* L^e (with a typical element e) one:

$$u ::= \top \mid \bot \mid p \mid \neg p \mid u \vee u \mid u \wedge u \mid \mathsf{A}\bigcirc u \mid \mathsf{A}\square u \mid \mathsf{A}(u\mathcal{U}u)$$
$$e ::= \top \mid \bot \mid p \mid \neg p \mid e \vee e \mid e \wedge e \mid \mathsf{E}\bigcirc e \mid \mathsf{E}\square e \mid \mathsf{E}(e\mathcal{U}e)$$

Say that we are given two Kripke structures: $K_1 = \langle S, S^0, R_1, V, \Phi, A, \alpha \rangle$ and $K_2 = \langle S, S^0, R_2, V, \Phi, A, \alpha \rangle$. We say that K_1 is a subsystem of K_2 and K_2 is a supersystem of K_1 (denoted $K_1 \sqsubseteq K_2$) if and only if $R_1 \subseteq R_2$. This yields the following observation which we will later use to prove some properties of our games.

Theorem 2.1 ([14]). *If $K_1 \sqsubseteq K_2$ and $s \in S$, then:*

$$\forall e \in L^e : K_1, s \models e \qquad \Rightarrow \qquad K_2, s \models e; \text{ and}$$
$$\forall u \in L^u : K_2, s \models u \qquad \Rightarrow \qquad K_1, s \models u.$$

Satisfaction of a formula φ in a state s of a structure K, $K, s \models \varphi$, is defined as follows:

$$K, s \models \top;$$
$$K, s \models p \text{ iff } p \in V(s);$$
$$K, s \models \neg\varphi \text{ iff not } K, s \models \varphi;$$
$$K, s \models \varphi \vee \psi \text{ iff } K, s \models \varphi \text{ or } K, s \models \psi;$$
$$K, s \models \mathsf{E}\bigcirc\varphi \text{ iff } \exists\pi \in \Pi(s) : K, \pi[1] \models \varphi;$$
$$K, s \models \mathsf{E}(\varphi\mathcal{U}\psi) \text{ iff } \exists\pi \in \Pi(s), \exists i \in \mathbb{N}, \text{s.t. } K, \pi[i] \models \psi$$
$$\text{and } \forall j, (0 \leq j < i) : K, \pi[j] \models \varphi;$$
$$K, s \models \mathsf{A}(\varphi\mathcal{U}\psi) \text{ iff } \forall\pi \in \Pi(s), \exists i \in \mathbb{N}, \text{s.t. } K, \pi[i] \models \psi$$
$$\text{and } \forall j, (0 \leq j < i) : K, \pi[j] \models \varphi.$$

2.2   Social Laws

A *social law* $\eta \subseteq R$ is a set of black-listed ("illegal") transitions, such that $R \setminus \eta$ remains serial. The set of all social laws over R is denoted as $N(R)$. We say that $K \dagger \eta$ is a structure with a social law η *implemented* on it, i.e.

for $K = \langle S, R, \Phi, V, A, \alpha \rangle$ and η, $K \dagger \eta = K'$ iff $K' = \langle S, R', \Phi, V, A, \alpha' \rangle$ with $R' = R \setminus \eta$ and:

$$\alpha'(s, s') = \begin{cases} \alpha(s, s') & \text{if } (s, s') \in R' \\ \text{undefined} & \text{otherwise.} \end{cases}$$

Also, $\eta \restriction C = \{(s, s') : (s, s') \in \eta \ \& \ \alpha(s, s') \in C\}$ for any $C \subseteq A$ – that is to account for agents that do not necessarily comply with the social law (i.e. we can consider a situation in which only those edges that are "owned" by members of C are blacklisted).

2.3   Cooperative Games

We now introduce some concepts from cooperative game theory. Again, definitions provided here, albeit complete, are necessarily terse. For a more detailed explanation of the concepts introduced below, see [7].

Definition 2.2. *A transferable utility* cooperative game *(sometimes also called a* coalitional, *or* characteristic function game*) is a tuple* $G = \langle N, \nu \rangle$, *where N is a non-empty set of* players, *and* $\nu : 2^N \to \mathbb{R}$ *is a* characteristic function *of the game which assigns a* value *to each coalition $C \subseteq N$ of players.*

We say a cooperative game $G = \langle N, \nu \rangle$ is *monotone* (or *increasing*) if $\nu(C) \leq \nu(D)$ whenever $C \subseteq D$ for $C, D \subseteq N$. A cooperative game is *simple* when each of the coalitions of players either wins or loses the game, in other words, when the characteristic function's signature is $\nu : 2^N \to \{0, 1\}$. Finally, we say that player i is a *veto player* in game G if $\nu(C) = 0$ for any $C \subseteq N \setminus \{i\}$.

3   Compliance Games

We now consider cooperative games in which agents are rewarded for satisfying formulas and punished for violating laws. We evaluate agents' actions based on how many of their respective *goal* formulas they are able to satisfy. Thus we say that, given a Kripke structure K, there is a set of goals:

$$\gamma_i = \{\varphi_1, \ldots, \varphi_m\}$$

associated with each agent $i \in A$ of K, where φ_j is a *goal formula* expressed in the language of CTL. We say that a Kripke structure K, a set of goals γ_i for each agent $i \in A$ of K and a social law η over R of K constitute a *social system* $S = \langle K, \gamma_1, \ldots, \gamma_n, \eta \rangle$.

Below we introduce the definition of the game. The idea behind it is that the value of a coalition C is the amount of goals it can achieve under restrictions minus the amount of goals achievable in a Kripke structure (without restrictions). This number can be negative, and the rationale behind such design of games is that behavior of agents would indicate to the system designer whether the laws he designed are optimal or not (i.e., if an agent can satisfy more of his goals while not complying than when complying then perhaps either the goals or the laws need to be adjusted).

Definition 3.1 (Compliance Game). *A social system $\mathcal{S}$ induces a coopera-tive game $G_{\mathcal{S}} = \langle \mathcal{A}, \nu_{\mathcal{S}} \rangle$, where $\mathcal{A}$ is a set of agents in K of $\mathcal{S}$, and*

$$\nu_{\mathcal{S}}(C) = \begin{cases} 1 & \text{if } \left(\sum_{\varphi \in \gamma_C} |\{\varphi : K \dagger (\eta \restriction C) \models \varphi\}| - \sum_{\varphi \in \gamma_C} |\{\varphi : K \models \varphi\}| \right) > 0 \\ 0 & \text{otherwise,} \end{cases}$$

where $C \subseteq \mathcal{A}$, and $\gamma_C = \bigcup_{i \in C} \gamma_i$.

We now analyze some properties of compliance games. First we observe that the characteristic function of said games is not always monotone.

Lemma 3.1. *Compliance games are not always monotone.*

Proof. The lemma above can be proved with a simple counter example shown in Fig. 1. As seen in the example, adding agents to a winning coalition can "break" the satisfiability of their goals.   □

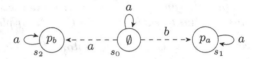

Fig. 1. A Kripke structure which induces a non-monotone compliance game, illus-trating Lemma 3.1. Here, $\gamma_a = \{E \bigcirc p_a\}$, $\gamma_b = \{E \bigcirc p_b\}$, $K \models \gamma_a$, $K \models \gamma_b$, and $K \dagger (\eta \restriction \{a\}) \models \gamma_a$, $K \dagger (\eta \restriction \{b\}) \models \gamma_b$, but $K \dagger (\eta \restriction \{a,b\}) \not\models \gamma_a \vee \gamma_b$.

The fact that compliance games are not always monotone is a negative result from a point of view of algorithmic game theory, because we cannot take compu-tational advantage of the monotonicity property of the characteristic function. In fact we present a Theorem below which states something even stronger:

Theorem 3.1. *Given an arbitrary function $\nu : 2^{\mathcal{A}} \rightarrow \{0,1\}$, there is always a social system $\mathcal{S} = \langle K, \gamma_1, \ldots, \gamma_n, \eta \rangle$ which induces a cooperative game $G_{\mathcal{S}} = \langle \mathcal{A}, \nu_{\mathcal{S}} \rangle$, where $\mathcal{A}$ is a set of agents in K of $\mathcal{S}$ and $\nu = \nu_{\mathcal{S}}$.*

Proof. We prove the theorem by providing a recipe for creating a social system $\mathcal{S} = \langle K, \gamma_1, \ldots, \gamma_n, \eta \rangle$ in which K is constructed of elements which "isolate" winning conditions for each winning coalition.

We construct $\mathcal{S}$ in the following way. Each agent is given the same goal: $E \Diamond A \Box p$, thus γ_i is a singleton set which contains one formula. We then construct the Kripke structure K starting from the initial state which is not labeled by any proposition and has a transition labeled by an arbitrary agent and not blacklisted by η (a "bridge") leading to another state s_C (again, not labeled by any proposition). The s_C state is the beginning of a construction which assures that coalition C wins. We then construct a sequence of states not labeled by any propositions with transitions labeled by all agents from $\mathcal{A} \setminus C$, one per agent, all of which are included in the social law η (this assures that the superset of C does not win along this path). Once we are done, we add a state labeled by all the goals of members of C and a reflexive loop labeled by an arbitrary agent. This state becomes the satisfied goal once members of C comply to η. Next, in order to assure subsets of C lose the game, we add a state and a transition per member of C leading to a state in which the negation of all the goals is satisfied, labeling transitions with respective agents and adding them to η – this way only if all members of C comply the transitions will be blacklisted and the goal satisfied. This whole construction from s_0 assures winning conditions for coalition C, and we can construct a separate such construction for each winning C'. Any C' that does not have a construction of this kind is a losing coalition, thus we can model *any* set of outcomes of the game. The construction is presented in Fig. 2.   □

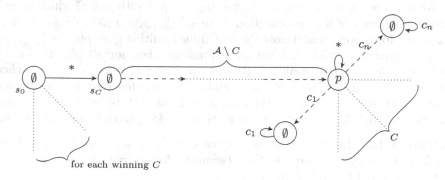

Fig. 2. Construction for the proof of Theorem 3.1. Dashed lines represent transitions in η, the $*$ symbol stands for an arbitrary agent.

The representation result presented in this section is more general, since it can easily be adapted to similar simple games. In [1], authors present social systems $S = \langle K, \varphi, \eta \rangle$ and induce simple cooperative games of the form

$$\nu_S(C) = \begin{cases} 1 & \text{if } K \dagger (\eta \restriction C) \models \varphi \\ 0 & \text{otherwise,} \end{cases}$$

in order to study power indices for agents. Since the game defined above is very similar to our compliance game, we immediately obtain the following result:

Corollary 3.1. *Given an arbitrary function $\nu : 2^{\mathcal{A}} \to \{0,1\}$, there is always a social system $S = \langle K, \varphi, \eta \rangle$ which induces a cooperative game $G_S = \langle \mathcal{A}, \nu_S \rangle$ as defined in [1], where $\mathcal{A}$ is a set of agents in K of S.*

Since monotonicity is a desirable property for most coalitional games, we are interested in identifying subclasses of our games that are actually monotone. Ågotnes et al. [3] identify social systems with universal goals as a subclass of monotone versions of their games. We can do the same for our compliance games.

Proposition 3.1. *Compliance games are monotone for* $\varphi \in L^u$.

Proof. Let $\mathcal{S} = \langle K, \eta, \gamma_1, \ldots, \gamma_n \rangle$ be a social system, and let $C \subseteq C' \subseteq \mathcal{A}$ be coalitions in K. Then from Theorem 2.1 we know that if $K \dagger (\eta \upharpoonright C) \models u$ then $K \dagger (\eta \upharpoonright C') \models u$. Thus if an agent's universal goal becomes satisfied by his compliance (removal of edges), another agent's compliance cannot break satisfiability of that goal. For the same reason if there is a universal goal satisfied in a Kripke structure, imposing a social law will not change its satisfiability. □

4   Stability – The Core

We concentrate on the most popular stability related solution concept, which is *the core*. In order to define it precisely, we need a few extra definitions.

We say that an *imputation* is a vector $(p_1, \ldots, p_n)$ with $p_i \in \mathbb{Q}$ which is such a division of gains of a grand coalition N that $\sum_{i=1}^{n} p_i = \nu(N)$. We say that p_i is a *payoff* for player i and denote the payoff for coalition C as $p(C) = \sum_{i \in C} p_i$.

An imputation satisfies *individual rationality* when for all players $i \in C$, we have $p_i \geq \nu(\{i\})$. A coalition B *blocks* a payoff vector $(p_1, \ldots, p_n)$ when $p(B) < \nu(B)$ – members of B can abandon the original coalition, with each member getting p_i and there is still some amount of $\nu(B)$ to be shared amongst players. The coalition is thus unstable when a blocking payoff vector is chosen.

Definition 4.1. *The* core *of a cooperative game is a set of such imputations which are not blocked by any coalition. Formally, for an imputation* $(p_1, \ldots, p_n)$, *and any coalition* C, $p(C) \geq \nu(C)$.

Intuitively, the core characterizes such a set of outcomes where no player has an incentive to abandon the coalition structure. Many games have an empty core, however simple games usually have a non-empty core, due to the following well-known result:

Lemma 4.1 ([10]). *A core of a simple cooperative game is non-empty iff there is at least one veto player in the game. And if there are veto players, any impu-tation that distributes payoffs only to them is in the core of the game.*

Thus checking non-emptiness of the core for a simple game boils down to finding whether there are veto players.

Before we attempt to identify outcomes in the core of compliance games, we need to discuss in detail what "stability" of said games actually means. Recall that in Definition 3.1 the value for a coalition is defined as the difference between how many goals a coalition can achieve while complying to a social law and the amount of goals achievable when not complying. There is an important detail in the semantics of $K \dagger (\eta \upharpoonright C)$ expression, though, that makes an interpretation of stability-capturing solution concepts somewhat problematic.

As mentioned in the paragraphs above, the core characterizes a set of stable outcomes, where stable means players have no incentives to "deviate" and pursue goals on their own. What does "deviating" mean in the context of compliance games? It means complying, but with other players. However, the expression $K \dagger (\eta \upharpoonright C)$ means that players in coalition C comply with η, but at the same time *no other players comply*. This means that if a proper subset of coalition C intends to abandon its coalition and form a new coalition C', the rationale behind its agents' behavior is to form a coalition in which they themselves comply, and at the same time they somehow force all other players to *not* comply. This aspect of compliance games is highly unusual and makes the interpretation of the core non-standard. The way we motivate and explain such design of compliance games is that we are interested in said games from a system designer's point of view. Reasoning this way, we may interpret a particular coalition structure of a compliance game as a set of *hypothetical scenarios*: each winning coalition is such a scenario, and in this scenario the coalition in question assumes no one but its members comply.

Proposition 4.1. *Compliance games can have empty cores.*

Proof. From Lemma 4.1 we know that the only situation when a compliance game has an empty core is when there are no veto players present in the game. From Theorem 3.1 we know that we can create a social system that induces a compliance game with a characteristic function that has an arbitrary output, so e.g. for a social system with two players a and b we can construct $\nu(\{a\}) = \nu(\{b\}) = 1$, but $\nu(\{a,b\}) = 0$ and $\nu(\mathcal{A}) = 0$.   □

In light of this negative result we would be interested in a relationship between the shape of elements of $\mathcal{S}$ and the non-emptiness of the core of the compliance game it induces, or more narrowly, we are interested in the relationship between the structure of $\mathcal{S}$ and the existence of veto players.

The first likely suspects to yield games with non-empty cores are social systems with only universal goal formulas, since these games will be monotone, as shown in Proposition 3.1. In monotone games it is easy to see that player i is a veto player iff $\nu(\mathcal{A} \setminus \{i\}) = 0$, thus any game with at least one winning and one losing coalition will have at least one veto player.

Proposition 4.2. *Let $\mathcal{S}$ be a social system containing only universal goals. If $\mathcal{S}$ induces a compliance game where there is at least one winning and one losing coalition, then this game's core is non-empty.*

Proof. Follows directly from the statement of the problem and Proposition 3.1.   □

5   Conclusions and Future Work

In this paper we presented a new, game theoretic approach to incentivizing agents' compliance to social laws. We analyzed properties of compliance games, studied their stability and relation between their properties and the underlying logical framework that induces them. For future work, we plan to first investigate complexity of decision problems and also try designing compliance games based on other classes of cooperative games. We think that the general idea of using cooperative game theory for modeling compliance to social laws is a naturally attractive and to a great degree unexplored idea, and we wish to pursue it further in the future.

Acknowledgments. The author would like to thank Pål Grønås Drange, Hannah Hansen, Truls Pedersen, and reviewers of EUMAS 2014 for helpful comments.

References

1. Ågotnes, T., van der Hoek, W., Tennenholtz, M., Wooldridge, M.: Power in normative systems. In: Proceedings of 8th International Conference on Autonomous Agents and Multiagent Systems (AAMAS 2009), pp. 145–152 (2009)
2. Ågotnes, T., van der Hoek, W., Wooldridge, M.: Normative system games. In: Proceedings of the 6th International Joint Conference on Autonomous Agents and Multiagent Systems (AAMAS 2007), pp. 1–8 (2007)
3. Ågotnes, T., van der Hoek, W., Wooldridge, M.: Robust normative systems and a logic of norm compliance. Log. J. IGPL **18**(1), 4–30 (2009)
4. Ågotnes, T., van der Hoek, W., Wooldridge, M.: Conservative social laws. In: Proceedings of the 20th European Conference on Artificial Intelligence (ECAI 2012), pp. 49–54 (2012)
5. Ågotnes, T., Wooldridge, M.: Optimal social laws. In: Proceedings of the 9th International Conference on Autonomous Agents and Multiagent Systems (AAMAS 2010), pp. 667–674 (2010)
6. Alur, R., Henzinger, T.A., Kupferman, O.: Alternating-time temporal logic. J. ACM **49**(5), 672–713 (2002)
7. Chalkiadakis, G., Elkind, E., Wooldridge, M.: Computational Aspects of Cooperative Game Theory. Synthesis Lectures on Artificial Intelligence and Machine Learning, vol. 16. Morgan & Claypool, San Rafael (2012)
8. Dyrkolbotn, S., Kaźmierczak, P.: Playing with norms: tractability of normative systems for homogeneous game structures. In: Proceedings of the 13th International Conference on Autonomous Agents and Multiagent Systems (AAMAS 2014), pp. 125–132 (2014)
9. Emerson, E.A.: Temporal and modal logic. In: van Leeuwen, J. (ed.) Handbook of Theoretical Computer Science Volume B: Formal Models and Semantics. Elsevier Science Publishers B.V., Amsterdam (1990)
10. Osborne, M.J., Rubinstein, A.: A Course in Game Theory. MIT Press, Cambridge (1994)
11. Pedersen, T., Dyrkolbotn, S., Kaźmierczak, P.: Big, but not unruly: Tractable norms for anonymous game structures. arXiv:1405.6899 (2013)
12. Shoham, Y., Tennenholtz, M.: On the synthesis of useful social laws for artificial agent societies. In: Proceedings of the 10th National Conference on Artificial intelligence (AAAI 1992), pp. 276–281 (1992)
13. Shoham, Y., Tennenholtz, M.: On social laws for artificial agent societies: off-line design. Artif. Intell. **73**, 231–252 (1995)
14. van der Hoek, W., Roberts, M., Wooldridge, M.: Social laws in alternating time: effectiveness, feasibility, and synthesis. Synthese **156**(1), 1–19 (2006)

Synthesis with Rational Environments

Orna Kupferman[1], Giuseppe Perelli[2]([⊠]), and Moshe Y. Vardi[3]

[1] The Hebrew University, Jerusalem, Israel
orna@cs.huji.ac.il
[2] University of Naples "Federico II", Naples, Italy
giuseppe.perelli@unina.it
[3] Rice University, Houston, USA
vardi@cs.rice.edu

Abstract. *Synthesis* is the automated construction of a system from its specification. The system has to satisfy its specification in all possible environments. The environment often consists of agents that have objectives of their own. Thus, it makes sense to soften the universal quantification on the behavior of the environment and take the objectives of its underlying agents into an account. Fisman et al. introduced *rational synthesis*: the problem of synthesis in the context of rational agents. The input to the problem consists of temporal-logic formulas specifying the objectives of the system and the agents that constitute the environment, and a solution concept (e.g., Nash equilibrium). The output is a profile of strategies, for the system and the agents, such that the objective of the system is satisfied in the computation that is the outcome of the strategies, and the profile is stable according to the solution concept; that is, the agents that constitute the environment have no incentive to deviate from the strategies suggested to them.

In this paper we continue to study rational synthesis. First, we suggest an alternative definition to rational synthesis, in which the agents are rational but not cooperative. In the non-cooperative setting, one cannot assume that the agents that constitute the environment take into account the strategies suggested to them. Accordingly, the output is a strategy for the system only, and the objective of the system has to be satisfied in all the compositions that are the outcome of a stable profile in which the system follows this strategy. We show that rational synthesis in this setting is 2ExpTime-complete, thus it is not more complex than traditional synthesis or cooperative rational synthesis. Second, we study a richer specification formalism, where the objectives of the system and the agents are not Boolean but quantitative. In this setting, the goal of the system and the agents is to maximize their outcome. The quantitative setting significantly extends the scope of rational synthesis, making the game-theoretic approach much more relevant.

O. Kupferman—The research leading to these results has received funding from the European Research Council under the European Union's Seventh Framework Programme (FP7/2007-2013) / ERC grant agreement 278410, by the Israel Science Foundation (grant 1229/10), and by the US-Israel Binational Science Foundation (grant 2010431).

G. Perelli—This research was partially done while visiting Rice University.

M.Y. Vardi—NSF Expeditions in Computing project "ExCAPE: Expeditions in Computer Augmented Program Engineering".

© Springer International Publishing Switzerland 2015
N. Bulling (Ed.): EUMAS 2014, LNAI 8953, pp. 219–235, 2015.
DOI: 10.1007/978-3-319-17130-2_15

1   Introduction

Synthesis is the automated construction of a system from its specification. The basic idea is simple and appealing: instead of developing a system and verifying that it adheres to its specification, we would like to have an automated procedure that, given a specification, constructs a system that is correct by construction. The first formulation of synthesis goes back to Church [Chu63]; the modern approach to synthesis was initiated by Pnueli and Rosner, who introduced LTL (linear temporal logic) synthesis [PR89]. The LTL *synthesis problem* receives as input a specification in LTL and outputs a reactive system modeled by a finite-state transducer satisfying the given specification — if such exists. It is important to distinguish between input signals, assigned by the environment, and output signals, assigned by the system. A system should be able to cope with all values of the input signals, while setting the output signals to desired values [PR89]. Therefore, the quantification structure on input and output signals is different. Input signals are universally quantified while output signals are existentially quantified.

Modern systems often interact with other systems. For example, the clients interacting with a server are by themselves distinct entities (which we call agents) and are many times implemented by systems. In the traditional approach to synthesis, the way in which the environment is composed of its underlying agents is abstracted. In particular, the agents can be seen as if their only objective is to conspire to fail the system. Hence the term "hostile environment" that is traditionally used in the context of synthesis. In real life, however, many times agents have goals of their own, other than to fail the system. The approach taken in the field of algorithmic game theory [NRTV07] is to assume that agents interacting with a computational system are *rational*, i.e., agents act to achieve their own goals. Assuming agents rationality is a restriction on the agents behavior and is therefore equivalent to softening the universal quantification on the environment.[1] Thus, the following question arises: can system synthesizers capitalize on the rationality and goals of agents interacting with the system?

In [FKL10], Fisman et al. positively answered this question by introducing and studying *rational synthesis*. The input to the rational-synthesis problem consists of LTL formulas specifying the objectives of the system and the agents that constitute the environment, and a solution concept, e.g., dominant strategies, Nash Equilibria, and the like. The atomic propositions over which the objectives are defined are partitioned among the system and the agents, so that each of them controls a subset of the propositions. The desired output is a strategy profile such that the objective of the system is satisfied in the computation that is the outcome of the profile, and the agents that constitute the environment have no incentive to deviate from the strategies suggested to them (formally, the profile is an equilibrium with respect to the solution concept). Fisman et al. showed

---

[1] Early work on synthesis has realized that the universal quantification on the behaviors of the environment is often too restrictive. The way to address this point, however, has been by adding assumptions on the environment, which can be part of the specification (cf., [CHJ08]).

that there are specifications that cannot be realized in a hostile environment but are realizable in a rational environment. Moreover, the rational-synthesis problem for LTL and common solution concepts used in game theory can be solved in 2ExpTime thus its complexity coincides with that of usual synthesis.

In this paper we continue the study of rational synthesis. We present the following three contributions. First, we suggest an alternative definition to rational synthesis, in which the agents are rational but not cooperative. Second, we study a richer specification formalism, where the objectives of the system and the agents are not Boolean but quantitative. Third, we show that all these variants of the rational synthesis problems can be reduced to model checking in fragments of *Strategy Logic* [CHP07]. Before we describe our contributions in more detail, let us highlight a different way to consider rational synthesis and our contribution here. *Mechanism design* is a field in game theory and economics studying the design of games whose outcome (assuming agents rationality) achieves some goal [NR01, NRTV07]. The outcome of traditional games depends on the final position of the game. In contrast, the systems we reason about maintain an *ongoing interaction* with their environment, and we reason about their behavior by referring not to their final state (in fact, we consider non-terminating systems, with no final state) but rather to the *language* of computations that they generate. Rational synthesis can be viewed as a variant of mechanism design in which the game is induced by the objective of the system, and the objectives of both the system and the agents refer to their on-going interaction and are specified by temporal-logic formulas. Our contributions here correspond to the classic setting assumed in mechanism design: the agents need not be cooperative, and the outcome is not Boolean.

We argue that the definition of rational synthesis in [FKL10] is *cooperative*, in the sense that the agents that constitute the environment are assumed to follow the strategy profile suggested to them (as long as it is in an equilibrium). Here, we consider also a *non-cooperative* setting, in which the agents that constitute the environment may follow any strategy profile that is in an equilibrium, and not necessarily the one suggested to them by the synthesis algorithm. In many scenarios, the cooperative setting is indeed too optimistic, as the system cannot assume that the environment, even if it is rational, would follow a suggested strategy, rather than a strategy that is as good for it. Moreover, sometimes there is no way to communicate with the environment and suggest a strategy for it. From a technical point of view, we show that the non-cooperative setting requires reasoning about *all* possible equilibria, yet, despite this more sophisticated reasoning, it stays 2ExpTime-complete. We achieve the upper bound by reducing rational synthesis to the model-checking problem for Strategy Logic (SL, for short). SL is a specification formalism that allows to explicitly quantify over strategies in games as first-order objects [CHP07]. While the model-checking problem for strategy logic is in general non-elementary, we show that it is possible to express rational synthesis in the restricted *Nested-Goal* fragment of SL, introduced in [MMPV14], which leads to the desired complexity. It is important to observe the following difference between the cooperative and the non-cooperative settings. In the cooperative one, we synthesize strategies for all agents, with the assumption that the agent that corresponds to the system always follows his suggested strategy and the agents that constitute the environment decide in a rational manner whether to follow their strategies. On the other hand, in the non-cooperative setting, we synthesize a strategy only for the agent that corresponds to the system, and we assume that the agents that constitute the environment are rational, thus the suggested strategy has to win against all rational behaviors of the environment.

Our second contribution addresses a weakness of the classical synthesis problem, a weakness that is more apparent in the rational setting. In classical synthesis, the specification is Boolean and describes the expected behavior of the system. In many applications, systems can satisfy their specifications at different levels of quality. Thus, synthesis with respect to Boolean specifications does not address designers needs. This latter problem is a real obstacle, as designers would be willing to give up manual design only after being convinced that the automatic procedure that replaces it generates systems of comparable quality. In the last years we see a lot of effort on developing formalisms that would enable the specification of such quality measures [BCHJ09, ABK13].

Classical applications of game theory consider games with quantitative payoffs. In the Boolean setting, we assumed that the payoff of an agent is, say, 1, if its objective is satisfied, and is 0 otherwise. In particular, this means that agents whose objectives are not satisfied have no incentive to follow any strategy, even if the profile satisfies the solution concept. In real-life, rational objectives are rarely Boolean. Thus, even beyond our goal of synthesizing systems of high quality, the extension of the synthesis problem to the rational setting calls also for an extension to a quantitative setting. Unfortunately, the full quantitative setting is undecidable already in the context of model checking [Hen10]. In [FKL10], Fisman et al. extended cooperative rational synthesis to objectives in the multi-valued logic LLTL where specifications take truth values from a finite lattice.

We introduce here a new quantitative specification formalism, termed *Objective* LTL, (OLTL, for short). We first define the logic, and then study its rational synthesis. Essentially, an OLTL specification is a pair $\theta = \langle \Psi, f \rangle$, where $\Psi = \langle \psi_1, \psi_2, \ldots, \psi_m \rangle$ is a tuple of LTL formulas and $f : \{0, 1\}^m \to \mathbb{Z}$ is a *reward function*, mapping Boolean vectors of length m to an integer. A computation η then maps θ to a reward in the expected way, according to the subset of formulas that are satisfied in η. In the rational synthesis problem for OLTL the input consists of OLTL specifications for the system and the other agents, and the goal of the system is to maximize its reward with respect to environments that are in an equilibrium. Again, we distinguish between a cooperative and a non-cooperative setting. Note that the notion of an equilibrium in the quantitative setting is much more interesting, as it means that all agents in the environment cannot expect to increase their payoffs. We show that the quantitative setting is not more complex than the non-quantitative one, thus quantitative rational synthesis is complete for 2ExpTime in both the cooperative and non-cooperative settings.

2   Preliminaries

2.1   Games

A *concurrent game structure* (CGS, for short) [AHK02] is a tuple $\mathcal{G} \triangleq \langle \varPhi, \Omega, (A_i)_{i \in \Omega}, S, \lambda, \tau, s_0 \rangle$, where $\varPhi$ and $\Omega = \{\alpha_0, \ldots, \alpha_k\}$ are finite sets of *atomic propositions* and *agents*, A_i are disjoint sets of *actions*, one for each agent α_i, S is a set of *states*, $s_0 \in S$ is a designated *initial state*, and $\lambda : S \to 2^\varPhi$ is a *labeling function* that maps each state to the set of atomic propositions true in that state. By $A \triangleq \bigcup_{i \in \Omega} A_i$ we denote the union of all possible action for all the agents. Let $D \triangleq A_0 \times \ldots \times A_k$ be the set of *decisions*, i.e., $(k+1)$-tuples of actions representing the choices of an action for each agent. Then, $\tau : S \times D \to S$ is a deterministic *transition function* mapping a pair of a state and a decision to a state.

A *path* in a CGS $\mathcal{G}$ is an infinite sequence of states $\eta = \eta_0 \cdot \eta_1 \cdot \ldots \in S^\omega$ that agrees with the transition function, i.e., such that, for all $i \in \mathbb{N}$, there exists a decision $\mathsf{d} \in D$ such that $\eta_{i+1} = \tau(\eta_i, \mathsf{d})$. A *track* in a CGS $\mathcal{G}$ is a prefix ρ of a path η, also denoted by $\eta_{\leq n}$, for a suitable $n \in \mathbb{N}$. A track ρ is *non-trivial* if $|\rho| > 0$, i.e., $\rho \neq \varepsilon$.

We use $\mathrm{Pth} \subseteq S^\omega$ and $\mathrm{Trk} \subseteq S^+$ to denote the set of all paths and non-trivial tracks, respectively. Also, for a given $s \in S$, we use Pth^s and Trk^s to denote the subsets of paths and tracks starting from $s \in S$. Intuitively, the game starts in the state s_0 and, at each step, each agent selects an action in its set. The game then deterministically proceeds to the next state according to the corresponding decision. Thus, the outcome of a CGS is a path, regulated by individual actions of the agents.

A *strategy* for Agent α_i is a tool used to decide which decision to take at each phase of the game. Formally, it is a function $\pi_i : \mathrm{Trk} \to A_i$ that maps each non-trivial track to a possible action of Agent α_i. By Π_i we denote the set of all possible strategies for agent α_i. A *strategy profile* is a $(k+1)$-tuple $\mathsf{P} = \langle \pi_0, \ldots, \pi_k \rangle \in \Pi_0 \times \ldots \times \Pi_k$ that assigns a strategy to each agent. We denote by $\mathcal{P} \triangleq \Pi_0 \times \ldots \times \Pi_k$ the set of all possible strategy profiles. For a strategy profile P and a state s, we use $\eta = \mathsf{play}(\mathsf{P}, s)$ to denote the path that is the outcome of a game that starts in s and agrees with P, i.e., for all $i \in \mathbb{N}$, it holds that $\eta_{i+1} = \tau(\eta_i, \mathsf{d}_i)$, where $\mathsf{d}_i = (\pi_0(\eta_{\leq i}), \ldots, \pi_k(\eta_{\leq i}))$. By $\mathsf{play}(\mathsf{P}) = \mathsf{play}(\mathsf{P}, s_0)$ we denote the unique path starting from s_0 obtained from P.

We model reactive systems by deterministic transducers. A *transducer* is a tuple $\mathcal{T} = \langle \mathrm{I}, \mathrm{O}, \mathrm{S}, s_0, \delta, \mathrm{L} \rangle$, where I is a set of input signals assigned by the environment, O is a set of output signals, assigned by the system, S is a set of states, s_0 is an initial state, $\delta : \mathrm{S} \times 2^\mathrm{I} \to \mathrm{S}$ is a transition function, and $\mathrm{L} : \mathrm{S} \to 2^\mathrm{O}$ is a labeling function. When the system is in state $s \in \mathrm{S}$ and it reads an input assignment $\sigma \in 2^\mathrm{I}$, it changes its state to $s' = \delta(s, \sigma)$ where it outputs the assignment $\mathrm{L}(s')$. Given a sequence $\varrho = \sigma_1, \sigma_2, \sigma_3, \ldots \in (2^\mathrm{I})^\omega$ of inputs, the *execution* of $\mathcal{T}$ on ϱ is the sequence of states $s_0, s_1, s_2, \ldots$ such that for all $j \geq 0$, we have $s_{j+1} = \delta(s_j, \sigma_j)$. The *computation* $\eta \in (2^\mathrm{I} \times 2^\mathrm{O})^\omega$ of S on ϱ is then $\langle \mathrm{L}(s_0), \sigma_1 \rangle, \langle \mathrm{L}(s_1), \sigma_2 \rangle, \langle \mathrm{L}(s_2), \sigma_3 \rangle, \ldots$.

2.2 Strategy Logic

Strategy Logic [CHP07, MMV10, MMPV12] (SL, for short) is a logic that allows to quantify over strategies in games as explicit first-order objects. Intuitively, such quantification, together with a syntactic operator called *binding*, allows us to restrict attention to restricted classes of strategy profiles, determining a subset of paths, in which a temporal specification is desired to be satisfied. Since nesting of quantifications and bindings is possible, such temporal specifications can be recursively formulated by an SL subsentence. From a syntactic point of view, SL is an extension of LTL with strategy variables $Var_0, \ldots, Var_k$ for the agents, existential ($\langle\!\langle x_i \rangle\!\rangle$) and universal ($[\![x_i]\!]$) strategy quantifiers, and a binding operator of the form (α_i, x_i) that couples an agent α_i with one of its variables $x_i \in Var_i$.

We first introduce some technical notation. For a tuple $t = s(t_0, \ldots, t_k)$, by $t[i \leftarrow d]$ we denote the tuple obtained from t by replacing the i-th component with d. We use $\vec{x}$ as an abbreviation for the tuple $(x_0, \ldots, x_k) \in Var_0 \times \ldots \times Var_k$. By $\langle\!\langle \vec{x} \rangle\!\rangle = \langle\!\langle x_0 \rangle\!\rangle \ldots \langle\!\langle x_k \rangle\!\rangle$, $[\![\vec{x}]\!] = [\![x_0]\!] \ldots [\![x_k]\!]$, and $b(\vec{x}) = (\alpha_0, x_0) \ldots (\alpha_k, x_k)$ we denote the existential and universal quantification, and the binding of all the agents to the strategy profile variable $\vec{x}$, respectively. Finally, by $b(\vec{x}_{-i}, y_i) = (\alpha_0, x_0) \ldots (\alpha_i, y_i) \ldots (\alpha_k, x_k)$ we denote the changing of binding for Agent α_i from the strategy variable x_i to the strategy variable y_i in the global binding $b(\vec{x})$.

Here we define and use a slight variant of the *Nested-Goal* fragment of SL, namely SL[NG], introduced in [MMPV14]. Formulas in SL[NG] are defined with respect to a set Φ of atomic proposition, a set Ω of agents, and sets Var_i of strategy variables for Agent $\alpha_i \in \Omega$. The set of SL[NG] formulas is defined by the following grammar:

$$\varphi ::= p \mid \neg\varphi \mid \varphi \wedge \varphi \mid \varphi \vee \varphi \mid X\varphi \mid \varphi \, U \, \varphi \mid \varphi \, R \, \varphi \mid \langle\!\langle x_i \rangle\!\rangle\varphi \mid [\![x_i]\!]\varphi \mid b(\vec{x})\varphi,$$

where, $p \in \Phi$ is an atomic proposition, $x_i \in Var_i$ is a variable, and $\vec{x} \in Var_0 \times \ldots \times Var_k$ is a tuple of variables, one for each agent.

The LTL part has the classical meaning. The formula $\langle\!\langle x_i \rangle\!\rangle\varphi$ states that there exists a strategy for Agent α_i such that the formula φ holds. The formula $[\![x_i]\!]\varphi$ states that, for all possible strategies for Agent α_i, the formula φ holds. Finally, the formula $b(\vec{x})\varphi$ states that the formula φ holds under the assumption that the agents in Ω adhere to the strategy evaluation of the variable x_i coupled in $b(\vec{x})$.

As an example, $\langle\!\langle x_0 \rangle\!\rangle [\![x_1]\!] b(\vec{x})(p \, U \, q) \vee [\![y_0]\!]\langle\!\langle y_1 \rangle\!\rangle b(\vec{y})(G \, F \, p \wedge G \, \neg q)$ is an SL[NG] formula stating that either the system α_0 has a strategy x_0 to enforce $p \, U \, q$ or, for all possible behaviors y_0, the environment has a strategy y_1 to enforce both $G \, F \, p$ and $G \, \neg q$.

We denote by $free(\varphi)$ the set of strategy variables occurring in φ but not in a scope of a quantifier. A formula φ is *closed* if $free(\varphi) = \emptyset$.

Similarly to the case of first order logic, an important concept that characterizes the syntax of SL is the one of *alternation depth* of quantifiers, i.e., the maximum number of quantifier switches $\langle\!\langle x_i \rangle\!\rangle [\![x_j]\!]$, $[\![x_i]\!]\langle\!\langle x_j \rangle\!\rangle$, in the formula.

A precise formalization of the concepts of alternation depth can be found in [MMV10, MMPV12].

Now, in order to define the semantics of SL, we use the auxiliary concept of assignment. Let $\mathrm{Var} = \bigcup_{i=0}^{k} \mathrm{Var}_i$ be a set of variables for the agents in Ω, an *assignment* is a function $\chi : \mathrm{Var} \cup \Omega \to \Pi$ mapping variables and agents to a relevant strategy, i.e., for all $\alpha_i \in \Omega$ and $x_i \in \mathrm{Var}_i$, we have that $\chi(\alpha_i), \chi(x_i) \in \Pi_i$. Let $\mathrm{Asg} \triangleq \Pi^{\mathrm{Var} \cup \Omega}$ denote the set of all assignments. For an assignment χ and elements $l \in \mathrm{Var} \cup \Omega$, we use $\chi[l \mapsto \pi] \in \mathrm{Asg}$ to denote the new assignment that returns π on l and the value of χ on the other ones, i.e., $\chi[l \mapsto \pi](l) \triangleq \pi$ and $\chi[l \mapsto \pi](l') \triangleq \chi(l')$, for all $l' \in (\mathrm{Var} \cup \Omega) \setminus \{l\}$. By $\mathsf{play}(\chi, s)$ we denote the path $\mathsf{play}(\mathsf{P}, s)$, for the strategy profile P that is compatible with χ.

We now describe when a given game $\mathcal{G}$ and a given assignment χ satisfy an SL formula φ, where $\mathsf{dom}(\chi)^2 = \mathsf{free}(\varphi) \cup \Omega$. We use $\mathcal{G}, \chi, s \models \varphi$ to indicate that the path $\mathsf{play}(\chi, s)$ satisfies φ over the CGS $\mathcal{G}$. For φ in LTL, the semantics is as usual [MP92]. For the other operators, the semantics is as follows.

1. $\mathcal{G}, \chi, s \models \langle\!\langle x_i \rangle\!\rangle \varphi$ if there exists a strategy π_i for α_i such that $\mathcal{G}, \chi[x_i \mapsto \pi_i], s \models \varphi$;
2. $\mathcal{G}, \chi, s \models [\![x_i]\!] \varphi$ if, for all strategies π_i for α_i, it holds that $\mathcal{G}, \chi[x_i \mapsto \pi_i], s \models \varphi$;
3. $\mathcal{G}, \chi, s \models \flat(\vec{x}) \varphi$ if it holds that $\mathcal{G}, \chi[\alpha_0 \mapsto x_0] \ldots [\alpha_k \mapsto x_k], s \models \varphi$.

Finally, we say that $\mathcal{G}$ satisfies φ, and write $\mathcal{G} \models \varphi$, if there exists an assignment χ such that $\mathcal{G}, \chi, s_0 \models \varphi$.

Intuitively, at Items 1 and 2, we evaluate the existential and universal quantifiers over a variable x_i by associating with it a suitable strategy. At Item 3 we commit the agents to use the strategy contained in the tuple variable $\vec{x}$.

Theorem 1. [MMPV14] *The model-checking problem for* SL[NG] *is* $(d + 1)$ ExpTime *with d being the alternation depth of the specification.*

2.3 Rational Synthesis

We define two variants of rational synthesis. The first, *cooperative rational synthesis*, was introduced in [FKL10]. The second, *non-cooperative rational synthesis*, is new.

We work with the following model: the world consists of a *system* and an environment composed of k agents: $\alpha_1, \ldots, \alpha_k$. For uniformity, we refer to the system as Agent α_0. We assume that Agent α_i controls a set X_i of propositions, and the different sets are pairwise disjoint. At each point in time, each agent sets his propositions to certain values. Let $X = \bigcup_{0 \le i \le k} X_i$, and $X_{-i} = X \setminus X_i$. Each agent α_i (including the system) has an objective φ_i, specified as an LTL formula over X.

This setting induces the CGS $\mathcal{G} = \langle \Phi, \Omega, (A_i)_{i \in \Omega}, S, \lambda, \tau, s_0 \rangle$ defined as follows. The set of agents $\Omega = \{\alpha_0, \alpha_1, \ldots, \alpha_k\}$ consists of the system and the agents that constitute the environment. The actions of Agent α_i are the possible assignments to its variables. Thus, $A_i = 2^{X_i}$. We use A and A_{-i} to

---

[2] By $\mathsf{dom}(\mathsf{f})$ we denote the domain of the function f.

denote the sets 2^X and 2^{X-i}, respectively. The nodes of the game record the current assignment to the variables. Hence, $S = A$, and for all $s \in S$ and $\langle \sigma_0, \ldots, \sigma_k \rangle \in A_0 \times A_1 \times \cdots \times A_k$, we have $\delta(s, \sigma_0, \ldots, \sigma_k) = \langle \sigma_0, \cdots, \sigma_k \rangle$.

A strategy for the system is a function $\pi_0 : \mathrm{Trk} \to A_0$. In the standard synthesis problem, we say that π_0 realizes φ_0 if, no matter which strategies the agents composing the environment follow, all the paths in which the system follows π_0 satisfy φ_0. In rational synthesis, on instead, we assume that the agents that constitute the environment are rational, which soften the universal quantification on the behavior of the environment.

Recall that the rational-synthesis problem gets a solution concept as a parameter. As discussed in Sect. 1, the fact that a strategy profile is a solution with respect to the concept guarantees that it is not worthwhile for the agents constituting the environment to deviate from the strategies assigned to them. Several solution concepts are studied and motivated in game theory. Here, we focus on the concepts of *dominant strategy* and *Nash equilibrium*, defined below.

The common setting in game theory is that the objective for each agent is to maximize his *payoff* – a real number that is a function of the outcome of the game. We use $\mathsf{payoff}_i : \mathrm{Pth} \to \mathbb{R}$ to denote the payoff function of Agent α_i. That is, payoff_i assigns to each possible path η a real number $\mathsf{payoff}_i(\eta)$ expressing the payoff of α_i on η. For a strategy profile P, we use $\mathsf{payoff}_i(\mathsf{P})$ to abbreviate $\mathsf{payoff}_i(\mathsf{play}(\mathsf{P}, s_0))$. In the case of an LTL goal ψ_i, we define $\mathsf{payoff}_i(\eta) = 1$ if $\eta \models \psi_i$ and $\mathsf{payoff}_i(\eta) = 0$, otherwise.

The simplest and most appealing solution concept is dominant-strategies solution [OR94]. A *dominant strategy* is a strategy that an agent can never lose by adhering to, regardless of the strategies of the other agents. Therefore, if there is a profile of strategies $\mathsf{P} = \langle \pi_0, \ldots, \pi_k \rangle$ in which all strategies π_i are dominant, then no agent has an incentive to deviate from the strategy assigned to him in P. Formally, P is a *dominant strategy profile* if for every $1 \leq i \leq k$ and for every (other) profile P', we have that $\mathsf{payoff}_i(\mathsf{P}') \leq \mathsf{payoff}_i(\mathsf{P}'[i \leftarrow \pi_i])$.

As an example, consider the game in Fig. 1(a), played by three agents, Alice, Bob, and Charlie, whose actions are $\{a_1, a_2\}$, $\{b_1, b_2\}$, and $\{c_1, c_2\}$, respectively. The arrows are labeled with the possible action of the agents. Each agent wants to visit a state marked with his initial letter, infinitely often. In this game, the strategy for Bob of always choosing b_2 on his node 2 is dominant, while all the possible strategies for Charlie are dominant. On the other hand, Alice has no dominant strategies, since her goal essentially depends on the strategies adopted by the other agents. In several games, it can happen that agents have not any dominant strategy. For this reason, one would consider also other kind of solution concepts.

Another well known solution concept is Nash equilibrium [OR94]. A strategy profile is a *Nash equilibrium* if no agent has an incentive to deviate from his strategy in P provided that the other agents adhere to the strategies assigned to them in P. Formally, P is a *Nash equilibrium profile* if for every $1 \leq i \leq k$ and for every (other) strategy π_i' for agent α_i, we have that $\mathsf{payoff}_i(\mathsf{P}[i \leftarrow \pi_i']) \leq \mathsf{payoff}_i(\mathsf{P})$. An important advantage of Nash equilibrium is that it is more likely

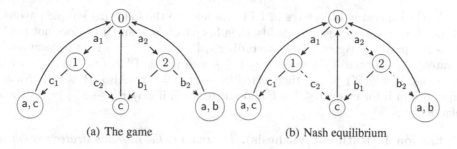

(a) The game   (b) Nash equilibrium

Fig. 1. A game.

to exist than an equilibrium of dominant strategies [OR94][3]. A weakness of Nash equilibrium is that it is not nearly as stable as a dominant-strategy solution: if one of the other agents deviates from his assigned strategy, nothing is guaranteed.

For the case of repeated-turn games like infinite games, a suitable refinement of Nash Equilibria is the *Subgame perfect Nash-equilibrium* [Sel75] (SPE, for short). A strategy profile $P = \langle \pi_0, \ldots, \pi_k \rangle$ is an SPE if for every possible history of the game, no agent α_i has an incentive to deviate from her strategy π_i, assuming that the other agents follow their strategies in P. Intuitively, an SPE requires the existence of a Nash Equilibrium for each subgame starting from a randomly generated finite path of the original one. In [FKL10], the authors have studied cooperative rational synthesis also for the solution concept of SPE. To do this, the synthesis algorithm in [FKL10] was extended to consider all possible histories of the game. In SL such a path property can be expressed combining strategy quantifiers with temporal operators. Indeed, the formula $\varphi = [\![\vec{x}]\!]\flat(\vec{x}) G \psi(\vec{y})$, with free$(\varphi) = \vec{y}$, states that, for all possible profile strategies the agents can follow, the game always reaches a position in which the formula $\psi(\vec{y})$ holds. Thus, for all possible paths that can be generated by agents, the property holds. By replacing $\psi(\vec{y})$ with the above formula, we then obtain a formula that represents SPEs. Hence, the cooperative and non-cooperative synthesis problems can be asserted in SL also for SPE, and our results hold also for this solution concept.

In rational synthesis, we control the strategy of the system and assume that the agents that constitute the environment are rational. Consider a strategy profile $P = \langle \pi_0, \ldots, \pi_k \rangle$ and a solution concept γ (that is, γ is either "dominant strategies" or "Nash equilibrium"). We say that P is *correct* if play(P) satisfies φ_0. We say that P is in a π_0-*fixed* γ-*equilibrium* if the agents composing the environment have no incentive to deviate from their strategies according to the solution concept γ, assuming that the system continues to follow π_0. Thus, P is a π_0-fixed dominant-strategy equilibrium if for every $1 \leq i \leq k$ and for every (other) profile P' in which Agent 0 follows π_0, we have that payoff$_i(P') \leq$ payoff$_i(P'[i \leftarrow \pi_i])$. Note that for the case of Nash equilibrium, adding the requirement that P is π_0-fixed does not change the definition of an equilibrium.

---

[3] In particular, all k-agent turn-based games with ω-regular objectives have Nash equilibrium [CMJ04].

In the context of objectives in LTL, we assume the following simple payoffs. If the objective φ_i of Agent α_i holds, then his payoff is 1, and if φ_i does not hold, then the payoff of Agent i is 0. Accordingly, $P = \langle \pi_0, \ldots, \pi_k \rangle$ is in a dominant-strategy equilibrium if for every $1 \leq i \leq k$ and profile $P' = \langle \pi_0', \ldots, \pi_k' \rangle$ with $\pi_0' = \pi_0$, if $\mathsf{play}(P') \models \varphi_i$, then $\mathsf{play}(P'[i \leftarrow \pi_i]) \models \varphi_i$. Also, P is in a Nash-equilibrium if for every $1 \leq i \leq k$ and strategy π_i', if $\mathsf{play}(P[i \leftarrow \pi_i']) \models \varphi_i$, then $\mathsf{play}(P) \models \varphi_i$.

Definition 1 (Rational synthesis). *The input to the rational-strategy problem is a set X of atomic propositions, partitioned into $X_0, \ldots, X_k$, LTL formulas $\varphi_0, \ldots, \varphi_k$, describing the objectives of the system and the agents composing the environment, and a solution concept γ. We distinguish between two variants of the problem:*

1. *In* Cooperative *rational synthesis [FKL10], the desired output is a strategy profile P such that $\mathsf{play}(P)$ satisfies φ_0 and P is a π_0-fixed γ-equilibrium.*
2. *In* Non-cooperative *rational synthesis, the desired output is a strategy π_0 for the system such that for every strategy profile P that includes π_0 and is a π_0-fixed γ-equilibrium, we have that $\mathsf{play}(P)$ satisfies φ_0.*

Thus, in the cooperative variant of [FKL10], we assume that once we suggest to the agents in the environment strategies that are in a γ-equilibrium, they will adhere to the suggested strategies. In the non-cooperative variant we introduce here, the agents may follow any strategy profile that is in a γ-equilibrium, and thus we require the outcome of all these profiles to satisfy φ_0. It is shown in [FKL10] that the cooperative rational synthesis problem is 2ExpTime-complete.

Note that the input to the rational synthesis problem may not have a solution, so when we solve the rational-synthesis problem, we first solve the *rational-realizability* problem, which asks if a solution exists. As with classical synthesis, the fact that SL model-checking algorithms can be easily modified to return a regular witness for the involved strategies in case an existentially quantified strategy exists, makes the realizability and synthesis problems strongly related.

Example 1. Consider a file-sharing network with the system and an environment consisting of two agents. The system controls the signal d_1 and d_2 (Agent α_1 and α_2 can download, respectively) and it makes sure that an agent can download only when the other agent uploads. The system's objective is that both agents will upload infinitely often. Agent α_1 controls the signal u_1 (Agent α_1 uploads), and similarly for Agent α_2 and u_2. The goal of both agents is to download infinitely often.

Formally, the set of atomic propositions is $X = \{d_1, d_2, u_1, u_2\}$, partitioned into $X_0 = \{d_1, d_2\}, X_1 = \{u_1\}$, and $X_2 = \{u_2\}$. The objectives of the system and the environment are as follows.

- $\varphi_0 = \mathsf{G}\,(\neg u_1 \rightarrow \neg d_2) \wedge \mathsf{G}\,(\neg u_2 \rightarrow \neg d_1) \wedge \mathsf{G}\,\mathsf{F}\,u_1 \wedge \mathsf{G}\,\mathsf{F}\,u_2$,
- $\varphi_1 = \mathsf{G}\,\mathsf{F}\,d_1$,
- $\varphi_2 = \mathsf{G}\,\mathsf{F}\,d_2$.

First, note that in standard synthesis, φ_0 is not realizable, as a hostile environment needs not upload. In the cooperative setting, the system can suggest to both agents the following TIT FOR TAT strategy: upload at the first time step, and from that point onward upload iff the other agent uploads. The system itself follows a strategy π_0 according to which it enables downloads whenever possible (that is, d_2 is valid whenever Agent α_1 uploads, and d_1 is valid whenever Agent α_2 uploads). It is not hard to see that the above three strategies are all dominant. Indeed, all the three objectives are satisfied. Thus, the triple of strategies is a solution for the cooperative setting, for both solution concepts.

What about the non-cooperative setting? Consider the above strategy π_0 of the system, and consider strategies for the agents that never upload. The tuple of the three strategies is in a π_0-fixed Nash equilibrium.

This ensures strategies for the environment to be dominant. Indeed, if Agent α_2 changes her strategy, φ_1 is still satisfied and vice-versa. Indeed, as long as Agent α_2 sticks to his strategy, Agent α_1 has no incentive to change his strategy, and similarly for Agent α_2. Thus, π_0 is not a solution to the non-cooperative rational synthesis problem for the solution concept of Nash equilibrium. On the other hand, we claim that π_0 is a solution to the non-cooperative rational synthesis problem for the solution concept of dominant strategies. For showing this, we argue that if π_1 and π_2 are dominant strategies for α_1 and α_2, then φ_0 is satisfied in the path that is the outcome of the profile $P = \langle \pi_0, \pi_1, \pi_2 \rangle$. To see this, consider such a path $\eta = \mathsf{play}(\pi_0, \pi_1, \pi_2)$. We necessarily have that $\eta \models \varphi_1 \wedge \varphi_2$. Indeed, otherwise π_1 and π_2 would not be dominant, as we know that with the strategies described above, α_1 and α_2 can satisfy their objectives. Now, since $\eta \models \varphi_1 \wedge \varphi_2$, we know that u_2 and u_1 hold infinitely often in η. Also, it is not hard to see that the formulas $\mathsf{G}\,(\neg u_1 \rightarrow \neg d_2)$ and $\mathsf{G}\,(\neg u_2 \rightarrow \neg d_1)$ are always satisfied in the context of π_0, no matter how the other agents behave. It follows that $\eta \models \varphi_0$, thus π_0 is a solution of the non-cooperative rational synthesis problem for dominant strategies.

3 Qualitative Rational Synthesis

In this section we study cooperative and non-cooperative rational synthesis and show that they can be reduced to the model-checking problem for SL[NG]. The cooperative and non-cooperative rational synthesis problems for several solution concepts can be stated in SL[NG].

We first show how to state that a given strategy profile $\vec{y} = (y_0, \ldots, y_k)$ is in a y_0-fixed γ-equilibrium. For $\alpha_i \in \Omega$, let φ_i be the objective of Agent α_i. For a solution concept γ and a strategy profile $\vec{y} = (y_0, \ldots, y_k)$, the formula $\varphi^\gamma(\vec{y})$, expressing that the profile $\vec{y}$ is a y_0-fixed γ-equilibrium, is defined as follows.

- For the solution concept of dominant strategies, we define:
  $\varphi^\gamma(\vec{y}) := [\![\vec{z}]\!] \bigwedge_{i=1}^{k} (\flat(\vec{z})\varphi_i \rightarrow \flat(\vec{z}_{-i}, y_i)\varphi_i)$.
- For the solution concept of Nash equilibrium, we define:
  $\varphi^\gamma(\vec{y}) := [\![\vec{z}]\!] \bigwedge_{i=1}^{k} (\flat(\vec{y}_{-i}, z_i)\varphi_i \rightarrow \flat(\vec{y})\varphi_i)$.
- For the solution concept of Subgame Perfect Equilibrium, we define:
  $\varphi^\gamma(\vec{y}) := [\![\vec{x}]\!] \flat(\vec{x}_{-0}, y_0)\mathsf{F} \bigwedge_{i=1}^{k} [\![z_i]\!] \flat(\vec{y}_{-i}, z_i)\varphi_i \rightarrow \flat(\vec{y})\varphi_i$.

We can now state the existence of a solution to the cooperative and non-cooperative rational-synthesis problem, respectively, with input $\varphi_0, \ldots, \varphi_k$ by the closed formulas:

1. $\varphi_{cRS}^{\gamma} := \langle\langle y_0 \rangle\rangle \langle\langle y_1 \rangle\rangle \ldots \langle\langle y_k \rangle\rangle (\varphi^{\gamma}(\vec{y}) \wedge \varphi_0);$
2. $\varphi_{noncRS}^{\gamma} := \langle\langle y_0 \rangle\rangle [[y_1]] \ldots [[y_k]] (\varphi^{\gamma}(\vec{y}) \rightarrow \varphi_0).$

Indeed, the formula 1 specifies the existence of a strategy profile $\mathsf{P} = \langle \pi_0, \ldots, \pi_k \rangle$ that is π_0-fixed γ-equilibrium and such that the outcome satisfies φ_0. On the other hand, the formula 2 specifies the existence of a strategy π_0 for the system such that the outcome of all profiles that are in a π_0-fixed γ-equilibrium satisfy φ_0.

As shown above, all the solution concepts we are taking into account can be specified in SL[NG] with formulas whose length is polynomial in the number of the agents and in which the alternation depth of the quantification is 1. Hence we can apply the known complexity results for SL[NG]:

Theorem 2 (Cooperative and non-cooperative rational-synthesis complexity). *The cooperative and non-cooperative rational-synthesis problems in the qualitative setting are 2EXPTIME-complete.*

Proof. Consider an input $\varphi_0, \ldots, \varphi_k$, X, and γ to the cooperative or non-cooperative rational-synthesis problem. As explained in Sect. 2.3, the input induces a game $\mathcal{G}$ with nodes in 2^X. As detailed above, there is a solution to the cooperative (resp., non-cooperative) problem iff the SL[NG] formula φ_{cRS}^{γ} (resp., $\varphi_{noncRS}^{\gamma}$) is satisfied in $\mathcal{G}$. The upper bound then follows from the fact that the model checking problem for SL[NG] formulas of alternation depth 1 is in 2EXPTIME-COMPLETE in the size of the formula (Cf., Theorem 1). Moreover, the model-checking algorithm can return finite-state transducers that model strategies that are existentially quantified.

For the lower bound, it is easy to see that the classical LTL synthesis problem is a special case of the cooperative and non-cooperative rational synthesis problem. Indeed, $\varphi(I, O)$ is realizable against a hostile environment iff the solution to the non-cooperative rational synthesis problem for a system that has an objective φ and controls I and an environment that consists of a single agent that controls O and has an objective *True*, is positive.

4 Quantitative Rational Synthesis

As discussed in Sect. 1, a weakness of classical synthesis algorithms is the fact that specifications are Boolean and miss a reference to the quality of the satisfaction. Applications of game theory consider games with quantitative payoffs. Thus, even more than the classical setting, the rational setting calls for an extension of the synthesis problem to a quantitative setting. In this section we introduce *Objective* LTL, a quantitative extension of LTL, and study an extension of the rational-synthesis problem for specifications in Objective LTL. As opposed to other multi-valued specification formalisms used in the context of synthesis of high-quality systems [BCHJ09, ABK13], Objective LTL uses the syntax and semantics of LTL and only augments the specification with a reward function that enables a succinct and convenient prioritization of sub-specifications.

4.1   The Quantitative Setting

Objective LTL (OLTL, for short) is an extension of LTL in which specifications consist of sets of LTL formulas weighted by functions. Formally, an OLTL *specification* over a set X of atomic propositions is a pair $\theta = \langle \Psi, f \rangle$, where $\Psi = \langle \psi_1, \psi_2, \ldots, \psi_m \rangle$ is a tuple of LTL formulas over X and $f : \{0,1\}^m \rightarrow \mathbb{Z}$ is a *reward function*, mapping Boolean vectors of length m to integers. We assume that f is given by a polynomial. We use $|\Psi|$ to denote $\sum_{i=1}^{m} |\psi_i|$. For a computation $\eta \in (2^X)^\omega$, the *signature of* Ψ *in* η, denoted $\mathsf{sig}(\Psi, \eta)$, is a vector in $\{0,1\}^m$ indicating which formulas in Ψ are satisfied in η. Thus, $\mathsf{sig}(\Psi, \eta) = \langle v_1, v_2, \ldots, v_m \rangle$ is such that for all $1 \leq i \leq m$, we have that $v_i = 1$ if $\eta \models \psi_i$ and $v_i = 0$ if $\eta \not\models \psi_i$. The *value of* θ *in* η, denoted $\mathsf{val}(\theta, \eta)$ is then $f(\mathsf{sig}(\Psi, \eta))$. Thus, the interpretation of an OLTL specification is quantitative. Intuitively, $\mathsf{val}(\theta, \eta)$ indicates the level of satisfaction of the LTL formulas in Ψ in η, as determined by the priorities induced by f. We note that the input of weighted LTL formulas studied in [CY98] is a special case of Objective LTL.

Example 2. Consider a system with m buffers, of capacities $c_1, \ldots, c_m$. Let full_i, for $1 \leq i \leq m$, indicate that buffer i is full. The OLTL specification $\theta = \langle \Psi, f \rangle$, with $\Psi = \langle F\,\mathsf{full}_1, F\,\mathsf{full}_2, \ldots, F\,\mathsf{full}_m \rangle$ and $f(v) = c_1 \cdot v_1 + \cdots + c_m \cdot v_m$ enables us to give different satisfaction values to the objective of filling a buffer. Note that $\mathsf{val}(\langle \Psi, f \rangle, \eta)$ in a computation η is the sum of capacities of all filled buffers.

In the quantitative setting, the objective of Agent α_i is given by means of an OLTL specification $\theta_i = \langle \Psi_i, f_i \rangle$, specifications describe the payoffs to the agents, and the objective of each agent (including the system) is to maximize his payoff. For a strategy profile P, the payoff for Agent α_i in P is simply $\mathsf{val}(\theta_i, \mathsf{play}(P))$.

In the quantitative setting, rational synthesis is an optimization problem. Here, in order to easily solve it, we provide a decision version by making use of a threshold. It is clear that the optimization version can be solved by searching for the best threshold in the decision one.

Definition 2 (Quantitative rational synthesis). *The input to the quantitative rational-strategy problem is a set* X *of atomic propositions, partitioned into* $X_0, \ldots, X_k$, OLTL *specifications* $\theta_0, \theta_1, \ldots, \theta_k$, *with* $\theta_i = \langle \Psi_i, f_i \rangle$, *and a solution concept* γ. *We distinguish between two variants of the problem:*

1. *In* cooperative quantitative rational synthesis, *the desired output for a given threshold* $t \in \mathbb{N}$ *is a strategy profile* P *such that* $\mathsf{payoff}_0(P) \geq t$ *and* P *is in a* π_0*-fixed* γ*-equilibrium.*
2. *In* non-cooperative quantitative rational synthesis, *the desired output for a given threshold* $t \in \mathbb{N}$ *is a strategy* π_0 *for the system such that, for each strategy profile* P *including* π_0 *and being in a* π_0*-fixed* γ*-equilibrium, we have that* $\mathsf{payoff}_0(P) \geq t$.

Now, we introduce some auxiliary formula that helps us to formulate also the quantitative rational-synthesis problem in SL[NG].

For a tuple $\Psi = \langle \psi_1, \ldots, \psi_m \rangle$ of LTL formulas and a signature $v = \{v_1, \ldots, v_m\} \in \{0,1\}^m$, let $\mathsf{mask}(\Psi, v)$ be an LTL formula that characterizes computations η for which $\mathsf{sig}(\Psi, \eta) = v$. Thus, $\mathsf{mask}(\Psi, v) = (\bigwedge_{i:v_i=0} \neg \psi_i) \wedge (\bigwedge_{i:v_i=1} \psi_i)$.

We adjust the SL formulas $\Phi^\gamma(\vec{y})$ described in Sect. 3 to the quantitative setting. Recall that $\Phi^\gamma(\vec{y})$ holds iff the strategy profile assigned to $\vec{y}$ is in a π_0-fixed γ-equilibrium. There, the formula is a conjunction over all agents in $\{\alpha_1, \ldots, \alpha_k\}$, stating that Agent α_i does not have an incentive to change his strategy. In our quantitative setting, this means that the payoff of Agent α_i in an alternative profile is not bigger than his payoff in $\vec{y}$. For two strategy profiles, assigned to $\vec{y}$ and $\vec{y}'$, an SL formula that states that Agent α_i has no incentive that the profile would change from $\vec{y}$ to $\vec{y}'$ can state that the signature of Ψ in $\mathsf{play}(\vec{y}')$ results in a payoff to Agent α_i that is smaller than his current payoff. Formally, we have that:

$$\Phi_i^{eq}(\vec{y}, \vec{y}') = \bigvee_{v \in \{1, \ldots, m_i\} : f_i(v) \leq \mathsf{payoff}_i(\vec{y})} \flat(\vec{y}') \mathsf{mask}(\Psi_i, v).$$

We can now adjust $\Phi^\gamma(\vec{y})$ for all the cases of solution concepts we are taking into account.

- For the solution concept of dominant strategies, we define:
  $\Phi^\gamma(\vec{y}) := \bigwedge_{i \in \{1, \ldots, n\}} [\![\vec{z}]\!] \Phi_i^{eq}(\vec{y}, (\vec{z}[\alpha_0 \leftarrow y_0]);$
- For the solution concept of Nash equilibrium, we define:
  $\Phi^\gamma(\vec{y}) := \bigwedge_{i \in \{1, \ldots, n\}} [\![\vec{z}]\!] \Phi_i^{eq}(\vec{y}, (\vec{y}[\alpha_i \leftarrow z_i]);$
- For the solution concept of Subgame Perfect Equilibrium, we define:
  $\varphi^\gamma(\vec{y}) := [\![\vec{x}]\!] \flat(\vec{x}[\alpha_0 \leftarrow y_0]) \mathsf{F} \bigwedge_{i \in \{1, \ldots, n\}} [\![\vec{z}]\!] \Phi_i^{eq}(\vec{y}, (\vec{z}[\alpha_0 \leftarrow y_0])).$

Once we adjust $\Phi^\gamma(\vec{y})$ to the quantitative setting, we can use the same SL formula used in the non-quantitative setting to state the existence of a solution to the rational synthesis problem. We have the following:

- $\Phi_{RS}^\gamma := \langle\!\langle y_0 \rangle\!\rangle \langle\!\langle y_1 \rangle\!\rangle \ldots \langle\!\langle y_k \rangle\!\rangle (\Phi^\gamma(\vec{y}) \wedge \varphi_0);$
- $\Phi_{nonRS}^\gamma := \langle\!\langle y_0 \rangle\!\rangle [\![y_1]\!] \ldots [\![y_k]\!] (\Phi^\gamma(\vec{y}) \rightarrow \varphi_0).$

Theorem 3. *The cooperative and non-cooperative quantitative rational-synthesis problems are* $2\mathrm{ExpTime}$-COMPLETE.

Proof. We can reduce the problems to the model-checking problem of the SL formulas Φ_{RS}^γ and Φ_{nonRS}^γ, respectively. We should, however, take care when analyzing the complexity of the procedure, as the formulas $\Phi_i^{eq}(\vec{y}, \vec{y}')$, which participate in Φ_{RS}^γ and Φ_{nonRS}^γ involve a disjunction over vectors in $\{0,1\}^{m_i}$, resulting in Φ_{nonRS}^γ of an exponential length.

While the above prevents us from using the doubly exponential known bound on SL model checking for formulas of alternation depth 1 as is, it is not difficult to observe that the run time of the model-checking algorithm in [MMPV14], when applied to Φ_{nonRS}^γ, is only doubly exponential. The reason is the fact that the inner exponent paid in the algorithm for SL model checking is due to the blow-up in the translation of the formula to a nondeterministic Büchi automaton over words (NBW, for short). In this translation, the exponentially many disjuncts are dominated by the exponential translation of the innermost LTL to NBW. Thus, the running time of the algorithm is doubly exponential, and it can return the witnessing strategies.

Hardness in 2EXPTIME follows easily from hardness in the non-quantitative setting.

5   Discussion

The understanding that synthesis corresponds to a game in which the objective of each player is to satisfy his specification calls for a mutual adoption of ideas between formal methods and game theory. In *rational synthesis*, introduced in [FKL10], synthesis is defined in a way that takes into an account the rationality of the agents that constitute the environment and involves and assumption that an agent cooperates with a strategy in which his objective is satisfied. Here, we extend the idea and consider also *non-cooperative* rational synthesis, in which agents need not cooperate with suggested strategies and may prefer different strategies that are at least as beneficial for them.

Many variants of the classical synthesis problem has been studied. It is interesting to examine the combination of the rational setting with the different variants. To start, the cooperative and non-cooperative settings can be combined into a framework in which one team of agents is competing with another team of agents, where each team is internally cooperative, but the two teams are non-cooperative. Furthermore, we plan to study rational synthesis with incomplete information. In particular, we plan to study rational synthesis with *incomplete information* [KV99], where agents can view only a subset of the signals that other agents output, and rational *stochastic* synthesis [CMJ04], which models the unpredictability of nature and involves stochastic agents that assign values to their output signals by means of a distribution function. Beyond a formulation of the richer settings, one needs a corresponding extension of strategy logic and its decision problems.

As discussed in Sect. 1, classical applications of game theory consider games with quantitative payoffs. We added a quantitative layer to LTL by introducing Objective-LTL and studying its rational synthesis. In recent years, researchers have developed more refined quantitative temporal logics, which enable a formal reasoning about the quality of systems. In particular, we plan to study rational synthesis for the multi-valued logics LTL[F] [ABK13], which enables a prioritization of different satisfaction possibilities, and LTL[D] [ABK14], in which discounting is used in order to reduce the satisfaction value of specifications whose eventualities are delayed. The rational synthesis problem for these logics induce a game with much richer, possibly infinitely many, profiles, making the search for a stable solution much more challenging.

References

[ABK13] Almagor, S., Boker, U., Kupferman, O.: Formalizing and reasoning about quality. In: Fomin, F.V., Freivalds, R., Kwiatkowska, M., Peleg, D. (eds.) ICALP 2013, Part II. LNCS, vol. 7966, pp. 15–27. Springer, Heidelberg (2013)

[ABK14] Almagor, S., Boker, U., Kupferman, O.: Discounting in LTL. In: Ábrahám, E., Havelund, K. (eds.) TACAS 2014 (ETAPS). LNCS, vol. 8413, pp. 424–439. Springer, Heidelberg (2014)

[AHK02] Alur, R., Henzinger, T.A., Kupferman, O.: Alternating-time temporal logic. JACM **49**(5), 672–713 (2002)

[BCHJ09] Bloem, R., Chatterjee, K., Henzinger, T.A., Jobstmann, B.: Better Quality in Synthesis through Quantitative Objectives. In: Bouajjani, A., Maler, O. (eds.) CAV 2009. LNCS, vol. 5643, pp. 140–156. Springer, Heidelberg (2009)

[CHJ08] Chatterjee, K., Henzinger, T.A., Jobstmann, B.: Environment Assumptions for Synthesis. In: van Breugel, F., Chechik, M. (eds.) CONCUR 2008. LNCS, vol. 5201, pp. 147–161. Springer, Heidelberg (2008)

[CHP07] Chatterjee, K., Henzinger, T.A., Piterman, N.: Strategy Logic. In: Caires, L., Vasconcelos, V.T. (eds.) CONCUR 2007. LNCS, vol. 4703, pp. 59–73. Springer, Heidelberg (2007)

[Chu63] Church, A.: Logic, arithmetics, and automata. In: Proceedings of the International Congress of Mathematicians, pp. 23–35. Institut Mittag-Leffler (1963)

[CMJ04] Chatterjee, K., Majumdar, R., Jurdziński, M.: On nash equilibria in stochastic games. In: Marcinkowski, J., Tarlecki, A. (eds.) CSL 2004. LNCS, vol. 3210, pp. 26–40. Springer, Heidelberg (2004)

[CY98] Courcoubetis, C., Yannakakis, M.: Markov decision processes and regular events. IEEE Trans. Autom. Control **43**(10), 1399–1418 (1998)

[FKL10] Fisman, D., Kupferman, O., Lustig, Y.: Rational synthesis. In: Esparza, J., Majumdar, R. (eds.) TACAS 2010. LNCS, vol. 6015, pp. 190–204. Springer, Heidelberg (2010)

[Hen10] Henzinger, T.A.: From boolean to quantitative notions of correctness. In: POPL 2010, pp. 157–158. ACM (2010)

[KV99] Kupferman, O., Vardi, M.Y.: Church's problem revisited. Bull. Symbolic Logic **5**(2), 245–263 (1999)

[MMPV12] Mogavero, F., Murano, A., Perelli, G., Vardi, M.Y.: What makes ATL* decidable? A decidable fragment of strategy logic. In: Koutny, M., Ulidowski, I. (eds.) CONCUR 2012. LNCS, vol. 7454, pp. 193–208. Springer, Heidelberg (2012)

[MMPV14] Mogavero, F., Murano, A., Perelli, G., Vardi, M.Y.: Reasoning about strategies on the model-checking problem. TOCL **15**(4), 1–47 (2014). doi:10.1145/2631917

[MMV10] Mogavero, F., Murano, A., Vardi, M.Y.: Reasoning about strategies. In: FSTTCS 2010, LIPIcs 8, pp. 133–144 (2010)

[MP92] Manna, Z., Pnueli, A.: The Temporal Logic of Reactive and Concurrent Systems - Specification. Springer, Heidelberg (1992)

[NR01] Nisan, N., Ronen, A.: Algorithmic mechanism design. Games Econ. Behav. **35**(1–2), 166–196 (2001)

[NRTV07] Nisan, N., Roughgarden, T., Tardos, E., Vazirani, V.V.: Algorithmic Game
          Theory. Cambridge University Press, Cambridge (2007)
  [OR94] Osborne, M.J., Rubinstein, A.: A Course in Game Theory. MIT Press,
          Cambridge (1994)
  [PR89] Pnueli, A., Rosner, R.: On the synthesis of a reactive module. In: POPL
          1989, pp. 179–190 (1989)
  [Sel75] Selten, R.: Reexamination of the perfectness concept for equilibrium points
          in extensive games. Int. J. Game Theory **4**(1), 25–55 (1975)

STIT Based Deontic Logics
for the Miners Puzzle

Xin Sun[(⊠)] and Zohreh Baniasadi

Faculty of Science, Technology and Communication, University of Luxembourg,
Walferdange, Luxembourg
xin.sun@uni.lu, zohreh.baniasadi.001@student.uni.lu

Abstract. In this paper we first develop two new STIT based deontic logics capable of solving the miners puzzle. The key idea is to use pessimistic lifting to lift the preference over worlds into the preference over sets of worlds. Then we also discuss a more general version of the miners puzzle in which plausibility is involved. In order to deal with the more general puzzle we add a modal operator representing plausibility to our logic. Lastly we present a sound and complete axiomatization.

1 Introduction

Research on deontic logic is divided into two main groups: the ought-to-be group and the ought-to-do group. The ought-to-do group originates from von Wright's pioneering paper [27]. Dynamic deontic logic [19,26], deontic action logic [6,22,24], and STIT-based deontic logic [11,13,23] belong to the "ought-to-do" family.

In recent years, the miners puzzle [12] quickly grabs the attention of lots of deontic logicians [4,5,7,9,28]. The miners puzzle goes like this:

> Ten miners are trapped either in shaft A or in shaft B, but we do not know which one. Water threatens to flood the shafts. We only have enough sandbags to block one shaft but not both. If one shaft is blocked, all of the water will go into the other shaft, killing every miner if they are inside. If we block neither shaft, both will be partially flooded, killing one miner.

Lacking any information about the miners' exact whereabouts, it seems acceptable to say that:

(1) We ought to block neither shaft.

However, we also accept that.

(2) If the miners are in shaft A, we ought to block shaft A.

(3) If the miners are in shaft B, we ought to block shaft B.

But we also know that.

(4) Either the miners are in shaft A or they are in shaft B.

© Springer International Publishing Switzerland 2015
N. Bulling (Ed.): EUMAS 2014, LNAI 8953, pp. 236–251, 2015.
DOI: 10.1007/978-3-319-17130-2_16

And (2)–(4) seem to entail.

(5) Either we ought to block shaft A or we ought to block shaft B.

Which contradicts (1).

Various solution to this puzzle has been proposed [4,5,7,9,28]. Willer [28] claims that any adequate semantics of dyadic deontic modality must offer a solution to the miners puzzle.

The existing STIT-based deontic logic [11,13,23] does not offer a satisfying solution to this puzzle: although the deduction from (2)–(4) to (5) is blocked by the dyadic deontic operator defined in Sun [23], but both Horty [11] and Sun [23] are unable to predict (1). We discuss this in detail in Sect. 2.2.

In this paper we first develop two new STIT-based deontic logics, referring them as pessimistic utilitarian deontic logic (PUDL$_1$ and PUDL$_2$), which are capable of blocking the deduction from (2)–(4) to (5) and are able to predict (1)–(4). We further consider a more general version of the miners puzzle in which the factor of plausibility is involved. Plausibility does not play a serious role in the original miners puzzle. It seems the plausibility of miners being in shaft A is equal to the plausibility of miner being in shaft B. If we are in a new scenario that the miners are more plausibly in shaft A, then in addition to statements (2) and (3), the following is acceptable:

(6) We ought to block shaft A.

A logic for the miners scenario should both solve the original miners puzzle and give right predictions in the plausibility involved scenario. In this paper we extend PUDL$_2$ to PUDL$_2^+$ by adding a modal operator representing plausibility. We show that PUDL$_2^+$ gives right predictions in the plausibility involved miners scenario.

The structure of this paper is as follows: in Sect. 2 we review the existing solutions to the miners puzzle and the existing STIT-based deontic logic. In Sect. 3 we develop PUDL$_1$ and PUDL$_2$ to solve the original miners puzzle. In Sect. 4 we develop PUDP$_2^+$ for the plausibility involved miners scenario. Section 5 is conclusion and future work.

2   Background

2.1   Solutions to the Miners Puzzle

Several authors have provided different solutions to the miners puzzle. We summarize the following approaches:

Kolodny and MacFarlane [12] give a detailed discussion of various escape routes. For example we may solve the paradox by rejecting (2) and (3) and instead accepting

(7) If we know that the miners are in shaft A, we ought to block shaft A.

(8) If we know that the miners are in shaft B, we ought to block shaft B.

Kolodny and MacFarlane [12] argue that such solution is not satisfying. Then they conclude that the only possible solution to the puzzle is to invalidate the argument from (2) to (5). To do this, Kolodny and MacFarlane state we have three choices: rejecting modus ponens (MP), rejecting disjunction introduction (∨I), rejecting disjunction elimination (∨E). Among these three Kolodny and MacFarlane further demonstrate that the only wise choice is to reject MP.

Willer [28] develops a fourth option to invalidate the argument form (2) to (5): falsify the monotonicity. In his solution MP can be preserved (there are very good reasons to do so) and we are unable to derive the inconsistency.

Cariani et al. [4] argue that the traditional Kratzer's semantics [14] of deontic conditionals is not capable of solving the puzzle. They propose to extend the standard Kratzer's account by adding a parameter representing a "decision problem" to solve the puzzle. Roughly, a decision problem contains a representation of action and a decision rule to select best action. Cariani et al. [4] use a partition of all possible worlds to represent actions, and the decision rule they used to select action is essentially the same as the MaxiMin principle–the decision theoretic rule that requires agents to evaluate actions in terms of their worst conceivable outcome and choose the "least bad" one among them. Such treatment shares some similarity with a special case of our logic to be in Sect. 3. In our logic every agent's actions are also represented by a partition of all worlds. And we use pessimistic lifting (to be introduced later) to compare actions, which is the same as MaxiMin.

Carr [5] argues that the proposal of Cariani et al. is still problematic. To develop a satisfying semantics, Carr uses three parameters to define deontic modality: an informational parameter, a value parameter and a decision rule parameter. According to Carr's proposal, (1) to (3) are all correct predictions and no contradiction arise within her framework.

Gabbay et al. [9] offers a solution to the miners puzzle using ideas from intuitionistic logic. In their logic "or" has an intuitionistic interpretation. Then the deduction from statement (2), (3) and (4) to (5) is blocked.

2.2 STIT-Based Deontic Logic

In STIT-based deontic logic, agents make choices and each choice is represented by a set of possible worlds. A preference relation over worlds is given as primitive. Such preference relation is then lifted to preference over sets of worlds. A choice is better than another iff the representing set of worlds of the first choice is better than the representing set of worlds of the second. A proposition ϕ is obligatory (we ought to see to it that ϕ) iff it is ensured by every best choice, i.e., it is true in every world of every best choice.

Therefore the interpretation of deontic modality is based on best choices, which can only be defined on top of preference over sets of worlds. Preference over sets of worlds is defined by lifting from preference over worlds. There is no standard way of lifting preference. Lang and van der Torre [15] summarize the following three ways of lifting:

- **strong lifting:** For two sets of worlds W_1 and W_2, W_1 is strongly better than W_2 iff $\forall w \in W_1$, $\forall v \in W_2$, w is better than v. That is, the worst world in W_1 is better than the best world in W_2.
- **optimistic lifting:** W_1 is optimistically better than W_2 iff $\exists w \in W_1$, $\forall v \in W_2$, w is better than v. That is, the best world in W_1 is better than the best world in W_2.
- **pessimistic lifting:** W_1 pessimistically better than W_2 iff $\forall w \in W_1$, $\exists v \in W_2$, w is better than v. That is, the worst world in W_1 is better than the worst world in W_2.

In Horty [11], Kooi and Tamminga [13] and Sun [23] strong lifting is adopted. Applying strong lifting to the miners scenario, all the three choices *block_neither*, *block_ A* and *block_ B* are the best choices. "we ought to block neither" is then not true in the miners scenario. To understand this more accurately, we now give a formal review of STIT-based deontic logic of Sun [23]. We call such logic utilitarian deontic logic (UDL).

The language of the UDL is built from a finite set $Agent = \{1, \ldots, n\}$ of agents and a countable set $\Phi = \{p, q, r, \ldots\}$ of propositional letters. Let $p \in \Phi$, $G \subseteq Agent$. The UDL language, $\mathcal{L}_{udl}$ is defined by the following Backus-Naur Form:

$$\phi ::= p \mid \neg\phi \mid \phi \wedge \phi \mid [G]\phi \mid \bigcirc_G \phi \mid \bigcirc_G(\phi/\phi)$$

Intuitively, $[G]\phi$ is read as "group G sees to it that ϕ". $\bigcirc_G \phi$ is read as "G ought to see to it that ϕ". $\bigcirc_G(\phi/\psi)$ is read as "G ought to see to it that ϕ under the condition ψ".

The semantics of UDL is based on utilitarian models, which is a non-temporal fragment of the group STIT model.

Definition 1 (Utilitarian Model). *A utilitarian model is a tuple $(W, Choice, \leq, V)$, where W is a nonempty set of possible worlds, Choice is a choice function, and $\leq$, representing the preference of the group Agent, is a reflexive and transitive relation over W. V is a valuation which assigns every propositional letter a set of worlds.*

The choice function $Choice : 2^{Agent} \mapsto 2^{2^W}$ is built from the individual choice function $IndChoice: Agent \mapsto 2^{2^W}$. IndChoice must satisfy the following conditions:

(1) for each $i \in Agent$ it holds that $IndChoice(i)$ is a partition of W;
(2) for $Agent = \{1, \ldots, n\}$, for every $x_1 \in IndChoice(1), \ldots, x_n \in IndChoice(n)$, $x_1 \cap \ldots \cap x_n \neq \emptyset$;

A function $s: Agent \mapsto 2^W$ is a selection function if for each $i \in Agent$, $s(i) \in IndChoice(i)$. Let Selection be the set of all selection functions, for every $G \subseteq Agent$, if $G \neq \emptyset$, then we define $Choice(G) = \{\bigcap_{i \in G} s(i) : s \in Selection\}$. If $G = \emptyset$, then we define $Choice(G) = \{W\}$.

$w \leq v$ is read as v is at least as good as w. $w \approx v$ is short for $w \leq v$ and $v \leq w$. Having defined utilitarian models, we are ready to review *preferences over sets of possible worlds*.

Definition 2 (Preferences over Sets of Worlds via Strong Lifting [23]). *Let $X, Y \subseteq W$ be two sets of worlds. $X \preceq^s Y$ (Y is at least as good as X) if and only if*

(1) *for each $w \in X$, for each $w' \in Y$, $w \leq w'$ and*
(2) *there exists some $v \in X$, some $v' \in Y$, $v \leq v'$.*

$X \prec^s Y$ (Y is better than X) if and only if $X \preceq^s Y$ and $Y \not\preceq^s X$. Here the superscript ^{s} in $\preceq^s$ is used to represent strong lifting.

Definition 3 (Dominance Relation [11]). *Let $G \subseteq Agent$ and $K, K' \in Choice(G)$. $K \preceq^s_G K'$ iff for all $S \in Choice(Agent - G)$, $K \cap S \preceq^s K' \cap S$.*

$K \preceq^s_G K'$ is read as "K' weakly dominates K". From a decision theoretical perspective, $K \preceq^s_G K'$ means that no matter how other agents act, the outcome of choosing K' is no worse than that of choosing K. $K \prec^s_G K'$ is used as an abbreviation of $K \preceq^s_G K'$ and $K' \not\preceq^s_G K$. If $K \prec^s_G K'$, then we say K' strongly dominates K.

Definition 4 (Restricted Choice Sets [11]). *Let G a groups of agents.*

$$Choice(G/X) = \{K : K \in Choice(G) \, and \, K \cap X \neq \emptyset\}$$

Intuitively, $Choice(G/X)$ is the collection of those choices of group G that are consistent with condition X.

Definition 5 (Conditional Dominance [23]). *Let G be a group of agents and X a set of worlds. Let $K, K' \in Choice(G/X)$.*

$$K \preceq^s_{G/X} K' \, iff \, for \, all \, S \in Choice((Agent - G)/(X \cap (K \cup K'))), K \cap X \cap S \preceq^s$$
$$K' \cap X \cap S.$$

$K \preceq^s_{G/X} K'$ is read as "K' weakly dominates K under the condition of X". And $K \prec^s_{G/X} K'$, read as "K' strongly dominates K under the condition of X", is used to express $K \preceq^s_{G/X} K'$ and $K' \not\preceq^s_{G/X} K$.

Definition 6 (Optimal and Conditional Optimal [11]). *Let G be a group of agents,*

- *$Optimal^s_G = \{K \in Choice(G) : there \, is \, no \, K' \in Choice(G) \, such \, that \, K \prec^s_G K'\}$.*
- *$Optimal^s_{G/X} = \{K \in Choice(G/X) : there's \, no \, K' \in Choice(G/X) \, such \, that \, K \prec^s_{G/X} K'\}$.*

In the semantics of UDL, the optimal choices and conditional optimal choices are used to interpret the deontic operators.

block_neither	in_A (9) w_1	w_2 (9) in_B
block_B	in_A (0) w_3	w_4 (10) in_B
block_A	in_A (10) w_5	w_6 (0) in_B

Fig. 1. $W = \{w_1, \ldots, w_6\}$, $w_3 \approx w_6 \leq w_1 \approx w_2 \leq w_4 \approx w_5$.

Definition 7 (Truth Condition). *Let* $M = (W, choice, \leq, V)$ *be a utilitarian model and* $w \in W$.

$M, w \models p$ *iff* $w \in V(p)$;

$M, w \models \neg\phi$ *iff it is not the case that* $M, w \models \phi$;

$M, w \models \phi \wedge \psi$ *iff* $M, w \models \phi$ *and* $M, w \models \psi$;

$M, w \models [G]\phi$ *iff* $M, w' \models \phi$ *for all* $w' \in W$ *such that there is* $K \in$ *Choice*(G), $\{w, w'\} \subseteq K$;

$M, w \models \bigcirc_G\phi$ *iff* $K \subseteq \|\phi\|$ *for each* $K \in Optimal_G^s$;

$M, w \models \bigcirc_G(\phi/\psi)$ *iff* $K \subseteq \|\phi\|$ *for each* $K \in Optimal_{G/\psi}^s$.

Here $\|\phi\| = \{w \in W : M, w \models \phi\}$.

Challenge from the Miners Puzzle. The miners scenario is described formally by a utilitarian model as $Miners = (W, Choice, \leq, V)$, where $W = \{w_1, \ldots, w_6\}$, $Choice(G) = \{\{w_1, w_2\}, \{w_3, w_4\}, \{w_5, w_6\}\}$, $Choice(Agent - G) = \{W\}$, $w_3 \approx w_6 \leq w_1 \approx w_2 \leq w_4 \approx w_5$, $V(in\_A) = \{w_1, w_3, w_5\}$, $V(in\_B) = \{w_2, w_4, w_6\}$, $V(block\_A) = \{w_5, w_6\}$, $V(block\_B) = \{w_3, w_4\}$, $V(block\_neither) = \{w_1, w_2\}$. We represent the miners scenario by Fig. 1:

Group G has three choices: *block_neither*, *block_A* and *block_B*. The group of other agents has one dummy choice: choosing W. According to the semantics based on strong lifting, all the three choices are optimal. Therefore $Miners, w_1 \not\models \bigcirc_G(block\_neither)$, which means UDL fails to solve the miners puzzle.

3 Pessimistic Utilitarian Deontic Logic

We now introduce pessimistic utilitarian deontic logic (PUDL) to solve the miners puzzle. We use such name because we adopt pessimistic lifting instead of strong lifting in PUDL. We develop two logics, call them PUDL$_1$ and PUDL$_2$ respectively. PUDL$_1$ is obtained from simply replacing strong lifting in UDL by pessimistic lifting. It turns out that PUDL$_1$ is sufficient to solve the miner puzzle. But it turns out that PUDL$_1$ is bothered by other problems in deontic logic. PUDL$_2$ also solves the miners puzzle, and it is less problematic than PUDL$_1$.

3.1   PUDL₁

Informally, according to the pessimistic lifting *block_neither* is the only optimal choice in the miners scenario. Therefore "we ought to block neither" is true. It can be further proved that both (2) and (3) are true while the deduction from (2)–(4) to (5) is not valid. Therefore PUDL₁ offers a satisfying solution to the miners paradox. We now start to explain these arguments formally.

Definition 8 (Preferences over Sets of Worlds via Pessimistic Lifting).
Let $X, Y \subseteq W$ be two sets of worlds. $X \preceq^p Y$ if and only if there exists $w \in X$, such that for all $w' \in Y$, $w \leq w'$. $X \prec^p Y$ if and only if $X \preceq^p Y$ and $Y \npreceq^p X$.

Proposition 1. $\preceq^p$ *is reflexive and transitive.*[1]

The pessimistic version of dominance ($\preceq_G^p$), conditional dominance ($\preceq_{G/X}^p$), optimal ($Optimal_G^p$) and conditional optimal ($Optimal_{G/X}^p$) are obtained by simply changing $\leq^s$ to $\leq^p$ in their strong version counterpart. We add $\bigcirc_G^{p_1}\phi$ and $\bigcirc_G^{p_1}(\phi/\psi)$ to $\mathfrak{L}_{udl}$ to represent "from the pessimistic perspective, G ought to see to it that ϕ" and "from the pessimistic perspective, G ought to see to it that ϕ in the condition ψ" respectively. The truth condition for $\bigcirc_G^{p_1}\phi$ and $\bigcirc_G^{p_1}(\phi/\psi)$ are defined as follows:

Definition 9 (Truth Conditions). *Let M be a utilitarian model and $w \in W$.*

$$M, w \models \bigcirc_G^{p_1}\phi \quad iff\ K \subseteq ||\phi||\ for\ each\ K \in Optimal_G^p;$$
$$M, w \models \bigcirc_G^{p_1}(\phi/\psi)\ iff\ K \subseteq ||\phi||\ for\ each\ K \in Optimal_{G/\psi}^p.$$

Now we return to the miners scenario. According to the pessimistic semantics, *block_neither* is the only optimal choice. So we can draw the prediction that "we ought to block neither" *i.e.* $Miners, w_1 \models \bigcirc_G^{p_1}(block\_neither)$. Moreover, given the condition of miners being in A, *block_A* becomes the only conditional optimal choice. Hence we have "if the miners are in A, then we ought to block A", *i.e.* $Miners, w_1 \models \bigcirc_G^{p_1}(block\_A/in\_A)$. The case for miners being in B are similar. Although we have both "if the miners are in A, then we ought to block A" and "if the miners are in B, then we ought to block B", by Proposition 2 below we can avoid the prediction that "we ought to block either A or B". Hence no contradiction arise. Therefore PUDL₁ gives right prediction meanwhile avoids contradictions. It therefore offers a viable solution to the miners puzzle.

Proposition 2. $\nvdash \bigcirc_G^{p_1}(p/q) \wedge \bigcirc_G^{p_1}(p/r) \rightarrow \bigcirc_G^{p_1}(p/(q \vee r))$.

3.2   PUDL₂

Although PUDL₁ solves the miners puzzle, it still has some drawbacks. On the intuitive side, PUDL₁ is not free from Ross' paradox. Ross' paradox [20] originates from the logic of imperatives, and is a well-known puzzle in deontic logic which can be concisely stated as follows:

---

[1] Due to the limitation of length, we present all proofs of propositions and theorems in the full version.

Suppose you ought to mail the letter. Since mail the letter logically entails mail the letter or burn it, you ought to mail the letter or burn it.

PUDL$_1$ validates the formula $\bigcirc_G^{p_1} p \rightarrow \bigcirc_G^{p_1}(p \vee q)$, which means it is not free from Ross' paradox.

On the technical side, PUDL$_1$ is difficult to be finitely axiomatized. This is because PUDL$_1$ contains group STIT. Herzig and Schwarzentruber [10] show that if $|Agent| \geq 3$ then group STIT is not finitely axiomatizable.

To fix these flaws, we develop PUDL$_2$. We show that PUDL$_2$ solves the miners puzzle and is free from the Ross's paradox. We further give an axiomatization of PUDL$_2$.

Language. Similar to $\mathcal{L}_{udl}$, the language of the PUDL$_2$ is built from *Agent* and Φ. But for the sake of axiomatization, we simplify group STIT in UDL to individual STIT. In order to define pessimistic lifting syntactically we add the preference and universal modality to our language. For $p, q \in \Phi$ and $i \in Agent$, the language $\mathcal{L}_{pudl}^2$ is given by the following Backus-Naur Form:

$$\phi ::= p \mid \neg\phi \mid \phi \wedge \phi \mid [i]\phi \mid \Box\phi \mid [\leq]\phi \mid [\geq]\phi \mid [<]\phi$$

Intuitively, $[i]\phi$ means "agent i sees to it that ϕ". $\Box\phi$ means "ϕ is true everywhere".[2] $[\leq]\phi$ means "ϕ is weakly preferable" while $[<]\phi$ means "ϕ is strictly preferable". $[\geq]\phi$ means "ϕ is unpreferable". We use $\Diamond$, $\langle\leq\rangle$ and $\langle<\rangle$ as the dual for $\Box$, $[\leq]$ and $[<]$ respectively.

Semantically the preference relation $\leq$ corresponding to $[\leq]$ is required to be a linear pre-order order. That is, $\leq$ is reflexive, transitive and total. The preference relation $<$ corresponding to $[<]$ is required to satisfy the following: $w < v$ iff $w \leq v$ and $v \not\leq w$. Lifting of preference can be defined in $\mathcal{L}_{pudl}^2$ only with these constrains. Liu [17] observes that it is sufficient to define optimistic lifting with $\leq$ being partial order. But to define strong and pessimistic lifting, $\leq$ is required to be linear.

- strong lifting: $\phi \leq^s \psi ::= \Box(\psi \rightarrow [<]\neg\phi)$. Intuitively, $\Box(\psi \rightarrow [<]\neg\phi)$ says that for all ψ-world, there is no ϕ world which is better. In other words, every ψ-world is at least as good as every ϕ-world. That is, the worst ψ-world is at least as good as the best ϕ-world.
- optimistic lifting: $\phi \leq^o \psi ::= \Box(\phi \rightarrow \langle\leq\rangle\psi)$. Intuitively, $\Box(\phi \rightarrow \langle\leq\rangle\psi)$ says that for all ϕ-world w there is a ψ-world which is at least as good as w. In other words, for the best ϕ-world w there is a ψ-world which is at least as good as w. That is, the best ψ-world is at least as good as the best ϕ-world.
- pessimistic lifting: $\phi \leq^p \psi ::= \Box(\psi \rightarrow \langle\geq\rangle\phi)$. Intuitively, $\Box(\psi \rightarrow \langle\geq\rangle\psi)$ says that for all ψ-world w, it is at least as good as some ϕ-world. That is, the worst ψ-world is at least as good as the worst ϕ-world.

---

[2] Bilbiani *et al.* [1] shows that as long as $|Agent| > 1$, then $\Box\phi$ is superfluous because $\Box\phi \leftrightarrow [i][j]\phi$ is valid for $i, j \in Agent$, $i \neq j$.

We use $\phi <^p \psi$ as an abbreviation of $(\phi \leq^p \psi) \wedge \neg(\psi \leq^p \phi)$. Obligation and conditional obligation are defined in our language as follows:

– $\bigcirc_i^{p2} \phi ::= \Diamond[i]\phi \wedge (\neg\phi <^p [i]\phi)$. Intuitively, agent i is obliged to see to it that ϕ iff it is possible for i to see to it that ϕ and seeing to it that ϕ is strictly better than $\neg\phi$ in the pessimistic sense.
– $\bigcirc_i^{p2}(\phi/\psi) ::= \Diamond[i]\phi \wedge ((\neg\phi \wedge \psi) <^p ([i]\phi \wedge \psi))$.

Semantics. The semantics of pessimistic utilitarian deontic logic is based on the pessimistic utilitarian model, which is a non-temporal individual fragment of the STIT model.

Definition 10 (Pessimistic Utilitarian Model). *A pessimistic utilitarian model is a tuple $M = (W, IndChoice, \leq, <, V)$, where W is a nonempty set of possible worlds, IndChoice is an individual choice function, $\leq$ is a reflexive, transitive and connected relation over W, representing the preference of the group Agent. $<$ is a sub-relation of $\leq$ such that for all $w, w' \in W$, $w < w'$ iff $w \leq w'$ and $w' \not\leq w$.*

The individual choice function $IndChoice : Agent \mapsto 2^{2^W}$ must satisfy the following conditions:

(1) for each $i \in Agent$ it holds that $IndChoice(i)$ is a partition of W;
(2) for $Agent = \{1, \ldots, n\}$, for every $x_1 \in IndChoice(1), \ldots, x_n \in IndChoice(n)$, $x_1 \cap \ldots \cap x_n \neq \emptyset$;

Let R_i be the equivalence relation induced by $IndChoice(i)$. Then $(w, w') \in R_i$ iff there is $K \in IndChoice(i)$ such that $\{w, w'\} \subseteq K$. $IndChoice(i) = \{R_i(w) : w \in W\}$, where $R_i(w) = \{w' \in W : (w, w') \in R_i\}$. The truth condition of formulas of $\mathcal{L}_{pudl}^2$ is defined as follows:

Definition 11 (Truth Conditions). *Let M be a pessimistic utilitarian model, $w \in W$.*
$M, w \models_{pudl_2} [i]\phi$ *iff* $M, w' \models \phi$ *for all w' such that $(w, w') \in R_i$;*
$M, w \models_{pudl_2} [\leq]\phi$ *iff* $M, w' \models \phi$ *for all w' such that $w \leq w'$;*
$M, w \models_{pudl_2} [\geq]\phi$ *iff* $M, w' \models \phi$ *for all w' such that $w' \leq w$;*
$M, w \models_{pudl_2} [<]\phi$ *iff* $M, w' \models \phi$ *for all w' such that $w < w'$;*
$M, w \models_{pudl_2} \Box\phi$ *iff* $M, w' \models \phi$ *for all $w' \in W$.*

The axiomatization of $PUDL_2$ is a fragment of the axiomatization of $PUDL^+$ in the next section. The following proposition shows that $PUDL_2$ is free from Ross' paradox.

Proposition 3. $\nvdash_{pudl_2} \bigcirc_i^{p2} p \rightarrow \bigcirc_i^{p2}(p \vee q)$.

Another Analysis to the Miners Puzzle. The miners scenario is described formally by a pessimistic utilitarian model as $Miners^p = (W, IndChoice, \leq, <, V)$, where $W = \{w_1, \ldots, w_6\}$, $IndChoice(i) = \{\{w_1, w_2\}, \{w_3, w_4\}, \{w_5, w_6\}\}$, $IndChoice(j) = \{W\}$ for all $j \neq i$, $w_3 \approx w_6 < w_1 \approx w_2 < w_4 \approx w_5$, $V(in\_A) =$

$\{w_1, w_3, w_5\}, V(in\_B) = \{w_2, w_4, w_6\}$, $V(block\_A) = \{w_5, w_6\}$, $V(block\_B) = \{w_3, w_4\}, V(block\_neither) = \{w_1, w_2\}$.

Agent i is able to see to it that: $block\_neither$, $block\_A$ and $block\_B$. $[i]block\_neither$ is true in worlds w_1 and w_2. According to the pessimistic semantics, $[i]block\_neither$ is strictly better than $\neg block\_neither$. Therefore i ought to block neither. That is, $Miners^p, w_1 \vDash \bigcirc_G^{p2}(block\_neither)$.

Moreover, given the condition of miners being in A, $[i]block\_A$ is better than $\neg block\_A$. Hence we have "if the miners are in A, then i ought to block A". That is, $Miners^p, w_1 \vDash \bigcirc_i^{p2}(block\_A/in\_A)$. The case for miners being in B is similar.

It remains to show that although we have both "if the miners are in A, then we ought to block A" and "if the miners are in B, then we ought to block B", but we cannot logically derive "we ought to block either A or B". This is done by the following proposition.

Proposition 4. $\nvDash_{pudl_2} \bigcirc_i^{p2}(p/q) \wedge \bigcirc_i^{p2}(p/r) \rightarrow \bigcirc_i^{p2}(p/(q \vee r))$

4   Plausiblity Involved Pessimistic Utilitarian Deontic Logic

The interplay of plausibility and preference are heavily discussed in qualitative decision theory [3,8]. Boutilier [2] uses the modality of plausibility and preference to define conditional goals. Langet $al.$ [16] use plausibility and preference to define hidden desire.

In this section we develop plausiblity involved pessimistic utilitarian deontic logic $PUDL_2^+$ to analyze the plausibility involved miners puzzle. The language of $PUDL_2^+$ is $\mathcal{L}_{pudl}^2$ extended with plausibility operators. Formally, for $p, q \in \varPhi$ and $i \in Agent$, the language $\mathcal{L}_{pudl}^{2+}$ is given by the following Backus-Naur Form:

$$\phi ::= p \mid \neg\phi \mid \phi \wedge \phi \mid [i]\phi \mid \Box\phi \mid [\leq]\phi \mid [\geq]\phi \mid [<]\phi \mid [\leq_p]\phi \mid [<_p]\phi$$

Plausibility involved pessimistic lifting is defined as follows:

$$\phi \leq_p^p \psi ::= (\phi \wedge [<_p]\neg\phi) \leq^p (\psi \wedge [<_p]\neg\psi)$$

Intuitively, $\phi \leq_p^p \psi$ says that the most plausible ψ worlds are better than the most plausible ϕ worlds from a pessimistic perspective. We use $\phi <_p^p \psi$ as an abbreviation of $(\phi \leq_p^p \psi) \wedge \neg(\psi \leq_p^p \phi)$. Plausibility involved obligation and conditional obligation are defined in $\mathcal{L}_{pudl}^{2+}$ as follows:

- $\bigodot_i \phi ::= \Diamond[i]\phi \wedge (\neg\phi <_p^p [i]\phi)$.
- $\bigodot_i(\phi/\psi) ::= \Diamond[i]\phi \wedge ((\neg\phi \wedge \psi) <_p^p ([i]\phi \wedge \psi))$.

block_neither	$in\_A_{(9)}$ w_1	w_2 $^{(9)}$ in_B
block_B	$in\_A_{(0)}$ w_3	w_4 $^{(10)}in\_B$
block_A	$in\_A_{(10)}$ w_5	w_6 $^{(0)}$ in_B

Fig. 2. $W = \{w_1, \ldots, w_6\}$, $w_3 \approx w_6 \leq w_1 \approx w_2 \leq w_4 \approx w_5$, $w_2 \approx_p w_4 \approx_p w_6 <_p$ $w_1 \approx_p w_3 \approx_p w_5$.

4.1   Semantics

Definition 12 (Plausibility Involved Pessimistic Utilitarian Model).
A plausibility involved pessimistic utilitarian model is a tuple $(W, IndChoice, \leq, <, \leq_p, <_p, V)$, where $(W, IndChoice, \leq, <, V)$ is a pessimistic utilitarian model. $\leq_p$ is a reflexive, transitive and connected relation over W, representing plausibility. $<_p$ is a sub-relation of $\leq_p$ such that for all $w, w' \in W$, $w <_p w'$ iff $w \leq_p w'$ and $w' \not\leq_p w$.

The truth condition of formulas in $\mathcal{L}^{2+}_{pudl}$ is the same as $\mathcal{L}^2_{pudl}$, except those formulas contains plausibility operators.

Definition 13 (Truth Conditions). *Let M be a pessimistic utilitarian model, $w \in W$.*
$M, w \models_{pudl_2^+} [\leq_p]\phi$ *iff* $M, w' \models \phi$ *for all w' such that $w \leq_p w'$;*
$M, w \models_{pudl_2^+} [<_p]\phi$ *iff* $M, w' \models \phi$ *for all w' such that $w <_p w'$;*

In the generalized miners puzzle. Since it is more plausible that miners are in shaft A, *block_A* is the only optimal choice. Therefore $\odot_i block\_A$ is true. Given the miner are in B, *block_B* is the conditional optimal choice, therefore $\odot_i(block\_B/in\_B)$ (Fig. 2).

4.2   Proof System

The proof system of PUDL$_2^+$ consists the following axioms and the rules of *modus pones*, and *necessitation* for $[1], \ldots, [n], \Box, [\leq], [\geq], [<], [\leq_p]$ and $[<_p]$. The following is the list of axioms:

1. S4.3 for $[\leq]$
    (a) $[\leq](\phi \to \psi) \to ([\leq]\phi \to [\leq]\psi)$
    (b) $[\leq]\phi \to \phi$
    (c) $[\leq]\phi \to [\leq][\leq]\phi$
    (d) $\langle\leq\rangle\phi \wedge \langle\leq\rangle\psi \to (\langle\leq\rangle(\phi \wedge \langle\leq\rangle\psi) \vee \langle\leq\rangle(\phi \wedge \psi) \vee \langle\leq\rangle(\psi \wedge \langle\leq\rangle\phi))$
2. S4.3 for $[\leq_p]$
    (a) $[\leq_p](\phi \to \psi) \to ([\leq_p]\phi \to [\leq_p]\psi)$
    (b) $[\leq_p]\phi \to \phi$
    (c) $[\leq_p]\phi \to [\leq_p][\leq_p]\phi$
    (d) $\langle\leq_p\rangle\phi \wedge \langle\leq_p\rangle\psi \to (\langle\leq_p\rangle(\phi \wedge \langle\leq_p\rangle\psi) \vee \langle\leq_p\rangle(\phi \wedge \psi) \vee \langle\leq_p\rangle(\psi \wedge \langle\leq_p\rangle\phi))$

3. Mutual converse for $[\leq]$ and $[\geq]$:
$$(\phi \rightarrow [\leq]\langle\geq\rangle\phi) \wedge (\phi \rightarrow [\geq]\langle\leq\rangle\phi)$$
4. K for $[<]$:
$$[<](\phi \rightarrow \psi) \rightarrow ([<]\phi \rightarrow [<]\psi)$$
5. K for $[<_p]$:
$$[<_p](\phi \rightarrow \psi) \rightarrow ([<_p]\phi \rightarrow [<_p]\psi)$$
6. Interaction
   (a) $[<]\phi \rightarrow [<][\leq]\phi$
   (b) $[<]\phi \rightarrow [\leq][<]\phi$
   (c) $[\leq]([\leq]\phi \vee \psi) \wedge [<]\psi \rightarrow \phi \vee [\leq]\psi$
   (d) $[<_p]\phi \rightarrow [<_p][\leq_p]\phi$
   (e) $[<_p]\phi \rightarrow [\leq_p][<_p]\phi$
   (f) $[\leq_p]([\leq_p]\phi \vee \psi) \wedge [<_p]\psi \rightarrow \phi \vee [\leq_p]\psi$
7. Inclusion
   (a) $[\leq]\phi \rightarrow [<]\phi$
   (b) $\Box\phi \rightarrow [\leq]\phi$
   (c) $[\leq_p]\phi \rightarrow [<_p]\phi$
   (d) $\Box\phi \rightarrow [\leq_p]\phi$
   (e) $\Box\phi \rightarrow [i]\phi$, for $i \in Agent$
8. S5 for $\Box$ and $[i]$, $i \in Agent$
9. Agent independent: $(\Diamond[1]\phi_1 \wedge \ldots \wedge \Diamond[n]\phi_n) \rightarrow \Diamond([1]\phi_1 \wedge \ldots \wedge [n]\phi_n)$

For every ϕ is derivable from the proof system of $PUDL_2^+$, then we say ϕ is a theorem of $PUDL_2^+$ and write $\vdash \phi$. For a set of formulas $\Gamma \cup \phi$, we say ϕ is derivable form Γ (write $\Gamma \vdash \phi$) if $\vdash \phi$ or there are formulas $\psi_1, \ldots, \psi_n \in \Gamma$ such that $\vdash (\psi_1 \wedge \ldots \wedge \psi_n) \rightarrow \phi$.

Theorem 1 (Soundness and Completeness). $\Gamma \vdash \phi$ *iff* $\Gamma \vDash_{pudl_2^+} \phi$

The proof of soundness is routine. For completeness, we adopt the canonical model method in addition with Bulldozing [21]: we first build a canonical model, then we transform the canonical model via Bulldozing to make a new model to satisfy the requirement of plausibility involved pessimistic utilitarian model. A similar proof can be found in van Benthem *et al.* [25]. We sketch the proof in the appendix.

5   Conclusion and Future Work

In this paper we first develop two new STIT based deontic logics capable of solving the miners puzzle. The key idea is to use pessimistic lifting to lift preference over worlds to preference over sets of worlds. To deal with the more general miners scenario we add modal operators representing plausibility. A complete axiomatization is given. Concerning future works, the most natural extension is to replace non-temporal STIT by temporal STIT logic [18].

Acknowledgment. We are grateful to the three reviewers of EUMAS 2014 for their valuable comments.

Appendix

Proposition 5. *If every consistent Γ is satisfiable on some model M, then $\Gamma \vDash_{pudl_2^+} \phi$ implies $\Gamma \vdash \phi$.*

Definition 14 (Maximal Consistent Set (MCS)). *A set of formulas Γ is maximally consistent if Γ is consistent and any proper extension of Γ is not consistent.*

For every consistent Γ, Γ can be extended to a MCS Γ^+, we then construct a canonical model for Γ^+.

Definition 15 (Canonical Model). *The canonical model $\mathfrak{M}^0$ for Γ^+ is a relational structure $(W^0, \{R_i^0\}_{i \in Agent}, \leq^0 <^0, \leq_p^0, <_p^0, V^0)$ where:*

- $W^0 = \{w | w$ *is a MCS and for all* $\Box\phi \in \Gamma^+, \phi \in w\}$;
- *For every $i \in Agent$, R_i^0 is a binary relation on W^0 defined by $wR_i^0 v$ iff for all ϕ, $[i]\phi \in w$ implies $\phi \in v$;*
- $\leq^0$ *is a binary relation on W^0 defined by $w \leq^0 v$ iff for all ϕ, $[\leq]\phi \in w$ implies $\phi \in v$;*
- $<^0$ *is a binary relation on W^0 defined by $w <^0 v$ iff for all ϕ, $[<]\phi \in w$ implies $\phi \in v$;*
- $\leq_p^0$ *is a binary relation on W^0 defined by $w \leq_p^0 v$ iff for all ϕ, $[\leq_p]\phi \in w$ implies $\phi \in v$;*
- $<_p^0$ *is a binary relation on W^0 defined by $w <_p^0 v$ iff for all ϕ, $[<_p]\phi \in w$ implies $\phi \in v$;*
- V^0 *is the valuation defined by $V^0(p) = \{w \in W^0 \mid p \in w\}$.*

Proposition 6. $\mathfrak{M}^0, \Gamma^+ \vDash_{pudl_2^+} \Gamma$.

Proposition 7. $\mathfrak{M}^0$ *has the following properties:*

(1) Both $\leq^0$ and $\leq_p^0$ are reflexive, transitive and connected relations.
(2) If $w \leq^0 v$ and $v \not\leq^0 w$ then $w <^0 v$.
(3) If $w \leq_p^0 v$ and $v \not\leq_p^0 w$ then $w <_p^0 v$.
(4) If $w <^0 v$ then $w \leq^0 v$.
(5) If $w <_p^0 v$ then $w \leq_p^0 v$.
(6) R_i^0 is an equivalence relation for each $i \in Agent$.
(7) For every $w \in W^0$, $R_1^0(w) \cap \ldots \cap R_n^0(w) \neq \emptyset$.

Deleting $<$-cluster. Note that converse of item (2) of Proposition 7 is not true because there may be two worlds w and v in W^0 such that $w <^0 v$ and $v <^0 w$. In this case we say that w and v are in the same $<^0$-clusters. To deal with this we follow Benthem [25] to use the technique called Bulldozing [21] to transform $\mathfrak{M}^0$ to a new model $\mathfrak{M}^1$ such that there is no $<$-cluster in $\mathfrak{M}^1$.

Definition 16 (Cluster). *A $<$-cluster is an inclusion-maximal set of worlds C such that $w < v$ for all worlds $w, v \in C$. Similarly for $\leq_p$-cluster.*

Let $\mathfrak{M}^1 = (W^1, \{R_i^1\}_{i \in Agent}, \leq^1, <^1, \leq_p^1, <_p^1, V^1)$ where:

- $W^1 = W^{0-} \cup \bigcup_{i \in I} C_i'$, here I is a set index of all $<$-clusters of W^0, $W^{0-} = W^0 - \bigcup_{i \in I} C_i$, $C_i' = C_i \times \mathbb{Z}$, $\mathbb{Z}$ is the set of natural numbers.
- R_i^1 is defined by wR_i^1v iff $\beta(w)R_i^0\beta(v)$, for every $i \in Agent$.
- $<^1$ is defined as follows: For each C_i, choose an arbitrary linear order $<^{1,i}$. Define a map $\beta : W^1 \to W^0$ by $\beta(x) = x$ if $x \in W^{0-}$ and $\beta(x) = w$ if x is a pair (w, n) for some world w and integer n. We define $<^1$ via the following cases:
  - Case 1: x or y is in W^{0-}. In this case we let $x <^1 y$ iff $\beta(x) <^0 \beta(y)$.
  - Case 2: $x \in C_i'$ and $y \in C_j'$, $i \neq j$. In this case we let $x <^1 y$ iff $\beta(x) <^0 \beta(y)$.
  - Case 3: $x \in C_i'$ and $y \in C_i'$. In this case, $x = (w, m)$ and $y = (v, n)$. There are two sub-cases:
    * Case 3.1: If $m \neq n$, we use the natural ordering on $\mathbb{Z}$: $(w, m) <^1 (v, n)$ iff $m < n$.
    * Case 3.2: If $m = n$, we use the linear ordering $<^{1,i}$: $(w, m) <^1 (v, m)$ iff $w <^{1,i} v$.
- $\leq^1$ is defined via the following cases:
  - Case 1: x or y is in W^{0-}. In this case we let $x \leq^1 y$ iff $\beta(x) \leq^0 \beta(y)$.
  - Case 2: Otherwise, we take the reflexive closure of $<^1$: $x \leq^1 y$ iff $x <^1 y$ or $x = y$.
- $\leq_p^1$ is defined by $w \leq_p^1 v$ iff $\beta(w) \leq_p^0 \beta(v)$.
- $<_p^1$ is defined by $w <_p^1 v$ iff $\beta(w) <_p^0 \beta(v)$.
- V^1 is defined by $w \in V^1(p)$ iff $\beta(w) \in V^0(p)$.

Definition 17 (Bounded Morphism). *A mapping $f : M = (W, \{R_i\}_{i \in Agent}, \leq, <, \leq_p, <_p, V) \to M' = (W, \{R_i'\}_{i \in Agent}, \leq', <', \leq_p', <_p', V')$ is a bounded morphism if it satisfies the following conditions:*

- *w and $f(w)$ satisfy the same proposition letters.*
- *if $w \leq v$ then $f(w) \leq' f(v)$. And similarly for $<, \leq_p, <_p, R_i$.*
- *if $f(w) \leq' v'$ then there exists v such that $w \leq v$ and $f(v) = v'$. And similarly for $<', \leq_p', <_p', R_i$.*

Lemma 1. *If f is a bounded morphism from M to M', then for all ϕ, for all $w \in M$, $M, w \vDash_{pudl_2^+} \phi$ iff $M', f(w) \vDash_{pudl_2^+} \phi$.*

Proposition 8. *For every consistent set Φ, if $\mathfrak{M}^0, \Gamma \vDash_{pudl_2^+} \Phi$, then there exists Γ' such that $\mathfrak{M}^1, \Gamma' \vDash_{pudl_2^+} \Phi$.*

Proposition 9. *$\mathfrak{M}^1$ has the following properties:*

(1) Both $\leq^1$ and $\leq_p^1$ are reflexive, transitive and connected relations.
(2) $w <^1 v$ iff $w \leq^1 v$ and $v \not\leq^1 w$
(3) If $w \leq_p^1 v$ and $v \not\leq_p^1 w$ then $w <_p^1 v$.
(4) If $w <_p^1 v$ then $w \leq_p^1 v$.
(5) R_i^1 is an equivalence relation for each $i \in Agent$.
(6) For every $w \in W^1$, $R_1^1(w) \cap \ldots \cap R_n^1(w) \neq \emptyset$.

Deleting $<_p$-cluster. Now we use Bulldozing again to delete $<_G$clusters.
  Let $\mathfrak{M}^2 = (W^2, \{R_i^2\}_{i \in Agent}, \leq^2, <^2, \leq_p^2, <_p^2, V^2)$ where:

- $W^2 = W^{1-} \cup \bigcup_{i \in I} C_i'$, here I is a set index of all $<_G$-clusters of W^1, $W^{1-} = W^1 - \bigcup_{i \in I} C_i$, $C_i' = C_i \times \mathbb{Z}$, $\mathbb{Z}$ is the set of natural numbers.
- R_i^2 is defined by $wR_i^2 v$ iff $\sigma(w)R_i^1\sigma(v)$, for every $i \in Agent$.
- $<_p^2$ is defined as follows: For each C_i, choose an arbitrary linear order $<_p^{2,i}$. Define a map $\sigma : W^2 \to W^1$ by $\sigma(x) = x$ if $x \in W^{1-}$ and $\sigma(x) = w$ if x is a pair (w, n) for some world w and integer n. We define $<_p^2$ via the following cases:
  - Case 1: x or y is in W^{1-}. In this case we let $x <_p^2 y$ iff $\sigma(x) <_p^1 \sigma(y)$.
  - Case 2: $x \in C_i$ and $y \in C_j$, $i \neq j$. In this case we let $x <_p^3 y$ iff $\sigma(x) <_p^2 \sigma(y)$.
  - Case 3: $x \in C_i$ and $y \in C_i$. In this case , $x = (w, m)$ and $y = (v, n)$. There are two sub-cases:
    * Case 3.1: If $m \neq n$, we use the natural ordering on $\mathbb{Z}$: $(w, m) <_p^2 (v, n)$ iff $m < n$.
    * Case 3.2: If $m = n$, we use the linear ordering $<_p^{2,i}$: $(w, m) <_p^2 (v, m)$ iff $w <_p^{2,i} v$.
- $\leq_p^2$ is defined via the following cases:
  - Case 1: x or y is in W^{1-}. In this case we let $x \leq_p^2 y$ iff $\sigma(x) \leq_p^1 \sigma(y)$.
  - Case 2: Otherwise, we take the reflexive closure of $<_p^2$: $x \leq_p^2 y$ iff $x <_p^2 y$ or $x = y$.
- $\leq^2$ is defined by $w \leq^2 v$ iff $\sigma(w) \leq^1 \sigma(v)$.
- $<^2$ is defined by $w <^2 v$ iff $\sigma(w) <^1 \sigma(v)$.
- V^2 is defined by $w \in V^2(p)$ iff $\sigma(w) \in V^1(p)$.

Proposition 10. *For every consistent set Φ, if $\mathfrak{M}^1, \Gamma \vDash_{pudl_2^+} \Phi$, then there exists Γ' such that $\mathfrak{M}^2, \Gamma' \vDash_{pudl_2^+} \Phi$.*

Proposition 11. $\mathfrak{M}^2$ *has the following properties:*

(1) Both $\leq^2$ and $\leq_p^2$ are reflexive, transitive and connected relations.
(2) $w <^2 v$ iff $w \leq^2 v$ and $v \not\leq^2 w$
(3) $w <_p^2 v$ iff $w \leq_p^2 v$ and $v \not\leq_p^2 w$
(4) R_i^2 is an equivalence relation for each $i \in Agent$.
(5) For every $w \in W^2$, $R_1^2(w) \cap \ldots \cap R_n^2(w) \neq \emptyset$.

References

1. Balbiani, P., Herzig, A., Troquard, N.: Alternative axiomatics and complexity of deliberative STIT theories. J. Philos. Log. **37**(4), 387–406 (2008)
2. Boutilier, C.: Toward a logic for qualitative decision theory. In: Doyle, J., Sandewall, E., Torasso, P. (eds.) Proceedings of the 4th International Conference on Principles of Knowledge Representation and Reasoning, Bonn, Germany, pp. 75–86. Morgan Kaufmann (1994)
3. Brafman, R., Tennenholtz, M.: Modeling agents as qualitative decision makers. Artif. Intell. **94**(1–2), 217–268 (1997)

4. Cariani, F., Kaufmann, M., Kaufmann, S.: Deliberative modality under epistemic uncertainty. Linguist. Philos. **36**(3), 225–259 (2013)
5. Carr, J.: Deontic modals without decision theory. Proceedings of Sinn und Bedeutung **17**, 167–182 (2012)
6. Castro, P., Maibaum, T.S.E.: Deontic action logic, atomic boolean algebras and fault-tolerance. J. Appl. Log. **7**, 441–466 (2009)
7. Charlow, N.: What we know and what to do. Synthese **190**(12), 2291–2323 (2013)
8. Doyle, J., Thomason, R.: Background to qualitative decision theory. AI Mag. **20**(2), 55–68 (1999)
9. Gabbay, D., Robaldo, L., Sun, X., van der Torre, L., Baniasadi, Z.: Toward a linguistic interpretation of deontic paradoxes. In: Cariani, F., Grossi, D., Meheus, J., Parent, X. (eds.) DEON 2014. LNCS, vol. 8554, pp. 108–123. Springer, Heidelberg (2014)
10. Herzig, A., Schwarzentruber, F.: Properties of logics of individual and group agency. In: Areces, C., Goldblatt, R. (eds.) Advances in Modal Logic 7, papers from the seventh conference on "Advances in Modal Logic," held in Nancy, France, 9–12 September 2008, pp. 133–149. College Publications (2008)
11. Horty, J.: Agency and Deontic Logic. Oxford University Press, New York (2001)
12. Kolodny, N., MacFarlane, J.: Ifs and oughts. J. Philos. **107**(3), 115–143 (2010)
13. Kooi, B., Tamminga, A.: Moral conflicts between groups of agents. J. Philos. Log. **37**, 1–21 (2008)
14. Kratzer, A.: The notional category of modality. In: Eikmeyer, H.J., Rieser, H. (eds.) Words, Worlds, and Contexts: New Approaches in World Semantics. de Gruyter, Berlin (1981)
15. Lang, J., van der Torre, L.: From belief change to preference change. In: Ghallab, M., Spyropoulos, C.D., Fakotakis, N., Avouris, N. (eds.) Proceedings of the 2008 Conference on ECAI 2008: 18th European Conference on Artificial Intelligence, pp. 351–355. IOS Press, Amsterdam (2008)
16. Lang, J., van der Torre, L., Weydert, E.: Hidden uncertainty in the logical representation of desires. In: Proceedings of IJCAI2003, pp. 685–690 (2003)
17. Liu, F.: Reasoning About Preference Dynamics. Springer, Dordrecht (2011)
18. Lorini, E.: Temporal stit logic and its application to normative reasoning. J. Appl. Non-class. Log. **23**(4), 372–399 (2013)
19. Meyer, J.J.: A different approach to deontic logic: deontic logic viewed as a variant of dynamic logic. Notre Dame J. Form. Log. **29**, 109–136 (1988)
20. Ross, A.: Imperatives and logic. Theoria **7**, 53–71 (1941)
21. Segerberg, K.: An Essay in Classical Modal Logic. Filosofiska Studier, vol. 13. Filosofiska foreningen och Filosofiska institutionen vid Uppsala universitet, Uppsala (1971)
22. Segerberg, K.: A deontic logic of action. Stud. Log. **41**, 269–282 (1982)
23. Sun, X.: Conditional ought, a game theoretical perspective. In: van Ditmarsch, H., Lang, J., Ju, S. (eds.) LORI 2011. LNCS, vol. 6953, pp. 356–369. Springer, Heidelberg (2011)
24. Trypuz, R., Kulicki, P.: On deontic action logics based on boolean algebra. J. Log. Comput. (2014, forthcoming)
25. van Benthem, J., Girard, P., Roy, O.: Evernthing else being equal: a modal logic approach for ceteris paribus preference. J. Philos. Log. **38**(1), 83–125 (2009)
26. van der Meyden, R.: The dynamic logic of permission. J. Log. Comput. **6**, 465–479 (1996)
27. von Wright, G.: Deontic logic. Mind **60**, 1–15 (1951)
28. Willer, M.: A remark on iffy oughts. J. Philos. **109**(7), 449461 (2012)

Arbitrary Announcements on Topological Subset Spaces

Hans van Ditmarsch, Sophia Knight, and Aybüke Özgün$^{(\boxtimes)}$

LORIA, CNRS - Université de Lorraine, Nancy, France
{hans.van-ditmarsch,sophia.knight,aybuke.ozgun}@loria.fr

Abstract. Subset space semantics for public announcement logic in the spirit of the effort modality have been proposed by Wang and Ågotnes [18] and by Bjorndahl [6]. They propose to model the public announcement modality by shrinking the epistemic range with respect to which a postcondition of the announcement is evaluated, instead of by restricting the model to the set of worlds satisfying the announcement. Thus we get an "elegant, model-internal mechanism for interpreting public announcements" [6, p. 12]. In this work, we extend Bjorndahl's logic PAL_{int} of public announcement, which is modelled on topological spaces using subset space semantics and adding the interior operator, with an arbitrary announcement modality, and we provide topological subset space semantics for the corresponding arbitrary announcement logic $APAL_{int}$, and demonstrate completeness of the logic by proving that it is equal in expressivity to the logic without arbitrary announcements, employing techniques from [2, 13].

1 Introduction

In [7], Dabrowski et al. introduce a bimodal modal logic called *subset space logic* (SSL) in order to capture the notions of knowledge and effort (to obtain knowledge). It has a knowledge modality K and an effort modality $\Box$. The authors proposed a 'topological semantics' called subset space semantics for this logic. This semantics is not necessarily based on topological spaces, however, topological reasoning provides the intuition behind the semantics and constitutes an important instance; [1] treats the more purely topological case. In the setting of [7], unlike the standard evaluation of K on Kripke models, both modal operators K and $\Box$ are evaluated not only with respect to a state but also with respect to a *neighbourhood* of a given possible world, i.e., with respect to pairs of the form (x, U), where the evaluation state x represents *the real/actual world* and the neighbourhood U serves as a *truthful observation*: we can think of the neighbourhood U as what an agent can observe from where she stands, that is, a set of states that the agent thinks the actual world may belong to. Hence, by following the idea of 'obtaining knowledge by means of an observation,' they propose to evaluate K 'locally' in a given neighbourhood of a subset space. Moreover, the effort is interpreted as *open-set-shrinking* on subset spaces where more effort corresponds to a smaller neigbourhood, thus, to a better approximation of where the real world is [1].

© Springer International Publishing Switzerland 2015
N. Bulling (Ed.): EUMAS 2014, LNAI 8953, pp. 252–266, 2015.
DOI: 10.1007/978-3-319-17130-2_17

More formally, the language used by Dabrowski et al. [7] is

$$\varphi ::= p \mid \neg\varphi \mid \varphi \wedge \varphi \mid K\varphi \mid \Box\varphi.$$

A *subset space* is a pair consisting of a non-empty set called the *domain* and a certain collection of subsets of the domain. These subsets are called *open* sets and a *neighbourhood of a state* x is any open set including x. The crucial effort operator $\Box$ is interpreted as

> *Pair* (x, U) *satisfies* $\Box\varphi$ *iff for all* V *containing* x *and contained in* U, (x, V) *satisfies* φ,

where U and V are neighbourhoods of x. On the other hand, the knowledge formula $K\varphi$ is interpreted 'globally' within the corresponding neighbourhood U in a standard way as truth of φ at all points in U (this is why knowledge in SSL is of **S5**-character). However, restriction to a particular neighbourhood makes the evaluation of $K\varphi$ 'local' within the model in the sense that only the states in a given neighbourhood U need to be checked for the truth of φ. More precisely,

> *Pair* (x, U) *satisfies* $K\varphi$ *iff for all* y *in* U, (y, U) *satisfies* φ.

A typical formula schema of this logic appearing in the SSL-literature (see, e.g., [1,6]) is

$$\varphi \to \Diamond K\varphi,$$

which says that if φ is true, then after some effort the agent comes to know that it is true. This formula is of particular importance since it links SSL to the notion of 'knowability/learnability' (more details below). Besides its epistemic importance, if we evaluate this formula on a topological space and if φ is not a modal formula, the schema is true on the topological model iff the truth set of φ is an open set [1,7]. Hence, SSL can be and is used to reason about elementary topology.

In [2], Balbiani et al. introduce a logic to quantify over announcements in the setting of epistemic logic. This *arbitrary public announcement logic* has (in the single agent version) the language

$$\varphi ::= p \mid \neg\varphi \mid \varphi \wedge \varphi \mid K\varphi \mid [\varphi]\varphi \mid \blacksquare\varphi$$

The construct $[\varphi]\psi$ stands for 'after public announcement of φ, ψ (is true)'. Throughout this work, we assume that announcements convey truthful, hard information. In a given model, the effect of the announcement of a formula in general is a model restriction to the subset satisfying the formula: $[\varphi]\psi$ is true iff after restriction of the model to the states satisfying φ, ψ is true in the restricted model. In this case the modality $\blacksquare$ quantifies over announcements and $\blacksquare\varphi$ means 'after any announcement, φ (is true)'. Its semantics is therefore

> *State* x *satisfies* $\blacksquare\varphi$ *iff for all announcements* ψ *true at* x *the model restriction to* ψ *satisfies* φ *at* x,

where the announcement ψ above does not contain $\blacksquare$.

A typical formula schema in this logic is again

$$\varphi \to \blacklozenge K\varphi,$$

which says that if φ is true, then there is an announcement after which the agent comes to know that it is true. This can be seen as an interpretation of 'knowability' à la Fitch [9,14] where 'knowable' is interpreted as 'known after an announcement' [2,14]. Clearly, the modality 'restriction to any submodel' (■) is very much related in motivation to the modality 'restriction to any smaller neighbourhood' (□)' and this has indeed become the topic of subsequent works.

The effort modality has a dynamic nature as does the arbitrary announcement modality. As mentioned, it is evaluated on subset spaces by shrinking the initial open neighbourhood where *open-set-shrinking* represents receiving new information by means of *any effort* such as measurement, observation, computation, approximation etc. [1,4,7,16]. More importantly for this work, the information intake represented by the effort modality is not necessarily via public announcements, however, it implicitly captures any kind of information gain including public announcements. Therefore, given such a dynamic operator on subset spaces, and extensive research on public announcement logics and the intuitive connection between the two, it is natural to investigate how to model public announcements on subset spaces and how to link the two in a formal setting. Proposals for the interpretation of public announcement on subset spaces as 'model restriction' include [3–5]. They propose to model public announcements on subset spaces by deleting the states and/or the neighbourhoods falsifying the announcement. However, this method is obviously not in the spirit of the effort modality in the sense that efforts do not lead to a global model change but lead to a 'local' neighbourhood shrinking. Hence, it is natural to search for an 'open-set-shrinking-like' interpretation of public announcements on subset spaces. To the best of our knowledge, Wang and Ågotnes [18] were the first to propose semantics for public announcements on subset spaces in the spirit of the effort modality, although this is not necessarily on topological spaces. Bjorndahl [6] then proposed a revised version of the [18] semantics. Bjorndahl's models are based on topological spaces and his topological usage of operators such as the interior operator $int(\varphi)$ we find quite natural and intuitive. This operation $int(\varphi)$ means 'φ is true and can be announced' (this will become clear below) and is therefore definable as $\langle \varphi \rangle \top$. Subject to this identity, Bjorndahl's language becomes

$$\varphi ::= p \mid \neg\varphi \mid \varphi \wedge \varphi \mid K\varphi \mid [\varphi]\varphi$$

where he mentions the arbitrary announcement as a future opportunity for research.

Our contribution to this emerging corpus of work is that we have extended Bjorndahl's proposal with such an arbitrary announcement modality so that we obtain (the language of [2])

$$\varphi ::= p \mid \neg\varphi \mid \varphi \wedge \varphi \mid K\varphi \mid [\varphi]\varphi \mid \blacksquare\varphi$$

and provide semantics for this language based on subset spaces rather than relational models, where we think that we have come close to the original [7] motivation for the effort modality. We then show completeness for this logic, by way of extending Bjorndahl's axiomatization with axioms and rules, and where the axioms are equivalences. The expressivity of the resulting logic is the same as that of the logic without the ■.

In Sect. 2 we review Bjorndahl's (topological) subset space logic with public announcements. This is the logical basis for our work. Section 3 contains our own contributions: we extend this logic with the effort-like arbitrary announcement modality and prove some of its properties, such as the **S4** character of this modality, and we demonstrate that this logic is complete and is not more expressive than the logic without the arbitrary announcement modality. Section 5 contains the conclusions and suggestions for further research.

2 Bjorndahl's Subset Space Logic with Public Announcements

In this section, we start by introducing the basic topological concepts that will be used throughout this paper. For a more detailed discussion of general topology we refer the reader to [8]. We then present Bjorndahl's epistemic and public announcement logics [6], denoted by EL_{int} and PAL_{int} respectively, and the corresponding topological-based subset space semantics.

Definition 1 (Structures). *A* topological space *is a pair* (X, τ)*, where* X *is a non-empty set and* τ *is a family of subsets of* X *containing* X *and* $\emptyset$ *and closed under finite intersections and arbitrary unions. The set* X *is called the* space. *The subsets of* X *belonging to* τ *are called* open sets *(or* opens*) in the space; the family* τ *of open subsets of* X *is called a* topology *on* X*. We denote the opens of a topological space by capital letters such as* U, V, W *etc. Complements of opens are called* closed sets*. An open set containing* $x \in X$ *is called an* (open) neighbourhood *of* x*. The* interior $Int(A)$ *of a set* $A \subseteq X$ *is the largest open set contained in* A*.*[1] *A* topological model *(or* topo-model*)* $\mathcal{X} = (X, \tau, \nu)$ *is a topological space endowed with a valuation map* $\nu : \text{Prop} \to \mathcal{P}(X)$*.*

We denote an *epistemic scenario of a topological space* by (x, U) where $x \in U \in \tau$ and let $ES(\mathcal{X}) = \{(x, U) \mid x \in U \in \tau\}$, the set of epistemic scenarios on $\mathcal{X}$. It is important to emphasize that, in [6], Bjorndahl works with an extension of subset space semantics first introduced in [7] and summarized in Sect. 1, however, he restricts his models to topological spaces rather than all subset spaces.

Syntax. In [6], Bjorndahl considers the language $\mathcal{L}_{PAL_{int}}$ defined by the following grammar

$$\varphi ::= p \mid \neg\varphi \mid \varphi \wedge \varphi \mid K\varphi \mid int(\varphi) \mid [\varphi]\varphi$$

where $p \in \text{Prop}$. Without the $[\varphi]$ operator, we get the language $\mathcal{L}_{EL_{int}}$. We employ the usual abbreviations for propositional operators and dual modalities, where in particular $\langle\varphi\rangle\psi$ is defined as $\neg[\varphi]\neg\psi$.

---

[1] Equivalently, for any $A \subseteq X$, $Int(A) = \bigcup\{U \in \tau : U \subseteq A\}$.

Definition 2 (Semantics for $\mathcal{L}_{PAL_{int}}$). *Given a topo-model $\mathcal{X} = (X, \tau, \nu)$ and an epistemic scenario (x, U) on $\mathcal{X}$, the semantics for the language $\mathcal{L}_{PAL_{int}}$ is defined recursively as follows:*

$$
\begin{aligned}
\mathcal{X}, (x, U) &\models p && \text{iff } x \in \nu(p) \\
\mathcal{X}, (x, U) &\models \neg\varphi && \text{iff } \mathcal{X}, (x, U) \not\models \varphi \\
\mathcal{X}, (x, U) &\models \varphi \wedge \psi && \text{iff } \mathcal{X}, (x, U) \models \varphi \text{ and } \mathcal{X}, (x, U) \models \psi \\
\mathcal{X}, (x, U) &\models K\varphi && \text{iff } (\forall y \in U)(\mathcal{X}, (y, U) \models \varphi) \\
\mathcal{X}, (x, U) &\models int(\varphi) && \text{iff } x \in Int[\![\varphi]\!]^U \\
\mathcal{X}, (x, U) &\models [\varphi]\psi && \text{iff } \mathcal{X}, (x, U) \models int(\varphi) \text{ implies } \mathcal{X}, (x, Int[\![\varphi]\!]^U) \models \psi
\end{aligned}
$$

where $p \in \text{Prop}$, and $[\![\varphi]\!]^U = \{y \in U \mid \mathcal{X}, (y, U) \models \varphi\}$.

We say that a formula φ is *valid in a topo-model* $\mathcal{X} = (X, \tau, \nu)$, denoted $\mathcal{X} \models \varphi$, iff $\mathcal{X}, (x, U) \models \varphi$ for all $(x, U) \in ES(\mathcal{X})$, and that φ is *valid*, denoted $\models \varphi$, iff for all topo-models $\mathcal{X}$: $\mathcal{X} \models \varphi$. Soundness and completeness with respect to the above semantics are defined as usual.

Let us now have a closer look at the public announcement semantics from Definition 2. As given in the semantic clause for $[\varphi]\psi$, the precondition of an announcement is assumed to be $int(\varphi)$ which is a stronger requirement for being able to announce φ than φ simply being true at the state/epistemic scenario in question (see [6] for differences between these two requirements). Moreover, unlike the standard approach where the announcement of a formula is interpreted as a model restriction that leads to a 'global' change of the initial model, the effect of an announcement of φ in the setting of [6] is 'local': it is a shrinkage of the initial evaluation neighbourhood U to $Int[\![\varphi]\!]^U$. Therefore, the effect of a public announcement is defined in such a way that it can be seen as information gain via a very *specific kind of effort*.

Theorem 3 ([6]). *The* epistemic logic EL_{int} *is axiomatized completely by the axioms and rules of propositional logic,* **S4** *for int,* **KD45** *for the knowledge modality and $K\varphi \rightarrow int(\varphi)$. The logic of public announcements PAL_{int} is axiomatized completely by the axioms of EL_{int} and the reduction axioms given in Proposition 5 (below).*

The system **KD45** for knowledge together with the axiom $K\varphi \rightarrow int(\varphi)$ yield $K\varphi \rightarrow \varphi$. Thus, the modality K in the logic EL_{int} unsurprisingly is of **S5**-type just like the one in SSL. We continue by reviewing some properties of these logics.

Proposition 4. *For any $\varphi, \chi, \psi \in \mathcal{L}_{PAL_{int}}$,*

1. $\models [\varphi]\psi \leftrightarrow [int(\varphi)]\psi$
2. $\models [\varphi][\psi]\chi \leftrightarrow [int(\varphi)][int(\psi)]\chi \leftrightarrow [int(\varphi) \wedge [int(\varphi)]int(\psi)]\chi \leftrightarrow [int(\varphi) \wedge [\varphi]int(\psi)]\chi$

Moreover, for any topo-model $\mathcal{X} = (X, \tau, \nu)$ and $(x, U) \in ES(\mathcal{X})$,

4. $[\![int(\varphi)]\!]^U = Int[\![\varphi]\!]^U$.
5. $[\![int(\psi) \wedge [\psi]int(\chi)]\!]^U = Int[\![\chi]\!]^{Int[\![\psi]\!]^U}$

Proof. The proofs have been removed from this presentation and can be found in [6].

Proposition 4.1 shows that there is no difference between announcing φ and $int(\varphi)$. In other words, $int(\varphi)$ constitutes the *core, essential* part of the information conveyed by the announcement of φ, that is, since $[\![int(\varphi)]\!]^U = Int[\![\varphi]\!]^U \subseteq [\![\varphi]\!]^U$ for any epistemic scenario (x, U), $Int[\![\varphi]\!]^U$ forms the set which represents exactly what an agent can learn from the announcement of φ.

We recall that in public announcement logic we have $[\varphi][\psi]\chi \leftrightarrow [\varphi \wedge [\varphi]\psi]\chi$. Hence, Proposition 4.2 shows that we have a similar principle of iterative announcements in PAL_{int}.

Proposition 5 ([6]). *The following $\mathcal{L}_{PAL_{int}}$ schemas are validities.*

1. $[\varphi]int(\psi) \leftrightarrow (int(\varphi) \rightarrow int([\varphi]\psi))$ 4. $[\varphi](\psi \wedge \chi) \leftrightarrow [\varphi]\psi \wedge [\varphi]\chi$
2. $[\varphi]p \leftrightarrow (int(\varphi) \rightarrow p)$ 5. $[\varphi]K\psi \leftrightarrow (int(\varphi) \rightarrow K[\varphi]\psi)$
3. $[\varphi]\neg\psi \leftrightarrow (int(\varphi) \rightarrow \neg[\varphi]\psi)$ 6. $[\varphi][\psi]\chi \leftrightarrow [\langle\varphi\rangle int(\psi)]\chi$

Proof. The first four are straightforward to prove and the proof of (5) is given in [6]. We only prove (6). It has been proven in [6] that $[\varphi][\psi]\chi \leftrightarrow [int(\varphi) \wedge [\varphi]int(\psi)]\chi$ is valid. Hence, here we only prove that $(int(\varphi) \wedge [\varphi]int(\psi)) \leftrightarrow \langle\varphi\rangle int(\psi)$ is valid.

Let $\mathcal{X} = (X, \tau, \nu)$ be a topo-model and (x, U) be an epistemic scenario in $\mathcal{X}$. Then:

$(x, U) \models int(\varphi) \wedge [\varphi]int(\psi)$

iff $x \in Int[\![\varphi]\!]^U$ and (if $x \in Int[\![\varphi]\!]^U$ then $(x, Int[\![\varphi]\!]^U) \models int(\psi)$)

iff $x \in Int[\![\varphi]\!]^U$ and $(x, Int[\![\varphi]\!]^U) \models int(\psi)$ (by tautology $p \wedge (p \rightarrow q) \leftrightarrow (p \wedge q)$)

iff $(x, U) \models \langle\varphi\rangle int(\psi)$

Therefore, by Proposition 4.2, we have that $[\varphi][\psi]\chi \leftrightarrow [\langle\varphi\rangle int(\psi)]\chi$. □

Note that the axiomatization of PAL_{int} in this paper is slightly different then the one in [6]. While the formula $[\varphi]\bot \leftrightarrow \neg int(\varphi)$, stating that $int(\varphi)$ can be defined in terms of the public announcement modality, is not an axiom but a derivable formula in PAL_{int} in our version, we also have a reduction rule for the formulas of the form $[\varphi]int(\psi)$.

3 The Logic $APAL_{int}$

We now provide topological subset space semantics for the arbitrary announcement operator $\blacksquare\varphi$. We do so by modifying the public announcement semantics proposed in [6] in a natural way, as a generalization of public announcements. We thus aim to give a semantics for $\blacksquare$ which does not represent global model change, as in [2], but interprets the arbitrary announcement operator $\blacksquare$ in the same initial model, *locally*, in a given *epistemic scenario* in a similar way to the effort modality modelled on subset spaces. By doing so, we link it to the *effort modality* $\Box\varphi$ of [7].

3.1 Syntax and Semantics

Syntax. We consider the language $\mathcal{L}_{APAL_{int}}$ obtained by extending $\mathcal{L}_{PAL_{int}}$ with the arbitrary announcement modality $\blacksquare$. In other words, $\mathcal{L}_{APAL_{int}}$ is defined by the following grammar

$$\varphi ::= p \mid \neg\varphi \mid \varphi \wedge \varphi \mid K\varphi \mid int(\varphi) \mid [\varphi]\varphi \mid \blacksquare\varphi$$

where $p \in \text{Prop}$. The formulas in $\mathcal{L}_{PAL_{int}}$ are called $\blacksquare$-free formulas.

Recall that the arbitrary announcement modality $\blacksquare\varphi$ is read 'after any announcement, φ is true'. Its semantics is as follows. For the semantics of the other operators, we refer to Definition 2.

Definition 6 (Semantics of arbitrary announcement). *Given a topo-model* $\mathcal{X} = (X, \tau, \nu)$ *and an epistemic scenario* (x, U) *on* $\mathcal{X}$, *the semantic clause for the arbitrary announcement modality* $\blacksquare$ *reads*

$$\mathcal{X}, (x, U) \models \blacksquare\varphi \quad \text{iff} \quad (\forall\psi \in \mathcal{L}_{PAL_{int}})(\mathcal{X}, (x, U) \models [\psi]\varphi).$$

Proposition 7 (S4 character of $\blacksquare$). *For any* $\varphi, \psi \in \mathcal{L}_{APAL_{int}}$,

1. $\models \blacksquare(\varphi \wedge \psi) \leftrightarrow \blacksquare\varphi \wedge \blacksquare\psi$
2. $\models \blacksquare\varphi \rightarrow \varphi$
3. $\models \blacksquare\varphi \rightarrow \blacksquare\blacksquare\varphi$
4. $\models \varphi$ *implies* $\models \blacksquare\varphi$

Proof. We only show the third item. These validities demonstrate the similarity of $\blacksquare$ to the arbitrary announcement modality in [2], and their proofs are similar. Instead of proving $\models \blacksquare\varphi \rightarrow \blacksquare\blacksquare\varphi$, we will prove $\models \blacklozenge\blacklozenge\varphi \rightarrow \blacklozenge\varphi$, which is equivalent. Let $\mathcal{X} = (X, \tau, \nu)$ be a topo-model and (x, U) be an epistemic scenario in $\mathcal{X}$. We omit $\mathcal{X}$ as it is obvious which model we are talking about.

$(x, U) \models \blacklozenge\blacklozenge\varphi$

iff $\exists\psi \in \mathcal{L}_{PAL_{int}} : (x, U) \models \langle\psi\rangle\blacklozenge\varphi$

iff $\exists\psi \in \mathcal{L}_{PAL_{int}} : (x, U) \models int(\psi)$ and $(x, Int[\![\psi]\!]^U) \models \blacklozenge\varphi$

iff $\exists\psi \in \mathcal{L}_{PAL_{int}} : x \in Int[\![\psi]\!]^U$ and $(x, Int[\![\psi]\!]^U) \models \blacklozenge\varphi$

iff $\exists\psi \in \mathcal{L}_{PAL_{int}} : x \in Int[\![\psi]\!]^U$ and $\exists\chi \in \mathcal{L}_{PAL_{int}} : (x, Int[\![\psi]\!]^U) \models int(\chi)$

 and $(x, Int([\![\chi]\!]^{Int[\![\psi]\!]^U})) \models \varphi$

iff $\exists\psi \in \mathcal{L}_{PAL_{int}} : x \in Int[\![\psi]\!]^U$ and $\exists\chi \in \mathcal{L}_{PAL_{int}} : x \in Int([\![\chi]\!]^{Int[\![\psi]\!]^U})$

 and $(x, Int([\![\chi]\!]^{Int[\![\psi]\!]^U})) \models \varphi$

iff $\exists\psi, \chi \in \mathcal{L}_{PAL_{int}} : x \in Int([\![\chi]\!]^{Int[\![\psi]\!]^U})$ and $(x, Int([\![\chi]\!]^{Int[\![\psi]\!]^U})) \models \varphi$

iff $\exists\psi, \chi \in \mathcal{L}_{PAL_{int}} : x \in Int[\![int(\psi) \wedge [\psi]int(\chi)]\!]^U$

 and $(x, Int[\![int(\psi) \wedge [\psi]int(\chi)]\!]^U) \models \varphi$

iff $\exists\psi, \chi \in \mathcal{L}_{PAL_{int}} : (x, U) \models int(int(\psi) \wedge [\psi]int(\chi))$

 and $(x, Int[\![int(\psi) \wedge [\psi]int(\chi)]\!]^U) \models \varphi$

iff $\exists\psi, \chi \in \mathcal{L}_{PAL_{int}} : (x, U) \models \langle int(\psi) \wedge [\psi]int(\chi)\rangle\varphi$

iff $\exists\theta \in \mathcal{L}_{PAL_{int}} : (x, U) \models \langle\theta\rangle\varphi$ (where $\theta : int(\psi) \wedge [\psi]int(\chi)$)

iff $(x, U) \models \blacklozenge\varphi$

3.2   Normal Forms for EL_{int}

In this section, we introduce normal forms for the logic EL_{int} and use the formulas in normal forms in order to provide the expressiveness results in Sect. 3.3. These normal forms are unique since they are based on subset space semantics and they are an extension of the normal form for basic epistemic logic given in [13] since we allow the modality int in our normal forms.

We denote the unimodal language having int as its only modality by $\mathcal{L}_{PL_{int}}$.

Definition 8 (Normal form for the language $\mathcal{L}_{EL_{int}}$). *We say a formula $\psi \in \mathcal{L}_{EL_{int}}$ is in* normal form *if it is a disjunction of conjunctions of the form*

$$\delta := \alpha \wedge K\beta \wedge \langle K \rangle \gamma_1 \wedge \cdots \wedge \langle K \rangle \gamma_n$$

where $\alpha, \beta, \gamma_i \in \mathcal{L}_{PL_{int}}$ for all $1 \le i \le n$.

Following the notation in [13], we call the formula δ *canonical conjunction* and the subformulas $K\beta$ and $\langle K \rangle \gamma_i$ *prenex formulas.*

Below we will prove that every formula in EL_{int} is equivalent to a formula in normal form, but first we need several results for this proof.

Lemma 9. *If $\psi \in \mathcal{L}_{EL_{int}}$ is in normal form and contains a prenex formula σ, then ψ can be written as $\pi \vee (\lambda \wedge \sigma)$ where π, λ and σ are all in normal form.*

The proof is similar to the proof of the same fact for epistemic logic found in [13, p. 35].

Before stating the next propositions, it is important to note that 'local' evaluation of formulas in $\mathcal{L}_{EL_{int}}$ with respect to a neighbourhood of a given state is completely reflected in the interpretation of the knowledge modality:

Observation 10. *For any topological model $\mathcal{X} = (X, \tau, \nu)$, any epistemic scenario (x, U) of $\mathcal{X}$ and any $\varphi \in \mathcal{L}_{APAL_{int}}$, $[\![K\varphi]\!]^U = U$ or $[\![K\varphi]\!]^U = \emptyset$, and $[\![\langle K \rangle \varphi]\!]^U = U$ or $[\![\langle K \rangle \varphi]\!]^U = \emptyset$.*

This observation follows from the fact that if there is any $y \in U$ such that $(y, U) \not\models \varphi$, then for all $x \in U$, $(x, U) \not\models K\varphi$, and otherwise, for every $x \in U$, $(x, U) \models K\varphi$. Observation 10 thus expresses that the modality K behaves like *a universal modality within the given neighbourhood.*

Proposition 11. *We have the following equivalences in EL_{int}:*

1. $\vdash int(K\varphi) \leftrightarrow K\varphi$
2. $\vdash int(\langle K \rangle \varphi) \leftrightarrow \langle K \rangle \varphi$
3. $\vdash int(\varphi \vee K\beta) \leftrightarrow int(\varphi) \vee K\beta$
4. $\vdash int(\varphi \vee \langle K \rangle \beta) \leftrightarrow int(\varphi) \vee \langle K \rangle \beta$
5. $\vdash int(\varphi \vee (\sigma \wedge K\beta)) \leftrightarrow int(\varphi \vee \sigma) \wedge (int(\varphi) \vee K\beta)$
6. $\vdash int(\varphi \vee (\sigma \wedge \langle K \rangle \beta)) \leftrightarrow int(\varphi \vee \sigma) \wedge (int(\varphi) \vee \langle K \rangle \beta)$

Proof. We use a semantic argument for this proof since we can obtain the result by the completeness of EL_{int} with respect to all topological spaces [6, p. 9]. Let $\varphi, \beta, \sigma \in \mathcal{L}_{EL_{int}}$, $\mathcal{X} = (X, \tau, \nu)$ be a topo-model and (x, U) be an epistemic scenario of $\mathcal{X}$.

1. ($\Rightarrow$) By the (T)-axiom for int.
   ($\Leftarrow$) Suppose $(x, U) \models K\varphi$. This means $x \in \llbracket K\varphi \rrbracket^U$, thus by Observation 10, $\llbracket K\varphi \rrbracket^U = U$. Then, as U is an open set, $Int\llbracket K\varphi \rrbracket^U = U$ and $x \in Int\llbracket K\varphi \rrbracket^U$. Therefore, by the semantics of int, $(x, U) \models int(K\varphi)$.
2. Similar to (1).
3. ($\Rightarrow$) Suppose $(x, U) \models int(\varphi \vee K\beta)$. We now have that $(x, U) \models int(\varphi \vee K\beta)$ iff $x \in Int\llbracket \varphi \vee K\beta \rrbracket^U$, and that $x \in Int\llbracket \varphi \vee K\beta \rrbracket^U$ iff $x \in Int(\llbracket \varphi \rrbracket^U \cup \llbracket K\beta \rrbracket^U)$. Then, by Observation 10, we have two cases:
   - [Case 1:] $\llbracket K\beta \rrbracket^U = U$
     Then, $(x, U) \models K\beta$, and thus $(x, U) \models int(\varphi) \vee K\beta$.
   - [Case 2:] $\llbracket K\beta \rrbracket^U = \emptyset$
     Then, $Int(\llbracket \varphi \rrbracket^U \cup \llbracket K\beta \rrbracket^U) = Int\llbracket \varphi \rrbracket^U$. Thus, $x \in Int\llbracket \varphi \rrbracket^U$, i.e., $(x, U) \models int(\varphi)$. Therefore, $(x, U) \models int(\varphi) \vee K\beta$.
   ($\Leftarrow$) Suppose $(x, U) \models int(\varphi) \vee K\beta$.
   - [Case 1:] $(x, U) \models int(\varphi)$
     $(x, U) \models int(\varphi)$ means $x \in Int\llbracket \varphi \rrbracket^U$. Since $\llbracket \varphi \rrbracket^U \subseteq \llbracket \varphi \vee K\beta \rrbracket^U$ and $Int\llbracket \varphi \rrbracket^U \subseteq Int\llbracket \varphi \vee K\beta \rrbracket^U$, we have that $x \in Int\llbracket \varphi \vee K\beta \rrbracket^U$. I.e., $(x, U) \models int(\varphi \vee K\beta)$.
   - [Case 2:] $(x, U) \models K\beta$
     This implies, by Observation 10, $\llbracket K\beta \rrbracket^U = U$. Thus, $Int\llbracket \varphi \vee K\beta \rrbracket^U = U$. Hence, $x \in Int\llbracket \varphi \vee K\beta \rrbracket^U$, i.e., $(x, U) \models int(\varphi \vee K\beta)$.
4. Similar to (3) as we have either $\llbracket \langle K \rangle \varphi \rrbracket^U = U$ or $\llbracket \langle K \rangle \varphi \rrbracket^U = \emptyset$.

$$int(\varphi \vee (\sigma \wedge K\beta)) \leftrightarrow int((\varphi \vee \sigma) \wedge (\varphi \vee K\beta))$$
$$\leftrightarrow int(\varphi \vee \sigma) \wedge int(\varphi \vee K\beta)$$
$$\leftrightarrow int(\varphi \vee \sigma) \wedge (int(\varphi) \vee K\beta) \quad \text{(by (3))}$$

5. Similar to (5), by using (4).

Lemma 12. *The following equivalence is a propositional tautology:*

$$(\varphi_1 \vee \cdots \vee \varphi_n) \wedge (\psi_1 \vee \cdots \vee \psi_m) \leftrightarrow ((\varphi_1 \wedge \psi_1) \vee \ldots (\varphi_1 \wedge \psi_m)) \vee ((\varphi_2 \wedge \psi_1) \vee \ldots$$
$$\cdots \vee (\varphi_2 \wedge \psi_m)) \vee \cdots \vee ((\varphi_n \wedge \psi_1) \vee \ldots (\varphi_n \wedge \psi_m)).$$

Theorem 13. *Every formula in EL_{int} is equivalent to a formula in normal form.*

Proof. The proof proceeds by induction on the complexity of φ.

- *Base Case* $\varphi := p$: In this case, as $p \in \mathcal{L}_{PL_{int}}$, φ is already in normal form. Now assume as an inductive hypothesis that ψ and χ can be written in an equivalent normal form.
- *Case* $\varphi := \neg\psi$: W.l.o.g. we can assume that ψ is in normal form. I.e., $\psi := \delta_1 \vee \cdots \vee \delta_m$ where each δ_i is a canonical conjunction. Thus, $\varphi = \neg\psi := \neg\delta_1 \wedge \cdots \wedge \neg\delta_m$. We can then distribute $\neg$ of each δ_i over the conjuncts. In other words, for each δ_i:

$$\neg\delta_i := \neg(\alpha \wedge K\beta \wedge \langle K \rangle \gamma_1 \wedge \cdots \wedge \langle K \rangle \gamma_n) = \neg\alpha \vee \langle K \rangle \neg\beta \vee K\neg\gamma_1 \vee \cdots \vee K\neg\gamma_n$$

where $\alpha, \beta, \gamma_i \in \mathcal{L}_{PL_{int}}$ for all $1 \leq i \leq n$. Let us call $\neg\delta_i$ *canonical disjunction*. Notice that each disjunct of $\neg\delta_i$ is still in the required form, i.e., each disjunct is either a prenex formula or in $\mathcal{L}_{PL_{int}}$. By using Lemma 12 repeatedly, we can write φ in normal form, i.e., as disjunctions of canonical conjuncts.

- *Case $\varphi := \psi \wedge \chi$:* W.l.o.g. we can again assume that ψ and χ are in normal form. I.e., $\psi := \delta_1 \vee \cdots \vee \delta_m$ and $\chi := \delta_1' \vee \cdots \vee \delta_k'$ where each δ_i and δ_j' is a canonical conjunct. Therefore, $\varphi := \psi \wedge \chi := (\delta_1 \vee \cdots \vee \delta_m) \wedge (\delta_1' \vee \cdots \vee \delta_k')$. Then, by Lemma 12, we easily obtain a formula in normal form.

- *Case $\varphi := int(\psi)$:* W.l.o.g. suppose ψ is in normal form. We also assume that ψ includes some prenex formulas, otherwise we are done. By Lemma 9, we can write $\psi := \pi \vee (\delta \wedge \sigma)$ where σ is a prenex formula occurring in ψ. Then, we have

$$int(\psi) \leftrightarrow int(\pi \vee (\delta \wedge \sigma))$$
$$\leftrightarrow int(\pi \vee \delta) \wedge (int(\pi) \vee \sigma) \quad \text{(by (5) or (6))}$$

By repeating this procedure, we can push every prenex formula in the scope of int to the top level, hence, obtain a formula in normal form.

- *Case $\varphi := K\psi$:* Proof of this case is quite similar to the case for int and the argument can be found in [13, Theorem 1.7.6.4, p. 37].

3.3 Expressiveness of $APAL_{int}$

This section includes the main result of this paper: we will prove that $APAL_{int}$ and EL_{int} are equally expressive and thus all $APAL_{int}$, PAL_{int} and EL_{int} are equally expressive. Moreover, this results yields the completeness of $APAL_{int}$.

Lemma 14. *For any $\varphi \in \mathcal{L}_{PL_{int}}$ and any topo-model $\mathcal{X} = (X, \tau, \nu)$ and any epistemic scenario (x, U) of $\mathcal{X}$, if $(x, V) \models \varphi$ for some $V \in \tau$ with $x \in V \subseteq U$, then $(x, U) \models \varphi$.*

Proof. It is elementary for propositional variables and boolean cases as their evaluation does not depend on the neighbourhood, but depends only on the evaluation state. Let us now by inductive hypothesis assume that the statement holds for χ.

Case $\varphi := int(\chi)$: Suppose $(x, V) \models int(\chi)$ for some $V \in \tau$ with $x \in V \subseteq U$. This means, $x \in Int[\![\chi]\!]^V$. By IH, $[\![\chi]\!]^V \subseteq [\![\chi]\!]^U$, and thus, $Int[\![\chi]\!]^V \subseteq Int[\![\chi]\!]^U$. Therefore $x \in Int[\![\chi]\!]^U$, i.e., $(x, U) \models int(\chi)$.

Lemma 15. *For any $\varphi \in \mathcal{L}_{APAL_{int}}$, $K\varphi \rightarrow K(int(\varphi))$ is valid.*

Proof. Let $\varphi \in \mathcal{L}_{APAL_{int}}$, $\mathcal{X} = (X, \tau, \nu)$ be a topo-model and (x, U) be an epistemic scenario of $\mathcal{X}$. Suppose $(x, U) \models K\varphi$. This means $[\![\varphi]\!]^U = U$. Thus, as U is open, $Int[\![\varphi]\!]^U = U$. Then, by Proposition 4.4, we have $[\![int\varphi]\!]^U = U$ meaning that for all $y \in U$, $(y, U) \models int(\varphi)$. Therefore, $(x, U) \models K(int(\varphi))$.

Lemma 16. *For any $\varphi \in \mathcal{L}_{PL_{int}}$, $int(\varphi) \rightarrow \langle\varphi\rangle K\varphi$ is valid.*

Proof. The proof proceeds by induction on the complexity of φ. Let $\mathcal{X} = (X, \tau, \nu)$ be a topological model and (x, U) be an epistemic scenario of $\mathcal{X}$. The cases for propositional variables and booleans are trivial since truth of those does not depend on the neighbourhood. The inductive hypothesis now is: $\models int(\psi) \rightarrow \langle \psi \rangle K \psi$.

Case $\varphi := int(\psi)$: Suppose $(x, U) \models int(\varphi)$, i.e., $(x, U) \models int(int(\psi))$. Thus, $(x, U) \models int(\psi)$. Then, by IH, $(x, U) \models \langle \psi \rangle K \psi$. This means, $(x, U) \models int(\psi)$ and $(x, Int[\![\psi]\!]^U) \models K\psi$. Then, by Lemma 15, $(x, Int[\![\psi]\!]^U) \models K(int(\psi))$. Thus, $(x, U) \models \langle int(\psi) \rangle K(int(\psi))$. Therefore, $(x, U) \models int(int(\psi)) \rightarrow \langle int(\psi) \rangle K (int(\psi))$, i.e., $(x, U) \models int(\varphi) \rightarrow \langle \varphi \rangle K \varphi$.

Proposition 17. *For any $\varphi \in \mathcal{L}_{PL_{int}}$, $\blacksquare \varphi \leftrightarrow \varphi$ is valid.*

Proof. Let $\mathcal{X} = (X, \tau, \nu)$ be a topological model and (x, U) be an epistemic scenario of $\mathcal{X}$. We will prove $\models \blacklozenge \varphi \leftrightarrow \varphi.(\Leftarrow)$ By Proposition 7-(2) $(\Rightarrow)$ Suppose $(x, U) \models \blacklozenge \varphi$. This means, there is a $\blacksquare$-free ψ such that $(x, U) \models \langle \psi \rangle \varphi$. Thus, $x \in Int[\![\psi]\!]^U$ and $(x, Int[\![\psi]\!]^U) \models \varphi$. $(x, Int[\![\psi]\!]^U) \models \varphi$ implies $(x, U) \models \varphi$ by Lemma 14. Therefore, $(x, U) \models \blacklozenge \varphi \rightarrow \varphi$.

Proposition 18. *For any $\varphi, \varphi_i \in \mathcal{L}_{PL_{int}}$,*

$$\models \blacklozenge (\varphi \wedge K\varphi_0 \wedge \bigwedge_{1 \leq i \leq n} \langle K \rangle \varphi_i) \leftrightarrow (\varphi \wedge int(\varphi_0) \wedge \bigwedge_{1 \leq i \leq n} \langle K \rangle (int(\varphi_0) \wedge \varphi_i))$$

$$(\text{NF}_n)$$

Proof. Let $\mathcal{X} = (X, \tau, \nu)$ be a topological model and (x, U) an epistemic scenario of $\mathcal{X}$.

W.l.o.g. we prove the required for $n = 1$. $(\Rightarrow)$ Suppose $(x, U) \models \blacklozenge (\varphi \wedge K\varphi_0 \wedge \langle K \rangle \varphi_1)$. Let us first see what this means.

$(x, U) \models \blacklozenge (\varphi \wedge K\varphi_0 \wedge \langle K \rangle \varphi_1)$

iff there exists a $\blacksquare$-free ψ s.t. $(x, U) \models \langle \psi \rangle (\varphi \wedge K\varphi_0 \wedge \langle K \rangle \varphi_1)$

iff $x \in Int[\![\psi]\!]^U$ and $(x, Int[\![\psi]\!]^U) \models \varphi \wedge K\varphi_0 \wedge \langle K \rangle \varphi_1$

iff $x \in Int[\![\psi]\!]^U$ and $(x, Int[\![\psi]\!]^U) \models \varphi$ and $(x, Int[\![\psi]\!]^U) \models K\varphi_0$

and $(x, Int[\![\psi]\!]^U) \models \langle K \rangle \varphi_1$

For simplicity, we enumerate the conjuncts of the last line as: ① $x \in Int[\![\psi]\!]^U$, ② $(x, Int[\![\psi]\!]^U) \models \varphi$, ③ $(x, Int[\![\psi]\!]^U) \models K\varphi_0$, and ④ $(x, Int[\![\psi]\!]^U) \models \langle K \rangle \varphi_1$. We want to show that $(x, U) \models \varphi \wedge int(\varphi_0) \wedge \langle K \rangle (int(\varphi_0) \wedge \varphi_1)$. Now ② and Lemma 14 imply $(x, U) \models \varphi$; and ③ implies that $(x, Int[\![\psi]\!]^U) \models int(\varphi_0)$, since in $\mathcal{L}_{PL_{int}}$, $K\varphi \rightarrow int(\varphi)$. Then, by Lemma 14, we have $(x, U) \models int(\varphi_0)$.

To show $(x, U) \models \langle K \rangle (int(\varphi_0) \wedge \varphi_1)$, we need to show that there is a $y \in U$ such that $(y, U) \models int(\varphi_0) \wedge \varphi_1$. ④ implies that there is a $z \in Int[\![\psi]\!]^U$ such that $(z, Int[\![\psi]\!]^U) \models \varphi_1$. Then, by Lemma 14, we have $(z, U) \models \varphi_1$. Moreover, ③ and Observation 10 imply that $[\![K\varphi_0]\!]^{Int[\![\psi]\!]^U} = Int[\![\psi]\!]^U$, and thus $(z, Int[\![\psi]\!]^U) \models K\varphi_0$. Hence, $(z, Int[\![\psi]\!]^U) \models int(\varphi_0)$. Then again by Lemma 14, $(z, U) \models int(\varphi_0)$. So, $(z, U) \models int(\varphi_0) \wedge \varphi_1$, and thus $(x, U) \models \langle K \rangle (int(\varphi_0) \wedge \varphi_1)$.

($\Leftarrow$) Suppose $(x, U) \models \varphi \land int(\varphi_0) \land \langle K \rangle (int(\varphi_0) \land \varphi_1)$. We unravel the assumption.

$(x, U) \models \varphi \land int(\varphi_0) \land \langle K \rangle (int(\varphi_0) \land \varphi_1)$

iff $(x, U) \models \varphi$ and $(x, U) \models int(\varphi_0)$ and $\exists y \in U$ s.t. $(y, U) \models int(\varphi_0)$

  and $(y, U) \models \varphi_1$

iff $(x, U) \models \varphi$ and $(x, U) \models int(\varphi_0)$ and $\exists y \in U$ s.t. $y \in Int[\![\varphi_0]\!]^U$

  and $(y, U) \models \varphi_1$

iff $(x, U) \models \varphi$ and $(x, U) \models int(\varphi_0)$ and $\exists y \in Int[\![\varphi_0]\!]^U$ s.t. $(y, U) \models \varphi_1$

We want to show $(x, U) \models \blacklozenge (\varphi \land K\varphi_0 \land \langle K \rangle \varphi_1)$, i.e., we want to show that there is a $\blacksquare$-free ψ such that $(x, U) \models \langle \psi \rangle (\varphi \land K\varphi_0 \land \langle K \rangle \varphi_1)$.

We now claim that $(x, U) \models \langle \varphi_0 \rangle (\varphi \land K\varphi_0 \land \langle K \rangle \varphi_1)$. To prove the claim, we need to show $x \in Int[\![\varphi_0]\!]^U$ and $(x, Int[\![\varphi_0]\!]^U) \models \varphi \land K\varphi_0 \land \langle K \rangle \varphi_1$. We have $(x, U) \models int(\varphi_0)$, i.e., $x \in Int[\![\varphi_0]\!]^U$, by assumption.

As $(x, U) \models \varphi$, we have $(x, U) \models \blacksquare \varphi$, by Proposition 17. This means, for all $\blacksquare$-free ψ if $x \in Int[\![\psi]\!]^U$ then $(x, Int[\![\psi]\!]^U) \models \varphi$. Therefore, as $x \in Int[\![\varphi_0]\!]^U$, we have $(x, Int[\![\varphi_0]\!]^U) \models \varphi$.

Since $(x, U) \models int(\varphi_0)$, by Lemma 16, $(x, U) \models \langle \varphi_0 \rangle K\varphi_0$. So $(x, Int[\![\varphi_0]\!]^U) \models K\varphi_0$.

Now suppose $(x, Int[\![\varphi_0]\!]^U) \not\models \langle K \rangle \varphi_1$, i.e., $(x, Int[\![\varphi_0]\!]^U) \models K\neg\varphi_1$. This means, for all $y \in Int[\![\varphi_0]\!]^U$, $(y, Int[\![\varphi_0]\!]^U) \models \neg\varphi_1$. Then, as $\neg\varphi \in \mathcal{L}_{PL_{int}}$, by Lemma 14, $(y, U) \models \neg\varphi_1$. This contradicts the main assumption, therefore, $(x, Int[\![\varphi_0]\!]^U) \models \langle K \rangle \varphi_1$.

Theorem 19. *Single agent $APAL_{int}$ and EL_{int} are equally expressive.*

Proof. We prove by induction on the number of occurrences of $\blacklozenge$ that every formula in $APAL_{int}$ is equivalent to a formula in EL_{int}. First of all, note that every formula in PAL_{int} is equivalent to formula in EL_{int} by Proposition 5. Hence, we do not need to consider this case: we can simply convert every subformula of a given formula in $APAL_{int}$ which includes a public announcement modality to a formula in EL_{int} by following the reduction axioms given in Proposition 5. Moreover, by Theorem 13, we can write every subformula of a given formula in EL_{int} in an equivalent normal form. Thus, put the epistemic formula in the scope of an innermost $\blacklozenge$ in normal form. Then, we can distribute $\blacklozenge$ over the disjunction, by Proposition 7-(1). We now get formulas of the form $\blacklozenge (\varphi \land K\varphi_0 \land \langle K \rangle \varphi_1 \land \langle K \rangle \varphi_2 \land \cdots \land \langle K \rangle \varphi_n)$ where $\varphi, \varphi_i \in \mathcal{L}_{PL_{int}}$ for all $0 \leq i \leq n$. Then, by Proposition 18, we can reduce these formulas to formulas of the form $\varphi \land int(\varphi_0) \land \langle K \rangle (int(\varphi_0) \land \varphi_1) \land \cdots \land \langle K \rangle (int(\varphi_0) \land \varphi_n)$. By repeating the same procedure as many times as the number of occurrences of $\blacklozenge$ in a given formula of $APAL_{int}$, we obtain an equivalent formula in EL_{int}.

Thus, we proved that every $APAL_{int}$ formula can be reduced to an EL_{int} formula. As EL_{int} and PAL_{int} are also equally expressive, we conclude by Theorem 19 that $APAL_{int}$, EL_{int} and PAL_{int} have the same expressive power, hence, the completeness of $APAL_{int}$ follows directly from the completeness of EL_{int} or from the completeness of PAL_{int}.

We would also like to point out that the semantics for the arbitrary announcement modality can also be directly given without reference to public announcements as

$$\mathcal{X},(x,U) \models \blacksquare\varphi \text{ iff } (\forall\psi \in \mathcal{L}_{PAL_{int}})(\mathcal{X},(x,U) \models int(\psi) \text{ implies } \mathcal{X},(x,Int[\![\psi]\!]^U) \models \varphi).$$

Therefore, if we define the fragment AEL_{int} as EL_{int} with the addition of only the arbitrary announcement modality $\blacksquare$, then we can extend above results to the fragment AEL_{int} of $APAL_{int}$. As a result of Theorem 13 and Proposition 18, AEL_{int} is also equally expressive as EL_{int}.

One of the advantages of having the arbitrary announcement modality in our logic is that it allows us to formulate realizability and goal directed reasoning. In public announcement logics with $[\psi]$ as their only dynamic modality (with standard semantics or with topological or subset space semantics) it is typical that announced formulas may become false after the announcement.[2] We therefore cannot formulate realizability or goal-directed reasoning in such logics. However, with the addition of arbitrary announcements, we can: $\blacklozenge K\varphi$ says that there is an announcement after which the agent knows φ, $K\varphi$ is the goal realized by the announcement (and, typically, the announcement is not the formula φ itself). In other words, epistemic logics with such quantifiers over information change can be used to solve planning problems.

4   Multi-agent Topological Subset Space

In the present paper we only focused on the single-agent subset space logic $APAL_{int}$. Multi-agent subset space logics have been investigated in, for example, [4,10,11,17]. Our ultimate goal is to define a multi-agent version of single-agent topological subset space logic $APAL_{int}$. There are many challenges with such a logic. Firstly, there are different options for the semantics of higher-order knowledge. Suppose for each of two agents i and j there is an open set such that the semantic primitive becomes a triple (x, U_i, U_j) instead of a pair (x, U). Now consider a formula like $K_i\langle K\rangle_j K_i p$, for 'agent i knows that agent j considers possible that agent i knows proposition p'. If this is true for a triple (x, U_i, U_j), then $\langle K\rangle_j K_i p$ must be true for any $y \in U_i$; but y may not be in U_j, in which case (y, U_i, U_j) is not well-defined: we cannot interpret $\langle K\rangle_j K_i p$! A solution to this dilemma is to consider neighbourhoods that are not only relative to each agent, as usual in multi-agent subset space logics, but that are also *relative to each state*, so that $K_i\langle K\rangle_j K_i p$ is true in (x, U_i^x, U_j^x) if and only if $\langle K\rangle_j K_i p$ is true in (y, U_i^y, U_j^y) for each $y \in U_i^x$, with some additional requirements on the neighbourhoods, in order to correctly generalize the single agent case to the multi-agent case. Secondly, given that we have quantification over announcements, this comes with additional complications for the axiomatization, similar to the complications for the logic APAL with relational semantics [2]. The obvious axiomatization will

---

[2] The classic example for such situations is the well-known Moore sentences (see e.g. [12,15] among others).

be infinitary, namely with a derivation rule saying that from $[\psi]\varphi$ for each ■-free formula ψ, we can derive ■φ; with a finitary version involving fresh variables. Also, we can expect the addition of ■ to make the logic more expressive, and the logic to be undecidable; this would already be of interest, but a result contrary to the expectation would be equally exciting: consider a subset space version of arbitrary public announcement logic that is decidable, unlike APAL, which is undecidable! This logic would have definite advantages for multi-agent systems modelling purposes.

5   Conclusions and Future Work

In this work, we proposed a topological subset space semantics for the arbitrary announcement modality as an extension of a proposal initially made by Wang and Ågotnes [18] and later adopted by Bjorndahl [6]. By providing a topological semantics for the arbitrary announcement modality, we linked it to the effort modality. We then demonstrated the completeness of $APAL_{int}$ by proving that $APAL_{int}$ and EL_{int} have the same expressive power. Our logic is as expressive as EL_{int}, and it has two major advantages. First, it is closely linked to the effort modality, as we represent, both syntactically and semantically, a particular kind of effort. On the syntactic side, we work with ■ intended to capture the information change brought about by any announcement. On the semantic side, we model ■ by shrinking the corresponding neighbourhood, rather than by deleting states or neighbourhoods. This interpretation of arbitrary announcements is close to the traditional interpretation of effort, connecting the two modalities. In the future, we intend more closely to investigate the exact relationship between the effort modality and our notion of arbitrary announcement. The second advantage of our logic is that we are able to naturally and concisely express information change via arbitrary public announcements in a topological setting.

For future research we envisage investigating the syntactic characterization of *knowable formulas* where 'knowable' means 'known after an announcement', but in the topological subset space setting. More precisely, we would like to give a syntactic characterization of those $\varphi \in APAL_{int}$ such that $\models \varphi \rightarrow \blacklozenge K\varphi$ [2,9,12]. Finally, as already discussed above, we intend to generalize our logic to multi-agent arbitrary announcement logic [4,10,11,17].

Acknowledgments. We thank the EUMAS reviewers and Philippe Balbiani for their valuable comments. Hans van Ditmarsch is also affiliated to IMSc (Institute of Mathematical Sciences), Chennai, as research associate. We acknowledge support from European Research Council grant EPS 313360.

References

1. Aiello, M., Pratt-Hartmann, I., van Benthem, J. (eds.): Handbook of Spatial Logics. Springer, Heidelberg (2007)
2. Balbiani, P., Baltag, A., van Ditmarsch, H., Herzig, A., Hoshi, T., de Lima, T.: 'Knowable' as 'known after an announcement'. Rev. Symb. Log. **1**(3), 305–334 (2008)

266   H. van Ditmarsch et al.

3. Balbiani, Philippe, van Ditmarsch, Hans, Kudinov, Andrey: Subset space logic with arbitrary announcements. In: Lodaya, Kamal (ed.) Logic and Its Applications. LNCS, vol. 7750, pp. 233–244. Springer, Heidelberg (2013)
4. Baskent, C.: Topics in Subset Space Logic. Master's thesis, University of Amsterdam, Amsterdam, The Netherlands (2007)
5. Baskent, C.: Public announcement logic in geometric frameworks. Fundam. Inform. **118**, 207–223 (2012)
6. Bjorndahl, A.: Subset space public announcement logic revisited. CoRR, abs/1302.4009 (2013)
7. Dabrowski, A., Moss, L.S., Parikh, R.: Topological reasoning and the logic of knowledge. Ann. Pure Appl. Logic **78**, 73–110 (1996)
8. Engelking, R.: General Topology. Heldermann, Berlin (1989)
9. Fitch, F.B.: A logical analysis of some value concepts. J. Symb. Log. **28**, 135–142 (1963)
10. Heinemann, Bernhard: Topology and knowledge of multiple agents. In: Geffner, Hector, Prada, Rui, Machado Alexandre, Isabel, David, Nuno (eds.) IBERAMIA 2008. LNCS (LNAI), vol. 5290, pp. 1–10. Springer, Heidelberg (2008)
11. Heinemann, B.: Logics for multi-subset spaces. J. Appl. Non Class. Log. **20**, 219–240 (2010)
12. Holliday, W.H., Icard, T.F.: Moorean phenomena in epistemic logic. Adv. Modal Log. **8**, 178–199 (2010)
13. Meyer, J.-J.C., van der Hoek, W.: Epistemic Logic for AI and Computer Science. Cambridge Tracts in Theoretical Computer Science, vol. 41. Cambridge University Press, Cambridge (1995)
14. van Benthem, J.: What one may come to know. Analysis **64**(2), 95–105 (2004)
15. van Ditmarsch, H., van der Hoek, W., Kooi, B.: Dynamic Epistemic Logic. Springer, Dordrecht (2007)
16. Vickers, S.: Topology via Logic. Cambridge Tracts in Theoretical Computer Science, vol. 5. Cambridge University Press, Cambridge (1989)
17. Wáng, Y.N., Ågotnes, T.: Multi-agent subset space logic. In: Proceedings of 23rd IJCAI, pp. 1155–1161 (2013)
18. Wáng, Yì N., Ågotnes, Thomas: Subset space public announcement logic. In: Lodaya, Kamal (ed.) Logic and Its Applications. LNCS, vol. 7750, pp. 245–257. Springer, Heidelberg (2013)

Theories in Practice and Real-World Problems

Direct Exchange Mechanisms for Option Pricing

Sarvar Abdullaev[✉], Peter McBurney, and Katarzyna Musial

Department of Informatics, King's College London, London, UK
{sarvar.abdullaev,peter.mcburney,katarzyna.musial}@kcl.ac.uk

Abstract. This paper presents the design and simulation of direct exchange mechanisms for pricing European options. It extends McAfee's single-unit double auction to multi-unit format, and then applies it for pricing options through aggregating agent predictions of future asset prices. We will also propose the design of a combinatorial exchange for the simulation of agents using option trading strategies. We present several option trading strategies that are commonly used in real option markets to minimise the risk of future loss, and assume that agents can submit them as a combinatorial bid to the market maker. We provide simulation results for proposed mechanisms, and compare them with existing Black-Scholes model mostly used for option pricing. The simulation also tests the effect of supply and demand changes on option prices. It also takes into account agents with different implied volatility. We also observe how option prices are affected by the agents' choices of option trading strategies.

Keywords: Mechanism design · Option pricing · Double auctions · Combinatorial exchanges · Prediction markets

1 Introduction

Standard financial theory provides a number of methods for calculating option prices based on the market performance of an underlying asset. But there are few models that take into account strategic agents playing in this market, and their role in forming the prices. It is commonly assumed that an individual trader is mostly a price-taker and therefore her influence to the market is insignificant. But in reality, traders with their aggregated utilities form the market prices. Although it is almost impossible to know how each individual agent would evaluate the risk in the market, we can still model them with reasonable properties such as rationality, strategic behaviour and risk-neutrality. This would provide a testable environment where various market mechanisms and trading behaviours can be simulated and used for taking analytical decisions.

There has been a growing interest in the research of markets as complex game-theoretic systems since Myerson coined *mechanism design* as a framework for strategic interactions between self-interested agents [1]. A new discipline of *auction theory* emerged as a part of mechanism design, and it found

© Springer International Publishing Switzerland 2015
N. Bulling (Ed.): EUMAS 2014, LNAI 8953, pp. 269–284, 2015.
DOI: 10.1007/978-3-319-17130-2_18

its applications in solving many of well-known problems such as resource allocation, scheduling, supply chain optimization, operations control and multi-agent system implementation [5]. The ultimate goal of any auction is the allocation of scarce resources to agents. The space of auction types is limitless, because they may vary in their initial settings, bidding rules, market clearing methods etc. Parsons describes more than 30 variations of auctions based on properties such as dimensionality, quantity and heterogeneity of traded items; direction, sidedness, openness of accepted bids; and kth order prices in determining winners [4].

There have been a number of researches accomplished in applying auction mechanisms to model prediction markets. One of the famous examples of such mechanisms is *Iowa Electronic Markets* used for aggregating predictions on political elections [12]. DeMarzo *et al.* have used regret minimisation of agent decisions on compiling a replicating portfolio which is equivalent to European option value [11]. King *et al.* has described a multi-agent model for derivatives market which used Gaia methodology [9] to match and coordinate agents. Espinosa has implemented a multi-agent system which uses options to allocate scarce resources through a market-like model [6].

We will focus more on Double Auctions (DA) and Combinatorial Exchanges (CE) in this paper. DA is an auction mechanism which involves sellers and buyers trading identical goods using single-item bids. McAfee laid the foundation of DA specifying the direct implementation of a DSIC mechanism which could match bids and asks efficiently [13]. CE is the generalisation of DA where traders are allowed to submit bids and asks as a bundle for heterogeneous goods. We will use DA and CE as prediction markets to evaluate option prices.

The paper is organised as follows. Section 2 provides the basic framework within which we will construct our mechanisms. We will define fundamental concepts used in auction theory and review the main aspects of option pricing. In Sect. 3 we will talk about how traders are going to produce bids and asks, and select option trading strategies (OTS). Then we will walk through the design of multi-unit DA and consequently the CE mechanisms. Section 4 provides experimental results obtained from the simulation of both proposed mechanisms. Finally, in Sect. 5 we conclude highlighting the important aspects of our work.

2 Preliminaries

In this section, we explain some of the key concepts that we use throughout this paper. This involves the basic framework for mechanism design and some brief overview of options and their intrinsic values.

2.1 Designing Mechanisms

The very idea of designing mechanisms imply making rules for given game settings that incentivise truthful revelation of agent types. In terms of auctions, it can be seen as the truthful bidding of agents. Myerson proved that if the allocation rule of the auction is monotone, then there is a unique and explicit payment rule which makes the mechanism *dominant strategy incentive compatible* (DSIC) [3]. This payment rule should include the *critical values* of each agent who has been allocated with goods. Critical value of an agent is the value that the agent needs to beat in order to get the good. For example, in terms of single-item auction, the payment rule corresponds to the second price, because agents must beat the second price to be the winner of the auction. In a continuous domain, Myerson's payment rule can be defined as follows:

Definition 1. For an auction with a monotone allocation rule $\chi(\mathbf{b})$, the *Myerson's payment rule* is

$$\rho_i(b_i, \mathbf{b_{-i}}) = \int_0^{b_i} z\chi_i'(z, \mathbf{b_{-i}})\mathrm{d}z \tag{1}$$

where b_i denote the agent i's bid, $\mathbf{b_{-i}}$ the bids of the rest of the agents, and χ_i' is the marginal allocation rule for bidder i.

Hence it is clear that we can calculate DSIC payments for agents given that we have a monotone allocation rule which never decreases as the bidder increases her bid. One economically fair way of allocating goods is giving it to the highest bidder, or in other words, maximise the social surplus. Indeed, *surplus maximisation* (SM) rule is monotone, because whenever bidder increases her bid, if it beats the other bids, the surplus maximising algorithm will select this bid and thus will increase the number of allocated items to this bidder. In case if it does not exceed the other bids, the bidder's allocation will remain unchanged. For this reason, we will use SM as our main allocation rule in our simulation model.

In double auction and exchange environments, the SM involves the maximisation of the utilities of buyers and sellers. We can define the utility for the agent as follows:

Definition 2. For given agent i, her *ex-post quasilinear utility* is

$$u_i(\mathbf{q}_i) = v_i(\mathbf{q}_i) - \mathbf{p}^\mathsf{T}\mathbf{q}_i \tag{2}$$

where v_i is the valuation function, $\mathbf{q}_i$ is the allocation result of a bidder i, and $\mathbf{p}$ represents the anonymous prices.

Thus utility function requires two types of outcomes from given mechanism: $\mathbf{q}_i$ the quantities allocated to agent i and $\mathbf{p}$ anonymous clearing prices. The agent i will buy (sell) the item j if $q_{ij} \in \mathbf{q}_i$ is positive (negative). So the quantities for a pure seller will be all negative, and for a pure buyer positive. We will assume that the valuation function $v_i(\mathbf{q}_i)$ will also reflect this relationship. Quasilinear utility assumption also implies that agents are risk-neutral as it changes linearly with no budget constraints. However, risk-neutrality in the context of option pricing must not be confused. We will later assume that every agent will have her own forecast on future price of an underlying asset (which might not be a risk-neutral estimate) and evaluate her own option price based on this factor.

2.2 Options

In this section, we will provide some basic notions about European options and how they are priced. An option is a financial contract which provides to its holder the right of buying or selling certain assets at an agreed future price (i.e. strike price). The one who sells (writes) them takes the liability to fulfil buy or sell requests in exchange for the premium he receives. European options are exercised upon their maturity date. An option allowing its holder to buy is named a *call option*, and allowing to sell is a *put option* [8]. Depending on the present value of its strike price K and the current price of its underlying asset S_t, options can be classified into *Out-of-The-Money* (OTM), *At-The-Money* (ATM) and *In-The-Money* (ITM) options. The table below illustrates the types of options that are traded in exchanges. We can also define the upper and lower boundaries for option valuation in Eqs. (3) and (4).

Option Types

	OTM	ATM	ITM
CALL	$K > S_t$	$K = S_t$	$K < S_t$
PUT	$K < S_t$	$K = S_t$	$K > S_t$

$$\max(S_t - K, 0) \leq c \leq S_t \quad (3)$$

$$\max(K - S_t, 0) \leq p \leq K \quad (4)$$

For simplicity reasons, we will assume that the risk-free interest rate is zero, so money has no time value. Also there is no friction in the market, so options can be sold and bought at the same price without any transaction costs involved.

There is an established relationship between put and call options with the same strike price and maturity date. This relationship results from the possibility of buying the one and selling the other. Consider a case, when trader buys a call option at K strike price, and at the same time sells a put option with K strike price, and both have the same maturity T. In some sense, it seems that trader can compensate the cost of a call option he bought for with the premium he received for selling put. So on maturity date, S_T turns out to be higher than strike price K, so the trader can benefit profit as a difference of $S_T - K$. However if S_T appears to be less than K, then trader has a liability to fulfil the put option that he sold, so he incurs a loss of $K - S_T$. This market position actually simulates a forward contract which could be obtained for free. This type of contract is free because it involves future possible liability or profit at the same time, so the risk for both parties is even. Once the combination of put and call options can replicate the liabilities of a forward contract, the prices for put and call options must hold the *put-call parity* relationship: $(c + K = p + S_T)$ [7]. Using the put-call parity relationship, we can easily convert call prices to put prices, and vice versa.

3   Design of Exchange Mechanisms

In this section, we will propose design of a multi-unit multi-type direct DA auction for pricing options and provide some future perspectives on its implementation using CE settings. We will start with McAfee's *Single-Unit Single-Type Double Auction* and gradually reduce it to an option pricing DA and CE mechanisms. In both mechanisms, we comply with the Myerson's lemma to make them DSIC, and thus the agent bids are equal to actual valuations ($\mathbf{b}_i = \mathbf{v}_i$). Vector $\mathbf{v}_i$ will represent the valuation of OTM, ATM and ITM call options by trader i. We will describe how trader valuations are drawn from the distribution, and used to determine the future forecast. We will also show an algorithm for selecting *option trading strategy* (OTS) based on agent's valuation vector. This will determine how demand and supply quantities are formed in the market.

3.1   Valuations and Bidding

In DA mechanism, we will be running a two-sided auction where traders can submit bids and asks to trade one type of option in multiple quantities. We can run several DAs in parallel to determine the pricing of different types of options independently from each other. Agents must represent their orders in terms of two matrices: $V = \{v_{ij} \in \mathbb{R}^+; \forall i \in N, \forall j \in G\}$ for valuations, and $Q = \{q_{ij} \in \mathbb{Z}; \forall i \in N, \forall j \in G\}$ for quantities requested.

Valuations are obtained from agent forecasts. We define agent i's forecast on the future price of underlying asset as a geometric Brownian motion without drift. We have already made an assumption that risk-free rate is zero which frees us from adjusting the prices for their time values. Below geometric process defines how agents obtain their forecasts.

$$S_{i,T} = S_0 e^{(-\frac{1}{2}\sigma^2 T + \sigma W_{i,T})} \quad \forall i \in N \tag{5}$$

Every agent calculates her own values for call options, and also translates those valuations to put options using put-call parity relationship mentioned earlier. Call options will be calculated for different strike prices K_j. It will form a valuation matrix $V = \{v_{ij} = (S_{i,T} - K_j)^+; \forall i \in N, \forall j \in G\}$.

For determining the quantities to be ordered for different types of options, first we need to consider option trading strategies (OTS). These are common combinations of options to be bought or sold in order to minimise the risk of loss. OTSs are frequently, if not every time, used by traders in major real-world option exchanges such as CBOT[1], Eurex[2], etc. Therefore we will assume that our virtual traders will use the same strategies while trading in the market. OTS can be represented as $\mathbf{q}_i \in Q$ for agent i, as it shows the units of options to be bought or sold. Some of the major OTSs, but not all of them, are listed in Table 1 where the quantity of option type to buy or sell is specified in positive or negative numbers respectively. The table also tells about the forecast direction of each OTS, so agents can choose OTS based on their forecast. For example if agent's forecast is in between some $S_0 - \epsilon \leq S_{i,T} \leq S_0 + \epsilon$, then agent will choose *neutral strategy*. If $S_{i,T} > S_0 + \epsilon$, then agent will choose *bullish strategy*. And finally if $S_{i,T} < S_0 - \epsilon$, the agent will choose bearish strategy. Traders pick random strategy among strategies with same direction. However some OTSs can be both bullish and bearish such as Long Straddle, so both bullish and bearish

---

[1] Chicago Board of Trade, http://www.cmegroup.com/company/cbot.html.
[2] Eurex Group, http://www.eurexchange.com/exchange-en/.

traders can be interested in this OTS. It is also possible that OTS is more bullish, than bearish, and vice versa. For example, Strip generates greater payoff when prices go up. Therefore there is a biased chance for a bearish trader to choose Strip among other bearish OTSs because it is less bullish.

Table 1. Option trading strategies

Name	c_{ATM}	p_{ATM}	c_{OTM}	p_{OTM}	c_{ITM}	p_{ITM}	Direction
Long Call	1	0	0	0	0	0	bullish
Long Put	0	1	0	0	0	0	bearish
Bull Call Spread	0	0	-1	0	1	0	bullish
Butterfly Put Spread	0	-2	0	1	0	1	neutral
Long Call Ladder	-1	0	-1	0	1	1	neutral
Long Put Ladder	0	-1	0	-1	0	1	neutral
Iron Butterfly	-1	-1	1	1	0	0	neutral
Long Straddle	1	1	0	0	0	0	bearish and bullish
Long Strangle	0	0	1	1	0	0	bearish and bullish
Strip	1	2	0	0	0	0	bullish > bearish
Strap	2	1	0	0	0	0	bearish > bullish

Also it is worth noting that we will regard option as ATM option if its strike price K_j is in ϵ vicinity of current asset price S_0. By definition of ATM option, its strike price must be equal to the current asset price, but because we only have discrete K_js in price line, we have to take this assumption. Strike prices beyond $[S_0 - \epsilon, S_0 + \epsilon]$ are either considered OTM or ITM.

We name the algorithm for selecting OTS as a $Strat(S_0, S_{i,T})$ function which returns $\mathbf{q}_i$ quantities to buy and sell. Thus the quantities matrix can be formed $Q = \{\mathbf{q}_i = Strat(S_0, S_{i,T}), \forall i \in N\}$. $Strat$ algorithm is defined below in Algorithm 1.

Algorithm 1. OTS Selection Algorithm

Require: $S_0, S_{i,T}, \epsilon$
  if $S_0 - \epsilon \leq S_{i,T} \leq S_0 + \epsilon$ **then**
    return random neutral OTS
  else if $S_{i,T} < S_0 - \epsilon$ **then**
    return random bearish OTS
  else if $S_{i,T} > S_0 + \epsilon$ **then**
    return random bullish OTS
  end if

3.2   Multi-Unit DA

In this section we will gradually extend McAfee's DA to a multi-unit auction, and apply it for option pricing using OTSs. McAfee's matching rule can be written as a greedy algorithm which sorts bids $b_{(1)} \geq b_{(2)} \geq \cdots \geq b_{(m)}$ and asks

$a_{(1)} \le a_{(2)} \le \cdots \le a_{(n)}$ to satisfy $k \le \min(m,n)$ such that $b_{(k)} \ge a_{(k)}$ and $b_{(k+1)} < a_{(k+1)}$ [13]. This rule assumes that bids and asks are for a single-unit of item. We can reformulate this rule to a LP problem defined below:

Definition 3. *For a given vector of valuations* **v**, *McAfee's SM allocation rule for DA is*

$$\max_{\lambda} \sum_i v_i q_i \lambda_i \tag{6}$$

$$s.t. \quad \lambda_i \in \{0,1\} \quad \forall i \tag{7}$$

$$\sum_i q_i \lambda_i = 0 \tag{8}$$

where $q_i \in \{-1,1\}$ *represents sell/buy action by trader* i, λ_i *is an allocation decision variable.*

Theorem 1. *Allocation rule* (6) *generates exactly same number of k efficient trades as McAfee's greedy matching rule.*

Proof. Given that the the supply and demand is matched in constraint (8), we can assume that the number of trades is $m = (\sum_i \lambda_i)/2$, hence we have to prove $m = k$. Let's assume that $m < k$, then it means that there is $b_{(m+1)} - a_{(m+1)} > 0$ and SM solver could add this difference to result greater surplus. So it is not the maximum surplus, and there is a contradiction. Let's assume that $m > k$, then it would mean that $b_{(m)} - a_{(m)} < 0$, and SM solver would be better off not including this match into allocation, as it decreases the objective. Hence there is a contradiction in this case too. Therefore $m = k$.   □

We will use McAfee's pricing rule to determine the clearing prices which conform with Myerson's payments.

Definition 4. *For a given vector of valuations* **v**, *McAfee's DSIC payment rule is:*

$$p = \begin{cases} p^0 & \text{if } p^0 \in [a_{(k)}, b_{(k)}] \\ p^1 & \text{otherwise} \end{cases}$$

where
$p^0 = (b_{(k+1)} + a_{(k+1)})/2,$ $p^1 = (b_{(k)} + a_{(k)})/2$
$b_{(k+1)} = \sup(v_i; \lambda_i = 0, q_i = 1, \forall i)$ $a_{(k+1)} = \inf(v_i; \lambda_i = 0, q_i = -1, \forall i)$
$b_{(k)} = \inf(v_i; \lambda_i = 1, q_i = 1, \forall i)$ $a_{(k)} = \sup(v_i; \lambda_i = 1, q_i = -1, \forall i)$

McAfee mechanism rejects $b_{(k)}$ and $a_{(k)}$ match when the clearing price is p^1, and thus it looses one efficient trade. This efficient trade makes the least portion of the overall surplus. However this makes the mechanism DSIC, individual rational and budget-balanced for single-unit single-type bids and asks. It is individual rational because whenever the p^0 exceeds the boundary of $[a_{(k)}, b_{(k)}]$, it uses p^1 price which is always in between the winning bid-ask spread. It is budget-balanced because it uses anonymous prices to clear the market along with fully matched supply and demand.

From the valuation of options (see the definition of matrix V), we know that traders value call options in monotonic strictly increasing function of their private prediction $S_{i,T}$. Then we can use *Revelation Principle* to convert McAfee's DSIC mechanism to another DSIC mechanism, let us name it *Predictions Matching* (PM) mechanism where traders disclose their private predictions to the mechanism designer, instead of submitting their valuations for every option. Hence we can find the aggregated predictions of asset price S_T at the maturity of option. Mechanism then can use this aggregated prediction to determine the price for any type of option, and clear the market. Also this would restore the lost information about predictions on the valuation of OTM calls, as they are valued zero if agent's prediction is below option's strike price.

Now let us extend McAfee's mechanism to multi-unit mechanism. For simplicity sake, we will assume that bids (asks) $b_i = S_{i,T}$ are agent i's prediction of asset prices at T. Then consider multi-unit bid as a tuple (b_i, q_i). We can split this tuple into set of same-valued bids $\mathbf{b}_i = \bigcup_{t=1}^{q_i} b_{i,t}$ where $b_{i,t} = b_{i,t'}, \forall = t, t'$. This can be done to asks as well. Then we will have complete set of bids $\mathbf{b} = \bigcup_{i=1}^{n} \mathbf{b}_i$ and asks $\mathbf{a} = \bigcup_{i=1}^{n} \mathbf{a}_i$. We can use single-unit McAfee's mechanism mentioned above to find SM allocation, and DSIC payments. However, we can observe below that not all bids/asks can be fully satisfied. If the bids are atomic then the mechanism will loose the efficiency from discarding partially satisfied bids. In case of OTS based bids, we assume that bids are indivisible, so the mechanism has to either satisfy fully or discard the bid. Moreover, by discarding the partially satisfied bids, mechanism also incurs into the cost of covering the exposed asks which has been matched to discarded bids. So it will make the mechanism not budget-balanced.

Lemma 1. *In extended multi-unit McAfee's mechanism, there exists at most one multi-unit bid/ask which is partially satisfied, and the remaining winning bids/asks are fully satisfied.*

Proof. Let us assume that we use McAfee's single-unit DA matching rule for expanded set of bids $\mathbf{b}$ and asks $\mathbf{a}$. Then we should have some k such that $b_{(k)} \geq a_{(k)}$ and $b_{(k+1)} < a_{(k+1)}$. We can also claim, without loss of generality, that there is a bid $\mathbf{b}_i$ such that $b_{(k)}, b_{(k+1)} \in \mathbf{b}_i$. This would imply that $b_{(k)} = b_{(k+1)}$. However, it cannot be $a_{(k)} = a_{(k+1)}$ because it contradicts $b_{(k+1)} < a_{(k+1)}$. Hence, $a_{(k)}$ and $a_{(k+1)}$ belong to different asks, and it must be the case that the multi-unit ask which owns $a_{(k)}$ is fully satisfied, and so do other preceding winning multi-unit bids and asks. $\qquad\square$

Using Lemma 1, we can formulate an LP problem for SM allocation of multi-unit bids and asks. This would involve changing decision variable from binary to continuous $\lambda_i \in [0, 1]$. Below is the definition.

Definition 5. *For given vectors of predictions and quantities* $(\mathbf{S}_T, \mathbf{q})$*, SM allocation rule for Multi-Unit DA is*

$$\max_{\lambda} \sum_i q_i \lambda_i S_{i,T} \tag{9}$$

$$s.t. \quad \lambda_i \in [0,1] \quad \forall i \tag{10}$$

$$\sum_i q_i \lambda_i = 0 \tag{11}$$

where $q_i \in \mathbb{Z}$ represents quantities, $S_{i,T}$ is the agent's prediction, λ_i is an allocation decision variable.

Given that the bids and asks are atomic, mechanism discards the partially satisfied bid/ask and covers the cost of exposed winning ask/bid. In this way, mechanism looses one partial multi-unit efficient bid. Without loss of generality, let us set $\mathbf{b}_l$ as the partially satisfied bid, and this implies the fact $b_{(k)} = b_{(k+1)}$ shown in Lemma 1. We can use p^0 defined in Definition 4 as long as it is within the bounds of winning bid-ask spread. However, mechanism has to reject both least winning multi-unit bid and ask, if p^0 exceeds the bounds. This may expose preceding bid $\mathbf{b}_{l-1}$ to be partially satisfied. Then mechanism will cover the cost of fully satisfying $\mathbf{b}_{l-1}$. The key difference in between the actions of mechanism for partially satisfied bids $\mathbf{b}_l$ and $\mathbf{b}_{l-1}$ is that it rejects the former, and covers the latter. In other words, the mechanism is responsible for covering the costs of rejecting the efficient trades. Rejecting both bid and ask at the edge would allow us to use them to compute the clearing price p^1 defined in Definition 4. As a matter of note, by p^0 and p^1 we mean not the price of an option, but the estimated predications $\hat{S}_T$ which can be used to determine the intrinsic value of any option.

Theorem 2. *Multi-Unit DA is DSIC, individual rational and at most looses one efficient multi-unit trade.*

Proof. Mechanism is DSIC is because it follows the Myerson's lemma, as it has monotonic SM allocation rule and its payment is the critical value of winning bids and asks. It is individual rational because it uses p^0 when it does not exceed the winning bounds. It discards efficient trade and use its prices to obtain p^1 when individual rationality bounds exceeded. There is only one case when mechanism discards both efficiently matched bid and ask, and this case is when the average of offsetting bid and ask is not individual rational. Therefore it approximates the efficiency of the mechanism up to a single efficient multi-unit trade.

As we have already mentioned, mechanism is not budget-balanced, and it may generate negative cash flow. However, we will closely examine how it progresses over the time if mechanism is allowed to keep record of its cash flows and inventory. For example, if mechanism discards partial multi-unit bid, then it will need to satisfy the exposed ask by buying out the remaining options. Mechanism then can use these bought options to satisfy exposed bids later in the time frame. For instance, when mechanism ends with over-supply having multi-unit ask partially satisfied. Mechanism will take options from its inventory to satisfy exposed bids. Below Algorithm 2 summarises the Multi-Unit DA:

Algorithm 2. Multi-Unit DA

Require: $\mathbf{S}_T, \mathbf{q}$

  Determine SM λ

  Discard λ_l bid or ask

  Calculate p^0 and p^1

  if $p^0 \in [b_k, a_k]$ **then**

    Clear the market with p^0

  else

    Discard remaining bid/ask at the edge

    Clear the market with p^1

  end if

  if Has inventory(cash) to cover exposed bid(ask) **then**

    Cover the exposed bid(ask) from inventory(cash)

  else

    Cover the exposed bid(ask) at mechanisms cost, update inventory(cash).

  end if

3.3 Multi-item Multi-Unit DA

In this section, we will extend our Multi-Unit DA further to accommodate multi-item bids and asks as well. In options case, traders would be interested in taking OTSs and this would involve different types of options such as OTM call, ATM put etc. We have defined several commonly used OTSs as a potential candidates for multi-item bids in Sect. 3.1. We will model a mechanism which is based on our previous multi-unit DA which also allows trading multiple heterogeneous items.

We will consider 2 cases of markets: multi-unit multi-item DA where traders can disclose their linear valuations of options to market maker; and CE where traders only disclose their valuation for the bundle. In both cases, traders would want to have their bids satisfied fully. In this multi-unit multi-item DA setup, we will have valuation and quantities matrices (V, Q) to represent the trader preferences. And in CE setting, traders will define their preferences as a tuple of valuation vector and quantities matrix $(\mathbf{v}, Q)$. We will again use Revelation Principle to turn option valuations into predictions in both cases, once we assert that both mechanisms are DSIC for valuations.

Let us consider several multi-unit DAs run in parallel for different items. Traders can simultaneously participate in all of them. In such setup, the overall SM outcome can be viewed as the sum of SM outcome for each DA. So let us construct LP allocation rule for this mechanism:

Definition 6. *For given valuations and quantities* (V, Q), *SM allocation rule for multi-unit multi-item DA is*

$$\max_{\lambda} \sum_i \sum_j v_{ij} q_{ij} \lambda_{ij} \tag{12}$$

$$s.t. \quad \lambda_{ij} \in [0, 1] \quad \forall i \in N, \forall j \in G \tag{13}$$

$$\sum_i q_{ij} \lambda_{ij} = 0, \quad \forall j \in G \tag{14}$$

where λ_{ij} *determines the allocation of each option to each trader.*

However it follows from Lemma 1 that there will be at most G number of partially satisfied bids/asks and the mechanism has to discard those multi-unit multi-item bids/asks in order to avoid traders partially executing their corresponding OTSs. It can use the same pricing method per option type as it has been described for multi-unit DA. Hence it can also inherit DSIC and individual rationality from multi-unit DA.

In CE mechanism, the valuations come for bundles and are usually expressed through indirect means such as bidding languages because communicating the valuation for all combination of possible bundles is exponentially large amount of data which requires much memory and computing resources to process. Nisan provides a good analysis of existing bidding languages [10] used in combinatorial auctions. But in order to avoid this complexity, we will assume that the trader's combinatorial bid space is a predefined list of OTSs and the trader can only choose one of them to participate in CE. Also, like in previous cases, trader want his OTS fully satisfied. In this way, we can represent traders preferences using one valuation vector $\mathbf{v} = \{v_i \in \mathbb{R}; \forall i \in N\}$, and one quantities matrix $Q = \{q_{ij} \in \mathbb{Z}; \forall i \in N, \forall j \in G\}$. If bidders use linear valuations for combinatorial bids, the CE problem can be reduced to multiple DAs. In case of options, the value of OTS is calculated through summing up the elements of the OTS. Moreover, every options' intrinsic value is dependent only on agent i's prediction $S_{i,T}$. Hence, mechanism designer can determine agent's prediction from the OTS value and quantities she submits. Below is the formula for calculating the value of OTS:

Definition 7. *If odd j represents call option, and even j represents put option, the linear value of OTS for agent i is*

$$v_i = \sum_j ((-1)^{j+1}(S_{i,T} - K_j))^+ q_{ij} \qquad (15)$$

Given all variables except $S_{i,T}$, the mechanism designer can numerically solve the Eq. (15), and find corresponding $S_{i,T}$ for every bidder. Then mechanism designer can use Revelation Principle to find estimated prediction $\hat{S}_T$ for calculating the individual prices of options. Below is the transformation of Definition 6 to a PM mechanism:

Definition 8. *For given predictions and quantities $(\mathbf{S}_T, Q)$, SM allocation rule for multi-unit multi-item DA and CE is*

$$\max_\lambda \sum_i \sum_j q_{ij} \lambda_{ij} S_{i,T} \qquad (16)$$

$$s.t. \quad \lambda_{ij} \in [0, 1] \quad \forall i \in N, \forall j \in G \qquad (17)$$

$$\sum_i q_{ij} \lambda_{ij} = 0, \quad \forall j \in G \qquad (18)$$

where λ_{ij} determines the allocation of each option to each trader.

It can be noted that allocation of G options will result at most G number of partially satisfied bids/asks. This would mean that we will have at most G estimated predictions $\hat{S}_T$ for every type of option. In order find the clearing estimated prediction we can calculate the weighted average of $\hat{S}_T$ by trade volume. In other words, we can have $\hat{S}_T$ adjusted based on the bullishness and bearishness of traders. This is the key part of our experiment, to observe how the use of OTSs may result in the change of overall estimated predication. We will provide series of experimental results to test this effect.

As a matter of caveat, we also admit that OTS can be valued in non-linear fashion, and options can be substitutes or compliments. In case if they are substitutes, then it has been shown by Roughgarden [2] that the above mechanism will beat the surplus produced from substitutes, and hence can be used to determine the SM allocation for combinatorial bids with substitute goods. However it is much more complex task and out of the scope of this paper to design a mechanism where goods are compliments, as it would require iterative rounds of price discovery and package bidding. Also it is important to note that options can be compliments and there is enough evidence to assert this assumption. There is an established phenomenon called *volatility smile* which exhibits abnormally higher prices for OTM options in major derivatives markets, whereas their intrinsic value is zero [8]. They can even be valued higher than ATM options. This forms a convex parabola for *implied volatility* as the strike price increases. Implied volatility can be calculated through finding the root of Black-Scholes formula for volatility σ using the resulted option price and other known parameters.

4   Experimental Setup and Results

We will conduct series of experiments to see how estimated predictions, and consequently the option prices change in multi-unit DA and CE mechanisms. In first set of experiments with multi-unit DA, we will simulate asset prices as Brownian process, and then use it for different market settings defined below:

- *Vol = Vol, Supply = Demand:* In this setting the real asset price volatility, and the implied volatility for agents are the same. Also supply and demand scalers are taken from a random variable $\lfloor 15 * z \rfloor$ where $z \sim \mathcal{N}(0,1)$. This balances the supply and demand the market around zero.
- *Vol = Vol, Supply > Demand* : The same as above, except supply and demand scalers are taken from $\lfloor 15 * z - 5 \rfloor$ where $z \sim \mathcal{N}(0,1)$. This balances the market around 5 oversupply.
- *Vol = Vol, Supply < Demand* : The same as above, except supply and demand scalers are taken from $\lfloor 15 * z + 5 \rfloor$ where $z \sim \mathcal{N}(0,1)$. This balances the market around 5 overdemand.
- *Vol ≠ Vol, Supply = Demand:* The same as above, except implied volatility of traders differ around real asset price volatility with lognormal standard deviation of 0.5.

We fix several other parameters for the experiment. For example, options have constant strike prices throughout the timeline. This means that agents will trade

Table 2. Parameters of the experiment

Name	Value	Name	Value
Initial Asset Price	$S_0 = 100$	Random Quantities Scaler Range	[-15, 15]
Strike Price	$K = 100$	Shift in Supply/Demand per Agent	5
Deviation from Strike price	$\epsilon = 10$	Random Implied Volatility Mean	0
Asset Price Volatility	$\sigma = 0.05$	Random Implied Volatility St.D	0.5
Risk-free rate	$r = 0$	Number of agents	$N = 100$
Time to maturity	$T = 100$	Number of option types	$G = 6$
Number of tests per mechanism	$w = 30$		

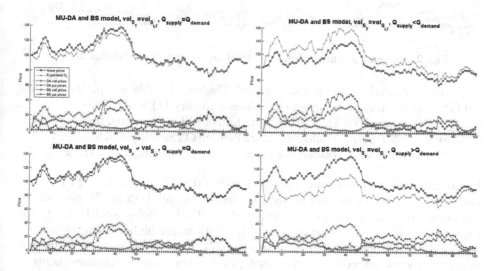

Fig. 1. Call and put prices from multi-unit DA mechanism and Black-Scholes model

only with predefined set of options at the beginning of the simulation, and no new type of option with new strike price will enter the market. Also option maturity date will be constant, and it will approach its maturity date through the timeline of the simulation. Asset price volatility will also be fixed (Table 2).

In Fig. 1 we can see estimated predictions change when implied volatility, supply and demand are different. It illustrates that multi DA mechanism can effectively simulate Black-Scholes prices, as long as the implied volatility is the same as the asset price volatility, and supply and demand are equal. However we can see that call prices drop blow Black-Scholes model when the supply exceeds demand, and vice versa. We can also observe that randomised implied volatility around real asset price volatility can better approximate option prices.

Another set of experiments reveals the key aspect of the research exhibiting the effect of OTSs on estimated predictions. In this experiment we simulate CE mechanism, and calculate the estimated predictions as weighted average of estimated predictions obtained for different option types through simultaneously executed multi-unit DAs. In this set, we consider following cases:

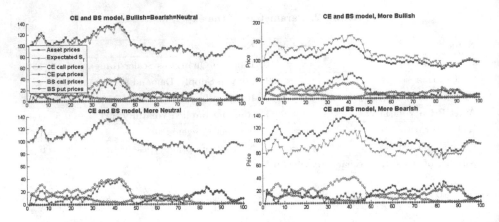

Fig. 2. Call and put prices from CE mechanism and Black-Scholes model

- *Balanced Bullish, Bearish and Neutral Traders*: In this setup, traders use OTSs equally having balanced quantities for every OTS.
- *More Bullish Traders*: Traders use more bullish OTSs compared to other OTSs.
- *More Bearish Traders*: Traders use more bearish OTSs compared to other OTSs.
- *More Neutral Traders*: Traders use more neutral OTSs compared to other OTSs.

Figure 2 illustrates the estimated predictions obtained from simulating CE mechanism where traders use OTSs to interpret their predictions. It also shows the corresponding option prices compared to Black-Scholes model. As it was expected, we can observe that estimated predictions are higher when traders are more bullish, and lower if they are more bearish. Also we can see that estimated predictions stick up well with the asset prices when traders are more neutral. This clearly shows that option prices are affected by the choice of OTSs in the market, although OTS is not purely a buy/ask order, but it is mixed combination of bids and asks for particular options.

As we have already mentioned, proposed mechanisms are not budget-balanced and it is worthwhile to view how they yield loss and profit from covering the partial bids/asks of rejected traders. Figure 3 shows the accumulated cost and revenue for multi-unit DA and CE mechanisms.

It can be seen from the Fig. 3 that in cases of oversupply in multi-unit DA or more bullish traders in CE the revenue of the mechanism is soaring, because there are fewer bids than asks, and the mechanism always ends up partially satisfying some seller. As a result it rejects that seller, and takes its role of selling options to exposed bidder. Hence it increase its revenue day after day. The opposite phenomena happens when there are more bids than asks, and mechanism has to spend money on behalf of rejected bidder to buy out exposed ask. Mechanisms are somewhat stabilised around zero when the balance of supply and demand is maintained. Also it is interesting to observe that in CE, the mechanism revenue/cost is more volatile and enormous because the volumes of options traded are at least G times bigger.

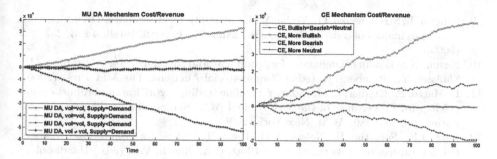

Fig. 3. Cost/Revenue for multi-unit DA and CE mechanisms

5   Concluding Remarks

In this paper, we have gradually designed two important mechanisms (multi-unit DA and CE) based on McAfee's description of single-unit DA. Although designed mechanisms are not budget-balanced, we have proved that they are DSIC, individual rational and approximately efficient. We have used these mechanisms to price options where traders not only bid in price and quantities, but also apply various commonly used OTSs to minimise their risks. The experiments gave us results where demand and supply can also affect the option prices, and more importantly, we saw that the OTSs have a considerable impact in forming option prices. We have also highlighted the revenue and cost of the mechanisms under various scenarios, and found out that mechanism is stable as long as the supply and demand in the market are balanced.

References

1. Satterthwaite, M.A., Myerson, R.B.: Efficient mechanisms for biliteral trading. J. Econ. Theor. **28**, 265–281 (1983)
2. Roughgarden, T.: Lectures on Combinatorial Auctions. Lecture Notes on Topics in Algorithmic Game Theory, Stanford (2008)
3. Myerson, R.: Optimal auction design. Mathematics of Operations Research **6**(1), 5873 (1981)
4. Parsons, S., Rodriguez-Aguilar, J.A., Klein, M.: Auctions and bidding. ACM Comput. Surv. **43**(2), 1–59 (2011). doi:10.1145/1883612.1883617
5. Shoham, Y., Crampton, P., Steinberg, R.: Combinatorial Auctions. MIT Press, Cambridge (2010)
6. Baqueiro Espinosa, O.: Agent Risk Management in Electronic Markets using Option Derivatives. PhD thesis, Department of Computer Science, University of Liverpool (2008)
7. Higham, D.: An Introduction to Financial Option Valuation: Mathematics, Stochastics and Computation. Cambridge University Press, Cambridge (2004)
8. Hull, J.C.: Options, Futures and Other Derivatives, 5th edn. Prentice Hall, Englewood cliffs (2001)

9. King, A.J., Streltchenko, O., Yesha, Y.: Using multi-agent simulation to understand trading dynamics of a derivatives market. Ann. Math. Artif. Intell. **44**–**3**, 233–253 (2005)
10. Nisan, N.: Bidding languages for combinatorial auctions. In: Crampton, P., Shoham, Y., Steinberg, R. (eds.) Combinatorial Auctions. The MIT Press (2006)
11. DeMarzo, P., Kremer, I., Mansour, Y.: Online trading algorithms and robust option pricing. In: Proceedings of the 38th Annual ACM Symposium on Theory of Computing, pp. 477–486. ACM, New York (2006)
12. Berg, J.E., Forsythe, R., Nelson, F.D., Rietz, T.A.: Results from a dozen years of election futures markets research. In: Plott, C.A., Smith, V.L. (eds.) Handbook of Experimental Economic Results, vol. 1, pp. 742–751. Elsevier, Amsterdam (2008)
13. McAfee, R.P.: A dominant strategy double auction. J. Econ. Theor. **56**, 434–450 (1992)
14. Shoham, Y., Leyton-Brown, K.: Multiagent Systems: Algorithmic, Game-Theoretic, and Logical Foundations. Cambridge University Press, Cambridge (2008)

A Study on the Influence of the Number of MTurkers on the Quality of the Aggregate Output

Arthur Carvalho[1]([✉]), Stanko Dimitrov[2], and Kate Larson[3]

[1] Rotterdam School of Management, Erasmus University,
Rotterdam, The Netherlands
`carvalho@rsm.nl`
[2] Department of Management Sciences, University of Waterloo,
Waterloo, Canada
`sdimitro@uwaterloo.ca`
[3] Cheriton School of Computer Science, University of Waterloo,
Waterloo, Canada
`kate.larson@uwaterloo.ca`

Abstract. Recent years have seen an increased interest in crowdsourcing as a way of obtaining information from a large group of workers at a reduced cost. In general, there are arguments for and against using multiple workers to perform a task. On the positive side, multiple workers bring different perspectives to the process, which may result in a more accurate aggregate output since biases of individual judgments might offset each other. On the other hand, a larger population of workers is more likely to have a higher concentration of poor workers, which might bring down the quality of the aggregate output.

In this paper, we empirically investigate how the number of workers on the crowdsourcing platform Amazon Mechanical Turk influences the quality of the aggregate output in a content-analysis task. We find that both the expected error in the aggregate output as well as the risk of a poor combination of workers decrease as the number of workers increases.

Moreover, our results show that restricting the population of workers to up to the overall top 40 % workers is likely to produce more accurate aggregate outputs, whereas removing up to the overall worst 40 % workers can actually make the aggregate output less accurate. We find that this result holds due to top-performing workers being consistent across multiple tasks, whereas worst-performing workers tend to be inconsistent. Our results thus contribute to a better understanding of, and provide valuable insights into, how to design more effective crowdsourcing processes.

1 Introduction

Recent technological advances have facilitated the outsourcing of a variety of tasks to "the crowd", *e.g.*, the development and testing of large software applications, the design of websites, professional translation of documents, transcription of audio, *etc.* Such a practice of obtaining relevant information or services from a large group of people is traditionally referred to as *crowdsourcing*.

© Springer International Publishing Switzerland 2015
N. Bulling (Ed.): EUMAS 2014, LNAI 8953, pp. 285–300, 2015.
DOI: 10.1007/978-3-319-17130-2_19

The crowdsourcing process, as considered in this paper, is as follows: a number of workers are asked to individually complete a common *task*. After completing the task, each worker must report back an *output*. The reported outputs are then aggregated to obtain an *aggregate output*. A crucial question that arises during this process is how many workers to include in the task. In particular, how does the number of workers influence the quality of the aggregate output?

Arguments can be made in favor and against the use of multiple workers. On the one hand, multiple workers bring diversity to the process so that biases of individual judgments can offset each other, which may result in a more accurate aggregate output. On the other hand, a larger population of workers might bring down the quality of aggregate outputs due to the likely inclusion of poor workers.

In this paper, we empirically investigate the above question through an experiment using one of the most popular crowdsourcing platforms: *Amazon Mechanical Turk* (AMT). In our experiment, we asked workers to solve three content-analysis tasks. Due to the nature of the tasks, we are able to derive *gold-standard outputs*, *i.e.*, outputs of high quality provided by experts with relevant expertise.

The existence of gold-standard outputs allows us to investigate how different combinations of workers affect the accuracy of aggregate outputs. We first analyze the accuracy of aggregate outputs as the number of workers increases. Focusing on simple averages to aggregate outputs, we find a substantial degree of improvement in expected accuracy as we increase the number of workers, with diminishing returns for extra workers. Moreover, the standard deviation of errors in the aggregate outputs decreases with more workers, which implies less risk when aggregating outputs.

Our experimental results also show that combining only the overall top-performing workers results in more accurate aggregate outputs, and these workers are consistent across multiple tasks. On the other hand, removing the overall worst-performing workers from the population of workers might result in less accurate aggregate outputs. The reason for this surprising result is that the overall worst-performing workers can produce good outputs on some tasks, which implies that they tend to be inconsistent across multiple tasks. Our results thus contribute to a better understanding on how to design more effective crowdsourcing processes.

2   Related Work

Many different research questions involving crowdsourcing have been recently addressed by the multi-agent systems community, *e.g.*, how to assign tasks to workers [5,13], how to design optimal workflows to coordinate the work of the crowd [7,15], how to induce honest behavior in crowdsourcing settings [1,4], *etc.* We refer the interested readers to the papers by Yuen *et al.* [14] and Quinn and Bederson [10] for comprehensive surveys on crowdsourcing-related works.

To the best of our knowledge, this paper is the first one to address the question of how the number of workers affects the quality of aggregate outputs in crowdsourcing settings. Similar studies have been performed in different domains. For example, it is well-known in decision analysis and operations research that combining multiple forecasts often leads to improved forecasting performance [3]. Sheng *et al.* [11] showed in a data mining/machine learning domain that labeling the same data set with different "labelers" might sometimes improve data quality.

However, some unexpected results are apparently specific to crowdsourcing. For example, our experimental results show that removing the overall worst-performing workers from the population of workers might result in less accurate aggregate outputs. Thus, we expect our work to shed light on how to design more effective crowdsourcing processes.

3   The Content-Analysis Experiment

In this section, we describe a content-analysis experiment designed to investigate the question of how the number of workers affects the quality of aggregate outputs. In the following subsections, we describe Amazon Mechanical Turk, the crowdsourcing platform used in our experiments, followed by the experimental design.

3.1   Amazon Mechanical Turk

Amazon Mechanical Turk[1] (AMT) is currently one of the most popular crowdsourcing platforms. AMT has consistently attracted thousands of workers, the so called *MTurkers*, willing to complete hundreds of thousands of outsourced tasks for relatively low pay. Most tasks posted on AMT are tasks that are relatively easy for human beings, but nonetheless challenging or even currently impossible for computers, *e.g.*, audio transcription, filtering adult content, extracting data from images, proofreading texts, *etc.*

AMT has also been widely used as a platform for conducting behavioral experiments [8]. The main advantage that AMT offers to behavioral researchers is the access to a large, diverse, and stable pool of workers willing to participate in the experiments for relatively low pay, thus simplifying the recruitment process and allowing for faster iterations between developing theory and executing experiments. Furthermore, AMT provides a built-in reputation system that helps requesters distinguish between good and bad workers and, consequently, to ensure data quality. AMT also provides an easy-to-use built-in mechanism to pay workers that greatly reduces the difficulties of compensating individuals for their participation in the experiments.

3.2   Experimental Design

We asked workers on AMT to review three short texts under three different criteria: *Grammar*, *Clarity*, and *Relevance*. The first two texts were extracts from published poems, but with some original words intentionally replaced by

---

[1] http://www.mturk.com.

misspelled words. The third text contained random words presented in a semi-structured way. Appendix A contains detailed information about the texts. For each text, three questions were presented to the workers, each one having three possible responses ordered in decreasing negativity order:

– Grammar: does the text contain misspellings, syntax errors, *etc.*?
  • A lot of grammar mistakes
  • A few grammar mistakes
  • No grammar mistakes
– Clarity: does the text, as a whole, make any sense?
  • The text does not make sense
  • The text makes some sense
  • The text makes perfect sense
– Relevance: could the text be part of a poem related to love?
  • The text cannot be part of a love poem
  • The text might be part of a love poem
  • The text is definitely part of a love poem

Words with subjective meaning were intentionally used so as to emphasize the subjective nature of content analysis, *e.g.*, "a lot", "a few", *etc.* In order to conduct numerical analysis, each individual response was translated into a *score* inside the set $\{0, 1, 2\}$. The most negative response received the score 0, the middle response received the score 1, and the most positive response received the score 2. Thus, each worker reported a vector of 9 scores (3 criteria for each of the 3 texts). Henceforth, we denote by *output* a vector of 3 scores for a given text. Thus, each worker reported 3 outputs.

A total of 50 workers were recruited on AMT, all of them residing in the United States of America and older than 18 years old. They were required to accomplish the task in at most 20 min. After accomplishing the task, every worker received a payment of $0.20. A study done by Ipeirotis [6] showed that more than 90 % of the tasks on AMT have a baseline payment less than $0.10, and 70 % of the tasks have a baseline payment less than $0.05. Thus, our baseline payment was much higher than the payment from the vast majority of other tasks posted on AMT.

Since the source and original content of each text were known *a priori*, *i.e.*, before the content-analysis experiment was conducted, we were able to derive gold-standard outputs for each text. In order to avoid confirmation bias, we asked five professors and tutors from the English and Literature Department at the University of Waterloo to provide their outputs for each text. We set the gold-standard score for each criterion in a text as the median of the scores reported by the professors and tutors. Coincidentally, each median value was also the mode of the underlying scores. We show the gold-standard outputs in Appendix A.

4   Accuracy of Aggregate Outputs by the Number of Workers

In this section, we study the influence of the number of workers on the quality of the aggregate output. In order to do so, we generated combinations of the 50 workers in our population. For $r \in \{1, \ldots, 4\}$ and $r \in \{46, \ldots, 50\}$, we calculated all possible combinations of workers, *i.e.*, $\binom{50}{r}$. For example, for $r = 2$, we generated all $\binom{50}{2} = 1225$ pairs of workers. Due to the intractable number of combinations for $r \in \{5, \ldots, 45\}$, we randomly generated 10^5 different combinations of workers for any $r \in \{5, \ldots, 45\}$.

For each combination of workers, we aggregated the outputs from the underlying workers by taking the average of them. For instance, for two workers, we calculated the average output for all $\binom{50}{2} = 1225$ possible pairs of workers.

We then measured the accuracy of each aggregate output. For each aggregate output, we calculated the *root-mean-square deviation* (RMSD) between the aggregate output and the gold-standard output. For example, suppose that a pair of workers report the outputs $(1, 2, 0)$ and $(2, 2, 1)$ for Text 1. Thus, the aggregate output is $(1.5, 2, 0.5)$. Given that the gold-standard output for Text 1 is $(1, 2, 2)$ (see Appendix A), the root-mean-square deviation between the aggregate output and the gold-standard output is:

$$\sqrt{\frac{(1.5 - 1)^2 + (2 - 2)^2 + (0.5 - 2)^2}{3}} \approx 0.9129$$

We denote by *error* the RMSD between the aggregate output and the gold-standard output. Clearly, the lower the error, the more accurate the aggregate output. In our experiments, the range of the error is $[0, 2]$. The resulting *average error* for a given r can be seen as the *expected error* when aggregating outputs using r workers. For instance, the average of the $\binom{50}{2} = 1225$ errors from all possible pairs of workers is the *expected error* when aggregating outputs using 2 workers chosen at random. The average error, the standard deviation of the errors, and the maximum error per text for each $r \in \{1, \ldots, 50\}$ are illustrated in Fig. 1. The complete numerical data is shown in Appendix B.

An interesting feature of Fig. 1 is that the influence of the number of workers on the quality of the aggregate output is qualitatively the same for all texts. That is, the average error decreases as the number of workers r increases, which means that the expected accuracy of the aggregate output increases with more workers.

Figure 2 shows the percentage of the reduction of the average error when one extra worker is added. From the starting point of one worker, adding a second worker reduces the average error by $3.6\%-16.5\%$. Given two workers, adding a third worker decreases the average error by $2\%-8.3\%$, and so on. Clearly, there are diminishing returns for extra workers. For example, while adding a fourth worker reduces the average error by $1.19\%-4.79\%$, adding a tenth worker reduces the average error by only $0.07\%-0.79\%$. After the sixth worker, adding another worker always decreases the average error by less than 2% for all texts.

Figure 1 also shows that the standard deviation of the errors decreases with the number of workers r. The initially high standard deviation indicates an opportunity to get considerably low error with a single worker. Of course, the other side of the coin is a greater risk of high error with a single poor worker.

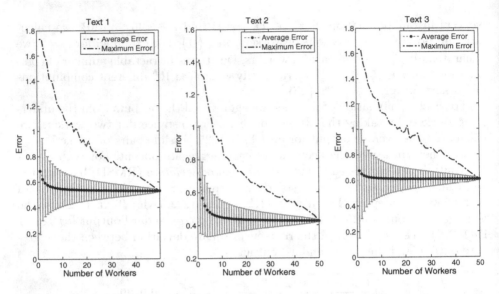

Fig. 1. The average error, the standard deviation of the errors, and the maximum error per text for each $r \in \{1, \ldots, 50\}$.

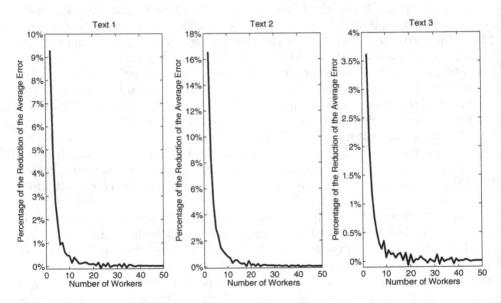

Fig. 2. The percentage of the reduction of the average error when one extra worker is added.

As the number of workers increases, this risk decreases because combinations of exclusively poor workers become less likely. This fact is also shown in the reduction of the maximum error when r increases, which implies less risk when aggregating outputs.

5   Accuracy of Outputs from the Top Workers

The analysis performed in the previous section is based on combinations of workers from the full population of workers. Two interesting follow-up questions are: (1) how much can accuracy be improved by restricting attention to combinations of the overall top-performing workers? and (2) how much can accuracy be improved by removing the overall worst-performing workers from the population of workers?

In order to answer these questions, we first sorted workers based on the *overall error*. Recall that each worker reported three outputs, each one consisting of three scores. We denote by *overall output* a vector of all nine reported scores. Likewise, we denote by *overall gold-standard output* the vector of all nine scores from the gold-standard outputs. Then, the *overall error* of a worker is the RMSD between his overall output and the overall gold-standard output. For example, suppose that a worker reports the following outputs for Text 1, 2, and 3: $(1, 2, 2)$, $(1, 2, 0)$, and $(1, 0, 0)$. Hence, his overall output is $(1, 2, 2, 1, 2, 0, 1, 0, 0)$. Recall that the gold-standard outputs for Text 1, 2, and 3 are, respectively, $(1, 2, 2)$, $(1, 2, 1)$, and $(0, 0, 0)$. Thus, the overall gold-standard output is $(1, 2, 2, 1, 2, 1, 0, 0, 0)$. Consequently, the worker's overall error is:

$$\sqrt{\frac{x}{9}} \approx 0.4714$$

where:

$$x = (1 - 1)^2 + (2 - 2)^2 + (2 - 2)^2 + (1 - 1)^2 + (2 - 2)^2$$
$$+ (0 - 1)^2 + (1 - 0)^2 + (0 - 0)^2 + (0 - 0)^2 = 2$$

For ease of exposition, in the following discussion we focus on the overall accuracy of the top 3 workers and on the accuracy of the population of workers without the 3 overall worst-performing workers, *i.e.*, the top 47 workers. We note, however, that the following results are qualitatively the same for the top k and the top $50 - k$ workers, for any $k \in \{2, \ldots, 20\}$. We return to this point later in this section, when we also suggest a different way of ordering workers.

After ordering workers in terms of overall errors, we considered all possible combinations of the top 3 workers, *i.e.*, we calculated the aggregate outputs and errors for all $\binom{3}{r}$ possible combinations of workers, for $r \in \{1, 2, 3\}$. Moreover, we removed the three overall worst-performing workers from the full population of workers and calculated the aggregate outputs and errors for all $\binom{47}{r}$ combinations of workers, for $r \in \{1, 2, 3\}$ in order to allow quantitative comparisons across different populations of workers. The resulting average error per text for different populations of workers is illustrated in Fig. 3. The complete numerical data is shown in Table 1 in Appendix B.

Focusing first on Text 1 and 3, any combination of the top 3 workers results in a perfect aggregate output with zero error, whereas removing the three overall worst-performing workers reduces the average error by 4.96 %–8.10 % in

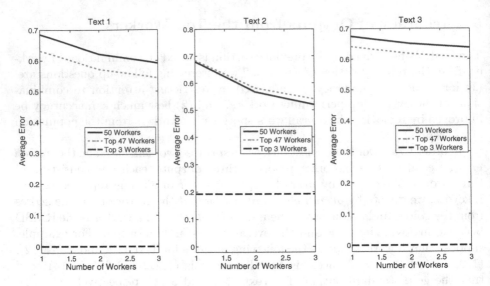

Fig. 3. The average error per text for different populations of workers and $r \in \{1, 2, 3\}$.

comparison with the complete population of workers, for the same group size $r \in \{1, 2, 3\}$.

Looking at the numerical values for Text 1 in Table 1 (see Appendix B), the average error for combinations of 1, 2, and 3 workers from the top 47 workers (*i.e.*, 0.632, 0.572, and 0.543) is less than the average error for combinations of 1, 4, and 11 workers from the complete population of workers (*i.e.*, 0.685, 0.575, and 0.544). In other words, the aggregate outputs of 1, 2, and 3 randomly selected workers from the top 47 workers are expected to be more accurate in Text 1 than the aggregate outputs of 1, 4, and 11 randomly selected workers from the complete population of workers. These numbers for Text 3 are, respectively, 2, 8, and 50. Thus, for Text 1 and 3, it is beneficial to remove some worst-performing workers from the full population of workers.

The striking result comes from Text 2, where the average error for the full population of workers is 0.69 %−3.85 % *lower* than the average error for the top 47 workers. The reason for this counter-intuitive result is that there were workers amongst the three overall worst-performing workers who excelled in Text 2, while performing poorly in Text 1 and 3. This shows that some workers are not consistent across multiple tasks. We return to this point in the next section.

For all populations of workers, the average error, the standard deviation of the errors, and the maximum error decrease as the number of workers increases, showing that combining multiple workers is always beneficial since it improves accuracy and reduces risks.

As stated before, for ease of exposition, our discussion in this section has been focused on the implications of restricting the population of workers to the overall top 3 workers and of removing the three overall worst-performing workers from the full population of workers. The obtained results are, however, more general. Any combination of up to k workers, for $k \in \{1, \ldots, 20\}$, from the top k

workers results in a lower average error than a combination of the same number of workers from both the complete population of workers and the top $50 - k$ workers. Moreover, removing any number $k \in \{2, \ldots, 20\}$ of worst-performing workers from the complete population of workers results in an increase of the average error for Text 2.

The above results are statistically significant for any $k \in \{3, \ldots, 20\}$ (rank-sum test, p-value ≤ 0.05). For combination of size $k \in \{1, 2\}$, the three populations of workers have many combinations of workers in common. In general, as k increases, the fraction of combinations of workers shared between the top k workers, the top $50 - k$ workers, and the full population of workers decreases, thus allowing us to make stronger statistical comparisons. For example, for $k \geq 4$, the p-values from the rank-sum tests are approximately 0.

It could be argued that the results in this section hold true because our experimental setting is biased, e.g., the overall top-performing workers are expected to be more accurate in all texts because the overall error contains information about errors from all individual texts. However, if such a bias existed, combinations of top-performing workers would always result in lower average errors than combinations of the same number of workers from the full population of workers, a fact which is not true for $k \in \{21, \ldots, 25\}$. For example, for $k \in \{23, 24, 25\}$ and Text 1 and 2, a random combination of workers from the complete population of workers results in a lower average error than a random combination of the same number of workers from both the top k workers and the top $50 - k$ workers. In general, we find no clear pattern for values of $k \in \{21, \ldots, 25\}$.

Another way to compute the overall error and, thus, of ranking workers is by using a leave-one-out cross-validation approach. That is, given n texts, each worker receives a *historical rank* based on his errors on $n - 1$ texts. Then, the performance of different populations of workers is measured on the left-out text. However, the leave-one-out cross-validation approach may not work well with small data sets, such as the one in this study. We tried this approach on our data set and had mixed results. For example, when defining workers' historical ranks based on their performance in Text 1 and 2, and measuring the performance of different populations of workers in Text 3, a random combination of workers from the top k workers resulted in *higher* average error than a random combination of the same number of workers from both the full population of workers and the top $50 - k$ workers, for some values of k. We conjecture that the above result is an artifact of having a small number of texts since the effect of a single text on the historical rank would likely be diluted if there was a larger number of texts.

To summarize, our results in this section imply that combining outputs from any number of the overall top 40 % workers yields substantial improvements in expected accuracy in comparison to a combination of the same number of workers from the full population of workers, whereas removing workers amongst the overall worst 40 % workers might result in less accurate aggregate outputs.

6 Consistency of Workers Across Multiple Tasks

Our previous analysis shows that the relative performance of some workers is not necessarily consistent across multiple tasks. In order to further investigate this issue, we first calculated the *overall ranking* of workers in terms of overall errors, *i.e.*, we sorted workers in ascending order according to their overall errors.

Next, we calculated the *individual rankings* of each worker in terms of individual errors, *i.e.*, for each reported output, we sorted workers in ascending order according to their errors. Thus, each worker was ranked three times according to his errors. Ties in rankings were allowed, *i.e.*, workers with similar (overall) errors received the same ranking.

In the following analysis, we use the standard deviation of a worker's individual rankings as a measure of how stable the overall ranking of that worker is, where a high standard deviation indicates more ranking inconsistency across multiple tasks. For example, suppose that the outputs of a worker result in the lowest error in Text 1, the third lowest error in Text 2, and the second lowest error in Text 3. Thus, the standard deviation of that worker's individual rankings is equal to 1, showing high consistency across multiple tasks. On the other hand, a worker with individual rankings equal to 5, 48, and 22 is much more inconsistent across multiple tasks since the standard deviation of his individual rankings is 21.66.

Fig. 4 shows the standard deviation of individual rankings as a function of the overall ranking of each worker. For the sake of a better visualization, we fit a quadratic function to the data in a least-squares sense (norm of residuals equal to 35.664). We note that 2 is the optimal degree for polynomial fitting according to the Akaike information criterion (AIC). The resulting quadratic function is:

$$f(x) = -0.018922 * x^2 + 1.1371 * x + 1.6287$$

where x is a worker's overall ranking, and $f(x)$ is the standard deviation of that worker's individual rankings. Figure 4 shows that the overall top-performing workers are more consistent across multiple tasks than the other workers.

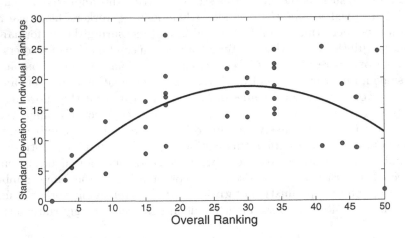

Fig. 4. The standard deviation of individual rankings as a function of the overall ranking of each worker.

For example, the standard deviations of the individual rankings of the top 7 workers are always less than 15, whereas 4 out of the 7 worst-performing workers have standard deviations greater than 15. In general, the most inconsistent workers are the workers with overall ranking between 15 and 35.

The results presented in this section, together with the results from the previous section, suggest that removing workers with high overall error from the population of workers might be a mistake since those workers can sometimes produce high quality outputs, as can be inferred from Fig. 4. Furthermore, restricting the population of workers to a few overall top-performing workers is likely to produce more accurate aggregate outputs because these workers consistently report outputs with low errors.

7   Conclusion

In this paper, we empirically studied the influence of the number of workers on the accuracy of aggregate outputs in a crowdsourcing setting. We first showed that adding more workers reduces the average error of the aggregate output, which was measured in terms of the root-mean-square deviation between the aggregate output and a gold-standard output. In other words, the expected accuracy of the aggregate output increases as the number of workers increases.

We also showed that there are diminishing returns for extra workers, where the reduction in the average error is always less than 2 % after the sixth worker. Adding extra workers also implies that the risk of obtaining a combination of exclusively poor workers decreases because both the standard deviation of errors in aggregate outputs and the maximum error decrease as the number of workers increases.

We then moved to analyze the benefits of removing the overall worst-performing workers from the population of workers as well as the benefits of restricting the population of workers to only the overall top-performing workers. We found that an aggregate output from any combination of up to k top-performing workers, for $k \in \{1, \ldots, 20\}$, is, in expectation, more accurate than an aggregate output from a random combination with the same number of workers from the complete population of workers.

Unexpectedly, removing any number $k \in \{2, \ldots, 20\}$ of worst-performing workers does not necessarily result in more accurate aggregate outputs. The reason for this unexpected result is that the worst-performing workers are not always consistent across multiple tasks, which implies that a poor worker can eventually produce an accurate output.

Based on our results, our first recommendation for an organization or a decision maker who wants to design a crowdsourcing process is: in the absence of prior knowledge about the accuracy of the workers, having more workers is always beneficial because both the expected error in the aggregate output and the risk of obtaining a poor combination of workers decrease as the number of workers increases. Clearly, the marginal costs as well as the marginal benefits of adding extra workers must be considered in practice. Our results showed that most of the benefit occurs with the first five to six workers. Thereafter, the marginal benefit of adding another worker is very low, and it might not outweigh the cost of adding the extra worker.

Our second recommendation for a more efficient design of crowdsourcing processes concerns the case when there exists prior knowledge about the accuracy of the workers. In this case, one should focus only on combinations of the overall top-performing workers since this greatly reduces the expected error in the aggregate output. We found that almost perfect accuracy can be achieved by using only combinations of the very top workers. In practice, however, workers have constraints on the number of outputs they are willing to provide. This issue can be addressed by increasing the pool of top-performing workers. Our results show that when the size of the pool is up to 40 % of the size of the full population, the aggregate outputs from the top-performing workers are, in expectation, still more accurate than the aggregate outputs from the full population of workers, for the same number of workers.

It is noteworthy that our study focused on simple averages to combine workers' outputs. More sophisticated combination procedures are available (e.g., see the work by Carvalho and Larson [2]), but simple averages have been shown to perform well empirically and to be robust when eliciting expert opinions in different domains [3]. In addition, an averaging approach is easy to use, requiring neither assessments regarding the worker's judgment process nor self-assessed confidence in the accuracy of the reported outputs.

An exciting open question is whether or not the results obtained in our study hold true in different settings, e.g., for different tasks, number of answers, etc. We argue that an answer to this question is of great importance to the crowdsourcing community given its potential to create less costly and more effective crowdsourcing processes.

Moreover, it would be of theoretical value to make stronger connections between our results in this paper and results from statistical theory. For example, an interpretation of our results in Sect. 4 is that we are estimating the population average error through empirical distributions of average errors, one for each group size $r \in \{1, \ldots, n\}$. Under this interpretation, the Central Limit Theorem then implies the reduction of the variance (risk) observed in our results. Exploring this connection might be useful to determine the optimal number of workers to hire, but now taking the risk of poor combinations of workers into account.

Acknowledgments. The authors acknowledge Craig Boutilier, Pascal Poupart, Daniel Lizotte, and Xi Alice Gao for useful discussions. The authors thank Carol Acton, Katherine Acheson, Stefan Rehm, Susan Gow, and Veronica Austen for providing gold-standard outputs for our experiment. The authors also thank the Natural Sciences and Engineering Research Council of Canada for funding this research.

A   Description of the Texts

We describe in this appendix the texts used in our experiments as well as the gold-standard scores.

Text 1

An excerpt from the "Sonnet XVII" by Neruda [9]. Intentionally misspelled words are highlighted in bold.

> "I do not love you as if you **was** salt-rose, or topaz
> or the **arrown** of carnations that spread fire:
> I love you as certain dark things are loved,
> secretly, between the **shadown** and the soul"

The gold-standard scores for the criteria *grammar*, *clarity*, and *relevance* are, respectively, 1, 2, and 2.

Text 2

An excerpt from "The Cow" by Taylor *et al.* [12]. Intentionally misspelled words are highlighted in bold.

> "THANK you, **prety** cow, that made
> **Plesant** milk to soak my bread,
> Every day and every night,
> Warm, and fresh, and sweet, and white."

The gold-standard scores for the criteria *grammar*, *clarity*, and *relevance* are, respectively, 1, 2, and 1.

Text 3

Words randomly generated in a semi-structured way. Each line starts with a noun followed by a verb in a wrong verb form. In order to mimic a poetic writing style, all the words in the same line start with a similar letter.

> "Baby bet binary boundaries bubbles
> Carlos cease CIA conditionally curve
> Daniel deny disease domino dumb
> Faust fest fierce forced furbished"

The gold-standard scores for the criteria *grammar*, *clarity*, and *relevance* are, respectively, 0, 0, and 0.

B   Experimental Results

Table 1 shows the numerical results from all the analysis performed in this paper.

Table 1. The average error, the standard deviation of the errors, and the maximum error per text for different populations of agents. All the values are rounded to 3 decimal places.

Population	r	Text 1			Text 2			Text 3		
		Avg	Std	Max	Avg	Std	Max	Avg	Std	Max
All	1	0.685	0.492	1.732	0.679	0.327	1.414	0.675	0.526	1.633
	2	0.621	0.322	1.732	0.567	0.220	1.323	0.650	0.348	1.633
	3	0.591	0.260	1.610	0.520	0.184	1.305	0.637	0.278	1.515
	4	0.575	0.225	1.555	0.495	0.162	1.199	0.630	0.237	1.451
	5	0.565	0.201	1.414	0.480	0.146	1.114	0.625	0.210	1.352
	6	0.560	0.183	1.398	0.469	0.135	1.045	0.622	0.189	1.305
	7	0.554	0.167	1.314	0.462	0.124	0.962	0.620	0.173	1.259
	8	0.550	0.155	1.220	0.457	0.116	0.944	0.618	0.161	1.242
	9	0.548	0.145	1.185	0.452	0.109	0.914	0.616	0.150	1.232
	10	0.545	0.135	1.158	0.449	0.102	0.920	0.616	0.140	1.134
	11	0.544	0.128	1.102	0.446	0.096	0.827	0.615	0.132	1.127
	12	0.542	0.121	1.063	0.444	0.092	0.814	0.614	0.124	1.120
	13	0.541	0.115	1.048	0.442	0.087	0.802	0.613	0.118	1.078
	14	0.540	0.110	1.067	0.440	0.083	0.768	0.613	0.111	1.042
	15	0.539	0.105	0.996	0.439	0.079	0.768	0.612	0.106	1.034
	16	0.538	0.100	1.026	0.438	0.076	0.744	0.611	0.102	1.032
	17	0.537	0.096	0.973	0.436	0.073	0.724	0.611	0.097	1.000
	18	0.537	0.092	0.911	0.436	0.069	0.726	0.610	0.093	1.012
	19	0.536	0.088	0.932	0.434	0.067	0.710	0.611	0.089	0.971
	20	0.536	0.084	0.877	0.434	0.064	0.694	0.610	0.086	0.979
	21	0.535	0.081	0.922	0.433	0.062	0.681	0.610	0.082	1.027
	22	0.535	0.078	0.860	0.433	0.059	0.660	0.610	0.079	0.923
	23	0.535	0.074	0.839	0.432	0.057	0.657	0.610	0.075	0.946
	24	0.534	0.072	0.835	0.432	0.055	0.650	0.609	0.073	0.950
	25	0.534	0.069	0.804	0.431	0.053	0.640	0.609	0.070	0.967
	26	0.534	0.066	0.824	0.431	0.051	0.629	0.609	0.067	0.890
	27	0.534	0.064	0.793	0.430	0.048	0.638	0.609	0.065	0.878
	28	0.534	0.061	0.791	0.430	0.047	0.627	0.609	0.062	0.850
	29	0.533	0.059	0.758	0.429	0.045	0.606	0.609	0.059	0.847
	30	0.533	0.056	0.752	0.429	0.043	0.600	0.609	0.057	0.852
	31	0.533	0.054	0.762	0.429	0.041	0.594	0.608	0.055	0.847
	32	0.533	0.052	0.738	0.428	0.040	0.578	0.609	0.052	0.823
	33	0.532	0.049	0.726	0.428	0.038	0.571	0.608	0.050	0.809
	34	0.532	0.047	0.718	0.428	0.036	0.567	0.608	0.048	0.837

(*Continued*)

Table 1. (*Continued*)

Population	r	Text 1			Text 2			Text 3		
		Avg	Std	Max	Avg	Std	Max	Avg	Std	Max
	35	0.532	0.045	0.709	0.428	0.035	0.575	0.608	0.046	0.813
	36	0.532	0.043	0.718	0.428	0.033	0.556	0.608	0.044	0.791
	37	0.532	0.041	0.692	0.427	0.031	0.542	0.608	0.041	0.785
	38	0.532	0.039	0.672	0.427	0.030	0.548	0.608	0.039	0.767
	39	0.531	0.036	0.677	0.427	0.028	0.537	0.608	0.037	0.757
	40	0.531	0.034	0.660	0.426	0.027	0.542	0.608	0.035	0.754
	41	0.531	0.032	0.647	0.426	0.025	0.518	0.608	0.033	0.727
	42	0.531	0.030	0.638	0.426	0.023	0.510	0.608	0.030	0.720
	43	0.531	0.028	0.623	0.426	0.021	0.513	0.607	0.028	0.706
	44	0.531	0.026	0.612	0.426	0.020	0.502	0.607	0.026	0.690
	45	0.531	0.023	0.598	0.426	0.018	0.491	0.607	0.023	0.675
	46	0.531	0.020	0.585	0.426	0.016	0.481	0.607	0.021	0.660
	47	0.531	0.017	0.570	0.425	0.013	0.470	0.607	0.018	0.646
	48	0.531	0.014	0.556	0.425	0.011	0.459	0.607	0.014	0.632
	49	0.530	0.010	0.543	0.425	0.008	0.442	0.607	0.010	0.620
	50	0.530	0.000	0.530	0.425	0.000	0.425	0.607	0.000	0.607
Top 47	1	0.632	0.456	1.732	0.684	0.318	1.414	0.641	0.525	1.633
	2	0.572	0.298	1.555	0.581	0.219	1.323	0.617	0.346	1.633
	3	0.543	0.241	1.503	0.541	0.182	1.305	0.604	0.275	1.515
Top 3	1	0.000	0.000	0.000	0.192	0.333	0.577	0.000	0.000	0.000
	2	0.000	0.000	0.000	0.192	0.167	0.289	0.000	0.000	0.000
	3	0.000	0.000	0.000	0.192	0.000	0.192	0.000	0.000	0.000

References

1. Carvalho, A., Dimitrov, S., Larson, K.: The output-agreement method induces honest behavior in the presence of social projection. ACM SIGecom Exch. **13**(1), 77–81 (2014)
2. Carvalho, A., Larson, K.: A consensual linear opinion pool. In: Proceedings of the 23rd International Joint Conference on Artificial Intelligence, pp. 2518–2524. AAAI Press (2013)
3. Clemen, R.T.: Combining forecasts: a review and annotated bibliography. Int. J. Forecast. **5**(4), 559–583 (1989)
4. Gao, X.A., Mao, A., Chen, Y.: Trick or treat: putting peer prediction to the test. In: Proceedings of the 1st Workshop on Crowdsourcing and Online Behavioral Experiments (2013)
5. Ho, C.J., Vaughan, J.W.: Online task assignment in crowdsourcing markets. In: Proceedings of the 26th AAAI Conference on Artificial Intelligence, pp. 45–51 (2012)

6. Ipeirotis, P.G.: Analyzing the amazon mechanical turk marketplace. XRDS Crossroads: ACM Mag. Stud. **17**(2), 16–21 (2010)
7. Lin, C.H., Weld, D.S.: Dynamically switching between synergistic workflows for crowdsourcing. In: Proceedings of the 26th AAAI Conference on Artificial Intelligence, pp. 132–133 (2012)
8. Mason, W., Suri, S.: Conducting behavioral research on amazon's mechanical turk. Behav. Res. Methods **44**(1), 1–23 (2012)
9. Neruda, P.: 100 Love Sonnets. Exile, Holstein (2007)
10. Quinn, A.J., Bederson, B.B.: Human computation: a survey and taxonomy of a growing field. In: Proceedings of the 2011 SIGCHI Conference on Human Factors in Computing Systems, pp. 1403–1412 (2011)
11. Sheng, V.S., Provost, F., Ipeirotis, P.G.: Get another label? improving data quality and data mining using multiple, noisy labelers. In: Proceedings of the 14th International Conference on Knowledge Discovery and Data Mining, pp. 614–622 (2008)
12. Taylor, J., Taylor, A., Greenaway, K.: Little Ann and Other Poems. Nabu Press, Charleston (2010)
13. Tran-Thanh, L., Stein, S., Rogers, A., Jennings, N.R.: Efficient crowdsourcing of unknown experts using multi-armed bandits. In: Proceedings of the 20th European Conference on Artificial Intelligence, pp. 768–773 (2012)
14. Yuen, M.C., King, I., Leung, K.S.: A survey of crowdsourcing systems. In: Proceedings of IEEE 3rd International Conference on Social Computing, pp. 766–773 (2011)
15. Zhang, H., Horvitz, E., Parkes, D.: Automated workflow synthesis. In: Proceedings of the 27th AAAI Conference on Artificial Intelligence, pp. 1020–1026 (2013)

Multi-Agent Cooperation for Optimizing Weight of Electrical Aircraft Harnesses

Stéphanie Combettes[1]([✉]), Thomas Sontheimer[2], Sylvain Rougemaille[2], and Pierre Glize[1]

[1] IRIT, Université Paul Sabatier-Toulouse III, Toulouse, France
stephanie.combettes@init.fr
[2] UPETEC, Ramonville-Saint-Agne, France

Abstract. This paper deals with minimizing aircraft electrical system weight. Because of technological advances that are spreading, electrical system of aircraft is more complex to design and requires new way to be conceived in order to reduce its weight. This paper describes how to optimize weight of harnesses thanks to the Adaptive Multi-Agent System approach. This approach is based on agent cooperation which makes global function of system emerge. Communication between agents is the focus of this approach. We will develop this approach and apply it to the weight optimisation problem. The developed software provides results that are either equivalent or better than those of classical approaches. Moreover, this software may be a precious help to engineer in charge of designing harnesses as it enables to make different tests in a quasi-real time.

Keywords: Multi-Agent System · Cooperation · Emergence · Adaptation · Criticality · Local decision

1 Introduction

The development and the use of new technologies as well as the increase of cabin space imply important changes in the field of aeronautics as aircraft have to integrate new characteristics to improve flight comfort. As part of the electrical system becomes larger in aircraft, cables routes are denser and electrical wiring intensifies.

As a consequence, defining new routes guaranteeing aircraft security becomes harder. Constraints are numerous and interdependent, and mainly concern environmental, electrical and thermic constraints (such as temperature, voltage drop, electromagnetic compatibility or EMC ...). They also depend on the flight phases: landing, parking, flying and taking off. Until now far margins taken to oversize cables ensured respect of constraints. The number of oversized elements is important as the structure of a cable harness is a complex electrical system. A harness is an assembly of cables being themselves an assembly of wires which transmit signals or electrical power through aircraft. Each element (harness, cable, wire) has several constraints to respect and an aircraft has a large number of harnesses: it implies an explosion of the number of elements and thus of constraints

© Springer International Publishing Switzerland 2015
N. Bulling (Ed.): EUMAS 2014, LNAI 8953, pp. 301–315, 2015.
DOI: 10.1007/978-3-319-17130-2_20

to respect. Indeed, as an aircraft may contain up to one thousand harnesses, each of them may contain dozens of cables having themselves up to four wires, there are about fifty thousand interdependent variables. For instance the A380 has about 350 Km of cables. Cables' diameter over-estimation leads to increase the weight of the harness (and thus the aircraft's one) implying an increase of operational costs (a more important fuel consumption for ex.) while current trends impose to reduce them.

The present challenge consists in decreasing harnesses weight: cables must be sized at their best while all constraints are not violated. As this problem is a first study in the framework of a French project, this paper will not take into account all constraints neither all elements of an aircraft. Since classical approaches of optimization lack performance to solve such problems, we tackle it by using Multi-Agents Systems. This approach is based on cooperation between agents in order to make global function of the system emerge. We focus our study on the cooperation between agents and the way they communicate.

The rest of this paper is divided into the following parts. Section 2 describes the structure of an electrical system and its constraints and gives a formalisation of this optimization problem. Section 3 gives an overview of meta-heuristics and develop the Adaptive Multi-Agents System (AMAS) approach. In Sect. 4, the AMAS approach is applied to the harness weight optimization problem. In this section the behaviour and the communication of agents are detailed. Section 5 gives some results and analyses them before concluding in Sect. 6.

2   Description of the Harness Weight Optimization Problem

Before formalizing this optimization problem, we give a detailed description of the harness architecture which has physical and functional points of view, as well as the constraints of its elements.

2.1   Electrical System Architecture

Electrical distribution in aircraft consists in bringing energy from production heart towards several consumer systems. Designing electrical systems must take into account the aircraft topology, pressure and non-pressure areas, electrical devices location within aircraft and possible routes for harnesses. Harnesses use paths reserved for electrical distribution in the aircraft structure. Moreover, for security reasons harnesses connecting sensitive equipments must be duplicated and follow different routes. Designing electrical system is a very complex task because of the harness structure which is an aggregation of several elements.

Electrical harness architecture is twofold: a physical point of view and a functional one. According to the physical point of view, equipments are at the lower level connected by *wires*; they are themselves aggregated into *cables* in order to reduce both weight and cost of cladding and shield. Cables are themselves gathered within a *harness*. A harness (connecting several equipments) forms an arborescence whose unit element is a *branch*. A branch, corresponding to space located between two nodes has homogeneous environmental conditions of temperature and pressure. Figure 1 shows a schematic representation of the harness physical view.

According to the functional point of view, production system is connected to consumer equipments via *links* going through the whole harness. A link is represented by wire succession: it has no physical reality but a functional one. The complexity of the problem also came from the fact that a link may run through several interlinked harnesses. Figure 2 shows a schematic representation of the harness functional view.

To sum up, a harness is composed of cables, wires and links. Wires are at the intersection of cables and links as they are related to these two elements.

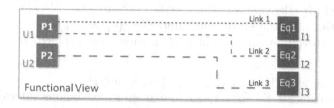

Fig. 1. A harness physical view

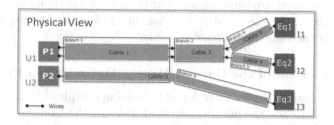

Fig. 2. A harness functional view

2.2 Harness Constraints

Besides structural constraints related to its architecture, the design of an electrical system has to take into account functional constraints which are numerous, manifold and interdependent in order to enable a secure functioning of an aircraft during its operation life. In the addressed problem we focus on electrical and thermal constraints detailed below.

A maximal voltage drop is associated with each link and it must not be exceeded at risk of dysfunction of the powered system. A maximal temperature and a maximal overheating are associated with each cable: they must not be exceeded at risk of melting. All of these constraints have to be checked for each flight phase (landing, parking, flying and taking off). Moreover, all wires that are gathered in a cable must have the same gauge. A gauge is a standardized measure representing section of a wire and in a cable (being an assembly of wires) all the wires must have the same section or gauge). Considering the harness sizing rules, increasing a cable gauge (denoting decreasing the cable diameter) means increase of its temperature and of its voltage drop. Thus selecting minimal diameter of cables to minimize harness weight does not mean respecting electrical and thermal constraints: this is not a solution!

Respecting those constraints is difficult task due to the data number (elements and constraints) to be processed. Indeed, in addition to the large number of interdependent variables (about fifty thousand), aircraft harness design has to consider voltage drop, overheating and temperature constraints and the objective of minimizing the electrical system weight. This optimization problem to solve is multi-constrained and mono-objective.

2.3   Formalization of the Harness Weight Optimization Problem

Different formalisms have been developed for solving complex optimization problems under constraints, the most widely studied being the Constraint Optimization Problem (COP) formalism. In this formalism, a set of variables (problem entities) must be assigned a value of a given domain in order to minimize or maximize an objective function. Solving such problems consists in exploring search space and finding the best assignment to those variables.

A COP is a triplet $\langle X, D, C \rangle$ where $X = \{x_1, \ldots, x_n\}$ is the set of variables to instantiate which take values in the specific domains $D = \{D(x_1), \ldots, D(x_m)\}$, and are restricted by the set of constraints $C = \{c_1, \ldots, c_k\}$.

Applying to the harness weight optimization, this problem is described as follows:

- Variables are wires $W = \{w_1, \ldots, w_m\}$ with $m \in \mathbb{N}$;
- Sets of domains are $\mathbb{R}^+$ for a range of diameter (continuous values) and a set of gauges $G = \{g_1, \ldots, g_{10}\}$ (discrete values); the gauges are standard cross sectional areas.
- Sets of constraints are:
  - A set of links $L = \{l_1, \ldots, l_n\}$ with $n \in \mathbb{N}$;
  - A set of connections $O = \{o_1, \ldots, o_j\}$ with $j \in \mathbb{N}$; a connection is a point connection between several wires belonging to the same links.
  - A set of cables $C = \{c_1, \ldots, c_p\}$ with $p \in \mathbb{N}$;
  - Let $ConnectedTo$ be a function giving connections of the considered wire: $ConnectedTo : W \longmapsto O$.
    Let $BelongToLink$ be a function giving links containing the considered wire $BelongToLink : W \longmapsto L$.
  - $\forall s \in [1..m], \forall l_i \in L$ and $\forall w_s \in W \mid BelongToLink(w_s = l_i), VoltageDrop(w_s) < MaxVoltageDrop$: terminal voltage drop of wires forming a link must be less than the authorized maximal voltage drop;

- $\forall k \in [1..p]$, $\forall c_k \in C$, $Temperature(c_k) < MaxTemperature$ and $Over$ $heating(c_k) < MaxOverheating$: each cable has to check temperature and overheating constraints;
- Let $BelongToCable$ be a function giving the cable containing considered wire: $BelongToCable : W \longmapsto C$.

  Let $Gauge$ be another function giving the gauge value of considered wire: $Gauge : W \longmapsto G$.

  $\forall r \in [1..m]$ and $\forall s \in [1..m]$ with $r \neq s$, $w_r \in W$ and $\forall w_s \in W$ | $BelongToCable(w_r) = BelongToCable(w_s)$, then $Gauge(w_r) = Gauge$ (w_s) (Gauge of each wire belonging to the same cable has to be identical);

The problem to solve is:

$$S = Min(\sum_{i=1}^{m} Weight(w_i))$$

with $Weight : W \longmapsto \mathbb{R}^+$ be a function giving the wire weight.

3   Optimization Methods

Complexity of optimization problem addressed in this paper is due to the number and interdependence of involved parameters. It is practically impossible to predict long-term consequences of the choice of a parameter value on the choice of values for others. Current applications having an important number of elements and constraints to be respected imply a combinatorial explosion of search space. Finding optimal solution of such applications becomes difficult even impossible or requires prohibitive computation times. If we consider n links and if each link has to choose a gauge among g gauges, the number of possibilities is g^n. Considering n = 1000 and g = 10, there are $g^n = 10^{1000}$ combinations. Some domain experts work on strategies to reduce this combination number but despite this, it remains large. Several methods have been developed among them Meta-heuristics, an approximated one, which we will focus on.

3.1   Brief Overview of Meta-heuristics

Meta-heuristics, the most important class among approximate methods, are uncertain and often non-deterministic solving algorithms. Their aim is to efficiently explore search space in order to find a solution close to the optimal one. Their strategy is to alternate between an exploration phase (which consists in discovering new zones of the search space) and an exploitation one (which consists in concentrating search in promising zones). Meta-heuristics are divided in two groups: trajectory meta-heuristics (such as Tabu search [6] or Simulated Annealing [10]) and population-based meta-heuristics (such as Genetic Algorithms [7], Particle Swarm Optimization [9] and Ant Colony [4]).

Those methods, based on a centered approach have shown their limits to cope with growing complexity of current applications because of system dynamics produced by unpredictable changes of events, and also by necessity to have a well-defined objective function that is sometimes missing. Furthermore those methods failed in resolving real problems with so many data because of required prohibitive computation time [11,13].

Hybrid meta-heuristics increase solving performance of problems with growing complexity as they combine trajectory meta-heuristics during exploitation phases and population-based ones during exploration phase. This association introduces parallelism (through computation distribution) and cooperation between several meta-heuristics (through control decentralisation).

Thus some solving methods, based on computation distribution and on control decentralisation were defined to bring these improvements to problems, and among them the Distributed Constraint Optimization Problem also called Multi-Agents Systems. In those MAS, each variable is managed by an autonomous entity called *agent*. Those agents have to cooperate by coordinating their choices and their actions, in order to satisfy global objective function. This global objective function is modelled as a set of constraints known by agents in which its variables are involved.

Multi-agent technology is pertinent for environments relatively dynamics (constraints and local objectives may evolve) and where search time is constrained (user waiting time). A comparative study realised in [8] shows scalability performances of MAS with regard to classical algorithms.

We propose to use the Adaptive Multi-Agent System (AMAS) approach [2,3] to solve harness weight optimization. This approach is based on cooperative self-organization of agents, and whose system's aim is to reach adequate collective function. For each agent the self-organization principle consists in satisfying its local criteria thanks to its skills and beliefs, and without being conscious of the global objective to reach. Thus each agent has its own local function and has to cooperate with its neighbour agents, thus enabling self-organization [12] to achieve its own local goal. Cooperation is defined as a social attitude of the agent.

3.2   The Adaptive Multi-Agent System Approach

The Adaptive Multi-Agent System (AMAS) approach is based on cooperative self-organization of agents of the system whose aim is to reach adequate collective function. Cooperation between agents having a local aim leads to emergence of the function at global (i.e. system) level. This emerging global behaviour is only visible by an observer outside the system. Explicitly defining the global function is not needed but it is necessary to lead agents to make this function emerge thanks to their cooperation.

This approach is based on the *functional adequacy theorem* [5] stating that: *For any functionally adequate system, there exists at least one system with cooperative internal medium that fulfils an equivalent function in the same environment.*

A cooperative internal medium system is a system having none Non Cooperative Situation (NCS): for this purpose each agent interacts with agents of its neighbourhood in a cooperative way. Life cycle of an agent being perception, decision and action non-cooperation is defined as follow:

$$NonCoop = \neg C_{perception} \lor \neg C_{decision} \lor \neg C_{action}$$

It means that an agent is in a NCS if (i) the signal it perceived is ambiguous or not understood, (ii) perceived information does not produce any new decision and (iii) consequences of its actions are not useful to others. An agent detecting a NCS should be able to solve it in order to come back into a cooperative state. During its life cycle an agent may face one or several of the seven types of NCS. During perception phase:

- *ambiguity*: the agent interprets the perceived signal in several ways;
- *incomprehension*: the agent does not understand the perceived message.

During decision phase:

- *unproductiveness*: the agent does not produce any conclusions from perceived information;
- *incompetence*: the agent is not able to exploit the perceived information.

During action phase:

- *uselessness*: the agent thinks that its action will neither help another agent nor come closer to its own objective;
- *conflict*: the agent thinks that its action and the one of another agent are antinomic;
- *concurrency*: the agent thinks its action and the one of another agent will end up in same result.

Solving NCSs may be regarded as learning adequate functionality and it represents the critical point of adaptation process. Besides its nominal behaviour related to its local objective, each agent needs a cooperative behaviour to detect and solve an NCS, or even to anticipate it.

3.3   Solving Non Cooperative Situations

In the AMAS approach, an autonomous agent owns a local objective that influences the function of decision of its life cycle. The agent has the capability to evaluate its non-satisfaction degree depending on its current situation with regard to its local aim. This non-satisfaction degree also called **criticality** represents the distance from its current situation to achievement of its local objective. Thus the further from its local objective an agent is, the more critical it is.

Cooperative attitude of an agent consists in achieving its local objective without increasing -but rather decreasing- criticalities of neighbourhood agents. It may even deteriorate timely its own situation, in order to help a neighbour agent with a too high criticality, thus offering a (temporary) discharge of constraints. The best solution is obtained when criticalities of all agents are minimum within the system. This cooperative attitude represents reorganization dynamics as it guarantees that the system will reach a functionally adequate state aimed by designer.

4   Applying the AMAS Approach to Minimize Harness Weight

Designing and sizing harness cables by minimizing their weight is a complex problem of combinatorial optimization under constraints. Since problem becomes more complex optimization tools come up against exponential increase of calculation times (see Sect. 3). This difficulty narrows use of these tools for sizing subsets of aircraft wiring and poses issue of coherence of the whole.

The AMAS approach leads to a strictly local resolution of problem. Thus search space is not totally explored but is guided by the cooperative principle. This paradigm change enables to break free of practical limits met by classical approaches of optimization such as increase of computation times. Thus cooperation between agents has to make the adequate function, i.e. minimizing the harness weight, emerge.

We now specify the different types of agents composing the system and their behaviours.

4.1   Agent, Local Aim and Nominal Behaviour

AMAS approach proposes a bottom-up analysis of the problem, the ADELFE methodology [1]. This methodology is based on *Unified Modelling Language* (UML) and *Rational Unified Process* (RUP) and uses Agent-UML to express interaction protocol between agents. Its aim is to guide complex system designers through development phase of systems based on AMAS approach and emergence concept. From domain and data model analysis, several Non Cooperative Situations (NCS) were identified and for each agent type encountering one of these situations, its behaviour has to be cooperative. Thus each agent type is endowed with a nominal behaviour and a cooperative one.

Applying ADELFE methodology to the harness weight problem, *agentification* phase has enabled to define four types of agents: the *Link*, *Cable*, *Wire* and *Connection* agents.

- the *Link* agent represents functional aspects of electrical system and its local goal is to respect voltage drop constraints.
- the *Cable* agent represents a cable and its local goal is to uniform diameter of its wires and to expose a current diameter. It also has to respect temperature and overheating constraints.
- the *Wire* agent represents a wire and it binds functional aspects (links) and physical ones (cables). Its local objective is to stabilize its diameter (whatever its initial value).
- the *Connection* agent represents a connection point between several wires belonging to a same link. Its local objective is to balance criticalities of *Wire* agents connected to it.

As constraints differ according to the four flight phases (landing, parking, flying and taking off) and as they must be respected at each of these phases, all *Link*,

Wire and *Connection* agents were cloned four times, once per flight phase. Only the *Cable* agent is not cloned as it is the central element which integrates all additional constraints of *Wire*, *Connection* and *Link* agents related to flight phases. Indeed, a *Cable* agent is the physical element shared by all flight phases and it seeks the optimized gauge value satisfying all its *Wire* agents, themselves constrained by *Connection* and *Link* agents.

For instance a cable made of three wires in a physical real system is thus represented by a *Cable* agent having three *Wire* agents for each flight phase, so twelve *Wire* agents in all. The *Cable* agent has to converge towards a common gauge satisfying constraints of all its *Wire* agents, and indirectly those of *Link* and *Connection* agents related to previous *Wire* agents. As each *Wire* agent is in relation with *Link* and *Connection* agents, a modification of its gauge perturbs voltage drop, criticalities balance etc. implying adaptation of other agents (chain reaction) but it also means that other agents may perturb it.

4.2 Steps of Resolution and Cooperative Behaviour

Problem resolution seeks the optimal diameter value and so is carried out on continuous values. For that purpose, *Wire* agents are at the heart of algorithm. Their own goal is to stabilize their diameter with *Link*, *Cable* and *Connection* agents satisfy electro-thermal and charge balance constraints.

First each *Wire* agent estimates its criticality degree according to its current diameter thank to a local computation. This criticality is then communicated to *Connection* agent to whom it is connected. Each *Link* agent checks that voltage drop between ends of *Wire* agents that form it is lower than the authorized one. When voltage drop exceeds the maximal authorized one the *Link* agent is in a Non Cooperative Situation (NCS) and more precisely an *incompetence* one since it is not able to change itself this situation. To become again cooperative, it informs the *Connection* agents connected to it. Each *Connection* agent retrieves criticalities of the *Wire* agents to whom it is connected to and it deduces which *Wire* agent may act in order to (i) solve *Link* agent NCS and (ii) make criticality degree decrease.

Each *Cable* agent checks that no temperature or overheating constraint is violated. Otherwise, incriminated *Wire* agents (the most critical contained by *Cable* agent) are informed and have to increase their current diameter. If none constraint is violated, the *Wire* agent decreases its criticality by reducing its diameter. The *Wire* agent ends up determining its optimal diameter through this play of modifications (successive increases and decreases) and through an internal learning mechanism. The selected diameter underlies the choice of the wire gauge.

During this solving phase, the notion of minimizing weight is not explicitly nor directly tackled. Weight of harness or of its elements is never computed. This is the succession of changes and the propagation of modification among agents that lead the system to have its global function that emerges. To show this clearly we will have a focus in the following section on communication between agents.

4.3   Focus on Communication Between Agents

Communication between agents is the crucial point that enables them to cooperate. To show how the cooperation occurs, we detail exchanges between agents by giving the algorithms of communication for each agent type. We consider here the first step of resolution, that is to say search of the optimal diameter of cables (continuous part). We clarify that the resolution has two steps: first computation of all diameters of cables (which are continuous values) and then once this first step achieved, gauges (which are discrete values) of cables are selected (according to the computed diameter) to size harnesses at their best. *Link* agent has to respect voltage drop constraints and it communicates with *Connection* agents connected to it.

```
if (voltage drop > Max. Voltage Drop) then
  send request to the Connection agents to reduce voltage drop
else
  send to them request to reduce weight
end
```

Connection agent has to balance criticalities of *Wire* agents who belong to it.

```
receive at least one query
if (request to decrease voltage drop) then
    send request to the Wire agents on less critical side to reduce
      voltage drop
else
  if (request to reduce weight) then
    send request to Wire agents on most critical side to reduce weight
  end
end
```

Wire agent has to stabilize its diameter according to the respect/non-respect of constraints and it may send a request to *Cable* agent to whom it belongs to.

```
receive at least one query
if (request to decrease  voltage drop) then
    send request to the Cable agent to reduce voltage drop
else
  if (request to reduce weight) then
      send request to the Cable agent to reduce weight
  end
end
```

Cable agent has to respect temperature and overheating constraints and to uniform diameter of its wires.

```
receive at least one query
if (request to decrease voltage drop, temperature or overheating) then
    increase its diameter
else
  if (request to reduce weight) then
```

```
        reduce its diameter
    end
end
```

First we could notice that during resolution step, the weight value is never used or calculated or exchanged between agents. Weight optimization is carried out indirectly by increasing or decreasing diameter of cables. This point shows that global objective is not explicitly *computed* but *emerges* from local actions of each agent achieving its own goal.

Second we notice that there is no *random* during algorithm execution as opposed to classical algorithms such as Ants Colony, or Tabu Search. An agent tries only to reduce its degree of criticality or the one of its neighbourhood. We also see in this algorithm that each agent decides at most one action during a cycle and may act in opposite way between cycles.

In this section we have detailed the problem solving process based on agent cooperation. This cooperation enables to find the smallest diameters (and gauges) of cables satisfying all addressed constraints and thus it entails an optimised weight of harnesses.

5   Results and Analysis

This work has been achieved within the French project SMART-HARNESS. As it was a first study on weight optimisation, addressed problem only considers few harnesses (up to 52). Data used to validate our solution were provided by expert Company. We have developed a software platform called Smart Harness

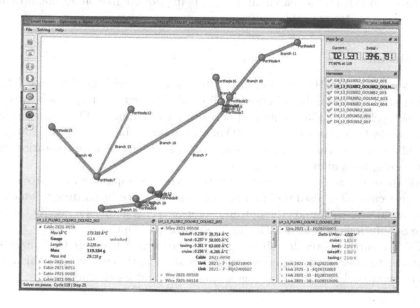

Fig. 3. The interface of the smart harness optimizer

Optimizer that implements AMAS approach using processes of local decision. Its interface may be visualized in Fig. 3 and shows the structure of a harness (center) and its elements and characteristics (below).

5.1   Outlines of Test Cases

Three categories of test cases were used to evaluate the developed tool. They correspond to three electrical systems constituted of respectively 3, 8 and 52 harnesses. Each category comes in several instances where charge required by equipments was changed. The two first instances are amperage uniformed loaded for all links in all flight phases with 1A, 4A and 20A (10A for the second case). The last instance has amperage modifications depending on flight phases. The 52-harness case has only one instance. Moreover we consider that there are 10 possibilities of gauge available per cables for all the instances and cases.

The first and simplest case contains 3 harnesses and is constituted of 9 cables crossing 9 branches and grouping together 18 wires realizing 6 links. Search space size of this case is 10^9.

The second case contains 8 harnesses and is constituted of 25 cables crossing 40 branches and grouping together 50 wires realizing 22 links. Search space size of this case is 10^{25}.

The third case contains 52 harnesses and represents an ATA (Air Transport Association). It is constituted of 404 cables crossing 406 branches and grouping together 643 wires realizing 200 links. Search space size of this case is 10^{404}.

We remind that size of these search spaces is huge but it is possible to reduce them by eliminating impossible values determined by experts. For instance, experts exclude from the search, all gauges being not eligible on ad-hoc problems considering constraints cables.

5.2   Results

Results with Smart Harness Optimizer tool are obtained on a laptop. The 3-harness case resolution lasts between 1600 and 4700 ms and requires between 60 and 160 cycles with 153 agents and according to instances. The 8-harness case resolution lasts between 2100 and 4700 ms and requires between 90 and 200 cycles with 425 agents and according to instances. The 52-harness case resolution, with 5548 agents, lasts about 2 min in 754 cycles.

All these cases were also tested by the expert company which provides us those test cases. The used tool first reduces search space (according to an experiment plan) and then finds the optimal solution. This enables to verify the relevance of solutions obtained with the Smart Harness Optimizer Tool.

Table 1 sums up results obtained with the Smart Harness Optimizer tool compared to ones of the expert company. Besides optimized weight, this tool is able to show each element violating a constraint and its characteristics.

Table 1. Test case results

	Agent number	Resolution time (ms)	Cycle number	Classical methods of optimization
3 harnesses	153	1600 to 4700	60 to 160	1000 ms
8 harnesses	425	2100 to 4700	90 to 200	2 min
52 harnesses	5548	about 120000	754	more than 2 h

5.3 Analysis

We compare here results of the Smart Harness Optimizer Tool with those obtained by the expert company using their own methods based on classical optimization algorithms. The main advantage with our tool using AMAS approach is the significant time saving particularly for the 52-harness case. Smart Harness Optimizer tool found a solution in a few minutes, while expert company methods require several hours. We underline that 52 harnesses represents an ATA and in an aircraft there may be more than 10 ATA. This first study is promising as time resolution is really short. Increasing the harness' number (or ATA) is now conceivable. Nevertheless we mention that for smaller cases (3 and 8 harnesses) results between our tool and expert company methods are quite similar, even better for the latter concerning the 3-harness case.

The second advantage is that our tool enables a fast adaptation in a real time to take into account dynamical changes and disruptions during resolution time or once a solution is provided. This is particularly interesting when an engineer needs to change a value to make tests or comparisons. For instance he may decide to block a gauge value, or to change another one. Once this modification is applied, resolution process does not start again from beginning, but from the current solution, i.e. from current computed values of variables. As the problem resolution is based on local objectives and on cooperation between agents, this value change has a direct impact on neighbourhood of agent whose value is modified is concerned and adapts itself to this new configuration. In other words the initiator agent of modification propagates around its neighbourhood change to other agents. This also leads to obtain new solutions in a quite short time.

The third advantage, consequence of the second one, is that our tool enables an analysis of obtained results. It is possible for engineer to visualize elements (it may be just one element) that prevent the problem to be solved because of constraint violation. An engineer is also able to test several versions for a harness: short time of response got with the tool facilitates such studies.

6 Conclusions

This paper addresses the weight optimization problem of aircraft harnesses. Minimizing harness weight consists in optimizing cable gauge: increasing gauges gives decreasing diameters and so lighter cables. An electrical system is mainly composed of harnesses, functional links, cables and wires of cables and lots of dependencies exist between these different elements. Additionally some environmental, electrical and thermal constraints must be respected and they depend on the four flight phases.

We show that considering the growing complexity of current applications, Adaptive Multi-Agent Systems enable to get systems being flexible, addressing scalability and being able to quickly adapt to the environment dynamics, thanks to the computation distribution and the control decentralization. The AMAS approach requires the implementation of local interactions between agents enabling them to coordinate locally their actions in order to produce a solution at the global level. In the used resolution techniques, we underline that cooperation is a fundamental notion that rules interactions and enhances quality of obtained solutions.

We have developed a platform to solve optimization problem using the AMAS approach. This tool enables harness designer (i) to obtain a solution in a relatively short time, (ii) to improve harness sizing by optimizing wire diameter and (iii) to focus on elements that do not satisfy constraints. Thus the optimized weight of harnesses enables to reduce operation costs of aircraft.

This work offers numerous perspectives for industrials. By improving and enriching this software, this tool may help designers to reconfigure harnesses by inverting or changing cables from their harness. For instance if one cable poses problem because of constraints imposed on its harness, moving it to a new harness may decrease its constraints as its nearby environment has changed.

Going one step further, the tool could help designers to co-design harnesses. This co-design may assist them to specify in real time the most appropriate characteristics and make designers save design time by avoiding going back and forth between services. Going one more step further, this kind of tool could help in routing harnesses within aircraft structure, by choosing the most appropriate way and it could also be coupled with assignment of cables within harnesses.

Considering performances of operational tool, we think that a commercial software may help designers to co-design harnesses. This co-design may assist them to specify in real time most appropriate characteristics like voltage drop.

Acknowledgements. This work was realized within the French national project 'Smart Harness'. This project is co-funded by the 'Ministère de l'Économie, des Finances et de l'Industrie' and the 'Région Midi-Pyrénées' and labeled by the pole of competitiveness Aerospace Valley. Upetec and Irit are specifically involved in the smart harness optimizer work package, in collaboration with the Labinal/Safran Engineering Services Company.

References

1. Bernon, C., Camps, V., Gleizes, M., Picard, G.: Engineering adaptive multi-agent systems: the ADELFE methodology. In: Henderson-Sellers, B., Giorgini, P. (eds.) Agent-Oriented Methodologies, pp. 172–202. Idea Group Publishing, New york (2005)

2. Camps, V.: Vers une théorie de l'auto-organisation dans les systèmes multi-agents basée sur la coopération: application à la recherche d'information dans un système d'information répartie. Ph.D. thesis, Université Paul Sabatier, Toulouse, France (1998)
3. Capera, D., Georgé, J., Gleizes, M., Glize, P.: The amas theory for complex problem solving based on self-organizing cooperative agents. In: TAPOCS Workshop at 12th IEEE WETICE, pp. 383–388 (2003)
4. Dorigo, M., Stützle, T.: Ant Colony Optimization. MIT Press, Cambridge (2004)
5. Glize, P.: L'Adaptation des Systèmes à Fonctionnalité Emergente par Auto-Organisation Coopérative. Ph.D. thesis (2001)
6. Glover, F., Laguna, M.: Tabu Search. Kluwer, Norwell (1997)
7. Holland, J.: Adaptation in Natural and Artificial Systems. MIT Press, Cambridge (1993)
8. Jorquera, T.: An adaptive multi-agent system for self-organizing continuous optimization. Ph.D. thesis (2013)
9. Kennedy, J., Eberhart, R.: Swarm Intelligence. Morgan Kaufmann, Burlington (2001)
10. Kirkpatrick, S., Gellat, C., Vecchi, M.: Optimization by simulated annealing. Science **220**(4598), 671–680 (1983)
11. Talbi, E.: Metaheuristics: From Design to Implementation. Wiley, Hoboken (2009)
12. Welcomme, J., Gleizes, M., Redon, R.: Self-organising multi-agent system managing complex system design application to conceptual aircraft design. Int. Trans. Syst. Sci. Appl. Systemics Inform. World Netw. (SIWN), Special issue: Self-organized Networked Syst. **5**(3), 208–221 (2009)
13. Yokoo, M., Durfee, E., Kubawara, K.: The distributed constraint satisfaction problem: formalization and algorithms. IEEE Trans. Knowl. Data Eng. **10**, 673–685 (1998)

Optimizing Emergency Medical Assistance Coordination in After-Hours Urgent Surgery Patients

Marin Lujak[✉], Holger Billhardt, and Sascha Ossowski

University Rey Juan Carlos, Madrid, Spain
marin.lujak@urjc.es

Abstract. This paper treats the coordination of Emergency Medical Assistance (EMA) and hospitals for after-hours surgeries of urgent patients arriving by ambulance. A standard hospital approach during night-shifts is to have standby surgery teams come to hospital after alert to cover urgent cases that cannot be covered by the in-house surgery teams. This approach results in a considerable decrease in staffing costs in respect to having sufficient permanent in-house staff. Therefore, coordinating EMA and the hospitals in a region with their outhouse staff with the objective to have as fast urgent surgery treatments as possible with minimized cost is a crucial parameter of the medical system efficiency and as such deserves a thorough investigation. In practice, the process is manual and the process management is case-specific, with great load on human phone communication. In this paper, we propose a decision support system for the automated coordination of hospitals, surgery teams on standby from home, and ambulances to decrease the time to surgery of urgent patients. The efficiency of the proposed model is proven over simulation experiments.

1 Introduction

Most hospitals that perform emergency surgery service provide also after-hours surgery for urgent patients whose conditions are not critical but might result in increased probability of morbidity or mortality. Out-of-hours is a period which is generally defined to be between 6 PM to 8 AM weeknights and the whole weekend, even though the definition might vary from one hospital to another. The growing demand of simultaneous multiple patients for emergency medical assistance (EMA) and urgent surgery treatment provided by hospitals puts a strong focus on the combined EMA and hospital surgery treatment coordination effectiveness and efficiency. The management of the hospital network and the emergency medical assistance in each region, city or town is challenged to deal with the seemingly conflicting objectives of fast, efficient and effective urgent patient response minimizing total system cost and maximizing the quality of care.

In this paper, we develop a decision-support system for the coordination of EMA and hospitals for after-hours urgent surgery patients. We assume that there are multiple hospitals available for urgent cases surgery treatment and

© Springer International Publishing Switzerland 2015
N. Bulling (Ed.): EUMAS 2014, LNAI 8953, pp. 316–331, 2015.
DOI: 10.1007/978-3-319-17130-2_21

for each hospital there is a sufficient number of in-house surgery teams needed to care for in-house and emergency patients safely. A surgery team consists of the individuals needed to adequately staff one operating room (OR) (e.g., a surgeon, an anesthetist, two nurses and a nurse anesthetist). Furthermore, we assume that there is a number of surgery teams on standby from home, coming to hospital after alert. The savings in staff expenditure between having sufficient staff in-house for urgent cases in respect to having them taking call from home might be considerable [5]. Hence, a good balance between the efficiency and the flexibility in hospital and EMA network management is a prerequisite for providing optimal care to patients.

The decision-support system proposed in this paper is based on the coordination of the assignment of idle ambulances to pending patients, and a simultaneous assignment of ambulances assisting patients in-situ to adequate hospitals together with the assignment of standby out-of-hospital surgery teams to the same. The multi-objective optimization of arrival times of multiple actors is solved for the minimization of patients' surgery waiting times. Responding to a possibility of occurrence of multiple simultaneous patients and based on the relative positions of the patients, surgery teams, and available hospitals, our approach is based on a system's view, not concentrating only on minimizing single patient delay, but concentrating on the system best solution in respect to the (temporal and spatial) multitude of patients. Simulated emergency scenarios demonstrate the efficiency of the coordination procedure and significant decrease in the urgent patients waiting time to surgery treatment.

This paper is organized as follows. In Sect. 2, we describe the State-of-the-Art practice in the EMA coordination for urgent surgery patients. In Sect. 3 we formulate the EMA coordination problem for urgent surgery patients arriving by ambulance. Section 4 describes briefly the proposed multi-agent architecture with the modified auction algorithm for EMA urgent surgery coordination. Section 5 contains simulation results comparing the proposed coordination approach and the benchmark urgent surgery coordination procedure first-come-first-serve. We draw conclusions in Sect. 6.

2 State-of-the-Art Practice and Related Work

The emergency medical system for the assistance of urgent surgery patients is made of the following participants: out-of-hospital patients, hospitals with after-hours urgent and emergency surgery option, Medical Emergency Coordination Center (ECC), ambulances staff, and standby out-of-hospital surgery teams. Usually, each hospital has assigned to it one or more out-of-hospital standby surgery teams positioned at alert outside hospital and obliged to come to the hospital in the case of emergency. The reason for their outside hospital position are staffing costs which make a large portion of costs in surgical care services [6]. Significant cost savings can be achieved by increasing staffing flexibility [3] and assignability to multiple hospitals.

The standard approach used in most of out-of-hospital after-hours urgent surgeries is the following. Patients are diagnosed in the place of emergency: at their momentary out-of-hospital location or at a health center without after-hours urgent surgery option. In both cases the ECC applies First-Come-First-Served (FCFS) strategy and locates the nearest available (idle) ambulance with ALS and dispatches it to pick up the patient. The use of ambulance for urgent patients is proven to increase patient chances in respect to the use of private transportation. The concrete example is infarct treatment [18] where ambulance should be considered a place for initial diagnosis, triage and emergency treatment since pre-hospital triage in the ambulance reduces infarct size and improves clinical outcome [16]. After the ambulance arrives to the scene and diagnoses the urgency at patient's momentary out-of-hospital location, ambulance confirms the diagnosis to the ECC which has a real time information of the states of ambulances. ECC sequently applies FCFS strategy for hospital assignment by locating the nearest available hospital with operating room working after-hours. The hospital then alerts the closest surgery team of the urgent surgery case.

The process for urgent surgery treatment coordination usually used in the ECCs is manual and the management is based on case by case principles with high human load necessary for telephonical arrangements to find a solution. This can significantly worsen the total delay time for patients awaiting surgery. In the case of a simultaneous presence of multiple urgent patients, hospitals and surgery teams located in multiple sites, support for optimized EMS coordination based on information updated in real time is necessary for efficient surgery planning and scheduling.

There is a vast Operations Research and Multi-Agent Systems literature in medical emergency assistance coordination. There exist different ambulance deployment, relocation and dispatch models, e.g., [9], operating room planning and scheduling, e.g., [3], and patient scheduling solutions, e.g., [15]. The proposed methods are mostly based on queuing theory, simulations and mathematical programming, e.g., [8,13,14,17].

Henderson in [8] outlines some of the key challenges EMS providers face, such as traffic congestion, increasing call volumes, hospital diversion, and increasing transfer times at emergency departments. Ingolfsson in [10] surveys research on planning and management for emergency medical services. In [1], Bandara et al. study optimal dispatch of paramedic units to emergency calls to maximise patients' survivability. Their computational results show that dispatching the closest vehicle is not always optimal and that dispatching vehicles considering the priority of the call leads to an increase in the average survival probability of patients.

Emergency medical assistance literature is abundant also in the multi-agent system community, e.g., [4,11]. Domnori et al. in [4] discuss the fitness of agent-based applications to managing healthcare emergences and large scale disasters and their application to problems where the main challenge is coordination and collaboration between components. López et al. in [11] propose a multiagent system using an auction mechanism based on trust to coordinate ambulances for emergency medical services. The auction mechanism here is based on three individual patient priority cases, where the winning ambulance is the one with the best estimated arrival time and a good trust degree. Lujak and Billhardt in [12] proposed an organization-based multi-agent application for emergency medical assistance (EMA) based on a distributed relaxation method for the assignment problem called auction algorithm [2] and the mechanism based on trust. The experiments results confirm the reduction of the average response times of EMA services.

Considering out-of-hours emergency surgery, in [19] the balance between hospital costs and patient safety was examined to determine the optimal size of emergency surgery teams that are on-call after-hours, including medical and nursing staff. The study found that the use of defined procedure-based safety intervals to plan on-call rosters can reduce the number of staff rostered on-call without jeopardising patient safety. The key premise of this argument is that fewer nighttime staff will be sufficient if patients wait a little longer for surgery, but not so long as to exceed safety intervals.

For the ambulance assignment problem, not infrequently applied dispatching method is first-come-first-served (FCFS) policy which is the method temporally discriminating patients and not considering the availability of hospitals or hospital staff. However, different centralized and distributed Operations Research optimization methods can be applied for the multi-agent task allocation and coordination problem encountered in this context. Since in this scenario, scalability, robustness and flexibility are of outermost importance, distributed methods, such as auction algorithm [2] are of preference. To the best of our knowledge, the literature on integrated mutual coordination of EMA, multiple hospitals operating rooms and out-of-hospital surgery teams is lacking which is the reason why in this paper we propose an integrated solution model for this problem.

3   Problem Formulation

In this paper, we treat the problem of after-hours out-of-hospital urgent surgery patient assignment to ambulance assistance, and consecutive patient transfer to adequate hospital with minimal waiting time for surgery. We assume that after transferring a patient to hospital, ambulance is redirected to the base station where it waits for the next emergency patient call.

In Fig. 1, we present patient delay time components:

- Call response and resource assignment time spent by the ECC (the time of analyzing the problem and giving it the highest priority category deciding on the ambulance and the hospital assignment);
- Mobilization of the ambulance and transportation time of the ambulance from its momentary position to the patient;
- Time of patient assistance in situ by ambulance staff;
- Transportation time of the ambulance with the patient to the hospital;
- Transportation time of the surgery team members from their momentary positions to the hospital;
- Expected waiting time due to the operating room occupancy of other prior pending patient(s) in the hospital (if any).

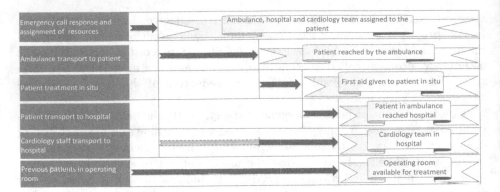

Fig. 1. Temporal sequence of six medical emergency events necessary for PCI treatment

Hesitation of patients to search for medical help together with the delays which are the result of the manual centralized coordination of multiple actors in EMA sometimes might average several hours and thus can prevent the early application of life-saving procedures and contribute substantially to a diminished effectiveness of surgery treatment. In the case of multiple simultaneous pending patients, the right combination and the individual choice of the ambulances to be assigned can significantly improve overall patients' chances and reduce the resulting morbidity and mortality. After a patient gets assisted in situ by ambulance staff, individually minimal expected time to surgery is the time resulting from the following three parameters, Fig. 1:

- transportation time of the ambulance with the patient from the initial patient location to assigned hospital,
- transportation time of the surgery team to the same,
- expected waiting time until the operating hall gets available.

The patient's and surgery team's arrival time to the hospital depends on their distance from the hospital and the driving conditions on the road. The availability of the operating hall depends on the previous patients (if any) booked for the operation hall with higher or equal urgency level to the patient in question.

In the case of multiple simultaneously appearing urgent patients, the objective is to find the minimum of the sum of all the patient delay times such that the system results in as high utilitarian value as possible. The objective is, therefore, twofold:

- to assign ambulances to simultaneous pending patients such that the assignment results in the minimum average time of transport of ambulances to simultaneous patients momentary locations considering their individual maximum allowed waiting times,
- to assign ambulances with patients to hospitals minimizing the combined times of patients transport to hospitals, and arrival times of surgery teams positioned outside hospitals, such that the difference between the expected arrival times of patients and surgery teams to hospitals is minimum.

In the following, we give the multi-agent system model and the mathematical programming definition of the problem inspired by [7].

Multi-agent System Representing EMS. Considering a time horizon made of T time periods, given are four distinct agent sets. Let $\Xi = \{\xi_1, \ldots, \xi_{N_p}\}$ be a pending patient set. Let $\Psi = \{\psi_1, \ldots, \psi_{N_c}\}$ be a set of surgery teams, each one made of at least one surgeon, one anaesthetist, two nurses and an anaesthetist assistant. Let $A = \{a_1, \ldots, a_{N_a}\}$ be the set of identical, capacitated ALS ambulance vehicles to be routed and scheduled to assist patients based on one-to-one assignment and let $H = \{h_1, \ldots, h_{N_h}\}$ be after-hours urgent surgery-capable hospitals. Furthermore, all agent sets are represented by points in the plane. N_p, N_c, N_a, N_h and N_b represent (not necessarily equal) cardinality of each set respectively. Agents initial coordinates are positioned, w.l.o.g., in a square environment $E = [0, l]^2 \subset \mathbb{R}^2$ of side length $l > 0$. The abbreviation $p(t)$ is used for the position of any kind of agent at time $t = 1, \ldots, T$; e.g., $p_a(t) \in E$ being the position of agent $a \in A$ at the beginning of each time period $t = 1, \ldots, T$, where T is the last period of the planning time horizon we are interested in.

Mathematical Formulation. We concentrate on the problem of the minimization of the average total delay time of urgent patients to get surgery treatment. No patient should be discriminated positively or negatively for his/her location. In the case that there is only one pending patient in the system, then the best ambulance is the ambulance which will arrive in the shortest time possible and the problem is to find ambulance $a \in A$, surgery team $\psi \in \Psi$ and hospital $h \in H$ that in combination minimize patient $\xi_k \in \Xi$ time to hospital:

$$\min_{a \in A} t(a, \xi_k) + \min_{h \in H_{av}} \left(\max_{h \in H_{av}} \left(t(\xi_k, h), \min_{\psi \in \Psi_{av}} t(\psi, h) \right), \min \rho_{h, \xi_k} \right), \quad (1)$$

where hospital h_{ξ_k} chosen for patient ξ_k, $k = 1, \ldots, N_p$ is

$$h_{\xi_k} = \arg\min \left(\max_{h \in H_{av}} \left(t(\xi_k, h), \min_{\psi \in \Psi_{av}} t(\psi, h) \right), \min \rho_{h, \xi_k} \right), \quad (2)$$

and Ψ_{av} is a set of available surgery teams and H_{av} set of available hospitals with necessary equipment. Furthermore, $t(x, y)$ is travel time from position x to position y and ρ_{h, ξ_k} available time periods of hospital h for patient ξ_k and $\min \rho_{h, \xi_k}$ is a first time period hospital h will be free for patient ξ_k. The objective for each patient $\xi_k \in \Xi$, thus, is to choose a triple $\langle a, h, \psi \rangle$ minimizing Eq. 1.

From the global point of view, multiple-patient problem is to assign patients in order to optimize the global waiting time for the treatment for all patients, i.e., find assignments of $a \in A$ and $h \in H$ such that:

$$\min_{a \in A} \sum_{k=1}^{N_p} t(a, \xi_k) + \min_{h \in H} \sum_{k=1}^{N_p} \left(\max_{h \in H_{av}} \left(t(\xi_k, h), \min_{\psi \in \Psi_{av}} t(\psi, h) \right), \min \rho_{h, \xi_k} \right). \quad (3)$$

Waiting time or patient delay is the sum of the time needed for the arrival of the ambulance to the patient, and the minimum value between the maximum of the arrival time of the patient to hospital and the arrival time of surgery team to the same (if not in-situ), and the minimum waiting time due to the pending patients booked for the operation room before patient ξ_k.

4 Solution Approach

To improve the response times of the emergency management system towards urgent surgery patients, we present the dynamic resource assignment model for ambulances, surgery teams and hospitals assignment to patients performed over iterative combinatorial auctions, e.g. [2,12]. The proposed solution is founded on the collaborative multi-agent system (MAS) organizational structure and MAS coordination model with four classes of agents seen as autonomous and independent decision makers. There exists a determined sequence of steps and message exchanges which is performed in order to resolve each urgent surgery case. The agents are described based on their characteristics and states as follows:

Patient: Each patient agent $\xi \in \Xi$ represents a real pending urgent surgery patient in the medical emergency assistance. When calling ECC, from his/her initial location, he/she gets assisted in-situ by ambulance crew, and gets transferred to hospital where he/she receives the urgent surgery treatment. Each patient is described over a tuple $\xi = \{p_\xi(t), \ \Delta_\xi, t_\xi^{in}\}$, where Δ_ξ is patient $\xi \in \Xi$ status which can be: pending patient waiting ambulance ξ_{wa}, being assisted in-situ ξ_{ais}, moving in ambulance to hospital ξ_{ath}, in hospital ξ_{inh}, and t_ξ^{in} is patient ξ detection time. The latter is defined as the time when the ECC is informed about the incident. New patient requests continuously unfold over time and must be assigned in real time to ambulances.

After-hour Urgent Surgery Capable Hospital: Hospital agents $h \in H$ collaborate with ambulances and emergency coordinator to receive patients for treatment. Furthermore, they are responsible of managing and coordinating their operation room(s) together with the assignable surgery team(s). Hospitals can be described over a touple $h = \{p_h, \ \rho_{h,\xi}\}$, where p_h is the position and $\rho_{h,\xi}$ is the temporal availability of hospital $h \in H$ for patient $\xi \in \Xi$. It is assumed that each hospital has a booking list for urgent and emergency surgery, i.e., information of the availability of the operation room within some future time. Hospitals have at the disposal the updated assignability of surgery teams $\rho_{\psi,h}(t)$ at every time period $t \in T$.

Ambulance: Ambulance agents $a \in A$ represent ALS ambulance vehicles (ambulances with advanced life support) together with their relative ambulance human crews. Ambulances communicate to ECC agent for patient and base station assignment and to hospitals for patient transfer. Furthermore, each ambulance is described over the touple $a = \{p_a(t), \ v_{avg}^{[a]}, s_a(t), b_a(t)\}$, where $p_a(t)$ is the current position at time period $t \in (1, \ldots, T)$ and $v_{avg}^{[a]}$ is the average velocity of ambulance a. $s_a(t)$ is its estimated end-of-service time with the current patient, if any. The dummy value -1 is used when the vehicle is free. $b_a(t)$ indicates the destination, i.e., the next station at which the ambulance vehicle will stop. Ambulances statuses can be: idle ambulance a_i, moving to incident position, a_{ip}, and ambulance moving to a hospital, a_h. At every time period t, idle ambulances a_i are considered for commitment to pending patients ξ_{wa}, and in case no patient assignment is made, they remain at their last assigned position.

In our model we assume that after arriving at patient location, the vehicle cannot be redirected elsewhere until transferring the patient to the hospital. However, at any time before getting to the patient location, the vehicle can be dispatched elsewhere.

Medical Emergency-Coordination Center: *ECC* receives emergency calls from patients and assigns the ambulance and hospital for each case, thus performing the high-level management of the urgent surgery logistic procedure.

Surgery Team: $\psi \in \Psi$ is responsible of the urgent surgery treatment. The team's members are positioned outside of hospital, generally at different locations, and move towards assigned hospital when needed. The combined arrival time to the hospital is the highest value of the members' arrival times. The touple which describes each surgery team is $\psi = \{p_\psi(t), \rho_{\psi,h}(t), b_\psi(t)\}$ where $\rho_{\psi,h}(t)$ is the temporal availability of surgery teams $\psi \in \Psi$ in hospital $h \in H$. It is assumed that each surgery team has its expected time of arrival to the hospital based on their momentary position $p_\psi(t)$ and the position of a hospital). The status of a surgery team can be: idle ψ_i, moving to an assigned hospital ψ_{mh}, in the assigned hospital ψ_{ih}. In general, the team can be assignable to different number of hospitals. Therefore, binary vector $\rho_{\psi,h}(t)$ expresses the assignability of the team for each time period $t \in T$ and for each hospital $h \in H$. Traditionally each surgery team is assigned to one hospital only. However, staff utilization and patient assistance can be significantly improved if all the regional surgery teams are at the disposal of all the region's hospitals.

4.1 Auction Algorithm

The relaxation method for the assignment problem called auction algorithm [2] is used to resolve the problem of the assignment of ambulances, hospitals and surgery teams to urgent surgery patients. Auction algorithm is a coordination mechanism guaranteed to find the best assignment solution for the system; furthermore, it is an effective method for solving the classical assignment problem. It admits an intuitive economic interpretation and is well suited for implementation in distributed and decentralized computing systems as is the one in emergency medical assistance. Moreover, it is an iterative procedure related to a sales auction where multiple bids are iteratively compared to determine the best offer for the system, with the final sales going to the highest bidders. The original form of the auction algorithm is an iterative method to find the optimal prices and an assignment that maximizes the net benefit in a bipartite graph, the maximum weight matching problem (MWM). This algorithm was first proposed by Dimitri Bertsekas [2].

In auctions, it is important that the number of bidders is equal or higher than the number of bided objects. This is why, if the number of patients is lower than the number of ambulances, and the number of hospitals, then patients bid for ambulances and hospitals in the iterative auction algorithm based on the starting available patient assistance time described above. Otherwise, i.e., if the number of ambulances is lower than the number of patients, then ambulances bid for patients, and similarly higher number of hospitals bid for lower number of patients.

In the patient hospital assignment, we consider all pending patients who called the ambulance and are waiting for ambulance or are in the process of ambulance assistance and/or arriving to hospital but still haven't reached the same. In the following, we present the algorithm steps for hospital patient assignment. The assignment of ambulances to patients is performed in a similar way.

In each iteration

- Each hospital receives updated pending patients virtual prices (those are dual variables of the primal problem).
- Each hospital gives a bid based on the virtual prices of the patients.
- The hospital with the highest bid wins in the momentary iteration.
- If at the end of the bidding, all the patients received at least one bid and the bidding hospitals don't bid for the same patients, then there are no more unassigned patients.
- The algorithm updates the patients' prices and continues in iterations until all the patients are assigned and all the conflicts are resolved.

If each surgery team is assignable to more hospitals, preferably all, then the combinatorial result of multiple assignments gives a globally optimal solution while if each team is assigned only to one hospital, this can limit significantly the arrival time of the team to the hospital and therefore, in the case of unexpected prolonged arrival times, jeopardize the urgent surgery success.

The additional parameters of the simulation algorithm are N_ξ^{sim} being the total number of patients in the simulation and $N_\xi(t)$ representing the number of patients assisted in hospital until time period $t \in [1, \ldots, T]$. The complete simulation algorithm for emergency medical assistance of angioplasty patients follows the proceeding steps.

At each time $t \in [1, \ldots, T]$

While $N_\xi(t) \leq N_\xi^{sim}$

- assign all pending patients ξ_{wa} to idle ambulances a_i using auction algorithm;
- assign patients moving in ambulance to hospital ξ_{ath} to hospitals and standby surgery teams considering the arrival times of the teams;
- move ambulances a_{ip} to unassisted patients one step*;
- move ambulances with assisted patients to hospitals one step*;
- move surgery teams outside hospitals to assigned hospitals one step*;

- when a patient gets assisted in hospital, inform ECC of the availability of ambulance;
- introduce new patients based on the frequency of patient appearance.

* the step is calculated based on the average ambulance velocity and the duration of a time period.

5 Simulation Experiments

In this Section, we describe the simulation setting, experiments, and results. The average patient waiting times resulting from the proposed optimized reassignment model are compared with the same based on the First-Come-First-Served principle used actually in many medical emergency coordination centers (e.g., SUMMA 112 in Madrid, Spain) and described previously.

In the simulation model, we follow a mesoscopic view of the emergency medical system and without loss of generality, ambulance velocities are set to an average system value. Together with the simplification of substituting the function of road travel time $t(\mathbf{x}, \mathbf{y})$ between positions $\mathbf{x} = (x_1, x_2)$ and $\mathbf{y} = (y_1, y_2)$ in Euclidean 2-space with Euclidean distance $d(\mathbf{x}, \mathbf{y}) = \sqrt{\sum_{i=1}^{2}(x_i - y_i)^2}$, we convert the road time minimization problem to Euclidean distance minimization problem which is independent of a road network structure different for each city and region.

Simulation Setting. We test the proposed strategy of optimized reassignment of ambulances and hospitals to patients looking at the average patient waiting times in the case of multiple pending patients and compare it with the benchmark First-Come-First-Served (FCFS) strategy of patient assignment. To demonstrate the scalability of our solution and possible application to small, medium and large cities and regions, in all of the experiments we vary the number of ambulances with ALS from 5 to 100 with increment 5 and the number of hospitals from 2 to 50 with increment 2. For simplicity and without the loss of generality, the number of surgery teams in each experiment equals the number of hospitals. The medical emergency system together with patients is positioned in the environment which dimensions are $[0, 50]^2 \subset \mathbb{R}$.

Each simulation is run over 300 patients. The number of experimented setup configurations combining different numbers of ambulances and hospitals with surgery teams sums up to 500. For each configuration, we simulate 5 instances of different random positions of ambulances, hospitals, surgery teams, and patients. Patients' positions are modeled based on the uniform distribution while patients' appearance frequency varies from low (1 new patient every 10 time periods) over medium (1 new patient every 2 time periods) to saturated one (1 new patient appearing in every time period). Time period can be considered here as a minimum time interval in which the assignment decisions are made; usually it is from 1 to 15 min.

In the proposed optimized reassignment model, surgery teams can be dynamically (re-)assigned to any hospital in every time period depending on the actual patient demand. Furthermore, we assume that the hospitals have at the disposal sufficient number of operating rooms so that the only optimization factor from the hospital point of view is the number of available surgery teams. If there are more patients with the same urgency already assigned waiting for treatment in the same hospital, they are put in a queue.

In the proposed model, surgery teams re-assignment to hospitals is performed as soon as an idle ambulance arrives to a pending patient. The former is made having in consideration all idle surgery teams, available hospitals, and new patients assisted by ambulances but still out of hospital.

For the surgery team arrival times to hospitals, we tested two assignment strategies: the first one minimizes the sum of the differences between the patients and the surgery teams arrival times to hospitals at the global level, while the second one concentrates only on the minimization of the arrival times of surgery teams to assigned hospitals independently of the arrival times of the assigned patients to the same.

We present the results of the latter since it gives significantly lower patient waiting times in all of the performed experiments. Even though the former considers a time window between surgery teams and patients arrival times, thus increasing the available time for surgery teams to arrive to the hospital when the patient has still not arrived, this strategy showed inferior to the minimization of arrival times of surgery teams without the reference to the assigned patients times. The reason for this is that without forecasting capabilities of new patients, the system is myopic towards new patients frequency appearance and positions and on the long run, the system suffers significant delays.

In the following, we present the results of the simulation tests.

Simulation Results. In the experiments, we test the performance of the proposed optimized reassignment strategy in respect to the FCFS benchmark model. For each out of 500 configurations, we use 5 instances of different patient, surgery team, hospital and initial ambulance coordinates. We compare the average patient waiting time of the proposed optimized reassignment method $\bar{t}_{OR}$ with the same of the benchmark FCFS model $\bar{t}_{FCFS}$. Relative performance function P of the proposed in respect to the benchmark model is calculated as:

$$P = \frac{\bar{t}_{FCFS} - \bar{t}_{OR}}{\bar{t}_{OR}} \cdot 100 \ , \ [\%]. \tag{4}$$

The simulation results of the performance function P for the three simulated cases of frequency of patient appearance of 1, 5, and 10 patients over 10 time periods are presented in Figs. 2, 3, 4, and Table 1. The Figures show the increase of performance in average as the number of hospitals increases from slightly negative values up to more than 1000 % as seen in Table 1.

Observing the performance dynamics in respect to the varying number of hospitals, it is evident from Figs. 2, 3, and 4 that with a relatively low number

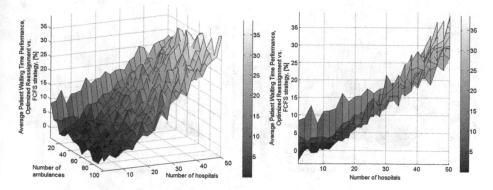

Fig. 2. Average patient waiting time performance of optimized reassignment strategy in respect to the FCFS strategy [%] for the frequency of appearance of 1 new patient every 10 time periods.

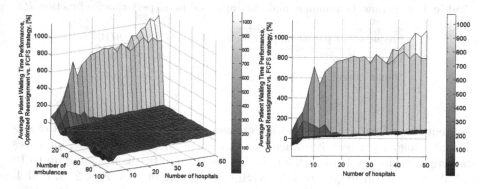

Fig. 3. Average patient waiting time performance of optimized reassignment strategy in respect to the FCFS strategy [%] for the frequency of appearance of 1 new patient every 2 time periods.

of after-hour urgent-surgery available hospitals, optimized reassignment gives similar results to the FCFS method. As the number of the hospitals increases, the performance increases in average up to the maximum of 38,52 % for the frequency of patient appearance of 1 new patient every 10 time periods, Fig. 2, and up to more than 1000 % in the cases with higher frequency of patient appearance, Figs. 3 and 4.

Looking at the optimized reassignment performance dynamics in respect to the varying number of ambulances, in Figs. 2, 3, and 4, two regions are evident: the first one with very low number of ambulances where the performance of the optimized reassignment is significantly better than the FCFS method, and the other region where the values do not change significantly in respect to the change of the number of ambulances. The performance values of the first region steeply decrease to the steady values of the valey region. It can be seen that as

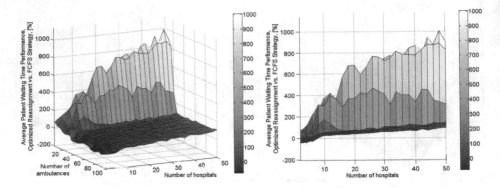

Fig. 4. Average patient waiting time performance of optimized reassignment strategy in respect to the FCFS strategy [%] for the frequency of appearance of 1 new patient every time period.

Table 1. Experiments minimum and maximum values of performance function P

Frequency of patient appearance	1/10	5/10	10/10
P min. value, [%]	$-2,92$	$-80,47$	$-74,62$
P max. value, [%]	38,52	1067,6	1004,1

the frequency of patient appearance increases, thus the size of the region of significantly higher performance when the number of ambulances is low, increases starting at frequency 1/10 with 5 ambulances, in 5/10 frequency going up to 10 ambulances, and in frequency 1/1 arriving to 20 ambulances, Figs. 2, 3, and 4. This implies that the optimized reassignment performance in respect to the FCFS method when the number of ambulances is low improves as the frequency of patient appearance increases.

From Figs. 2, 3, and 4, it is also visible that when the number of hospitals is low, minimum values of the optimized reassignment method performance increase as the patient appearance frequency increases. The number of hospitals for which the first two cases show strictly positive performance is 8, while for the case 3, it is 10. Proportionally to the increase of the number of hospitals, there is a constant increase of performance up to the maximum values as seen in Table 1.

Furthermore, as can be seen from Fig. 2, when the frequency of new patient appearance is relatively low, 1 over every 10 consecutive time periods, the performance of the proposed optimized reassignment method increases in average proportionally to the increase of the number of hospitals. However, when the number of hospitals is relatively low, i.e., lower than 8, the optimized reassignment approach does not necessarily give a better patient waiting time solution. The reason is that by reassignment of surgery teams, they move from one hospital to the other, and are in the time of travel unavailable for patient assistance which worsens the patient waiting time. However, when the number of ambulances is relatively low, (lower than 20), the reassignment approach gives better results since with high number of ambulances, their geographical distribution compensates for the availability of surgery teams at all hospitals at all times and no additional combinatorial technique is necessary to improve the assignment performance. With lower number of ambulances and hospitals, since ambulances are not equally distributed in the area, the reassignment method compensates for their unequal distribution thus giving better results. This tendency is even more emphasized in the cases of higher new patient appearance frequency as seen in Figs. 3 and 4 reaching up to more than 1000 % of improvement, Table 1.

6 Conclusions

In this paper, we proposed a heterogeneous multiagent system coordination model that facilitates a seamless coordination among the participants in the emergency medical assistance for the minimization of delay times of after-hours urgent surgery patients. The proposed model implies the change of the current functioning based on a manual coordination through communications via phone calls, towards an automated coordination process where the basic decisions are taken (or proposed) by software agents. The proposed multi-agent system model enables a better control of the availability of stand-by surgery teams and gives a decision making tool for ambulance and hospital assignment.

In order to reduce the transfer and waiting times of after-hours urgent surgery patients, we integrated in the multiagent model a multi-objective optimisation tool based on iterative auctions for the minimization of ambulances and surgery teams arrival times. The proposed solution results in the provably increased flexibility and responsiveness of the emergency system.

Simulation results prove the efficiency of the proposed solution resulting in significantly lower urgent surgery waiting times. The proposed auction mechanism enables spatially and temporally optimized resource assignment in the cases with multiple patients.

In real life, assumption on ambulances' equal velocities cannot be made so the estimation of arrival times should be made based on the more sophisticated methods and tools as, e.g., Google maps. For the usage of our technology, ambulances should have a GPS and a navigator for localizing the patient and navigating the way to him/her. ECC should have a digitalized map with localized ambulances, patients and hospitals and hospitals should have a receptionist service or personnel for admittance of patients.

As a future work, we plan to develop heterogeneous MAS coordination model for participants in Emergency Medical Assistance with integrated future patients forecast over a receding horizon.

Acknowledgements. This work was supported in part by the Spanish Ministry of Science and Innovation through the projects "AT" (Grant CONSOLIDER CSD2007-0022, INGENIO 2010) and "OVAMAH" (Grant TIN2009-13839-C03-02) co-funded by Plan E, and by the Spanish Ministry of Economy and Competitiveness through the project iHAS (grant TIN2012-36586-C03-02).

References

1. Bandara, D., Mayorga, M.E., McLay, L.A.: Optimal dispatching strategies for emergency vehicles to increase patient survivability. Int. J. Oper. Res. **15**(2), 195–214 (2012)
2. Bertsekas, D.P.: The auction algorithm: a distributed relaxation method for the assignment problem. Ann. Oper. Res. **14**(1), 105–123 (1988)
3. Cardoen, B., Demeulemeester, E., Beliën, J.: Operating room planning and scheduling: a literature review. Eur. J. Oper. Res. **201**(3), 921–932 (2010)
4. Elton, D., Giacomo, C., Letizia, L.: Coordination issues in an agent-based approach for territorial emergence management. In: 2011 IEEE Workshops of International Conference on Advanced Information Networking and Applications (WAINA), pp. 184–189. IEEE (2011)
5. Dexter, F.: Influence of staffing and scheduling on operating room productivity. In: Kaye, A.D., Fox, C.J., Urman, R.D. (eds.) Operating Room Leadership and Management, pp. 46–66. Cambridge University Press, New York (2012)
6. Guerriero, F., Guido, R.: Operational research in the management of the operating theatre: a survey. Health Care Manag. Sci. **14**(1), 89–114 (2011)
7. Haghani, A., Hu, H., Tian, V.: An optimization model for real-time emergency vehicle dispatching and routing. In: 82nd Annual Meeting of the Transportation Research Board, Washington (2003)
8. Henderson, S.G.: Operations research tools for addressing current challenges in emergency medical services. In: Wiley Encyclopedia of Operations Research and Management Science (2011)
9. Henderson, S.G., Mason, A.J.: Ambulance service planning: simulation and data visualisation. In: Brandeau, M.L., Sainfort, F., Pierskalla, W.P. (eds.) Operations Research and Health Care: A Handbook of Methods and Applications, vol. 70, pp. 77–102. Springer, Boston (2004)
10. Ingolfsson, A.: Ems planning and management. In: Zaric, G.S. (ed.) Operations Research and Health Care Policy, pp. 105–128. Springer, New York (2013)
11. López, B., Innocenti, B., Busquets, D.: A multiagent system for coordinating ambulances for emergency medical services. IEEE Intell. Syst. **23**(5), 50–57 (2008)
12. Lujak, M., Billhardt, H.: Coordinating emergency medical assistance. In: Ossowski, S. (ed.) Agreement Technologies, pp. 597–609. Springer, Dordrecht (2013)
13. Maxwell, M.S., Restrepo, M., Henderson, S.G., Topaloglu, H.: Approximate dynamic programming for ambulance redeployment. INFORMS J. Comput. **22**(2), 266–281 (2010)
14. Mielczarek, B., Uziałko-Mydlikowska, J.: Application of computer simulation modeling in the health care sector: a survey. Simulation **88**(2), 197–216 (2012)
15. Patrick, J.M., Puterman, L., Queyranne, M.: Dynamic multipriority patient scheduling for a diagnostic resource. Oper. Res. **56**(6), 1507–1525 (2008)
16. Postma, S., Jan-Henk, E., Dambrink, M.-J., de Boer, A.T., Gosselink, G.J., Eggink, H., van de Wetering, F., Hollak, J.P., Ottervanger, J.C.A., Hoorntje, E.K., et al.: Prehospital triage in the ambulance reduces infarct size and improves clinical outcome. Am. Heart J. **161**(2), 276–282 (2011)
17. Rais, A., Viana, A.: Operations research in healthcare: a survey. Int. Trans. Oper. Res. **18**(1), 1–31 (2011)
18. Song, L., Yan, H., Hu, D.: Patients with acute myocardial infarction using ambulance or private transport to reach definitive care: which mode is quicker? Intern. Med. J. **40**(2), 112–116 (2010)

19. van Oostrum, J.M., Van Houdenhoven, M., MJ Vrielink, M., Klein, J., Hans, E.W., Klimek, M., Wullink, G., Steyerberg, E.W., Kazemier, G.: A simulation model for determining the optimal size of emergency teams on call in the operating room at night. Anaesth. Analg. **107**(5), 1655–1662 (2008)

Spatial Coordination Games for Large-Scale Visualization

Andre Ribeiro[✉] and Eiko Yoneki

The Computer Lab, University of Cambridge, William Gates Building,
15 JJ Thomson Ave, Cambridge CB30FD, UK
{Andre.Ribeiro,Eiko.Yoneki}@cl.cam.ac.uk

Abstract. Dimensionality reduction ('visualization') is a central problem in statistics. Several of the most popular solutions grew out of interaction metaphors (springs, boids, neurons, etc.) We show that the problem can be framed as a game of coordination and solved with standard game-theoretic concepts. Nodes that are close in a (high-dimensional) graph must coordinate in a (low-dimensional) screen position. We derive a game solution, a GPU-parallel implementation and report visualization experiments in several datasets. The solution is a very practical application of game-theory in an important problem, with fast and low-stress embeddings.

Keywords: Dimensionality reduction · Visualization · Game-theory · Belief revision · Spatial coordination

1 Introduction

Most of the current practical visualization solutions make use of interaction metaphors (springs, boids, self-organizing neurons, etc.) among data-points. In this paper we give agents more strategic intelligence and consider whether a multi-agent perspective can bring in new connections and solutions to the problem.

Namely, the problem is to take a graph or high-dimensional distance matrix between data points as input and calculate a lower dimensional embedding of these points as output. General data practitioners, from diverse areas of knowledge, often use, for example, force-directed graph visualization, which is the main element in most popular graph visualization tools. Scientific practitioners and statisticians, on the other hand, tend to prefer less scalable and less exploratory solutions that have, instead, stronger guarantees. We depart from Multi-Dimensional Scaling (MDS), a classical statistical dimensionality reduction technique, and reach a solution that is as practical as force-directed systems, while maintaining (or improving) the quality of statistical solutions.

We look at the problem as a game where players have to decide which screen position to occupy. Given that they want to be far away on the screen to far away players on the graph (or distance matrix), their chosen position will depend

© Springer International Publishing Switzerland 2015
N. Bulling (Ed.): EUMAS 2014, LNAI 8953, pp. 332–345, 2015.
DOI: 10.1007/978-3-319-17130-2_22

on their expectations about what others will do. To solve the problem we thus study games, which we call Spatial Coordination Games, where player payoffs vary with mutual distances in a player-to-player basis. Players keep probability distributions over each others positions and update them with each individual movement.

2 Spatial Coordination Games

More precisely, we consider a game $G = [N, M, a_{ij}]$ with N players over a finite set of M positions and a pairwise distance-based payoff function, $a_{ij}(m, k)$ - with m and k as players i and j's respective positions, $i, j \in [N]^1$, $m, k \in [M]$, $a : [N]^2 \times [M]^2 \to \mathbb{R}$ and $M, N \in \mathbb{N}^+$.

When $M = 1$, the Spatial Coordination Game is reduced to the consensus problem [24] (the solution is a single consensual position and players have incentive to conglomerate). The problem has applications in agent (spatial) sensing, formation, rendezvous, alignment, evacuation, flocking, coordinated decision making, etc.

When a_{ij} is uniform across players, $a_{ij}(m, .) = 1/N$, the game is reduced to a congestion game [21] (all players have the exact same amount of influence on individual decisions, making payoffs proportional to the number of players using a resource and giving them incentive to disperse). The problem has applications in network routing (especially over wireless networks) and analysis.

We are interested in the general case when payoffs a_{ij} are not constant, but player-specific, and the game is played over a large set of positions and players, $M \gg 1$ and $N \gg 1$. This is the case of visualization - where players choose where to go based on where other individual players are, and not, for example, an absolute count of players (as in general congestion or the El-Farol Bar problem [20]). In this game a pure strategy profile specifies a player's position given all others' possible movements. A mixed profile assigns a probability (or belief) to each possible position, which players can review after observing others' beliefs.

Consider that player i has a probability distribution over positions m, $p_i(m)$, as mixed strategy. The player starts with a prior distribution and calculates its strategy based on the expected actions of all others $p_1(m), p_2(m), ..., p_N(m)$ a posteriori.

Player i can calculate the (expected) utility of choosing a position m as the probability of player j choosing a position k and the resultant (joint) utility $a_{ij}(m, k)$ in that case, $m, k \in [M]$. The expected utility reflects proximities across all possible *likely* placements. In a best-reply fashion, it is rational for the player to update its distribution at any point in the game proportional to its expected payoff,

$$p_i(m) \propto \sum_{j,k} p_j(k) a_{ij}(m, k) \qquad (1)$$

---

[1] $[c]$ denotes a set with $c \in \mathbb{N}^+$ elements.

which is iterated, with some prior distribution $p_i^0(m)$. The mutual, synchronous updates then create a coupled dynamical system that can be analyzed with game-theory.

The model has three parts: the players' utility functions, their belief revision strategy and their communicative strategy. We first formulate the payoff function $a_{ij}(m, k)$, then how players update their beliefs (i.e., the inherited dynamics of the game) and then how players can intervene (manipulate their private beliefs) to change the outcome of the game. We finally move on to implementation notes and experiments.

2.1   Stress Payoffs

The payoff for a player i varies with its distance to each other player j individually, and is derived from an input (weighted) graph or distance matrix D_{ij} - which we simply call 'graph' for short.

Specifically, the payoff $a_{i,j}(m, k)$ is the embedding's normalized stress [18], the difference between the (low-dimensional) spatial distance $d(m, k)$ and the (high-dimensional) distance $D(i, j)$ across placements.

$$a_{ij}(m, k) = \frac{\sum_{ij}[d_{ij}(m, k) - D(i, j)]^2}{\sum_{ij} d_{ij}(m, k)^2} \qquad (2)$$

The measure explicitly indicates the difference between the distances in the input (high-dimensional) and the output (low-dimensional) positions. The values lie between zero and one (assuming a normalized input); the smaller, the better an embedding represents the high-dimensional data. This quantity can be calculated once and independently of the next equations (and thus can be pre-calculated and stored in look-up tables during the game). The squared euclidean distance is used for $d(m, k)$ in all experiments.

2.2   Update Strategy

A central issue is how exactly players change their distributions (redistribute their probabilistic mass) after observing others' beliefs, while keeping their own beliefs altogether stochastic. If the payoffs are normalized $a_{ij} \in [0, 1]$, symmetric and do not change, then

$$p_i(m) = \sum_{j,k} \frac{1}{\sum_l p_j(k)a_{ij}(l, k)} p_j(k)a_{ij}(m, k) \qquad (3)$$

with $l \in [M]$.

A player using Eq. (3) change its beliefs according to expected payoffs. For the type of problem studied here (where payoffs are coordinative), Eq. (3) using expected payoffs has advantages. This is because in these problems it's advantageous for players to readjust not based on their immediate gains but also considering what others might actually do, which seemingly allows them to explore further opportunities for coordination.

We want to derive next a differential equation $\dot{p}_i(m)$ which gives players iterative updating rules and allow us to better understand the asymptotic game behavior. The solution can be derived (with regularity assumptions) by enforcing that $\sum_i p_i(m) = 1$ and thus that $\sum_i \dot{p}_i(m) = 0$.

The denominator in Eq. (3) unfortunately makes updates impractical in large games. We can simplify the relationship between players strategies by assuming parametric forms to the belief distributions. Let players' beliefs have an exponential form with constant rate of change (derivative) $a_{ij}(m, k)$.

$$\sum_{j,k} \frac{1}{\sum_l p_j(k)e^{a_{ij}(l,k)}} p_j(k)e^{a_{ij}(m,k)} \tag{4}$$

This, together with the second-order regularity assumption, leads to a simpler form $\dot{p}_i(m) = p_i(m)(v_i(m, k) - \alpha(m, k))$, where $v_i(m, k)$ is the right-hand-side likelihood of Eq. (1) and $\alpha(m, k)$ is a renormalizing constant. Under these conditions, the normalizing constant $\alpha(m, k)$ exists and can be derived with a few simple logarithmic operations, leading to the final form of the belief updating strategy[2] and the multi-population replicator dynamics [30]:

$$\dot{p}_i(m) = p_i(m)[\sum_{i \neq j}\sum_k a_{ij}(m, k)p_j(k) - \sum_{i \neq j}\sum_{l,k} a_{ij}(l, k)p_i(l)p_j(k)], \tag{5}$$

with $i, j \in [N]$ and $l, m, k \in [M]$. The interpretation, however, is slightly different from typical multi-population replicator dynamics. We view the dynamics as a model of learning where the population m frequency correspond to an individual player's probability of playing m at time t. Thus $p_i(m)$ is its mixed strategy at t. And the payoff received from the rest of the players, α, is a renormalizing constant.

For analysis, we are interested in the situation in which *every* player chooses a pure strategy - i.e., for every player i, $p_i(m)$ is concentrated on a single position. That is, while having the choice from the set of mixed strategies, players choose a particular position with little uncertainty. These are "corners" of the M-dimensional probability vectors $p(m)$ simplex. Corners are trivially equilibrium points. Other equilibria, that are not corners, are sometimes named interior equilibria. A further attractiveness of the replicator dynamic is that it is typically well behaved. All asymptotically stable attractors must include corners, and if compact, these are the game Nash equilibria [13]. That is, a trajectory either converges to a corner, or eternally moves around in the interior of the simplex. However, when asymptotically stable corners do exist, their basin of attraction typically cover most of the simplex. Although we do not require equilibrium to reach the final game solution (see Implementation Section) and currently focus on demonstrating the practically of the game, we observe this empirically (the game typically converges to a corner).

---

[2] See [1,12] for a similar derivation and further details on the relationship between the exponential family and the replicator dynamics.

2.3   Communication Strategy

We introduce the notion of a player's probabilistic intervention in this game. An intervention [11] is an experimental change on a player's model (e.g., a player clamping of the variable m to a value k). Causal interventions are often notated as $P(X|do(y))$ [25], we use $p_j(m|do(i,k))$ to denote player j's distribution when i's distribution is clamped to a value k. Because an intervention affects the game outcome simply by changing others' mental models, it's natural to think of it as a model for communication ('I will be at position x').

If players are distributed on the graph and will favor positions according to (5), it is then the order of interventions that remains to be optimized. We define the player's risk in the game in terms of its uncertainty across positions. We then propose a minmax criterion that chooses the intervention with minimum risk across players at each step. In the resulting game, a competitive game is progressively modified through 'communication' (a cycle of intervention followed by equilibrium calculation, repeated to a desired uncertainty level). This way, an embedding is defined incrementally.

We imagine players incur a risk when they have to settle for a given position (i.e., it's beneficiary to keep their individual options open, or their own position uncertainty high). We then take the individual risk to be

$$R(i) = -log_2 p_i(m) \tag{6}$$

The intervention $do(i,k)$'s collective risk is the maximal risk across all players, $argmax_{(i,k)}R(j|do(i,k))$. Players then choose the intervention with minimum collective risk at each iteration,

$$do(i,k)^* = minargmax_{(i,k)}R(j|do(i,k)) \tag{7}$$

The criterion has a cooperative interpretation, in which all players incur the risk of the worst player in a given intervention. Below we show how to calculate Eqs. (5) and (7) in a parallel GPU [28] implementation. We also explore the spatial nature of the problem to devise probability distributions with increasing resolution (i.e., a multi-level scheme that alleviates the solution's computational requirements). Finally, we show how to use the model for visualization and report results.

3   Related Work

'Classic' (or Torgerson) metric MDS is often done by transforming distances into similarities and performing PCA (e.g., singular-value-decomposition) on those. PCA is sometimes taken as the simplest possible MDS algorithm. In particular for real world data, which is typically nonlinear, nonlinear techniques may offer a definite advantage. In the spatial domain, spatial data with local correlations are especially problematic for PCA, and it is similar to simply taking a Fourier transform and filtering out low-frequency components [23]. Linear methods (like classical MDS) are generally not good at modeling curved manifolds, often only preserving distances between widely separated points and loosing local structure [27]. Currently, Kruskal's stress [18] is the most common measure of goodness-of-fit for a non-metric MDS embedding, and serves as objective function to minimize in majorization approaches ('smacof') [9], which perform well in a wider range of domains.

Spring layout algorithms are probably the most practical and popular algorithms for drawing general graphs, as proposed by Eades [6]. Since, his method has been revisited and improved in a variety of ways [16]. In general, force-directed algorithms can produce good results for small graphs, but do not scale well. Large graphs often result in the energy function been trapped in local minima. Additionally, force-directed algorithms lack predictability, two different runs with the same input may lead to disparate results. This inconsistency can be a serious problem in visualization. Annealing [15] has show to be a uniquely effective way to globally optimize both force-directed [4] and stress majorization schemes [2]. The player-guided, progressive reduction of uncertainty studied here provides an alternative to annealing schedules. In the experimental section, we compare the performance of these methods to the suggested.

Self-organizing maps (SOMs) [17] also use the metaphor of a competitive process ('game') between agents, inspired by neural behavior. A neural network is trained to produce a low-dimensional (typically 2D), discretized representation of the training samples input space. For each training point, a neuron is selected, and weights in its neighborhood are moved in the same direction ('similar items tend to excite adjacent neurons'). More neurons go to regions with high training sample concentration, and fewer where the samples are scarce. SOMs have been shown to have advantages [31] over more conventional feature extraction methods such as PCA. The neurons' exact location in the grid/graph, however, constrain their interaction and capture completely their mutual model. If players are given the latitude to move around freely, they require foresight (and a model) on others' behavior to coordinate. In Boids [22,26], players calculate individual positions using simple following and flocking behaviors. Players are homogeneous (have no preferential proximity among them) and need not to reason about each other actions.

In a polymatrix games [14], there is a utility matrix for every pair of players (i, j), each a separate component of player i's utility. Polymatrix games always have at least one mixed Nash equilibrium. Erdem and Pelillo [7] solved a generic polymatrix game using evolutionary game-theory (i.e., the replicator dynamics) to estimate a classification decision over partially-observed values in a set of prior graph-structured exemplars (i.e., transduction) with interesting results.

Congestion games were first proposed by Rosenthal [21]. In them, the payoff of each player depends on the resources it chooses and the number of players choosing the same resource. In general, players cannot communicate and have no uncertainty over each other's actions (only an observed and determined congestion on the chosen resource). More recently, the notion of uncertainty over a resource's congestion was explored [10]. Uncertainties are, however, static (i.e., cannot change or be strategically manipulated) - the inverse assumption of the current approach.

4   Implementation

4.1   Parallel Implementation

We implement a parallel GPU [28] version of the game where each thread-row correspond to players' probabilities $p_i(m)$ under a different intervention. Each individual intervention $y = do(i, k)$ is described jointly by a player i and a (clamped) position k, and we have C interventions.

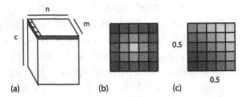

Fig. 1. (a) Player/threads layout, (b) radial prior, (c) multi-level prior.

The resulting thread layout for the game is a 3-dimensional $C \times N \times M$ matrix (Fig. 1a). Each row (i, m) correspond to an intervention in i and each column to a player j. A tread-cell contains the likelihood that player j (column) will go to a given position m when the intervention (i, m) is applied (i.e., that an arbitrary player will go to an arbitrary position). The value of $d(m, k)$ in Eq. (2) is fixed for each cell. We use the Euclidian distance between the centers of a 2-dimensional $\sqrt{M} \times \sqrt{M}$ cells regular grid (Fig. 1b). The value for a cell $p(i, k, m)$ can then be calculated from this constant, $D(i, j)$, and $N - 1$ vectors $p(i, k, .)$, where $D(i, j)$ is taken from the input distance-matrix and $p(i, k, .)$ from neighboring cells. Since this corresponds to $N \times M$ parallel vector multiplications, common GPU vector-vector optimizations can be used [3]. The individual values can then be made stochastic again by a depth (i.e., across m values) and row prefix-sums and a parallel division. We let the system run for T cycles, with values $p^t(i, j, m)$. We do not require, however, for players to reach equilibrium to stop the game, although we have observed that for a value $t > 10$ they often do. We look at T, instead, as a time constraint on the solution.

For visualization, interventions are exhaustively enumerated and an optimal intervention is selected according to the risk criterion, Eq. (7). This correspond to a row selection, based on a calculated property f over rows, $argmin f[p^t(i, j, m)]$. This row selection can be implemented trivially with parallel arithmetic operations and prefix-sums.

4.2   Priors and Multi-level Games

For realtime performance, we employ a second set of optimizations. Instead of playing the game over all M positions, we first play the game over a small grid $M' \ll M$. Then play the game again in each individual grid position, limited to players there but with further M' positions. We repeat this D_{max} times, generating an increasingly finer grid. The probabilistic priors serve to connect the levels, allowing players to take a summarized version of the previous (higher-level) game into consideration.

In practice, it's hard however to specify the prior distribution parametrically. We imagine then that the grid is a metal plate with discrete heat sources (each located in the middle position of two cell's border and with temperatures varying $[0, 1]$) [5]. With the sources positions and the heat equation, it's easy to calculate the temperatures at plate positions (i.e., the new level prior probabilities) by interpolating temperatures in parallel (Sanders and Kandrot, 2011) (Fig. 2).

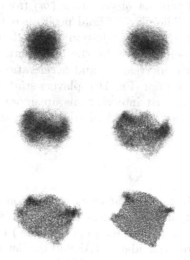

Fig. 2. 4.5M players in a synthetic dataset (subsequent interventions).

Let c^d denote a game's congestion - the number of players who intervened to position m in a game at level d, and with $c^{D_{max}} = N$. For the first-level prior, we place a single heat source at the grid center with temperature 0.5. For subsequent priors, we place sources at the middle positions of each adjacent square side with temperatures

$$1 - \frac{c^d(m)}{c^{d-1}(m)},$$

the normalized congestion on the prior level. Figure 1b shows a first-level prior and Fig. 1c a prior with two previous neighbours (each with equal congestion) in a grid with $5 \times 5 = 25$ positions. By breaking large games into independent smaller ones, we are able consider the exhaustive set of interventions C' in a level, for each position m ($C' = C^d(m) \times M'$).

4.3   Rendering

For rendering, players have no single, determinate position in this game (only a mixture of positions). We render player i's screen position $x_i \in \mathbb{R}^2$ (vector) as the average position across all M positions, weighted by the mixed strategy profile:

$$x_i = \sum_m p_i(m)x_c(m) \qquad (8)$$

where $x_c(m)$ is the vector from the grid center to the position m in the regular, squared grid. Each intervention (and subsequent competitive play) changes incrementally others' mixtures, and thus positions.

Each level has a different set of vectors $x_c(m)$ from the level cell center to all lower level positions. The player's final position is then the sum of vectors across all levels. The metaphor of single-body attraction and repulsion between nodes, for example, is then replaced by the interventions on players' probability distributions. And players' velocity and acceleration are 'replaced' by their uncertainty. With a radial prior (Fig. 1b), players start at the screen center and spread out. Typically, the first interventions are more 'catastrophic' and very noticeable, with latter ones barely. And equilibrium states are apparent (i.e., players halt movement).

5   Experiments

A difficulty with visualization is that there are no consensual benchmark measures (and often no comparison measures at all are given). We start with a few synthetic data. We then test the game ('coord-game') in several machine learning datasets and compare to standard-MDS and the deterministic annealing approach of [2] which do report stress measures. We also report results in a Facebook dataset with three networks. To reveal the structure of the output embedding more explicitly, we additionally reproduce the MNIST characters visualization of [29]. We finally briefly discuss running times. Experiments ran on an Intel Core 2 3 GHz CPU with 4 GB of memory and an nVidia 8800GTX graphics card with 512 MB of texture memory. Timings do not include file loading time.

We started by generating a batch of synthetic datasets, consisting of 4.5 million players distributed in a 2D grid embedded in 7 dimensions. We also tested the effects of adding noise to this grid (5 % noise in a third dimension). Figure 3a shows one run, comparing the performance (expected stress through number of interventions) of the min-max criterion, Eq. (7) compared to a greedy criteria, $min_{(i,k,j)}R(j|do(i,k))$. By avoiding riskier placements (i.e., ones that would constraint unfavorably individual, future others) the criterion leads to an overall layout that is closer to the high-dimensional, more quickly. The min-max criterion seems very resistant to local minima, when compared to annealing. This is reflected on the stress results reported below.

The Iris dataset (available on the UCI ML Repository) has 150 points in 4 dimensions (4 attributes over 3 classes of flowers). It's one of the most famous datasets in both machine learning and statistics [8]. Its dimensionality is speculated to be marginally greater than the embedding dimension (with two of the

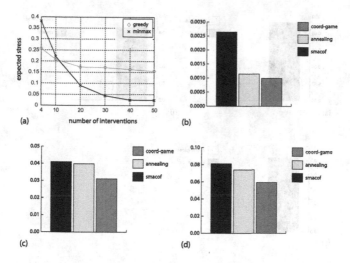

Fig. 3. (a) stress trough time, (b) iris dataset stress, (c) yeast dataset stress, (d) metagenomics dataset stress.

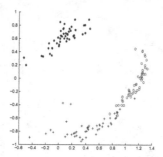

Fig. 4. Iris dataset scatterplot (crosses, circles, asterisk coding from ground truth).

classes linearly separable), both the global structure and the local proximity of the data may be important but neither can be reconstructed without some distortion (not being perfectly separable). Some cluster structure can be distinguished.

Figure 4 shows the output map as a scatterplot (all experiments and figures ran with radial prior distribution in Fig. 1c, $M = 5 \times 5 = 25$, $D_{max} = 3$ and $T = 10$). There is class information with each datapoint, but it is only used to label players in the figure (and no way influences their positions). Symbols (asterisk, cross and circle) clarifies how well the map preserves the similarities within each class. Qualitatively, the spatial embedding clearly separates the symbol-coded groups.

The yeast dataset has approximately three time more data points (1,484 points) than Iris, each 8-dimensional. The metagenomics data has twenty times more points (30,000 points). Figure 3 lists the obtained normalized stress ('coord-game'), together with those obtained with classical Scaling by Majorizing a Convex Function [9] ('smacof') and the more recent Deterministic Annealing

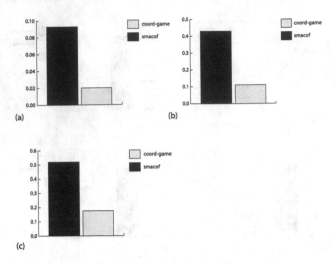

Fig. 5. (a) facebook friends network-1 stress, (c) network-2 stress, (d) network-3 stress.

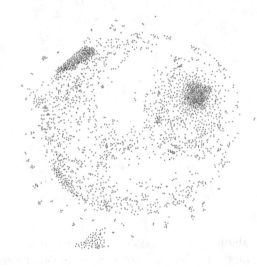

Fig. 6. Facebook friends network scatterplot with 10078 nodes.

with Iterative Majorization [2] ('annealing'). Since the later two algorithms have randomizations, these are average performances over 50 trial runs. For Iris, the stress obtained with coord-games is over twice as low as smacof and outperforms deterministic annealing, with a final normalized stress of 0.00111. This suggests that coord-game generates low-dimensional embeddings that are more accurate representations of these high-dimensional data-sets. Error bars across trials in [2] indicate variation across the trials for smacof and annealing which is not observed for coord-game (Fig. 4).

Next, we run the algorithm in a set of 3 collegiate facebook social graphs with 1005, 10078 and 13455 nodes. We only consider users with at least 10 friends, and all information but the plain friendship graph is ignored. The gain in performance is more dramatic, Fig. 5. Force-directed and MDS algorithms tend to look like a ball of yarn - a dense mess with no visually discernible structure - for networks with over 1000 nodes. We can however see structure in placements for these graphs using coord-game, Fig. 6. This is described more precisely by the stress measures in Fig. 5. MDS Algorithms [9] are $O(N^2)$ and obtaining comparison measures for networks larger than 10000 nodes is difficult without further optimization schemes.

The MNIST database of 28×28 (scaled and centered) handwritten digits (training set) has 60,000 examples. Although it's used mostly on classification tasks, it's interesting to take advantage of the visual difference between digits

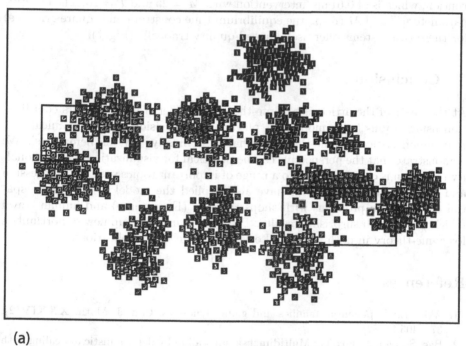

(a)

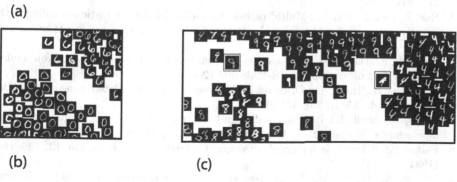

(b)   (c)

Fig. 7. MNIST dataset.

to make the mapped relationships clearer [29]. We downsampled and Gaussian smoothed digits to 16×16 bitmaps. We then selected 900 of the images, the 100 first examples for each digit in the original distribution [19]. Figure 5a contains the overall resulting embedding. Figure 5b,c show two bordering regions in detail (between 0–6 and 8–9–4 clusters). The separation between the digit classes is very clear. The few digits close to the wrong cluster are distorted, almost unrecognizable characters (Fig. 5c highlights, with rectangles, two examples, both from the '9' training subset).

The coord-game system is an order of magnitude faster than others with comparable performance (see, for example, [29]). It takes approximately 0.8 s, 1.9 and 8.3 s for the final placement of the Iris, Yeast and Metagenomics datasets. The visualization is iterative, and, perhaps more relevant, is the time per intervention, which is of 0.61 ms/intervention with $M = 25$ and $T = 10$. The effective parameters T and M (resp., the equilibrium time constrain and square grid size) for these two systems offer useful speed-quality tradeoffs (Fig. 7).

6   Conclusion

At the heart of the article is a game-theoretic model of many-players coordination using graphs (with models for players belief revision and communication). A common critic of game-theory is that it is mostly 'toy mathemathics'. We demonstrate that the perspective can be practical for visualization. Dimensionality reduction is closely related to a range of important topics such as compression and discriminant analysis. We have also applied the model to large-scale spatial coordination problems with shops check-in (Foursquare) and human travel (Flickr) data with surprising results. The work thus opens up new opportunities for game-theory in both Machine Learning and in new applications.

References

1. Akin, E.: Exponential families and game dynamics. Can. J. Math. **XXXIV**(2), 374–405 (1982)
2. Bae, S., Qiu, J., Fox, G.: Multidimensional scaling by deterministic annealing with iterative majorization algorithm. In: Proceedings of IEEE eScience 2010 Conference (2010)
3. Bell, N., Garland, M.: Efficient sparse matrix-vector multiplication on cuda. NVIDIA Technical report NVR-2008-004 (2008)
4. Davidson, R., Harel, D.: Drawing graphs nicely using simulated annealing. ACM Trans. Graph. **15**(4), 301–331 (1996)
5. Doyle, P., Snell, L.: Random walks and electric networks. Carus mathematical monographs. Mathematical Association of America, Washington, D.C (1984)
6. Eades, P.: A heuristic for graph drawing. Congressus Numerantium **42**, 149–160 (1984)
7. Erdem, A., Pelillo, M.: Graph transduction as a noncooperative game. Neural Comput. **24**(3), 700–723 (2012)

8. Fisher, R.: The use of multiple measurements in taxonomic problems. Annu. Eugenics, Part II **7**, 179–188 (1936)
9. Hong, Seok-Hee, Eades, Peter: A linear time algorithm for constructing maximally symmetric straight-line drawings of planar graphs. In: Pach, János (ed.) GD 2004. LNCS, vol. 3383, pp. 307–317. Springer, Heidelberg (2005)
10. Georgiou, C., Pavlides, T., Philippou, A.: Network uncertainty in selfish routing. In: IPDPS (2006)
11. Halpern, J. Pearl, J.: Causes and explanations: a structural-model approach. Part I: Causes. In: UAI (2001)
12. Harper, M.: Information geometry and evolutionary game theory. In: CoRR (2009)
13. Hofbauer, J., Sigmund, K.: Evolutionary Games and Population Dynamics. Cambridge University Press, Cambridge (1998)
14. Howson, J.: Equilibria of polymatrix games. Manag. Sci. **18**(5), 312–318 (1972)
15. Kirkpatrick, S., Gelatt, C., Vecchi, M.: Optimization by simulated annealing. Science **220**(4598), 671–680 (1983)
16. Kobourov, S.: Force-Directed Drawing Algorithms (2012)
17. Kohonen, T.: Self-organized formation of topologically correct feature maps. Biol. Cybern. **43**(1), 59–69 (1982)
18. Kruskal, J.: Nonmetric multidimensional scaling: a numerical method. Psychometrika **29**(2), 115–129 (1964)
19. LeCun, Y., Bottou, L., Bengio, Y., Haffner, P.: Gradient-based learning applied to document recognition. Proc. IEEE **86**(11), 2278–2324 (1998)
20. Lus, H., Aydn, C.O., Keten, S., Unsal, H.I., Atlgan, A.R.: El farol revisited. Physica A Stat. Mech. Appl. **346**(3), 651–656 (2005)
21. Milchtaich, I.: Congestion games with player-specific payoff functions. Games Econ. Behav. **13**(1), 111–124 (1996)
22. Moere, A.: Time-varying data visualization using information flocking boids. In: Information Visualization (InfoVis) (2004)
23. Novembre, J., Stephens, M.: Interpreting principal component analyses of spatial population genetic variation. Nat. Genet. **40**, 646–649 (2008)
24. Olfati-Saber, R., Fax, A., Murray, R.: Consensus and cooperation in networked multi-agent systems. Proc. IEEE **95**(1), 215–233 (2007)
25. Pearl, J.: Causality. Cambridge University Press, Cambridge (2000)
26. Reynolds, C.: Flocks, herds, and schools: a distributed behavioral model. In: Computer Graphics, SIGGRAPH, p. 25 (1987)
27. Roweis, S., Saul, L.: Nonlinear dimensionality reduction by locally linear embedding. Science **290**(5500), 2323–2326 (2000)
28. Sanders, J., Kandrot, E.: CUDA by Example: An Introduction to General-Purpose GPU Programming. Addison-Wesley, Upper Saddle River (2011)
29. van der Maaten, L., Hinton, G.: Visualizing high-dimensional data using t-sne. J. Mach. Learn. Res. **9**, 2579–2605 (2008)
30. Weibull, J.: Evolutionary Game Theory. MIT Press, Cambridge (1995)
31. Yonggang, L., Weisberg, R., Christopher, M.: Performance evaluation of the self-organizing map for feature extraction. J. Geophys. Res. **111**, (2006)

Decision Making, Conflicts and Agreements

Modeling a Multi-issue Negotiation Protocol for Agent Extensible Negotiations

Samir Aknine[1], Souhila Arib[2], and Djamila Boukredera[3][✉]

[1] LIRIS Laboratory, Université Claude Bernard Lyon 1, Lyon, France
samir.aknine@univ-lyon1.fr
[2] LAMSADE Laboratory, Université Paris Dauphine, Paris, France
souhila.arib@dauphine.fr
[3] LMA Laboratory, Université de Bejaia, Bejaia, Algeria
boukredera@hotmail.com

Abstract. In this paper, we study how to achieve more effective negotiations by extending during the negotiation process, the negotiation object with new relevant items. Indeed, the possibility to extend the initial set of items defined by the requester agent with other items related to the original query can help find an agreement. In doing so, with extended proposals, the requester agent may be incentivized to be more flexible, e.g., by making concessions or relaxing some constraints on the issues. This may help to achieve an agreement which is more beneficial for both parties than breaking down the negotiation. Such extensible negotiations may lead to win-win outcomes which otherwise can not be achieved with some usual negotiation strategies where it is hard to dynamically alter the set of items under negotiation during the course of the process. In this paper, we first outline a negotiation strategy which allows the extension of the negotiation space by extending the negotiation object with new relevant items. Based on this, we then propose a new multi-issue negotiation protocol which relies on the bidding-based mechanism and deals with such extensible negotiation strategies.

Keywords: Negotiation · Multi-agent · Protocols

1 Introduction

The worldwide expansion of the Internet has considerably contributed to changing the way people use Internet. They become heavy Internet commerce users who always ask for more sophisticated services involving automated and flexible data processing systems. Indeed, the emergence of several more advanced e-commerce service clients and providers has led to an increasing demand for more complex systems composed of software agents representing individuals or organizations capable to conduct automated negotiations on behalf on their human owners. In such context, automated negotiation has proved to be more efficient and promises higher quality of agreements. Complex automated negotiations have been widely studied in the field of multi-agent systems and different

© Springer International Publishing Switzerland 2015
N. Bulling (Ed.): EUMAS 2014, LNAI 8953, pp. 349–359, 2015.
DOI: 10.1007/978-3-319-17130-2_23

negotiation mechanisms have been proposed. These are based on game theoretic models (see e.g. [8]), heuristic approaches (see e.g. [4]) and argumentation [5]. Lot of negotiation systems have been produced to solve collective and distributed problems but the use of such technology on the web is still under investigation and experimentation and much further work has to be done especially in the young field of automated negotiation on multiple issues with incomplete information [1–3,9]. Negotiation strategies depend heavily on the specific characteristics of the environment under consideration such as the cardinality of the negotiation (single issue, multiple issues, one-to-one, multi-party, etc.), agents characteristics and information parameters. Most of the traditional models achieve coordination through specification of the negotiation space: the issues agents negotiate over, and their possible values that determine the set of alternative solutions. The central focus of this study is to achieve more effective negotiations where agents would move towards agreements by searching new alternatives allowing agents to reach a compromise when a failure seems to be unavoidable in the first phase. To fulfill such objective, deliberative mechanisms seems to be more suitable than responsive mechanisms [6]. Indeed, responsive mechanisms, widely used in current negotiation models, are simple and uncostly responses to the environment, but they rely on a straightforward response mechanism to generate proposals and counterproposals by assigning new values to the issues determined by the user's query (called support of the query). In this case, the only feedback to a proposal is a counter-proposal (if any) which is another point in the negotiation space, an acceptance or a withdrawal. However, in a deliberative mechanism with issue manipulation mechanism, participants are allowed to dynamically extend the structure of the negotiation object by adding new relevant items to clinch the deal. This mechanism aims to increase the likelihood of an agreement by adding (or removing) issues in the negotiation set. With such extensible proposals, the requester agent would be more incentivized to make concessions or to relax some constraints specified in the initial request. This variant, denoted extensible negotiation, authorizes the dynamic extension of the set of items concerned with the negotiation in order to widen the negotiation space of possible solutions. Against this background, this paper proposes a new multi-issue negotiation protocol relying on a negotiation strategy where the issue manipulation mechanism is adopted. Based on the alternating offers model, the protocol deals with the specific characteristics of such extensible negotiations where: (1) the negotiation object is composed of multiple issues, (2) the negotiating agent may dynamically alter the set of issues by adding new relevant items in the case of an inevitable negotiation failure. In doing so, this agent may send either a counter-proposal or an extended counter-proposal going beyond the limited set of items specified in the support of the query especially when new compromising points between the applicant and the suppliers could be reached. The proposed protocol which operates in three main phases namely exploration, commitment and termination, include time deadlines to ensure that in the case of no convergence it will terminate. The remainder of the paper is organized as follows. Section 2 presents the negotiation protocol and details the communication primitives and their semantics. Section 3 describes the behaviors of the agents. Section 4 concludes and gives some perspectives.

2 Negotiation Protocol

Let us consider the example of an Internet user who wishes to organize his trip by the means of an electronic agency. The Internet user sends to this agency a query describing the list of services he wants to get in his trip, including plane tickets, a room reservation and museum tickets. This set of items is called the support of the query. The user also adds his list of preferences (e.g. dates of travel) and his constraints (e.g. hotel and room categories, budget, etc.). Let us outline an illustrative scenario: once the query of the user has been received and processed by the suppliers, if they do not have proposals to submit on this support, the failure of the negotiation will be imminent. The same situation also happens if the proposals on these items are not accepted by the applicant, the failure of the negotiation will be also inevitable. Based on the set manipulation mechanism, our negotiation model allows the openness of the negotiations with respect to the items which have not been mentioned in the support initially fixed by the user. Thus the negotiation started with the items: "plane tickets, room reservation and museum tickets" could be extended by the suppliers with new items, not initially specified in the query of the user, but which would interest him if they are related to the items listed in his query. In our example, the user could possibly agree to modify his constraints on his travel dates if the suppliers provide him additional services, e.g. guided tours of historic sites. Note that this new item would be generated dynamically in the particular scenario where the negotiation seems to move towards an unavoidable failure, extending hence the negotiation object of the requester agent in order to reach an agreement. To formally model this situation, we use two types of agents: supplier agents and agencies. Agencies are represented by a set A such that: $A = \{a_1, a_2, \ldots, a_n\}$ and the set of suppliers is denoted F such that: $F = \{f_1, f_2, \ldots, f_m\}$. The queries the agencies submit for the suppliers in F are represented by the set Q, such that: $Q = \{q_1, q_2, \ldots, q_p\}$. Each q_i considers a set of items in S such that: $S = \{s_1, s_2, s_3, \ldots, s_r\}$. The constraints C_i on items s_j of a query q_i are indicated by each agency at the submission of the query. Our protocol uses three phases: exploration, commitment and termination (cf. Fig. 1).

- *Phase 1: Exploration*: This first phase starts when an agency sends the query of the Internet user to the suppliers. The agency specifies the requirements needed for the acceptance of the bids and waits for the reception of the proposals. The suppliers reply with their proposals, detail their own conditions and wait for the answers of the agency. If the agents decommit they will not be penalized since their proposals are not committing them. The whole negotiation process is only delimited with a fixed duration but there is not a specific duration for this first phase of exploration.

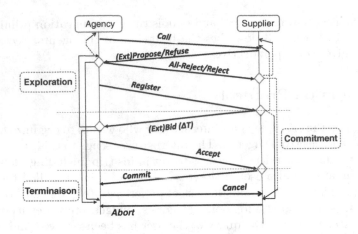

Fig. 1. Behaviors of the agency and the supplier agents in the negotiation.

- *Phase 2: Commitment*: This phase starts when the agency accepts a proposal made by a supplier. After that if this supplier applies definitely, it should clarify the constraints on its proposal, in particular, its period of validity. Then it waits for the confirmation of the agency in the next period. If the agency desists before the end of this period, it will not be penalized. However if it desists after the expiration of the negotiation, it will be penalized. By the same way, a supplier which accepts the registration of an agency cannot cancel its proposal and if it does, even before the end of the validity period of the proposal, it will be penalized. Among the constraints associated with a bid, we have the period of validity *(ΔT)* which indicates the moment after which this proposal could be canceled automatically if the agency does no answer. Each agency should manage this kind of constraints on the bids. Once this validity period expires, the supplier can, if necessary, propose new proposals of higher or lower values compared to the proposals made in preceding iterations.
- *Phase 3: Termination*: This phase starts once the agency confirmed to the supplier the acceptance of its proposal or its withdrawal from the negotiation. Any withdrawal must be performed before the end of the validity period of the bid; otherwise the agency will be penalized. After the agency accepts a bid, the acceptance of the supplier is expected. If a compromise between the participants has not been reached the negotiation fails.

Communication Primitives of the Protocol: These primitives allow an interpretation of the exchanged messages between the agents. Let K_f and K_a be respectively the knowledge bases of the supplier agents f and the agencies a:

- *Cfp (a, f, Items, Conditions)*: The initiator of the negotiation, which is the agency a sends a message to the suppliers in which it declares its intention to negotiate the items described in its query. This query is completed with a set of specifications and constraints on the items. The pre and post conditions associated with the *cfp* are:

Pre-conditions(Cfp): $\exists x \subseteq Items \wedge satisfied(x, a) \notin K_a \wedge wait(x) \notin K_a$

Post-conditions(Cfp): $\exists x \subseteq Items \wedge wait(x) \in K_a \wedge satisfied(x, a) \notin K_f \wedge wait(x) \in K_f$

- wait(x) means that the items in x are under negotiation.
- satisfied(x,a) means that a owns a promising proposal for the set x.
- *Propose (f, a, Proposal, Cfp, Conditions)*: With this answer, the supplier f indicates for the agency a the proposals it can provide and for which a can register if it accepts them. Up till now f specifies only the proposals it owns, it is still not committed with a.

Pre-conditions(Propose): $\exists x \subseteq Items \wedge \exists y Proposal(x, y) \in K_f \wedge satisfied(x, a) \notin K_f \wedge know(y) \notin K_a \wedge wait(x) \in K_f$

Post-conditions(Propose): $\exists x \subseteq Items \wedge \exists y Proposal(x, y) \in K_f \wedge y \in K_a \wedge sender(y, f) \in K_a$

- *Ext-Propose (a, f, Ext-Proposal, Cfp, Conditions)*. With this primitive, the supplier f indicates for the agency a that it has formulated a new proposal for the query. However, the new proposal is an extended proposal since it contains new items that will probably interest the agency. Recall that the agency has not explicitly required them. It has thus to re-evaluate the new proposal taking into account this additional knowledge.

Pre-conditions(Ext-Propose): $\exists x \subseteq Items \wedge \exists y Ext - Proposal(x, y) \in K_f \wedge satisfied(x, a) \notin K_f \wedge know(y) \notin K_a \wedge wait(x) \in K_f$

Post-conditions(Ext-Propose): $\exists x \subseteq Items \wedge \exists y Ext - Proposal(x, y) \in K_f \wedge y \in K_a \wedge sender(y, f) \in K_a$

To build an extended proposal, the supplier agents compute the semantic distance between the items indicated in the user's query and the items they own in their domain ontology [7]. The constraints fixed by the user are also used to delimit the search space of possible proposals. This distance is used to identify the closest items to propose for the agents and which could interest the user.

- *Refuse (f, a, Cfp)*: The supplier declares that it is not able to satisfy the original query in its *Cfp*. It has no proposal to submit in this exploration phase.

Pre-conditions(Refuse): $\exists x \subseteq Items \wedge satisfied(x, a) \notin K_f \wedge \rceil \exists y Proposal(x, y) \in K_f \wedge wait(x) \in K_f$

Post-conditions(Refuse): $\exists x \subseteq Items \wedge wait(x) \notin K_f$

- *Register (a, f, (Ext)Proposal, Items, Conditions)*: The agency a notifies to the supplier f that its proposal (possibly extended) is in a favorable position compared to all the received proposals either of f or other suppliers. The agency a may also provide more precise details on the conditions it would see improved by the supplier f. Up till now a is not committed with f even with this registration for its items. Both agents can withdraw in this stage of the negotiation without being penalized.

Pre-conditions(Register): $\exists x \subseteq Items \wedge \exists y(Ext)Proposal(x,y) \in K_a \wedge sender$
$(y,f) \in K_a \wedge satisfied(x,a) \in K_a \wedge preferred(x,a,f) \notin K_a$

Post-conditions(Register): $\exists x \subseteq Items \wedge preferred(x,a,f) \in K_a \wedge satisfied$
$(x,a) \in K_f$

- preferred(x,a,f) denotes that the agency a considers the supplier f as the agent with the best proposal on x. -satisfied(x,a,f) signifies for f that its proposal on x interests a.
- *Reject (a, f, Items, (Ext)Proposal, Favored (Ext)Proposal)*: The agency *a* informs the supplier *f* that its proposal (possibly extended) is not the best preferred compared to those received. Here the proposal *Favored (Ext)Proposal* is the one likely to be accepted. *f* may thus improve its proposal by making some modifications on it (either in its extensions or not).

Pre-conditions(Reject): $\exists x \subseteq Items \wedge \exists y(Ext)Proposal(x,y) \in K_a \wedge \exists z sender$
$(y,z) \in K_a \wedge z \neq f \wedge satisfied(x,a) \in K_a \wedge preferred(x,a,z) \in K_a$

Post-conditions(Reject): $\exists x \subseteq Items \wedge rejected(x,y,a) \in K_f \wedge rejected$
$(x,y,f) \in K_a$

- *All-Reject (a, f, Items, Refused (Ext)Proposal, Best Refused (Ext)Proposal)*. This message is sent by the agency and informs the suppliers that it has not selected a proposal among those received. It rejects all these agents and indicates for them the best refused proposal so as it allows them to improve their next proposals.

Pre-conditions(All-Reject): $\exists x \subseteq Items \wedge \exists y Proposal(x,y) \in K_a \wedge satisfied$
$(x,a) \notin K_a$

Post-conditions(All-Reject): $\exists x \subseteq Items \wedge \rceil \exists y Proposal(x,y) \in K_a$

- *Reject-and-new-Cfp (a, f, (Ext)Proposal, new Cfp)*. The agency sends this message when all the proposals previously received are not compatible with its specified constraints. It should thus prepare a new call more adapted to the current context and send it to all the suppliers which have already answered with their proposals.

Pre-conditions(Reject-and-new-Cfp): $\exists x \subseteq Items \wedge \exists y Proposal(x,y) \in K_a \wedge$
$satisfied(x,a) \notin K_a$

Post-conditions(Reject-and-new-Cfp): $\exists x \subseteq Items \wedge satisfied(x,a) \notin K_f \wedge \rceil$
$\exists y Proposal(x,y) \in K_a \wedge wait(x) \in K_f$

- *Bid (f, a, Cfp, Proposed Conditions)*: The supplier sends this message to the agency as an answer for its registration. The difference between the proposal which it has submitted in the exploration phase and the current *Bid* lies only on the validity conditions added to this proposal. These conditions specify, the expiry time period of the proposal, for instance. The agency knows now, that it should commit (or give up its registration) before reaching the expiry limit. If it exceeds this limit, it will lose its registration (and can be possibly penalized if the conditions agreed on authorize that). Even if the agency carried out a registration for the items of the supplier f, it is not yet committed.

Pre-conditions(Bid): $\exists x \subseteq Items \wedge satisfied(x, a, f) \in K_f \wedge Timeout(x) \notin K_f$
$\wedge \exists y Bid(x, y) \notin K_a \wedge sender(y, f)$

Post-conditions(Bid): $\exists x \subseteq Items \wedge \exists y Bid(x, y) \in K_a \wedge sender(y, f) \wedge committed$
$(x, f, a) \in K_a$

– Timeout(x) denotes the expiration of the decommitment phase.
– Committed(x,f,a) signifies that the bid on x has committed agent f to a.

The semantics of the primitive *Ext-Bid* is same than *Bid*, the only difference is in the set of items which becomes wider since the extension of the initial proposal.

– *Accept (a f, Items, (Ext)Bid):* With this message, the agency *a* accepts the *Bid* or the *Ext-Bid* of the supplier and it starts a termination phase with *f*.

Pre-conditions(Accept): $\exists x \subseteq Items \wedge \exists y(Ext)Bid(x, y) \in K_a \wedge sender(y, f) \in$
$K_a \wedge satisfied(x, a) \in K_a$

Post-conditions(Accept): $\exists x \subseteq Items \wedge preferred(x, a, f) \in K_a \wedge satisfied$
$(x, a, f) \in K_f \wedge committed(x, f, a) \in K_a \wedge committed(x, a, f) \in K_f$

– *Commit (f, a, Cfp, (Ext)Bid):* The supplier *f* sends this message when it receives an acceptance of *a* on the bid the latter received previously and when the conditions of validity, such as validity period, are not violated. Once this message is sent, *f* is definitely committed and cannot decommit if it does not satisfy the conditions for a decommitment, for instance by accepting the payment of a penalty to the agency.

Pre-conditions(Commit): $\exists x \subseteq Items \wedge committed(x, a, f) \in K_f \wedge \exists y(Ext)Bid$
$(x, y) \in K_a \wedge sender(y, f)$

Post-conditions(Commit): $\exists x \subseteq Items \wedge \exists y(Ext)Bid(x, y) \in K_a \wedge sender(y, f) \wedge$
$committed(x, f, a) \in K_f$

– *Abort (f, a, Cfp, (Ext)Bid, Reason):* f can end its negotiation on a failure if for instance the validity period of a proposal has expired before receiving the answer. It thus sends a message to the agency explaining the failure. This message ends the negotiation.

Pre-conditions(Abort): $\exists x \subseteq Items \wedge committed(x, a, f) \notin K_f \wedge \exists y(Ext)Bid$
$(x, y) \in K_a \wedge sender(y, f) \wedge \rceil Condition(y, a)$

Post-conditions(Abort): $\exists x \subseteq Items \wedge (Ext)Bid(x, y) \notin K_a \wedge sender(y, f) \wedge$
$committed(x, a, f) \notin K_f \wedge wait(x) \notin K_f$

– Condition (y,a) signifies that the conditions on y have been respected by a.

Recall that we try to define a faithful protocol that guarantees coherent behaviors for the agents as done currently with human negotiations in the usual electronic systems (in plane reservation systems, for instance). The aim is certainly to facilitate use of this kind of protocols for the applications based on automatic negotiation.

3   Behaviors of the Agents in the Negotiation

- **Behaviors of the Agency:** The protocol enables several series of exchanges for an agency with its different suppliers. Once the agency receives the users' query, it contacts the suppliers it knows. Based on their proposals, the agency seeks to obtain the intended utility and to satisfy all the constraints on the items in the query. At the beginning, the agency makes a call for proposals, *Cfp*, to each supplier agent it considers as able to provide one or more required items (cf. Fig. 2). Initially, suppliers are not necessarily informed about the other agents involved in the same negotiation. The agency is now in *the state 1* where it waits for the answers of the contacted suppliers in the form of *Propose* messages. If these suppliers refuse to take part in the negotiation, the agency either ends its negotiation or makes some concessions (i.e. accepts to change the constraints on the items, for instance). Then the agency has to wait for the new answers of the suppliers. These two states are respectively involved by the transitions Tr_5 and Tr_8. Once the suppliers have answered with their proposals, the agency goes to the state generated by the transition Tr_4 in order to process their messages. In this state, the agency analyzes the received proposals using its predefined strategy. Based on the received *Propose* messages and possibly extended proposals in the form of *(Ext)Propose*, it tries to build a solution which satisfies its constraints. If the agency succeeds, it starts its registrations with the Register messages it sends to its best supplier agents owning these proposals. It also sends *Pre-Reject* messages to the other suppliers. The agency reaches the *state 7* resulting from Tr_7. This step continues until the agency satisfies the query of the user. Once the exploration phase finished, the agency waits for the final proposals of the potential suppliers. During the exploration phase, the agency can also receive temporary proposals of other suppliers it has only pre-rejected. These suppliers may indeed decide to make concessions and thus improve their previous proposals. In this case, the agency reaches the next state following the transition Tr_{16}. In this state the agency processes its proposals based on its own strategies. It may decide to choose a new potential supplier agent for which it asks a final proposal and cancels its previous registration with the other potential suppliers. However after reaching a certain level of satisfaction of its utility function, the agency should only wait for final proposals from the potential suppliers. This is shown on the transition Tr_{10} in the protocol description. If a supplier agent has received a *Register* message and decided to decommit -or does not answer within a specific time period- the agency can prefer the transition Tr_{11} where it selects a new potential supplier. However if the supplier agent answers with a final proposal in a *Bid* message or possibly an *(Ext)Bid* message, the

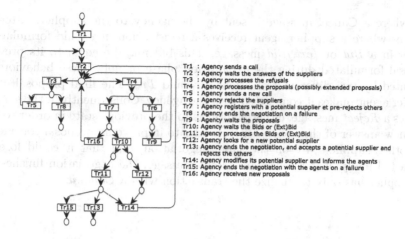

Tr1 : Agency sends a call
Tr2 : Agency waits the answers of the suppliers
Tr3 : Agency processes the refusals
Tr4 : Agency processes the proposals (possibly extended proposals)
Tr5 : Agency sends a new call
Tr6 : Agency rejects the suppliers
Tr7 : Agency registers with a potential supplier et pre-rejects others
Tr8 : Agency ends the negotiation on a failure
Tr9 : Agency waits the proposals
Tr10: Agency waits the Bids or (Ext)Bid
Tr11: Agency processes the Bids or (Ext)Bid
Tr12: Agency looks for a new potential supplier
Tr13: Agency ends the negotiation, and accepts a potential supplier and
        rejects the others
Tr14: Agency modifies its potential supplier and informs the agents
Tr15: Agency ends the negotiation with the agents on a failure
Tr16: Agency receives new proposals

Fig. 2. Internal behavior of the agency agent.

agency analyzes the different allowed choices. If this *Bid* seems overestimated compared to the previous proposal received in the exploration phase, the agency may decide to definitively reject the potential supplier, or reject it temporarily, or to maintain it in its current state as long as the allowed negotiation time has not expired. Before rejecting the supplier, the agency makes sure that there is at least one other interested potential supplier having a better proposal. It should then send a registration message to this potential supplier for the items it proposes. Once these messages sent, the agency waits for the final proposal. When it receives from a supplier a *Bid* or *(Ext)Bid* which satisfies it conditions, it sends an *Accept* message to this supplier where it announces that its proposal is definitively selected and that any negotiation concerning these items is closed. It waits for a *Commit* message from this supplier. This message results in the broadcast of the *Cancel* messages for all other suppliers. Thus the negotiation finishes successfully. However in case that the agency has been unsatisfied by all its suppliers, it ends the negotiation on a failure. This state results from the transition Tr_{15} on the protocol description.

- Behaviors of the Supplier Agent: After the supplier agent receives a *Cfp* on its items, it analyzes it in *state 1* (cf. Fig. 3) where it prepares the proposal to give for the agency. It has to send a *Refuse* message if it considers that the query is not interesting or that the conditions of the query are unreachable. If it is able to meet these requirements, it sends its proposal in a *Propose* message and reaches then the *state 3* where it waits for an answer from the agency. The supplier can receive a rejection message from the agency. It then behaves in different ways. If it builds a new proposal, it reaches the *state 10*. It can also decide to end the negotiation, and attains then the *state 11*. In this case, it waits temporarily until the agency revises some of its constraints and yields on some of its requirements. The supplier becomes temporarily accepted with a registration of the agency, this enables it to attend the *state 6*. The negotiation stops in the case where a Cancel message is sent by the agency to the supplier. After the moment where a supplier agent receives a registration, it should formulate an answer in a *Bid* or *(ext.)Bid* message. This bid may be equal to its previous proposal formulated during the exploration phase or not. These behaviors are generated by two different transitions Tr_8 and Tr_9. The final proposal of the supplier agent makes it committed with the agency. Consequently, if the supplier receives a *Reject* message, either it returns to the previous state in order to wait for a new answer of the agency, or it decides to improve its proposal considering that other suppliers are on the same negotiation, and that it could lose the contract. Finally, if it receives an *Accept* message, the negotiation finishes and the supplier has only to finalize the transaction with a *Commit*.

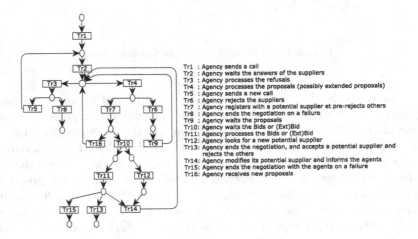

Tr1 : Agency sends a call
Tr2 : Agency waits the answers of the suppliers
Tr3 : Agency processes the refusals
Tr4 : Agency processes the proposals (possibly extended proposals)
Tr5 : Agency sends a new call
Tr6 : Agency rejects the suppliers
Tr7 : Agency registers with a potential supplier et pre-rejects others
Tr8 : Agency ends the negotiation on a failure
Tr9 : Agency waits the proposals
Tr10: Agency waits the Bids or (Ext)Bid
Tr11: Agency processes the Bids or (Ext)Bid
Tr12: Agency looks for a new potential supplier
Tr13: Agency ends the negotiation, and accepts a potential supplier and rejects the others
Tr14: Agency modifies its potential supplier and informs the agents
Tr15: Agency ends the negotiation with the agents on a failure
Tr16: Agency receives new proposals

Fig. 3. Internal behavior of the supplier agent.

4 Conclusion and Perspectives

In this paper, we have proposed a novel protocol designed for the important challenge of automated negotiation on multiple issues with incomplete information and time constraints. We have specified this protocol with its three main negotiation phases as well as the communication primitives used by the agents and their semantics. The direction for future work will be primarily focused at the modeling, the verification and the analysis of the proposed protocol using formal methods such as high level Petri nets which have proved their effectiveness in performing formal verification and validation.

References

1. Zheng, R., Chakraborty, N., Dai, T., Sycara, K.: Multiagent negotiation on multiple issues with incomplete information. In: Proceedings of the Twelfth International Conference on Autonomous Agents and Multiagent Systems, pp. 1279–1280 (2013)

2. Kattan, A., Ong, Y., Lopez, E.G.: Multi-agent multi-issue negotiations with incomplete information: a genetic algorithm based on discrete surrogate approach. In: IEEE Congress on Evolutionary Computation, pp. 2556–2563 (2013)
3. An, B., Lesser, V., Sim, K.M.: Strategic agents for multi-resource negotiation. Auton. Agent. Multi-Agent Syst. **23**(1), 114–153 (2011)
4. Faratin, P., Sierra, C., Jennings, N.R.: Using similarity criteria to make issue trade-offs in automated negotiation. Artif. Intell. **142**, 205–237 (2001)
5. Dimopoulos, Y., Moraitis, P.: Advances in argumentation-based negotiation. In: Lopes, F., Coelho, H. (eds.) Negotiation and Argumentation in Multi-agent Systems: Fundamentals, Theories, Systems and Applications, pp. 82–125. Bentham Science Publishers (2014)
6. Faratin, P., Sierra, C., Jennings, N.R., Buckle, P.: Designing responsive and deliberative automated negotiators. In: Proceedings of AAAI Workshop on Negotiation, Orlando, FL, pp. 12–18 (1999)
7. Resnik, P.: Using information content to evaluate semantic similarity in a taxonomy. In: IJCAI, pp. 448–453 (1995)
8. Rosenschein, J.S., Zlotkin, G.: Rules of Encounter. MIT Press, Cambridge (1994)
9. Lai, G., Sycara, K.: A generic framework for automated multi-attribute negotiation. Group Decis. Negot. **18**(2), 169–187 (2009)

Conflict Resolution
in Assumption-Based Frameworks

Martin Baláž[1]($\boxtimes$), Jozef Frtús[1], Giorgos Flouris[2], Martin Homola[1],
and Ján Šefránek[1]

[1] Comenius University in Bratislava, Bratislava, Slovakia
balaz@ii.fmph.uniba.sk
[2] FORTH-ICS, Heraklion, Greece

Abstract. We show how defeasible reasoning can be embedded into
ABF. Differently from other proposals, we do not encode the conflict resolution mechanism for defeasible rules into the ABF's deductive systems.
Instead, we formalize the notions of conflict and conflict resolution and
make them part of the extended ABF framework (XABF). This improves
the control over the conflict resolution process, and allows to devise
and compare different domain-dependent conflict resolution strategies.
We also show, that no matter which conflict resolution strategy is used,
our framework is able to guarantee certain desired properties.

1 Introduction

A number of logics from Non-Monotonic Reasoning (NMR) were investigated
and tried for agent reasoning capabilities in logic-based multi-agent systems,
especially to deal with incompleteness, uncertainty, inconsistency, and other
practical aspects of knowledge. Many of these formalisms can be captured in
the Assumption-Based Framework (ABF) [3,6]. ABF is particularly well suited
for capturing default reasoning, which is useful to deal with incomplete knowledge. In this case some of the statements are *assumptions* (i.e., hypothetical
statements) which can be possibly uprooted if a contrary statement is strictly
derived. Such conflicts, called *undermining*, are naturally captured and resolved in
ABF (by dropping the assumption and upholding the strictly derived statement).

Defeasible reasoning, which is also often associated with ABF, is useful to
deal with inconsistent knowledge. In this case conflicts arise between two conflicting statements that are supported by two different derivations. Such conflicts,
called *rebutting*, may be resolved by tracing the respective derivations and finding a derivation rule or an assumption that is to be dropped. However, there
is often more than one possibility to do this, therefore multiple conflict resolution strategies (CRS) may be applied, sometimes depending on the application
domain. Two such strategies are known as last-link principle and weakest-link
principle [9].

Defeasible reasoning can also be embedded into ABF, however, since rebutting conflicts are not resolved directly by the ABF semantics, workarounds are
often used, e.g., to use names of rules as new assumptions and to encode the

N. Bulling (Ed.): EUMAS 2014, LNAI 8953, pp. 360–369, 2015.
DOI: 10.1007/978-3-319-17130-2_24

conflict resolution strategy using the ABF's deductive system [2,7]. One of the advantages of ABF is its employment of argumentation semantics which allows not only to compute the solution, but also to provide intuitive explanations why necessary assumptions had to be dropped. As we show in Sect. 2, by relying upon workarounds as cited above such explanations are no longer easily found.

We propose the eXtended Assumption-Based Framework (XABF) in which CRS need not to be encoded into the deductive system; it is elevated to a first-class citizen of the formalism. Our main results are summarized as follows:

- CRS is a parameter of the framework, a number of different CRSs may be defined and used according to the specific needs of the application domain.
- Treatment of the CRS in XABF enables to identify the reasons why conflicts were resolved in any particular way much more clearly, in comparison to encoding a CRS into the deductive system.
- Consistency and closure [4], two widely accepted desiderata for defeasible reasoning, are satisfied in our approach in general, for any given CRS.
- Unlike the ASPIC$^+$ framework [8,9] we avoid using transposed rules which cause problems when embedding formalisms with strictly directional rules whose meaning is affected by transposition (see Sect. 7 for details).

2   Motivating Example

To motivate our approach, we will use a running example borrowed from [4]:

Example 1 (Marriage Example). Consider the following set of rules:

| $\rightarrow$ *wears_ring* | $r_1:$ *wears_ring* $\Rightarrow$ *married* | *married* $\rightarrow$ *has_wife* |
| $\rightarrow$ *goes_out* | $r_2:$ *goes_out* $\Rightarrow$ *bachelor* | *bachelor* $\rightarrow$ $\sim$ *has_wife* |

The rules in the above example lead us to conclude conflicting knowledge that a man wearing a ring is married, and therefore has a wife, whereas a man that goes out is a bachelor and therefore does not have a wife. Note that some of the rules are strict ($\rightarrow$) whereas others are defeasible ($\Rightarrow$), and that defeasible rules are associated with a name of the form r_i.

To obtain an argumentative semantics for the program, it is not sufficient to directly embed ABF into Dung's abstract argumentation framework [5]. The following arguments are respective to the program above:

$$A_1 = [\rightarrow wears\_ring] \quad A_3 = [A_1 \Rightarrow married] \quad A_5 = [A_3 \rightarrow has\_wife]$$
$$A_2 = [\rightarrow goes\_out] \quad A_4 = [A_2 \Rightarrow bachelor] \quad A_6 = [A_4 \rightarrow \sim has\_wife]$$

We can see that A_5 and A_6 are the only conflicting arguments since they have contradictory conclusions. However, defeating only one of them does not resolve the conflict. Since the remaining arguments are not conflicting, we should accept each literal in {*wears_ring, goes_out, married, bachelor*}. Futhermore, since strict rules have to be always satisfied, we should also believe in *has_wife* and $\sim$ *has_wife* and the original conflict reappears. The problem is that the conflict has to be resolved by defeating one of the arguments A_3 or A_4 which are not directly involved in the conflict.

There exist other approaches [2,7] which encode conflict resolutions into deductive system. All rules are treated as strict, and for each defeasible rule r_i an additional literal of the form r_i is added. The meaning of r_i is "r_i is defeated", and the meaning of $\sim r_i$ is "r_i is undefeated". The encoding of the program is as follows:

$$
\begin{array}{c|c}
\rightarrow wears\_ring & wears\_ring, \sim r_1 \rightarrow married \\
\rightarrow goes\_out & goes\_out, \sim r_2 \rightarrow bachelor \\
married \rightarrow has\_wife & \sim r_1 \rightarrow r_2 \\
bachelor \rightarrow \sim has\_wife & \sim r_2 \rightarrow r_1 \\
\end{array}
$$

Now, application of each formerly defeasible rule r_i is guarded by the new assumption $\sim r_i$. The rules $\sim r_1 \rightarrow r_2$ and $\sim r_2 \rightarrow r_1$ serve as implementation of the conflict resolution strategy: in order to resolve the conflict between possible derivation of has_wife and its contrary $\sim has\_wife$ only one of $\sim r_i$ may hold while the other must be defeated.

However, the link between has_wife and $\sim r_1$ is hard to see from the two rules $\sim r_1 \rightarrow r_2$ and $\sim r_2 \rightarrow r_1$. Therefore it is not straightforward to obtain an explanation.

3 Preliminaries

A *language* is a set $\mathcal{L}$ of well-formed sentences. An *inference rule* over a language $\mathcal{L}$ is an expression r of the form $\varphi_1, \ldots, \varphi_n \rightarrow \varphi_0$ where $0 \leq n$ and each φ_i, $0 \leq i \leq n$, is a sentence in $\mathcal{L}$. The sentences $prem(r) = \{\varphi_1, \ldots, \varphi_n\}$ are called the *premises* of r and the sentence $cons(r) = \varphi_0$ is called the *consequence* of r. A *deductive system* is a pair $(\mathcal{L}, \mathcal{R})$ where $\mathcal{L}$ is a language and $\mathcal{R}$ is a set of inference rules over $\mathcal{L}$.

A *default derivation for* a sentence $\varphi \in \mathcal{L}$ is an expression of the form $D = [\varphi]$. The consequence of D is the sentence $cons(D) = \varphi$. A default derivation has only one premise $prem(D) = \{\varphi\}$ and only one subderivation $subderiv(D) = \{D\}$. A *deductive derivation for* a sentence φ is defined as an expression $D = [D_1, \ldots, D_n \rightarrow \varphi]$ where D_i is a default or deductive derivation for φ_i, $0 < i \leq n$, and $\varphi_1, \ldots, \varphi_n \rightarrow \varphi$ is an inference rule in $\mathcal{R}$. The consequence of D is the sentence $cons(D) = \varphi$, the premises of D are the sentences $prem(D) = prem(D_1) \cup \cdots \cup prem(D_n)$, and the subderivations of D are $subderiv(D) = \{D\} \cup subderiv(D_1) \cup \cdots \cup subderiv(D_n)$. A *derivation for* a sentence φ is a default or deductive derivation for φ. We will say that derivation D' is a *subderivation* of D (denoted by $D' \sqsubseteq D$) iff $D' \in subderiv(D)$; similarly, we will say that derivation D' is a *proper subderivation* of D (denoted by $D' \sqsubset D$) iff $D' \sqsubseteq D$ and $D' \neq D$. A *theory* is a set S of sentences. A sentence φ is a *consequence* of a theory S iff there exists a derivation D for φ such that $prem(D) \subseteq S$. By $Cn_{\mathcal{R}}(S)$ we will denote the set of all consequences of S.

An *assumption-based framework* is a tuple $\mathcal{F} = (\mathcal{L}, \mathcal{R}, \mathcal{A}, ^{-})$ where $(\mathcal{L}, \mathcal{R})$ is a deductive system, $\mathcal{A} \subseteq \mathcal{L}$ is a set of *assumptions*, and $^{-} : \mathcal{A} \mapsto \mathcal{L}$ is a mapping called *contrariness function*. We say that the sentence $\overline{\alpha}$ is the *contrary* of an assumption α. A *context* is a set Δ of assumptions. We say that Δ is *conflict-free* iff $\{\alpha, \overline{\alpha}\} \not\subseteq Cn_{\mathcal{R}}(\Delta)$ for each assumption α; and that Δ is *closed* iff $Cn_{\mathcal{R}}(\Delta) \cap \mathcal{A} \subseteq \Delta$. An assumption-based framework is *flat* iff each context is closed. A context Δ *attacks* an assumption α iff $\overline{\alpha} \in Cn_{\mathcal{R}}(\Delta)$. A context Δ *defends* an assumption α iff each closed context attacking α contains an assumption attacked by Δ. A closed context Δ is *attack-free* iff Δ does not attack an assumption in Δ. An attack-free context Δ is *admissible* iff Δ defends each assumption in Δ. A closed context Δ is *complete* iff Δ is admissible and contains all assumptions defended by Δ; *grounded*[1] iff Δ is a subset-maximal admissible context contained in all complete contexts; *preferred* iff Δ is a subset-maximal admissible context; *ideal* iff Δ is a subset-maximal admissible context contained in all preferred contexts; *stable* iff Δ is an attack-free context attacking each assumption which does not belong to Δ.

4 Conflict Resolution Strategies

Conflict resolution in standard ABF is performed using sets of assumptions (i.e., contexts). Other formalisms, like ASPIC^{+} [8,9], or the framework proposed in [12] use structures similar to derivations. Here, we propose to use derivations to define conflicts and conflict resolution in ABF. Thus, each different pair of derivations (that allow us to conclude an assumption and its contrary) leads to a different conflict, even if these different conflicts are all generated by the same pair of contexts. Consequently, a conflict resolution deals with one possible "cause" of conflict (where "cause" here means a pair of derivations). This approach allows a very fine-grained treatment of conflicts and resolutions, as motivated in Sect. 2, as well as the distinction between different kinds of conflicts (rebutting, undermining). Formally:

Definition 1 (Conflict). *We say that derivation D_1 is in conflict with derivation D_2 iff there is some $\alpha \in \mathcal{A}$ such that $cons(D_1) = \alpha$ and $cons(D_2) = \overline{\alpha}$. A conflict is a pair (D_1, D_2) such that D_1 is in conflict with D_2.*

Now let's consider two conflicts (D_1, D_2) and (D_1', D_2'). It is clear that if $D_1 \sqsubseteq D_1'$ and $D_2 \sqsubseteq D_2'$, then by resolving the first conflict, the second is automatically resolved as well. Therefore, it makes sense to resolve "smaller" conflicts first. This leads us to introduce the notion of *subconflict*, as follows:

Definition 2 (Subconflict). *Let (D_1, D_2) and (D_1', D_2') be conflicts. We say that (D_1', D_2') is a subconflict of (D_1, D_2) (denoted by $(D_1', D_2') \sqsubseteq (D_1, D_2)$) iff $D_1 \sqsubseteq D_1'$ and $D_2 \sqsubseteq D_2'$. We say that (D_1, D_2) is a proper subconflict of (D_1', D_2') (denoted by $(D_1, D_2) \sqsubset (D_1', D_2')$) iff $(D_1, D_2) \sqsubseteq (D_1', D_2')$ and $(D_1, D_2) \neq (D_1', D_2')$.*

---

[1] Grounded context is called well-founded in [3]; we call it grounded to be consistent with [5].

Conflict resolution can be simply defined as a triple, where the first two elements indicate a conflict, whereas the third indicates the assumption chosen to abandon in order to eliminate that conflict. Formally:

Definition 3 (Conflict Resolution). *A conflict resolution is a triple $\rho = (D_1, D_2, \alpha)$ such that D_1 is in conflict with D_2 and $\alpha \in prem(D_1) \cup prem(D_2)$. The contrary of α is called the* resolution *of ρ, and denoted by $res(\rho)$. The context of a conflict resolution, denoted by $ctx(\rho)$, is the set:*

$$ctx(\rho) = \begin{cases} prem(D_1) \cup prem(D_2) & \text{whenever } \alpha \in prem(D_1) \cap prem(D_2) \\ (prem(D_1) \cup prem(D_2)) \setminus \{\alpha\} & \text{otherwise} \end{cases}$$

In Definition 3, $res(\rho)$ intuitively refers to the contrary of an assumption that the conflict resolution chose to drop from our set of assumptions, whereas the set $ctx(\rho)$ refers to the assumptions that essentially "cause" the chosen assumption to be dropped. Note that this is true only as far as the specific ρ is concerned; the interplay between different conflict resolutions and the choices they encode need also to be considered, as explained in detail in Sect. 5.

Definition 4. *A conflict resolution strategy σ is a mapping which assigns to an ABF a set of conflict resolutions of this ABF.*

Intuitively, a conflict resolution strategy takes an ABF and returns a set of conflict resolutions; note that a conflict resolution strategy does not necessarily resolve all conflicts that appear in an ABF, i.e., it may opt to leave some of the conflicts unresolved. In the following example, we explain the notions of conflict, conflict resolution and conflict resolution strategy:

Example 2 (Marriage Example Revisited). Continuing Example 1, we note that the following derivations can be created:

$$D_1 = [[[\to goes\_out], [\sim r_2] \to bachelor] \to \sim has\_wife]$$
$$D_2 = [[[\to wears\_ring], [\sim r_1] \to married] \to has\_wife]$$

We can see that there are two alternatives for resolving the conflict (D_1, D_2). We defeat either $\sim r_2$ or $\sim r_1$. Thus, we can define the following conflict resolutions: $\rho_1 = (D_1, D_2, \sim r_2)$, $\rho_2 = (D_1, D_2, \sim r_1)$. It follows that $ctx(\rho_1) = \{\sim r_1\}$, $res(\rho_1) = r_2$, and $ctx(\rho_2) = \{\sim r_2\}$, $res(\rho_2) = r_1$. We define a conflict resolution strategy that includes both resolutions, i.e., $\sigma(\mathcal{F}) = \{\rho_1, \rho_2\}$.

5   Argumentation Semantics

In this section, we will show how we can model conflict resolution and conflict resolution strategies. In the following, by XABF we mean an arbitrary, but fixed, ABF $\mathcal{F}$ and the set of conflict resolutions $\mathcal{P} = \sigma(\mathcal{F})$, for an arbitrary, but fixed, conflict resolution strategy σ. Each conflict resolution ρ in $\mathcal{P}$ represents a choice as to how a conflict should be resolved; this choice actually determines the assumption to be dropped in order for the conflict to disappear. This essentially implies that certain assumptions invalidate other assumptions (more precisely, the assumptions in $ctx(\rho)$ invalidate $res(\rho)$). This idea can be captured nicely using the notion of "attack" appearing in ABFs [3,6], where a context Δ "attacking" an assumption α intuitively means that $\Delta \subseteq \mathcal{A}$ would imply that $\alpha \notin \mathcal{A}$. This is of course generalized to all super-contexts of Δ, which attack contexts including α.

However, the above viewpoint considers only the effects of a single conflict resolution, not taking into account the interplay between conflict resolutions in the conflict resolution strategy. In effect, the choices made by the different conflict resolutions in the strategy are not independent, because the resolution proposed by a conflict resolution may implicitly resolve other conflicts as well, thereby making another conflict resolution void. As a result, a certain context (that is causing a certain conflict, which is being resolved in a manner prescribed by the chosen strategy), may prevent another conflict from appearing, therefore it may *defend* some assumption (resulting from the corresponding conflict resolution) from attack. This notion of defence can also be described using ABFs, via their inherent notion of defence.

In Definitions 5, 6 we formally define the notions of attack and defence, which depend on the actual conflict resolution strategy considered and are thus an extension of the corresponding notions described in Sect. 3 and in [3,6].

Definition 5 (Attack-Freeness). *A context Δ attacks an assumption α iff there exists some $\rho \in \mathcal{P}$ with $ctx(\rho) \subseteq \Delta$ and $res(\rho) = \overline{\alpha}$. We denote:*

$$Attack_{\mathcal{P}}(\Delta) = \{\alpha \in \mathcal{A} \mid \exists \rho \in \mathcal{P}: res(\rho) = \overline{\alpha} \wedge ctx(\rho) \subseteq \Delta\}$$

A context Δ is attack-free iff Δ does not attack any assumption in Δ, i.e. iff $Attack_{\mathcal{P}}(\Delta) \cap \Delta = \emptyset$.

Definition 6 (Admissibility). *A context Δ defends an assumption α iff Δ attacks an assumption in each context attacking α. We will denote*

$$Defence_{\mathcal{P}}(\Delta) = \{\alpha \in \mathcal{A} \mid \forall \rho \in \mathcal{P}: res(\rho) = \overline{\alpha} \Rightarrow ctx(\rho) \cap Attack_{\mathcal{P}}(\Delta) \neq \emptyset\}$$

An attack-free context Δ is admissible iff Δ defends each assumption in Δ, i.e. iff $\Delta \subseteq Defence_{\mathcal{P}}(\Delta)$.

Definition 7 (Extension). *A context Δ is*

- complete *iff Δ is admissible and $Defence_{\mathcal{P}}(\Delta) \subseteq \Delta$*
- grounded *iff Δ is a subset-maximal admissible context contained in all complete contexts*
- preferred *iff Δ is a subset-maximal admissible context*
- ideal *iff Δ is a subset-maximal admissible context contained in all preferred contexts*
- stable *iff $\Delta = \mathcal{A} \setminus Attack_{\mathcal{P}}(\Delta)$*

If Δ is a $\Sigma_{\mathcal{P}}$-context then $\mathcal{E} = Cn_{\mathcal{R}}(\Delta)$ is a $\Sigma_{\mathcal{P}}$-extension of $\mathcal{F}$ for each $\Sigma \in \{complete, grounded, preferred, ideal, stable\}$.

In the following, we will use the term *standard semantics* to refer to any of the semantics of extensions that appear in Definition 7. An extension corresponds to a set of assumptions (aka, context) that is acceptable, under the given conflict resolution strategy. This extension is essentially the result of the conflict resolution process, where all different conflict resolutions in the strategy, as well as their interplay, have been considered in selecting what to drop and what to keep. Recall that this process does not guarantee a conflict-free set of assumptions $\mathcal{A}$, as, by design, we allow some conflicts to remain unresolved. An important difference of the above viewpoint compared to standard approaches is that the actual reason for defeating an assumption is not an argument, but the conflicts themselves (and their resolutions), which force us to drop some of the assumptions.

Example 3 (Marriage Example Continued). If we take the ABF $\mathcal{F}$ with the set $\mathcal{P}$ of conflict resolutions from Example 2, we have three complete contexts, namely $\Delta_1 = \{\sim r_1, \sim bachelor\}$, $\Delta_2 = \{\sim r_2, \sim married, \sim has\_wife\}$, and $\Delta_3 = \{\}$. They correspond to three extensions $\mathcal{E}_1 = Cn_{\mathcal{R}}(\Delta_1) = \Delta_1 \cup \{married, has\_wife\}$, $\mathcal{E}_2 = Cn_{\mathcal{R}}(\Delta_2) = \Delta_2 \cup \{bachelor\}$, and $\mathcal{E}_3 = Cn_{\mathcal{R}}(\Delta_3) = \{\}$. In the context Δ_1, the conflict resolution ρ_1 explains why the assumption $\sim r_2$ is defeated. Since $ctx(\rho_1) \subseteq \Delta_1$ and $res(\rho_1) = r_2$, the assumption $\sim r_2$ is defeated in order to resolve conflicts between derivations D_1 and D_2. Similarly, the conflict resolution $\rho_2 \in \mathcal{P}$ is an explanation for defeating $\sim r_1$ in the context Δ_2.

6   Properties

In this section, we show the properties of the constructions defined in Sect. 5. In particular, we show that XABF behaves in a reasonable manner, according to well-established properties present in [4] (Propositions 1, 2, 3). Finally, we show the role of "minimal" subconflicts (see Definitions 9, 10 and Propositions 4, 5).

In the rest of this section, we assume an arbitrary, but fixed, ABF $\mathcal{F}$ and the set of conflict resolutions $\mathcal{P} = \sigma(\mathcal{F})$ for an arbitrary, but fixed, conflict resolution strategy σ, as well as any given standard semantics $\Sigma_{\mathcal{P}}$.

As already mentioned, a conflict resolution strategy does not need to resolve all conflicts. However, strategies that do resolve all conflicts have some interesting properties and will be called *total*. Formally:

Definition 8. *A set of conflict resolutions $\mathcal{P}$ is total iff for each context Δ, which is not conflict-free, there is a resolution ρ with $ctx(\rho) \subseteq \Delta$ and $res(\rho) \in \Delta$.*

The following results show that our framework satisfies a generalized version of the rationality conditions proposed in [4]. Note that for Proposition 1, the hypothesis of totality is crucial.

Proposition 1. *If $\mathcal{P}$ is total then each $\Sigma_{\mathcal{P}}$-extension is conflict-free.*

Proposition 2. *If $\emptyset$ is not conflict-free then each $\Sigma_\mathcal{P}$-extension is not conflict-free.*

Proposition 3. *Each $\Sigma_\mathcal{P}$-extension is closed under $Cn_\mathcal{R}$.*

Subconflicts (Definition 2) were introduced to capture the intuition that the resolution of "smaller" conflicts (in the sense of $\sqsubseteq$) also resolves "larger" ones. Thus, resolutions resolving the $\sqsubseteq$-minimal conflicts are of special interest.

Definition 9. *The bottom of $\mathcal{P}$ is a set $\lfloor \mathcal{P} \rfloor = \{(D_1, D_2, \alpha) \in \mathcal{P} \mid \forall (D_1', D_2') \sqsubset (D_1, D_2) \colon (D_1', D_2', \alpha) \notin \mathcal{P}\}$.*

Proposition 4. *A theory $\mathcal{E}$ is a $\Sigma_\mathcal{P}$-extension iff $\mathcal{E}$ is a $\Sigma_{\lfloor \mathcal{P} \rfloor}$-extension.*

Proposition 4 implies that all conflict resolutions that are not in the bottom of the original set can be dropped without changing the semantics. If the set $\mathcal{P}$ of conflict resolution is in addition downward closed then $\sqsubseteq$-minimal conflicts take precedence during resolution. As a special case, undermining takes precedence over rebutting as already suggested by Prakken and Sartor [10]. In our case, the same precedence in conflict resolutions is given also in the case of two $\sqsubseteq$-related rebutting conflicts (i.e., the subconflict of the two should be removed).

Definition 10. *We say that a set $\mathcal{P}$ of conflict resolutions is* downward closed *iff for each conflict resolution $(D_1, D_2, \alpha) \in \mathcal{P}$ there exists a minimal subconflict (D_1', D_2') of (D_1, D_2) with $(D_1', D_2', \alpha) \in \mathcal{P}$.*

Proposition 5. *The bottom of a downward closed set $\mathcal{P}$ of conflict resolutions contains only $\sqsubseteq$-minimal conflicts.*

An important consequence of Proposition 5 is that, for constructing a conflict resolution strategy, one only needs to be concerned with minimal conflicts. This is a very useful property from the practical viewpoint, as it allows not dealing with all conflicts during the construction of a strategy, only with minimal ones. Note that this intuition cannot be extended to minimal derivations, as they do not always lead to minimal conflicts: a pair of minimal derivations for an assumption could "hide" a subconflict on another assumption.

7   Related Work

The formal notion of CRS occurs in previous works [1,2], where the focus was however entirely on DeLP. In the current work, these ideas are largely pushed forward resulting into the extension of ABF as a generic framework with improved capabilities and properties, capable to embed any non-monotonic formalism, not only DeLP.

ASPIC$^+$ [8,9] also enables general purpose defeasible reasoning and it satisfy the both consistency and closure properties, though it relies on the addition of transposed rules. XABF offers more flexible notion of CRS than ASPIC$^+$ and, in addition, it does not rely in transposition of rules which may introduce undesired consequences. For instance rules in logic programming (LP) are directional. Rule

$\neg b \rightarrow \neg a$ does not allow to derive anything from the theory $\{a\}$, after the addition of the transposed rule $a \rightarrow b$ we derive b as a consequence of the theory $\{a\}$. This does not allow to directly embed[2] of LP into ASPIC$^+$. In XABF we avoid this problem.

The generalized ABF of Toni [11] also assure closure and consistency. On the other hand, the properties of generalized ABF are not investigated in detail on the abstract level. While sharing several goals with Toni, we proposed a principal extension of ABF with well motivated and useful generalizations, such as flexible CRSs (which also capture domain specific preferences), which are not investigated by Toni.

8   Conclusions

We proposed XABF, an extended ABF framework that enables improved treatment of defeasible reasoning via assumption-based argumentation. Lifting the CRS to a first-class citizen in XABF enables multiple CRSs to be formalized and used with XABF. Moreover, it provides a customized choice of the CRS to use, based on the specific needs of the application domain. Furthermore, it is possible to identify the reasons why conflicts were resolved in any particular way and thus to provide for explanations. The semantics we proposed for XABF takes care that the widely accepted properties of consistency and closure [4] are satisfied *for any given CRS*. These properties are important, as they guarantee that conflicts are not resolved just cosmetically and then consequently derived again by the deductive system.

Our approach also allows to compare different CRSs and to study their formal properties. To demonstrate this, we formally characterized a class of CRSs which are minimal in the sense that resolution of superconflicts can be propagated to resolving their minimal subconflicts; that is, in these CRSs all conflicts can be resolved more effectively by considering a smaller number of cases.

Acknowledgements. This work resulted from the Slovak–Greek bilateral project co-financed by APVV (as SK-GR-0070-11) and GSRT together with the EU (as 12SLO_ET29_1087). The Slovak side further acknowledges support from the VEGA project no. 1/1333/12. Martin Baláž and Martin Homola are also supported by the APVV project no. APVV-0513-10.

References

1. Baláž, M., Frtús, J., Homola, M.: Conflict resolution in structured argumentation. In: LPAR-19 (Short Papers), EPiC, vol. 26, pp. 23–34. EasyChair (2014)

---

[2] Direct embedding is such that LP rules will become the rules of the deductive system in ASPIC$^+$. Note that we do not claim that a more complex, indirect embedding cannot be done.

2. Baláž, M., Frtús, J., Homola, M., Šefránek, J., Flouris, G.: Embedding defeasible logic programs into generalized logic programs. In: WLP, vol. 1335 of CEUR-WS (2014)
3. Bondarenko, A., Dung, P.M., Kowalski, R.A., Toni, F.: An abstract, argumentation-theoretic approach to default reasoning. Artif. Intell. **93**(1–2), 63–101 (1997)
4. Caminada, M., Amgoud, L.: On the evaluation of argumentation formalisms. Artif. Intell. **171**(5–6), 286–310 (2007)
5. Dung, P.M.: On the acceptability of arguments and its fundamental role in non-monotonic reasoning, logic programming and n-person games. Artif. Intell. **77**(2), 321–357 (1995)
6. Dung, P.M., Mancarella, P., Toni, F.: Computing ideal sceptical argumentation. Artif. Intell. **171**(10–15), 642–674 (2007)
7. Kowalski, R.A., Toni, F.: Abstract argumentation. Artif. Intell. Law **4**(3–4), 275–296 (1996)
8. Modgil, S., Prakken, H.: Revisiting preferences and argumentation. In: IJCAI (2011)
9. Prakken, H.: An abstract framework for argumentation with structured arguments. Argum. Comput. **1**(2), 93–124 (2010)
10. Prakken, H., Sartor, G.: Argument-based extended logic programming with defeasible priorities. J. Appl. Nonclassical Log. **7**(1), 25–75 (1997)
11. Toni, F.: Assumption-based argumentation for closed and consistent defeasible reasoning. In: Satoh, K., Inokuchi, A., Nagao, K., Kawamura, T. (eds.) JSAI 2007. LNCS (LNAI), vol. 4914, pp. 390–402. Springer, Heidelberg (2008)
12. Vreeswijk, G.A.W.: Abstract argumentation systems. Artif. Intell. **90**(1–2), 225–279 (1997)

Decision Making in Agent-Based Models

Guillem Francès[1]($\boxtimes$), Xavier Rubio-Campillo[2],
Carla Lancelotti[3], and Marco Madella[4]

[1] Artificial Intelligence Group, Universitat Pompeu Fabra, Barcelona, Spain
guillem.frances@upf.edu
[2] Barcelona Supercomputing Centre, Barcelona, Spain
xavier.rubio@bsc.es
[3] CaSEs Research Group, Department of Humanities, Universitat Pompeu Fabra,
Barcelona, Spain
carla.lancelotti@upf.edu
[4] CaSEs Research Group, Department of Humanities,
ICREA, Universitat Pompeu Fabra and IMF-CSIC, Barcelona, Spain
marco.madella@icrea.cat

Abstract. Agent-Based Models (ABM) are being increasingly applied
to the study of a wide range of social phenomena, often putting the
focus on the macroscopic patterns that emerge from the interaction of
a number of agents programmed to behave in a plausible manner. This
agent behavior, however, is all too often encoded as a small set of rules
that produces a somewhat simplistic behavior. In this short paper, we
propose to explore the impact of decision-making processes on the outcome of simulations, and introduce a type of agent that uses a more
systematic and principled decision-making approach, based on casting
the simulation environment as a Markov Decision Process. We compare
the performance of this type of agent to that of more simplistic agents
on a simple ABM simulation, and examine the interplay between the
decision-making mechanism and other relevant simulation parameters
such as the distribution and scarcity of resources. Our preliminary findings show that our novel agent outperforms the rest of agents, and, more
generally, that the process of decision-making needs to be acknowledged
as a first-class parameter of ABM simulations with a significant impact
on the simulation outcome.

Keywords: Agent-based modeling · Social simulation · Model-based
behavior · Markov Decision Process

1 Introduction and Motivation

Recent years have witnessed a remarkable increase in the use of computer simulation methods and, more specifically, Agent-Based Model simulations, to enhance
our understanding of an extremely wide array of social processes, from the emergence of social norms [1] to population dynamics [19], through all sorts of cul-
tural [6], economic [20], or archaeological processes [10]. One of the reasons of

© Springer International Publishing Switzerland 2015
N. Bulling (Ed.): EUMAS 2014, LNAI 8953, pp. 370–378, 2015.
DOI: 10.1007/978-3-319-17130-2_25

this momentum is the fact that simulation stands as a compelling and affordable paradigm for the analysis of complex, highly non-linear environments involving the interaction of heterogeneous entities. Indeed, central to the development of ABM simulations and to the broader notion of complexity theory is the ambition to explain the emergence of certain regularities at the macroscopic level from the microscopic-level interaction of agents. These agents are generally programmed to behave in a plausible manner, often in the form of a fixed set of simple condition-action rules [2,13]. However, the plausibility of this type of behavioral strategy remains somewhat problematic, in particular, but not exclusively, when the simulation agents are meant to model human beings [21].

As a matter of fact, the problem of intelligent behavior, *i.e.* of choosing what action to perform next, has been one of the core concerns of Artificial Intelligence (AI) almost since the dawn of the discipline, with the General Problem Solver [12] being at the same time one of the first automated planners and one of the first AI programs. Geffner [8] classifies the different solutions historically used to address this problem into three categories or approaches. In the *programming-based* approach, a human programmer reflects on the characteristics of the problem, devises an *ad-hoc* way of solving it, and expresses this solution as a computer program. In the *learning-based* approach, the behavior is learnt from the experience of past actions and their associated rewards, as in reinforcement learning [18]. Finally, in the *model-based* approach, the behavior is derived from a model of the world, *i.e.* a formal description of its possible states, the actions that can be performed and the goals to be achieved. As we suggested before, the approach usually employed to define the behavior of ABM simulation agents is the first one, as it offers the advantage of being simple and computationally inexpensive [21]. However, the only way in which this approach can be considered to model intelligent behavior is insofar as it embodies the intelligence of a human programmer. The model-based approach, in contrast, offers a more generic and principled method for the generation of behavior that can be considered intelligent and cognitively more plausible, thus fitting much better the objectives of ABM simulations.

The motivation of the present work is twofold. On the one hand, we aim at exposing the fundamental but seldom recognized affinity between agent-based modeling and AI, framing the problem of deriving the behavior of simulation agents in the context of well-studied model-based planning techniques. Incidentally, this will allow us to provide a generic mechanism where the modeler needs only specify the utility function that should govern the agent behavior, and let the actual behavior be automatically derived. On the other hand, we aim at exploring the impact of different decision-making strategies on the actual outcome of simulations, and check if the use of these more sophisticated (and computationally expensive) AI techniques pays off, not only conceptually and theoretically but also empirically, thus producing significantly different outcomes. We hypothesize that the use of different decision-making mechanisms can radically affect macro-level indicators (such as the carrying capacity of the simulated environment) that are frequently used for the analysis of emergent phenomena.

Outline of the Paper. The remainder of this paper is organized as follows. The next section offers a brief account of Markov Decision Processes and of the UCT algorithm, which form the basis of the novel type of ABM agent we present. Section 3 describes a simple ABM model that we put to work in order to evaluate the impact of different decision-making strategies and compare them to this novel type of agent, and Sect. 4 discusses some preliminary empirical results. Finally, Sect. 5 concludes the paper and outlines some ideas for future research.

2   Model-Based Behavior

2.1   Model-Based Planning and Markov Decision Processes

The alternative to traditional rule-base behavior that we propose is based on *finite-horizon* Markov Decision Processes (MDPs). In a nutshell, these are fully-observable, stochastic state models where the objective is to find a suitable policy of action that maximizes the expected reward that can be accumulated in a fixed number of timesteps, the so-called *horizon* of the problem. MDPs have been widely used and studied in several fields, from artificial intelligence to operational research and economics [4,18], but to the best of our knowledge this work constitutes the first attempt to use them in the context of agent-based models and social simulations. The basic idea is to cast the simulation environment as an MDP and automatically derive the behavior of each simulation agent by selecting at each time step the action that best suits her interests, suitably defined through a utility function. Formally, a finite-horizon MDP is defined by *(i)* a set S of possible states of the world, *(ii)* an initial state $s_0 \in S$, *(iii)* a set $A(s)$ of actions that can be applied in each state $s \in S$, *(iv)* transition probabilities $P_a(s'|s)$ that encode the probability of transitioning from state s to state s' when the action $a \in A(s)$ is applied, and, finally *(v)* a utility or reward function $r : S \times A \to \mathbb{R}$ that models the agent interest by specifying the reward $r(s, a)$ obtained by applying action $a \in A(s)$ when s is the actual state of the world.

2.2   The UCT Algorithm

In order to choose the adequate action in an MDP, we employ the UCT algorithm [9], an anytime optimal algorithm [3] for finite-horizon MDPs that is guaranteed to converge to the optimal sequence of actions when given enough time. Being one of the most popular Monte-Carlo Tree Search methods [5], UCT successfully tackles extremely large state spaces by running a number of stochastic simulations from the initial state of the problem that help building incrementally a partial search tree containing the most promising nodes. The algorithm has been empirically proven to excel at finding an adequate balance between the *exploitation* of actions that are believed to offer the highest reward and the *exploration* of actions that appear to be sub-optimal but might emerge as better options when sufficiently explored. For a more thorough discussion on UCT and

Monte-Carlo Tree Search methods, we refer the interested reader to [5]; for the purpose of this work, it suffices to note that the two parameters of the algorithm that are relevant to our simulations are the planning *horizon h* and the number of stochastic simulations run from the initial state, which we call the *width w* of the algorithm.

3   Model Description

We next describe a simple Sugarscape-like model [7] that we have designed and implemented on top of the Pandora simulation framework [17] in order to test the different decision-making mechanisms that we consider.[1]

3.1   Resource Distribution and Dynamics

Agents interact in a 50×50 grid-like resource map where each map cell contains an amount of resources between 0 and a maximum that depends on the particular cell. These per-cell maximum values are spatially autocorrelated, meaning that the value of each cell relates to that of neighboring cells, following a standard ecological model of resource distribution in which spatial autocorrelation is a key feature that adapted foraging strategies need to take into account [11]. The higher the autocorrelation factor we use, the more clustered the map resources are. At the beginning of the simulation all map cells start at their maximum amount of resources. Whenever this amount is diminished by the action of agents, each cell increases one amount of resources per timestep, up to its maximum.

3.2   Agent Dynamics

Agents are basic resource-accumulating entities, and start the simulation at random map locations. At each time step, they can either remain in their current cell or move to one of the 8 neighboring cells (for a total of 9 possible actions, diagonal moves are allowed). After the move, each agent collects from her current cell an amount of resources which is distributed uniformly between 1 and the resources available on the cell. After the resource collection, agents consume a fixed amount of resources λ, a simulation parameter intended to model resource scarcity. If the total amount of resources accumulated by an agent is less than λ, the agent dies; if, on the contrary, this amount surpasses a certain threshold value (currently 20λ), the agent gives birth to a new agent, which will be located in the same cell, and both agents see their amount of resources set to a fixed value 5λ.

---

[1] The model, implemented in C++, can be downloaded from https://github.com/gfrances/model-based-social-simulations/releases/tag/eumas2014.

3.3   Agent Behavior

We examine a number of possible decision-making strategies to choose among the 9 possible actions. We first consider a baseline `random` agent that chooses uniformly at random between the available actions. Second, we consider a `greedy` agent that chooses among the 9 possible destination cells the one with the highest amount of available resources, breaking ties at random. We also consider a `lazy` agent that only moves whenever the current cell does not satisfy her needs, *i.e.* when the amount of resources in the cell multiplied by a certain slack parameter α $(0 < \alpha \leq 1)$ is less than the agent's daily consumption requirements. In that case, the agent moves to the first satisfactory cell, according to a random ordering; in case none of the 9 possible destinations is satisfactory, a random action is chosen. Finally, we consider a novel `MDP`-based agent, which we describe more in detail next.

3.4   Modeling the World as a Markov Decision Process

As previously mentioned, the decision-making process of an `MDP` agent is based on choosing the optimal action according to a specific utility function and to the evaluation performed by the `UCT` algorithm on an `MDP` model of the world that is constructed by each agent at each timestep. The states of the `MDP` contain information regarding *(i)* the position of the agent, *(ii)* the amount of resources held by the agent, and *(iii)* the availability of resources in each cell of the map. The initial state of the `MDP` is derived from the actual state of the world in the current time step, and the transition probabilities between states are given by the simulation dynamics described above, the only stochasticity arising from the resource recollection process. Most relevantly, the utility function of the agent is designed to strongly penalize those states in which the agent is dead, and otherwise is proportional to the amount of resources held by the agent. It is important to note that at this stage, the presented `MDP` model does not take into account the indirect competition of other agents that might be consuming resources from neighboring cells.

4   Experiment Design and Empirical Results

4.1   Assessing the Impact of UCT Parameters

Before discussing the fully multi-agent simulations, and in order to calibrate the width and horizon parameters of the `UCT` algorithm discussed in Sect. 2, we first run some single-agent (only one agent, no agent reproduction) simulations, measuring the amount of resources that the agent is able to accumulate over time. To simplify things, we only explore moderate resource consumption factors $\lambda \in \{2, 3\}$, and fix the map autocorrelation factor to 25. We examine the performance of `MDP` agents using varying horizon $(h \in \{2, 4, 6, 8, 10, 12\})$ and width $(w \in \{50, 100, 500, 1000, 5000\})$, running simulations with the agent starting in a number of different random locations that are consistently the same for the different combinations of values of w and h. We expect the amount of accumulated resources to grow with both the allowed width and horizon. The results of these simulations, not shown here for the sake of brevity, are not entirely consistent for the lower width values, which do not permit a sufficient exploration of the search tree. For higher values $w \in \{1000, 5000\}$, however, the amount of accumulated resources slightly increases as the horizon grows, although the differences are not significant. Because of this, and since the computation time required by UCT increases with both the width and horizon, we stick with an intermediate combination $\langle h = 8, w = 1000 \rangle$ for the remainder of our experiments.

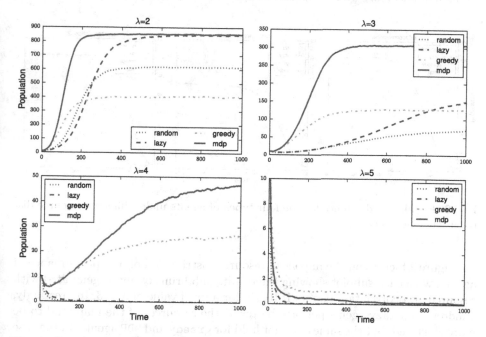

Fig. 1. Population dynamics for the four types of agents under different resource scarcity conditions λ.

4.2   Comparative Performance

We now turn to compare MDP agents with the other decision-making strategies that we consider in multi-agent simulations. We have run a number of simulations comparing the four decision-making strategies under varying values of the resource scarcity parameter $\lambda \in \{2, 3, 4, 5\}$ and resource autocorrelation factor *autocorrelation* $\in \{1, 10, 25\}$. Each subplot in Fig. 1 shows the population growth for the 4 agent types, averaged over 50 runs on 5 different randomly generated maps with a fixed resource autocorrelation value of 25. As expected, resource scarcity has a big impact on population growth for all types of agents:

as the value of λ increases, resources are more scarce and the total population achieved by any agent type sharply decreases, with $\lambda = 5$ simulations being hardly able to sustain any agent. For the remaining values of λ, we note that the carrying capacities for different agents vary broadly, and that the MDP agent outperforms the rest of agents by a large margin. In general, the population of greedy agents increases more rapidly than that of lazy and random agents, although the carrying capacity of the system for this type of agent is lower in some contexts. This is due to the fact that many greedy agents located in nearby cells will tend to overpopulate the same cell if its amount of resources is higher than that of the neighbors, whereas random and lazy agents will tend to disseminate more over the available space.

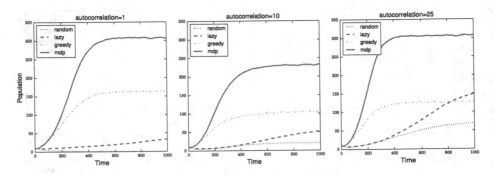

Fig. 2. Population dynamics for the four types of agents under different resource distribution conditions.

Figure 2 focuses on the impact of resource distribution on the performance of agents, with each subplot showing the results of 50 runs on maps generated with resource autocorrelation factors $1, 10, 25$, for a fixed value of $\lambda = 3$. Interestingly, random and lazy agents perform better as the resources of the map tend to be more clustered, but the same does not hold for greedy and MDP agents. In the case of greedy agents, a more uniform distribution of resources, might help overcome the negative effects of their myopic nature; in the case of MDP agents, the way in which the clusterization of resources affect population dynamics is not entirely clear from the results of this experiment, and deserves further examination.

5   Conclusions

We have presented a preliminary examination of the use of sound and principled model-based AI techniques to handle the problem of decision making in ABM simulations, in an attempt to bridge the large and (to our opinion) inexplicable gap between the two disciplines. Our empirical findings show that agents employing these techniques adapt to the simulation environment significantly better, and that this holds irrespective of resource distribution and scarcity issues. Due to the exploratory nature of this work, however, we have put aside a large number of issues that deserve further analysis. Coupling the UCT algorithm with a base policy that exploits the particular characteristics of the simulation model, for instance, should be a straight-forward manner to improve the efficiency of MDP agents — exploring discretization strategies in order to reduce the size of the state space should be another. More relevantly, the possibility of linking the use of model-based techniques to the systematic analysis of the role of bounded rationality (both as bounded information and bounded complexity [14]) in ABM simulations, on the one hand, and the stimulus posed by ABM simulations to develop truly multi-agent planning techniques [8], on the other, constitute, in our opinion, promising areas for future research.

Acknowledgments. This research is part of the SimulPast Project (CSD2010-00034) funded by the CONSOLIDER-INGENIO2010 program of the Spanish Ministry of Science and Innovation. The implementation of MDP agents relies on Blai Bonet's mdp-engine library (Available at https://code.google.com/p/mdp-engine/, the implementation of the UCT algorithm that we use is described in [3]). Resource maps were generated using the R statistical environment [16] and *gstat* package for geostatistical analysis [15].

References

1. Axelrod, R.: An evolutionary approach to norms. Am. Polit. Sci. Rev. **80**(4), 1095–1111 (1986)
2. Bandini, S., Manzoni, S., Vizzari, G.: Agent based modeling and simulation: an informatics perspective. J. Artifi. Soc. Soc. Simul. **12**(4), 4 (2009). http://jasss.soc.surrey.ac.uk/12/4/4.html
3. Bonet, B., Geffner, H.: Action selection for MDPs: anytime AO* versus UCT. In: Proceedings of the Twenty-Sixth AAAI Conference on Artificial Intelligence (2012)
4. Boutilier, C., Dean, T., Hanks, S.: Decision-theoretic planning: structural assumptions and computational leverage. J. Artif. Intell. Res. **1**, 1–93 (1999)
5. Browne, C.B., Powley, E., Whitehouse, D., Lucas, S.M., Cowling, P.I., Rohlfshagen, P., Tavener, S., Perez, D., Samothrakis, S., Colton, S.: A survey of monte carlo tree search methods. IEEE Trans. Comput. Intell. AI. Games **4**(1), 1–43 (2012)
6. Epstein, J.M.: Generative Social Science: Studies in Agent-Based Computational Modeling. Princeton University Press, Princeton (2006)
7. Epstein, J.M., Axtell, R.: Growing Artificial Societies: Social Science From the Bottom Up. Brookings Institution Press, Washington, D.C. (1996)
8. Geffner, H., Bonet, B.: A concise introduction to models and methods for automated planning. Synt. Lect. Artif. Intell. Mach. Learn. **8**(1), 1–141 (2013)
9. Kocsis, L., Szepesvári, C.: Bandit based monte-carlo planning. In: Fürnkranz, J., Scheffer, T., Spiliopoulou, M. (eds.) ECML 2006. LNCS (LNAI), vol. 4212, pp. 282–293. Springer, Heidelberg (2006)
10. Lake, M.: Trends in archaeological simulation. J. Archaeol. Meth. Theory **21**(2), 258–287 (2014)
11. Legendre, P.: Spatial autocorrelation: trouble or new paradigm? Ecology **74**(6), 1659–1673 (1993)

12. Newell, A., Shaw, J.C., Simon, H.A.: Report on a general problem-solving program. In: Proceeding of the International Conference on Information Processing, pp. 256–264 (1959)
13. O'Sullivan, D.: Complexity science and human geography. Trans. Inst. Br. Geogr. **29**(3), 282–295 (2004)
14. Papadimitriou, C.H., Yannakakis, M.: On complexity as bounded rationality. In: Proceeding of the 26th ACM Symposium on Theory of Computing, pp. 726–733 (1994)
15. Pebesma, E.J.: Multivariable geostatistics in S: the gstat package. Comput. Geosci. **30**, 683–691 (2004)
16. R Development Core Team: R: A Language and Environment for Statistical Computing. R Foundation for Statistical Computing, Vienna, Austria (2008). http://www.R-project.org, ISBN: 3-900051-07-0
17. Rubio-Campillo, X.: Pandora: a versatile ABM platform for social simulation. In: Sixth International Conference on Advances in System Simulation. IARIA (2014)
18. Russell, S., Norvig, P.: Artificial Intelligence: A Modern Approach. Prentice Hall, Englewood Cliffs (2010)
19. Schelling, T.C.: Dynamic models of segregation. J. Math. Sociol. **1**(2), 143–186 (1971)
20. Tesfatsion, L.: Agent-based computational economics: a constructive approach to economic theory. In: Handbook of Computational Economics, vol. 2, pp. 831–880 (2006)
21. Wellman, M.P.: Putting the agent in Agent-Based Modeling (2014). http://web.eecs.umich.edu/srg/wp-content/uploads/2014/08/transcript.pdf, talk from the 13th International Conference on Autonomous Agents and Multi-Agent Systems (AAMAS 2014)

Strategic Argumentation Under Grounded Semantics is NP-Complete

Guido Governatori[1]([⊠]), Michael J. Maher[2], Francesco Olivieri[3],
Antonino Rotolo[4], and Simone Scannapieco[3]

[1] NICTA, Brisbane, QLD, Australia
guido.governatori@nicta.com.au
[2] UNSW, Canberra, Australia
[3] University of Verona, Verona, Italy
[4] CIRSFID and Law Faculty, University of Bologna, Bologna, Italy

Abstract. We study the complexity of the Strategic Argumentation Problem for 2-player dialogue games where a player should decide what move to play at each turn in order to prove (disprove) a given claim. We shall prove that this is an NP-complete problem. The result covers one the most popular argumentation semantics proposed by Dung [4]: the grounded semantics.

1 Introduction

Consider the following argument exchange due to [12], where two players are involved, a proponent Pr and an opponent Op:

Pr$_0$: "You killed the victim."
Op$_1$: "I did not commit murder! There is no evidence!"
Pr$_1$: "There is evidence. We found your ID card near the scene."
Op$_2$: "It's not evidence! I had my ID card stolen!"
Pr$_2$: "It is you who killed the victim. Only you were near the scene at the time of the murder."
Op$_3$: "I didn't go there. I was at facility A at that time."
Pr$_3$: "At facility A? Then, it's impossible to have had your ID card stolen since facility A does not allow a person to enter without an ID card."

The peculiarity of this argument game is that the exchange of arguments reflects an asymmetry of information between the two parties. First, each player does not know the other player's knowledge, thus she cannot predict neither which arguments will be attacked, nor which counterarguments may be employed for attacking the arguments. Second, the private information disclosed by a party might be eventually used by the adversary to construct and play justified counterarguments. In the previous setting, Pr$_3$ attacks Op$_2$, but only after Op$_3$ has

---

NICTA is funded by the Australian Government through the Department of Communications and the Australian Research Council through the ICT Centre of Excellence Program.

N. Bulling (Ed.): EUMAS 2014, LNAI 8953, pp. 379–387, 2015.
DOI: 10.1007/978-3-319-17130-2_26

been given. That is to say, the attack Pr_3 of the proponent is possible only when the opponent discloses some private information through the move Op_3.

The scenario above exemplifies argument games with *incomplete informa-tion*, i.e., dialogues where the structure of the game is *not* common knowledge among the players. Dialogues with incomplete information are typical in domains such as the *legal domain* where a disputant does not know what arguments her opponent will employ. As argued in [6], players have different logical theories which constitute their private knowledge, being unknown by the opposite party. A player may build an argument supporting her claim by using some of her private knowledge; in turn, the other party may then re-use such rules and others (again from her own private knowledge) to construct a new argument defeating the previously constructed argument. In other words, the set R of rules that are used to build arguments is partitioned into three subsets: a set R_{Com} known by both players and two subsets R_{Pr} and R_{Op} corresponding, respectively, to Pr's and Op's private knowledge. Consider a setting where $F = \{a, d, f\}$ is the known set of facts, $R_{Com} = \emptyset$, and the players have the following rules:

$$R_{Pr} = \{a \Rightarrow b, \quad d \Rightarrow c, \quad c \Rightarrow b\}$$
$$R_{Op} = \{c \Rightarrow e, \quad e, f \Rightarrow \neg b\}.$$

If Pr's intent is to prove b and she plays $\{a \Rightarrow b\}$, then Pr wins the game. If Pr plays $\{d \Rightarrow c, c \Rightarrow b\}$ (or even R_{Pr}), this allows Op to succeed. Here, a minimal subset of R_{Pr} is successful. The situation can be reversed for Pr. Replace the sets of private rules with

$$R_{Pr} = \{a \Rightarrow b, \quad d \Rightarrow \neg c\}$$
$$R_{Op} = \{d, c \Rightarrow \neg b, \quad f \Rightarrow c\}.$$

In this second case, the move $\{a \Rightarrow b\}$ is not successful for Pr, while playing with the whole R_{Pr} ensures victory.

Reference [6] has considered standard propositional Defeasible Logic [2] in a dialogue game to represent the knowledge of the players, the structure of the arguments, and to perform reasoning. In this setting, it has been proved that the problem of deciding what set of rules to successfully play (called Strategic Argumentation Problem) at a given turn is NP-complete. That result was offering an interesting starting point, but it covers a non-standard argumentation semantics [5]. In this paper, we shall extend that result by considering one of the most popular argumentation semantics proposed by Dung [4], i.e., grounded semantics.

The layout of the paper is as follows. Section 2 recalls the basics of [4]'s grounded semantics and a framework for argumentation with logically struc-tured arguments for that semantics. Section 3 considers the strategic argumen-tation framework introduced in [6] and offers a formulation of the Strategic Argumentation Problem. Section 4 outlines Defeasible Logic and, in particular, the Ambiguity Propagating Defeasible Logic variant that corresponds to Dung's grounded semantics. Section 5 presents an implementation of the strategic argu-mentation game with Defeasible Logic as the underlying logical framework, and Sect. 6 proves the main complexity results. Some conclusions end the paper.

2   Abstract Argumentation and Grounded Semantics

The well-known, abstract argumentation paradigm was originally proposed by Dung [4] to study the general aspects of argumentation without specifying the internal structure of arguments. In this perspective, an argumentation framework AF is a structure $\langle \mathscr{A}, \gg \rangle$, where $\mathscr{A}$ is a non-empty set of arguments and $\gg$ is a binary attack relation on $\mathscr{A}$. For any pair or arguments A and B in $\mathscr{A}$, $A \gg B$ means that A attacks B. If the goal is to determine whether an argument can be accepted, this cannot be done by only choosing between two arguments that directly conflict with each other. We need to understand how arguments can be indirectly defended by other arguments. The corresponding literature flourishes [3] with different formalisations among which Dung's grounded semantics is perhaps the most popular one.

Let us recall the basic formal concepts of abstract argumentation and the basic features of Dung's grounded semantics. An argument A is *acceptable* w.r.t. a set of arguments $\mathscr{S}$ if and only if any argument defeating A is defeated by an argument in $\mathscr{S}$. The function F_{AF}, for an argumentation framework $AF = \langle \mathscr{A}, \gg \rangle$, is defined as $F_{AF} : 2^{\mathscr{A}} \Rightarrow 2^{\mathscr{A}}$ and $F_{AF}(\mathscr{S}) = \{A \mid A \text{ is acceptable w.r.t. } \mathscr{S} \subseteq \mathscr{A}\}$. A *grounded extension* $GE(AF)$ of an argumentation framework AF is the least fixed-point of F_{AF}. An argument A and its conclusion are *justified* w.r.t. an argumentation framework AF if, and only if, $A \in GE(AF)$.

As is done in [5,11,13], given the above framework the (internal) logical structure of arguments can be specified in such a way that arguments are logical inference trees.

Definition 1. *The language consists of* literals *and* rules. *Given a set* PROP *of propositional atoms, the set of* literals *is* Lit = PROP $\cup \{\neg p \mid p \in$ PROP$\}$. *We denote with* $\sim p$ *the* complementary *of literal* p; *if* p *is a positive literal* q, *then* $\sim p$ *is* $\neg q$, *and if* p *is a negative literal* $\neg q$, *then* $\sim p$ *is* q.

Let Lab *be a set of unique* labels. *A rule* r *with* $r \in$ Lab *describes the relation between a subset of* Lit, *called the* antecedent *or the* premises *of* r *and denoted by* $A(r)$ *(which may be empty) and a literal in* Lit, *called the* consequent *or* head *of* r *and denoted by* $C(r)$. *Three kind of rules are allowed:* strict rules *of the form* $r : A(r) \rightarrow C(r)$, defeasible rules *of the form* $r : A(r) \Rightarrow C(r)$, *and* defeaters *of the form* $r : A(r) \rightsquigarrow C(r)$. *An undisputed fact is represented as a strict rule with empty antecedent.*

A strict rule is a rule in the classical sense: whenever the antecedent holds, so is the conclusion. A defeasible rule is allowed to assert its conclusion unless there is contrary evidence to it. A defeater is a rule that cannot be used to draw any conclusion, but can provide contrary evidence to complementary conclusions.

Definition 2. *An argumentation theory* D *is a structure* $(R, >)$, *where* R *is a (finite) set of rules and* $> \subseteq R \times R$ *is a binary relation on* R *called the* superiority *relation.*

The relation $>$ describes the relative strength of rules, that is to say, when a single rule may override the conclusion of another rule, and is required to be irreflexive, asymmetric and acyclic (i.e., its transitive closure is irreflexive).

By combining the rules in a theory, we can build arguments (we adjust the definition in [11] to meet Definition 2). In what follows, for a given argument A, Conc returns its conclusion, Sub returns all its sub-arguments, Rules returns all the rules in the argument and, finally, TopRule returns the last inference rule in the argument.

Definition 3 (Argument). *Let $D = (R, >)$ be an argumentation theory and $\Rightarrow \in \{\rightarrow, \Rightarrow, \rightsquigarrow\}$. An argument A constructed from D has the form $A_1, \ldots, A_n \Rightarrow_r \phi$, where*

- *A_k is an argument constructed from D, for $1 \leq k \leq n$, and*
- *$r : \mathsf{Conc}(A_1), \ldots, \mathsf{Conc}(A_n) \Rightarrow \phi$ is a rule in R.*

With regard to argument A, the following holds:

$$\mathsf{Conc}(A) = \phi$$
$$\mathsf{Sub}(A) = \mathsf{Sub}(A_1), \ldots \mathsf{Sub}(A_n), A$$
$$\mathsf{TopRule}(A) = r : \mathsf{Conc}(A_1), \ldots, \mathsf{Conc}(A_n) \Rightarrow \phi$$
$$\mathsf{Rules}(A) = \mathsf{Rules}(A_1) \cup \cdots \cup \mathsf{Rules}(A_n) \cup \{\mathsf{TopRule}(A)\}$$
$$\mathsf{Rules}(A_1) \cup \cdots \cup \mathsf{Rules}(A_n) \ does \ not \ contain \ a \ defeater$$

The following example illustrates the notions just introduced.

Example 1. Given the set

$$R = \{r_1 : \quad \rightarrow a, \quad r_2 : \quad \Rightarrow b, \quad r_3 : a, b \Rightarrow c\}$$

we have arguments:

$$A_1 : \quad \rightarrow_{r_1} a \qquad \text{(strict argument)}$$
$$A_2 : \quad \Rightarrow_{r_2} b \qquad \text{(defeasible argument)}$$
$$A_3 : A_1, A_2 \Rightarrow_{r_3} c \qquad \text{(defeasible argument)}$$

Let us now consider conflicts between arguments. In grounded semantics we just need to consider rebuttals. Hence, conflicts between contradictory argument conclusions are resolved on the basis of preferences over arguments using a simple last-link ordering according to which an argument A is stronger than another argument B, denoted as $A > B$, if, and only if, the rule $\mathsf{TopRule}(A)$ is stronger than the rule $\mathsf{TopRule}(B)$ (i.e. $\mathsf{TopRule}(A) > \mathsf{TopRule}(B)$).

Definition 4 (Defeats). *An argument B defeats an argument A if, and only if $\exists A' \in \mathsf{Sub}(A)$ such that $\mathsf{Conc}(B) = \sim\mathsf{Conc}(A')$, and $A' \not> B$.*

We can now define the argumentation framework that is determined by an argumentation theory.

Definition 5 (Argumentation Framework). *Let $D = (R, >)$ be an argumentation theory. The argumentation framework determined by D is $\langle \mathscr{A}, \gg \rangle$ where $\mathscr{A}$ is the set of all arguments constructed from D, and $\gg$ is the defeat relation defined above.*

Given this definition of argumentation framework, if D is an argumentation theory, we can abuse notation somewhat and write $GE(D)$ to denote the grounded extension of the argumentation framework determined by D.

The following is thus a standard result that can be obtained:

Theorem 1. *Given a theory D, a conclusion ϕ is justified by D under the grounded semantics iff there is an argument A in $GE(D)$ such that $\mathsf{Conc}(A) = \phi$.*

3 Strategic Argumentation

We herein consider the strategic argumentation framework introduced in [6]. The dialogue games proposed in that work involves an alternating sequence of interactions between two players, the *Proponent* Pr and the *Opponent* Op. The content of the dispute being that Pr attempts to assess the validity of a particular claim, whereas Op attacks Pr's claims in order to refute such a claim. In that setting, Op has the burden of proof on the opposite claim, and not just the duty to refute Pr's claim.

The challenge between the parties is formalised by means of argument exchange. In the majority of concrete instances of argumentation frameworks, arguments are defined as chains of reasoning based on facts and rules captured in some formal language. Each party adheres to a particular set of game rules as defined below.

The players partially share knowledge of a logical theory, which includes common facts and rules to put forward arguments. Each participant has a private knowledge regarding some rules of the theory. Other rules are known by both parties, but the set of such rules may be empty. These rules along with all the facts of the theory represent the common knowledge of both participants.

The repertoire of moves at each turn just includes either putting forward an argument, or passing. By putting forward a private argument during a step of the game, the agent increases the common knowledge by the rules used within the argument just played. Essentially, the agent chooses a subset of her private knowledge which, along with the current common knowledge, justifies her claim. On the other hand, when a player passes, she declares her defeat and the game ends. This happens when there is no combination of the remaining private rules which proves her claim.

We now provide the formal definition of a dialogue game. The state of the game at turn i is denoted by a theory $D^i = (R^i_{com}, >)$ and by two sets R^i_{Pr} and R^i_{Op}. R^i_{Com} is the set of rules known by both participants at turn i (which may be empty when $i = 0$), and R^i_{Pr} (R^i_{Op}) is the private knowledge of Pr (Op) at turn i. We assume that each player is informed about the restriction of $>$ to the rules that she knows. We assume that the private theories of the proponent and the opponent are conflict-free.

We now formalise the game rules which establish how the theory D^{i-1} and the sets R^{i-1}_{Pr}, R^{i-1}_{Op} are modified based on the move played at turn i.

The parties start the game by choosing the content of dispute l (in our case, a literal) to discuss about. At turn i, Pr has the burden to justify l (under the grounded semantics) by using the current common knowledge along with a subset of R_{Pr}^{i-1}, whereas Op's final goal is to justify $\sim l$ (under the grounded semantics) using R_{Op}^{i-1} instead of R_{Pr}^{i-1}. We point out that at turn i, Pr (Op) may put forward an argument whose terminal literal differs from l ($\sim l$).

Let R_{Com}^0, R_{Pr}^0 and R_{Op}^0 be respectively the common knowledge, and the private knowledge of Pr and Op at the beginning of the game, and $D^0 = (R_{com}^0, >)$. If l is justified by D^0 then Op starts the game. Otherwise, Pr does so.

At turn i, if Pr plays R^i, then

- $\sim l$ is justified by D^{i-1} under the grounded semantics;
- $R^i \subseteq R_{\mathsf{Pr}}^{i-1}$;
- $D^i = (R_{\mathsf{Com}}^i, >)$;
- $R_{\mathsf{Pr}}^i = R_{\mathsf{Pr}}^i \setminus R^i$, $R_{\mathsf{Op}}^i = R_{\mathsf{Op}}^{i-1}$, and $R_{\mathsf{Com}}^i = R_{\mathsf{Com}}^{i-1} \cup R^i$;
- l is justified by D^i under the grounded semantics.

At turn i, if Op plays R^i, then

- l is justified D^{i-1} under the grounded semantics;
- $R^i \subseteq R_{\mathsf{Op}}^{i-1}$;
- $D^i = (R_{\mathsf{Com}}^i, >)$;
- $R_{\mathsf{Pr}}^i = R_{\mathsf{Pr}}^{i-1}$, $R_{\mathsf{Op}}^i = R_{\mathsf{Op}}^{i-1} \setminus R^i$, and $R_{\mathsf{Com}}^i = R_{\mathsf{Com}}^{i-1} \cup R^i$;
- $\sim l$ is justified by D^i under the grounded semantics.

The corresponding decision problem can be formulated as follows:

Strategic Argumentation Problem Under Grounded Semantics

> Pr's INSTANCE FOR TURN i: Let l be the content of dispute, R_{Pr}^{i-1} be the set of the private rules of Pr, and D^{i-1} be such that $\sim l$ is justified by D^{i-1} under the grounded semantics.
> QUESTION: Is there a subset R^i of R_{Pr}^{i-1} such that l is justified by D^i under the grounded semantics?

Op's instance of the problem is similar, asking for $\sim l$ to be justified.

Later, we will show that both Pr's and Op's version of this problem is NP-complete.

4   Defeasible Logic

Defeasible Logic is a rule-based skeptical approach to nonmonotonic reasoning. It is based on a logic programming-like language and is simple, efficient but flexible formalism capable of dealing with many intuitions of non-monotonic reasoning in a natural and meaningful way [1].

The language of Defeasible Logic consists of literals and rules. In order to avoid notational redundancies, from now on we use the same definitions of PROP, Lit, complementary literal, and the same rule types, structure and notation as already introduced in Definition 1.

A defeasible theory D is a triple $(F, R, >)$, where $F \subseteq \text{Lit}$ is a set of indisputable statements called *facts*, R is a (finite) set of rules, and $> \subseteq R \times R$ is a superiority relation on R as introduced in Definition 2.

The proof theory of a defeasible logic can draw two main types of conclusions. A conclusion $+df\ q$ expresses that the literal q can be proven defeasibly, while a conclusion $-df\ q$ expresses that a proof has established that q cannot be proven defeasibly. df is known as a *tag*. Different tags are used to characterize the conclusions of different defeasible logics. In this paper, there are two defeasible logics of interest, characterized by the tags ∂ and δ.

The logics are denoted by $\text{DL}(\partial)$ and $\text{DL}(\delta)$. There is no room here to provide the full inference rules for these logics; we refer the reader to [5] (where ∂_{ap} is used instead of δ).

In a series of papers [7,8] Maher investigates the relative expressiveness of variants of Defeasible Logic. Briefly, two (defeasible) logics L_1 and L_2 have the same expressiveness iff the two logics can simulate each other. A defeasible logic L_2 *simulates* a defeasible logic L_1 if there is a polynomial time transformation T that transforms a theory D_1 of L_1 to a theory $D_2 = T(D_1)$ of L_2 such that, for any set of additional facts F, $D_1 + F$ and $D_2 + F$ have the same conclusions in the language of D_1[1]. Reference [8] provides polynomial time transformations from $\text{DL}(\partial)$ to $\text{DL}(\delta)$ and the other way around.

Theorem 2. *[8] $\text{DL}(\delta)$ can simulate $\text{DL}(\partial)$, and vice versa.*

5 Strategic Argumentation in DL

A defeasible logic implementation of the game introduced in Sect. 3 follows the same structure, but some specifics are expressed in terms of the defeasible logic. From now on, the content of the dispute discussed by the players will be called the *critical literal*, and the arguments brought about by the players will be in the form of defeasible derivations. We state that the players may not present arguments in parallel, that is to say, they take turns in making their move.

The state of the game at turn i is now denoted by a defeasible theory $D^i = (F, R^i_{com}, >)$ and by two sets R^i_{Pr} and R^i_{Op}. R^i_{Com} is the set of rules known by both participants at turn i (which may be empty when $i = 0$), and R^i_{Pr} (R^i_{Op}) is the private knowledge of Pr (Op) at turn i. We assume that each player is informed about the restriction of $>$ to the rules that she knows. D^i is assumed to be coherent and consistent for each i, i.e., there is no literal p such that: (i) p is at the same time defeasibly proved and refuted in D^i, and (ii) both p and $\sim p$ are defeasibly proved in D^i.

The game rules discussed in Sect. 3 are instantiated as follows. In place of requiring that a literal is justified under the grounded semantics, we instead require that it can be inferred defeasibly from the defeasible theory under the given logic.

---

[1] $D + F$ denotes the addition of the facts F to the facts in the defeasible theory D.

Thus we formulate the strategic argumentation problem under a defeasible logic as follows.

Strategic Argumentation Problem Under DL(df)

Pr's INSTANCE FOR TURN i: Let l be the critical literal, R_{Pr}^{i-1} be the set of the private rules of Pr, and D^{i-1} be such that either $D^{i-1} \vdash -df\, l$ if $i = 1$, or $D^{i-1} \vdash +df \sim l$ otherwise.
QUESTION: Is there a subset R^i of R_{Pr}^{i-1} such that $D^i \vdash +df\, l$?

6   NP-Completeness Result

We are now ready to give the result of the paper, namely deciding what argument to play in a given turn of a dialogue game under Dung's grounded semantics is an NP-complete problem even when the problem of deciding whether a conclusion follows from an argument is computable in polynomial time.

Governatori et al. [6] proved that the same problem is NP-complete for DL with ambiguity blocking, i.e., DL(∂).

Theorem 3. *[6] The strategic argumentation problem under* DL(∂) *is NP-complete.*

While it is possible to define DL(∂) in terms of an argumentation semantics, the logic corresponding to Dung's grounded semantics is DL(δ) [5]. Thus the next step is to determine the computational complexity of the problem at hand for DL(δ).

We cannot employ Theorem 2 directly, because it only applies to addition of facts. However, it is shown in [9] that every strategic argumentation problem involving addition of *rules* can be easily transformed into an equivalent strategic argumentation problem only involving addition of *facts*. Thus we can apply Theorem 2 to show that the transformed strategic argumentation problem for DL(∂) can be reduced to the corresponding transformed problem for DL(δ). The NP-completeness of the strategic argumentation problem under DL(δ) now follows.

Theorem 4. *The strategic argumentation problem under* DL(δ) *is* NP-*complete.*

In [5] the equivalence of derivations in DL(δ) and justified conclusions under grounded semantics has been established.

Theorem 5. *[5] Given a defeasible theory D, $D \vdash +\delta l$ iff l is justified by D under the grounded semantics.*

We can solve the strategic argumentation problem by non-deterministically choosing a set R^i of rules and then verifying whether the critical literal l is justified in the argumentation framework determined by D^i, or not. Further, the literals justified by the grounded semantics are computable in polynomial time. Thus the strategic argumentation problem is in NP.

Now, from Theorems 4 and 5 we obtain the main result of this contribution.

Theorem 6. *The strategic argumentation problem under the grounded semantics is NP-complete.*

7 Conclusions

Almost all research in AI on argumentation assumes that strategic dialogues are games of complete information, that is where the structure of the game is common knowledge among the players (see [6] for a review of the literature). Following [10,12], we argued that argument games work under incomplete information: by not knowing the other player's knowledge, each player cannot predict neither which arguments will be attacked, nor which counterarguments will be employed for attacking her arguments. We proved that the problem of deciding what set of rules to play at a given move is NP-complete, even if the problem of deciding whether a given theory (defeasibly) entails a literal can be computed in polynomial time.

References

1. Antoniou, G.: A discussion of some intuitions of defeasible reasoning. In: Vouros, G.A., Panayiotopoulos, T. (eds.) SETN 2004. LNCS (LNAI), vol. 3025, pp. 311–320. Springer, Heidelberg (2004)
2. Antoniou, G., Billington, D., Governatori, G., Maher, M.J.: Representation results for defeasible logic. ACM Trans. Comput. Log. **2**(2), 255–286 (2001)
3. Baroni, P., Giacomin, M.: Semantics of abstract argument systems. In: Simari, G., Rahwan, I. (eds.) Argumentation in Artificial Intelligence, pp. 25–44. Springer, Heidelberg (2009)
4. Dung, P.M.: On the acceptability of arguments and its fundamental role in non-monotonic reasoning, logic programming and n-person games. Artif. Intell. **77**(2), 321–358 (1995)
5. Governatori, G., Maher, M.J., Antoniou, G., Billington, D.: Argumentation semantics for defeasible logic. J. Log. Comput. **14**(5), 675–702 (2004)
6. Governatori, G., Olivieri, F., Scannapieco, S., Rotolo, A., Cristani, M.: Strategic argumentation is NP-complete. In: Proceedings of the ECAI 2014, IOS Press (2014)
7. Maher, M.J.: Relative expressiveness of defeasible logics. Theor. Pract. Log. Program. **12**(4–5), 793–810 (2012)
8. Maher, M.J.: Relative expressiveness of defeasible logics II. Theor. Pract. Log. Program. **13**, 579–592 (2013)
9. Maher, M.J.: Complexity of exploiting privacy violations in strategic argumentation. In: Pham, D.-N., Park, S.-B. (eds.) PRICAI 2014. LNCS, vol. 8862, pp. 523–535. Springer, Heidelberg (2014)
10. Okuno, K., Takahashi, K.: Argumentation system with changes of an agent's knowledge base. In: IJCAI 2009, pp. 226–232 (2009)
11. Prakken, H.: An abstract framework for argumentation with structured arguments. Argum. Comput. **1**(2), 93–124 (2010)
12. Satoh, K., Takahashi, K.: A semantics of argumentation under incomplete information. In: Proceedings of Jurisn 2011 (2011)
13. Toni, F.: A generalised framework for dispute derivations in assumption-based argumentation. Artif. Intell. **195**, 1–43 (2013)

Deliberative Argumentation for Service Provision in Smart Environments

Juan Carlos Nieves[✉] and Helena Lindgren

Department of Computing Science, Umeå University,
SE-901 87 Umeå, Sweden
{jcnieves,helena}@cs.umu.se

Abstract. In this paper, we introduce an inquiry dialogue approach for supporting decision making in a smart environment setting. These inquiry dialogues have as topic either *agreement atoms* or *agreement rules*, which capture services in a smart environment. These services are provided and supported by three rational agents with different roles: *Environment Agent*, *Activity Agent* and *Coach Agent*. These three agents have different capabilities and represent different data sources; however, they have to collaborate in order to deliver services in a smart environment.

The knowledge base of each agent is captured by extended logic programs. Therefore, the construction of arguments is supported by the *Well-Founded Semantics* (WFS). The outcome of the inquiry dialogues is supported by well-known argumentation semantics.

1 Introduction

In this paper the cooperative layer of a multi-agent system is presented. This multi-agent system aims to find the *optimal actions* in the presence of partial and inconsistent information in a particular situation. Consequently, providing supportive services by synthesizing the relevant sources of data, possibly represented using a variety of formats, represents a fundamental challenge in the information management. This challenge is addressed by a *formal dialogue-based approach* in a multi-agent setting. Formal argumentation dialogues have been intensively explored on the last years [1,3,6,8,10] in the community of formal argumentation theory. Most of these approaches have been suggested as general frameworks for setting up different kinds of dialogues. By having in mind these frameworks, we introduce an argumentation dialogue approach for supporting decision making in a smart environment setting in terms of *agreement rules*.

From the structure point of view, our argumentation dialogues follow the dialogue style suggested by [3]. However, since we support our specification language on default theories (*i.e.*, *extended logic programs*) and default theories can be mapped into Assumption-Based Argumentation (ABA) [4], our approach is close to ABA-dialogue inference [6]. Indeed, the inferences of our argumentation dialogues in terms of *x-committed agreement rules* (Definition 9) are based on argumentation semantics as it is done on ABA-dialogues [6]. Moreover, we

© Springer International Publishing Switzerland 2015
N. Bulling (Ed.): EUMAS 2014, LNAI 8953, pp. 388–397, 2015.
DOI: 10.1007/978-3-319-17130-2_27

want to point out that both our arguments (Definition 3) and attack relations (Definition 4) can be regarded as particular definitions of arguments and attacks in ABA. In this sense, our dialogues can be seen as a specialization of ABA dialogues.

The article is organized as follows. Section 2 describes a multi-agent approach designed to deliver personalized services in a smart environment. Section 3 introduces our argumentation-based deliberative method; moreover, we show some relevant properties of our approach. In the last section, conclusions and future work are presented.

2   A Multi-agent System for Providing Intelligent Services

In [9], we introduced a multi-agent approach designed to deliver personalized services in a smart environment. To this end, three agents were designed: the *Environment Agent*, *Activity Agent* and *Coach Agent*. In [9], these agents were motivated from an activity-theoretical point of view. In this section, these three agent are instantiated from the point of view of a particular intelligent infrastructure called *As-A-Pal*.

Kitchen As-A-Pal is a smart environment, which serves as a living laboratory environment for designing and developing a range of different knowledge-based applications intended to be deployed as part of a holistic approach to ambient assisted living. Kitchen As-A-Pal is augmented with sensors and passively tagged objects. The physical and ambient interfaces provide access to information and services.

Three agents have been partially implemented in the As-A-Pal environment: *Environment Agent*, *Activity Agent* and *Coach Agent*. These three agents have different roles and needs therefore to collaborate on providing support to the human actor in conducting activities in the As-A-Pal smart environment.

The **Environment Agent** is responsible for facilitating interaction in smart environments. Since the human actor is mobile, the context and conditions for interaction is changing with the human actor's and objects' physical position, the Environment Agent is expected to handle the dynamic availability of environmental resources. In an activity-theoretical perspective, the Environment Agent organizes and provides the *tools* for activity execution, e.g., the *mediators* when smart services are provided by the actor.

A *rule-based knowledge base* has been defined as the knowledge base of the Environment Agent. This knowledge base contains a set of predicates, which are turned grounded by considering readings from sensors embedded in the As-A-Pal environment.

The **Activity Agent** is responsible for supporting and enhancing the ongoing activities and the activities predicted to be performed in the near future. The Activity Agent recognizes activities (which have an objective) and actions (which are goal-oriented) performed in smart environments. The Activity Agent filters the available services to the ones that impact and enhance the ongoing activity.

Like the Environment Agent, the Activity Agent has a rule-based knowledge base. The Activity Agent has an extended knowledge base whose predicates are turned grounded by different activity recognition processes.

The **Coach Agent** enhances the human actor's ability to perform the activities perceived as important to the human, with assistance from the other agents. It is the Coach Agent's responsibility to guard the human actor's interests, so that the smart environment provides the desired support and services. It is responsible for maximizing the quality of activity execution, consequently, it needs to evaluate the performance, the human actor's satisfaction with her performance, and her satisfaction with how the ambient support is supporting her in activities. The quality of interaction service and satisfaction with activity performance can be obtained by continuously keeping track of the human actor's emotions and experiences.

Like the Environment and Activity Agents, Coach Agent has a rule-based knowledge base. The predicates of the extensional knowledge base of the Coach Agent are turned grounded by different emotions processes, *e.g.*, *emotions recognition* and questionnaires.

3   A Deliberative Argumentation Approach

In this section, an argumentation approach will be presented in order to manage agreements between the As-A-Pal architecture's agents. This argumentation approach will be basically an operational implementation of *deliberation dialogues*. A deliberation dialogue is characterized as a dialogue occurring when two or more parties attempt to agree on an action to be performed in some situation.

In a deliberation dialogue, all the participants use their knowledge to inform their contributions. A procedural approach for reaching agreements between the parties, which are taking part of a deliberation dialogue is by the considering *agreement rules* [9]. An agreement rule is basically *a consensus* in which the different participant of a deliberation dialogue agree.

3.1   Knowledge Bases of the Agents

We start defining the components of the knowledge base of each agent. To implement deliberation dialogues between the As-A-Pal agents, we provide each agent with a set of *agreement rules*. Agreement rules will be associated to specific *goals* related to *the services*, which As-A-Pal may provide. Hence, an agreement rule is defined as follows:

Definition 1. *An agreement rule[1] is of the form:* $\alpha : a_0 \leftarrow a_1, \ldots, a_j, not$ $a_{j+1}, \ldots, not\ a_n$ *in which* $\alpha \in \mathbb{N}$, $a_i (0 \leq i \leq n)$ *is an atom such that for each* $a_i (1 \leq i \leq n)$ *either exists an agent Ag such that its logic-based knowledge base*

---

[1] This definition of an agreement rule extends our previous definition of agreement rules introduced in [9].

is Σ and $a_i \in \mathcal{L}_\Sigma{}^2$ or $a_i \in \mathcal{L}_{AR}$ such that AR is a set of agreement rules, and $a_0 \neq a_i(1 \leq i \leq n)$.

Observing Definition 1, we can see that the atoms, which appear in the body of an agreement rule, a.i. $a_i(1 \leq i \leq n)$, are either beliefs, which belong to different agents, or atoms, which appear in other agreement rules. As we will see in Definition 2, the knowledge base of each agent is private. This means that an agent itself cannot know if an agreement rule holds true in a given moment. Hence, for knowing the trueness of agreement rules, the collaboration of all the agents whose knowledge is part of an given agreement rule is required.

The head of an agreement rule, a.i. a_o, will be associated to a particular belief which will be held by an As-A-Pal agent. For instance, this believe can be a service for the end user. This means that by considering the trueness of an agreement rule, different agents will agree on a particular service for a user.

According to Definition 1, each agreement rule has a natural number attached. This number will be used for attaching a preference level to each agreement rule. We will assume that smaller number capture high preferences. In the As-A-Pal smart environment, these preferences levels will initially be set up based on user-studies. However, we will expect that the As-A-Pal architecture will update these preference levels by considering the user-satisfiability, which is managed by the *Coach Agent*.

In the As-A-Pal architecture, each of the agents which belong to the As-A-Pal architecture is supported by a knowledge base, which is split mainly in three components.

Definition 2. *An As-A-Pal agent Ag is defined by the following structure $Ag = \langle \Sigma, AR, CS \rangle$ in which Σ is an extended logic program which denotes the knowledge base of agent Ag, AR is a set of agreement rules and CS is a set of normal clauses which is called a commitment store.*

We will assume that Σ and AR keep private information for each agent. In other words, other agents do not have access to Σ and AR. On the other hand, the commitment store of each agent keeps public information that other agents could access. AR and CS will be relevant structures for dealing with the dialogues between the As-A-Pal's agents.

In order to identify the atoms which only appear in agreement rules, let $Ag = \langle \Sigma, AR, CS \rangle$ and $\mathcal{L}_{Agreement} = \mathcal{L}_{AR} \setminus (\mathcal{L}_\Sigma)$. The atoms which appears in $\mathcal{L}_{Agreement}$ are called *agreement-atoms*.

3.2   Arguments

Now that we have defined the structure of the knowledge base of each agent in the As-A-Pal architecture, we will move on how to come up with agreements between the different agents which take part of the As-A-Pal architecture. To this end, we will introduce a basic definition of an argument.

---

[2] By $\mathcal{L}_P$, we denote the set of atoms in the language of P.

Well-Founded Semantics (WFS) [7] provides a reasoning engine for inferring information from a logic programs. In the context of the As-A-Pal's agents, WFS will support the construction of arguments from the knowledge bases. The definition of an argument is as follows:

Definition 3 (Argument). *Let Σ be a logic program. $A_D = \langle S, c \rangle$ is an argument if the following conditions holds: 1.- $WFS(S) = \langle T, F \rangle$ and $c \in T$; 2.- $S \subseteq \Sigma$ such that S is a minimal set (w.r.t. set inclusion) of Σ satisfying 1; 3.- $WFS(S) = \langle T, F \rangle$ such that $\nexists a \in \mathcal{L}_P$ and $\{a, \neg a\} \subseteq T$. $\mathcal{A}_\Sigma$ denotes the set of arguments built from Σ.*

As we can observe in Definition 3, an argument $\langle S, c \rangle$ is composed by two components a *support* S and a *conclusion* a. An argumentation can be regarded as an explanation of a particular claim. We have implemented an argumentation engine which constructs arguments from a logic program according to Definition 3[3]. Now, let us define an attack relationship between arguments as follows:

Definition 4 (Attack Relationship Between Arguments). *Let $A = \langle S_A, g_A \rangle$, $B = \langle S_B, g_B \rangle$ be two arguments, $WFS(S_A) = \langle T_A, F_A \rangle$ and $WFS(S_B) = \langle T_B, F_B \rangle$. We say that A attacks B if one of the following conditions holds: 1.- $a \in T_A$ and $\neg a \in T_B$; and 2.- $a \in T_A$ and $a \in F_B$. $At(\mathcal{A}rg)$ denotes the set of attack relations between the arguments which belong to the set of arguments $\mathcal{A}rg$.*

3.3   Inquiry Dialogues

Now that we have defined how the knowledge base of each agent is structured, our dialogue approach will be presented. The general idea of our approach is to apply *inquiry dialogues* in order to validate the trueness of either an agreement atom or an agreement rule. For instance, if an agreement atom holds true in an given state of the As-A-Pal architecture, then the given agreement atom holds the trueness of a particular belief in the whole As-A-Pal system.

Inspired by [3], we will consider a combination between *argument inquiry dialogues* and *warrant inquiry dialogues*. Hence, our inquiry dialogues are based on three basic moves: open - $\langle x, open, dialogue(\theta, \gamma) \rangle$; assert - $\langle x, assert, \langle S, a \rangle \rangle$ and close - $\langle x, close, dialogue(\theta, \gamma) \rangle$ in which x denotes an agent, $\langle S, a \rangle$ is an argument, $\theta \in \{wi, ai\}$, if $\theta = wi$ then γ is an agreement atom and if $\theta = ai$ then γ is an agreement rule. wi means "*warrant inquiry dialogue*" and ai means "*argument inquiry dialogue*". $\mathcal{M}$ denotes set of moves defined above. Let us observe that the format of these moves are not exactly the same as the ones introduced by [3]. Our moves are personalized in terms of agreement atoms and agreement rule. Moreover, the arguments asserted by assert-modes will be constructed according to Definition 3. According to Black and Hunter [3] a dialogue is defined as follows:

---

[3] This argumentation engine can be download from: http://esteban-guerrero.tumblr.com/argengine.

Definition 5. *A dialogue, denoted* D_r^t, *is a sequence of moves* $[m_r, \ldots, m_t]$ *involving a set of participants* $\mathcal{I}$, *where* $r, t \in \mathbb{N}$ *and* $r \leq t$, *such that: 1.- the first move of the dialogue,* m_r, *is a move of the form* $\langle x, open, dialogue(\theta, \gamma)\rangle$; *2.- Sender*$(m_s) \in \mathcal{I}$ $(r \leq s \leq t)$; *3.- Sender*$(m_{s1}) \neq$ *Sender*(m_{s2}) *such that* $(p \leq s1 < s2 \leq q)$, $(q - p) + 1 = |A|^4$ *and* $(r \leq p < q \leq t)$. *In which, Sender :* $\mathcal{M} \longmapsto \mathcal{I}$ *is a function such that Sender*$(\langle Agent, Act, Content\rangle) = Agent$.

The only difference between Definition 5 and the original definition presented in [3] is that the set of participants is not restricted to two participants. In the As-A-Pal architecture, we have identified three main agents; hence, these agents will take part of the dialogue.

As in [3], a dialogue terminates whenever all the participants of a dialogue have made a close move, *w.r.t.* the topic of the dialogue, in a consecutive form. A dialogue allows us to manage multi nested dialogues; hence, the nested dialogues terminate before the outermost dialogue terminates.

Whenever an agent takes part of a dialogue, its commitment store will be updated. The update of the commitment stores of each agent is done as follows:

Definition 6. *Let* D_r^t *be the current dialogue and* $\mathcal{I}$ *be the set of participants. For all agent* $\in \mathcal{I}$: *1.-* $CS_{agent}^t = \emptyset$ *iff* $t = 0$; *2.-* $CS_{agent}^t = CS_{agent}^{t-1} \cup S$ *iff* $m_t = \langle agent, assert, \langle S, a\rangle\rangle$, *3.-* $CS_{agent}^t = CS_{agent}^{t-1}$ *if the previous cases do not hold.*

According to Definition 6, the commitment store of each agent is updated whenever it performs an *assert* move; moreover, the information, which is added to the commitment store, is the support of the argument which is asserted. An important consequence of this update is that the information, which is added to the commitment store, is turned public; hence, the other agents which are taking part of the dialogue have access to this information. Therefore, this information can be used by other agents in order to construct their own arguments. It is worth mentioning that the commitment store of each agent basically is *an extended normal logic program*.

In order to deal with argument inquiry dialogues, a query store is attached to a dialogue. A query store is basically a set of atoms.

Definition 7. *Let* D_r^t *be the current dialogue and* $\mathcal{I}$ *be the set of participants such that agent* $\in \mathcal{I}$. *A query store* QS_r *is a finite set of positive literals such that:* $QS_r = \begin{cases} \mathcal{B}^+ \cup \mathcal{B}^- & \text{iff } m_t = \langle agent, open, dialogue(ai, a_0 \leftarrow \mathcal{B}^+, not \ \mathcal{B}^-)\rangle, \\ \emptyset & \text{otherwise.} \end{cases}$

Let us observe that although the topic of an argument inquiry dialogue can have negative literal, these literals are updated into the query store as positive literals.

The protocol of an argument inquiry dialogue will be presented as a sequence of general steps. To this end, some notation is introduced: let $\mathcal{I}$ be the finite set of participants of a dialogue. We identify each agent from $\mathcal{I}$ by a natural number this means that $\mathcal{I} = \{1, \ldots, n\}$ and $i \in \mathcal{I}$ such that $i = \langle \Sigma^i, AR^i, CS^i\rangle$. Hence, an argument inquiry dialogue works as follows:

---

[4] We are assuming that A has at least two participants.

Step	Argument Inquiry Dialogue
1	One of the participant agents starts the argumentation inquiry dialogue with the move $\langle x, open, dialogue(ai, \gamma) \rangle$.
2	The query store QS is updated according to Definition 7.
3	Each participant agent i performs one of the following moves:

    1. $\langle i, assert, \langle S, a \rangle \rangle$ if $\langle S, a \rangle \in \mathcal{A}_\Sigma$, $a \in QS$ in which $\Sigma = \Sigma^i \cup \bigcup_{j \in \mathcal{I} and i \neq j} CS^j$ and none of the participants have asserted the argument $\langle S, a \rangle$ in the dialogue before. The commitment store of the agent i is updated according to Definition 6.

    2. $\langle i, open, dialogue(ai, a_0 \leftarrow \mathcal{B}^+, not\ \mathcal{B}^-) \rangle$ if $a_0 \in QS$, $\alpha : a_0 \leftarrow \mathcal{B}^+, not\ \mathcal{B}^- \in AR^i$ and there is no previous open move in the dialogue with $a_0 \leftarrow \mathcal{B}^+, not\ \mathcal{B}^-$ as its topic. The dialogue go to Step 1 in a recursive way.

    3. $\langle i, close, dialogue(ai, \gamma) \rangle$ if the agent i is unable to perform one of the previous steps.

There are formal conditions *w.r.t. well-formed argument inquiry dialogues*, which basically argue that all the moves *extend* an initial dialogue and all the participants of the dialogue have the opportunity to perform a move (see [3] for its definition).

In order to define the outcomes of dialogues, let us introduce the following notation: Given a dialogue D_r^t: $AR_{D_r^t} = \{\gamma | \langle x, open, dialogue(ai, \gamma) \rangle$ is a open-move that appears in $D_r^t\}$.

As we can observe, $AR_{D_r^t}$ contains basically the agreement rules which appear in the dialogue D_r^t. Considering $AR_{D_r^t}$, the outcome of an argument inquiry dialogue is defined as follows:

Definition 8. *Let D_r^t be a well-formed argument inquiry dialogue. The outcome of D_r^t is: $Outcome_{ai}(D_r^t) = \mathcal{A}_\Sigma$ such that $\Sigma = \bigcup_{i \in \mathcal{I}} CS^i \cup AR_{D_r^t}$.*

As we can see in Definition 8, the outcome of an argument inquiry dialogue is basically the set of arguments which we can build from the commitment stores of each of its participants and the agreement rules which appear in the dialogue D_r^t. Let us point out that $Outcome_{ai}(D_r^t)$ contains arguments which their conclusions can be agreement atoms. These arguments are the main outcomes of an argument inquiry dialogue since these arguments cannot be built by an agent itself.

Considering the arguments from $Outcome_{ai}(D_r^t)$ and the attack relation introduced by Definition 4, an argumentation framework *w.r.t.* an argument inquiry dialogue D_r^t is $AF_{D_r^t} = \langle Outcome_{ai}(D_r^t), At(Outcome_{ai}(D_r^t)) \rangle$.

An agreement rule γ will be called *x-committed* ($x \in \{s, p, c, g, i, ss, sg\}$) by a set of agents $\mathcal{I}$ as follows[5]:

Definition 9. *Let D_r^t be a well-formed argument inquiry dialogue involving a set of participant $\mathcal{I}$ and $m_r = \langle x, open, dialogue(ai, \gamma) \rangle$ such that $x \in \mathcal{I}$ and $\gamma = a_0 \leftarrow \mathcal{B}^+, not\ \mathcal{B}^-$ is an agreement rule. γ is s-committed by $\mathcal{I}$ w.r.t. D_r^t iff $\langle S, a_0 \rangle \in E$ and E is a stable extension of $AF_{D_r^t}$. γ is p-committed by $\mathcal{I}$ w.r.t. D_r^t iff $\langle S, a_0 \rangle \in E$ and E is a preferred extension of $AF_{D_r^t}$. γ is c-committed by $\mathcal{I}$ w.r.t. D_r^t iff $\langle S, a_0 \rangle \in E$ and E is a complete extension of $AF_{D_r^t}$. γ is g-committed by $\mathcal{I}$ w.r.t. D_r^t iff $\langle S, a_0 \rangle \in E$ and E is the grounded extension of $AF_{D_r^t}$. γ is i-committed by $\mathcal{I}$ w.r.t. D_r^t iff $\langle S, a_0 \rangle \in E$ and E is the maximal (w.r.t. set inclusion) ideal extension of $AF_{D_r^t}$. γ is ss-committed by $\mathcal{I}$ w.r.t. D_r^t iff $\langle S, a_0 \rangle \in E$ and E is a semi-stable*

---

[5] Due to lack of space, we omit the formal definition of the argumentation semantics. Please find their definitions in [2].

extension of $AF_{D_r^t}$. γ is sg-committed by $\mathcal{I}$ w.r.t. D_r^t iff $\langle S, a_0 \rangle \in E$ and E is a stage extension of $AF_{D_r^t}$.

It is straightforward to observe that by considering the subset relations between argumentation semantics, there are some relations that hold true between the different x-commitments ($x \in \{s, p, c, g, i, ss, sg\}$).

Proposition 1. *Let D_r^t be a well-formed argument inquiry dialogue involving a set of participant $\mathcal{I}$ and γ be an agreement rule. If γ is g-committed by $\mathcal{I}$ w.r.t. D_r^t then γ is $\{p,c\}$-committed by $\mathcal{I}$ w.r.t. D_r^t. If γ is s-committed by $\mathcal{I}$ w.r.t. D_r^t then γ is $\{ss,p,c,sg\}$-committed by $\mathcal{I}$ w.r.t. D_r^t. If γ is i-committed by $\mathcal{I}$ w.r.t. D_r^t then γ is $\{g,p,c\}$-committed by $\mathcal{I}$ w.r.t. D_r^t. If γ is ss-committed by $\mathcal{I}$ w.r.t. D_r^t then γ is $\{p,c\}$-committed by $\mathcal{I}$ w.r.t. D_r^t. If γ is p-committed by $\mathcal{I}$ w.r.t. D_r^t then γ is c-committed by $\mathcal{I}$ w.r.t. D_r^t.*

We observe that deciding whether an agreement rule is g-committed is decidable in polynomial time.

Proposition 2. *Let γ be an agreement rule, $\mathcal{I}$ be a set of agents and D_r^t be an argument inquiry dialogue. Deciding whether γ is g-committed agreement rule by $\mathcal{I}$ w.r.t. D_r^t is decidable in polynomial time.*

So far, we have introduced dialogues for committing agreement rules; however, it can be the case that a given agent knows a particular agreement atoms a_0 and wants to commit this given agreement atom. Hence, the agent needs to identify an agreement rule γ which has a_0 as its head atom and to validate weather γ is x-committed or not. To this end, we introduce *warrant inquiry dialogues*. Warrant inquiry dialogues will be introduced by a simple protocol. Like argument inquiry dialogues, we identify each agent from $\mathcal{I}$ by a natural number this means that $\mathcal{I} = 1, \ldots, n$ such that $i = \langle \Sigma^i, AR^i, CS^i \rangle$. Hence, a warrant inquiry dialogue works as follows:

Step	Warrant Inquiry Dialogue
1	One of the participant agents starts the warrant inquiry dialogue with the move $\langle x, open, dialogue(wi, a_0) \rangle$.
2	Each participant agent i performs one of the following moves:

    1. $\langle i, open, dialogue(ai, a_0 \leftarrow \mathcal{B}^+, not\ \mathcal{B}^-) \rangle$ if $\alpha : a_0 \leftarrow \mathcal{B}^+, not\ \mathcal{B}^- \in AR^i$ and there is no previous open move in the dialogue with $a_0 \leftarrow \mathcal{B}^+, not\ \mathcal{B}^-$ as its topic.
    2. $\langle i, close, dialogue(wi, a_0) \rangle$ if the agent i is unable to perform the previous step.

Let us observe that a warrant inquiry dialogue basically allow the participant to suggest agreement rules which could infer the topic of the warrant inquiry dialogue. Hence, the outcome will be, like argument inquiry dialogues, a set of arguments and the commitment of the topic will depend on this set of arguments.

Definition 10. *Let D_r^t be a well-formed warrant inquiry dialogue involving a set of participant $\mathcal{I}$ and $m_r = \langle x, open, dialogue(wi, \gamma) \rangle$ such that $x \in \mathcal{I}$ and $\gamma = a_0$ is an agreement atom. $Outcome_{ai}(D_r^t) = \mathcal{A}_\Sigma$ such that $\Sigma = \bigcup_{i \in \mathcal{I}} CS^i \cup AR_{D_r^t}$.*

Since both warrant and argument inquiry dialogues induce an argumentation framework $AF_{D_r^T}$, let us abuse of Definition 9 and say that: given a well-formed warrant inquiry dialogue D_r^t and $x \in \{s, p, c, g, i, ss, sg\}$, a_0 is x-committed by $\mathcal{I}$ w.r.t. D_r^t iff $\delta = a_0 \leftarrow \mathcal{B}^+$, not $\mathcal{B}^- \in AR_{D_r^T}$ and δ is x-committed by $\mathcal{I}$ w.r.t. D_r^t. Due to lack of space, a whole example of the dialogues process is not presented.

4   Conclusions and future work

In the state of the art of formal argumentation dialogues, we can find different approaches for setting up different kinds of dialogues [1,3,6,8,10]. Since these approaches have been defined as general frameworks, they do not offer guidelines for splitting the knowledge base of each agent in order to identify the knowledge which is particularly managed at the level of dialogues. In this sense, we argue for identifying a particular vocabulary for capturing agreements. In our suggested approach, this particular vocabulary is materialized by the *agreement atoms*. We point out that all the commitments of our dialogues are expressed in terms of these agreement atoms (which also give place to agreement rules).

From the practical point of view, by identifying sets of agreement atoms (and their respective agreement rules), the design of dialogues in real application domains is guided by these agreement atoms and agreement rules.

From the technical point of view, the consideration of logic programs and logic programming semantics such as WFS has allowed us to have an efficient construction of arguments. Currently we are using implementations of WFS as the one suggested by XSB. However, our argumentation approach can take advantage of new approaches for inferring WFS in a setting of Big Data [11] in order to have a really faster argumentation builder. Moreover, since it is known that the grounded semantics is characterized by WFS [5], the implementation of a g-committed agreement solver can be implemented in a very efficient way. As we have observed, deciding whether an agreement rule is g-committed is decidable in polynomial time (Proposition 2). Part of our future work is to explore the characterization of WFS suggested by [11] in our argumentation setting.

References

1. Amgoud, L., Prade, H.: Reaching agreement through argumentation: a possibilistic approach. In: Principles of Knowledge Representation and Reasoning: Proceedings of the Ninth International Conference (KR2004), Whistler, Canada, 2–5 June 2004, pp. 175–182. AAAI Press (2004)
2. Baroni, P., Caminada, M., Giacomin, M.: An introduction to argumentation semantics. Knowl. Eng. Rev. **26**(4), 365–410 (2011)
3. Black, E., Hunter, A.: An inquiry dialogue system. Auton. Agents Multi-Agent Syst. **19**(2), 173–209 (2009)
4. Bondarenko, A., Dung, P.M., Kowalski, R.A., Toni, F.: An abstract, argumentation-theoretic approach to default reasoning. Artif. Intell. **93**, 63–101 (1997)
5. Dung, P.M.: On the acceptability of arguments and its fundamental role in non-monotonic reasoning, logic programming and n-person games. Artif. Intell. **77**(2), 321–358 (1995)

6. Fan, X., Toni, F.: A general framework for sound assumption-based argumentation dialogues. Artif. Intell. **216**, 20–54 (2014)
7. Gelder, A.V., Ross, K.A., Schlipf, J.S.: The well-founded semantics for general logic programs. J. ACM **38**(3), 620–650 (1991)
8. Kraus, S., Sycara, K.P., Evenchik, A.: Reaching agreements through argumentation: a logical model and implementation. Artif. Intell. **104**(1–2), 1–69 (1998)
9. Nieves, J.C., Guerrero, E., Baskar, J., Lindgren, H.: Deliberative argumentation for smart environments. In: Dam, H.K., Pitt, J., Xu, Y., Governatori, G., Ito, T. (eds.) PRIMA 2014. LNCS (LNAI), vol. 8861, pp. 141–149. Springer, Heidelberg (2014)
10. Prakken, H.: Formal systems for persuasion dialogue. Knowl. Eng. Rev. **21**(2), 163–188 (2006)
11. Tachmazidis, I., Antoniou, G., Faber, W.: Efficient computation of the well-founded semantics over big data. TPLP **14**(4–5), 445–459 (2014)

Priority-Based Merging Operator Without Distance Measures

Henrique Viana[✉] and João Alcântara

Departamento de Computação, Universidade Federal do Ceará,
P.O.Box 12166, Fortaleza, Ceará 60455-760, Brazil
{henriqueviana,jnando}@lia.ufc.br

Abstract. This paper proposes a refinement of the PS-Merge merging operator, which is an alternative merging approach that employs the notion of partial satisfiability rather than the usual distance measures. Our approach will add to PS-Merge a mechanism to deal with a kind of priority based on the quantity of information of the agents. We will refer to the new operator as Pr-Merge. We will also analyze its logical properties as well its complexity by conceiving an algorithm with a distinct strategy from that presented for PS-Merge.

1 Introduction

Information fusion or *merging* consists in techniques of how to merge or combine information provided by multiple sources, taking into account possible inconsistencies and letting the result as reliable as possible. Different kinds of information may be merged: knowledge, belief, preference, rule, etc.; each one with its own specificity and intuition [8].

Most of the works introduced in the literature focus especially on belief and preference merging [1,3,8,13]. Belief (preference) merging is concerned with the process of combining the information contained in a set of belief (preference) bases obtained from different sources to produce a single consistent belief (preference) base. It is an important issue in Artificial Intelligence and Databases, and its applications are many and diverse [2].

There is a slight difference between the approaches of belief and preference merging. Beliefs are information held by human or artificial agents about the world. Preferences represent human or artificial agents' goals, desires and plans about the world. They both can be false, uncertain, exhibit an elementary nature, susceptible to changes or involve a complex logical structure. Syntactically, they can be represented in the same way, but semantically, it is needed to consider their own characteristics, inherited by the nature of its information.

Under this assumption, several merging operators have been defined and characterized in a logical way. Among them, model-based merging operators [13] obtain a belief/preference base from a set of interpretations with the help of a

---

This research is supported by CNPq (Universal 2012 - Proc. n° 473110/2012-1), and CNPq Casadinho/PROCAD Project (n° 552578/2011-8).

N. Bulling (Ed.): EUMAS 2014, LNAI 8953, pp. 398–413, 2015.
DOI: 10.1007/978-3-319-17130-2_28

distance measure on interpretations and an aggregation function. Other merging operators, syntax-based (or formula-based) ones [13], are based on the selection of some consistent subsets of the set-theoretic union of the belief/preference bases.

The major problem with distance-based merging operators is that evaluating the closeness between interpretations as a number may lead to lose too much information [7]. For example, the widely used Hamming distance [4] (also known as Dalal distance) assumes not only that propositional symbols are equally relevant to determining a distance between interpretations, but also that they are independent from each other and that nothing else is relevant to the determination of the distance between interpretations. These assumptions are restrictive and give the Hamming distance very little flexibility [14].

To overcome this issue, some characterizations of model-based merging operators were achieved by modifying the distance measure [6,7,10,14]. In addition, merging operators without distance measures were also conceived. An alternative method of merging was proposed in [16–18], which uses the notion of Partial Satisfiability instead of a distance measure, to define PS-Merge, a model-based merging operator which depends on the syntax of the belief bases [15].

In this paper, we will consider mainly the problem of preference merging without distance measures, by refining the definition of PS-Merge (which is characterized originally considering belief merging) through the weighting of the information in the preference bases. We will name our approach of Pr-Merge. Intuitively, we are concerned in representing priority information among the agents, that will be provided according of how the preference bases are organized.

The paper is organized as follows: in Sect. 2, we will introduce the Pr-Merge. In Sect. 3, we will discuss about its logical properties. In Sect. 4, we will exhibit its computational complexity results. Finally, in Sect. 5 we will conclude the paper.

2   Priority-Based Merging Operator

In this section we introduce the priority-based merging operator Pr-Merge. Basically, the idea of priority consists in ranking the importance of each outcome, based on the preferences of each agent. In our work, we will measure the importance of an outcome by considering the number of propositions' appearance in the agents' goal bases.

Example 1. The application of this merging is relevant in the following scenario: suppose that three friends are going to share a meal in a restaurant, which is constituted of a main dish and a drink. One person is very restrictive with relation to his/her preferences, e.g., he/she prefers vegetarian food, while the others two have more choices to make than the first one, since they are non-vegetarian and there is a greater diversity of choices to make for both, and these possible options are considered equally satisfactory for them. Since the choices are more restricted and objective for the first person, it is natural that we need to give more priority to his/her desires, but without forgetting completely the desires of the other two people.

The merging operator introduced in this section will consider this aspect: it will give more importance and priority to the agents which express their preferences in a simplified, objective or restricted way. On the other hand, it is extremely plausible to think in a context where we should give more priority to the agents that express more preferences (this kind of view can be achieved later by changing a definition in the merging operator). The details about this approach will be explained during this section.

In the following lines, we will present some preliminary notions and the definition of the Pr-Merge. As said previously, we considered the definitions and intuitions of PS-Merge to define our approach. More details about PS-Merge can be found in [16–18].

First, we will consider a propositional language $\mathcal{L}$ defined from a finite set of propositional variables $\mathcal{P}$ and the usual connectives $\neg, \wedge$ and $\vee$. A literal is a propositional variable from $\mathcal{P}$ or its negation.

Definition 1. *A profile $E = \{K_1, \ldots, K_n\}$ represents sets of goal bases K_i, for $1 \leq i \leq n$. For a goal base $K_i = \{c_1, \ldots, c_m\}$, each c_j, where $1 \leq j \leq m$, denotes the set of preferences of the agent i.*

A goal base K_i is a finite and consistent set of propositional formulas. In this work, we restrict each goal base K_i to a DNF (Disjunctive Normal Form) formula, i.e., it can be viewed as $K_i = (c_1 \vee \cdots \vee c_m)$ and $c_l = (x_1 \wedge \cdots \wedge x_k)$, where $x_1, \ldots, x_k$ are literals. We chose the DNF format in order to represent the agents' preferences/choices of a simplified way.

Example 2 (Borrowed from [19]). Let us consider the academic example of a teacher who asks his three students which among the following languages SQL (denoted by s), O_2 (denoted by o) and *Datalog* (denoted by d) they would like to learn. The first student wants to only learn SQL or O_2, that is, $K_1 = (s \vee o) \wedge \neg d$. The second wants to learn either *Datalog* or O_2 but not both, i.e., $K_2 = (\neg s \wedge d \wedge \neg o) \vee (\neg s \wedge \neg d \wedge o)$. For the last, the third one wants to learn the three languages: $K_3 = (s \wedge d \wedge o)$.

First of all, we need to convert these preferences to the DNF format. We shall have $K_1 = (s \wedge \neg d) \vee (o \wedge \neg d)$, and consequently, $K_1 = \{c_1, c_2\}$, where $c_1 = (s \wedge \neg d)$ and $c_2 = (o \wedge \neg d)$. For the goal bases K_2 and K_3, we shall have $K_2 = \{c_3, c_4\}$ and $K_3 = \{c_5\}$, where $c_3 = (\neg s \wedge d \wedge \neg o)$, $c_4 = (\neg s \wedge \neg d \wedge o)$ and $c_5 = (s \wedge d \wedge o)$. We can view in this example that the third agent has only one preferable choice $(s \wedge d \wedge o)$, while the first and second ones have both two preferable choices (for K_1, it is $(s \wedge \neg d)$ or $(o \wedge \neg d)$, and for K_2, it is $(\neg s \wedge d \wedge \neg o)$ or $(\neg s \wedge \neg d \wedge o)$). We can say that K_3 is more certain/restricted about his/her choices.

Definition 2. *An outcome or interpretation is a function $\omega : \mathcal{P} \to \{0, 1\}$. The values 0 and 1 are identified with the classical truth values false and true, respectively.*

For instance, when $\omega(s) = 1$, we say that the interpretation of the propositional variable s is true, whereas when $\omega(s) = 0$, we say that its interpretation is false. We have that $\omega(s) = 1 \Leftrightarrow \omega(\neg s) = 0$.

Example 3. With respect to the previous example, we have three propositional variables: s, d and o. The set of all possible outcomes/interpretations is $\Omega = \{\omega_1, \ldots, \omega_8\}$, where: $\omega_1 = \neg s \neg d \neg o$, $\omega_2 = \neg s \neg d o$, $\omega_3 = \neg s d \neg o$, $\omega_4 = \neg s d o$, $\omega_5 = s \neg d \neg o$, $\omega_6 = s \neg d o$, $\omega_7 = s d \neg o$ and $\omega_8 = s d o$.

Slightly abusing the notation, the interpretation $\omega_1 = \neg s \neg d \neg o$ may be viewed as $\omega_1(\neg s) = 1, \omega_1(\neg d) = 1$ and $\omega_1(\neg o) = 1$.

Before proceeding with the rest of the definitions, let us make a little detour in the subject. As said previously, several merging operators have been defined and characterized in a logical way. Among them, model-based merging operators [13] obtain a belief/preference base from a set of interpretations with the help of a distance measure on interpretations and an aggregation function. Formally, a distance measure between an interpretation and a goal base is defined as $d(\omega, K) = \min_{\omega' \models K} d(\omega, \omega')$, where $d(\omega, \omega')$ is the distance between interpretations. In the first works on model-based merging, the distance used was the Hamming distance between interpretations [4], but any other distance may be used as well.

To be considered a distance measure, a function needs to satisfy the following conditions:

Definition 3 (Distance). *A distance measure between interpretations is a total function d from $\Omega \times \Omega$ to $\mathbb{N}$ such that for every $\omega_1, \omega_2 \in \Omega$,*

– $d(\omega_1, \omega_2) = d(\omega_2, \omega_1)$, *and*
– $d(\omega_1, \omega_2) = 0$ *if and only if* $\omega_1 = \omega_2$.

The Hamming distance between interpretations characterizes the number of propositional variables that they differ. For example, the Hamming distance (denoted d_H) between $\omega_1 = \neg s \neg d \neg o$ and $\omega_6 = s \neg d o$ is $d_H(\omega_1, \omega_6) = 2$ (i.e., they differ in two propositional variables).

Basically, the distance gives the closeness between an interpretation and each formula of a goal base. However, this measure between interpretations may lead to lose information and not to discriminate them [6,7]. In order to try to avoid this problem, merging operators without distance measures were conceived. An alternative method of merging was proposed in [16–18], which uses the notion of Partial Satisfiability instead of a distance measure. In this work, we will exploit the notion of Partial Satisfiability for the purpose of describing the priority preferences.

We can now begin with the notion of preference priority. In order to do this, we will work in two levels: the partial satisfiability of a specific agent (to each $K_i \in E$) and the preference priorities of a group of agents E (based on the partial satisfiability of each agent). These definitions are inspired in the work of the PS-Merge operator [16–18].

Definition 4 (Partial Satisfiability). *Let $K = \{c_1, \ldots, c_m\}$ be a goal base. The partial satisfiability of the interpretation ω w.r.t. K is given by:*

$$\omega(K) = max\{\omega(c_1), \ldots, \omega(c_m)\},$$

where for each $c_i = (x_1 \wedge \cdots \wedge x_k)$, $1 \leq i \leq k$:

$$\omega(c_i) = \sum_{l=1}^{k} \left\{ \frac{\omega(x_l)}{k} \right\}.$$

The partial satisfiability of an interpretation in a clause indicates the rate of the occurrences of its literals in the DNF formula. The higher an interpretation appears in a clause the higher will be its partial satisfiability. We assume that each literal in a clause must have the same weight in the evaluation, i.e., no propositional variable has priority over another one. For example, in the clause $(s \wedge d \wedge o)$ of K_3, the propositions s, d and o have the same weight of $\frac{1}{3}$, since the sum of the weights of propositional variables needs to be equal to 1; and in the clause $(s \wedge \neg d)$ of K_1, the propositions s and $\neg d$ have the same weight of $\frac{1}{2}$.

Example 4. From the *Example 2*, we have $K_1 = \{(s \wedge \neg d), (o \wedge \neg d)\}$, $K_2 = \{(\neg s \wedge d \wedge \neg o), (\neg s \wedge \neg d \wedge o)\}$ and $K_3 = \{(s \wedge d \wedge o)\}$. The partial satisfiability of each interpretation w.r.t. K_1, K_2 and K_3 is computed as:

Ω	$\omega(K_1)$	$\omega(K_2)$	$\omega(K_3)$
$\omega_1 = \neg s \neg d \neg o$	1/2	2/3	0
$\omega_2 = \neg s \neg d o$	1	1	1/3
$\omega_3 = \neg s d \neg o$	0	1	1/3
$\omega_4 = \neg s d o$	1/2	2/3	2/3
$\omega_5 = s \neg d \neg o$	1	1/3	1/3
$\omega_6 = s \neg d o$	1	2/3	2/3
$\omega_7 = s d \neg o$	1/2	2/3	2/3
$\omega_8 = s d o$	1/2	1/3	1

To define the preference priority in our framework, we will assume that each clause of a goal base shares the same weight in the preference evaluation. For example, the formula $(s \wedge d \wedge o)$ of the goal base K_3 will have a priority weight 1 (because there is only one clause in the goal base), while the clauses $(s \wedge \neg d)$ and $(o \wedge \neg d)$ of the goal base K_1 will have both the priority weight $\frac{1}{2}$ (the sum of weights needs to be equal to 1). Formally, we will define this idea in two different ways.

Definition 5 (Preference Priority (Sum)). *Let* $E = \{K_1, \ldots, K_n\}$ *be a profile and* ω *an interpretation. The priority of* ω *w.r.t.* E *is given by:*

$$\omega_+(E) = \sum_{i=1}^{n} \frac{1}{a_i} \times \omega(K_i),$$

where a_i *is the number of clauses in the goal base* K_i.

This step reflects the preference priority of the group of agents, which will be a prioritized sum of the partial satisfiability of each individual goal base of the group. Intuitively, The higher is the number of choices made by an agent, the lower will be his/her preference priority among the group of agents. Another characterization of the preference priority can be defined as:

Definition 6 (Preference Priority (Product)). *Let $E = \{K_1, \ldots, K_n\}$ be a profile and ω an interpretation. The priority of ω w.r.t. E is given by:*

$$\omega_\times(E) = \prod_{i=1}^{n} (\omega(K_i))^{\frac{1}{a_i}},$$

where a_i is the number of clauses in the goal base K_i.

Example 5. Finally, considering the sum operation, the preference priority of the profile $E = \{K_1, K_2, K_3\}$ is:

Ω	$\omega_+(E)$
$\omega_1 = \neg s \neg d \neg o$	$1/4 + 1/3 + 0 = 7/12 \simeq \mathbf{0.583}$
$\omega_2 = \neg s \neg do$	$1/2 + 1/2 + 1/3 = 4/3 \simeq \mathbf{1.333}$
$\omega_3 = \neg sd \neg o$	$0 + 1/2 + 1/3 = 5/6 \simeq \mathbf{0.833}$
$\omega_4 = \neg sdo$	$1/4 + 1/3 + 2/3 = 5/4 = \mathbf{1.25}$
$\omega_5 = s \neg d \neg o$	$1/2 + 1/6 + 1/3 = 6/6 = \mathbf{1}$
$\omega_6 = s \neg do$	$1/2 + 1/3 + 2/3 = 3/2 = \mathbf{1.5}$
$\omega_7 = sd \neg o$	$1/4 + 1/3 + 2/3 = 5/4 = \mathbf{1.25}$
$\omega_8 = sdo$	$1/4 + 1/6 + 1 = 17/12 \simeq \mathbf{1.416}$

By considering the product, the preference priority of the profile E is:

Ω	$\omega_\times(E)$
$\omega_1 = \neg s \neg d \neg o$	$0.707 \times 0.816 \times 0 = \mathbf{0}$
$\omega_2 = \neg s \neg do$	$1 \times 1 \times 0.333 \simeq \mathbf{0.333}$
$\omega_3 = \neg sd \neg o$	$0 \times 1 \times 0.333 = \mathbf{0}$
$\omega_4 = \neg sdo$	$0,707 \times 0.816 \times 0.666 \simeq \mathbf{0.384}$
$\omega_5 = s \neg d \neg o$	$1 \times 0.577 \times 0.333 \simeq \mathbf{0.192}$
$\omega_6 = s \neg do$	$1 \times 0.816 \times 0.666 \simeq \mathbf{0.544}$
$\omega_7 = sd \neg o$	$0,707 \times 0.816 \times 0.666 \simeq \mathbf{0.384}$
$\omega_8 = sdo$	$0,707 \times 0.577 \times 1 \simeq \mathbf{0.407}$

For the sake of information, if we consider in giving more priority to the agents that are expressing more choices, we must make a little change in the definitions above. In this case, we shall have $\omega_+(E) = \sum_{i=1}^{n} a_i \times \omega(K_i)$ and

$\omega_\times(E) = \prod_{i=1}^{n}(\omega(K_i))^{a_i}$, we will follow the examples using the former definitions, but we want to highlight that, although these two approaches express different ideas, they share similar properties (the logical properties of the merging operator will be explored in the next section).

After compute the preference priorities, we can rank the interpretations and decide which one is the best option for the group.

Definition 7. *The binary relations $\leq_E^{pr,+}$ and $\leq_E^{pr,\times}$ are defined as*

$$\omega \leq_E^{pr,+} \omega' \text{ if and only if } \omega_+(E) \leq \omega'_+(E) \text{ and}$$
$$\omega \leq_E^{pr,\times} \omega' \text{ if and only if } \omega_\times(E) \leq \omega'_\times(E)$$

Here, an outcome ω' is preferred to ω if the preference priority of ω' is greater or equal to the priority of ω.

Example 6. After computing the preference priority of the group of agents we can rank the interpretations as:

$$\omega_1 \leq_E^{pr,+} \omega_3 \leq_E^{pr,+} \omega_5 \leq_E^{pr,+} \{\omega_4, \omega_7\} \leq_E^{pr,+} \omega_2 \leq_E^{pr,+} \omega_8 \leq_E^{pr,+} \omega_6 \text{ and}$$
$$\{\omega_1, \omega_3\} \leq_E^{pr,\times} \omega_5 \leq_E^{pr,\times} \omega_2 \leq_E^{pr,\times} \{\omega_4, \omega_7\} \leq_E^{pr,\times} \omega_8 \leq_E^{pr,\times} \omega_6.$$

The best outcome in this example is the interpretation ω_6. Comparing our approach (with the sum operation) to the one presented by the PS-Merge (which is defined with the help of the sum), we will have:

Ω	Pr-Merge $\omega_+(E)$	PS-Merge $\omega(E)$
$\omega_1 = \neg s \neg d \neg o$	0.583	1.16
$\omega_2 = \neg s \neg d o$	1.333	**2.33**
$\omega_3 = \neg s d \neg o$	0.833	1.5
$\omega_4 = \neg s d o$	1.25	1.83
$\omega_5 = s \neg d \neg o$	1	1.67
$\omega_6 = s \neg d o$	**1.5**	**2.33**
$\omega_7 = s d \neg o$	1.25	1.83
$\omega_8 = s d o$	1.416	1.83

Note that, in general, the preferences between the outcomes are very similar. The difference appears in the results of the outcomes ω_2 and ω_8. The goal base $K_3 = (s \wedge d \wedge o)$ have a preference priority greater than the other bases, which will influence in the result of ω_8 (an interpretation that satisfies K_3), increasing its final result, whereas it will decrease the result of the outcome ω_2, because it is not a good outcome to K_3 (ω_2 satisfies only one propositional variable of K_3). We can define this process as a merging operator in the following model-theoretical way:

Definition 8 (Pr-Merge). *Let $E = \{K_1, \ldots, K_n\}$ be a profile and μ an integrity constraint, the merging operator $\Delta_\mu^{pr,op}(E)$ is defined as:*

$$Mod(\Delta_\mu^{pr,op}(E)) = max(Mod(\mu), \leq_E^{pr,op}),$$

where $op \in \{+, \times\}$ and $max(Mod(\mu), \leq_E^{pr,op})$ is the set of interpretations that satisfy μ and are the maximal with respect to the relation $\leq_E^{pr,op}$.

An integrity constraint μ is a formula that the result of the merging process has to obey, i.e., they cannot be inconsistent. When we do not consider an integrity constraint in the process, we assume that $\mu = \top$.

Example 7. The merging operator $\Delta_\mu^{pr,op}(E)$ for the previous example, when $\mu = \top$ and $op \in \{+, \times\}$, shall result in:

$$Mod(\Delta_\mu^{pr,op}(E)) = \omega_6 = (s \wedge \neg d \wedge o).$$

If we restrict the result of merging, considering that only one programming language will be taught, i.e., $\mu_1 = (s \wedge \neg d \wedge \neg o) \vee (\neg s \wedge d \wedge \neg o) \vee (\neg s \wedge \neg d \wedge o)$, the result is:

$$Mod(\Delta_{\mu_1}^{pr,op}(E)) = \omega_2 = (\neg s \wedge \neg d \wedge o).$$

To conclude this section, we want to emphasize our choice with respect to the partial satisfiability approach. The approach introduced in this paper is not restricted only to PS-Merge, i.e., it can be used with distance-based merging operators too. Indeed, the distance-based merging with priorities may be viewed as a particular case of the weighted sum aggregation function [9].

Formally, it can be defined in the following way: as said previously, the distance measure between an interpretation and a goal base is defined as $d(\omega, K) = \min_{\omega' \models K} d(\omega, \omega')$, where $d(\omega, \omega')$ is the distance between interpretations. Using the *sum* as an aggregation function we define the distance measure between an interpretation and a profile $E = \{K_1, \ldots, K_n\}$ as $d(\omega, E) = \sum_{i=1}^{n} \{d(\omega, K_i)\}$. When the weighted *sum* is considered as the aggregation function we have $d(\omega, E) = \sum_{i=1}^{n} a_i \times d(\omega, K_i)$, where a_i is the number of clauses in the goal base K_i in our work. Consequently, the merging operator $\Delta_\mu^{d,op}(E)$, where $op \in \{sum, wsum\}$, is defined as $Mod(\Delta_\mu^{d,op}(E)) = min(Mod(\mu), \leq_E^{d,op})$. The comparison between distance-based and partial satisfiability merging is showed below (when $d = d_H$):

Ω		$\Delta_\mu^{d_H,sum}$	$\Delta_\mu^{ps,+}$	$\Delta_\mu^{d_H,wsum}$	$\Delta_\mu^{pr,+}$
$\omega_1 = \neg s \neg d \neg o$	5		1.16	4	0.583
$\omega_2 = \neg s \neg do$	2		**2.33**	2	1.333
$\omega_3 = \neg sd \neg o$	4		1.33	3	0.833
$\omega_4 = \neg sdo$	3		1.83	2	1.25
$\omega_5 = s \neg d \neg o$	4		1.66	3	1
$\omega_6 = s \neg do$	2		**2.33**	1.5	**1.5**
$\omega_7 = sd \neg o$	3		1.83	2	1.25
$\omega_8 = sdo$	3		1.83	**1.5**	1.416

In short, we can see that a partial satisfiability-based merging is richer than a distance-based merging, since it gives us a more detailed evaluation of the interpretations. Another important point that we want to highlight is that the partial satisfiability allows us to employ the product as an aggregation function, which is not possible when a distance is considered.

3   Logical Properties

A main requirement for adhering to a merging operator is that it offers the expected properties of what intuitively merging means. This calls for sets of rationality postulates and this has been addressed in several papers [5–7,10,11]. The more postulates satisfied the more rational the operator. We will look in the sequence the characterization of Integrity Constraints (IC) merging operators.

Definition 9 (IC Merging Operators [11]). *Let E, E_1, E_2 be profiles, K_1, K_2 be consistent goal bases, and μ, μ_1, μ_2 be propositional formulas. Δ is an IC merging operator if and only if it satisfies the following postulates:*

- **(IC0)** $\Delta_\mu(E) \models \mu$.
- **(IC1)** If μ is consistent, then $\Delta_\mu(E)$ is consistent.
- **(IC2)** If $\bigwedge E$ is consistent with μ, then $\Delta_\mu(E) \equiv \bigwedge E \wedge \mu$.
- **(IC3)** If $E_1 \equiv E_2$ and $\mu_1 \equiv \mu_2$, then $\Delta_{\mu_1}(E_1) \equiv \Delta_{\mu_2}(E_2)$.
- **(IC4)** If $K_1 \models \mu$ and $K_2 \models \mu$, then $\Delta_\mu(\{K_1, K_2\}) \wedge K_1$ is consistent if and only if $\Delta_\mu(\{K_1, K_2\}) \wedge K_2$ is consistent.
- **(IC5)** $\Delta_\mu(E_1) \wedge \Delta_\mu(E_2) \models \Delta_\mu(E_1 \sqcup E_2)$.
- **(IC6)** If $\Delta_\mu(E_1) \wedge \Delta_\mu(E_2)$ is consistent, then $\Delta_\mu(E_1 \sqcup E_2) \models \Delta_\mu(E_1) \wedge \Delta_\mu(E_2)$.
- **(IC7)** $\Delta_{\mu_1}(E) \wedge \mu_2 \models \Delta_{\mu_1 \wedge \mu_2}(E)$.
- **(IC8)** If $\Delta_{\mu_1}(E) \wedge \mu_2$ is consistent, then $\Delta_{\mu_1 \wedge \mu_2}(E) \models \Delta_{\mu_1}(E)$.

The meaning of the properties is the following: **(IC0)** ensures that the result of merging satisfies the integrity constraint. **(IC1)** states that, if the integrity constraint is consistent, then the result of merging will be consistent. **(IC2)** states that if there is no inconsistencies among the goal bases, the result of merging is simply the conjunction of the goal bases with the integrity constraint. **(IC3)** is the principle of irrelevance of syntax: the result of merging has to depend only on the expressed opinions and not on their syntactical presentation. **(IC4)** is a fairness postulate meaning that the result of merging of two goal bases should not give preference to one of them. It is a condition that aims at ruling out operators that can give priority to one of the bases. **(IC5)** expresses the following idea: if profiles are viewed as expressing the beliefs/preferences of the members of a group, then if E_1 (corresponding to a first group) compromises on a set of alternatives which A belongs to, and E_2 (corresponding to a second group) compromises on another set of alternatives which contains A too, then A has to be in the chosen alternatives if we join the two groups. **(IC5)** and **(IC6)** together state that if one could find two subgroups which agree on at least one alternative, then the result of the global merging will be exactly those alternatives the two groups agree on. **(IC7)** and **(IC8)** state that the notion of closeness is well-behaved, i.e., that an alternative that is preferred among the possible alternatives will remain preferred if one restricts the possible choices.

Proposition 1. $\Delta_\mu^{pr,op}$ *satisfies (IC0)–(IC3) and (IC5)–(IC8).*

Proof. **(IC0)** By definition, $Mod(\Delta_\mu^{pr,op}(E)) \subseteq Mod(\mu)$.

(IC1) The functions $\omega_+(E)$ and $\omega_\times(E)$ map to values in $\mathbb{R}$, so if $Mod(\mu) \neq \emptyset$, there is a model ω of μ such that for every model ω' of μ, $\omega_+(E) \geq \omega'_+(E)$ (or $\omega_\times(E) \geq \omega'_\times(E)$). So $\omega \models \Delta_\mu^{pr,op}(E)$ and $\Delta_\mu^{pr,op}(E) \not\models \bot$.

(IC2) By assumption, $\bigwedge E$ is consistent and without loss of generality let $E = \{K_1, \ldots, K_n\}$. There exists ω such that $\omega \models (c_{11} \vee \cdots \vee c_{1k}) \wedge \cdots \wedge (c_{n1} \vee \cdots \vee c_{nm})$, where $K_1 = \{c_{11}, \ldots, c_{1k}\}, \ldots, K_n = \{c_{n1}, \ldots, c_{nm}\}$. By definition, $\omega(K_1) = max\{\omega(c_{11}), \ldots, \omega(c_{1n})\}$ and as $\omega \models (c_{11} \vee \cdots \vee c_{1n})$, there is a clause c_{1j} such that $\omega \models c_{1j}$. It is easy to see that this clause has the maximum value, i.e. $\omega(c_{ij}) = 1$ (see the Definition 4). Thus, $\omega(K_1)$ will also receive the maximum possible value. The same idea holds for every K_i, $1 \leq i \leq n$. Hence, as $\omega_+(E) = \sum_{i=1}^{n} \frac{1}{a_i} \times \omega(K_i)$, for every ω', $\omega_+(E) \geq \omega'_+(E)$ (the same holds for $\omega_\times(E)$). So $\omega \models \Delta_\mu^{pr,op}(E)$ if and only if $\omega \models \bigwedge E \wedge \mu$.

(IC3) Assume that $E_1 \equiv E_2$ and $\mu_1 \equiv \mu_2$, where $E_1 = \{K_1, \ldots, K_n\}$ and $E_2 = \{K'_1, \ldots, K'_n\}$. We want to prove that $\Delta_{\mu_1}^{pr,op}(E_1) \equiv \Delta_{\mu_2}^{pr,op}(E_2)$. For this, it is sufficient to guarantee that $\omega(K_i) \leq \omega'(K_i) \Rightarrow \omega(K'_i) \leq \omega'(K'_i)$, for any ω, ω'. It is possible to show this using the notion of Hamming distance [10]. The Hamming distance between interpretations, denoted as $d_H(\omega, \omega')$, characterizes the number of propositional variables that they differ. The distance between an interpretation and a goal base is defined as: $d(\omega, K_i) = \min_{\omega' \models K_i} d(\omega, \omega')$.

We have that if $\omega(K_i) \leq \omega'(K_i)$ then $d(\omega', K_i) \leq d(\omega, K_i)$ (it is easy to show this by contradiction). By hypothesis, $K_i \equiv K'_i$, and therefore we have $\omega(K_i) \leq \omega'(K_i)$ then $d(\omega', K'_i) \leq d(\omega, K'_i)$. We need to show now that $d(\omega', K'_i) \leq d(\omega, K'_i) \Rightarrow \omega(K'_i) \leq \omega'(K'_i)$. By contradiction, suppose that $d(\omega', K'_i) \leq d(\omega, K'_i)$ and $\omega(K'_i) > \omega'(K'_i)$. In this case we would have $d(\omega', K'_i) > d(\omega, K'_i)$ (by the consequence of $\omega(K'_i) > \omega'(K'_i)$), which is a contradiction.

To end this proof, note that definition of $\omega_+(E) = \sum_{i=1}^{n} \frac{1}{a_i} \times \omega(K_i)$ (and

$\omega_\times(E) = \prod_{i=1}^{n}(\omega(K_i))^{\frac{1}{a_i}})$does not alter the results showed above, i.e., $\omega_+(E_1) \leq$
$\omega'_+(E_1) \Rightarrow \omega_+(E_2) \leq \omega'_+(E_2)$ (resp. $\omega_\times(E_1) \leq \omega'_\times(E_1) \Rightarrow \omega_\times(E_2) \leq \omega'_\times(E_2)$),
due the properties of the sum (resp. product). As $\mu_1 \equiv \mu_2$, finally we have that
$\Delta^{pr,op}_{\mu_1}(E_1) \equiv \Delta^{pr,op}_{\mu_2}(E_2)$.

(IC5) In order to show that the operator satisfy (IC5), it is enough to
guarantee that the following property holds: if $\omega_{op}(E_1) \geq \omega'_{op}(E_1)$ and $\omega_{op}(E_2) \geq$
$\omega'_{op}(E_2)$, then $\omega_{op}(E_1 \sqcup E_2) \geq \omega'_{op}(E_1 \sqcup E_2)$, for $op \in \{+, \times\}$. We can see clearly
that this is satisfied.

(IC6) In order to show that the operator satisfy (IC6), it is enough to
guarantee that the following property holds: if $\omega_{op}(E_1) > \omega'_{op}(E_1)$ and $\omega_{op}(E_2) \geq$
$\omega'_{op}(E_2)$, then $\omega_{op}(E_1 \sqcup E_2) > \omega'_{op}(E_1 \sqcup E_2)$, for $op \in \{+, \times\}$. We can see clearly
that this is satisfied.

(IC7) Suppose that $\omega \models \Delta^{pr,op}_{\mu_1}(E) \wedge \mu_2$. For any $\omega' \models \mu_1$, we have $\omega_{op}(E) \geq$
$\omega'_{op}(E)$. Hence, for any $\omega' \models \mu_1 \wedge \mu_2$, we have $\omega_{op}(E) \geq \omega'_{op}(E)$. Subsequently
$\omega \models \Delta^{pr,op}_{\mu_1 \wedge \mu_2}(E)$.

(IC8) Suppose that $\Delta^{pr,op}_{\mu_1}(E) \wedge \mu_2$ is consistent. Then there exists a model
ω' of $\Delta^{pr,op}_{\mu_1}(E) \wedge \mu_2$. Consider a model ω of $\Delta^{pr,op}_{\mu_1 \wedge \mu_2}(E)$ and suppose that $\omega \not\models$
$\Delta^{pr,op}_{\mu_1}(E)$. In this case $\omega'_{op}(E) > \omega_{op}(E)$, and since $\omega' \models \mu_1 \wedge \mu_2$, we have
$\omega \notin Mod(\Delta^{pr,op}_{\mu_1 \wedge \mu_2}(E)) = max(Mod(\mu_1 \wedge \mu_2), \leq^{pr,op}_E)$, hence $\omega \not\models \Delta^{pr,op}_{\mu_1 \wedge \mu_2}(E)$.
Contradiction.   □

Proposition 2. $\Delta^{pr,op}_{\mu}$ *does not satisfy* **(IC4)**.

Proof. In general, $\Delta^{pr,op}_{\mu}$ does not satisfy (IC4). Let us give a counter-example:
suppose that $\mu = \top$, $K_1 = \{(a \wedge \neg b) \vee (\neg a \wedge b)\}$ and $K_2 = \{(a \wedge b)\}$. The result of
the merging is $\Delta^{pr,op}_{\mu}(\{K_1, K_2\}) = (a \wedge b)$, when $op \in \{+, \times\}$. $\Delta^{pr,op}_{\mu}(\{K_1, K_2\}) \wedge$
K_2 is consistent, but $\Delta^{pr,op}_{\mu}(\{K_1, K_2\}) \wedge K_1$ is not.   □

Since (IC4) is not satisfied, it means that this merging operator tends to give
preference to some specific goal bases. This is not a bad result, since we intended
from the beginning to give more priority to some agents.

The merging operators $\Delta^{pr,+}_{\mu}$ and $\Delta^{pr,\times}_{\mu}$ share the same logical properties so
far, but intuitively, they express different ideas. Two main subclasses of merging
operators are described by analyzing others characteristics: majority operators
which are related to utilitarianism, and arbitration operators which are related to
egalitarianism. In other words, majority operators solve conflicts using majority wishes, i.e., they try to satisfy the group as a whole. Whereas arbitration
operators have a more consensual behavior, trying to satisfy each agent as far
as possible.

Besides these nine postulates presented above, we will also consider these
two important sub-classes of merging operators: IC majority operator and IC
arbitration operator. We will show in the sequel that $\Delta^{pr,+}_{\mu}$ and $\Delta^{pr,\times}_{\mu}$ do not
agree with both postulates.

Definition 10 (IC Majority Operator). *A merging operator is a majority operator if it satisfies*

– **(Maj)** $\exists n \Delta_\mu(E_1 \sqcup \underbrace{E_2 \sqcup \cdots \sqcup E_2}_{n}) \models \Delta_\mu(E_2)$.

This postulate states that if an information has a majority audience, then it will be the choice of the group.

Proposition 3. $\Delta_\mu^{pr,+}$ *satisfies* **(Maj)**.

Proof. Showing that the operator satisfies **(Maj)** is easy from the properties of sum. Since $w_+(E) = \sum_{i=1}^{n} \frac{1}{a_i} \times w(K_i)$, without loss of generality we can assume two cases: (i) let w be a model for $\Delta_\mu^{pr,+}(E_1 \sqcup E_2)$ and for all w', $w_+(E_2) \geq w'_+(E_2)$. In this case, we also have that w is a model for $\Delta_\mu^{pr,+}(E_2)$, and for every n, $\Delta_\mu^{pr,+}(E_1 \sqcup E_2^n) \models \Delta_\mu^{pr,+}(E_2)$; (ii) let w be a model for $\Delta_\mu^{pr,+}(E_1 \sqcup E_2)$ and there is a w' such that $w_+(E_2) < w'_+(E_2)$. In this case we can always find a number n of repetitions to E_2 such that w' will be a model for $\Delta_\mu^{pr,+}(E_1 \sqcup E_2^n)$, i.e., $w'_+(E_2) \times n + w'_+(E_1) > w_+(E_2) \times n + w_+(E_1)$. Consequently, $\Delta_\mu^{pr,+}(E_1 \sqcup E_2^n) \models \Delta_\mu^{pr,+}(E_2)$. □

As a consequence of this postulate, we can state that although it is given more priority to some goal bases in the merging process of $\Delta_\mu^{pr,+}$, it will not be always the case that these goal bases will be satisfied by the results of the merging operator.

Proposition 4. $\Delta_\mu^{pr,\times}$ *does not satisfy* **(Maj)**.

Proof. We can find a counter-example where the repetition of one base does not change the result. Consider the following counter-example: Let $\mu = \top$, $E_1 = \{K_1\} = \{\{a \wedge b\}\}$ and $E_2 = \{K_2\} = \{\{\neg a \wedge \neg b\}\}$. Clearly, we have $\Delta_\mu^{pr,\times}(E_1 \sqcup \underbrace{E_2 \sqcup \cdots \sqcup E_2}_{n}) \neq \Delta_\mu^{pr,\times}(E_2)$ for any $n \in \mathbb{N}$. □

Definition 11 (IC Arbitration Operator). *A merging operator is an arbitration operator if it satisfies*

– **(Arb)**

$$\Delta_{\mu_1}(\{K_1\}) \equiv \Delta_{\mu_2}(\{K_2\})$$
$$\Delta_{\mu_1 \leftrightarrow \neg \mu_2}(\{K_1, K_2\}) \equiv (\mu_1 \leftrightarrow \neg \mu_2) \Rightarrow \Delta_{\mu_1 \vee \mu_2}(\{K_1, K_2\}) \equiv \Delta_{\mu_1}(\{K_1\}).$$
$$\mu_1 \not\models \mu_2$$
$$\mu_2 \not\models \mu_1$$

Unlike the majority operator, an arbitration operator tries to satisfy each agent as possible. According to [12] this postulates ensures that this is the median of possible choices that are preferred.

Proposition 5. $\Delta_\mu^{pr,+}$ *does not satisfy* **(Arb)**.

Proof. To show that $\Delta_\mu^{pr,+}$ does not satisfy **(Arb)**, consider the following counter-example: $K_1 = \{\{a \wedge b\}\}, K_2 = \{\{\neg a \wedge \neg b\}\}, \mu_1 = \neg(a \wedge b)$ and $\mu_2 = a \vee b$. We have that $\Delta_{\mu_1 \vee \mu_2}^{pr,+}(\{K_1, K_2\}) \not\equiv \Delta_{\mu_1}^{pr,+}(\{K_1\})$.   □

We can note that, it may be the case where a goal base has more priority than the other ones, and the result of the merging will only favor it rather than the others.

Proposition 6. $\Delta_\mu^{pr,\times}$ *satisfies* **(Arb)**.

Proof. We can see that **(Arb)** holds since the stronger following property is true: if $\Delta_{\mu_1}^{pr,\times}(K_1) \equiv \Delta_{\mu_2}^{pr,\times}(K_2)$, then $\Delta_{\mu_1 \vee \mu_2}^{pr,\times}(\{K_1, K_2\}) \equiv \Delta_{\mu_1}^{pr,\times}(K_1)$.   □

The weighted product considers relevant the partial satisfiability of each agent to compute the preference priority of the group. It is different from the weighted sum in the sense that every agent is relevant to the final result and this result tries to satisfy the whole group as much as possible. In other terms, we can say that, although the merging gives priority to some specific agents, the product operator tries to consider important the opinion of each agent to the result of the merging.

To finish this section, we remind that regardless the strategy used in the priority merging, the logical properties remain the same, i.e., we can use the same proofs of this section to the case where we give more priority to the agents with more clauses in the goal bases.

4   Computational Complexity

Let us now consider the complexity issue of the merging operator $\Delta_\mu^{pr,op}$. Formally, the decision problem $\text{MERGE}(\Delta_\mu^{pr,op})$ is defined as:

– **Input:** A triple $\langle E, \mu, \alpha \rangle$ where $E = \{K_1, \ldots, K_n\}$ is a profile and μ and α are propositional formulas.
– **Question:** Does $\Delta_\mu^{pr,op}(E) \models \alpha$ hold?

In this section, we will give an alternative algorithm to Pr-Merge, instead of using the one presented for PS-Merge in [16].

Proposition 7. $\text{MERGE}(\Delta_\mu^{pr,op})$ *is PTIME*.

This result is consequence of the following two lemmas:

Lemma 1. *For any* $\omega \in \Omega$ *the number of possible values of* $\omega_{op}(E)$ *is bounded by the value* $h(|E|)$ *(where* h *is a function with values in* $\mathbb{N}$*), which is polynomial.*

Proof. Let $E = \{K_1, \ldots, K_n\}$ be a profile and $|V| = m$ be the number of propositional variables of E. For each $K_i \in E$, the number of possible values that $\omega(K_i)$ may receive is bounded by $m + (m-1) + \cdots + 1 = m.(m+1)/2 = O(m^2)$, i.e., the scenario where K_i has clauses of size $m, m-1, \ldots, 2$ and 1 (if a clause has size m, then the quantity of values that it can obtain is m). Thus, for the profile E, the number of possible values is $O(n.m^2)$.   □

Lemma 2. *Given a profile E and an integrity constraint μ, the problem of determining the $\max_{\omega \models \mu} \omega_{op}(E)$ is PTIME.*

Proof. $\max_{\omega \models \mu} \omega_{op}(E)$ can be computed using binary search on $L = \{0, \ldots, h(|E|)\}$ (the list of possible values for $\omega_{op}(E)$), but first we shall change slightly the representation of L. Assuming that $E = \{K_1, \ldots, K_n\}$, each $l_i \in L$ is represented as $l_i = [l_{i1}, \ldots, l_{in}]$, where l_{ij} denotes a possible value of the base K_j and $l_i = l_{i1} + \cdots + l_{in}$ (when $op = +$) or $l_i = l_{i1} \times \cdots \times l_{in}$ (when $op = \times$). For instance, considering $op = +$, we have that the first element of the list is $0 = [0, 0, \ldots, 0]$, and according to *Example 2*, the last element of the list would be $2 = [\frac{2}{4}, \frac{2}{4}, \frac{3}{3}]$ (the maximum value of ω for $K_1 = \{(s \wedge \neg d), (o \wedge \neg d)\}$ is $\frac{2}{4}$, $K_2 = \{(\neg s \wedge d \wedge \neg o), (\neg s \wedge \neg d \wedge o)\}$ is $\frac{2}{4}$ and $K_3 = \{(s \wedge d \wedge o)\}$ is $\frac{3}{3}$).

Generating the list L can be made in the following way: Consider $E = \{K_1, \ldots, K_n\}$, and $(K_i) = [m, [m_1, \ldots, m_m]]$, where m is the number of clauses of K_i and for $1 \leq j \leq m$, m_j is the number of literals in the j-th clause. With respect to the weighted sum operator, the set of possible values of K_i is $\{0, \frac{1}{m \cdot m_1}, \frac{2}{m \cdot m_1}, \ldots, \frac{m_1}{m \cdot m_1}, \ldots, \frac{1}{m \cdot m_m}, \ldots, \frac{m_m}{m \cdot m_m}\}$. In consideration with the weighted product, the set of possible values of K_i is $\{0, (\frac{1}{m_1})^{\frac{1}{m}}, (\frac{2}{m_1})^{\frac{1}{m}}, \ldots, (\frac{m_1}{m_1})^{\frac{1}{m}}, \ldots, (\frac{1}{m_m})^{\frac{1}{m}}, \ldots, (\frac{m_m}{m_m})^{\frac{1}{m}}\}$. For instance, in the *Example 2*, for $op = +$, the set of possible values of $K_1 = \{(s \wedge \neg d), (o \wedge \neg d)\}$ is $(K_1) = [2, [2, 2]]$ is $\{0, \frac{1}{4}, \frac{2}{4}, \frac{1}{4}, \frac{2}{4}\} = \{0, \frac{1}{4}, \frac{2}{4}\}$.

Let us assume now that L is ordered by the value of the l_i, where $l_i = l_{i1} + \cdots + l_{in}$ or $l_i = l_{i1} \times \cdots \times l_{in}$ (this sorting can be done in polynomial time) and that $E = \{K_1, \ldots, K_n\}$ is also ordered by the number of clauses in the bases (i.e., K_1 is the base with the least number of clauses), in order to simplify the execution of the algorithm.

It is sufficient to consider the following algorithms:

1. The first step is ask whether $\max_{\omega \models \mu} \omega_{op}(E) \geq l$, for a given $l \in L$.

2. For a given $l = [l_1, \ldots, l_n]$, pick K_1 and find the interpretations ω in which $\omega(K_1) = l_1$ and $\omega \models \mu$. As each l_i is a number of the form $(p/q.m)$, an interpretation ω is given by the outcome that satisfies p elements in the clause with q literals. These interpretations can be found in polynomial time, since K_1 is in DNF.

3. For every $K_j \in E$, check if $\omega(K_j) = l_j$, for any ω found in the previous step. If it is true, then $\max_{\omega \models \mu} \omega_{op}(E) \geq l$. This step can be done in polynomial time.

4. To compute $\max_{\omega \models \mu} \omega_{op}(E)$, we can make a binary search on $L = \{0 = [0, \ldots, 0], \ldots, l_k = [l_{k1}, \ldots, l_{kn}]\}$. We start with l_k and ask if $\max_{\omega \models \mu} \omega_{op}(E) \geq l_k$. The $\max_{\omega \models \mu} \omega_{op}(E)$ will be the highest l_i which $\max_{\omega \models \mu} \omega_{op}(E) \geq l_i$ holds. Consequently all ω that satisfies this statement are results from merging. Clearly, we can see that this step is polynomial, since the binary search needs at most $log_2 h(|E|)$ steps and the procedure of $\max_{\omega \models \mu} \omega_{op}(E) \geq l$ is polynomial.

5. Lastly, we only have to check if $\omega \models \alpha$, for any ω found in the previous step. This can be done in linear time.   □

This result shows that Pr-Merge is computationally easier (as well as the PS-Merge) than usual merging operators, which are usually at the first level of the polynomial hierarchy [10]. This is given mainly because the goal bases are represented in DNF formulas and the computation of the preference priority ω can be done in polynomial time.

5 Conclusion

In this work, we described a refined version of the merging operator PS-Merge by introducing the notion of priority information between goal bases. This new operator was named Pr-Merge, which was defined in two versions: one with a weighted sum and another one with a weighted product. The weighted sum has a characteristic of majority priority, whereas the weighted product shows the characteristic of priority combined with some aspects of egalitarianism. We analyzed their logical properties and computational complexity. With respect to the complexity, we exhibited an alternative algorithm from that presented to PS-Merge, which has a polynomial time complexity.

Regarding the logical properties, Pr-Merge satisfies all postulates in general, except **(IC4)**. The loss that we have in using Pr-Merge is that our approach does not satisfy the fairness condition, i.e., our merging approach can give priority to some goal bases, which is an expected result to us. When the weighted sum is considered as the aggregation function, Pr-Merge satisfies **(Maj)**. In other terms, we can say that, even the priority given to some agents, a group of agents can influence the result of the merging. When the weighted product is considered, Pr-Merge satisfies **(Arb)**, i.e., the priority merging tries to satisfy each agent as far as possible.

Following the proposal presented by PS-Merge, this paper focus in researching a merging operator without using distance measures. There is still too much to be done in this area. A possible line of research is to characterize a family of merging operators using the notion of partial satisfiability employed by PS-Merge, through different aggregation functions, and their relationships. Another open question is to discover the relationship between Partial Satisfiability-based and distance-based merging. Lastly, another interesting subject is to find out other alternative ways of doing information merging without using distance measures.

References

1. Arrow, K.J., Sen, A., Suzumura, K.: Handbook of Social Choice & Welfare, vol. 2. Elsevier, New York (2010)
2. Bloch, I., Hunter, A., Appriou, A., Ayoun, A., Benferhat, S., Besnard, P., Cholvy, L., Cooke, R., Cuppens, F., Dubois, D., et al.: Fusion: general concepts and characteristics. Int. J. Intell. Syst. **16**(10), 1107–1134 (2001)

3. Chevaleyre, Y., Endriss, U., Lang, J., Maudet, N.: A short introduction to computational social choice. In: van Leeuwen, J., Italiano, G.F., van der Hoek, W., Meinel, C., Sack, H., Plášil, F. (eds.) SOFSEM 2007. LNCS, vol. 4362, pp. 51–69. Springer, Heidelberg (2007)
4. Dalal, M.: Investigations into a theory of knowledge base revision. In: Proceedings of the Seventh American National Conference on Artificial Intelligence (AAAI 1988), pp. 475–479 (1988)
5. Everaere, P., Konieczny, S., Marquis, P.: Quota and gmin merging operators. In: Proceedings of 19th International Joint Conference on Artificial Intelligence (IJCAI 2005) (2005)
6. Everaere, P., Konieczny, S., Marquis, P.: Conflict-based merging operators. In: KR, pp. 348–357 (2008)
7. Everaere, P., Konieczny, S., Marquis, P.: A diff-based merging operator. In: Proceedings of the NMR, vol. 8, pp. 19–25 (2008)
8. Grégoire, E., Konieczny, S.: Logic-based approaches to information fusion. Inf. Fus. 7(1), 4–18 (2006)
9. Konieczny, S., Lang, J., Marquis, P.: Distance-based merging: a general framework and some complexity results. KR 2, 97–108 (2002)
10. Konieczny, S., Lang, J., Marquis, P.: DA^2 merging operators. Artif. Intell. 157(1), 49–79 (2004)
11. Konieczny, S., Pino Pérez, R.: Merging with integrity constraints. In: Hunter, A., Parsons, S. (eds.) ECSQARU 1999. LNCS (LNAI), vol. 1638, pp. 233–244. Springer, Heidelberg (1999)
12. Konieczny, S., Pérez, R.P.: On the frontier between arbitration and majority. In: KR, pp. 109–120 (2002)
13. Konieczny, S., Pérez, R.P.: Logic based merging. J. Philos. Logic 40(2), 239–270 (2011)
14. Lafage, C., Lang, J.: Propositional distances and preference representation. In: Benferhat, S., Besnard, P. (eds.) ECSQARU 2001. LNCS (LNAI), vol. 2143, pp. 48–59. Springer, Heidelberg (2001)
15. Macías, V.B., Parra, P.P.: Model-based belief merging without distance measures. In: Proceedings of the 6th International Joint Conference on Autonomous Agents and Multiagent Systems, p. 154. ACM (2007)
16. Macías, V.B., Parra, P.P.: Implementing PS-merge operator. In: Aguirre, A.H., Borja, R.M., Garciá, C.A.R. (eds.) MICAI 2009. LNCS, vol. 5845, pp. 39–50. Springer, Heidelberg (2009)
17. Pozos Parra, P., Borja Macías, V.: Partial satisfiability-based merging. In: Gelbukh, A., Kuri Morales, Á.F. (eds.) MICAI 2007. LNCS (LNAI), vol. 4827, pp. 225–235. Springer, Heidelberg (2007)
18. Pozos-Parra, P., Perrussel, L., Thevenin, J.M.: Belief merging using normal forms. In: Batyrshin, I., Sidorov, G. (eds.) MICAI 2011, Part I. LNCS, vol. 7094, pp. 40–51. Springer, Heidelberg (2011)
19. Revesz, P.Z.: On the semantics of theory change: arbitration between old and new information. In: Proceedings of the 12th ACM SIGACT-SIGMOD-SIGART Symposium on Principles of Database Systems, pp. 71–82. ACM (1993)

A Dialogical Model for Collaborative Decision Making Based on Compromises

Dimitra Zografistou[1], Giorgos Flouris[1(✉)], Theodore Patkos[1],
Dimitris Plexousakis[1], Martin Baláž[2], Martin Homola[2], and Alexander Šimko[2]

[1] FORTH-ICS, Heraklion, Greece
{dzograf,fgeo,patkos,dp}@ics.forth.gr
[2] Comenius University in Bratislava, Bratislava, Slovakia
{balaz,homola,simko}@fmph.uniba.sk

Abstract. In this paper, we deal with group decision making and propose a model of dialogue among agents that have different knowledge and preferences, but are willing to compromise in order to collaboratively reach a common decision. Agents participating in the dialogue use internal reasoning to resolve conflicts emerging in their knowledge during communication and to reach a decision that requires the least compromises. Our approach has significant potential, as it may allow targeted knowledge exchange, partial disclosure of information and efficient or informed decision-making depending on the topic of the agents' discussion.

Keywords: Group decision making · Multi-agent systems · Conflicts · Conflict resolution · Preferential reasoning · Dialogues

1 Introduction

The effectiveness of any community of autonomous agents is highly contingent on the interaction schemes of its members. Even when decision making within the community is collaborative, conflicts frequently arise for a multitude of reasons, e.g., because the agents may be heterogeneous (i.e., they perceive the world in different ways), self-interested (i.e., they pursue atomic objectives), etc. Negotiation is inevitable and takes the form of an exchange of offers and positions attempting to find the best mutually beneficial deal in the space of possible deals or of bargaining based on the exchange of richer information (such as arguments), attempting to persuade the other parties to modify their positions.

The relevant literature is rich with approaches that propose elegant protocols for many different cases, especially when finding the optimal solution is a well-defined, as well as highly desirable goal. Nevertheless, many real-world multi-agent systems resemble in complexity the social interactions of humans; as such, adopting typical human negotiation attitudes in certain types of automated dialogues can prove to be more appropriate. Imagine the following example:

© Springer International Publishing Switzerland 2015
N. Bulling (Ed.): EUMAS 2014, LNAI 8953, pp. 414–423, 2015.
DOI: 10.1007/978-3-319-17130-2_29

Example 1. Mary and Anne, each with her own knowledge and preferences, want to decide whether to go to a party (go_party or ¬ go_party). Mary is positive, as she knows that the whole class will be invited. She would also like to go if there is a live band, even though she has no such information. Unlike Mary, Anne prefers going to the theatre than going to the party. If the party is far away, she does not want to go, even though knowing that transport to the party is available could make her reconsider. She also knows that the party will have a live band. The individual Knowledge Bases (KBs) are presented below:

Mary	Anne
r_1: live_band $\Rightarrow$ go_party	r_7: long_distance $\Rightarrow$ ¬ go_party
r_2: class_invited $\Rightarrow$ go_party	r_8: ¬ go_party $\Rightarrow$ theatre
r_3: go_party $\Rightarrow$ meet_new_people	r_9: transport $\Rightarrow$ go_party
r_4: live_band > long_distance	r_{10}: theatre > go_party
r_5: $\Rightarrow$ transport	r_{11}: $\Rightarrow$ live_band
r_6: $\Rightarrow$ class_invited	r_{12}: $\Rightarrow$ long_distance

To decide, the girls engage in the following dialogue:

M: *The whole class will be invited so we should go to the party.*
A: *Yes, but the party is a long distance from here so we shouldn't go.*
M: *Do you know whether the party will have a live band?*
A: *Yes, it will.*
M: *We should go to the party, since there will be a live band.*
A: *Do you know whether there will be transportation to the party?*
M: *Yes there will be.*
A: *Ok, I agree going to the party, as there is transportation.*   □

Even in this simple example, there are complex features that constitute traditional negotiation schemes less preferable in approaching how to reach agreement. Notice, for instance, that both parties typically desire to come to a common decision without having to disclose all their local information (e.g., r_3), which is often impractical. More importantly, decision making is not a take-it-or-leave-it kind of information exchange, but typically involves some degree of *compromise* by each involved party, decided in the course of the discussion. These compromises are driven by the desire to accommodate each other's preferences until an agreement is acceptable to all (i.e., the best for the group), even if this agreement is not optimal for any individual agent. In this sense, negotiations of this type can be seen as a combination of what Walton describes as *persuasion* and *information-seeking* dialogues [14]: information exchange is equally important to being convincing, in order to resolve conflicts.

In this paper, we present an initial attempt towards a formal framework that enables complex negotiations among collaborative agents that are willing to compromise by putting forward partial, yet justifiable positions of their mindset. The compromise per decision is quantified, facilitating the evaluation of individual and group compromise under various alternative methods. To support message exchange, we propose a dialectical model. Our work will enable modelling agents' willingness to compromise, the definition of strategies allowing targeted message exchange, and the support of efficient (quick) decisions.

The paper proceeds with an introduction to the basic notions of our model. Then, Sect. 3 explains different types of internal reasoning related to decision-making, while Sect. 4 defines the protocol of the dialogue. We conclude with a discussion on related work and a description of the currently pursued extensions.

2 Preliminaries

Agents use a common *language* ($\mathcal{L}$), generated by a set of *positive literals* $\mathcal{L}_0 = \{\alpha_1, \alpha_2, \dots\}$, and defined as $\mathcal{L} = \{\alpha, \neg \alpha \mid \alpha \in \mathcal{L}_0\}$. We also consider a set of *rules* $\mathcal{R} = \{r_1, r_2, \dots, \}$, which represents all the rules that can be used by the agents. Rules may be either *inference* or *preference* rules. *Inference rules* are of the form $\ell_1, \dots, \ell_n \leadsto \ell_0$, where $\leadsto \in \{\to, \Rightarrow\}$, $n \geq 0$, $\ell_1, \dots, \ell_n, \ell_0 \in \mathcal{L}$. An inference rule is called *strict* iff $\leadsto = \to$, *defeasible* iff $\leadsto = \Rightarrow$; it is called a *fact* iff $n = 0$. For an inference rule r, we set $body(r) = \{\ell_1, \dots, \ell_n\}$, $head(r) = \ell$. *Preference rules* are of the form $\ell_1 > \ell_2$, where $\ell_1, \ell_2 \in \mathcal{L}$. We denote by $\mathcal{R}^F, \mathcal{R}^\to, \mathcal{R}^\Rightarrow, \mathcal{R}^>$ the set of facts, strict rules, defeasible rules and preference rules in $\mathcal{R}$ respectively.

A literal ℓ is *inferred from* $T \subseteq \mathcal{L}$ given a set of rules $R \subseteq \mathcal{R}$, iff $\ell \in T$ or there is some $r \in R \cap (\mathcal{R}^\to \cup \mathcal{R}^\Rightarrow)$ such that $head(r) = \ell$ and ℓ_i is inferred from T given R for all $\ell_i \in body(r)$. We denote by $Cn^R(T)$ the set of literals inferred from T given R (or simply Cn^R when $T = \emptyset$). A set of rules $R \subseteq \mathcal{R}$ will be called *inconsistent* iff there is some $\alpha \in \mathcal{L}_0$ such that $\alpha, \neg \alpha \in Cn^R$; *consistent* otherwise. We require that $\mathcal{R}^\to$ is consistent, but $\mathcal{R}$ may be inconsistent.

3 Decision-Making Using Compromises

3.1 Setting and Basic Concepts

Our framework assumes two agents, say ag_1, ag_2 who are faced with a binary decision (e.g., "go to the party"/"not go to the party"), which they have to take collaboratively. Thus, a decision-making process is about the truth value of a positive literal α and the two related *choices* are α and $\neg \alpha$. Both agents use the same, arbitrary but fixed, language and set of rules ($\mathcal{L}, \mathcal{R}$). Agent ag_i has a KB $K_i \subseteq \mathcal{R}$ ($i = 1, 2$), containing all the rules that he *is aware of*. The agents are aware of all the strict rules, i.e., $K_i \supseteq \mathcal{R}^\to$.

An agent's KB contains all the knowledge (rules) that the agent has acquired, including *both* his own (original) rules (e.g., strict rules, or rules acquired from personal observation, K^*), *and* the knowledge acquired by other agents via message exchange (communicating a rule makes the recipient aware of it). The KB is finite, which implies that the set of facts in $\mathcal{R}^\to$ is also finite. As the agents' KBs may contain contradicting knowledge, this exchange of rules may result to inconsistencies. Agents tolerate inconsistency in their KBs, but reasoning and decision-making should be based on a consistent subset of the KB. The following subsection, describes the way an agent handles inconsistencies and results to a decision.

3.2   Conflict Resolution and Compromises

The main idea behind conflict resolution, is that when an agent's KB is inconsistent, the agent "ignores" some rules so as to achieve consistency. Note that "ignoring" does not mean dropping the rules from the KB, just considering the subset which makes the KB consistent for the purposes of decision-making. The end result should be conflict-free and "compatible" with the preferences encoded in preference rules. Compatibility in this respect means that the agent cannot ignore rules in such a way that his final knowledge implies a less preferred literal but does not imply a more preferred one. Formally:

Definition 1 (Inferable). A literal ℓ is called *inferable* by a set of rules R iff there is a consistent subset of R, say R', such that $\ell \in Cn^{R'}$.

Definition 2 (Conflict Resolution). Given a KB K, a set of rules $\widehat{K}$ is called a *conflict resolution (CR)* for K iff:

- $\mathcal{R}^{\rightarrow} \subseteq \widehat{K} \subseteq K$.
- $\widehat{K}$ is consistent.
- If $\ell_1 > \ell_2 \in \widehat{K}$, $\ell_2 \in Cn^{\widehat{K}}$ and ℓ_1 is inferable, then $\ell_1 \in Cn^{\widehat{K}}$.

Each KB is amenable to several, but not equally desirable, CRs, as each ignored rule corresponds to a compromise on behalf of the agent. In particular, each CR is associated with a *level of compromise* determined by the amount and type of rules the agent ignores. Formally, this is determined by an arbitrary asymmetric (i.e., irreflexive and antisymmetric) ordering ($\triangleright$) between sets of rules, that we will call *conflict resolution policy (CRP)*. Intuitively, $\widehat{K}_1 \triangleright \widehat{K}_2$ means that $\widehat{K}_1$ is "more preferred" than $\widehat{K}_2$, so $\widehat{K}_1$ requires a lower compromise.

Definition 3 (Compromises). Let ag be an agent and K his KB. ag *accepts* $\widehat{K}_1$ *with* 0-*compromise* iff $\widehat{K}_1$ is a CR of K, and there is no CR of K, say $\widehat{K}_2$, such that $\widehat{K}_2 \triangleright \widehat{K}_1$. ag *accepts* $\widehat{K}_1$ *with* i-*compromise* $(i > 0)$ iff $\widehat{K}_2 \triangleright \widehat{K}_1$, where $\widehat{K}_2$ is a CR of K, implies that $\widehat{K}_2$ is accepted with j-compromise and $j < i$.

3.3   Defining a Conflict Resolution Policy

Our model is agnostic as to the actual CRP used, and we don't require any specific properties for it (e.g., transitivity). However, some of the proposed extensions of this work (namely strategies) require a fixed CRP, so in this subsection we propose a specific ordering, which is based on the idea that the agents should ignore as few rules as possible; to resolve ties, we differentiate the significance of each rule type, so we aim to ignore as little of the "important" information as possible. To formalize these ideas we need the following definitions:

Definition 4 (Contribution). Given a set of rules R and some $r \in R$, the *contribution* of r in R, denoted $Ctr^R(r)$, is defined as $Ctr^R(r) = Cn^R \setminus Cn^{R \setminus \{r\}}$.

Intuitively, the contribution of r determines the inferred literals that would be "missed" if r was removed from R, i.e., it is an indicator of the amount of new knowledge that r helps infer. The following relations, that we call *CRP heuristics*, can be used to rank two CRs, $\widehat{K}_1, \widehat{K}_2$ based on different dimensions:

h_1. **Total rules:** $\widehat{K}_1 \succ_1 \widehat{K}_2$ iff $|\widehat{K}_1| > |\widehat{K}_2|$

h_2. **Own preferences:** $\widehat{K}_1 \succ_2 \widehat{K}_2$ iff $|\widehat{K}_1 \cap \mathcal{R}^> \cap K^*| > |\widehat{K}_2 \cap \mathcal{R}^> \cap K^*|$

h_3. **Contribution:** $\widehat{K}_1 \succ_3 \widehat{K}_2$ iff $\sum_{r \in CR_1} |Ctr^K(r)| > \sum_{r \in CR_1} |Ctr^K(r)|$

h_4. **Defeasible facts:** $\widehat{K}_1 \succ_4 \widehat{K}_2$ iff $|\widehat{K}_1 \cap \mathcal{R}^\Rightarrow \cap \mathcal{R}^F| > |\widehat{K}_2 \cap \mathcal{R}^\Rightarrow \cap \mathcal{R}^F|$

h_5. **Defeasible rules:** $\widehat{K}_1 \succ_5 \widehat{K}_2$ iff $|(\widehat{K}_1 \cap \mathcal{R}^\Rightarrow) \setminus \mathcal{R}^F| > |(\widehat{K}_2 \cap \mathcal{R}^\Rightarrow) \setminus \mathcal{R}^F|$

h_6. **Others' preferences:** $\widehat{K}_1 \succ_6 \widehat{K}_2$ iff $|(\widehat{K}_1 \cap \mathcal{R}^>) \setminus K^*| > |(\widehat{K}_2 \cap \mathcal{R}^>) \setminus K^*|$

Definition 5 (Proposed CRP). Given two conflict resolutions, $\widehat{K}_1, \widehat{K}_2$, and the relations $\succ_i, i = 1, \ldots, 6$ as defined above, we set $\widehat{K}_1 \rhd \widehat{K}_2$ iff $\widehat{K}_1 \succ_i \widehat{K}_2$ for some $i \in \{1, \ldots, 6\}$ and there is no $j \in \{1, \ldots, 6\}$, $j < i$, such that $\widehat{K}_2 \succ_j \widehat{K}_1$.

Intuitively, these definitions imply that the optimal CR will be the one that ignores the least number of others' preferences (h_6) and nothing else; followed by those that ignore defeasible rules, facts or rules with a small contribution (h_5, h_4, h_3); and so on.

3.4   Single-Agent Decision Making Using Compromises

Decision making is a cognitive skill that initially happens internally to each agent (to select the optimal decision) before extending to a group of participants. The process of conflict resolution is just the first step in this process. Obviously, each agent would prefer the choice that requires the least compromise. Formally:

Definition 6 (Beliefs). An agent believes a literal ℓ with i-compromise ($i \geq 0$) iff there is a CR $\widehat{K}$ that the agent accepts with i-compromise such that $\ell \in Cn^{\widehat{K}}$ and for all CRs $\widehat{K}'$ that the agent accepts with j-compromise ($0 \leq j < i$), $\ell \notin Cn^{\widehat{K}'}$. If there is no CR $\widehat{K}$ such that $\ell \in Cn^{\widehat{K}}$, then we say that the agent *does not believe* ℓ, or that he believes it with ∞-compromise.

Definition 7 (Optimal Choice). Given a pair of choices $\alpha, \neg \alpha$, the choice that is *optimal* for an agent is the one that is believed with the least compromise; if both are believed with the same compromise, we say that the agent is *indifferent* between the two choices.

Example 2. In Example 1, assume that Anne has become aware of $\{r_2, r_6\}$ (sent by Mary). Then her KB (say K_A^1) will be conflicting; a partial list of conflict resolutions, compromises and choices believed per CR are shown below.

CR_{ID}	Conflict Resolution	Compromise	Choice believed (for the given CR)
$\widehat{K}_1$	$K_A^1 \setminus \{r_2\}$	0-compromise	$\neg$ go_party
$\widehat{K}_2$	$K_A^1 \setminus \{r_6\}$	1-compromise	$\neg$ go_party

4   Dialectical Model and Protocol

Our previous analysis described the internal reasoning performed by agents to perform conflict resolution, compromise computation and optimal choice selection. Here, we describe the dialectical model that the agents use to communicate their choices and justifications, in order to reach a consensus. In particular, we consider two interlocutor agents, ag_1, ag_2; for an agent ag, we will use $\overline{ag}$ to denote the other agent. The discussion consists of *locutions*, each of which allows an agent to communicate some rule(s). These rules are internalized in the other agent's KB, allowing him to reconsider his ignored rules in future conflict resolution if adequate support for a rejected rule appears. This fact differentiates a cooperative dialogue from classic argumentative, where agents support their own position and counter-argue [13].

Table 1. Locution summary

Locution	Description
Ask(ℓ)	Used by an agent to ask for justification about a literal ℓ
Believe(ℓ, JUST)	Used in response to an "Ask" locution, to state an agent's belief in literal ℓ (of the form α or $\neg\alpha$), along with a justification (JUST), which is a set of rules such that $\ell \in Cn^{\text{JUST}}$. In case that the agent's KB contains no justification for either α or $\neg\alpha$, then Believe($\sim\alpha, \emptyset$) should be returned. Finally, if the agent's KB contains justification for both α and $\neg\alpha$, then Believe($\pm\alpha$, JUST) should be returned, such that $\alpha, \neg\alpha \in Cn^{\text{JUST}}$
Propose(ℓ, JUST)	Used to exchange rules (JUST) in favour of a choice ($\ell \in Cn^{\text{JUST}}$) that the agent proposes. The justification may optionally contain preference rules that affected his conflict resolution process
Agree(ℓ)	Used to express agreement with the last proposed literal
Pass	Used when the agent has nothing to add to the discussion

The different locution types and their intuition are shown in the Table 1. The type of a locution LOC is denoted by $type($LOC$)$. A *dialectical move* is a pair (ag, LOC), which states that agent ag made the locution LOC. A *dialogue* D is a sequence of dialogical moves; the ith dialectical move will be denoted by D_i. We will denote by K_{ag}^i the KB of agent ag after D_i. The dialogue is governed by a *protocol*, inspired by [13], which indicates conditions regarding dialogue initialization, message exchange and dialogue termination:

Initialization. The dialogue starts by agent ag_1, with a Propose or an Ask move. Thus, $D_1 = (ag_1, \text{LOC})$, where $type(\text{LOC}) \in \{\text{Ask, Propose}\}$.

Message Exchange. The conditions below determine the allowable moves:

- *Turn-taking:* the agents should alternate in providing locutions, i.e., if $D_i = (ag, \text{LOC})$, $D_{i+1} = (ag', \text{LOC}')$, then $ag' = \overline{ag}$.
- *Move succession:* each move type can be followed by specific move types, in particular, if $D_i = (ag, \text{LOC})$, $D_{i+1} = (ag', \text{LOC}')$, then:
  - If $type(\text{LOC}) = $Ask, then $type(\text{LOC}') = $Believe
  - If $type(\text{LOC}) = $Believe, then $type(\text{LOC}') \in \{\text{Ask, Propose, Pass, Agree}\}$
  - If $type(\text{LOC}) = $Propose, then $type(\text{LOC}') \in \{\text{Ask, Propose, Agree}\}$
  - If $type(\text{LOC}) = $Pass, then $type(\text{LOC}') \in \{\text{Ask, Propose}\}$
- *Agreement:* an agreement cannot be reached unless there was a specific proposal. Formally, if $D_i = (ag, \text{LOC})$ and $type(\text{LOC}) = $Agree, then there is some $1 \le j < i$ such that $D_j = (ag^*, \text{LOC}^*)$, $ag^* = \overline{ag}$ and $type(\text{LOC}^*) = $Propose.
- *Effects:* locutions containing a justification cause these rules to be incorporated in the KB of the recipient agent. Formally, if $D_i = (ag, \text{LOC})$ then:
  - If $\text{LOC} = $Propose($\ell$,JUST) then $K_{\overline{ag}}^{i+1} = K_{\overline{ag}}^i \cup \text{JUST}$
  - If $\text{LOC} = $Believe($\ell$,JUST) then $K_{\overline{ag}}^{i+1} = K_{\overline{ag}}^i \cup \text{JUST}$
- *Move uniqueness:* an agent cannot make the same move twice, i.e., if $i \ne j$ then $D_i \ne D_j$.
- *Honesty:* agents communicate rules they are aware of, i.e., if $D_i = (ag, \text{LOC})$ and $\text{LOC} = $Believe($\ell$,JUST) or $\text{LOC} = $Propose($\ell$,JUST) then $\text{JUST} \subseteq K_{ag}^{i-1}$.

Termination. The dialogue terminates when an Agree locution has been made, or when both agents use a Pass in succession. Formally, we say that the dialogue *terminates in step i* in the following two cases:

- *Consensus:* $D_i = (ag, \text{LOC})$ and $type(\text{LOC}) = $Agree. In this case, we say that the dialogue *terminates with a consensus*, and the *decision* of the dialogue is determined by the last Propose locution. Specifically, if j is the maximum integer for which $D_j = (ag^*, \text{LOC}^*)$, $ag^* = \overline{ag}$ and $type(\text{LOC}^*) = $Propose, then the decision is the literal ℓ in the first parameter of LOC^*.
- *No consensus:* $D_i = (ag, \text{LOC})$, $D_{i-1} = (ag', \text{LOC}')$ and $type(\text{LOC}) = type(\text{LOC}') = $Pass. In this case, we say that the dialogue *terminates with no consensus*.

The termination of the dialogue is guaranteed by the conditions of move uniqueness and honesty, as well as by the fact that the agents' KBs are assumed finite.

5   Related Work

Dialogues for reaching agreement have been studied in other frameworks, too. Prakken [13] formally models dialogue games for argumentation. The framework is flexible enough to capture different protocols. A approach similar to ours, is described in [1], where agents engage in a collaborative dialogue to achieve consensus, conformed to a predefined protocol allowing the dialogue to end up with no agreement.

The system described in [3] represents a cooperative dialectical model for practical reasoning equipped with a formalization about opponent's preferences and a strategic selection mechanism. None of the previous models have features of information seeking that enhance the notion of collaboration. A dialectical protocol targeting in agreement that supports this feature is presented in [10], where the agents negotiate to agree in a common ontology. However, in our model we additionally focus on the process of single-agent decision making through the notion of compromise.

Fan et al. [8] rely on the assumption-based framework to model decision making as a setting of two communicating agents, each one equipped with a decision making framework that respectively resolves conflicts according to the trustworthiness between agents, but ignoring preferences. In [11] a dialogue protocol between cooperative agents is presented, although it is based on three-valued non-monotonic modal logic in order to reason with incomplete knowledge. Cooperative agents aiming for a common goal, are also presented in [12]. The main differentiations lie in the outcome of the dialogue which, in their approach is a common plan, whilst in our model is a final decision, as well as in the protocol of the dialogue.

6   Discussion and Possible Extensions

The current study sets the foundations for enabling agents to engage in complex negotiations. This is just the first step towards a more ambitious aim; in essence, our framework will be the substrate on top of which different extensions are going to be investigated. First, we plan to expand the expressiveness of the underlying language with more complex features, such as contextual preferences of the form $a \Rightarrow (b > c)$ or even $(a > b) \Rightarrow (c > d)$, similar in style to [4].

A topic we are currently working on is to enhance the reasoning capacity of the agents with *strategies* that would make them "smarter" in selecting their next moves. Note that the protocol defined in Sect. 4 gives the allowable moves, but does not provide any algorithm for selecting the next move. Such an algorithm would include targeted information seeking, in order to satisfy preferences and lighten the compromise, or "smart" rule exchange to decrease the total number of messages exchanged before terminating the dialogue. In this respect, the work in [2] is relevant, which uses argumentation and relies on preferences on arguments to perform decision making, even though the setting is not distributed, as in our case. Our strategies will be inspired by the persuasion field [5,9], exploiting knowledge about other agents' KBs, or applying the notion of *relevant* literals or rules, which should be communicated first.

Additionally, we plan to accommodate more complex dialogues with more than two agents that negotiate over more involved decisions (e.g., choosing among a set of diverse choices), use more complex locutions (e.g., stating reasons for ignoring rules), and have different and more complex CRPs (e.g., using trust considerations, or ideas from utility theory and heuristics like utilitarian, egalitarian, elitist, etc. [6]). Multi-party dialogues demand more complex models regulating turn-taking, termination, different roles or ways of cooperation and other issues highlighted in [7]. In such models it will be challenging how the interplay of different strategies and CRPs will affect the course of the dialogue and possibly also the notion of *group compromise*.

Another possible extension would be to incorporate the notion of *willingness to compromise*, which would make agents more (or less) receptive to accepting a decision that requires more compromise than the optimal one, or even forcing them to reject optimal decisions that are above a certain level of compromise. This would prevent from prematurely taking decisions with large compromises when it comes to important topics. It could also be coupled with a mechanism for successively lowering the threshold; the latter would prohibit quick decisions on important matters, and would force the agents to engage in longer dialogues.

Finally, our future work includes studying formal properties of dialogues, such as the rate of reaching consensus with different strategies, or how decisions reached by agents are related to the optimal (and informed) decision obtained by an omniscient agent. A prolog-based implementation is under way, so as to couple the theoretical properties with experimental evaluations, which would consider, apart from performance, also issues of dialogue quality, such as the length of the dialogue or the quality of the decision taken under different strategies or settings.

Acknowledgements. This work was partially funded from the Slovak–Greek bilateral project "Multi-context Reasoning in Heterogeneous environments", registered on the Slovak side under no. SK-GR-0070-11 with the APVV agency and co-financed by the Greek General Secretariat of Science and Technology and the EU. It was further supported by the Slovak national VEGA project no. 1/1333/12. Martin Baláž and Martin Homola are also supported by APVV project no. APVV-0513-10.

References

1. Amgoud, L., Belabbes, S., Prade, H.: Towards a formal framework for the search of a consensus between autonomous agents. In: Parsons, S., Maudet, N., Moraitis, P., Rahwan, I. (eds.) argmas 2005. LNCS (LNAI), vol. 4049, pp. 264–278. Springer, Heidelberg (2006)
2. Amgoud, L., Prade, H.: Using arguments for making and explaining decisions. Artif. Intell. **173**(3–4), 413–436 (2009)
3. Black, E., Atkinson, K.: Choosing persuasive arguments for action (2011)
4. Brewka, G.: Logic programming with ordered disjunction. In: Eighteenth National Conference on Artificial intelligence, pp. 100–105 (2002)
5. Budzynska, K., Kacprzak, M.: Formal models for persuasive aspects of argumentation. Stud. Logic, Grammar and Rhetoric **16**(29), 159–187 (2009)
6. Chevaleyre, Y., Dunne, P.E., Endriss, U., Lang, J., Lemaitre, M., Maudet, N., Padget, J., Phelps, S., Rodriguez-aguilar, J.A., Sousa, P.: Issues in multiagent resource allocation. INFORMATICA **30**, 3–31 (2006)

7. Dignum, F.P.M., Vreeswijk, G.A.W.: Towards a testbed for multi-party dialogues. In: Dignum, F.P.M. (ed.) ACL 2003. LNCS (LNAI), vol. 2922, pp. 212–230. Springer, Heidelberg (2004)

8. Fan, X., Toni, F., Mocanu, A., Williams, M.: Dialogical two-agent decision making with assumption-based argumentation. In: AAMAS 2014, pp. 533–540 (2014)

9. Hunter, A.: Making argumentation more believable. In: AAAI 2004 (2004)

10. Morge, M., Routier, J.C., Secq, Y., Dujardin, T.: A formal framework for inter-agents dialogue to reach an agreement about a representation. In: Proceedings of the Workshop on Formal Ontologies for Communicating Agents (FOCA 2006) (2006)

11. Moubaiddin, A., Obeid, N.: Partial information basis for agent-based collaborative dialogue. Appl. Intell. 30(2), 142–167 (2009)

12. Pardo, P., Pajares, S., Onaindia, E., Godo, L., Dellunde, P.: Multiagent argumentation for cooperative planning in DeLP-POP. In: The 10th International Conference on Autonomous Agents and Multiagent Systems, AAMAS 2011, vol. 3 (2011)

13. Prakken, H.: Coherence and flexibility in dialogue games for argumentation. J. Logic and Comput. 15(6), 1009–1040 (2005)

14. Walton, D., Krabbe, E.C.W.: Commitment in Dialogue: Basic Concepts of Interpersonal Reasoning. State University of New York Press, Albany (1995)

Author Index

Printed in the United States
by Bookmasters

Printed in the United States
By Bookmasters